W9-CNH-959

CONSULS OF THE LATER ROMAN EMPIRE

PHILOLOGICAL MONOGRAPHS

OF THE

AMERICAN PHILOLOGICAL ASSOCIATION

Number 36

Accepted for Publication by the Editorial Board for Monographs

of the American Philological Association

Ludwig Koenen, Chairman

CONSULS OF THE LATER ROMAN EMPIRE

By

Roger S. Bagnall
Alan Cameron
Seth R. Schwartz
Klaas A. Worp

Published for

The American Philological Association

by

Scholars Press

Atlanta, Georgia

1987

The publication of this book was aided by
a grant from the Stanwood Cockey Lodge Foundation
of Columbia University

Library of Congress Cataloging in Publication Data:

Consuls of the later Roman Empire.

    (Philological monographs of the American
Philological Association ; no. 36)
        Bibliography: p.
        Includes index.
        1. Consuls, Roman. 2. Chronology, Roman.
I. Bagnall, Roger S.   II. American Philological
Association.   III. Series: Philological monographs ;
no. 36.
DG83.5. C7C68 1987   937'.00202   86-31452
ISBN 1-55540-099-X (alk. paper)

Printed on acid-free paper in the United States of America

Preface

We are perhaps unduly interested in consuls.
--Peter Brown, *Society and the Holy*, 137

Consuls, to be sure, offer various points of interest. This book is not so much concerned with these men as figures in the society of late antiquity as it is devoted to their utility for identifying years: consulates as a means of reckoning time. The compilation of lists of consuls was actively pursued in antiquity, and modern listmakers have not been lacking. But only two scholars have sought, since the development of Latin epigraphy in the later nineteenth century,[1] to compile the evidence for each consulate--Vaglieri and Liebenam, seven decades ago--and their work is simply no longer current with the evidence. Recent works on late antiquity have sometimes suffered from the lack of a comprehensive listing of the evidence. Compiling this evidence was our first concern.

The full assemblage of evidence has provided quite a number of opportunities to alter views in the modern literature about the recognition of consuls and the dissemination of their names (two phenomena which must be distinguished), and the comments appended to the evidence in the central part of this work set out briefly our conclusions for individual years. Beyond this, the assembled evidence also made possible a number of inquiries into various aspects of the functioning of the consulate as a chronological system. These, along with discussions of the character and limitations of the various types of documentation, form the introduction.

No one can assemble thousands of ancient documents--on any subject--without finding out things their editors and past commentators have not seen. The catalogue of our attempts to improve readings and interpretations, coupled with the list of documents we have rejected as useless for our purposes, form the Critical Appendix--a section for consultation rather than for reading, even more than the main body of the book. It also includes a number of extended discussions for which there was insufficient space on the pages for the years in question.

The bulk of the work of compilation was done during 1982-83, when Worp was able to spend a year at Columbia University. For the funds which made this year possible we are grateful to the Faculty of Letters of the University of Amsterdam, to the Netherlands Organization for the Advancement of Pure Scientific Research (ZWO), and to the National Endowment for the Humanities. To the Endowment we also owe the means for Schwartz's participation in the project. We are indebted to the Dunning Fund of the Department of History and to the Graduate School of Arts and Sciences of Columbia University, for small grants toward the cost of computer time, laser printing, and photocopying.

To avoid the cost of entirely recomposing this book from a final manuscript, we created it from the start on computer. We thank here the staff of the Columbia University Center for Computing Activities for their help in the early stages of this process. Technology has continued to change over the years we have

---

[1]There is a thorough documentation of the literary sources attesting consulates in H.F. Clinton, *Fasti Romani* (Oxford 1845), 2 vols., but Clinton's work antedates not only the development of epigraphy and papyrology, but modern editions of the ancient chronicles.

been at work, and our final camera-ready pages were produced on a Hewlett-Packard Laserjet Plus printer using Nota Bene on an IBM PC-AT computer; these facilities were made possible by an equipment grant from the IBM Corporation to Columbia University through Project Aurora and by funds from the Stanwood Cockey Lodge Foundation of Columbia University. The assistance of Steven Siebert and Jonathan Gumport of Dragonfly Software was essential in the final stages of our work.

        We also owe a debt of gratitude to many persons who have helped us in scholarly matters: Thomas Drew-Bear checked the reading of an inscription in Lyon for us; Werner Eck, Hermann Harrauer and Johannes Diethart provided us with references and copies of some items of documentation otherwise unavailable or unknown to us; Brian Croke and Steven Muhlberger read drafts of and commented usefully on Chapter 4. R.A. Coles sent us Oxyrhynchos material before publication; Richard W. Burgess sent us prepublication copies of two articles and helped us in correspondence to clarify our views on several points; Diane Schauer helped us immeasurably with the collection of numismatic evidence; and Timothy Barnes, Werner Eck, Denis Feissel, and Antonio Ferrua, S.J., all read the work in various versions, offering numerous improvements. Barnes and Eck in addition read the penultimate version as readers for the American Philological Association and contributed many improvements at that stage. That even with the unselfish help of all of these this work is free of errors and omissions would be too much to hope, but it owes much of what it does contain to their generosity.

May, 1987

CONTENTS

PART I

INTRODUCTION

Chapter 1

History of the Consulate

1. The Evolution of the Consulate

"At the end of a thousand years two consuls were created by the
sovereigns of Rome and Constantinople for the sole purpose of
giving a date to the year and a festival to the people..."[1]

It is true that the consulate of the late empire was, as one of the consuls of 362 observed, "honos sine labore" (Mamertinus, *Grat. Actio* 2.2), but it was nonetheless the supreme goal of any Roman citizen and the supreme mark of imperial favor. If anything, its prestige actually increased with the passage of the centuries.

It is instructive to trace the evolution of the consulate from the early to the late empire. With the establishment of the principate, though formally still elected, consuls were in reality nominated by the princeps.[2] Their original powers were drastically reduced, though they retained their (alternating) presidency of the senate and some judicial functions[3]--and acquired the expensive honor of providing games.[4]

The consulate was no longer sought for the powers it gave to the holder in office, but for the openings it gave for advancement in the imperial administration.[5] It was less to satisfy ambition than to generate a larger pool of candidates for consular governorships that Augustus institutionalized the suffect consulate, thus making room for many more than the two *ordinarii*. There might be anything from two to ten suffects in one year, rising to an extraordinary high of 25 in 190.[6]

Despite this proliferation of suffect consuls, many of them *novi homines*, the lustre of the ordinary consulate remained untarnished. It was the only office[7] the emperor deigned to share with his subjects, and those openings left free by the imperial family[8] were for the most part filled by patricians and descendants of consuls.

In the second half of the third century some major changes took place in the senatorial career. In the first two centuries, the consulate had come to a man about halfway through his career, in the early 30's for patricians, the early 40's for most others.[9] It determined whether or not he was going to advance to the

---

[1]E.Gibbon, *Decline and Fall of the Roman Empire*, ed. J.B. Bury, IV (London 1909) 285.

[2]This much is agreed, though the exact means used by the emperor to make his preferences known are hotly disputed: see (for example) B. Levick, "Imperial Control of the Elections under the Early Principate," *Historia* 16 (1967) 207-30; R. Frei-Stolba, *Untersuchungen zu den Wahlen in der römischen Kaiserzeit* (Zürich 1967).

[3]R.J.A. Talbert, *The Senate of Imperial Rome* (Princeton 1984) 21-22.

[4]Consuls were not required to provide games during the Republic, and it was not perhaps till the fifth century that this became their main function. But as early as Augustus they were at least expected to contribute to the cost of games, at whatever time of the year they assumed office: Talbert, 60.

[5]See R. Syme, *Tacitus* (Oxford 1958), *passim*; W. Eck, "Beförderungskriterien innerhalb der senatorischen Laufbahn," *ANRW* II.1 (Berlin 1974) 158-228; G. Alföldy, "Consuls and Consulars under the Antonines," *Ancient Society* 7 (1976) 263-99 and *Konsulat und Senatorenstand unter den Antoninen* (Bonn 1977), with the reservations of G.P. Burton, *JRS* 70 (1980) 204-06; K. Hopkins, *Death and Renewal* (Cambridge 1983); and for a useful recent summary of the position of the consulate in early imperial career patterns, see A.R. Birley, *The Fasti of Roman Britain* (Oxford 1981) 24-32.

[6]For the variation in number from reign to reign, see the brief account in Talbert, 21.

[7]Unless we count the censorship and priesthoods.

[8]Fifteen emperors before the tetrarchs held the consulate four or more times, six of them seven or more times.

[9]The general assumption, though there is still no satisfactory discussion.

more prestigious senior posts, the consular legateships and proconsulships of Asia and Africa, the major urban curatorships and the prefectship of the city of Rome. Those who continued to distinguish themselves might win a second or even (very rarely) a third consulate. Before the first (normally suffect) consulate a man would typically have served in the vigintivirate, the military tribunate, two or three of the old Republican offices (aedile, quaestor, tribunus plebis, praetor) and at least two praetorian posts. That is to say, a man of non-patrician birth would already have a substantial active career behind him before his first consulate.

By the close of the third century, all pre-consular functions except for the quaestorship and praetorship disappeared from the senatorial career. Praetorian posts were taken over by equites, and senators disappear from military careers. This is not the place to explore the reasons for this change.[10] But with nothing left for senators to do before the consulate, it was inevitable that it should be held earlier and (with the passage of time) valued less highly. Already by the last quarter of the third century it was sometimes omitted from cursus inscriptions, a clear sign of its decreasing importance.

One consequence was that second consulates, always now ordinary, became commoner, while first consulates were normally suffect.[11] From the beginning of the third century, praetorian prefects were occasionally allowed, on being appointed to the (ordinary) consulate, to count the earlier award of *ornamenta consularia* as a first consulate, so that they could style themselves cos. II--a clear hint of the progressive devaluation of the first, suffect consulate.[12] The award of the consulate to praetorian prefects in office was itself one of the more conspicuous signs of the assimilation of the equestrian and senatorial orders at this period. Senators had finally lost their monopoly on the consulate.

As late as 289 we still find at least six suffects named in a fragmentary consular list from Cales (*CIL* X 4631). And a further twenty, of unknown date, are attested from the period covered by this book, but only five or six are later than the reign of Constantine.[13] By the early decades of the fourth century the status of the suffect consulate had sunk so low that it was normally held in the 20's and seldom even recorded on cursus inscriptions.[14] A law of (probably) 329 implies that it might be held at the age of sixteen.[15]

The change in the nature and status of the office was formalized when the emperor transferred the election of suffects from himself to the senate. It was perhaps Constantine who did this, or at any rate Constantius II.[16] Early in 385 Symmachus sent to court the nominations of those "subeundis fascibus destinatos" (*Rel.* 45). These nominations were made at the meeting of the senate held on 9 January;[17] the suffect consulate had become a *munus*, like the quaestorship and praetorship.[18] We may guess that only two were elected for this purpose.[19]

---

[10]For which see now M. Christol, *Tituli* 4 (1982) 143-66 and *Essai sur l'évolution des carrières senatoriales dans la 2e moitié du IIIe siècle ap. J.-C.* (Paris 1986).
        [11]R. Syme, *Tacitus* I (Oxford 1958) 643-44; H.G. Pflaum, *REL* 28 (1951) 47-48; A. Chastagnol, *Revue historique* 219 (1958) 221-31.
        [12]In earlier times the award of *ornamenta consularia* to praetorian prefects did not even confer active membership of the senate: see W. Ensslin, *RE* 22.2399; A. Chastagnol, *Recherches sur l'Histoire Auguste* (Bonn 1970) 40f.; B.Rémy, *REA* 78/79 (1976/77) 166-82.
        [13]Since they cannot be assigned to particular years, there is no point in including them in a work such as ours. For the list, see *PLRE* I 1046-47; M.T.W. Arnheim, *The Senatorial Aristocracy of the Later Roman Empire* (Oxford 1972) 225-26; and (with full discussion and bibliography) W. Kuhoff, *Studien zur zivilen senatorischen Laufbahn im 4 Jdt. n. Chr.* (Frankfurt 1983) 29-39; 279-91.
        [14]Chastagnol argued that it was no longer held at all by aristocrats of the bluest blood, who often moved directly from the praetorship, held in the late teens, to the most junior senatorial governorship--with the title *consularis*: see *Revue historique* 219 (1958) 231-37 and, in more detail, replying to the criticisms of Arnheim, 15f., in *Atti dell' Accademia Costantiniana: 2o Convegno Internazionale 1975* (Perugia 1975) 58-59; Kuhoff (p.37) could find no evidence for the sort of social distinctions alleged by Chastagnol.
        [15]*CTh* 6.4.1; on the date, Seeck, *Regesten* 60.
        [16]For recent discussions of this controversial issue, see Chastagnol, *Atti Acc.Cost.* (n.14) 66-67 and D. Vera, *Commento storico alle Relationes di Q. Aurelio Simmaco* (Pisa 1981) 330-32.
        [17]Polemius Silvius, *CIL* I^2 p.257; cf. Vera (above, n.16) 332.
        [18]The three are linked (for example) in *CTh* 6.4.1 of 329.
        [19]And perhaps only one by the fifth century: see Cameron, "A Note on the Suffect Consulate in the Late Empire," forthcoming. On their duties (probably nothing more than standing in for the ordinary consuls when the latter were absent) see below, pp.20-21.

Knowledge of this change helps to expose a forged item in the *Historia Augusta*. The Emperor Tacitus is alleged to have asked the senate for a consulate for his brother Florianus. He was refused, on the grounds that "the senate had already fixed the terms of office of the suffects" (*Tac.* 9.6). Since it was undoubtedly the emperor who appointed suffects in the third century, the anachronism is patent.[20]

Two early indications of the decline of the suffect consulate have recently been underlined by W. Eck.[21] First, from the beginning of the third century the names of suffect consuls disappear from the dating formulas of official documents, which begin to be dated by ordinary consuls alone throughout the year. Dating by suffects had never been universal or widespread, even in Italy, but it had been standard practice throughout the first two centuries on all documents emanating from the imperial chancellery. The change can be dated fairly precisely: in the 180's suffects still seem to be the norm; from 203 on ordinary consuls alone become the norm.[22]

Second, it is from the beginning of the third century again that we find men drawing attention to the fact that they had been ordinary (ex kal. Ian.) rather than suffect consuls on their cursus inscriptions.[23] The distinction itself was not new, of course; but, perhaps surprisingly, the countless cursus inscriptions of the first two centuries never draw attention to it. The first examples of this phenomenon are from 212 and 214.

But the decline of the suffect consulate did not in itself automatically affect the position or prestige of the ordinary consulate. Right up to the age of the Tetrarchs the first consulate remained the beginning of the consular career, the prelude to the highest offices, normally suffect but still occasionally ordinary. For example, the first consulates of Anullinus and Tuscus in 295 were both ordinary; it was not till later that Anullinus became proconsul of Africa (303-304) and prefect of Rome (306-307 and again in 312) and Tuscus *curator aquarum* and prefect of Rome (302). These are typical traditional careers. So too probably Gallus cos. 298 and Nepotianus cos. 301. It is a decade later that the change comes. From 311 on the ordinary consulate became, for private citizens, the equivalent of the second consulate of the early empire, the culmination of a distinguished career. It normally came to a man around or after his tenure of the urban or praetorian prefecture, or (for military men) the mastership of the soldiers.[24] No longer were the two prefectures the summit of a man's ambition. By the second half of the century the consulate was officially ranked above both prefectures.[25]

Titianus cos. 301 seems to be the last securely documented case of a man officially styled *bis consul* (in both fasti and inscriptions; for the papyri see note *ad annum*) on the strength of an early suffect consulate. Volusianus cos.ord. 311 under the usurper Maxentius and again under Constantine in 314 is styled *bis ordinarius consul* on the private inscription *ILS* 1222 (but not in the fasti or in *CPR* VIII 22, which gives I explicitly), evidently so as to make it clear that he was *not* counting a devalued suffect consulate. One Roman inscription (*CIL* VI 1748 = *ILS* 1238) describes Nummius Albinus cos. 345 as *consul ordinarius iterum*, and since he appears only once on the fasti, it has usually been inferred that the other consulate was suffect.[26] De Rossi, followed more recently by Chastagnol,[27] suggested an ordinary consulate held under the usurpers Magnentius or even Nepotian. There are certainly serious objections to this hypothesis,[28] but at the same time it would be improbably late for a man to be equating suffect and ordinary consulates, and the wording of the inscription appears (as in the case of Volusianus) to imply two

---

[20]So "Vopiscus"; "Lampridius" (*Alex.* 43.2) had only dared to claim that, when appointing both ordinary and suffect consuls, the emperor followed senatorial recommendations ("ex senatus sententia nominavit"). Different authors, perhaps, one better informed than the other? Not necessarily. It depends whether the author of the life of Tacitus was trying unsuccessfully to deceive-- or simply playing with his readers.

[21]*Heer und Integrationspolitik: Die römischen Militärdiplome als historische Quelle*, ed. W. Eck and H. Wolff (Köln 1986).

[22]The last extant date given by suffect consuls in any text is from 289; see *ad annum*.

[23]So already Mommsen, *Staatsrecht* II.1³ 92.

[24]Since the consulate now carried no serious duties beyond the provision of games, it could be and often was held concurrently with these posts.

[25]*CTh* 6.7.1 (372); cf. 6.4.12 (361).

[26]E.g., with full bibliography, Kuhoff, *Studien* 36.

[27]*Rev.hist.* 219 (1958) 234.

[28]*PLRE* I 37; Kuhoff, loc.cit.

ordinary consulates. Another possibility is that Albinus died while designated to a second ordinary consulate; the inscription might then (like *ILS* 1257 in the case of Symmachus cos.des. for 377) have simply anticipated his honor.

It has often been assumed that it was Constantine who 'reformed' the ordinary consulate.[29] But if so, he did no more than regularize an obvious tendency. In the twenty years between 302 and 322, no fewer than thirty of the forty ordinary consulates went to emperors (see section II). With the loss of prestige of the suffect, first consulate, that meant only ten consulates worthy of the name available for private citizens during those two decades. It was inevitable that they should rise in prestige, marking the culmination rather than the beginning of a man's career.[30]

2. The Consuls

In the first three centuries of the empire, according to Burton and Hopkins, "about half of all senators surviving to consular age became consuls".[31] Even if this is a (slight) exaggeration, the consulate was clearly a reasonable ambition for any well-connected young man.[32] By the fourth century it was no longer an honor that even a distinguished man could count on winning. Since most emperors continued to reserve the fasces fairly regularly for themselves, their colleagues and their sons, there was seldom more than one ordinary consulate a year available for subjects, often not even that. For example, Diocletian and Maximian held ten and nine consulates respectively; the family of Constantine no fewer than nineteen during his thirty-year reign; Honorius and Theodosius II, thirteen and eighteen. In addition to members of the imperial college, brothers, uncles, cousins and even in-laws of emperors might also be so honored. As a result, in the first century of our period (284-395) almost exactly half the available consulates were held by emperors and kin (126, as against 127 held by subjects[33]). Between 396 and 450 the proportion changes, with 40 imperial consulates as against 70 held by subjects; and between 451 and 541 there were only 24 imperial consulates as against 110 held by subjects. This increase of non-imperial consulates is in part explained by the absence of western emperors after 476, but also by the growing reluctance of eastern emperors after 450 to hold repeated consulates. For example, in seventeen years Zeno held only two; in 28 years (491-518) Anastasius held three; in 38 (527-565) Justinian too only three.

Over 1800 subjects held the consulate between 30 B.C. and A.D. 235, of whom we know the names of about 1400. The number is high enough to permit useful study of senatorial career patterns, for example the controversial recent claim of Burton and Hopkins[34] that "three quarters of all consuls who held office A.D. 18-235 are not known to have had a single consular direct descendant in the next three generations." For our period, with only 311 non-imperial consuls over a longer period, no comparable results should be expected. In order to give some idea what sort of men were appointed by different emperors in different periods, we have supplied brief summaries of the careers of non-imperial consuls, in effect dividing them into three categories: generals, aristocrats and bureaucrats.[35] Even such broad categories as these are not altogether satisfactory. For while aristocrats and bureaucrats never became generals, aristocrats sometimes

[29]See Chastagnol, *Rev.hist.* 219 (1958) 229-30.
[30]The few fourth-century exceptions are usually explained by some imperial connection: for example, Hypatius cos. 359, PVR 379 and PPO 382-383, brother-in-law of Constantius II and consul jointly with his own older brother Eusebius. In the Ostrogothic age it became common for the consulate to be held very young by members of the much shrunken nobility, for quite different reasons; see section 3 below. For the case of 395, see section 2 below.
[31]In Keith Hopkins, *Death and Renewal* (Cambridge 1983) 124.
[32]On the criteria of selection, much disputed in recent years, see Hopkins, 152f.
[33]For this purpose counting nominations of and by usurpers, since it is category rather than legality that is at issue here.
[34]See n.31 above. Against, W. Eck, *Gnomon* 57 (1985) 624-31; G. Alföldy, *Die römische Gesellschaft* (Stuttgart 1986) 139-61.
[35]The same three categories are given by Ausonius: "viros gloriae militaris...viros nobilitatis antiquae...viros fide inclitos et officiis probatos" (*Grat.actio* 4).

led bureaucratic careers and descendants of bureaucrats and generals sometimes became aristocrats. A "pure" aristocratic career would include brief tenure of a governorship of an Italian province, the proconsulship of Africa, and the prefecture of Rome. A "pure" bureaucratic career would consist of service at court, culminating in often extended tenure of one or more of the great palatine ministries, the *comitiva sacrarum largitionum* (CSL), *magisterium officiorum* or praetorian prefecture (PPO). Symmachus cos. 391 falls into the first category, Rufinus cos. 392 into the second. But how do we categorize Petronius Probus cos. 371, head of the wealthiest and most powerful of aristocratic families, the Anicii, whose career culminated in no fewer than four praetorian prefectures, one lasting at least eight years? Whereas Symmachus' consulate can be construed as a gesture to the Roman aristocracy, Probus' was at least as much a reward for his loyal services at court.

With so high a degree of imperial monopolization of the fasti, it is inevitably harder to detect trends and patterns in the later empire, especially over short periods. But a few obvious trends can be identified.[36]

For example, there were eighteen subject consuls during the first eleven of Constantius II's 21 years as senior Augustus (340-361), but only six in his more troubled and suspicious second decade. During the eleven years of joint reign by Valentinian and Valens (364-375) there were only eight subject consuls. During the sixteen years of Theodosius I (379-395) there were 21. To analyse the Valentinianic statistics rather differently, out of the 26 places available between 364 and Valens' death in 378, no fewer than seventeen went to the imperial family; seven to generals; one to an aristocrat; and one to a praetorian prefect. Since the aristocrat was Probus, the fasti are at any rate consistent with the traditional picture of a clash between the dynasty and the aristocracy. They also lend some support to the traditional picture of Diocletian, who appointed only four aristocrats to the consulate, as "hammer of the aristocracy,"[37] in contrast with Constantine, who appointed ten.

To look more closely now at the Theodosian statistics, Theodosius I took only three consulates himself, and two and three respectively for his two sons. It might be added that his own second (388) and the second and third of his sons' (394) were clearly taken as political gestures, to advertise his repudiation of illegal consulates proclaimed by western usurpers. In general, Theodosius seems to have been more concerned than his immediate predecessors to treat the consulate as a reward for deserving subjects rather than a prerogative of the ruling house--a fact noted and praised by contemporaries. "Renuntiantur amici ante filios tuos consules, quia non poterant plus esse quam consules" (Pacatus, *Pan.Theod.* 16.4). Themistius praised him repeatedly for giving to a general the consulate he was expected to take in celebration of his own quinquennalia in 383 (see p.15). He also appointed three aristocrats (Symmachus in 391; Olybrius and Probinus in 395), though on both occasions he was attempting to restore good relations with the aristocracy after prominent members had supported the two western usurpers he had just suppressed. In 395 there was the additional factor of the pagan element in the rebellion, for Olybrius and Probinus were members of the great Christian family of the Anicii. The symbolic potential of the consulate, now completely dissociated from the old concept of "career", emerges very clearly from examples like these.

The accession of Theodosius' feeble son Arcadius in the East (395) brought a series of civilian ministers to power and the consulate. One of the complaints of the Gothic general Gainas who rebelled in 400 was apparently that he was being kept out of the consulate.[38] Theodosius had appointed seven generals, three of them barbarians, and the half-Vandal Stilicho was western consul that very year. Gainas' victor Fravitta (another Goth) became consul for 401, but thereafter the next eastern general to win the fasces was Varanes in 410, and the next German was Plinta in 419. Thus the attempt of the eastern goverment to keep power in civilian hands stands reflected in the consular fasti.

---

[36]There is no comprehensive analysis of the consuls of this period; for the period of the tetrarchy and Constantine, see Barnes, *New Empire*, Chapter 6.

[37]M.T.W. Arnheim, *The Senatorial Aristocracy in the Later Roman Empire* (Oxford 1972) Ch.II.

[38]See Cameron, "Barbarians and Politics at the Court of Arcadius," forthcoming.

It is harder to detect any significant pattern in the appointment of citizen consuls in the long reign of Theodosius II (408-450), not least because he took no fewer than 18 consulates himself. But one interesting development in the East is the emergence of consular dynasties spanning many reigns. For example, Taurus cos. 361, his sons Caesarius cos. 397 and Aurelian cos. 400, Aurelian's son Taurus cos. 428, and a later descendant, Taurus Clementinus cos. 513. The first four all held the praetorian prefecture. More interesting still, we find military dynasties: Plinta cos. 419, his son-in-law Ardabur cos. 427, Ardabur's son Aspar cos. 434 and grandson Ardabur junior cos. 447. In the fourth century such dynasties are only to be found in the West. For example, the father and grandfather of Probus cos. 371 had held the fasces in 322 and 341; his three sons after him in 395 and 406.[39] Perhaps the most consistently successful of all Roman families throughout our period is the Symmachi, with consuls in 330, 391, 446, 485 and 522, not to mention a consul designate for 377 who died a few months before assuming office. By the sixth century, the consulate is often the only office held by such nobles.

This is not to say that every name on the fasti is a household word. Given our poor documentation for so much of the period, it is hardly surprising that some are otherwise unknown to us. Some may be unidentified scions of noble houses, some may be court favorites of lowly origin. With generals, the consulate is often said to be a reward for victories won. With bureaucrats it was a reward for loyal service. And Studius cos. 454 is stated in an inscription to have won his as a reward for building a famous church of St. John the Baptist.[40] In general, however, with ancestral wealth the balance of obligation might run the other way. It was prudent to secure the goodwill of those whose wealth gave them a power even emperors could not ignore, and how better than with the supreme honor at the emperor's disposal.

There was little that mattered more to the Byzantine than protocol and precedence. The modern student is bewildered by the constant proliferation of titles, no sooner invented than devalued by promiscuous distribution.[41] The key to the enduring status of the ordinary consulate at the very top of the pyramid lay in its restriction (amazingly enough never extended) to two per calendar year. Even the most distinguished candidate, with the most pressing claim, might simply have to wait a year--or perhaps two. No exception was ever made.

Two last texts, one eastern the other western, will sufficiently illustrate the supreme standing of the consulate in our period. First Jordanes' comment (written *ca* 551 in Constantinople) that it was "summum bonum primumque in mundo decus" (*Get.* 289). Secondly, that fascinating series of acclamations recorded at the meeting of the Roman senate that "debated" the acceptance of the Theodosian Code one day in December 438,[42] the consulate of Anicius Acilius Glabrio Faustus. "Fauste aveas," "Hail Faustus," cried the senate 17 times, followed by "bis consulem te," "a second consulate for you," 15 times. A little later, addressed to Paul the urban prefect (not in fact destined to reach the consulate), "Paule aveas" (12 times), followed by "consulem te" (11 times). Finally, the acclamations to Aetius, now consul for the second time and effective ruler of the West: "Aeti aveas" (15 times) and "*ter* consulem te" (13 times). Whatever his achievements, the highest honor that could be wished for a man was the consulate. And if he had won it already, what remained but to win it a second or even third time?

---

[39]For further examples of western consular dynasties, see below, p.7.

[40]τῶν κάμεν εὕρετο μίσθον, ἐλὼν ὑπατηΐδα ῥάβδον, 1.3 of the epigram originally inscribed on the church, preserved as *Anth.Pal.* i.4.

[41]Jones, *Later Roman Empire* I 543-45.

[42]Printed at the beginning of Mommsen's edition of the Code.

3. The End of the Consulate[43]

The eventual disappearance of the consulate has evoked little curiosity. When Anicius Faustus Albinus Basilius assumed the fasces at Constantinople in January 541 it was after all one thousand and forty-nine years on the traditional reckoning since L. Junius Brutus was elected the first consul (509 B.C.). Quite long enough, it might seem, for an office without power whose only duty now--at ruinous cost--was to provide games.

As a means of numbering the years it had always been cumbersome. A fully maintained consular list must have been required for even the most elementary calculations. And by the fifth century the delay in disseminating the names of new consuls--sometimes not until they were already out of office!--must have made it a constant source of error and confusion. A single example will suffice. Basilius cos. 480 was not announced in Egypt till (at earliest) April 481. The scribe of *BGU* XII 2155 may therefore be pardoned for supposing "that the newly announced name meant the consul of the current year" and so misdating his document.[44] For day-to-day purposes most people used the more convenient fifteen-year indiction cycle; by itself, however, this was useless for long term reckoning. In 537 Justinian laid down that all legal documents were henceforth to be dated not only by consuls and indiction number but also by his regnal year (*Nov.* 47), and the consulate did not long survive.[45]

But it would be quite wrong to suggest that the consulate was abolished because of its (long obvious) shortcomings as a chronological system. Hardly less of an oversimplification is the influential view of J.B.Bury,[46] that the honor simply became too expensive. Nor should we lightly assume that there was the same shortage of candidates in the West as there may have been in the East. Least of all should we see the fact that it lasted longer in the East as a sign of its greater health there.

There had in fact long been more gaps in the eastern consular fasti. Between 480 and 534 (the last western consul) there were 21 years without a consul in the East as against ten in the West.[47] Of the 47 western consuls in this period, 46 were private citizens, the 47th being Theoderic's heir-apparent Eutharic. Of the 36 eastern consuls only 21 were private citizens (counting kin of emperors with emperors). And of that 21 only nine were civilians, as against twelve generals. In the West all 46 private citizens were civilians (military commands being reserved for Goths). We may contrast the 53 western consuls in a corresponding period in the early fifth century (400-455): 18 imperial consulates, 16 for generals and only 19 for civilians, of whom about 14 were aristocrats.

So in the early fifth century Roman aristocrats filled just over a quarter of the western consulates, while by the turn of the sixth century they were filling 46 out of 47. In the reigns of Odoacar and Theoderic the burden of the consulate came to fall on the aristocracy of Rome as never before--or at least as not since the days of the Republic. There are no signs that this development was beyond their means or even against their wishes. Families like the Decii and Corvini continued to furnish consuls generation after generation: three sons of Basilius cos. 463 (himself a consul's son) became consul, six grandsons and at least three great-grandsons.[48]

---

[43]This section is a revised version of the concluding section of Cameron and Schauer, *JRS* 72 (1982) at 137-42. The classic study is that of Mommsen, *Ges.Schr.* VI 363-87.

[44]Bagnall and Worp, *BASP* 17 (1980) 7-8.

[45]On the competing chronological systems in use in early Byzantine Egypt see Bagnall and Worp, *GRBS* 20 (1979) 279-95; on the survival of the consulate, Worp, *BASP* 22 (1985) 359.

[46]*Later Roman Empire* II² (London 1923) 346-48.

[47]And it must be borne in mind that the lack of western consuls in 491-2 and 496-7 may have been due to the failure of Theoderic and Anastasius to come to terms; there is no reason to believe that there were no candidates in these years, as the apparently withdrawn consulship of Speciosus in 496 indicates: see *PLRE* II 1024-25. There may have been similar political reasons for the lack of western consuls in the 530's: see J. Sundwall, *Abhandlungen zur Geschichte des ausgehenden Römertums* (Helsinki 1919) 274.

[48]See the stemma in *JRS* 72 (1982) 143.

There is no indication that the Decii were finding it harder to make ends meet by the 530's. Indeed, by a lucky chance we have the letter in which King Athalaric congratulated Venantius cos. 508 on the promotion of his son Paulinus to what was to prove the last western consulate (534), and (more generally) on the honestly won wealth that had allowed him to finance the consulates of so many other sons already.[49] After his capture of Rome in 546, Totila called the senate together and reproached them for their ingratitude to the Goths after "amassing vast wealth" under both Theoderic and Athalaric[50]. If there were occasional gaps in the western fasti, this was not because the western aristocracy, though reduced in numbers, was becoming impoverished. It was just that, with no emperors and generals to help them out, there were not quite enough aristocrats to provide a consul every single year.

Nobody was forcing these families to continue so expensive a tradition. It is true that, for obvious reasons of convenience, the German kings of Italy took over most of the Roman administrative framework, but they cannot have had any motive to perpetuate so useless an office as the consulate. It was the aristocrats themselves who refused to let it lapse. There had been no western consuls for three years before Odoacar's deposition of the last legitimate western emperor Romulus in 476, and it would not have been at all surprising if the office had lapsed for good with what amounted to the political disappearance of the western empire. It seems to have been a senatorial embassy that included recognition of western consuls (from 480) among the terms Odoacar was negotiating with the Emperor Zeno.[51]

Nor is there any mystery why. Leading Roman senators were powerful landowners who wielded extensive power. It was essential for them to maintain their prestige in the traditional way as patrons and providers of public entertainments. The correspondence of Symmachus cos. 391 reveals what his less perceptive commentators have felt to be a disproportionate concern for the games he put on--two years of preparation and 2000 pounds of gold for the praetorian games of his son in 401.[52] Symmachus' *Letters* and the *History* of Ammianus also underline the importance to the aristocracy of the urban prefecture--no less vividly documented in the age of Odoacar and Theoderic by the careers revealed in the inscriptions of the Colosseum. Venantius cos. 484 served as urban prefect in his consular year, and in that capacity, on top of the expense of his consular games, rebuilt *de sumptu suo* the podium and arena of the Colosseum after an earthquake.[53] It was vital to the aristocracy to maintain good relations with the people of Rome, where the Gothic kings allowed them a free hand--well worth the expense of the consulate. This is why the western consulate continued to thrive until it was suspended by Justinian--and then made impossible by the destruction of senatorial wealth in the Gothic wars.

There is nothing to suggest that Odoacar or Theoderic discouraged such competitive personal expenditure among the Roman aristocracy. Quite the contrary. Here is King Theoderic's form letter (courtesy of Cassiodorus) to the new consul of the year:[54]

It becomes consuls to be generous. Do not be anxious about your private fortune, you who have elected to win the public favor by your gifts. It is for this cause that we make a difference between your dignity and all others. Other magistrates we appoint, even though they do not ask for the office. To the consulship we promote only those who are candidates for the dignity, those who know that their fortunes are equal to its demands; otherwise we might be imposing a burden rather

[49]Cassiodorus, *Var.* ix.23.

[50]Procopius, *BG* iii.21.2.

[51]See Mommsen, *Ges.Schr.* VI 380ff.; E.A. Thompson, *Romans and Barbarians* (Madison 1982) 64f. and Cameron's forthcoming paper "Odoacar's Consuls." According to Procopius (*BG* i.1.8), Odoacar took a third of the land of Italy for his followers. Whether or not this is true (cf. Jones, *Later Roman Empire* I 250-51), the continuing prosperity of the great landowners seems beyond question: see W. Goffart, *Barbarians and Romans* (Princeton 1980) 70-182, with Thompson, l.c.

[52]For the details see J.A. McGeachy, *Q. Aurelius Symmachus and the Senatorial Aristocracy of the West* (Chicago 1942) 103f.; S.Roda, *Commento storico al libro IX dell'epistolario di Q. Aur. Simmaco* (Pisa 1981) 44f., 116f. On the cost, Cameron, *GRBS* 25 (1984) 193-96.

[53]Chastagnol, *Le sénat romain sous le règne d'Odoacre* (Bonn 1966) 44.

[54]*Var.* vi.1, in the paraphrase of T. Hodgkin, *The Letters of Cassiodorus* (London 1886) 295.

than a favor. Enjoy therefore, in a becoming manner, the honor *which you wished for*. This mode of spending money is a legitimate form of bribery (*hic est ambitus qui probatur*). Be illustrious in the world, be prosperous in your life, leave an example for the happy imitation of your posterity.

And this was his exhortation to Felix cos. 511:[55]

> This is an occasion where extravagance earns praise; where it is a kind of virtue not to love one's own possessions; and where one gains in good opinion all that one loses in wealth.

In *Var.* iv.51 Theoderic congratulates Symmachus cos. 485 at length on rebuilding from his own pocket (among other decaying ancient monuments) the theatre of Pompey--and closes by reimbursing him from the royal treasury.

The situation was altogether different in the East. The aristocracy of Rome ruled supreme in Rome, far from king and court at Ravenna. But Constantinople was the permanent seat of both the emperor and his administration. The common assumption that eastern aristocrats were less wealthy than their western counterparts is no doubt true enough,[56] but it is not the only relevant factor.

First, there is one illuminating statistic. According to Procopius, the consulate cost at least 2000 pounds of gold, though he adds that only a small portion of this was the consul's own money, most being supplied by the emperor (*Anecd.* xxvi.12). In 401 Symmachus spent 2000 pounds of gold entirely from his own pocket, and a generation later the senator Maximus spent double that sum.[57] So not only were eastern consuls expected to spend far less than their western colleagues; it was common knowledge that the emperor footed most of the bill and deserved most of the credit.

Second (and more important), it was not prudent for a private citizen, however rich, to make the same sort of bid for popular favor in Constantinople as was customary in Rome. No eastern emperor would tolerate that sort of competition, least of all the insecure Justinian. A study of A.H.M. Jones's collection of eastern laws relating to the provision of games over nearly two centuries[58] suggests a conclusion not explicitly drawn by Jones: that, unlike the Ostrogothic kings, successive eastern governments did their best to discourage lavish private expenditure on public entertainments.[59] There was a persistent attempt to get first praetors and later consuls to contribute instead (or as well) to more essential public services, such as the aqueduct fund.

It was not only in the West that the consulate seemed in danger of extinction in the years after the fall of the western empire. In a reign of 17 years the Emperor Zeno (474-491) appointed only four subject consuls, taking two years for himself and entrusting a further two to his brother Longinus.

Not unconnected with his attitude to the ordinary consulate was Zeno's introduction of the honorary consulate, conferred in return for a contribution of 100 pounds of gold to the aqueduct fund. Holders were entitled to style themselves ex-consul, but not to give their name to a year--and had to yield in precedence to ordinary consuls of whatever year. An "unwise vulgarization of the supreme magistracy," according to Jones, which "probably hastened its decline."[60] Yet both emperor and consul were surely well satisfied; the consul acquired the highest of titles at a bargain rate and the treasury reaped the full benefit. It was only

---

[55]*Var.* ii.2, p.172 Hodgkin. *Var.* iii.39 actually reproaches Felix for being remiss in his consular largess. Asterius cos. 494 reflected ruefully on the cost of his consular games and their compensating immortality in a poem he wrote in his manuscript of Vergil (the Medicean) on the very day of the games: *Anth.Lat.* I.1², ed. A. Riese (1894), pp.18-19, with J.E.G. Zetzel, *Latin Textual Criticism in Antiquity* (New York 1981) 217-18.

[56]Jones, *Later Roman Empire* II (1964) 554-57, 706, 782-84.

[57]Olympiodorus, frag. 44 (*FHG* iv.67-8 = R.C. Blockley, *Fragmentary Classicising Historians of the Later Roman Empire* II (Liverpool 1983) 206-07, frag. 41.2), with Cameron, *GRBS* 25 (1984) 193-96. For the expenses of the consulate, cf. M.H. Hendy, *Studies in the Byzantine Monetary Economy c. 300-1450* (Cambridge 1985) 192-93.

[58]*Later Roman Empire* II 538-39.

[59]Cameron, *AJA* 86 (1982) 126.

[60]*Later Roman Empire* II 533.

the people who suffered, losing the games an ordinary consul would have provided at 10 or 20 times the cost. At Constantinople the honorary consulate soon became widespread.[61] Significantly enough, it is not attested and surely never existed at Rome.

Both Zeno and Justinian (who also appointed very few ordinary consuls) seem to have thought that it was a dangerous opportunity for self-advertisement to give a potential rival. Zeno suffered from two rebellions, led respectively by his brother-in-law Basiliscus and the generalissimo Illus--both of them former consuls (465, 478). Hypatius and Pompeius, the ill-fated beneficiaries of the Nika revolt against Justinian (532), had also both been consuls (500, 501). And (rightly or wrongly) Justinian eventually came to suspect that he had been played false by the two most conspicuous of his few consuls, Belisarius (535) and John the Cappadocian (538). While still a private citizen in 521, not yet sure of the succession, Justinian himself had given the most extravagant consular games remembered in Constantinople,[62] and he had no intention of encouraging emulation. In the first ten years of his reign Belisarius was the only citizen consul appointed.

Novel 105 of 28.xii.537, which reduces the scale and duration of consular games, has often been interpreted as a straightforward attempt "to rescue the endangered institution."[63] This is only half the story.

In the first place, we are not entitled to assume that the few consuls appointed in Justinian's first ten years (in the West as well as the East) reflect a lack of candidates rather than Justinian's reluctance to appoint them. It is true that *Novel* 105 gives as the emperor's motive the wish that all men he judged worthy of the consulate might in future be able to afford it. But in the preamble he also says that in the past some have used it to advertise their own generosity. And having laid down the modest, seven-day consular program he thinks appropriate, he goes on to state that these limits are under no circumstances to be exceeded. Anyone who does exceed them will have to pay a fine of 100 pounds of gold "for having destroyed the entire purpose of the law," that is to say "frightening off" others because of the expense. So no one, he repeats, is to exceed these limits, whether he is an official or a senator or holds no office at all. There are to be no exceptions whatever, he thunders yet again.

Clearly the problem was not just a lack of candidates able to afford the honor. Justinian was evidently afraid that there might be some only too ready to exceed his newly imposed limits.[64] The law was issued shortly before John the Cappadocian became consul in January 538, and no more consuls were appointed after John's fall in May 541. E. Stein long ago connected the reform of the consulate with John,[65] but failed to provide any satisfactory overall explanation of its purpose. There was no need for Justinian to change the law just to help John afford the consulate; he could simply have contributed to John's expenses, something emperors often did anyway. Nor is it obvious why the ambitious John should have wished to make it easier for others after him to hold the consulate. It is not John's motives we need to fathom, but Justinian's. And they are surely obvious enough: not merely to restore so popular an institution, but to restore it on an altogether more modest scale in the furtherance of two quite separate aims. First in the interests of economy, so that it could be afforded by private citizens without the huge imperial subsidy which Procopius tells us had been necessary in the past. And second, so that it no longer provided ambitious individuals with an opportunity of currying favor with the masses on a large scale.

The source of this last anxiety is not hard to identify. Belisarius' consulate had closely followed on his Vandalic triumph, the first triumph awarded to a subject for more than half a millennium. His consulate had been celebrated with extraordinary munificence:

[61]C. Courtois, "Ex-consul: observations sur l'histoire du consulat à l'époque byzantine," *Byzantion* 19 (1949) 37f.; cf. R. Guilland, *Byzantion* 24 (1954) 545f. and Cameron, *GRBS* 17 (1976) 183; for a list of those known down to 527, *PLRE* II 1246.

[62]*Chron.Min.* II 101. It is interesting that Marcellinus should specify that Justinian was the most extravagant of all *eastern* consuls, as though aware that his display might not have been thought exceptional at Rome. He goes on to say that Justinian spent 4000 pounds of gold (288,000 solidi)--the same figure spent on praetorian games by Maximus a century before at Rome (cf. above, n.57).

[63]Bury, *Later Roman Empire* II² 347.

[64]As rightly pointed out by Averil Cameron, *Fl. Cresconius Corippus: In Laudem Iustini Augusti Minoris libri IV* (London 1976) 175, cf. 196.

[65]*BZ* 30 (1929/30) 379-81; *Histoire du Bas-Empire* II (Paris/Bruges 1949) 461-62.

He was borne aloft by the captives, and as he was thus carried in his curule chair, he threw to the populace those very spoils of the Vandalic war. For the people carried off the silver plate *and golden girdles* and a vast amount of the Vandals' wealth of other sorts as a result of Belisarius' consulship, and it seemed that after a long interval of disuse an old custom was being revived.[66]

It is not surprising that the people were pleased if Belisarius distributed gold. In this context it is easy to see why *Novel* 105 expressly bars civilian (but not imperial) consuls from making distributions in gold. The restriction of the consular games (and so in effect the consulate itself) to the first week of January was also surely inspired by Belisarius' consulate. The first move of Belisarius' Italian expedition of 535 had been to seize Sicily, which he did in a rapid and brilliant campaign, entering Syracuse on December 31, the last day of his consular year. Procopius' account is instructive:

> There fell to Belisarius a piece of good fortune beyond the power of words to describe. For having received the dignity of the consulship because of his victory over the Vandals, while he was still holding this honor, and after he had won the whole of Sicily, on the last day of his consulship he marched into Syracuse, loudly applauded by the army and by the Sicilians *and throwing gold coins to all*. This coincidence, however, was not intentionally arranged by him, but it was a happy chance which befell the man, that after having recovered the whole of the island for the Romans he marched into Syracuse on that particular day; and so it was not in the senate house in Byzantium, as was customary,[67] but there that he laid down the office of the consuls and so became an ex-consul. Thus then did good fortune attend Belisarius (*BG* i.5.18-19).

Whether or not Belisarius did plan this spectacular conclusion to his consulate, it is plain that Procopius is defending him against precisely that charge. Justinian saw to it that no future consul should be able to exploit his office for twelve months--or while campaigning abroad. *Novel* 105 makes it clear that the new restrictions do not apply to the emperor. There was to be no question in future of ambitious subjects rivalling or even exceeding their emperor's generosity. By keeping the limits low and forcing consuls to pay all their expenses themselves, Justinian could easily outspend subject consuls whenever he chose to take the consulate himself.

On the face of it the reform worked. For the first time in more than half a century there were four consecutive subject consuls in the East: John the Cappadocian (538), Apion (539), Justinus (540) and Basilius (541). Why then no more thereafter? Not (it seems) because there were no more candidates, since Procopius implies that suspending the consulate was a deliberate act of policy by Justinian for which he was widely criticized:

> But although at first a consul was appointed for the Romans after a long interval, yet finally the people never saw that official even in a dream, and consequently mankind was being most cruelly pinched by a kind of poverty, since the emperor no longer provided his subjects with what they had been wont to receive (*Anecd.* xxvi.15).

The first "after a long interval" must be Belisarius' consulate of 535; that is to say Procopius is not counting Justinian's own second, third and fourth consulates in 528, 533 and 534. In his second (according to *Paschal Chronicle* 617.20B), the first since his accession in 527, Justinian made more spectacular distributions than any previous emperor, but there was apparently nothing special about the other two.

---

[66]Procopius, *BV* ii.9.15-16.

[67]This passage makes clear that (at this period anyway) eastern consuls were appointed for the full twelve months. There is no evidence that the suffect consulate ever existed at Constantinople. See Chapter 2, section 3, on the duration of the consulate.

Stein thought that since (on his view) the restoration of the consulate was John the Cappadocian's idea, Justinian naturally discontinued it on John's fall. There was surely more to it than this. None of John's three successors was the sort of man who, but for the new law, would not have been able to afford the consulate. Justinus was the emperor's own grandnephew, son of the great general Germanus and (as it must have seemed at the time) a possible future emperor. Apion came from one of the oldest and wealthiest of eastern families; Basilius from one of the oldest and wealthiest of western families. Whether or not they kept within the new limits for their games, they did not stint themselves in other ways. All three issued ivory commemorative diptychs, the only extant sequence of three consecutive consular diptychs.[68] And if Basilius unwittingly entertained on anything approaching the usual Roman scale, he is bound to have aroused Justinian's apprehensions.

There were also two external factors that may have influenced the emperor. First, there was Belisarius' triumphant return in 540 from what for the moment seemed another brilliantly successful victory. Justinian refused him a second triumph, but Belisarius both behaved and was treated like royalty, parading around the city with (for a subject) an unprecedented and exotic retinue--Vandals, Goths and Moors.[69] The other factor was the arrest and disgrace of John the Cappadocian on the charge of treason, soon after his return from a triumphant procession through the eastern provinces making his own unwise bid for popular favor, boasting of the way he was taxing the rich and flaunting his allegiance to the more rowdy Green circus faction.[70] Each of the two great ministers saw the other as his rival, and Justinian was suspicious of both. It would not be surprising if they had confirmed his worst fears about the dangers of the consulate. Justinian naturally became more anxious about the possibility of rivals for popular favor the more his own popularity declined. The continuation of wars on all fronts and increasing austerity at home left less money for games, and in the remaining 25 years of his reign Justinian never took the consulate again himself. If the emperor could not afford to be consul, it was clear that no one else could be allowed to.

The new Emperor Justin II won himself great popularity, skilfully exploited, by reverting to the tradition of taking the consulate in the first January after his accession (i.e. 566). In Corippus' panegyric (II.35lf.) the emperor himself is presented as proclaiming at his accession:[71]

> ditabo plebes opibus, nomenque negatum
> consulibus consul post tempora tanta novabo,
> gaudeat ut totus Iustini munere mundus.

At the "unexpected name of consul" the people burst out in joy! Every emperor followed suit down to Constans II in 642.[72] But the last subject consul, appropriately enough, was a senator of Rome, Anicius Faustus Albinus Basilius.

---

[68]For details, see Cameron and Schauer, *JRS* 72 (1982) 126f.
[69]Procopius, *BG* ii.1.
[70]John the Lydian, *De Magg.* iii.62f., with Stein, *Bas-Empire* II 480-83 and Cameron, *Circus Factions* (Oxford 1976) 102-03.
[71]See Averil Cameron's commentary here and elsewhere on Corippus' treatment of Justin's consulate.
[72]E. Stein, *Mélanges J. Bidez* (Brussels 1934) 894-96 = *Op.Min.Sel.* (Amsterdam 1968) 342-44.

Chapter 2

Proclamation and Dissemination

1. Proclamation

Up till the early years of the fifth century, the names of both consuls were always proclaimed simultaneously (and in the same sequence) as a pair.[1] Naturally it was the emperor who chose them. But what happened when there were two (or more) emperors? According to an influential study by J.R. Palanque, up till 383 (the death of Gratian) there was no ambiguity or problem: "le collège consulaire a été constitué chaque année par la volonté exclusive du premier Auguste".[2] But Mommsen had allowed three alternative possibilities: either the senior Augustus alone, or each in alternation, or both in some form of cooperation.[3] Seeck too believed in some form of alternation or cooperation, at any rate by the reign of Theodosius (379-395).[4]

Palanque's thesis is certainly unacceptable in its most extreme form. For example, the fasti of 318-320 clearly suggest cooperation between Constantine and Licinius (see § 4 below). When relations deteriorated, each proclaimed his own consuls (321-324). Between 307-313 there were often as many as three different sets of consuls proclaimed in the territories of different Augusti. Each was claiming recognition as Augustus, but hardly as senior Augustus.[5] Least of all can the usurper Magnentius have been making any such claim when he proclaimed his own consuls in 351-352. It is worth emphasizing that in all cases of rival proclamations up to the reign of Theodosius I, it is always both consuls that are proclaimed. Never do we find an emperor proclaiming just one consul, as though leaving the other place for his co-emperor.

It looks as if any and every ruling Augustus[6] might claim the right to proclaim consuls,[7] though in practice it was not a right that could be exercised without the cooperation of the rest of the imperial college, since there could only be two consuls in any one year. The senior Augustus might claim the decisive voice, but only if he was strong enough to dominate his colleagues. A good example of this is provided by the situation after the death of Constantine.

After a delay of nearly four months in which all dynastic rivals were eliminated, Constantine's three sons met and proclaimed themselves joint Augusti (9.ix.337). This meeting must also have decided the

---

[1]The basic work is Mommsen, "Die Consuldatirung des getheilten Reiches," *Neues Archiv* 14 (1890) 226-49 = *Ges.Schriften* VI (1910) 363-87.

[2]"Collégialité et partages dans l'empire romain aux IVe et Ve siècles," *REA* 46 (1944) 47-64 and 280-98, here 283. Contrast the more prudent verdict of W. Liebenam, *Fasti consulares* (Bonn 1909) 6: "wie die ernennung im 4 Jahrh. geschah, wenn mehrere kaiser regierten, ist öfters problematisch."

[3]*Ges.Schr.* VI 363-64, unfortunately without detailed argumentation.

[4]*Geschichte des Untergangs der antiken Welt* V (1919) 183, 506-07.

[5]Note also the plural in the provisional formula *consules quos iusserint dd.nn.Augusti* (308, 311, 317).

[6]We are adopting here Palanque's distinction between ruling emperors with a specific sphere of command, and "Augusti sans terre" (op.cit. 48f.), sons elevated to the rank of Augustus to mark them out as heirs presumptive but with no territory: for example (at the beginning of their reigns) Gratian, Valentinian II, Arcadius, Honorius, Theodosius II. Palanque's categories (including his mistaken theory about the status of Constans) were applied to the coinage by M. Woloch, "Indications of Imperial Status on Roman Coins A.D.337-383," *Numismatic Chronicle* 7 ser. 6 (1966) 171-78. Note already J.W.E. Pearce's observation that "By the time of Valentinian I it had become a fixed convention that a reigning Emperor always had a "broken" legend" (*Num.Chron.* 5 ser. 14 [1934] 115). As he points out, that the unbroken legend does not (as Alföldi had originally suggested) imply mere juniority is proved by the case of Theodosius I, who was junior to both Gratian and Valentinian II on his accession, but is never shown with unbroken legend.

[7]Just as every Augustus could issue laws (Barnes, *New Empire* 48, nn.10-11), another privilege mistakenly restricted by

consuls for the coming year, contrary to all precedent *none* of the new Augusti, but two private citizens, probably generals.[8] The obvious explanation is that the brothers could not agree[9] which of the three[10] should take the two available places. In effect that must mean that Constantine, the eldest, could not persuade Constans, the youngest, to wait his turn. By the following year the situation had been resolved-- but in Constans' favor, not Constantine's. The consuls for 339 were Constantius and Constans, and barely a year later[11] Constantine was dead, destroyed by Constans. So the consuls of 339 appear to show the senior Augustus overruled and excluded by his junior colleagues.

After this it was not likely that the aggressive Constans would allow the new senior Augustus Constantius to monopolize consular nominations. Of the consuls appointed between 340 and Constans' death in 350, those of 344 were both easterners, and those of 346 (the two emperors) were clearly proclaimed by Constantius, since Constans refused to recognize them in the West. But in 347 and 348 we find one eastern and one western consul:

> 347: Rufinus PPO Ital. and Eusebius eastern MVM
> 348: Philippus PPO Or. and Salia western MVM.

And in 341 and 349 it looks as if both consuls were westerners:

> Marcellinus PPO Ital. and Probinus PVR 345-6.
> Limenius PVR and PPO Ital. and Catullinus, ex PPO Ital. and PVR.[12]

It can at least be said that Constans' current PPO was consul prior on no fewer than three occasions during this period. It is difficult to doubt that he was playing a part in the consular nominations. The extent of this part surely exceeds Palanque's concession that the senior Augustus might occasionally act "pour être agréable à son collègue, sans que celui-ci ait été appelé à faire des propositions" (referring to the appearance of two kinsmen of Theodosius as consuls while Gratian was senior Augustus).

We might expect to find similar results during the joint reign of Valentinian and Valens, another pair of emperors of almost equal standing who ruled the West and East respectively more or less independently. Like Constans, Valens must surely have felt entitled to use the consulate as a reward for his most deserving prefects and generals. Excluding joint consulates of the emperors themselves (365, 368, 370, 373), we find:

> 366: Valentinian's son Gratian and mag.peditum Dagalaifus
> 367: Lupicinus and Iovinus, mag.equitum in East and West
> 369: Valens' son Valentinianus Galates and magister equitum Victor
> 371: Gratian II and Valentinian's PPO Probus
> 372: Valens' PPO and mag.peditum, Modestus and Arinthaeus
> 374: Gratian III and Valentinian's MVM Equitius

Palanque to the senior Augustus, at any rate under the tetrarchy (p.50).

[8]Ursus and Polemius: see Barnes, *Constantine and Eusebius* 398, n.17.

[9]We might compare the way they delayed their proclamation as Augusti till they had eliminated the competition; that way they did not have to eliminate fellow Augusti.

[10]We reject Seeck's view, elaborated by Palanque (pp.56-58) and now generally accepted (e.g. Stein, *Bas-Empire* I [1959] 131-32, 484-85; Paschoud, *Zosime* I [1971] 245) that the settlement of 337 divided the empire between only Constantine and Constantius, with Constans remaining an "Auguste sans terre." This claim relies on a dubious interpretation of the latest and least reliable of our five ancient sources (Zos. 2.39.2); the others all clearly imply threefold division, as correctly assumed by Barnes, *Phoenix* 34 (1980) 160-66. Constans must already have had a comitatus of his own as Caesar of Italy, Africa and Illyricum since 335, and it is inconceivable that he agreed to give it up on Constantine's death. Indeed, it was Constans and Constantius who divided Dalmatius' portion between them, while Constantine was left with the same territory as in 335 (Barnes, *Constantine and Eusebius* 262). The emphasis in the modern literature on the "seniority" of Constantine II obscures his obvious failure to sieze the reins of power, well illustrated in the matter of the consular nominations for 338-340.

[11]Note too that not even in 340 did Constantine become consul.

[12]The possibility that Probinus and Catullinus had served Constantius in the East cannot be excluded, but the extant evidence for their careers is entirely western. It should be borne in mind that Constantius did not visit the West till two years after

It looks as if Valentinian was responsible for 366, 371 and 374, Valens for 369 and 372, with both naming one each for 367. Once again, the extent of their cooperation goes beyond what Palanque allowed. Moreover, in one year at least we have more than just names to go on. In 372 our most reliable contemporary evidence, Egyptian papyri and Roman inscriptions, bear witness to unusually early dissemination in Egypt (three papyri with the new consuls as early as January or February) and unusually late dissemination in Rome (p.c. in use as late as 18 March). This is the exact converse of the usual situation. But if it were Valens who proclaimed these two eastern consuls in person, all would be explained.[13] For he was wintering at Antioch in January 372, close to Egypt and (in winter) a long way from Rome by land. It should be noted that, with only one exception, whichever emperor it was still proclaimed both consuls.

Between 376 and 378 Valens was senior Augustus, but in 377 we find Gratian IV and Merobaudes, western magister peditum already under Valentinian. We know from Ausonius (*Grat.actio* 9; 10; 12) that it was (as we should expect) Gratian (senior Augustus 378-383) who appointed both consuls for 379, Ausonius and Olybrius. But in 381, 382 and 383 we find a new departure. It seems that Gratian and Theodosius nominated one consul each: Gratian the two Syagrii and Merobaudes (II), all men with exclusively western careers; and Theodosius his uncle Eucherius, his more distant kinsman Antonius[14] and his general Saturninus. That the three last-named all owed their consulates to Theodosius happens to be expressly stated by Themistius, in his congratulatory speech on Saturninus' consulate (*Or.* 16). Theodosius "transferred to a private citizen the honor offered to himself by his partner in empire" (202d), repeating the point a few lines later: "no one but Theodosius transferred the consulate allotted to himself to another" (203a). The terminology used, "offered" (προσενενηγμένην) and "allotted" (λαχοῦσαν) might be held consistent with Palanque's thesis, but the fact remains that Theodosius evidently could and did transfer to someone else this consulate that (on whatever basis[15]) was rightfully his. Furthermore, Themistius goes on to claim that, by so doing, Theodosius "has numbered the name of his general after those of his uncle and kinsman, without any interval [i.e. in consecutive years] joining excellence to relationships," for he had "previously honored the proximity of his kin" (203d). Whatever the constitutional position, clearly Theodosius was perceived as having directly appointed one consul each year from 381-383.

On Gratian's death (383) the young Valentinian II (elevated in 375 at the age of four) was theoretically senior Augustus, but in practice Theodosius soon took over the role.[16] Valentinian's name was allowed to stand first in imperial legislation,[17] but as early as 384 we find two easterners proclaimed consul (Richomer and Clearchus), as again in 389 (Timasius and Promotus).[18] From now on Palanque regarded Theodosius as senior Augustus, and would not allow Valentinian any say in the selection of consuls.[19] But in 384 the westerner Praetextatus was designated as colleague to Theodosius' son Arcadius, and when he died another westerner, the magister militum Bauto, was appointed. As we shall see (section 2), Praetextatus died so late in the year that there would not have been time to consult with Theodosius (then in Constantinople). There can be no doubt that Bauto was not merely recommended but directly appointed by Valentinian. The same pattern was followed in 386 too: Theodosius' other son Honorius and Evodius, PPO of Gaul; in 387 Valentinian with Eutropius, last in office as prefect of Illyricum; in 390 Valentinian again with Neoterius, prefect of Gaul; 391 the eastern PPO Tatianus and the westerner Symmachus. The distribution of consuls between East and West between 384 and 391 may thus be

---

Constans' death.

[13]It is also possible that cos. in one or more of the papyri is an error for p.c., cf. comments *ad annum*.

[14]On the relationship, see J.R. Martindale, *Historia* 16 (1967) 254-56.

[15]Two pages later (205bc) Themistius adds the further information that the consulate Theodosius made over to Saturninus was to have commemorated his *quinquennalia*.

[16]Palanque, 284-85.

[17]Though he is treated on the coinage "as standing in the same relation to [Theodosius] as his own son Arcadius" (J.W.E. Pearce, *RIC* IX [1953] xx; cf.xvii).

[18]And 388, but this was a response to Maximus' usurpation in the West, and cannot be counted in the sequence shared with Valentinian.

[19]Note that in the original (1928) text of his *Histoire du Bas-Empire* I 220 (= German ed. p.339) E. Stein wrote that "depuis les dernières années du IVe siècle, chacun des deux gouvernements nomme régulièrement l'un des deux consuls." The 1959 revision

represented as following: 384 EE; 385 WE; 386 EW; 387 WE; 389 EE; 390 WW; 391 EW. Theodosius appointed both consuls twice, Valentinian once; but usually they appointed one each. Valentinian was the symbol of imperial power in the West, and it was vital that Theodosius should publicly maintain his prestige.[20]

Mommsen was right after all. Well before the death of Theodosius in 395, there was a clear tendency for East and West to name one consul each, presumably by prior arrangement in time for joint proclamation, since there is no sign yet of the separate proclamation that was to become the norm in the fifth century. The clearest proof is provided by the conduct of the two western usurpers of Theodosius' reign. Unlike Magnentius in the 350's, both proclaimed only one consul: Maximus, himself in 388; Eugenius, Nicomachus Flavianus in 394. Theodosius signalled his repudiation by proclaiming two consuls rather than the pair to the nominees of his new colleagues. The case of 393 is a little more complex. The western formula was Theodosius III et Eugenius; the eastern Theodosius III et Abundantius. Did Theodosius at first recognize Eugenius? Hardly, to judge from his own rival proclamation, followed by the elevation of Honorius to the rank of Augustus on 23 January. Did Eugenius add Theodosius' name to his own simply in the hope of obtaining recognition by flattery? The truth is surely that Theodosius was already known to be consul designate for 393 when Eugenius assumed the purple on 22 August 392. It was almost inevitable that he would take the consulate to celebrate his third *quinquennalia*, especially since he had missed the one destined to celebrate his first when he yielded place to Saturninus in 383. So Eugenius simply did what Valentinian would have done if he had still been alive: he proclaimed the expected Theodosius III together with a nomination of his own. Theodosius made his answer clear by adding another name to the proclamation he had originally planned.

It is important to establish this point, since it helps to explain the development of separate proclamations in East and West in the fifth century. For Palanque, this was an entirely new development of the post-Theodosian age;[21] he speculates about its introduction at some moment in the cold war between East and West in 395-9. So too E. Demougeot, in the fullest study so far published of the "division" of the empire in the years after 395: "Ce fut encore peut-être à la demande de Stilichon qu'Arcadius renonça à son droit de choisir les consuls comme *Augustus senior*..."[22] Few less likely moments could be imagined for such a concession. In fact no major change in procedure took place at all, whether in 395 or 399. For several years eastern and western consuls continued to be proclaimed simultaneously, as in the 380's. When Claudian was writing his panegyric on Honorius' third consulate for 1 January 396 (presumably late in 395) he already knew that Arcadius was to be his colleague. When writing his panegyric on Theodorus for 1 January 399, he knew that Eutropius' name had not been accepted in the West. Similarly in 400 it seems clear that the decision not to recognize Aurelian's name had already been taken by 1 January. In fact right down to 411 there seems no reason to doubt that both names either were or could have been proclaimed simultaneously as in the past.[23] The only unusual feature is that Stilicho several times refused to recognize the consuls proclaimed by his political enemies at the eastern court, though the East continued to recognize western consuls in the usual way. It was not till 411 that we find either court proclaiming its own consul without waiting for the other.

Recent papyrus finds have revealed that in 411 the eastern court proclaimed a joint consulate of Honorius IX and Theodosius IV--in error, for Honorius did not in fact take his ninth consulate until the following year, 412 (so at any rate all western consular lists).[24] In 1978 Bagnall and Worp suggested (without explanation) that the "first" Honorius IX was cancelled, and in 1979 Cameron speculated that the cancellation was made because of the confusion caused by the late proclamation. That is to say, we assumed that both proclamation and cancellation were western. Yet confusion would surely be worse

---

(by Palanque) refers to Palanque's study of 1944 without comment.

[20]At any rate so long as his own sons were minors.

[21]"Rien n'indique que Théodose ait procédé, de son vivant ou par testament, à ce partage du consulat" (pp.286-87).

[22]*De l'unité à la division de l'empire romain: 395-410* (Paris 1951) 161.

[23]For example, most eastern consuls who were recognized at all are attested as early as January on Roman inscriptions.

[24]In 412 both East and West proclaimed Honorius IX and Theodosius V, the East ignoring the fact that they had already

compounded by cancellation of a consulate once proclaimed, nor is there any parallel for cancellation of a consulate *except* in association with *damnatio memoriae* (e.g. Proculus in 325; Eutropius in 399; Vitalian in 520). R.W. Burgess[25] has pointed out that the evidence for this premature Honorius IX of 411 is exclusively eastern. It is the result, not of western cancellation, but of eastern error.

How did the eastern court come to make such a mistake? Burgess suggests that it arose from an earlier misapprehension, namely that Honorius was planning to celebrate his *vicennalia* (due in 412) a year early so as to synchronize with Theodosius' *decennalia*. It was established practice for emperors to advance such celebrations so as to synchronize with a co-emperor's vota years (see section 5), and according to Marcellinus (s.a. 411), "Theodosius iunior decennalia, Honorius Romae vicennalia dedit." In view of the Gothic occupation of Italy, it is hardly likely that the timid Honorius ventured the journey to Rome for such a purpose, and it may be doubted whether he celebrated his *vicennalia* at all during such a crisis. But Marcellinus' entry may reflect eastern expectations (perhaps based on a provisional agreement), especially since solidi were minted at Constantinople for Theodosius' *decennalia* and Honorius' *vicennalia*, stylistically and typologically very similar.[26] Since the *dies imperii* of both Honorius and Theodosius fell in January, it seems logical to suppose that both issues were struck in December 410.

This (Burgess suggests) was the origin of the second error. For it was common practice for emperors to hold the consulate in their vota years, especially in conjunction with co-emperors (see again section 5). But the eastern misapprehension cannot have been quite so simple as this. For the first law of the year, *CTh* 5.16.33, is dated to the Ides (or some day preceding the Ides) of June, Theodosius IV *et qui fuerit nuntiatus*. This section of the Code is badly damaged, and an instance of the common corruption of IAN/IVN cannot be excluded, in which case the date would be in early January rather than early June. But in either case we would be faced with a unilateral proclamation, the first on record.

So whatever misapprehension the eastern court may have entertained about Honorius' *vicennalia* and the likelihood of an impending consulate, they did *not* simply proclaim Honorius IX in January 411. It seems clear that they did not receive the usual notification from the western court (presumably because of the dislocation in Italy), and, rather than guess, they took the unprecedented step of proclaiming the eastern consul alone, adding the cumbersome saving formula "and whoever shall have been announced." The surprise is that, having thus far reacted so cautiously and carefully, when they finally made a proclamation it should have been incorrect. The simplest guess is that they received a letter announcing Honorius' intentions for 412 which they misinterpreted as referring to the current year, and hastily proclaimed Honorius IX at once.

It was an embarrassing error--and the source of endless confusion in consular dates for 411-412 (see the comments *ad annos* and in the Critical Appendix). But there is no sign that steps were taken to prevent a recurrence, no sign of an effort by each court to notify the other in good time for a restoration of simultaneous proclamation. On the contrary, it was apparently decided that unilateral proclamations were simpler. The very next year opened with the formula Theodosius V *e.q.f.n.*, and such formulas immediately became standard (see the table on p.27). Simultaneous proclamation of eastern and western consuls together from each court was in fact never restored.

As the fifth century progressed, the dissemination of the new consular names took longer and longer (section 7), not only between East and West but even within the two halves of the empire. By mid century it was often quite late in the year before the new western name first appeared in eastern dates. As a consequence of the increasing bureaucratic delays, we find as many as four different formulas in use in (say) fifth or sixth century Egypt: first by the postconsulate (p.c.) of the preceding year; then either by the new eastern consul *et qui (de Occidente) nuntiatus fuerit* or by just the one local name without any qualification; and finally by both new names together. But despite all provisional formulas, the consular pair remained the theoretical ideal. The more carefully executed consular lists continue to include both

proclaimed Honorius IX the year before. For full details, see commentary *ad annum*.

[25]*ZPE* 65 (1986) 211-21.

[26]Cf. A.A. Boyce, "A New Solidus of Theodosius II and Other Vota Solidi of the Period," *Festal and Dated Coins of the Roman Empire; Four Papers, Numismatic Notes and Monographs* 153 (New York 1965) 43-45, with the comments of W.E. Kaegi,

names, and the p.c. formula normally likewise includes both names of the previous year, however late the second was added (except in 496 and 503). As a consequence, it is necessary to survey the totality of the evidence for a given year before reaching any conclusion about the non-recognition of a western consul in the East on the basis of the laws and the papyri, especially if there are no laws and papyri from the end of the year itself.

There are, however, a number of years in the fifth and even sixth centuries when the consuls were again proclaimed as pairs from only one court. This is proved by the following three considerations: (a) in each case the consuls (if citizens) are either both eastern or both western; (b) the names appear in the same sequence in both east and west; and (c) there is none of the usual evidence that one name was published separately from or earlier than the other. In these years we must conclude that, after consultation, one court allowed the other to nominate both consuls, presumably on condition that the favor would be reciprocated when desired. The reason may have varied--one emperor anxious to honor two subjects (or one with himself), another unable to find even one worthy, willing or wealthy enough. These years are as follows:

417	W	Honorius XI et Constantius II
419	E	Monaxius et Plinta
425	E	Theodosius Aug. XI et Valentinianus Aug.
427	E	Hierius et Ardabur
429	E	Florentius et Dionysius
436	E	Isidorus et Senator
437	W	Aetius II et Sigisvultus
443	W	Maximus II et Paterius
446	W	Aetius III et Symmachus
450	W	Valentinianus Aug. VII et Avienus
454	E	Aetius et Studius
457	E	Constantinus et Rufus
464	E	Rusticius et Olybrius
467	E	Pusaeus et Iohannes
476	E	Basiliscus Aug. II et Armatus
488	W	Dynamius et Sifidius
492	E	Anastasius Aug. et Rufus
494	W	Asterius et Praesidius
500	E	Patricius et Hypatius
512	E	Paulus et Moschianus
522	W	Symmachus et Boethius
530	W	Lampadius et Orestes

2. Designation

Despite the often protracted use of postconsulates, there seems no reason to suppose that the consuls actually assumed office later than the first of January in those years--at least as a rule.[27] After all, their principal duty was to provide games that began on that very day. They must also have had a fair amount of advance warning; even the richest would need some time to raise the cash for those games. In fourth century Rome, where the praetorian games were still the big occasion, praetors were designated ten years in advance to allow the necessary budgeting.[28] Consuls too must have wanted as much notice as

---

[27]In times of political turmoil, of course, exceptions could arise: see 307, 308, 311 and 317.
[28]*CTh* 6.4.13.2 (361); 6.4.22 (373); 6.4.21 (372). Cf. above, p.8.

possible, though there is no evidence of formal designation years in advance. Both L. Aur. Avianius Symmachus and Vettius Agorius Praetextatus died as *consul designatus*, in 376 and 384, both apparently only a month or so before taking office in 377 and 385 respectively. Seeck argued[29] that in both years it was an emperor who replaced the dead man (Gratian in 377, Arcadius in 385), observing:

"cum consulatus functio eum apparatum requireret, qui nisi ab imperatore brevi tempore confici non posset, honorem demortui in privatum conferre ultimis anni mensibus iam non licebat."

He may well have been right about Gratian in 377, but in 384 it must have been Bauto who was the replacement, since Arcadius, promoted Augustus on 19.i.383, might have been expected to hold his first consulate in 384, and must surely have been one of the original pair designated for 385.

D. Vera points out that the unnamed conqueror of the Sarmatae praised by Symmachus in *Rel.* 47 must be Bauto.[30] The expedition took place in the autumn, and Vera argues that the games to which the *Rel.* alludes are those that began on 2 December. While listing the honors the emperors have heaped on Bauto, Symmachus says not a word of the supreme honor of the consulate, which he could hardly have failed to do if Bauto had already then been consul designate. It follows (as Vera acutely observes) that Praetextatus was still alive at the time. It cannot have been till after this (though obviously not long after) that Praetextatus died and Bauto was unexpectedly designated consul in his place--evidently by Valentinian, since there would not have been time to consult with Theodosius in Constantinople, and Bauto was duly inaugurated on 1 January in Milan, as we know from Augustine, who pronounced the consular panegyric that day in his capacity as professor of rhetoric.[31]

Symmachus cannot have been designated long when he died, since it was only in the course of 376 that the senate successfully petitioned Gratian so to honor him.[32] It is interesting to discover from this instance that the initiative might come from the senate in this way.

Constantius' magister officiorum Fl. Eugenius also died as consul designate, probably in 349. His posthumous cursus begins: *ex praefecto praetorio consuli designato magistro officiorum* (*ILS* 1244), implying by the sequence that the (clearly honorary) rank of PPO came later than his designation as consul. But that need not imply designation earlier than (say) September, 349.

A rather longer period of designation is implied in the case of Lollianus *qui et* Mavortius, to whom, as *ordinario consuli designato*, Firmicus Maternus dedicated his astrological work *Mathesis*. The problem here is that Lollianus did not become consul till 355, while the *Mathesis* was undoubtedly written before Constantine's death in May, 337. There seems no objection to the usual solution: that Lollianus was designated consul by Constantine, but the designation was revoked by his successors.[33] If so, then he must have been designated as early as Spring, 337.[34] Cyrus cos. 441 is addressed as *PPO et consuli designato* in a law of 5.iv.440 (*CJ* 1.14.7). Ausonius' designation for 379 is known to have taken place in September, 378.[35]

There are three other references that help to fill out the picture. Olympiodorus describes the future Emperor Constantius III as πάλαι δησιγνάτος when he entered on his first consulship in 414 (frag.23), but with no indication how long.[36] Vincomalus, the future consul of 453, is described as ὕπατος δησιγνάτος in a document dated 13.iii.452 (*ACO* II.1.3.120). This is the more interesting in that, despite such early designation, Egypt was nonetheless dating by the postconsulate of 452 as late as 17.ii.453. And according to Theophanes (a.m.5988, p.140.6 de Boor), it was in 496 that Anastasius honored John the Scythian and John

[29]*Symmachi quae supersunt* (Berlin 1883) xliii-xliv.
[30]*Commento storico alle Relationes di Q. Aurelio Simmaco* (Pisa 1981) 341-42; *Koinonia* 7 (1983) 140.
[31]*Contra litt. Petiliani* 3.25-30; cf. P. Courcelle, *Recherches sur les Confessions de S. Augustin*[2] (Paris 1968) 79f.
[32]Seeck, l.c.
[33]Perhaps specifically by Constans, whose influence on the consular nominations for 338-340 we have already noted. It may be significant that Lollianus had to wait till after Constans' death before finally winning his consulate.
[34]T.D. Barnes, *JRS* 65 (1975) 40; cf. *PLRE* I 513.
[35]Seeck, *Regesten* 250.
[36]And to add to the uncertainty, like Latin *olim*, πάλαι can in effect mean "recently" as well as "a long time ago".

the Hunchback with the consulate for their successful suppression of the Isaurian rebellion. Now Anastasius himself took 497; the two Johns had to wait till 498 and 499 respectively. If we can press both Theophanes' date and his linking of the two names (which is doubtful), it looks as if Anastasius designated both men well in advance.

In some cases it was certainly a last-minute decision. For example, the consulate for 401 was given to the Gothic general Fravitta as a reward for defeating his fellow Goth Gainas, in a battle off the Thracian Chersonnese dated (by Marcellinus s.a.) to 27.xii.400. Since the man previously designated for 401 was none other than Gainas,[37] a replacement was certainly needed. A rather different case concerning a general is Saturninus' consulate of 383, which Themistius, in his speech congratulating Saturninus (*Or.* 16, 203a), claims to have been originally destined for the Emperor Theodosius himself. This time it was not a victory but the Gothic peace treaty of 3.x.382 that won Saturninus his consulate:[38] pointedly to renounce his own claim in Saturninus' favor was a clever way for Theodosius to emphasize the importance of the much criticised Gothic settlement--and deflect criticism from himself. At any rate, also a last-minute appointment.[39]

In the first three centuries the emperors often designated themselves, sometimes years in advance, from the moment they laid down their current consulate. For example, Claudius, cos. III in 43 and cos. IV in 47, appears as *cos. III designatus IV* in 44-46 (*ILS* 204; *CIL* X 1558); Gallienus as *cos. VI designatus VII* in 264-265 (*ILS* 542-543).[40] There is no trace of this practice in the late empire.

3. Duration of the Consulate

According to Polemius Silvius (*CIL* I² p.263), writing in the middle of the fifth century, the ordinary consuls laid down the *fasces* on 21 April, and we know from Symmachus (*Epp.* 6.40) that in 401 the suffect consul was expected[41] to preside at the games given for the Natalis Urbis Romae on the 21 April. It might therefore seem that up till the mid fifth century, the ordinary consuls held office for less than four months. According to E. Stein, it was not till the second half of the fifth century that "la durée du consulat ordinaire fut étendue à l'entière année"[42] and the suffect consulate abolished. There is no basis for either of these propositions--still less for Stein's arbitrary connection of both measures with the eastern emperor Zeno.[43]

In all probability ordinary consuls held office for the entire year already by the mid fourth century.[44] There are two relevant passages in Ausonius' *Gratiarum actio*, delivered before Gratian at Trier near the end of Ausonius' own consular year of 379. The speech would ordinarily have been given at the beginning of the year, but Gratian was far away in Sirmium at the time, and could not be in Trier before September.[45] First, Ausonius quotes from the beginning of Gratian's letter of appointment: "cum de consulibus in annum creandis solus mecum volutarem..."(§ 9, 43). It could be argued that this need only mean "for the year" in the sense "of the year," rather than "for the entire year." But then there is § 18, 82, where Ausonius describes how Gratian hastened across the frontiers of the empire "ut consulem tuum, quamvis desideratus, anticipes," well rendered by Evelyn White "to surprise (how welcome the surprise!) your own consul while still in office." This is not an otherwise attested sense for *anticipare*, but the context clearly requires

[37]So at least we infer from Theodoret, *HE* 5.32.6.
[38]*Or.*16, 208af.; see G.Dagron, *Travaux et Mémoires* 3 (1968) 105.
[39]A man appointed so late in the year would have little time to raise the cash for his games or make the necessary arrangements. Presumably the emperor helped out.
[40]See B.W. Jones, *Domitian and the Senatorial Order* (MemPhilSoc 132, Philadelphia 1979) 56-58.
[41]In the event the unfortunate man was involved in a street accident on the way to the games and was carried off with a broken leg--a dreadful omen, remarks Symmachus.
[42]*Histoire du Bas-Empire* II (1949) 68; cf. also I.2 417 n.99.
[43]As we have seen (p.11, n.67), there is no evidence that the suffect consulate ever existed at Constantinople.
[44]So, without arguing the point at any length, Chastagnol, *Rev.hist.* 219 (1958) 236.
[45]Seeck, *Regesten* 252.

something of the sort. At all events, it is certain from the tenor of the speech as a whole and especially its concluding sections that Ausonius was addressing his thanks to the emperor as consul still in office.

For the East we have John Chrysostom's *Homilia in Eutropium consulem* (*PG* 52.391f.), which clearly implies that the eunuch was still consul at the time of his disgrace and deposition in August 399. And Synesius *Epp.* 61 implies that Aurelian cos. 400 was still in office when Synesius left Constantinople in September of the year[46] (as too does his *de providentia* 2.4). A law of the Emperor Zeno distinguishes the new title of honorary consul from those "qui per annale tempus consularium editione munerum gloriantur."[47] Lastly, we have the case of Belisarius, who is expressly stated to have laid down his consulate on the last day of his year (Procopius, *BG* i.5.19; cf. above, p.11).

Stein's mistake was to assume that the continued existence of suffect consuls implied a curtailed tenure of the ordinary consulate. For by the death of Constantine the suffect consulate had lost more than its earlier parity with the ordinary consulate. Once Constantine had transferred the nomination of suffects to the senate, the nature of the office must have changed entirely. Teenagers[48] nominated by the senate could not possibly take over the duties of men singled out by the emperor for the highest honor at his disposal. On two occasions in the early fourth century one of the ordinary consuls seems to have been disgraced and removed from office (in 325 and 344; cf. also notes to 359). On both occasions he was replaced, not by a devalued suffect, but by a new ordinary consul,[49] obviously appointed by the emperor.

The function of the new, devalued suffects was surely no more than to stand in for the ordinary consuls on ceremonial occasions when they could not be present in Rome themselves. Their duties were surely limited to the city of Rome.[50] During the fourth and fifth centuries the ordinary consuls were normally praetorian prefects in office, generals on active service or (of course) the emperors themselves. Their other duties must often have made it difficult for them to get to Rome for their inaugurations. In fact it became normal for the consul to be inaugurated at court, in the nearest convenient capital. We happen to known from Claudian's panegyrics that the consuls of 396, 398, 399 and 400 all held their inaugurations at Milan. Ausonius held his at Trier, though his colleague Olybrius, a Roman aristocrat, may well have held his at Rome. In another passage[51] Claudian claims (writing in 404) that Rome has been visited by an emperor only three times in the last 100 years (in fact by Constantine in 312, by Constantius II in 353 and by Theodosius in 389).

The year Symmachus mentions the suffect who set out so inauspiciously to preside at the Natalis Urbis games was 401, when the western consul was Vincentius, PPO of the Gauls from 397 till at least 9 December 400,[52] and so probably absent from Rome in the early part of his consular year. When the consul was a Roman aristocrat, resident in Rome for much of the year, there would have been no call for a suffect. Suffects were no doubt duly nominated each year, but did not necessarily serve. It is perhaps no coincidence that there is no mention of suffects in our sources for Ostrogothic Italy. Not because (as Stein supposed) they had been formally abolished, but simply because the western consul was now invariably a Roman aristocrat, in no need of a stand-in.

What then of Polemius Silvius' statement that the ordinary consuls laid down their fasces on 21 April? Polemius wrote in mid fifth century Gaul,[53] and though he did his best to produce an up to date calendar, he may never have been to Rome and had no way of knowing how many of the entries he copied from his source were still operative. As Chastagnol has put it: "la déposition des faisceaux par les consuls ordinaires est toute théorique et n'a de sens--purement symbolique--qu'à Rome; c'est probablement le 21

---

[46]See Cameron, "Earthquake 400," forthcoming.
[47]*CJ* 12.3.3 (undated; wrongly assigned by Chastagnol, *Rev.hist.* 219 [1958] 236 n.4, to 452).
[48]For their age already by the end of Constantine's reign, see above, p.2.
[49]As proved by the fact that in each case the new consul's name was at once added to the consular formula of they year, something that had not happened to a suffect for more than a century (above, p.3).
[50]So Chastagnol, l.c.
[51]*VI cons.Hon.* 392-97.
[52]*PLRE* II 1169.
[53]Mommsen, *Ges.Schriften* VII (1909) 635-36.

avril que les consuls ordinaires se retiraient au IIIe siècle et on a conservé jusqu'à la fin de l'Empire d'Occident la formule alors en usage."

4. Seniority

There were clearcut rules for determining seniority between the two consuls: (1) Augusti and Caesars took precedence over all subjects; (2) Augusti took precedence over Caesars and senior over junior Augusti; between subjects (3) former consuls (suffect consulate not counting) took precedence; otherwise (4) the senior emperor would decide whose name would be entered first in the fasti. Ausonius (cos. 379) several times refers to the fact that, thanks to the favor of Gratian, he was "prior renuntiatus" (*Grat.Actio* 3; 9; 12; *carm*. 3.37)--as consular documents of the year bear out. Gratian's reason, he adds, was that Ausonius was already senior to his future colleague Olybrius as PPO (ib. 12).

In only two years does there seem to have been uncertainty as to which was the "prior consul", 381 and 428, both probably genuine contemporary disputes. In 381 it looks as if Gratian and Theodosius disagreed about who should be consul prior, each naming his own candidate first in his own territory, with Theodosius presumably arguing that his, being his uncle, must be given seniority for that reason. Gratian evidently conceded the point, since another kinsman of Theodosius (Antonius) was consul prior the very next year.[54] Every other consul related (even by marriage) to an emperor is given priority: Iulius Constantius (335), Vulcacius Rufinus (347), Stilicho (400) and Basiliscus (465). But the Empress Eudocia's brother Valerius is not given priority in the West.[55] In 428 the evidence implies that Felix was given seniority over Taurus in the course of the year, presumably after appealing to Gratian's law of 382 (*CTh* 6.6.1) giving seniority among consuls to those with the patriciate:[56]

> We decree that all the highest ranking dignities must yield precedence to the consulate...If any person is distinguished by the consulate and either the prefecture [= PPO] or the supreme height of military rank [= MVM], it has not been doubtful for some time that he shall take precedence over men of consular rank <alone>. Furthermore, if it should happen that to these two prerogatives the glory of the patriciate also should happen to be added, who would doubt that such a man should be exalted above all others? For one honor alone is not able to take precedence over two or more, provided that any one of those dignities should be associated with the consulate.[57]

The first three rules continued to apply after 411, but in other respects the concept of priority between subject consuls virtually disappeared. Instead, the name of the western consul (if a subject) was written first in western consular documents, the name of the eastern consul first in eastern documents. The first example of this practice occurs in 421; then 423, 431, 432 and regularly thereafter. This was presumably less a deliberate change of policy than a practical consequence of the new situation, in which the name of the local consul was always known first. When the name of the second consul was announced, it was simply added after the first--unless (of course) it was an emperor's name. So from 421 it becomes possible to distinguish eastern from western consular formulas at a glance from the sequence of names.

---

[54]The very next year Gratian issued a law on the status of the consulate, quoted below. The surviving extract (*CTh* 6.6.1) deals only with the relative standing of consuls, prefects, MVMs and patricians, but the full text was surely more comprehensive and may well have ruled on the seniority of imperial kinsmen.

[55]Since Zeno's brother Longinus (cos. I 486) is so poorly attested in the West (see *ad annum*), it would be hard to say whether or not his priority was acknowledged--perhaps an unrealistic question at this date anyway.

[56]See too the case of 465, where the western inscriptions, a novel of Severus, and several western lists all give Hermenericus first; but a Dalmatian inscription (which could be a p.c.), Eastern (and a few western) lists, the *Liber Pontificalis* and Hilary's letters plus the *CJ* give Basiliscus first. It is not clear to us what the contemporary situation was, but it should be noted that Basiliscus was a kinsman of the emperor Leo.

[57]A law of Valentinian III in 443 recapitulates the provisions of Gratian's law and adds that the award of a second consulate shall confer precedence over "those who have given their name to the calendar for only one year, even though at a prior time they had obtained the consulate as well as the patriciate" (*NovVal* 11).

5. Imperial Consulates

There were three main sorts of occasions on which emperors took consulates. First, following a tradition that can be traced all the way back to Vespasian, new Augusti and Caesars normally took the consulate in the first January after their elevation. For example: Diocletian, Constantius, Galerius, Gallus, Julian, Jovian, Valentinian and Valens, Valentinian II, Theodosius I, Honorius, Theodosius II, Valentinian III, Marcian, Avitus, Leo I, Majorian, Severus, Anthemius, Leo II, Zeno, Basilicus, Anastasius, Justin I, Justinian. Usurpers naturally did the same: Carausius, Magnentius, Maximus, Eugenius--though Johannes (425) was a year late. Three of the tetrarchs were also a year late. Maximinus had to wait two years (307), as did Maximinian and Severus (at least from the date of their proclamation as Caesars: 287, 307). Maxentius chose to wait a year (308).

Sometimes there is an obvious explanation for the delay. For example, Constantine's two sons Crispus and Constantine junior and Licinius' son Licinius junior were all made Caesars together in 317. All three could not be consuls together in 318, and Licinius could not be expected to allow both Constantine's sons (although older) to take precedence over his own. The compromise agreed on was for Crispus to go first in 318 with Licinius as colleague; and then Licinius junior in 319 with Constantine as colleague. This is why Constantine junior had to wait two years longer than usual. Arcadius waited two years (385); cf. above, p.19. Gratian (like Honorius) held his first consulate while merely *nobilissimus puer*, but then had to wait four years after his proclamation as Augustus for his second (371). But the one real puzzle is Constans. Though proclaimed Caesar in 333, he did not become consul till after he became Augustus, in 339. The explanation can hardly be his youth (ten in 333), for his two brothers had held their first consulates at the age of four and nine respectively. Another curiosity is the fact that none of the last three western emperors, Glycerius (473-474), Nepos (474-475) and Romulus Augustulus (475-476) took a consulate at all.[58]

Emperors also regularly took consulates when their co-emperors did, whether to introduce sons or new colleagues in their first consulates, or to accompany brothers or colleagues of long standing, whatever the reason for their consulates (victory or vota). For example, Diocletian and Maximiam held six joint consulates, Constantius I and Galerius five, Valentinian and Valens four. Constantine and his four sons shared a number of consulates in various combinations. Constantius II shared one consulate with his brother Constantine, and three each with his other brother Constans, and his nephews Gallus and Julian; Arcadius three with Honorius, Honorius six with Theodosius II, and Theodosius II four with Valentinian III. When Theodosius took his first consulate after his accession in 380, it was with Gratian as his colleague. Usurpers naturally followed suit: e.g. Maxentius and Romulus, Magnentius and Decentius. But there were exceptions. Theodosius did not hold a consulate with either of his sons,[59] and Gratian held no fewer than three during his father's reign, on every occasion with a private citizen.

Third, the emperor regularly, though not invariably, took a consulate in his quinquennial or decennial years. For example, Diocletian and Maximian held joint consulates for their *decennalia* and *vicennalia* in 293 and 303; Constantius and Galerius for their *decennalia* in 302. Licinius was consul in his quinquennial and decennial years 313 and 318. Constantine celebrated his *decennalia* (315), *tertia quinquennalia* (320) and *vicennalia* (326; cf. notes *ad annum*) with consulates. But not his first *quinquennalia*--or his *tricennalia*, the first celebrated by any emperor since Augustus. Valentinian and Valens held consulates in their quinquennial and decennial years, Theodosius I for his *decennalia* and *tertia*

---

[58]Olybrius (who had been consul as a private citizen in 464) was only emperor from ?April to November 472, and so did not have a chance to become consul as emperor.
[59]A fact praised by his panegyrist Pacatus: "cui cum essent domi filii...dilatis eorum magistratibus amicos consulatus ornavit" (*Pan.Theod.* 16.4).

quinquennalia. In addition, the passage from Themistius 16 discussed above (p.15) shows that he was expected to take another for his first *quinquennalia* in 383, when he gave it to Saturninus instead. On the other hand, the fact that he did this does not suggest that he set any great store by being consul in his quinquennial year.

It might seem a simple task to correlate quinquennial celebrations and consulates throughout our period.[60] Unfortunately, vota were not celebrated with absolute regularity. They were often held a year early or late: in fact "celebrations might be as many as six or as few as three years apart."[61] There are abundant vota coins, but relatively few can be dated independently. Those that show consular imagery in addition to vota legends naturally suggest coincidence with consular years, but even then the year is not always certain. The vota of Theodosius II (402-450) are a good illustration of the problems. On the one hand no fewer than five are precisely (if surprisingly) dated by Marcellinus: to 406, 411, 430, 439 and 444. Theodosius was consul in 411, 430, 439 and 444--but not in 406. It is tempting to accept the Paschal Chronicle's date of 407 (when he was consul) for the first *quinquennalia*, but in general Marcellinus is an incomparably more reliable witness to the common source he shares with the Paschal Chronicle.[62] It might also seem tempting to assign the vota celebrations missing in Marcellinus to 420, 425 and 435, when Theodosius was consul. But the irregularity of the other attested dates hardly entitles us to assume such regularity where we have to guess. To take another example, are we entitled to assume that Valentinian III (425-455) held vota celebrations regularly in 425, 430, 435, 440, 445, 450 and 455, simply because he was consul in those years? Vota coins for his *decennalia* and *tricennalia* bear consular imagery,[63] but there is no evidence that he celebrated quinquennia at all. The case of Arcadius counsels caution. He was consul in 392 and 402, which would suit his presumed (but not attested) *decennalia* and *vicennalia*. But not in his quinquennial years 387 or 397, and then a year early in 406. Honorius too was not consul in the year of his first (presumed) *quinquennalia* (397), nor in 411, where Marcellinus places his *vicennalia*.[64] The evidence of the coinage also counsels caution. On the one hand there are a few fifth century consular solidi that also commemorate *decennalia*, *vicennalia* and *tricennalia*, though not the less important quinquennial vota. On the other, most consular solidi do not. And the mass of fourth century vota issues do not bear any consular imagery. As for the synchronization of imperial consulates to celebrate the vota of one emperor, consider the apparent example of 422, when Honorius celebrated his *tricennalia* and both he and Theodosius II minted consular solidi. Yet neither minted any in the name of the other or even included his name on the reverse. It does not look as if either attached much importance to the synchronization.

Obviously there is a considerable degree of coincidence between vota years and consulates. But hardly enough to enable us to use the consular fasti to fix otherwise undated vota celebrations. There seems no reason why two such different occasions should be linked in any rigorous way.

6. Non-Recognition

For one emperor to refuse to recognize the consuls of a co-emperor was a standard sign of hostility. It would take too long even to summarize the complicated consular politics of the reign of Constantine. Full details are given in the commentaries to 307, 308, 309, 310, 311, 312, and 313. The uneasy concord of the following decade was broken when the joint consulate of Crispus and Constantine iunior in 321 was not accepted in the East.

---

[60]The most elaborate attempt to do just this is R.W. Burgess, "Quinquennial Vota and the Consulship in the Fourth and Fifth Centuries," to appear in *Numismatic Chronicle*. We are very grateful to Mr. Burgess for showing us a draft of his paper before publication.
[61]J.P.C. Kent, *RIC* VIII (1981) 50. See too A.A. Boyce, *Festal and Dated Coins of the Roman Empire: Four Papers* (Numismatic Notes and Monographs 153, New York 1965) 46 n.11.
[62]See *YCS* 27 (1982) 259-62.
[63]Boyce, *Festal and Dated Coins* 75f.
[64]On which see p.17.

Legitimate emperors naturally refused to acknowledge the consuls of usurpers: thus the three consular pairs of Magnentius (351-353) were not proclaimed in the East. In 351 Constantius II proclaimed no new consuls at all; in 352-353 he proclaimed himself and his new Caesar Gallus. In such circumstances[65] consular lists and the dates in official documents tended to be retroactively corrected to reflect the consuls of the winning side, though of course inscriptions and private documents (which means most papyri) kept their original dates. Licinius' name has been eliminated from the heading of all laws in *CTh* (and all but two in *CJ*), but only his title Augustus is removed from the consular dates (cf. 313 and 315); his traces still remain in the so-called *Fragmenta Vaticana*, an unofficial collection completed before Licinius' fall.

In 346 Constans refused to recognize the consuls of his brother Constantius, and from the end of the fourth century on, the West refused to acknowledge eastern consuls in 399, 400, 404, 405, 424, 451, 452, 453, and 459; the East refused western consuls in 424, 451, 452, 456, 458, and 459. But caution is necessary. Sometimes consuls repudiated at the beginning of the year were later recognized (e.g. in 405, 456, and 461); sometimes non-recognition has been wrongly inferred from mere paucity of evidence (e.g. in 420). Sometimes the contemporary documentation is too slight for the picture to be clear; for inclusion by chronicles and compilers after the fact is not a sure guide to contemporary practice. Hence again the importance of assembling all the relevant evidence, as we have attempted to do in this book. In the absence of detailed narrative sources, the documentation of consulates can often cast welcome light on the darkness of fifth century politics.

Some distinctions may be drawn. Simply not to recognize the consul(s) of a co-emperor seems to have been a less drastic step than to proclaim rival consuls in their place. Proclamation of rival consuls usually indicated readiness to go to war, whereas simple non-recognition was often just a sign of temporary bad relations, sometimes no more than a bargaining counter. From the late fifth century on we find a third phenomenon, non-dissemination, where a consul is not named in the documents issued by one court or disseminated to its provinces, but where there seems no reason to believe in formal repudiation. Non-dissemination is evidently a consequence less of political decision than of bureaucratic indecision.

Most delicate of all is the question of recognition of western consuls in the late fifth century East. Several western consuls do not appear in either consular or postconsular dates in the papyri, and there are sometimes few or no laws to offer a check. The case of 440, while the system was in general still functioning properly, shows that in some years the central administration simply failed to send out a revised formula after receipt of the western name (in 440, Valentinian III). In this case, his iteration numbers in subsequent consulates in the eastern documents suffice to put his recognition in 440 beyond doubt. But in the case of citizen consuls we have only the eastern lists to turn to for the question of recognition (as opposed to contemporary dissemination). In cases where all three main eastern lists (Heracl., Marcell., Pasch.) are in agreement, rejecting their testimony entails two important assumptions: first, that these lists, independent of one another, were all edited to include names from western lists but do not otherwise conform to them; and second, that the eastern court recognized or repudiated western consuls on a year-by-year basis. Both assumptions are difficult to accept. It is hard to suppose that relations between barbarian Ravenna and Constantinople fluctuated quite this much. It was as a courtesy to the western aristocrats rather than to Odoacar and Theoderic that eastern emperors (anomalously enough) recognized them as Roman consuls. Since Italy was now to all intents and purposes a separate country with a foreign policy of its own, withholding recognition of consuls was no longer a realistic bargaining counter.

The problem is the fitfulness of dissemination of western names in the late fifth-century East. In the West there is no problem; though generally entered in western consular lists, eastern names were *never* disseminated for general use, except sometimes perhaps in Gaul. Most westerners dated by the western consul alone for all practical purposes. The puzzle is therefore not the absence of western consuls' names from the papyri in some years, but rather their inclusion in others:[66] Is there a rationale behind this

---

[65]See 388, 393, 409, 425, 456 and 476 for other instances.
[66]The western consuls of 480, 495, and 498 are attested in papyri.

inconsistency? In some years there may have been, but in general we cannot identify any. We turn to the details of practices of dissemination.

7. Dissemination

The promulgation of the new consuls each year was obviously quite an occasion, as the following excerpts from fourth-century laws illustrate:

> "Whenever victories are announced, whenever occasions of public rejoicing, or when the names of the new consuls are conveyed throughout the Empire..." (*CTh* 8.11.2 of 365)

> "Whenever the joy of auspicious announcements is made known to the provincials and whenever any message is disseminated throughout the world, whether the illustrious victories of Our soldiers and the slaughter of Our enemies and Our triumphs are reported throughout the Empire, or the announcement of those consulates which We either hold Ourselves or bestow on others..." (*CTh* 8.11.3 of 369; cf. 8.11.1, 364)

The Egyptian evidence makes it clear (as we should expect) that an official formula was officially disseminated. In the first place there is the remarkable uniformity in the formula used throughout Egypt, even down to unusual embellishments of titulature. For example, all nine papyri dated by the consulate of Constantius and Albinus in 335 add after Constantius' name "patrician and brother of our Lord Constantius Augustus," as does the date added by an editor to the Festal Letter of Athanasius for the year and that in a letter addressed to the prefect. In 340 seven out of nine papyri add the remarkably full formula "prefect of the sacred praetorium" after Acyndinus' name and--even more remarkable, onomastically speaking--his signum Populonius before Proculus' name. Secondly, there is only very rarely any overlap between use of the postconsulate of the preceding year and the current formula (cf. below, pp.29, 68). For example, the formula for Constantius and Albinus continued in use during the first three months of 336, the last examples being documents dated 25 and 26 March. The new formula is first found on documents dated 22 April and (two) 26 April. The pattern is standard throughout our period. As time passes the formula gets shorter, but uniformly shorter. There is hardly any sign that the scribes varied the formula substantially according to personal whim (see Chapter 6 for minor variations), and they seldom even abbreviated it, both common occurrences on private funerary inscriptions.

Who were these scribes? Not employees of the state. They were for the most part largely self-employed, and spent most of their time drafting contracts, official documents that were intended, if necessary, to stand up in court. It was obviously important that they be fully and accurately dated, and it seems clear that scribes took the trouble to check with the local government official to ascertain the latest formula (we have seen [above, p.17] that it might change up to three times in the course of the year). The uniform adoption of the new formula in a number of different cities suggests that, inside Egypt at any rate, the news was disseminated uniformly and promptly.

So where did the delays arise? Presumably in some office in Alexandria, Constantinople, and other locations of imperial offices.

1. Constantinople

Unfortunately there is only one papyrus from Constantinople with a consular date (*P.Cair.Masp.* III 67126, of 541) and (astonishingly enough) only one inscription bearing a consular date (to 351). But for almost 150 years (395-541) the overwhelming bulk of eastern legislation was issued from Constantinople.

Unfortunately again an immediate qualification has to be added. For reasons to be explained more fully in Chapter 7, the dates to these laws were systematically corrected by the compilers of the Theodosian and (once again) Justinianic Codes. So although many years show laws dated by the new consuls from the early days of January, these dates cannot be relied upon. Since (fortunately, for once) the compilers missed many of the anomalies they were trying to eliminate, in a number of years we have some means of getting behind the false uniformity imposed by the compilers. What follows is a list of years where provisional formulas of one sort or another have survived:[67]

Latest attestation of provisional formula		*First attestation of current full formula*
e.q.n.f.	*Eastern name alone*	
411 (6-13.vi)		17.viii
412 (28.i)		28.i
	415 (17.ii)	5.iii
416 (8.ii)		20.i
420 (18.ix)		30.xii (5.v *CJ*)
428 (20.ii)		31.i
430 (16.iv)		31.xii
431 (23.iii)		--
432 (28.iii)		11.vi
435 (9.x)		14.xi
438 (15.ii)	9.v	4.xi
439 (7.iv)	19.iv	8.vi (20.i *CJ*)
	440 (20.v)	21.ix (22.i *CJ*)
	444 (20.vii)	29.xi (26.ii *CJ*)
447 (i.x)		--
450 (3.iv)		11.x
452 (6.vii)	18.vi	--
	455 (24.iv)	1.viii
	472 (23.xii)	16.xii

It cannot be emphasized too strongly that these are random cases that eluded correction. There is no reason to believe that they are the latest provisional formulas used at court that year, or that there were none in other years.

Why (for example) was the name of the western consul proclaimed consistently late at Constantinople in (e.g.) 430-432, 435, 438, 439, 444, 447, 450 and 452? C. Pharr explained that "communication between the two capitals...was slow and often interrupted,"[68] but the journey could be accomplished in a month, and there seems no good reason why it should have taken longer in the fifth century than the fourth. And while there were factors (political and military) that might on occasion lead to an interruption in communications (e.g. in 411-412 and 420), in most of the years listed above there were not. In any case, if consuls were usually designated by September, there should have been plenty of time for the news to reach all the main centers in time for January.

We are in fact quite well informed about the transmission of official documents across the Roman Empire, thanks to a number of double dated laws, that is to say laws with subscriptions that record both the date of issue at one end and the date of receipt or posting at the other.[69] For example, the trip from

[67]Formulas with p.c. are not included here. See Chapter 7 for a full discussion.
[68]*The Theodosian Code* (Princeton 1952), p.14, n.33.
[69]The evidence is assembled by A.H.M.Jones, *Later Roman Empire* I 402-03, with III 91-93.

Ravenna to Rome could be done in 5 days; but it could also take as long as 33 days, desk to desk. Milan to Constantinople could be done in 4 weeks, but 80 days is also on record--and not in winter either. One law dated 17 April at Sirmium reached Carthage on 18 May, but many took 3 months, not a few 6 or more, and one almost a year. Sea travel was normally suspended during the winter months, but in general it is difficult to believe that the major source of delay was the journey itself. Jones has pointed to numerous cases of 2 or 3 weeks' delay "when the document had merely to go from one office to another in the same town." It is difficult to resist the conclusion that many laws spent more time gathering dust in successive out-trays and in-trays than on the road. There is no reason to believe that consular proclamations fared better than other official mail.

But this in turn suggests another conclusion, perhaps more important from our point of view. It is difficult to believe that the emperors of the fifth and sixth centuries could not have exchanged consular nominations by January if they had considered it important enough. It seems clear that they did *not* consider it important enough. Taking their cue from above, those responsible for disseminating the information at successive stages gave their respective tasks correspondingly low priority. For practical purposes it was no more inconvenient to use a postconsulate--in one respect actually easier, since there were no new names to learn. Paradoxically enough, while the consulate continued to be venerated by all as an honor, no one felt the same respect for it as a dating system. For that purpose any formula would do provided that its reference was clear.

This is nicely illustrated in 449, when we have a substantial number of uncorrected consular dates in the Acta of the "Robber" Council of Ephesus. According to both Greek and Syriac sources, the Emperor Theodosius himself wrote a letter to the Council dated by the p.c. of 448 as late as 30 March 449. As we shall see in Chapter 7, it is difficult to believe that p.c.'s were ever used at court, where the name of the local consul at least must always have been known from 1 January. The p.c. is more likely to be the date on which the letter was received in Ephesus (official documents were always dated both on dispatch and on arrival; see again Chapter 7 below). Other correspondence to the Council from Constantinople was still being dated by *Protogene et qui nuntiatus fuerit* as late as 13 June. But the western consul Astyrius was inaugurated with due pomp in the regular way, presumably in January (Sidonius Apoll., *Epp.* 8.6.5), and it is difficult to believe that the eastern court had really not heard by 13 June. Chalcedon being virtually a suburb of Constantinople, the Acta of the Council held there in October 451 and Marcian's letter in December to Pope Leo provide valuable contemporary proof that, right up till almost the end of the year, Marcian refused to acknowledge the western consul of the year (see *ad annum*).

For the last few years of the consulate we are lucky enough to have some welcome precision. In 535, there is Justinian *Nov.* 1.4, dated by the new consul of the year already on 1.i; in 538, *Nov.* 64.2, dated by the new consul on 19.i. And for 541 we have our one Constantinopolitan papyrus, dated by the new consul on 7.i. There is also *Nov.* 105 of 537, restricting the consular games to the first week of the year, beginning on 1 January, "when the consul assumes his consulate and receives its codicils." It is clear too from Corippus (*Laud.Iust.* 4.103; 139 f.) that Justin II assumed his consulate of 566 on 1 January. If proof were needed, it is obvious that the consular inauguration still normally took place on 1 January.

2. Greek Cities of the East

There is simply not enough evidence to attempt any comprehensive account of consular dating in the other cities of the East. The paucity of inscriptions with consular dates is obviously significant, given the total bulk of inscriptions still yielded by the Greek East in late antiquity. The habit never really caught on (cf. below, p.60 n.5).

In fact the best evidence here too comes from the Acta of the two Councils of Ephesus (431 and 449[70]). The Emperor Theodosius wrote to Ephesus on 29 June 431, dating by *Antiocho et qui nuntiatus*

---

[70]The evidence is quoted in full *ad annos*.

fuerit. Despite having so authoritative a document before them, the bishops at Ephesus continued to date by the p.c. of 430 until as late as 31 August.

But nowhere is the disjunction between consul as office and consul as date more clear than in the acclamations against Ibas, bishop of Edessa, copied down verbatim in the chapel of St. Zacharias at Edessa on 12 April 449.[71] The acclamations are prefaced by a series of appeals, beginning with the emperors, continuing with Protogenes, prefect of the East and consul, and finishing with the new governor Chaereas. It is clear that the people of Edessa were well aware that Protogenes was consul, as too was Chaereas, who addressed Protogenes in his report as PPO II and consul. Yet the protocol of the acclamations is dated by the p.c. of 448!

3. Egypt

Here at last we have an abundance of original documents with uncorrected consular dates.[72] Within reasonable limits, evidence from any part of Egypt can be used to determine when consulates were announced.[73] The most useful tool is usually the date of the last attestation of the *previous* consulate for each year. These dates provide a rough *terminus post quem* for the announcement of the new consuls; in any given case, new evidence may of course come to move the *terminus* later (or, in cases of overlap, earlier). The following tabulation includes years from 310 to 541; in cases where the exact day is not known but the range can be narrowed, the year is listed under the *earliest* month possible (in the cases of 364, 441, 451, and 508, it is the date of earliest attestation of the new consulate; there is overlap of p.c. and consulate in those years):

January: 310, 311, 315, 316, 319, 325, 328, 330, 334?, 342, 355, 359, 371, 373, 374, 392, 480, 496a[74], 500, 523
February: 314, 339, 340, 345, 350, 360, 377, 442, 453, 463, 492, 497, 517, 518, 534, 538, 539
March: 336, 337, 393, 397, 409, 418, 445, 455, 471, 481a, 498, 503, 530, 535
April: 383, 395, 427, 428, 493, 524
May: 346, 380, 387, 389, 403, 410, 475, 484, 489, 509
June: 386, 399, 400, 407, 417, 448, 458, 478, 499
July: 364, 382, 396, 398, 419, 421, 423, 439, 451, 501, 505, 513, 516, 540
August: 402, 415, 422, 432, 449, 454, 456, 483, 487, 506, 527
September: 412, 429, 431, 434, 435, 441, 452, 459, 461, 462, 470, 473, 486, 488, 508, 510, 526, 541
October: 379, 426, 443, 465, 468, 476, 481b, 482, 491, 504, 514, 533
November: 385, 420, 430, 436, 444, 446, 464, 495, 496b
December: 413, 447, 472, 485, 494

Although no great reliance can be placed in statistics based on this sort of evidence, the distribution seems sufficiently spread out to suggest that the news of new consuls could arrive at any time of year. A breakdown by centuries, however, modifies this conclusion:

	IV	V	VI	Total
January	16	2	2	20
February	7	5	5	17

[71]J. Flemming and G. Hoffmann, *Akten der ephesinischen Synode vom Jahre 449* (Abhandl.Gesell.Wiss.Göttingen N.F. 15 (1917) 15f.; cf. O.Seeck, *RheinMus* 73 (1920/24) 86f.
[72]This discussion excludes material from Athanasius and the *Hist.Aceph.*, which may contain useful information for 356, 362, and 366, on the grounds that we cannot tell if the dates have been editorially altered at a later date.
[73]This section is a revised version of remarks by Bagnall and Worp in *BASP* 17 (1980) 32-36; it takes for granted some facts established earlier in that article, 27-32; and see below, p.68.
[74]Years followed by *a* or *b* refer to years in which a p.c. of an earlier year was replaced by a p.c. of the immediately preceding year during the course of the year.

March	4	7	3	14
April	2	3	1	6
May	4	5	1	10
June	2	7	0	9
July	4	5	5	14
August	0	9	2	11
September	0	14	4	18
October	1	8	3	12
November	1	8	0	9
December	0	5	0	5

It is obvious that in the fourth century more *termini* fell in January-February than in all other months together, and this picture is consistent with a situation in which the consuls were normally designated in the Autumn, proclaimed on 1 January, and disseminated rapidly. In the fifth century, on the other hand, the median is between July and August, and in the sixth it is July: there is no longer any preference for the early months of the year, quite the reverse in fact. It is difficult to avoid the conclusion that the news of the new consuls reached Egypt much later than in the fourth century (as the high number of fifth century postconsulates shows in itself) and that the amount of delay followed no observable pattern.

In eleven years we find in the papyri provisional formulas (X καὶ τοῦ δηλωθησομένου/ἀποδειχθησομένου or its more familiar Latin equivalent):[75] 451 (24.vii); 453 (17.ii); 460; 461 (1.ix); 463 (p.c. possible); 464 (17.iii, 7.x, 20.xi); 466; 472 (8.xi); 473 (14.ix); 481 (22.vi); 482 (13?.x); 483 (27.viii).[76] Curiously enough, in none of these cases was a second consul ever subsequently disseminated in Egypt, despite the formula.

If the dissemination of consular names within Egypt seems to have been fairly uniform, why the curiously even distribution of these termini post quem over the whole julian year? With full awareness of its shortcomings, we have compiled a list of years where the *latest* reference to the p.c. of the (or a) preceding year in the papyri is two months or more later than the *earliest* attestation of the current formula in the laws (including for this purpose formulas with just one current consul). All early dates from *CTh* and (even more) *CJ* must be viewed with suspicion, but dates from *Novels* seem to be uncorrected.

Year	Latest reference to p.c.	Earliest reference to cos.
379	*P.Lips.* 13.1 (23.x)	*CTh* 10.1.12 (17.vi)
380	*CPR* VII 19.1 (6.v)	*CTh* 9.27.1 (15.i)
382	*SB* IV 7445.1 (12.vii)	*CTh* 14.10.1 (12.i)
385	*P.Lips.* 62 ii.17 (4.xi)	*CJ* 1.55.4 (2-5.i)
386	*ZPE* 61 (1985) 74.1 (26.vi)	*CTh* 9.34.9 (19.i)
387	*SB* XIV 11285.1 (28.v)	*CTh* 10.10.19 (2.iii)
395	*ZPE* 56 (1984) 82.11 (17.iv)	*CTh* 2.1.8 (6.i)
396	*CPR* X 107a.1 (25.vii)	*CTh* 15.13.1 (6.i)
398	*P.Herm.* 52.1, 53.1 (4.vii)	*CTh* 7.1.16 (28.i)
399	*P.Giss.* 104.1 (30.vi)	*CTh* 11.24.4 (10.iii)

[75]We distinguish these instances from cases where the complete pair was yet to be announced, such as p.c. plus καὶ τοῖς ἀποδειχθησομένοις in 336, or the era with various formulas in the period 322-324.

[76]The text of 501, *P.Amst.* I 45, is a peculiar case. The scribe has written μετὰ τὴν ὑπατείαν Φλ. Πατρικίου τοῦ μεγαλοπρεπεστάτου καὶ ἐνδοξοτάτου στρατηγοῦ καὶ ὑπάτου καὶ τοῦ δηλωθησομένου. The scribe has thus transformed the name of the second consul Hypatius (already known in Egypt on 15.ix.500, *SB* XVI 12583.1) into the title ὑπάτου, consul (nonsensically: who but a consul would be consul!); he has then felt the need of a second consul and added the "to be designated" phrase.

402	*P.Grenf.* II 80.1 (4.viii)	*CTh* 14.17.14 (22.iii)
407	*P.Oxy.* VIII 1122.1 (9.vi)	*CTh* 6.26.13 (25.i)
409	*SB* I 1540.8 (19.iii)	*CTh* 13.5.32 (19.i)
410	*P.Herm.* 69.1 (5.v)	*CTh* 16.5.48 (21.ii)
412	*P.Mich.* XI 611.1 (27.ix)	*CTh* 7.17.1 (28.i)
413	*P.Heid.* IV 306.1 (16.xii)	*CTh* 6.13.1 (21.iii)
415	*P.Mich.* XI 613.1 (19.viii)	*CTh* 3.1.9 (17.ii)
417	*P.Berl.Zill.* 5.1 (15.vi)	*CTh* 8.12.9 (14.iii)
418	*P.Köln* II 102.1 (30.iii/9.iv)	*CTh* 16.2.43 (3.ii)
419	*PSI* XIII 1365.2 (6.vii)	*CTh* 11.30.66 (8.iii)
420	*PSI* XIII 1340.1 (18.xi)	*CJ* 8.10.10 (5.v)
422	*SPP* XX 118.3 (29.viii)	*CTh* 6.32.2 (12.i)
423	*P.Köln* III 151.1 (24.vii)	*CTh* 7.4.35 (14.ii)
426	*P.Oslo* II 35.1 (6.x)	*CTh* 9.42.24 (23.i)
428	*P.Flor.* III 314.1 (27.iv)	*CTh* 6.2.26, 27.22 (31.i)
429	*P.Rainer Cent.* 122.1 (19.ix)	*CTh* 1.1.5 (26.iii)
430	*BGU* XII 2138.1 (16.xi)	*CTh* 10.10.34 (22.ii)
431	*P.Köln* V 234.1 (1.ix)	*CTh* 9.45.4 (23.iii)
432	*PSI XVII Congr.* 29.1 (31.viii)	*CTh* 9.45.5 (28.iii)
434	*P.Lond.* V 1777.1 (7.ix)	*CTh* 5.12.3, 11.28.15 (18.vi)
435	*P.Flor.* III 315.1 (ix-x?)	*CTh* 6.28.8 (29.i)
436	*PSI* VI 708.1 (2.xi)	*CTh* 10.20.18 (8.iii)
439	*CPR* VI 6.1 (8.vii)	*NovTheod* 7.1 (20.i)
443	*P.Oxy.* VI 913.1 (16.x)	*CJ* 1.46.3 (28.i)
444	*P.Oxy.* L 3583.1 (13.xi)	*NovTheod* 25 (16.i)
447	*P.Rainer Cent.* 97.1 (3.xii)	*NovTheod* 2 (1.x)
448	*P.Flor.* III 311.1 (24.vi)	*CJ* 1.1.3 (16.ii)
449	*P.Flor.* III 313.1 (12.viii)	*CJ* 5.17.8 (9.i)
452	*P.Rainer Cent.* 100.1 (21.ix)	*CJ* 1.1.4 (7.ii)
454	*SB* X 10523.1 (4.viii)	*NovMarc* 4 (4.iv)
456	*P.Yale* I 71.1 (28.viii)	*CJ* 1.4.13 (25.iii)
459	*P.Rainer Cent.* 102.1 (ix-xii)	*CJ* 8.53.30 (3.iii)
468	*P.Wisc.* I 10.1 (10.x)	*CJ* 1.14.10 (8.ii)
470	*SB* XVI 12486.2 (30.ix)	*CJ* 5.27.4 (1.i)
472	*P.Lond.* V 1793.2 (1.xii)	*CJ* 8.37.10 (1.i)
473	*Mneme Petropoulos* II 204.1 (14.ix)	*CJ* 6.61.5 (1.vi)
478	*P.Rainer Cent.* 123.1 (15-23.vi)	*CJ* 5.9.7 (1.iii)
486	*CPR* V 16.2 (16.ix)	*CJ* 4.20.14 (21.v)
491	*P.Flor.* I 94.1 (18.x)	*CJ* 7.39.4 (29/30.vii)
496	*P.Oxy.* XVI 1975.1 (30.xi)	*CJ* 6.21.16 (13.ii)
499	*P.Mich.* XV 731.1 (vi-vii)	*CJ* 5.62.25 (1.i)
505	*P.Stras.* 471 bis.1 (16.vii)	*CJ* 1.4.19 (19.iv)
513	*SB* I 5175.1 (9.vii)	*CJ* 1.42.2 (8.ii)
527	*P.Lond.* V 1690.1 (30.viii)	*CJ* 1.31.5 (22.iv)
533	*CPR* X 27.1 (8.x)	*NovIust* 155 (1.ii)
535	*P.Giss.* I 121.1 (17.iii)	*NovIust* 1.4 (1.i)
541	*SB* XIV 12051.1 (ix)	*P.Cair.Masp.* II 67126 (7.i)

It was little more than a week from Constantinople to Alexandria by sea.[77] There are no figures for the land route, but pilgrims presumably stopping every night could get from Constantinople to Jerusalem in 8 weeks,[78] and official couriers must have travelled much faster. It is true that navigation was suspended between October and April,[79] but it should not have taken more than the two months we allow by land. And after April communication would once more have been cut to less than two weeks.

It will be obvious that, even when all due allowance has been made for the possibility of corrected dates in the laws, the gap between the two columns is much larger than can be explained by delays in transportation. It is again difficult to avoid the conclusion that significant delays occurred in the bureaucracy, whether in Constantinople or Alexandria or (more probably) both.

In one year, our last, we are in a position to measure the delay exactly. Basilius is attested in office at Constantinople already on 7.i.541. The news took nine months to reach Upper Egypt, with the first mention of Basilius dated to 10.ix.541 and the last p.c. of 540 a few days earlier.

4. Rome and the West

For the city of Rome we have more original consular dates than anywhere else in the Empire. Since most are funerary inscriptions, they do not permit such precise inferences as the papyri. At best, in years with many inscriptions in which there is a sharp division between postconsulates and current consuls, approximate dates for the arrival of information can be suggested. Unfortunately, almost all such years fall in the relatively unproblematic fourth century, when consulates were normally in use by the first to third months of the year, at least at Rome. Though the evidence from Italy usually coincides with that from Rome in this period, on rare occasions consulates seem to have been known somewhat later outside Rome.[80] In the table below, the years in all three centuries for which Italian p.c. dates are known are arranged (as above for Egypt) by the latest month in which such a date occurs.[81]

January: 366, 395, 399 (*?), 402 (Italy), 403 (Italy), 408, 417 (pope) (*?), 431, 434 (Italy), 461 (Italy), 473, 477 (pope), 487 (Italy), 488 (Italy), 538* (Italy)

February: 367*, 429, 464 (pope), 492* (Italy)

March: 350* (Italy) (?), 372*, 385*, 386 (Italy), 392* (Italy), 395* (Italy), 418* (Italy), 423* (Italy), 425* (Italy), 478 (Italy), 540 (Italy) (*?)

April: 370*, 381* (Italy), 384*, 457, 484* (Italy), 491 (Italy), 533, 538*

May: 384* (Italy), 393* (Italy), 439* (Italy), 453 (Italy) (*?)

June: 454*, 479* (pope)

July: 350*, 409* (Italy), 411 (Italy) (*), 427 (Italy), 441 (Italy), 447* (Italy)

August: 410*

September: none

October: 409* (Italy), 466* (Italy)

November: none

December: 533 (Italy)

One can see immediately that Roman epigraphical p.c. dates after April are rare (one each in June, July, and August), and even Italian are clustered in the first four months of the year, a striking contrast to

---

[77]L. Casson, *Ships and Seamanship in the Ancient World* (Princeton 1971) 287-94, gives a useful tabulation of voyages in this part of the Mediterranean, oddly omitting the only documented voyage from Constantinople to Alexandria: 9 days, according to Theophylact Simocatta, *Hist.* 8.13.14. This is clearly in line with other figures recorded by Casson, e.g. Constantinople to Rhodes and Gaza in 5 and 10 days respectively (Marcus Diac., *V.Porph.* 55 and 27).

[78]E.D. Hunt, *Holy Land Pilgrimage in the Later Roman Empire* (Oxford 1982) 56.

[79]For details, Casson 270-71; cf. for an opposing view F.J. Meyer, *Hermeneus* 55 (1983) 1-20.

[80]In Capua, 381; Piano Laroma, 384; Genosa, 395. The scattered late uses of postconsular dates in the fourth century inscriptions are usually of no significance; cf. below, p.65.

[81]In this and the following tables, inscriptions, papyri, church councils and papal correspondence are all included, but imperial laws are not. The provenance is given only when it is not Rome. An asterisk indicates an overlap of consulate and p.c.; overlaps take western imperial laws into account. Years which never had a proclaimed consulate are not included.

the Egyptian pattern described above. It is obvious that the transmission problems evidently responsible for the situation in Egypt did not normally occur in Italy.

With Africa, however, the situation is different. Whenever evidence from Carthage and such places is available, it seems to attest later dissemination there than in Rome and Italy.[82]

January: none
February: 418* (council)
March: 373*
April: 399*
May: none
June: 401*, 410*, 411 (*)
July: 419*
August: none
September: none
October: none
November: 419*
December: none

The bulge falls in the middle of the year, and if the evidence of African *accepta* and *proposita* dates in imperial laws discussed in Chapter 7 were added to the table, the concentration would be still more visible. This is hardly surprising. When sailing was suspended between October and April, there was no land route to Africa. As Jones has pointed out, laws issued "in the autumn, whether at Milan, Paris, Trier, or Constantinople, practically never reached Africa till the following spring or early summer."[83]

In the fifth century, not only was proclamation often later than it had been in the fourth, but there are signs that dissemination, especially of the names of eastern consuls, was less thorough, or that people more routinely disregarded information at their disposal. In relatively few years between 395 and 476 are eastern consuls attested in western inscriptions in January through March of the year; and even in these cases, some tombstones may carry anachronistic formulas.[84] Inscriptions with the western consul and *e.q.n.f.* are found in 439 and 452 (cf. below, p.66). But the carving is in general unlikely to have been more than a month or so later than burial, and dates of burial have a certain rough value. Early attestation of eastern consuls at Rome is found in 396, 397, 398, 402, 403, 407, 408, 422, 423, 428, 430, 432,[85] 434, 435, 465,[86] 466,[87] 467 and 474. Western consuls are attested in January-March far more frequently: 401, 402, 403, 407, 408, 416, 422, 423,[88] 425, 428,[89] 430, 432, 435, 439,[90] 447,[91] 449, 450,[92] 451, 453 (?), 458, 459, 461, 463, 469, 470 and 472.

Though consular dating remained in use under Odoacar and Theoderic, in practice there was a drastic change.[93] Of the 48 eastern consuls appointed between 476 and 541, 25 are never attested in a

---

[82]See the ostraca of 359 and 373 and the laws of 380 and 382. Interestingly, in all these years dissemination was also late in Egypt.

[83]*Later Roman Empire* I 403; see further below, pp.79f.

[84]On the other hand, given the extreme paucity of evidence after 410, it is likely that proclamation and dissemination were earlier than the evidence allows us to determine in some years.

[85]Valerius is not attested at Rome before April: an inscription from 10.iii omits him. He is attested in Acqui (Italy) on 5.iii.

[86]Basiliscus and Hermenericus are attested on all western inscriptions, the earliest a Milanese inscription from the second half of February. The earliest Roman inscription with a certain date is of 25.vii.

[87]The situation resembles that of 465; this time, however, the earliest inscription is from Lyons. A Milanese inscription from 9.x, however, has a p.c.

[88]A Syracusan inscription from 3.iii, however, has a p.c.

[89]But p.c. seems possible for the inscription from 15?.iii.

[90]A Syracusan inscription from 24.v, however, has a p.c.

[91]At Rome; Italian inscriptions are postconsular as late as July.

[92]A Dalmatian inscription from 17.ix, however, has a p.c.

[93]Mommsen, *Ges.Schr.* VI 381, noted the disappearance from the fasti after 461 of the formula "et qui de oriente nuntiatus fuerit," implying that the proclamation of the other consul was no longer routinely expected. The papyri, however, tell a different story for the East; see p.30.

western inscription.[94] Of the remaining 23, only 4 (Basiliscus Aug. and Armatus, coss. 476, Zeno Aug., cos. 479, and Basilius, cos. 541) are attested in the West early in the year or with any regularity. The remaining 19 are attested late (sometimes only in p.c.'s) and sporadically.[95] If there was no new western consul, the year was dated by the p.c. of the last western consul, whether or not there was a new eastern consul. Yet the reason for this western neglect of eastern information was not nonrecognition, for the German kings of Italy seem to have had no consistent policy of nonrecognition of eastern consuls, as some of their Roman imperial predecessors had. Indeed, some western consular lists regularly include eastern consuls, though never comprehensively.[96]

But to blame the general ignorance of eastern consuls on dissemination would be to imply that it was slow or ineffective, when in most years there was probably none at all. Use of the western consul alone hardened into official practice, as may be most clearly seen from the subscriptions to the letters of late fifth and sixth century Popes. In 519, for example, when Justin I had gone out of his way to conciliate Theoderic by recognizing his designated heir as consul with himself as colleague (eastern documents being dated *Iustino Augusto et Eutharico consulibus*), Pope Hormisdas (*Coll.Avell.* 168; 190) dated only by the name of Eutharic, even when writing to Justin himself! In the circumstances, it seems impossible to believe that this was intended to be the slight it might appear. In the following year also, eastern correspondence received at the papal court early in the year is all dated by the new consular pair, while Hormisdas' replies are all dated by the western consul alone.

It is not difficult to see why the eastern government, which still claimed and ultimately reconquered Italy, was keener than the Ostrogoths to maintain the collegiality of the consulate and with it the fiction of a Roman Italy. But if it was not Ostrogothic policy to ignore eastern consuls, there was perhaps a touch of Italian nationalism behind it. In 536, after the Byzantine reconquest, the official consular proclamation (there being no new consuls that year) was the p.c. of Belisarius, eastern consul in 535. But the second p.c. of Paulinus, western consul in 534, was also widely employed, as it was again in 537 (again no new consuls). The new eastern consul was fairly widely proclaimed in 538, but, perhaps significantly, he sometimes appears as 'Iohannes orientalis' (*ILCV* 318) or 'cons. per Oriente' (*ILCV* 217 adn.). Apion, the new eastern consul of 539, never appears on an Italian inscription, but the (by now fifth) p.c. of Paulinus is as well attested as p.c. Iohannis. Throughout the late fifth and sixth centuries, new western consuls continue to be well and regularly attested in Italy.

The situation in Gallia Narbonensis and Lugdunensis, the only areas outside Italy where a relatively large body of evidence is available in most of our period,[97] was sometimes very different, as can be seen from the following table:

January: 405, 503, 519 (*?), 529, 530
February: 441, 467, 516, 523
March: 493, 495, 505 (*?)
April: 541*
May: 486*, 533, 538
June: 540*
July: 487*
August: 454*, 491, 520
September: 485*

---

[94]Years: 484, 493, 496, 497, 498, 499, 500 (both consuls are eastern), 501, 502, 503, 505, 506, 508, 511, 512 (both eastern), 513, 518, 521, 524, 525, 528, 534, 539.

[95]478, 482, 486, 489, 490, 491, 492, 507, 515, 517, 519, 520 (Vitalian does not appear in the western evidence until *after* he had suffered damnatio memoriae in the East), 533, 535, 538, 540.

[96]See e.g. the situation between 496 and 503: not a single western inscription names an eastern consul, but the consuls always appear in at least some of the lists. Admittedly, it is not always clear what constitutes a western list; cf. below, pp.52 (Victor), 54 (Hyd.). Nevertheless, relations between Theoderic and Anastasius were friendly in this period, so there is no reason eastern consuls should *not* have been recognized and listed in the West.

[97]There is not enough Spanish or Dalmatian material to draw any conclusions.

October: 508
November: none
December: 510*

There is a concentration early in the year, as in Rome and Italy. But in Gaul, news of *western* consuls often did not arrive until late in the year and was not well disseminated. Symmachus, cos. 485, though well attested in Italy and named on one Narbonese inscription (18.v), is absent from three other Narbonese inscriptions dated 9?.v, 1.vi and 18.ix, all dated p.c. 484. (Oddly, a p.c. Symmachi era was used at Arles as late as 495.) Once again, in 486, the western consul is attested in Rome from 22.iii, while a Narbonese inscription dated 19.v uses a p.c. Another Narbonese inscription (30.i), however, knows not only the western but the eastern consul (it is possible that it is an error for p.c., to be sure). The one inscription from Lyons of 488 (19.vi) gives only one of the two western consuls and mangles his name ('Dedamius'). The two inscriptions from the same city from 493 are ignorant of the western consul (admittedly, the Italian evidence for that year is also late). The western consul of 495, attested in Rome on 23.i, first appears in Gaul in October. Venantius ('alius iunior') is never attested in Gaul, where 508 is either a p.c. or an iterum p.c. Likewise, a Lyonnaise inscription of 510 (2.xii) is ignorant of the western consul of the year, well-attested in Italy. See also 520, 523, 540, and 541.

More remarkable than this slow and incomplete dissemination of western consulates in Gaul is the occasional dissemination of eastern information there in years when the same information was unknown in Italy. This phenomenon occurs in 486 (Narbo, 30.i), 489 (Marseille, undated), 491 (Vezeronce, 28?.xi), 508 (a Narbonese p.c., 1.vi, names the eastern consul of 507), 515 (Vienne, 14.ii-15.iii; cf. the p.c. in 516), 517 (Aix, Narbonensis, 24.xii--the eastern consul is named alone; he is also attested in a p.c. from Lodi dated 20.i.518); the eastern consul of 519 (Justin) is attested on two Narbonese p.c.'s (2.viii.520 and undated), while Vitalian (cos. 520) is attested in a Lyonnaise inscription (19.ix) and one from Grenoble (2.xi; all Italian inscriptions of 520 date by Rusticius alone). Strikingly, though in these years knowledge of the eastern consuls is restricted (of the western areas) to Gaul, it is not widespread even there. Often inscriptions from the same area differ, one knowing and one ignorant of the eastern consul. It is presumably through some connection with Gaul that we are to explain the possibility that the consulate (or postconsulate) of the eastern consul of 540 is attested in Wales (see the Critical Appendix for 540).

How is this curious situation to be explained? Informal distribution of information along trade routes? But Gallic trade with Levantine cities like Alexandria was more important than trade with Constantinople, and dissemination in Egypt was often late enough. These cities had plenty of trade with other areas in the West, particularly Rome, where the names of eastern consuls do not appear. Moreover, Arles, the most important focal point for this trade, has not one example of an eastern consul in an inscription of the period.

On the other hand, the almost chaotic situation in the Gallic inscriptions is difficult to reconcile with any explanation which involves systematic official proclamation and dissemination. The answer may lie in a deliberate decision of the Gallic kingdoms to proclaim eastern consuls, coupled with progressive disintegration of governmental institutions in the West in general which made such decisions less than fully effective.

Chapter 3

Points of Nomenclature:

Flavius and Junior

1. Flavius

The name Flavius enjoyed a sudden and permanent vogue in the Roman world from the early fourth century on. At one level, the reason is obvious; it was the *gentilicium* of the Emperor Constantine. Up to the early third century, adoption of the *gentilicium* of the reigning emperor was the hallmark of the newly enfranchised citizen. But a meticulous study by J.G. Keenan[1] has shown that this cannot be the sole or main explanation for the massive explosion of Flavii in the best documented area of Constantine's realm, Egypt--still less for the continuing popularity of the name right down to the Arab conquest (and later, cf. *CPR* VIII, pp.196-97). Too many of the new Flavii were people of consequence who cannot have been *peregrini* as recently as 325. Keenan concludes that

> The name Flavius appears to have served, in a sense, as a dignity, a status marker setting off the group of imperial civil servants and soldiers from the general populace. In Egypt, the masses of the population--farmers, craftsmen, etc.--remained Aurelii.

With one or two qualifications, this seems to be true of the civil servants and soldiers of Byzantine Egypt. But they were pretty small beer compared with the governing class of the empire as a whole. What role did Flavius play in the higher reaches of late Roman society?

A recent study cites Flavius Anicius Probus Faustus cos. 490 as a typical example of a Roman aristocrat under the Ostrogothic kingdom in Italy, adding: "as his title Flavius indicates, he was among the very highest ranks of the Roman nobility."[2] But there is no reason to believe that Flavius was a status marker inside the governing class of Italy. Far too many men of the noblest birth and highest rank are *not* Flavii. For example, of the 100 prefects of Rome included by A. Chastagnol in his *Fastes de la préfecture de Rome au Bas-Empire* (1962) after 325, only 10 are Flavii.

Yet a great many important people (among them Roman aristocrats) are attested as Flavii, especially in the fifth and sixth centuries. The principal addition A. Degrassi made to the names of consuls from this period in his *Fasti consolari* of 1952 was Flavii culled from the papyri. But there are two peculiarities about the documentation of these names that seem not to have been noticed, peculiarities which must cause us to doubt their status as genuine, integral elements in a man's nomenclature.

The first is that almost without exception they come from inscriptions and papyri that do not record the full name of the person in question; simply Fl(avius) and the last, "diacritical" name.[3] Second, these

---

[1] "The names Flavius and Aurelius as status designations in later Roman Egypt," *ZPE* 11 (1973) 33-63 and 13 (1974) 283-304, together with his later thoughts in *ZPE* 53 (1983) 245-50. A.Mócsy, "Der Name Flavius als Rangbezeichnung in der Spätantike", *Akten des IV. Internationalen Kongresses für griechische und lateinische Epigraphik* (Vienna 1964) 257-63, is undocumented and inaccurate.

[2] T.S.Burns, *A History of the Ostrogoths* (Bloomington 1984) 84, quoting not Keenan, but Mócsy, who at p.258 made the confident but quite false statement that "Flavii waren z.B. alle Mitglieder der vornehmen Familie der Anicii". The truth is that of the 30 Anicii listed in the two volumes of *PLRE*, only three bear the name Flavius.

[3] The name a man was known by in one-name contexts, normally his last name: see *JRS* 75 (1985) 164-82.

documents are almost all consular dates. Now since there were normally two consuls, the documents normally give two names presented as a pair: that is, they are each given either one name (the last) or two; but whichever it is, both consuls are virtually always given in the same style, a matching pair.[4] No one who has worked his way through the thousands of consular inscriptions and papyri could doubt that a Flavius is often added to one of the pair to make it match the other.

Thus the more than 30 consular inscriptions for 397 (all Italian) give either "Caesarius et Atticus" or "Fl. Caesarius et Nonius Atticus." But eastern documents (the papyri) give "Fll. Caesarius et Atticus." On the strength of the papyri, Degrassi added a Flavius to Atticus' name, i.e. "Flavius Nonius Atticus."[5] But is it likely that Egyptian papyri preserve a genuine name for this Italian unknown to more than 30 Italian inscriptions? For a clearer example we may turn to 391, where the Italian inscriptions give either "Fl. Tatianus et (Q.) Aurelius Symmachus" or "Tatianus et Symmachus," while the papyri give "Fl. Tatianus et Fl. Symmachus." Degrassi did not hesitate to add a Flavius to Symmachus' nomenclature. But it is hard to believe that the papyri preserve genuine information not recorded in the heading to Symmachus' writings or on local inscriptions that give his name and career in full, in particular *CIL* VI 1699 = *ILS* 2946, from the base of a statue in Symmachus' own house on the Caelian hill, dedicated by his son. All these sources agree in giving his full name as Q. Aurelius Symmachus.

By the sixth century this use of Fl. plus diacritical becomes common on Italian consular inscriptions too, even on inscriptions from Rome (isolated earlier examples occur in 344, 372, 379, and 382). For example, Fl. Mavortius on *ICUR* n.s. VIII 22979 = *ILCV* 344. This is the consul of 527, who signed himself Vettius Agorius Basilius Mavortius in his famous "edition" of Horace's *Epodes*. It is hardly likely that we should add a Flavius to this total. Similarly with Fl. Orestes on *ICUR* n.s. II 5053 = *ILCV* 591 for Rufius Gennadius Probus Orestes cos. 530. We must therefore be doubtful whether the consul of 529, unfortunately known to us only as Decius iunior but a member (like Mavortius) of the polyonymous clan of the Decii, was really called Flavius as *CIL* IX 1384 and 1385 allege. The nomenclature of this prolific family happens to be particularly well documented,[6] and there is not a Flavius to be seen in five generations.

PLRE pursues no consistent policy. While not giving Flavii to Atticus or Symmachus, they do add them more or less routinely to consuls otherwise known by only one name: for example, Fl. Caesarius cos. 397, Fl. Timasius and Fl. Promotus coss. 389, and scores of others. Occasionally also to polyonymi as well. For example, Fl. Anicius Probus Faustus cos. 490 (quoted above) or, to take a more familiar case, Fl. Magnus Aurelius Cassiodorus Senator cos. 514. His last four names are well known from Cassiodorus' writings; once more, the Fl. is known only from papyri. Are we justified in combining these two sources into one composite name? If not, what *is* the status of the Flavii in the consular inscriptions and papyri? Are they just errors? Or guesses? If so, why always the same guess?

We may suggest that in such cases Flavius is little more than a courtesy title functioning something like Mr in modern English usage. That is to say, it was no doubt both correct and desirable to refer to Symmachus in certain contexts as Fl. Symmachus, just as it would be both correct and desirable in certain contexts to style John Smith Mr Smith. But the Mr would normally be dropped for an entry in a telephone directory or biographical dictionary. In narrative contexts Smith alone would suffice; in personal contexts John alone; in yet other contexts John Smith, with or without the Mr; and in certain official contexts John Paul William Smith, without the Mr. Bewildering though these distinctions might appear to (say) a Korean, they present no problems to us--nor are they really status designations either. In upper class British usage of a generation ago there were indeed one or two additional refinements of protocol (now fast disappearing) that in practice did act as status designators. For example, a gentleman would never have

---

[4] On rare occasions a consul is given his full names, however long and regardless of what is given for the other consul: cf. e.g. 408.

[5] We are here disregarding the Maximus erroneously added to his name on the strength of the bungled inscription *ICUR* n.s.II 6058 = *ILCV* 3781: see *Epigraphica* 47 (1985) 109-10 for fuller discussion.

[6] See the stemma in *JRS* 72 (1982) 143 or *PLRE* I 1324.

introduced himself (at least to his equals) as Mr Smith (always Smith or John Smith). By the same token he would never have introduced his wife as Mrs Smith (always Mary or my wife). Nor would he have addressed an equal as Mr Smith (with or without the John) on an envelope (always John Smith, or perhaps rather J. Smith, Esq.). Nor would he have addressed in person a social equal to whom he had been introduced as Mr Smith (always Smith, whatever the difference in age or rank); though for a different reason he would not have dignified his social inferiors with a Mr either. This too would not have puzzled his peers, though it might convey a false impression of egalitarianism to a later generation.

It was not the purpose of this digression on British usage to suggest that Flavius shared all these functions and implications in late Roman usage. But in so class-conscious a society it is intrinsically probable that there was a correct and an incorrect way to employ a title that is agreed to be a status designator. And there is in fact (for antiquity) an unusually large and unanimous body of evidence suggesting that Flavius was correctly used with the diacritical name alone. Thus Fl. Symmachus, but not Fl. Q. Aurelius Symmachus; Fl. Senator, but not Fl. Magnus Aurelius Cassiodorus Senator.

If this is so, it would follow that hundreds of entries in *PLRE* and other prosopographies are in error--or at any rate ignore a nicety of contemporary protocol. To add Flavii in those cases where they happen to be attested (disproportionately for consuls) would be as if some future prosopographer of our own age added a Mrs to his entry for (say) Margaret Thatcher because he had seen her styled Mrs Thatcher in a contemporary newspaper report. This would be not so much incorrect as misleading, inasmuch as it would falsely imply some difference in rank from other women whom our prosopographer happened not to have seen so styled in contemporary newspapers. For everybody mentioned in *Who's Who* could be styled Mr, Miss or Mrs. By the same token surely everybody rating an entry in *PLRE* must have reached the modest level of what Keenan calls "the Flaviate." In most cases we simply do not happen to have the evidence.

There is one category that deserves special mention: barbarians. According to E.A.Thompson,[7] citing (of course) consular documents, the Gothic deserter Fravitta "took upon himself the Roman name of Flavius." The statement is true but misleading, inasmuch as it implies that Fravitta acted deliberately--and differently from other barbarians in Roman service. For *all* officers in the Roman army were routinely entitled to the "Flaviate", whatever their origin.[8] To quote a handful of examples, the Frankish generals Fll. Nevitta, Merobaudes, Ricomer and Bauto, consuls in 362, 377, 384 and 385. Nor is it any mystery why later barbarian kings often bore the name Flavius, for example Theoderic and Odoacar. Both had (of course) been Flavii since their days in Roman service. For Theoderic we have the usual documentary evidence, since he happened to win himself a consulate while still a subject of Zeno (484).[9]

If this analysis is correct, how should the situation be handled in our prosopographies? No monolithic policy would accommodate all the local and social variations. In the case of those otherwise known by only one name, it seems best to follow the contemporary practice attested in the inscriptions and papyri, and to go on including the Flavius. In the case of polyonymous Italian aristocrats[10] it seems best not to combine it with what appears to be a full local style. Thus Fl. Caesarius, but Q. Aurelius Symmachus. But the eastern governing class (a group with very different social and political traditions[11]) do seem to have combined it with their other names, however many: e.g. Fl. Marianus Petrus Theodorus Valentinus Rusticius Boraides Germanus Iustinus cos. 540.

There seems to have been a clear distinction of usage between East and West here. We are quite well informed about the nomenclature of the Roman aristocracy, both in the fourth century and then again under the Ostrogothic kingdom. For the earlier period we have a great many inscriptions from Italy and

---

[7]*Romans and Barbarians: The Decline of the Western Empire* (Madison 1982) 41.
[8]For Flavii in the army, Keenan, *ZPE* 11 (1973) 39-40.
[9]For later examples, see Keenan, *ZPE* 11 (1973) 38-39.
[10]Using the term aristocrat here fairly loosely to include any well to do family that could trace its roots beyond the age of Constantine.
[11]See *GRBS* 19 (1978) 276.

North Africa; for the latter period inscribed seats in the Flavian amphitheatre and consular diptychs. It is therefore the more significant that Flavii are so rare in the cursus inscriptions of these normally polyonymous dignitaries. Eastern dignitaries are much less well served; a few sixth century consular diptychs and a mere handful of inscriptions. Even so, there are many examples of easterners including Flavius in their full nomenclature. For example, Fl. Anthemius Isidorus cos. 436; Fl. Taurus Seleucus Cyrus (Hierax) (the poet) cos. 441; Fl. Flor. Romanus Protogenes cos. 449; Fl. Appalius Illus Trocundes cos. 482; Fl. Theodorus Petrus Demosthenes, many times city and praetorian prefect under Justinian. And the evidence from eastern diptychs is abundant and unanimous: Fl. Areobindus Dagalaifus Areobindus cos. 506; Fl. Taurus Clementinus Armonius Clementinus cos. 513; Fl. Anastasius Paulus Probus Sabinianus Pompeius Anastasius cos. 517; and the no less polyonymous eastern consuls of 518, 521, 525, 539 and 540.

By contrast, the diptychs of the western consuls of 487, 488 and 530 proclaim their honorands Mar. Manlius Boethius, Rufius Achilius Sividius and Rufius Gennadius Probus Orestes respectively. There are two apparent exceptions that seem to prove the rule. First there is the fragmentary panel from a diptych of Severus, western consul in 470. Both Delbrueck and Volbach supplemented the inscription: [Fl. M]essius Phoeb(us) Sever(us). But anyone who takes a careful look at their photographs will see that there is just no room for the Fl. And then there is the diptych of the last citizen consul, Anicius Faustus Albinus Basilius, eastern consul, but himself a doyen of the aristocracy of old Rome. There are in fact good reasons to believe that the surviving diptych was carved and issued in the West, where he returned after his consulate.[12]

There is at least one other subtle difference in the use of titles between East and West, one that it will prove relevant to survey together with Flavius. By the fifth century the once proud title of *vir clarissimus* counted for little; it did not even carry active membership of the senate.[13] And yet the highest western dignitaries, those whose offices entitled them to the rank of *vir inlustris*, clung to the old formula.[14] Their reason is obvious: its antiquity, certified by the classics of Roman literature. There are almost one hundred examples in the works (mainly orations) of Cicero,[15] and a fair number in the newly fashionable *Letters* of the younger Pliny.[16] To start with, aristocrats simply ignored the new styles *vir spectabilis* and *vir inlustris*. If we may turn again to the fasti of the prefects of Rome, a well documented group of mainly aristocratic birth, the first prefect to use the curious compromise style (retaining the lower along with the higher rank) *v(ir) c(larissimus) et inl(ustris)*, and then in only one out of three dedications, is Postumius Lampadius, PVR 403/7. Anicius Acilius Glabrio Faustus cos.438, is simply *v.c.* in all six of his extant inscriptions. By contrast, he appears seven times as *v.c. et inl.* in the official record of the meeting of the senate that endorsed the publication of the *Theodosian Code* in the West. We may surely assume that the simpler style of his own dedications was his own preference.

For the late fifth and early sixth centuries we have the seats of the Flavian amphitheatre and the *Variae* of Cassiodorus. About 31 seats survive inscribed with the (often fragmentary) names and titles of men of illustrious rank. Of these no fewer than six still maintain a bare *v.c.*; 21 compromise with *v.c. et inl.*; and only six have gone all the way to a bare *v.i.* By contrast, there are some 70 *v.i.*s and not a single *v.c.* among the *viri illustres* addressed in Cassiodorus' *Variae*. Once again, the explanation is presumably that, in official documents from the royal chancellery addressing office-holders by their current rank, Cassiodorus felt obliged to use the official style. Even letters addressed to himself (I.3; III.28) are headed *v.i.* But on the title page of the collection he styled himself *v.c. et inl.*

---

[12]See *JRS* 72 (1982) 136-37.

[13]A.H.M. Jones, *Later Roman Empire* I 529.

[14]This point is made briefly in *JRS* 72 (1982) 135.

[15]For the list, see M. Gelzer, *Kleine Schriften* I (Wiesbaden 1962) 50f. = *The Roman Nobility*, tr. R. Seager (1969) 40-43.

[16]H.U. Instinsky, "Formalien im Briefwechsel des Plinius mit Kaiser Trajan," *Abh. der Akademie der Wiss. und Literatur in Mainz, Geistes- und sozialwiss. Klasse* 1969, no.12, 12-22. For the "rediscovery" of Pliny's *Letters* in the late fourth century, see *CQ* n.s. 15 (1965) 289-98; *CQ* 17 (1967) 421-22; C.P. Jones, *Phoenix* 21 (1967) 301.

In the East there is little trace of this archaizing affectation for *v.c.* or even *v.c. et inl.*[17] Nothing comparable to the inscriptions from Italy and North Africa survives from the fifth and sixth century East, but the usage of the consular diptychs once again makes a clear and telling contrast. We have six western diptychs (from Felix in 428 to Basilius, the westerner who was eastern consul in 541): Felix, the earliest, is *v.c.*; all the others are *v.c. et inl.* The seven eastern diptychs run from Areobindus in 506 to Justinus in 540: every one is a bare *v.i.* or *v.inl.*

If *v.c.* had a comforting antique ring in the ears of a Roman aristocrat, Flavius conspicuously did not. Any Italian notable with a family tree that went back beyond the age of Constantine knew that Flavius was not a particularly common name in the higher reaches of the old nobility.[18] He also knew that it was as common as dirt in the lower reaches of the new municipal elites. Flavius was above all things the hallmark of the *newly* important. It is understandable that the old nobility of the West did not wish to risk confusion with the newly emerging nobility of the East. In the East, however, people were less sensitive to names and titles with a history behind them, and there the conquest of Flavius was complete.

2. Junior

The use of *iunior* with the names of consuls is a peculiarity of protocol in the second half of our period. In western (but not eastern[19]) dating formulas and lists several western consuls of the late fifth and early sixth centuries are styled iunior.[20] In 1873 Mommsen stated in a footnote what we believe to be the true explanation, that such indications had no genealogical value, but served only to distinguish identically-named years.[21] Twenty-five years later, without referring to his own earlier view, he stated no less succinctly a quite different doctrine: "non raro reperitur nominibus adiectum ad distinguendos opinor filium nepotemve a patre vel avo cognomine."[22] Mommsen's final thoughts have prevailed, and it has come to be generally believed that the iunior does after all denote a genealogical relationship. As a result, it appears fairly systematically in prosopographies, as a fixed element in the consul's nomenclature.

Mommsen's article of 1873 dealt only with one consular list (the Fasti Veronenses, of which more below, p.42), and those who have touched on the subject since have likewise been concerned with particular cases. We do not claim to have collected all the evidence bearing on the use of iunior, especially from the earlier period,[23] but we do at least attempt to find an explanation that fits all well-attested cases of junior consuls.

The following are designated iunior in one or more of the ten surviving consular lists:[24] Basilius (cos. 480); Severinus (482); Faustus (483); Symmachus (485); Decius (486); Faustus (490); Olybrius (491); Avienus (501); Avienus (502); Venantius (507); Venantius (508); Inportunus (509); Probus (525); Olybrius (526); Decius (529); Paulinus (534); and Basilius (541). Other evidence suggests that some of these names are mistakes. Naturally we must eliminate the mistakes before we can reach a satisfactory explanation. On

---

[17]V.c. survives in fossilized use in papyrus formulas, but alongside a range of other, more grandiose epithets. For a full list of these, see *CSBE* 132 and cf. *P.Rainer Cent.* 92.

[18]It is perhaps significant that, in one of the very few cases where a Flavius does appear regularly in the full nomenclature of a prominent aristocrat, Q. Flavius Maesius Egnatius Lollianus cos. 355, it is not in first place and normally written out in full (the inscriptions are set out in full by A. Chastagnol, *Les Fastes de la préfecture de Rome au Bas-Empire* (Paris 1962) 114-21; some use the abbreviated style Fl. Lollianus). Note too that he passed the name on to his son, Q. Flavius Maesius Cornelius Egnatius Severus Lollianus (*ILS* 1226). Surely this is (so to speak) a "genuine" Flavius, reflecting a family connection going back before Constantine.

[19]In genuine contemporary contexts, that is. Consular lists of a normally eastern character (in 491, 510, and 540) and two *CJ* laws (in 480 and 502) have picked *iunior* up, presumably by the use of western lists in editing; cf. also below, n.30.

[20]A longer version of this section first appeared in *ZPE* 56 (1984) 159-72.

[21]"Veroneser Fastentafel von 439-494 n.Chr.," *Hermes* 7 (1873) 474-81, reprinted in his *Röm. Forschungen* II (1879) 87 ff.

[22]*Chron.Min.* III 497.

[23]For the careers of the consuls here discussed, reference may be made to *PLRE* II; but for information specifically about the consulates, we refer to our own year-by-year compilation below.

[24]See the year-by-year compilation below for detail. It should be noted that the index to *Chron.Min.* is not fully representative of the actual state of the individual chronicles and lists.

the other hand, we need a working hypothesis before we can begin to eliminate the mistakes with any confidence. Explanation and elimination must proceed hand in hand.

The natural assumption (it might seem) is that iunior was a device to distinguish fathers and sons, especially if they were exact or close homonyms. And the two earliest examples do fit such a hypothesis: Basilius iunior (cos. 480) and Severinus iunior (cos. 482), whose homonymous fathers were consuls respectively in 463 and 461. Then there is Boethius iunior (the philosopher), cos. 510, whose father was consul in 487. But none of these can be shown to be a close homonym. The full name of Boethius iunior, Anicius Manlius Severinus Boethius, is quite different from that of his father, Marius Manlius Boethius.[25] The full name of Basilius iunior--Caecina Decius Maximus Basilius--is closer to his father's--Caecina Decius Basilius--but still not the same. Unfortunately, we do not know the full names of either of the Severini.[26]

Other cases show that the father-son explanation simply cannot be correct. The father of Avienus iunior (cos. 502) was not even called Avienus, but Faustus (cos. 490). It is hardly likely that the iunior was meant to distinguish him from his long dead grandfather, Gennadius Avienus (cos. 450). There can in fact be little doubt that the point was to distinguish him from a cousin called Avienus, who had been consul the year before, 501.[27] Similarly his father, Fl. Anicius Probus Faustus (cos. 490), is surely styled iunior in consular documents to distinguish him from Anicius Acilius Aginantius Faustus (cos. 483), who may not have been related to him at all.[28]

There was a reason for the development of what was certainly a new practice. Up till the deposition of the last western emperor in 476 there had normally been two consuls each year and whenever they were known, both names were used in dating formulas. But under Odoacar and Theoderic things changed. On the one hand there was often only one consul a year; and on the other, even when there was an eastern consul, it became customary in the West to date by the western consul alone. In theory it should have been easy to distinguish between the homonymous western consuls of 501 (*Avieno et Pompeio*) and 502 (*Avieno et Probo*) by their different eastern colleagues. In practice, the names of Pompeius and Probus are never found in western consular documents. Instead we have one batch of inscriptions dated 'Avieno v.c. consule' (presumably 501) and another batch 'Avieno iuniore v.c. consule' or 'consulatu Avieni iunioris v.c.' (presumably 502). Probus iunior, cos. 525, was presumably so styled to distinguish him from Probus, cos. 513, who is not known to have been related to him. Once again, both had eastern colleagues, but the western inscriptions give either 'Probo v.c. cons.' alone (presumably 513), or 'Probo iun. v.c. cons.' (presumably 525). That in some cases at least Probus iunior is the consul of 525 rather than 513 is proved by the indiction numbers of *ILCV* 2890 and 1162A.

There were also two consuls called Paulinus and two called Decius in our period, again not at all closely related. The later Decius was sole consul in his year (529) and the eastern colleague of Decius cos. 486 is only once mentioned in a western formula (in Gaul: *AE* 1928, 83 = *I.Lat.Gaul.Narb.* 606).[29] The eastern colleagues of the two Paulini (498 and 534) are also ignored in western consular documents; in addition, ignoring the eastern consuls of both years, 499 and 500 (when there were no new western consuls) were known in the West as 'p.c. Paulini' and 'iterum p.c. Paulini' respectively. It was thus essential to distinguish between the consular years of the two Decii and the two Paulini, and it is surely no coincidence

---

[25]For the name, see *ZPE* 44 (1981) 181-83.

[26]According to Chastagnol, the point of the iunior was to indicate that the father was still alive when the son became consul (*Le sénat romain sous le règne d'Odoacre* [Bonn 1966] 40). There is no way of disproving this hypothesis for the Basilii and the Severini, but it is certainly not true of the Boethii; Boethius iunior is known to have been left an orphan and brought up by another family, probably the Symmachi.

[27]Mommsen wrongly dated the first session of the council quoted below to 501 (in his edition of Cassiodorus, *MGH*, AA 12 [1898] 416) and so wrongly identified the consuls of 501 and 502. For the correct identifications, following Sundwall, see now *PLRE* II 192-93.

[28]Albinus cos. 493 is called *iunior* by one inscription (*CIL* XI 4163) but by no other source--to distinguish him from the consul of 444? The latter may have been his great-grandfather.

[29]Inscriptions from Gaul--beyond the borders of the Ostrogothic kingdom of Italy--show wider (though spasmodic) knowledge of eastern consuls: see above, pp.34-35.

that once again we find the two sets of formulas in inscriptions: 'Decio/p.c. Decii' (13 times) and 'Decio iun./p.c. Decii iun.' (6), 'Paulino' (10, one of them a papyrus) and 'Paulino iun.' (dozens including the p.c.'s). One of the 'Decio' inscriptions gives the correct indiction number for 486 (*CIL* V 5423 = *ILCV* 1445A adn.); and many of the 'Paulino iun.' bear the correct indiction number for 534 (or the proper postconsular year).

Despite their undoubted father-son relationship, this explanation also fits the cases of the two Severini and the two Basilii. For various reasons, the elder Severinus and the elder Basilius were the only consuls generally recognized in the West during their years (461 and 463). Since the younger Severinus and the younger Basilius were sole consuls in their years, without some mark of differentiation the years of father and son would have been indistinguishable, both 'Severino v.c. cons.' and 'Basilio v.c. cons.' The two Boethii (487 and 510) were likewise both sole consuls in their years. This use of iunior is an exclusively western phenomenon. None of these consuls is styled iunior (or νέος, the Greek equivalent) in eastern consular documents (e.g., the papyri), where the same possibilities of confusion did not exist.[30]

A few entries in some of the fasti do not fit this explanation. No one familiar with the multitude of errors to be found in these lists will be in much doubt that in most if not all cases the entries in question are simply mistaken. For example, it is only the erratic Victor Tunnunensis who calls Inportunus, cos. 509, iunior. Since this is the only known occurrence of the name in the Roman aristocracy let alone the consular fasti, here at least we may safely disregard the iunior. The commonest error is a tendency for fasti to duplicate iunior consuls. For example, some fasti (oddly followed by *PLRE* II) style the consul of 501 'Avienus iunior' as well as the consul of 502. It is difficult to believe that, when homonyms were consuls in successive years, contemporaries so far further compounded confusion as to call both iunior. The obvious explanation is that the first iunior was mistakenly added in retrospective anticipation.[31]

Less clearcut is the case of Olybrius, sole eastern consul in 491--and the only eastern consul to figure in this discussion. Five western lists[32] call him iunior, but there seems no pressing reason to distinguish him from his grandfather, who was eastern consul (with an eastern colleague) in 464 (the year is mostly cited in the fasti as 'Rusticio [or Rustico] et Olybrio' or with wrong inverted order; only Hyd. and Aq. (Q) give Olybrius alone). In 526 another Olybrius was consul (in the west), and two of the same lists that had called Olybrius cos. 491 iunior call this later Olybrius iunior also. Erroneous duplication might be postulated here, but the two other lists--the Fasti Augustani and Cassiodorus--both stop before 526. It is true that one other list that stops before 526, the Fasti Veronenses, a list (as we shall see) very prone to add false iuniors, does not so style Olybrius 491, but there is also one Gallic inscription (*ILCV* 1734), where the indiction number proves that 'Olibrius iunior' there at least must refer to 491 rather than to 526. But in this case there may be another explanation altogether. The Chronicon Paschale, while styling Olybrius 491 just 'Olybrius' under his own consular year, elsewhere calls him Olybrios ὁ μικρός without reference to his consulate (p.594.10, s.a. 464). And one usually accurate eastern list, the Fasti Heracliani (*Chron. Min.* III 406), calls him Olybrios ναίος (i.e. νέοςᾱ. It may be that, alone among the consuls here discussed, Olybrius was actually known as 'Olybrius the young (or younger)' in social as well as consular contexts. Nor is it hard to think of the reason: he became consul as a mere child, barely ten years old, perhaps even less.[33]

The most perplexing single document is the Fasti Veronenses. Not only does it give Basilius (480) and Severinus (482) as iunior, but also Faustus (483), Symmachus (485), and Decius (486). Not one other consular list styles this Decius iunior, while several so style Decius cos. 529. There is similar differentiation in the inscriptions. Surely only the latter of the two was really called 'Decius iunior.'

---

[30]There are, however, examples of νέος used in eastern documents referring to emperors being distinguished from earlier homonyms: cf. e.g. the Egyptian documents in 376-377 and 474-476, as well as Heracl. on 352, 378; Marcell. on 418; Pasch. on 411/412, 416, 420, 426, 430, 435; Scal. on 320 (cf. below, p.53), 353, 354, 377, 378.

[31]Cf. S. Timpanaro, *The Freudian Slip* (London 1976) 97.

[32]For the list see below s.a. 491.

[33]See *PLRE* II 795, Olybrius 5. For Iunior as a proper name, see *PLRE* I 486, especially 'v.c. Iunior' in Symm., *Rel.* 31.2.

Only one other list calls Faustus cos. 483 iunior, the Fasti Augustani. Once again, there seems no reason so to style him, and there is an undoubted Faustus iunior a few years later in 490. Once again, too, there are four inscriptions 'Fausto v.c. cons.' and six 'Fausto iun. (v.c.) cons.' There is also one inscription 'cons. Aginanti Fausti' (*ICUR* n.s. II 4985), and one 'post cons. Probi Fausti'; another offers the interesting (but strictly unnecessary) combination 'Probo Fausto iun.' (*ICUR* n.s. VII 17598; cf. *CIL* XI 4333, without iun.). Clearly these important contemporaries--in full Anicius Acilius Aginantius Faustus (483) and Anicius Probus Faustus (490)--were concerned not to be confused.[34] Writers of the age differentiate them as 'Faustus albus' (Ennodius, *Epp.* 6.34) and 'Faustus niger' (Anon.Val. 12.57). One contemporary consular list (the Fasti Aug.) gives 490 as 'Fausto nigro cons.', another (the Fasti Veron.) uses yet another formula (to which we shall be returning), 'Fausto alio et Longino.' There are in addition five postconsular references to 491 or 492 that include the eastern consul of the year (Longinus II: from Italy, *CIL* V 5210; 5656; 7531; from Gaul, *AE* 1965, 141; *CIL* XII 2058). Naturally this rendered a iunior unnecessary, and it is therefore the more significant that it is not to be found in a single one of these cases. The addition of a iunior was just one of several alternative ways of differentiating homonymous consulates.

But there is a problem with the hypothesis of simple confusion between homonyms in the Fasti Veronenses here. For these fasti are generally supposed to have been compiled before even the second Faustus let alone the second Decius had become consul. They comprise one venerable folium on which a fine half uncial hand listed the consuls from 439 to 486; another hand has added the consuls from 487 to 494.[35] It appears to be the last page of a list originally completed in 486 and then brought up to date in 494. But contemporary or not, the compiler was an ignorant fellow: he gives the consul of 479 as 'Zeno v.c.', apparently unaware that this was the eastern emperor. Mommsen plausibly suggested that he was under the impression that 'iun. v.c. cons.' was the standard style for the new phenomenon of sole consul.[36] So far as can be judged from his 8 entries, the continuator was rather better informed: he gives three eastern consuls and no false iuniors. Did he perhaps write 'Fausto alio et Longino' under 490 because he saw that 'Faustus iunior' might be taken for the same man as the 'Faustus iunior' already entered under 483?

For this use of alius we have four other examples, all applied to Venantius cos. 508--and for the same reason. The first Venantius to appear on western lists as sole consul was in 484. It is presumably he to whom most of a dozen inscriptions (some dated by a postconsulate) and one Ravenna papyrus refer as just 'Venantius v.c.' Then came the consular Venantii of 507 and 508. In the ordinary way we might have expected a iunior for 507, and it seems natural to guess that some of the inscriptions that offer 'Venantius iunior' refer to him. But what was to be done when a third Venantius became sole western consul in the very next year? The lists cope with the problem in various ways. Cassiodorus (*Chron.Min.* II 160) gives each his eastern colleague, adding a iunior for 508:

507: Anastasio Augusto III et Venantio
508: Venantio iuniore et Celere

The Paschale Campanum (*Chron.Min.* I 747) offer 'Venantio' for 507 and adds another of the consul's names, 'Basilio Venantio,' for 508; the various continuators of Victor of Aquitaine (*Chron.Min.* I 728) offer (leaving v.c. aside) 'Venantio' for 507 and for 508 (1) 'Venantio Basilio iun.' (Q), (2) 'Basilio Venantio iun.' (N), and (3) 'Venantio Basilio' (LS); Victor Tunn. (*Chron.Min.* II 194) distinguishes them as 'Venantio et Celere' and 'Venantio iun.', though he ruined his efforts by transposing 507 and 508! That is to say, Victor's source must have given 'Venantius iunior' for 507 and added the eastern colleague to distinguish the third Venantius. *ICUR* I 935 = n.s. II 4278 discloses another way of distinguishing 507 from 508 without using another name: '[Ven]antio alio iun.', a usage also found in an anonymous but

[34]See their entries in *PLRE* II, Faustus 4 and 9, for all the details.
[35]In addition to Mommsen's original publication (supra, n.21), see the improved text in *Chron. Min.* III 382-83.
[36]Above, n.21, 480-81.

authoritative continuation of Prosper Tiro, offering 'Venantio iun.' for 507 and 'alio Venantio' for 508 (*Chron.Min.* I 331).[37] The clear implication is that this was the second Venantius iunior--and so inescapably the consul of 508. Bearing in mind the 'Fausto alio' of Fasti Veronenses s.a. 490, we should probably interpret in the same way *CIL* XI 4978 (add. on p.1376), 'Venantio cons. alio.' It should also be noted that the eastern Fasti Heracliani offer Καίλλερος καὶ ἄλλου Βεναντίου (*Chron.Min.* III 406) under 508.

   But it might be rash to insist on a consistent threefold division of the extant Venantius formulas on these lines: that is to say 'Venantius' (484), 'Venantius iunior' (507) and 'Venantius alius' or 'alius iunior' (508). For example, we have a letter from King Theoderic to the senate of Rome written by Cassiodorus, dated just 'Venantio v.c. consule' (p.392 Mommsen). Now 484 is impossibly early for Cassiodorus (and Theoderic), so this has to be the consul of either 507 or 508. Mommsen left it an open question which, but it is difficult to believe that anyone writing in 508 would not have taken some steps to differentiate 508 from 507. On the other hand, the Roman senate was not in much danger of supposing in 507 that Theoderic's letter was written in 484--a year before the earliest possible date for Cassiodorus' birth. For such a document, 'Venantio' alone was quite sufficient. But if the same document had been publicly inscribed, to compete for the reader's attention with the monuments of centuries past and to come, then more precision would surely have been added to the dating formula. We may compare a legal papyrus from Ravenna listing a series of *cautiones*, securities for fairly substantial loans made to different parties at different times.[38] For this purpose it was obviously essential that there should be no possibility of error or dispute about the dates. And yet there is not one reference to an eastern consular collegue in the 16 consular dates given in the list. Instead, we find no fewer than 8 references to iunior consuls. Seven are to 'Boethius iunior' (510), evidently to be distinguished from the one loan (line 13) made 'Boethio consul.' (487). Then there is the one loan each made 'Venantio' (line 27) and 'Venantio iun. consul.' (line 24). Those who have paid any attention to this document have so far assumed that these lines refer to the successive consuls of 507 and 508. But since at least one of the loans in this incompletely preserved list is as early as 487 ('Boethio consul.'), a reference to the first consular Venantius of 484 is clearly within the bounds of possibility. Indeed, it is surely mandatory. Given the consistency of his practice, how else is this writer likely to have designated 484? So 'Venantio' refers to 484 and 'Venantio iun.' to 507; if he had needed to refer to 508 he would presumably have added either an alius or some other element in the consul's name. It is curious but nonetheless a fact that only one extant inscription differentiates between the three Venantii by adding (to the third) an eastern colleague, and that one comes from Narbonne (*ILCV* 3555, A.D. 508; cf. above, p.35).

   There is only one other case where three homonyms held sole consulates: the Basilii of 463, 480, and 541.[39] There can be no doubt that the consuls of 480 and 541 were both styled iunior in the western documents. There is no sign of any consistent attempt to differentiate them, though of course the possibility of confusion was minimized by the interval of more than 60 years between them. Since Basilius 463 seems not to have been proclaimed in the East (as the p.c.'s in 464 in the papyri show), naturally there was no need for Basilius 480 to be consistently styled iunior in the East.[40] But it is interesting to note that Basilius 541 was not a iunior in the East either, although, like Basilius 480, he was sole consul in his year. Since he happened also to be the last non-imperial consul, his name appears more often in the papyri than that of any previous consul, in the p.c. formulas of the 25 years following his own, and not once is he iunior or νέος. Once again the explanation is presumably the 60 year interval; there was no serious risk of confusion. It should also be noted that the use of indictions and the addition of regnal formulas helped avoid any possible uncertainty.

[37]This same list gives 502 as 'Avieno alio iun.', though his entry for 501 is simply 'Avieno,' not 'Avieno iun.'
[38]J.O. Tjäder, *Nichtliterarische lateinische Papyri Italiens* II 47-48A.
[39]On these three consuls see Alan Cameron and Diane Schauer, "The Last Consul: Basilius and his Diptych," *JRS* 72 (1982) 126-45.
[40]Cf. the exceptional (and no doubt corrected) *CJ* 6.23.22 from 1.v.480.

But rather more has to be said about the 'Symmachus iunior' (485) of the Fasti Veronenses. On the one hand it makes no obvious sense on any hypothesis: the last Symmachus to hold the consulate was in 446: Not only did he have a western colleague (the year is always styled 'Aetio III et Symmacho'); if he was really (as usually assumed) the father of Symmachus cos. 485,[41] he is hardly likely still to have been alive for his son's consulate, forty years after his own. Furthermore, there are numerous inscriptions from Rome which offer only 'cons. Symmachi v.c.' or 'Symmacho v.c. cons.' and Symmachus cos. 485 is the only Symmachus ever to be sole consul in his year.

On the other hand, there is a certain amount of solid support for the iunior: two inscriptions and an anonymous epitaph. First, *CIL* XII 2487 (= *ILCV* 1421A): 'se[xie]s post cons. Sym. iuni[oris],' i.e. 491; *CIL* XII 932 (= *ILCV* 4420), 'decies p.c. Sy[mma]chi iun. v.c. i[ndic]tione tertia,' i.e. 495. Then there is the statement in the epitaph that a bishop called Namatius died 73 years after the consulate of "Symmachus iunior" (i.e. 558):[42]

> septies hic denos et tres compleverat annos,
> post fasces posuit vel cingula Symmachus alma
> iunior...

These three texts have two points in common: all are unusually long periods of time reckoned after Symmachus' consulate; and all are from Narbonensis. But most Gallic inscriptions (including p.c.'s) offer just 'Symmacho' (*ILCV* 2888 adn.; 1340, 2765; 1118; 2889A) like those from Italy. Nor is there any reason to assign the Fasti Veronenses to Gaul: on palaeographical grounds E.A. Lowe classified the MS̩ 'origin uncertain, presumably North Italy.'[43] And 'Symmachus iunior' is also found in one Roman inscription (*ICUR* n.s. II 5869) and one late Italian chronicle, *Haun.* (*Chron.Min.* I 313). On any hypothesis it must remain an anomaly. All other inscriptions from the year simply have v.c. after the name. Why should anyone have wanted to distinguish the consul of 485 from his consular forebears when there was no real likelihood of confusion? Or from some living homonym; for this hypothetical homonym could not have been consul, and the evidence for 'Symmachus iunior,' such as it is, is limited to consular documents. The nomenclature--Q. Aurelius Memmius Symmachus--and titles of this well known figure are transmitted in full by a number of other contemporary documents of unimpeachable authority, notably the works of his son-in-law Boethius, never with a iunior. If it was an error, it was a contemporary error[44]--and not isolated. But whatever the explanation, it is certain that Symmachus was never styled iunior in any but a consular context.

The evidence cannot be reduced to perfect harmony, but the view here offered seems to explain most of our evidence and (apart from the errors of the Fasti Veronenses) encounters serious difficulty only with Symmachus. The suffix iunior was not used or intended to distinguish consuls as individuals but as consular dates.

It follows that iunior is not to be treated as a standing element in the nomenclature of the consuls discussed in these pages. Had it become a fixed element in a man's name, the problem of differentiating him from his son in turn would soon have arisen. The consul of 510 is entered in *PLRE* II as 'Anicius Manlius Severinus Boethius iunior.' In fact, he is either 'Anicius Manlius Severinus Boethius' (as he always styled himself in the headings to his books) or, as a consular date, 'Boethius iunior.' The conclusion that these are alternative styles, not to be combined, is perfectly illustrated by the acta of two sessions of a church council held at Rome in 502, the second of two successive years with an Avienus as consul. The first proceedings are dated 'Rufio Magno Fausto Avieno v.c. consule' (Mommsen's edition of Cassiodorus, pp. 420.14; 426.6); the second 'Fl. Avieno iun. v.c. cons.' (ibid., p.438.4). Writing the man's name out in full was

---

[41]*PLRE* II, Symmachus 3 and 9, with *JRS* 72 (1982) 144.
[42]Avitus, App. 11.29-30, p.189 Peiper.
[43]*Codices Latini Antiquiores* IV (1947) 30 no. 508.
[44]Mommsen suggested that this was thought to be the correct style for a sole consul; cf. n.36.

one way of identifying him (and so the year); adding iunior to his last name was another (and briefer) way. What might have seemed the obvious way--adding the name of his eastern colleague--is just not found.[45]

   There is indeed a letter to Avitus of Vienne published together with the correspondence of Pope Symmachus dated 13 October 'Avieno et Pompeio consulibus' (*Epp.Pont.Rom.* I, ed. A. Thiel [1867-68] 657). By October the names of the consuls designated for 502 could have been known, and it might seem tempting to conjecture that it was to forestall the possibility of confusion next year that, against the normal practice of the papal chancellery at this period, a secretary added the name of the eastern consul. Unfortunately for so plausible a hypothesis, the letter is an outright modern forgery, fabricated by the eccentric Abbé Vignier *ca* 1660. De Rossi had already expressed doubts about the consular date when J. Havet recognized it as simply one more telltale trace of the forger.[46]

[45]The names of eastern consuls are found in Gaul in a number of years in this period, but hardly ever in Rome. In 490, for example, Rome uses Faustus iun., while Gaul has Longinus II and Faustus. Cf. above, pp.35 and 43.

[46]"Questions mérovingiennes II: les découvertes de Jérôme Vignier," *Bibliothèque de l'école des Chartes* 46 (1885) 205-71 (256-61 on the letter of Symmachus). J. Sundwall, *Abhandlungen zur Geschichte des ausgehenden Römertums* (Helsinki 1919) 206 n.4, made light of Havet's 'doubts,' but there can be no question that Vignier simply fabricated it, together with a small corpus of other documents, from genuine material that Havet was able to track down. Nothing but Vignier's own papers (certainly no manuscript evidence) was ever found. It may be helpful to list the other papal documents Vignier forged: Leontius of Arles to Pope Hilarius (Hil., *Ep. 5*, p.138 Thiel); Pope Gelasius to Rusticus of Lyons (*Ep. 13*, p.358 Thiel); Pope Anastasius to Clovis the Frank (*Ep. 2*, p.623 Thiel). On the alleged letter of Pope Symmachus (also printed in R. Peiper's edition of Avitus of Vienne, p.63; cf. Jaffé no.756) see too E. Caspar, *Geschichte des Papsttums* II (1933) 90 n.9. Whatever questions Havet left unanswered have been dealt with exhaustively by H. Rahner, *Die gefälschten Papstbriefe aus dem Nachlass von Jérôme Vignier* (Munich 1935).

Chapter 4

Chronicles and Consular Lists

Only one consular list engraved on stone (common in the early empire) has so far been found, the *Fasti Caleni*, and (as preserved) it goes no further than 289 or a little later (see notes *ad annum*). But a great many have been preserved by MS tradition, most conveniently available in the three incomparable volumes of Mommsen's *Chronica Minora* (1892, 1894, 1898).[1] Some are bare consular lists; some chronicles (of varying compass) dated by consuls.

It will be obvious that no list covering more than 30 years or so can be attributed to the care or carelessness of any one individual. The work of many hands must lie behind lists covering many centuries. Naturally enough the early part of later lists is usually copied from earlier lists, which can sometimes be identified. But the copy is never exact or complete. Over and above the likelihood of simple error (on the part of both original compiler and later copyist), and correction or contamination from another list, once the compiler reached his own day he maintained his list himself. Old chronicles may delight historians, but lawyers and administrators need them kept up to date. Several of the extant lists bear clear traces of year by year maintenance (retention of provisional or superseded formulas), traces which sometimes help to explain some anomaly in the papyri or inscriptions.

These scrappy, tantalizing but often important texts stand in urgent need of comprehensive research.[2] The following brief characterizations are intended to do no more than provide the basic facts relevant to their value and accuracy *as consular lists*. For example, our praise of the Paschal Chronicle's consular list should not be taken to imply that it is accurate *as a chronicle*, which it is not;[3] but it does reproduce consular names in more or less recognizable form and accurate sequence. Note also that our remarks apply only to those parts of the works discussed that cover the period 284-541. To take the same example, the Paschal Chronicle's consular list for the Republic is worthless.

1. Western Lists

1. *Chronographer of 354*, 288-410 (*Chr. 354*)

The misleadingly entitled "Chronographer of 354" consists of a series of lists (Christian and pagan, some illustrated) put together at Rome in or about 354 (Mommsen, *Chron.Min.* I 15-148, with more details in *Ges.Schriften* VII [1909] 536-79; for the illustrations, H. Stern, *Le calendrier de 354* [Paris 1953], and in *ANRW* 12.2 [1981] 431-75; M. Salzman, *AJA* 88 [1984] 43-50). For our purposes, the relevant items are: (1) a consular list from the beginning to 354; (2) a list of praefecti urbis, also including a consular list for every year from 254 to 354; (3) a Paschal Cycle with consular dates for every year from 312 to 354, which was subsequently maintained (with the exception of 359-367) up to 410; (4) a list of bishops of Rome (a vital document for the history of the Papacy) with consular dates for those years in which a pope died or was

---

[1]Near the end of his labors (in a letter of 16.vii.1893), Mommsen ruefully referred to his "chronische Krankheit" (*Mommsen und Wilamowitz: Briefwechsel 1872-1903* [Berlin 1935] 473).
[2]Forthcoming books by Steven Muhlberger on Prosper, Hydatius and the Gallic Chronicle of 452 and by Brian Croke on Marcellinus Comes will do much to fill this gap.
[3]For example, see Cameron, *YCS* 27 (1982) 259-62.

elected. Of these, the most interesting is the list of prefects, which preserves two consular pairs of the usurper Magnentius (351-352) retroactively eliminated from the other lists--and from all other extant lists.

Given the importance of consular annals[4] as a subliterary genre from the late fourth century on, it is significant (as Muhlberger has emphasised) that the consular list of Chr. 354 contains no historical entries. Indeed, their absence was felt in later times, and in two extant MSS (Vindobonensis 3416 and Sangallensis 878) excerpts from such a work going down to the sixth century have been added (the Fasti Vindobonenses, discussed below). As we shall see, the genre seems to have evolved at Constantinople in the 360's, with the Fasti Hydatiani. No one had yet thought to take this step at Rome in 354.

2. Consularia Italica

This was the title Mommsen gave to a group of texts which share a number of common features and entries (*Chron.Min.* I 251-339):

> I: *Anonymi Valesiani pars posterior*, 474-526 (*Val.*)
> II: *Fasti Vindobonenses priores* (*VindPr.*)
> III: *Fasti Vindobonenses posteriores* (*VindPost.*)
> IV: *Paschale Campanum*, 464-541 (*Camp.*)
> V: *Continuatio Hauniensis Prosperi*, 388-523 (*Haun.*)
> VI: *Excerpta ex Barbaro Scaligeri*
> VII: *Excerpta ex Agnelli Libro Pontificali Ecclesiae*
>   *Ravennatis*[5]

What Mommsen called the *Vindobonenses priores* (Anonymus Cuspiniani in the earlier literature) are a set of consular annals going from 44 B.C. to A.D. 403 and (after a gap) 455 to 493 (where they break off abruptly). They are found in only one MS, Vindobonensis 3416 (f.47-53), together with Chr. 354 (*Chron.Min.* I 263). The latter section shows local knowledge of Ravenna, and signs of year by year maintenance. Curiously enough they were edited twice in the same year (and never since): *Chron.Min.* I 274f.; C. Frick, *Chron.Min.* I 375f.

The *Vindobonenses posteriores* are to be found in the same MS (f.15-24), and go (as extant) from 44 B.C. to 387 (with omissions before our period), 439 to 455 and 495 to 539. Though less full, they are closely related to the *priores*, but neither copy nor source. The *priores* are in general more accurate, though the *posteriores* often preserve titles more fully. Here as with many other chronicles preserved in medieval manuscripts, we have not bothered to record the often preposterous distortions of proper names. For example, the *priores* tend to write Constantius indiscriminately, the *posteriores* Constantinus. Like the *Fasti Augustani* (see below), the *posteriores* also have a tendency to get one consul out of step over long stretches, as though miscopying a text where one name was written below rather than beside the other.

The *Excerpta Sangallensia* are a selection of closely related though sometimes fuller entries between 390 and 573, transmitted again in a MS that contains (excerpts from) Chr. 354 (Sangallensis 878).

What Mommsen put together under the title *Prosperi Continuatio Hauniensis* (*Chron.Min.* I 266-71) consists of a fragmentary series of overlapping extracts in the form of supplements to the Chronicle of Prosper in a 12th/13th century MS (Haun. 454), evidently taken by a seventh century compiler from a

---

[4]That is to say, consular lists that include brief historical entries, in the main restricted to imperial births, deaths and accessions, victories won, and natural disasters. On the development of the genre, see Steven Muhlberger, *The Fifth Century Chroniclers: Prosper, Hydatius and the Gallic Chronicler of 452* (forthcoming) and Brian Croke, *Count Marcellinus* (forthcoming).
[5]Nothing need be said here about Agnellus, since he quotes no consular dates.

related but fuller chronicle covering (at least) 388 to 523. Some years are covered more than once, while 458-473 are entirely omitted. Consular dates are given with all the trimmings, sometimes in unusual detail: e.g. the formula *perpetuo Augusto* at 479 and 492. A full analysis and a new edition of the text is provided by R. Cessi in *Archivio muratoriano* 22 (1922) 587-641; see too M.A. Wes, *Das Ende des Kaisertums* (The Hague 1967) 57-66 and S. Muhlberger's useful study (together with a translation of the text) in *Florilegium* 6 (1984) 50-95. For Prosper, see below, no.3.

To these we must now add the illustrated fragment of a fifth century chronicle published, under the title *Annales Ravennates (Rav.)*, by B. Bischoff and W. Koehler, "Un'edizione illustrata degli Annali Ravennati del basso impero," *Studi Romagnoli* 3 (1952) 1-17 (originally published in German in *Medieval Studies in Memory of A. Kingsley Porter*, ed. W.R.W. Koehler I [Cambridge 1939] 125-38): the bottom half of one page from an eleventh century MS in Merseburg containing illustrated entries for the years 411-413, 422-423, 427-429, 434-437, 440-443 and 452-454, though the names of the consuls for 412 and 422 have been omitted (and those for 452 cut off by the tear in the page). It contains a number of entries related to the preceding texts and was clearly written in Ravenna.

It was O. Holder-Egger[6] who first worked out in detail the theory that the first four texts (and many others) derive from officially maintained "Annals of Ravenna". His main argument for the official nature of these annals, repeated as though decisive by R.Cessi,[7] is the fact that emperors are always styled *dominus noster*. But this is also true of countless private consular documents (papyri, tombstones and the like). Decisive on the other side is the fact that the accession and death of usurpers is regularly recorded in the same style as that of legitimate emperors: e.g. "eo die levatus Eugenius imp. xi kl. Sept." (VindPr. s.a. 391, cf. 394). The very triviality and sparseness of the notices is also against such a hypothesis; why should the government officially record earthquakes? The truth is surely that these are no more than the variously memorable events by which people orient their lives. We tend to forget how difficult this must have been in the absence of a uniformly progressive dating system. Earthquakes, wars and major imperial events were far more memorable than consular names; combine the two and you had a genuinely practical document.

It is in fact only a brief stretch (*ca* 456-495) of the annals that lie behind the first four texts that may with any confidence be claimed to have been maintained at Ravenna. The notice in VindPost. under 495, "fiunt ergo ab adventu Domini usque ad consulatum Viatoris anni D, ab Adam autem anni VI milia," suggests a redaction that stopped in 495. According to Holder-Egger, there is no reason why the entry in VindPost. under 443 describing the effects of an earthquake at Rome should not have been recorded at Ravenna. Unfortunately, the Merseburg fragment records the effects of the same quake at Ravenna. It follows that the years before *ca* 450 in the other four texts must have been maintained at Rome (as other references to Rome confirm).

Mommsen ignored the debate about "Ravenna Annals" and instead simply set out in parallel columns seven obviously related texts that were undoubtedly compiled or maintained in Italy. He did not mean to suggest (nor are we entitled to assume) that an item found in only one of the seven is a lone survival from some "Urchronik" rather than a later interpolation. It is not so much the ultimate existence, in some sense, of a common source that is in doubt, as the centrality of its role in the tradition. Nor by calling this group *Consularia Italica* did Mommsen mean to distinguish them sharply from the other group he called *Consularia Constantinopolitana*. The two groups are indeed very closely related for the fourth century and earlier. The difference turns on where they were maintained on a year by year basis. Thus defined, Mommsen's groupings and parallel columns are a helpful way of setting out the texts. But since our business is less with the similarities than the differences between the various lists, we cite each one separately throughout. This is the more necessary with the large Italian group in that all its components are fragmentary, and for any given year the consensus implied by the label "Ital." might amount to as little as one list--or as many as three or four all in conflict.

---

[6]*Neues Archiv* 1 (1877) 215-368, building on G. Waitz, *Nachrichten Göttingen* (1865) 81-114.
[7]Holder-Egger, 241; R. Cessi, *Archivio muratoriano* 17-18 (1916) 377.

In addition to the five already listed, Mommsen also included the two following more marginally related texts:

Paschale Campanum: This text is to be found a few leaves after Victor of Aquitaine (no.6 below) in a seventh century Vatican manuscript (*Vat.Reg.* 2077, f.96-98), with a consular list going from 464 to 543 (*Chron.Min.* I 744-50). It may have been maintained in Campania at some time (Mommsen, p.744). There are almost no eastern consuls, none at all between 494 and 536, where 'quod est consulatu Vili[sari]' is written in the margin by 'it. p.c. Paulini.' Since no consulate of the Emperor Anastasius later than 492 is noted, 'Anastasius Inportuno' in 509 (also in N of AqS: *Chron.Min.* I 728) is puzzling--unless Anastasius is simply one of Inportunus' names (cf. 'Basilio Venantio' in 508; Anastasius is found as a Roman aristocratic name at this period: cf. *PLRE* II 81-82).

The *Anonymi Valesiani pars posterior* is a work of an altogether different order from the others (and cited by us under "other"), a detailed narrative of the reign of Theoderic the Goth (in fact from 474-526) drawing (among other sources) on Italian consular annals and containing only a few consular dates. In addition to Mommsen's edition (cf. *Chron.Min.* I 259-62) there is the Teubner edition of J. Moreau, rev. V. Velkov (1968), with useful bibliography.

Mommsen also included among his *Ital.* the chronicle known as "Scaliger's Barbarian." This is, however, no more than a Latin translation of an Alexandrian chronicle, and is treated below with that group.

3. Prosper Tiro, 284-455 (Prosp.); Add. ad Prosp., 446-466

Prosper Tiro wrote in Gaul an *epitoma chronicon* which abbreviates Jerome's *Chronicle* (with the insertion of consular dates) and continues it up to (in the first instance) 433 (*Chron.Min.* I 343-499). Subsequently he published continuations up to 445, 451, and (finally) 455 (Mommsen, p.345). According to Mommsen, *post Adelfi consolatum* in the heading to the recension in *Par.Lat.* 4871 (Mommsen, p.346) implies an edition that was completed in 451 before the news of the consulate of the new eastern emperor Marcian arrived. The truth is that Valentinian III did not recognize Marcian's first consulate. Steven Muhlberger has shown that there is no basis for Mommsen's further suggestion (based on a mistaken interpretation of Victor Tunn.'s preface) that there was also an edition going down to 443.[8]

Prosper got his consuls from the same inaccurate source as the 'Italian' chronicles discussed above, and for the early centuries his list is full of errors (Mommsen, pp. 354-55 with his judgment at p.355: "ex parentibus prodigiosis monstrum informe natum esse consentaneum est"). For our period it is more reliable, but there are errors at 307, 311, 330 and eastern consuls (included in other western lists) omitted at 404, 414, 451 and 452. There are several brief anonymous continuations of Prosper, none going later than 466 (*Chron.Min.* I 486-99).

4. Marius of Aventicum, 455-581 (Marius)

Marius, Bishop of Aventicum (Avenches, near Lausanne), compiled a chronicle from 455 to 581 in continuation of Prosper (*Chron.Min.* I 227-39). While drawing a number of entries from the *Consularia Italica*, he also consulted an eastern chronicle, and includes the following eastern consuls[9] generally omitted in the representatives of Mommsen's "Italic" tradition: 490, 500, 505, 506, 508, 511, 512, 513, 515, 517, 518,

---

[8]*CP* 81 (1986) 240-44.
[9]See Chapter 5 for the fact that the dated inscriptions of Gaul often show knowledge of eastern consuls.

519, 520, 521, 524 and 525 (e.g. for 500, 'Patricio et Hypatio' rather than 'iterum p.c. Paulini' as in regular western consular documents and lists); cf. also 528 and 533. But he does not include all eastern consuls (e.g. 'p.c. Paulini' for 499).

While in general Marius gives his consuls in the western sequence, in 490, 505, 513, 517, 519, 521 and 524 the eastern name comes first (e.g. 'Longino et Fausto' for 490). Marius also includes information of eastern origin (e.g. the Nika revolt and Belisarius' Vandalic triumph in Constantinople under 532 and 534). He also regularly includes indiction numbers, likewise absent from the lists of Mommsen's "Italic" tradition.

Catherine Morton ("Marius of Avenches, the 'Excerpta Valesiana', and the Death of Boethius," *Traditio* 38 [1982] 107-36) has recently republished from the unique tenth century MS (BM Add. 16974) the years 489-540, together with a photograph and a commentary sternly critical of Marius' accuracy. Her purpose was to cast doubt on his dates for the execution of Boethius (524) and Symmachus (525). To be sure, Marius' Chronicle is a poor piece of work, but many of the faults she finds should be imputed rather to his copyists, and it is going too far to say that he "often...assigns events to the wrong year" (p.114). There is not a single indisputable example of this. It is only because the consuls of 493 have been omitted (surely by a copyist) that the extant text appears to assign Odoacar's defeat to 492, and Marius has not "incredibly prolonged" the life of Justin I (s.a. 540); he has simply confused him with Iustinus cos. 540.

5. *Liber Paschalis codicis Cizensis 447*, 365-388 (*Ciz.*)

Four leaves of a fifth century Easter treatise (the consuls of 447 are mentioned in its preface) listing the consuls for 365 to 388 (*Chron.Min.* I 503-10; cf. Taff. I and II). Valentinian II and Honorius are styled *n.p.* s.a. 369 and 386, and there is only one error, the classification of Valentinian II's first consulate of 376 as Valentinian I's fifth.

6. Victorii Aquitani *Cursus Paschalis*, 284-457 (*Aq*); *AqS* (458-541)

Victorius of Aquitaine published in 457 another Easter treatise, incorporating a consular list going up to that year (*Chron.Min.* I 669-735; cf. II 493, no.7). It is entirely derivative from his fellow-Aquitanian Prosper (published only two years before), and so of virtually no independent value. Of far more value are his continuators (*Chron.Min.* I 672). Victorius calculated the dates of Easter up till 559, and the blanks 458-541 left for future consulates have been filled in (independently for the most part) in six different manuscripts, denoted by Mommsen GLSQX and N (*Chron.Min.* I 722-32). The main differences tend to be inclusion (not always in the correct order) or omission of Eastern consuls and the title iunior, but for wider divergences see 508 (cf. p.43); s.a. 528 GSQN offer 'p.c. Mavorti', while X has 'Iustinianus Aug. II v.c.' (sic).

7. *Cyclus Paschalis Annorum LXXXIIII*, 354-437 (*Cycl.*)

The seventh century *Vat.Reg.* 2077 preserves (at f.79-81) a Paschal Cycle incorporating a consular list from 354-437 (*Chron.Min.* I 371-72; 739-43; E.A. Lowe, *CLA* I [1934] 114: probably of Italian origin). Given its early date, the names are often barbarously written, but the information is fairly accurate except for the omission of eastern consuls (414, 424, 428, 433; 399-400 and 404-405 were of course not recognized). A subscription suggests that the list originally went down to 428 and was subsequently continued by a later hand (Mommsen, p.739), which mixed up the consuls of 431 and 432. 360 has the unusual formula 'dnis nostris' alone (cf. 'p.c. VIIII et V' for 413); 'Hon. X et Theod. Aug. p.c. Paulini' in 415 is inexplicable (there is no 'p.c. Paulini' till 499).

8. *Fasti Veronenses*, 439-494 (*Ver.*)

One folium in the fifth-century *Veron.* 55 (53) lists the consuls from 439-486 in a half-uncial hand (f.88; *CLA* IV [1947] 508). Another hand then added the consuls from 487-494 (*Chron.Min.* III 382ff.). That is to say, what we have here is the last page of a list originally completed in 486 and then continued by someone else to 494. It is weak on eastern consuls and inconsistent in its use of *iunior* (see pp.42-43).

9. Fasti Augustani, 379-498 (Aug.)

This is a consular list taking up from the close of Jerome's *Chronicle* (378) and going down to 498 (*Chron.Min.* III 384-85). There are signs of year by year maintenance in its sources: 'p.c. id est Teracliano et Lucio' in 413; 'p.c. id est Isidoro et Senatore' in 436. In 434, 447 and 448, Aug. gives the eastern order of names; and s.a. 496 Aug. is alone among all consular documents in preserving knowledge of an apparently withdrawn consulate of Speciosus (*PLRE* II 1024-25; cf. *JRS* 72 [1982] 138 no. 90). On the other hand, 452-472 are hopelessly confused.

10. Cassiodori Senatoris Chronica, 284-519 (Cass.)

In 519, the consulate of the heir to the throne of Italy, Cassiodorus published a *Chronicle* that went from the Creation down to that year (*Chron.Min.* II 111-61). His consular list (the only extant list compiled by an ex-consul) is entirely dependent on Prosper up to 445, though through the intermediary of Victorius (Mommsen, *Ges.Schr.* VII [1909] 685-87). Cassiodorus invariably sides with Victorius where the two diverge (e.g. 309, 310, 358). Thereafter he used some continuation of Prosper or Victorius (not identical with any extant) and is naturally of independent value for the concluding section. He includes more eastern consuls than other western lists, but (surprisingly enough, given his access to official sources) by no means all (e.g. 482, 490, 493). Almost alone among western consular lists, Cassiodorus was tactful enough to make his master Theoderic consul prior in 484--and Eutharic consul prior over even the Emperor Justin in 519.

11. Victoris Tunnunnensis Chronica, 444-541 (Victor)

Victor, Bishop of Tunnuna in North Africa, compiled a Chronicle from the beginning of the world to A.D. 566, though what we possess begins only with 444 (*Chron.Min.* II 178-206; cf. S. Muhlberger, *CP* 81 [1986] 240-44). He wrote in exile at various places, finally ending up in Constantinople in 564/5 (B. Croke, *GRBS* 24 [1983] 81f.). This no doubt explains the hybrid nature of his consular pairings, now in western, now in eastern sequence. From 444 to 457 the western name comes first (except for emperors); from 458-500 the eastern name (except in 460 and 465); from 501-521 the western name again except in 519, when the emperor's name comes first; and in 525 again the eastern. There are some bad errors (e.g. 468, 473, 490 and 518), and Victor has the peculiarity of counting the consular year in his reckoning of postconsular eras: e.g. 536 is 'p.c. Belesarii anno secundo' (for this way of reckoning, see *BASP* 18 [1981] 33-38).

2. Eastern Lists

1. Alexandrian Chronicles

Scal., 296-387   *Gol.*, 385-392   *Berol.*, 252-338

First a text included by Mommsen in his 'Italici', the bizarrely but not inappropriately titled "Scaliger's Barbarian", more prosaically *Excerpta Barbari*. In addition to the edition of the relevant parts in *Chron.Min.* (cf. I 272), there are the complete editions in A. Schoene's *Eusebii Chronicorum liber prior*

(Berlin 1875) 177-239 and C. Frick's *Chronica Minora* I (Leipzig 1892) 183-371; and see the comprehensive discussion by F. Jacoby in *RE* VI 1566-1576 = *Griechische Historiker* (Stuttgart 1956) 257-62.

This is a late and barbarous Latin translation of a Greek chronicle going down to 387 that, though undoubtedly drawing on a common source with the *Vindobonenses*, was clearly written in Alexandria, early in the fifth century (Frick's edition includes his own backtranslation into Greek). Though full of the grossest errors (and not a few fictitious consuls), the translation nonetheless on occasion preserves, albeit in garbled form, a text that reflects fuller consular entries than most other fasti. For example, it gives Gallus the style *novus* s.a. 353 and 354, reflecting νέος in the Greek original, which in turn represents *iunior* in contemporary Latin usage. This must be authentic survival rather than medieval fancy (see Chapter 3). So too the entries *Valentinianus novus* s.a.377 and *Licinio minimo* s.a.320. While the names of consuls are always given (following Latin usage) in the ablative, the titles *Augustorum* and *clarissimorum* faithfully reflect the original Greek genitives; in fact *clarissimorum* exactly represents the Greek formula τῶν λαμπροτάτων rather than Latin *viris clarissimis*. Note too *Valentiniano Augusto V et Valente filio eius Augustorum* under 376, an impeccably full formula except for the grammar and the reversal of the names. Scal. also uses *novus* in a quite different way before imperial titles, where it appears to be a misunderstanding of the abbreviation *nob.* for *nobilissimus*: e.g. s.a. 319 *novo Caesare* for the correct *nobilissimo Caesare*. Note too the frequent *novorum Augustorum*, not an authentic fourth century formula but probably to be explained as a backtranslation of Greek ἐνδοξότατος, properly represented in contemporary Latin by *gloriosissimus*.[10] Inasmuch as these errors are based on a misunderstanding in Latin (*nob./nov.*), Scal. cannot (as usually implied or stated) have been the first Latin translation made directly from the Greek original.

Not the least interesting feature about the Greek original is that it was illustrated. The "Barbarian" did not attempt to reproduce the illustrations, but he did leave spaces for them (marked in Schoene's edition). This at once links him to the late fourth-century illustrated chronicle fragments Gol. and Berol. discussed below, both of which also have entries related to Scal. and the Vindobonenses.

In 1906 A. Bauer and J. Strzygowski published extensive papyrus fragments of a work which must have borne a very close relationship to this lost Alexandrian original, a profusely illustrated Alexandrian chronicle of the early fifth century (*Gol.*).[11] The text is more badly damaged than the illustrations, only the last few consular names being (in part) legible (385-392). Then in 1937 H. Lietzmann published a perhaps slightly earlier (*ca* 400) papyrus fragment from an illustrated chronicle now in Berlin (*Berol.*), including the consuls for 252-270, 306, 312-317 and 326-338 ("Ein Blatt aus einer antiken Weltchronik," *Quantulacumque: Studies Presented to Kirsopp Lake* [London 1937] 339-48 = *Kleine Schriften* I [Berlin 1958] 419-29). The Berlin chronicle has the same entry for the passion of S. Cyprian (s.a. 258) as both the Vindobonenses (p.289 Mommsen) and the same entry for the arrival of the relics of SS. Andrew and Luke into Constantinople (s.a. 336) as Scal. and both the Vindobonenses (p.293). These are hardly items one would expect to occur independently to the compilers of such brief chronicles. It is fairly clear that a common source lies behind this group, but that does not mean that they all copied it carefully or exactly. For example, the consular names in the badly damaged Gol. have been heavily restored. Of the two names for 384 only one final genitive termination survives; of 389, only an "and" and an initial "P". Bauer's restorations were based on what no doubt seemed the reasonable assumption that the copyist of so early a text must have got the names right. Yet the perhaps even earlier Berol. not only badly misspells a number of names; the consuls for 307-311 are entirely omitted and at least two names are completely wrong. For Faustinianus s.a. 262 it offers Maximus; for Nepotianus s.a. 336 Pompeianus; and for Symmachus s.a. 330 apparently Valerius (see ad annum). It is also interesting to note that while Scal. and Gol. both give consuls' titles fairly meticulously, Berol. gives no titles at all, not even differentiating emperors from subjects.

---

[10]This interpretation is put beyond doubt by an example of *nobilium Augustorum* (*Chron.Min.* I 290 [s.a. 303]).

[11]*Eine Alexandrinische Weltchronik. Text und Miniaturen eines griechischen Papyrus der Sammlung W. Golenischev*, *Denkschrift der kaiserlichen Akademie der Wissenschaften zu Wien*, Philos.-Histor. Klasse 51, 1906.

The links between Berol. and Mommsen's Italici are highly illuminating. But we should beware of attributing too precise a significance to them. We should not (for example) rush to the conclusion that Italian consular annals were directly influenced by a chance Alexandrian import. For the entry on the passion of S. Cyprian also appears in the Fasti Hydatiani (no.3 below) of Constantinople, as too (though differently dated) does the entry on the relics of SS. Luke and Andrew.[12] We shall see that Hyd. is the earliest extant annotated consular list. In all probability both the Italian and Alexandrian consular annals descend from a version that originated in Constantinople and circulated everywhere at the turn of the fifth century. Most people no doubt copied the early years (complete, for example, with the Cyprian entry) fairly mechanically, not making additions of their own (e.g. Alexandrian magistrates in the case of Scal.) till near the time of composition. This would explain why most of these texts begin the same way but end up as local annals of Constantinople, Alexandria, Rome, Ravenna or wherever the owner happened to live.

2. *Theon*, 138-372 (*Theo*)

A careful consular list from 138-372 was compiled at Alexandria by the astronomer Theon (ed. H. Usener, *Chron.Min.* III 359-81). Usener pointed out that the closing entry, Μοδέστος καὶ ᾿Αρινθέου, suggests that Theon himself closed his list early in 372 with the only consular name then proclaimed in Egypt, the second being added later by someone else who did not notice that Theon (unusually) gave his names in the nominative. The papyri, however, indicate that both names were disseminated together, and it may be that a more trivial explanation of the facts is warranted. Theon's list is complete for our period, carefully distinguishing Augusti from Caesares. In 325, alone among the consular lists, he preserves ("Proculus or Paulinus and Iulianus") the traces of the replacement of Proclus by Paulinus.

Unlike the illustrated Alexandrian consular annals discussed above (to which it appears to be unrelated) Theon includes no historical entries. The vogue for amplifying consular lists with illustrations and historical entries may not have reached Alexandria till the end of the century, perhaps spreading from Constantinople (see next item).

3. *Fasti Hydatiani*, 284-468 (*Hyd.*)

This composite consular chronicle mistakenly attributed to the fifth century Spanish bishop Hydatius[13] (*Chron.Min.* I 197-247[14]) falls into three parts:
a) from the establishment of the consulate to the foundation of Constantinople, presumably originating in Rome;
b) from 330 to 389, compiled (with abundant historical entries) in Constantinople (Mommsen, p.200);
c) from 390 to 468, compiled or completed in Spain by Hydatius (Mommsen, p.201).
The Constantinopolitan section is not only accurate and informative; it coincides to a considerable degree with the material preserved in the *Chronicon Paschale* or *Alexandrinum* (see below) of *ca* 630. On the assumption that both derive from a fuller common source (discussed below under Pasch.), Mommsen printed the text of Pasch. in parallel columns with Hyd. under the composite title *Consularia Constantinopolitana* (his Const.). Pasch. continues at the same level of accuracy after 395, but Hyd. at once deteriorates in quality, occasionally offering provisional formulas such as *et qui de Oriente* (459, 461), or omitting the second consul (446, 453, 464). In 458 it alone of the lists preserves Avitus' consulate.

---

[12]On which see H.Lietzmann, *Kleine Schriften* I (1958) 429.
[13]On Hydatius' own chronicle (*Chron.Min.* II 3-36; A. Tranoy, *Hydace: Chronique* [Paris 1974]), which is not consular, see E.A. Thompson, *Romans and Barbarians* (Madison 1982), Chapter 8 and forthcoming studies by S. Muhlberger and R.W. Burgess.
[14]Although in its present form this text was compiled in fifth century Spain, we have discussed it here in view of the importance of its central section; we quote its entries for 330-388 with the eastern evidence, the rest with the western evidence.

The central section has considerable interest and importance as perhaps the earliest extant example of that characteristic late Roman phenomenon, consular annals. An important study by O. Seeck[15] established year by year maintenance from about 365, after when imperial births, deaths and accessions, battles, earthquakes and local events of Constantinople were all recorded and dated to the day--and usurpers designated *tyrannus*. Earlier events back to Constantine were retroactively entered, often inaccurately.

The Constantinopolitan material breaks off abruptly in 389, and the reason may easily be conjectured. The entry for 388 runs as follows:

> Theodosio Aug.II et Cynegio cons. his conss. defunctus est Cynegius praefectus Orientis in consulatu suo Constantinopolim. hic universas provincias longi temporis labe deceptas in statum pristinum revocavit et usque ad Egyptum penetravit et simulacra gentium evertit. unde cum magno fletu totius populi civitatis deductum est corpus ad Apostolos die xiiii kal. Apr. et post annum transtulit eum matrona eius Achantia ad Hispanias pedestre.

So extravagant and tendentious a eulogy of a private citizen (albeit a consul) is without parallel in the spare style of the genre. As Seeck acutely saw, our MS derives from the very copy that was custom made for Cynegius himself--or rather for his widow Achantia, who must have taken it back with her as a memento to Spain the following year (*post annum*[16]). There is indeed one more year after 388 with a substantial entry--and a corresponding entry in Pasch.

It follows that Hyd. does not (as some have supposed) derive from officially maintained public records. It is rather "die speculation eines findigen buchhändlers" (Seeck, p.619). It is tempting to conjecture that it may also have been illustrated. Cynegius' widow must surely have been a grander patron than the man who commissioned Berol., well able to afford the best. And the Merseburg fragment has revealed that the vogue for illustrated consular annals was not limited to Alexandria. It also reveals that the illustrations were stereotyped; the same allegorical figure illustrates two different earthquakes, and stylized wrapped corpses illustrate deaths and executions no fewer than three times.[17] It may be that illustrations and historical entries went together from the beginning. For de luxe illustrated editions of such utilitarian texts we have the slightly earlier Chr. 354 prepared in Rome (but lacking either annotated or illustrated consular list) and also the *Notitiae Dignitatum*, that for the West compiled in the western court, that for the East in Constantinople. The extant redactions are slightly later than Hyd. and characterized above all by the endless repetition of stereotyped illustrations for the various insignia and personifications of provinces.

We should not expect correctness of text to be the primary feature of an illustrated chronicle, an expectation (as Muhlberger points out) borne out by the extant specimens. This is conspicuously true of Berol., a leaf from an original book of *ca* 400. The care with which the illustrations are reproduced in Rav. suggests that the omissions in the text are to be blamed on the original rather than the copyist. And while most of the shortcomings in Scal. are doubtless to be laid at the Barbarian's door, the original can hardly have been perfect. Most extant lists are not illustrated, but some may owe their gaps and blunders to derivation from sources that were.[18]

---

[15]"Idacius und die Chronik von Constantinopel," *Neue Jahrbücher für Philologie und Pädagogik* 139 (1889) 601-35; more succinctly in *RE* 3 (1899) 2454-60 s.v. Chronica Constantinopolitana.

[16]She will have waited a year until "the road to the West was open after the suppression by Theodosius of the usurper Maximus" (John Matthews, *Western Aristocracies and Imperial Court A.D. 364-425* (Oxford 1975) 142.

[17]See Koehler's discussion, *Medieval Studies...Porter* I (1939) 130-32.

[18]In view of the suggestion made above that the original text of Hyd. was illustrated, it should be observed that it is not characterized by errors of this sort. But a book produced for so important a person may have been executed with more care.

4. Marcellinus, 379-534 (Marcell.); MarcellS., 535-548

Marcellinus *comes* compiled a Chronicle from 379 to 518 in continuation of Jerome's Chronicle, though within a consular framework. He worked at Constantinople, and subsequently published a continuation up to 534 (*Chron.Min.* II 39-101; B. Croke, *Phoenix* 38 [1984] 77-88). A further continuation up to 548, though of good quality, is by a later hand (Mommsen, p.42).

There are numerous parallels between Marcellinus' historical entries and Chron.Pasch. between 395 and 469 (the texts are again printed in parallel columns by Mommsen), and there can be no doubt that both drew on local consular annals. Marcellinus' sources (entirely eastern, not western as once thought) are discussed (with full bibliography) by B. Croke, *Chiron* 13 (1983) 87f. Apart from one inexplicable (463) and one mechanical error (446), his consular list is accurate. Under 399 he includes the name of the deposed and disgraced Eutropius, but not from his main annalistic source, since he quotes it in the wrong sequence-- and with a quotation from Claudian's *In Eutropium*. This is a unique case of a chronicler supplementing his annalistic source from a literary work.

5. Chronicon Paschale, 284-541 (Pasch.)

This chronicle (ed. L. Dindorf, Bonn 1832), completed in 630, incorporates (save for the accidental omission of 508-517) perhaps the most complete consular list for our period. No other eastern list gives more western consuls.

It was evidently compiled in Constantinople, and (as we have seen) has many parallel entries with the earlier Constantinopolitan chronicles, Hyd. and Marcellinus. A common source is clearly indicated, whether or not it was a publicly maintained city chronicle (Croke, *Chiron* 13 [1983] 87). All three extant witnesses (and the *Fasti Heracliani*) share anomalous errors we should not expect to find in an official list. For example, Marcellinus, Pasch., and Heracl. all preserve the name of Vitalian (s.a. 520), who suffered *damnatio memoriae* during his year. Marcellinus and Heracl. likewise preserve the name of Eutropius in 399, this time correctly deleted in Pasch. More puzzlingly, both Pasch. and Marcellinus have the name of Castinus, unrecognized nominee of the western usurper Johannes in 424. In addition, Hyd. and Pasch. both give the incorrect "western" sequence for the consuls of 381. There are indications (occasional mistranslations and Latin idioms) that this source was written in Latin (Seeck, *Neue Jahrbücher* 139 [1889] 621).

A peculiarity of Pasch. is that the compiler, living as he did after the end of the consulate as a functioning dating system, evidently did not understand the use of the p.c. formula. Either he simply repeated the preceding year (e.g. 350 = 351; 476 = 477) or added an iteration number after; e.g. 375 (p.c. Gratiani III et Equitii) appears as Gratiani IV et Equitii II. When confronted with a sequence of two p.c.'s (530-532; 535-537), on each occasion he omitted one, thus destroying his indiction sequence. Only under 532 do we find the μετὰ ὑπ. formula, though with the addition of an iteration number.

Because he had printed the text of Pasch. (which he cited as Alex.) for 330-395 with Hyd. and for 395-469 with Marcellinus, Mommsen did not cite it as an independent witness in his *index consulum* (*Chron.Min.* III 497ff.) until 470, evidently misleading W. Liebenam (*Fasti consulares* 3) as to its true compass. In view of its consistent excellence, we cite it in its own right throughout.

Du Cange's claim that a lost MS stopped at 354 seems to be based on a misunderstanding: see Clinton, *Fasti Romani* II 209; Grumel (below) 83-84.

Pasch. has generated quite a substantial bibliography, of which the following may be singled out: H. Gelzer, *Sextus Julius Africanus und die Byzantinische Chronologie* I (Leipzig 1885) 138-76; E. Schwartz, *RE* III.2 (1899) 2460-77; V. Grumel, *La chronologie* (Paris 1958) 73-84; H. Hunger, *Die hochsprachliche profane Literatur der Byzantiner* I (Munich 1978) 328-30; but still no satisfactory edition.[19]

---

[19]A new edition is in preparation by O. Mazal (Vienna), cf. *JÖB* 35 (1985) 341.

6. Fasti Heracliani, 222-630 (*Heracl.*)

The *Fasti Heracliani* were drawn up in Constantinople, in all probability by Stephanus of Alexandria, *ca* 630 (ed. H. Usener, *Chron.Min.* III 386-410). He claims to have used a consular list appended to a law code (see the scholion printed by Usener, p.392). They begin our period disastrously enough with six pairs of interpolated consuls in the second decade of the fourth century (one between 312 and 313; two between 317 and 318; two between 318 and 319; cf. Usener, pp.387-88). Thereafter they are generally accurate as far as they go, chiefly of interest for the unusually detailed traces they preserve of their manner of compilation over a long period. The new consular names seem to have been entered each year when proclaimed in Constantinople, with the result that western consuls not known till later in the year are either omitted (463, 482, 484) or else added as afterthoughts to entries presumed complete: e.g. 472, "Marcianus alone--and Festus" (see Usener, pp.387-91). Another good example is 440, Anatolius et Valentinianus: for whatever reason, Valentinian III's fifth consulate was not known in the East until late in the year (see *ad annum*), and the fact that, though an emperor, he appears here in second place, is clear proof of subsequent addition. For the same reason, the names of consuls who suffered *damnatio memoriae* in the course of their year have not been removed (e.g. 399, 520). Like Pasch., Stephanus seems not to have understood the p.c. formula: 475, 477, 483, 531-532 and 536-537 he designated ἀνύπατα, and though he does use the formula μετὰ ὑπατείαν at 351 and 375, he prefixed a definite article, which makes no sense.

3. Varia Minora

There are in addition several other chronicles and lists (all of western origin) which contain only a handful of consular references each. These are cited (where not with full title) by Mommsen's abbreviations, which we repeat here, along with volume and page references to his edition. For their character, we refer to his prefaces.

1. The *Prologus Paschae* of 395 (*Chron.Min.* I 737f.).
2. The *laterculus* of Polemius Silvius of 449 (*Chron.Min.* I 511f.). See *ad annum*.
3. Comput.: The *computatio anni 452* (*Chron.Min.* I 149f.).
4. Chr.Gall.: The *Chronica Gallica* of 511 (*Chron.Min.* I 615f.).
5. Reges Vand.: The *laterculus Regum Vandalorum* of *ca* 534 (*Chron.Min.* III 456f.).
6. Caesaraug.: The *Chronica Caesaraugustana* of *ca* 580 (*Chron.Min.* II 221f.).
7. Gildas, *De excidio Britanniae*, 6c. (*Chron.Min.* III1f.).
8. Beda, *Chronica*, *ca* 725 (*Chron.Min.* III 223f.).
9. Hist.Britt.: *Historia Brittonum cum add. Nennii*, 859. (*Chron.Min.* III 111f.).
10. Geneal.: *Liber genealogus*, 5c. (*Chron.Min.* I 154-96).
11. Dionys.: *Adnotationes antiquiores ad cyclos Dionysianos*, 8c. (*Chron.Min.* I 751-56).
12. Isidoriana: Addenda in a 12c Paris MS of Isidore (*Chron.Min.* II 493).

Chapter 5

Inscriptions

Christian funerary inscriptions constitute the overwhelming majority of the epigraphic evidence for consular dating. Aside from them, there is a group of 58 (out of our total of 2462) dedicatory inscriptions, most from the city of Rome, fourth century and pagan, though a few are non-Roman or Christian. There are, in addition, three Jewish funerary inscriptions (*ICUR* n.s. I 2804 = *CIJ* 482, Rome, 330; *ILCV* 4987 = *CIJ* 528, Rome, 387; *CIJ* 650, Catania, 383),[1] and a few inscriptions which are neither funerary nor dedicatory: *CIL* VI 31075, Rome, 362, a *descriptio feriarum*; *ICUR* n.s. II 4770, Rome, 390,[2] commemorating the construction of the Ecclesia S. Pauli extra Muros; Grégoire 314 = *ILCV* 23, Constantinople, 527, an imperial rescript; *MAMA* VII 305, Orkistos, 331, an imperial rescript; *I.Kalchedon* 22, 452, a commemoration of the construction of a church of St. Christopher in Chalcedon; *IG* XIV 455, Catania, 434, an edict concerning the administration of the local baths; *AE* 1971, 454, of 413, commemorating the foundation of a bathhouse on Lesbos; *CIL* III 5670a, Noricum, 370, construction of a burgus; *IG* XIV 956B, Rome, 313, on the appointment of priests; *IG*[2] II-III 1121, Athens, 305, a constitutio; *CIL* X 3698, Cumae, 289, on the appointment of priests.

1. Quantity, Chronological, and Geographical Distribution of Inscriptions

In the tables below, the evidence is distributed by five-year periods and by six more or less broad geographical categories. The purpose of the tables is to provide the reader with a good idea of chronological and geographical trends, not with information on year-by-year, province-by-province distribution.

First, a few words about the geographical categories used in the tables. Europe includes the Gauls, the Germanies, Raetia, Noricum, Spain and Lusitania. Danube includes Dalmatia, the Moesias, the Pannonias and Thrace. The East is Greece, the Aegean islands, Anatolia, Cyprus, Syria, Phoenicia, Palestine, Arabia, Egypt and Cyrenaica. Africa is all of Latin-speaking North Africa.

N.B. The numbers refer only to usable evidence; dubious material is excluded.

1. 284-410

	ROME	ITALY	EUROPE	DANUBE	EAST	AFRICA	TOTAL
284-290	10	5	-	4	1	3	23
291-295	7	-	1	-	-	-	8
296-300	8	2	1	3	-	2	16
301-305	5	1	-	3	4	1	14
306-310	5	1	1	1	-	-	8

[1]The small number is explained by the fact that the Roman Jews gave up the custom of burial in catacombs in the early fourth century; this emerges from a study of the brick stamps from the catacombs, see *CIJ* pp. 10-11, 51, 55, 212-227. As the tables below show, epigraphical evidence for consular dating is not abundant until the mid fourth century.
[2]The editors and Chastagnol date to 391; see the Critical Appendix under 390.

	ROME	ITALY	EUROPE	DANUBE	EAST	AFRICA	TOTAL
311-315	1	1	1	2	1	-	6
316-320	6	-	-	3	3	-	12
321-325	14	4	1	1	1	1	22
326-330	7	-	-	-	2	-	9
331-335	8	1	1	-	4	1	15
336-340	25	8	1	-	-	1	35
341-345	39	14	-	1	-	1	55
346-350	46	7	2	-	1	1	57
351-355	25	2	2	1	3	-	33
356-360	45	10	-	5	2	1	63
361-365	83	8	-	1	1	-	93
366-370	77	7	1	-	-	-	85
371-375	82	9	3	4	1	-	99
376-380	79	12	1	3	-	-	95
381-385	117	13	1	3	1	-	135
386-390	79	6	1	-	1	-	87
391-395	93	14	2	1	-	-	110
396-400[3]	112	11	-	1	-	-	124
401-405	88	14	2	2	-	-	106
406-410	78	17	1	2	1	1	100
TOTAL	1139	167	23	41	27	13	1410

2. 411-475

	ROME	ITALY	EUROPE	DANUBE	EAST	AFRICA	TOTAL
411-415	12	4	-	4	1	-	21
416-420	12	10	-	2	-	-	24
421-425	23	12	2	5	-	-	42
426-430	24	7	-	2	-	1	34
431-435	31	17	2	4	1	-	55
436-440	18	101	1	8	-	1	38
441-445	25	12	2	9	-	-	48
446-450	28	9	3	1	1	-	42
451-455	37	8	9	2	1	3	60
456-460	17	4	3	3	1	-	28
461-465	28	11	1	3	3	-	46
466-470	18	11	6	-	2	-	37
471-475	26	6	3	1	-	-	36
TOTALS	299	121	32	44	10	5	511

[3]7 of these may belong in 401-405.

3. 476-541

	ROME	ITALY	EUROPE	DANUBE	EAST	AFRICA	TOTAL
476-480	11	6	1	1	-	-	19
481-485	20	9	9	-	-	-	38
486-490	24	22	9	-	1	-	56
491-495	16	11	10	-	1	-	38
496-500	12	2	2	-	-	-	16
501-505	10	6	15	-	-	-	31
506-510	17	9	4	-	1	-	31
511-515	12	12	7	1	-	-	32
516-520	23	14	13	2	3	-	55
521-525	20	22	8	-	3	-	53
526-530	24	18	9	1	2	-	54
531-535	35	19	3	1	6	-	64
536-541	20	18	9	2	5	-	54
TOTALS	244	168	99	8	22	0	541
TOTALS 284-541	1682	456	154	93	59	18	2462

A few observations are in order. Throughout the period 284-541, the city of Rome provides us with the most evidence of all six geographical areas. The paucity of evidence from North Africa and the Orient may be due in part to accidents of preservation, but it seems more reasonable to suppose that consular dating never caught on in these areas, which normally used a variety of local or provincial eras[4] with the advantage of being traditional and much easier to keep track of than consular dates.[5] For example, even at so well and consistently documented a site as Ephesos, only three consular dates have been preserved out of several thousand inscriptions; and none of these three dates comes from our period.

Perhaps the most striking observation--aside from the fluctuations in the quantity of the Roman evidence, due to such major events as the sack of the city in 410 and the fall of the Western Empire in 476 (though the effect of the latter was much slighter than might be supposed[6])--is the sudden emergence, starting in the 450's and 460's, of Gallia Narbonensis and Gallia Lugdunensis as significant sources of evidence.

2. The Character of the Evidence

There are certain problems peculiar to the epigraphical evidence. Since the overwhelming majority of the documents are private and unofficial, the stonecutters were under no constraint to use a full and absolutely correct formula: their goal was merely comprehensibility. Hence, the name of one member of a

[4]E.J. Bickerman, *Chronology of the Ancient World*[2] (London 1980) 71ff.; A.E. Samuel, *Greek and Roman Chronology* (Munich 1972) 245f. and 280.

[5]For the African era, see *ILCV* III pp.268-72; there are slightly more than 200 examples. For the Spanish era, see *ILCV* III, pp.273-75, with about 60 examples from our period, and cf. J. Vives, *Inscripciones Cristianas de la España Romana y Visigoda* (Barcelona 1942) 257ff. In the East, the Seleucid era was still in use. Cf. Grumel, *La chronologie* 209ff., and for other eras, Grumel, 211-18.

[6]Cf. Chapter 1, section 3, for continued use of consular dating in Italy after 476. This conservatism contrasts with the behavior of the areas under Visigothic kings, such as Spain and North Africa.

consular pair, iteration numbers, and similar elements could be omitted. It is also to be supposed that most stonecutters were not as accustomed as were, say, the scribes of large Egyptian villages or the metropoleis of the nomes to consular dating, so all sorts of random errors could occur. Only in rare cases, to be discussed below, do these omissions or oddities hint at anything more serious than the ineptitude of their perpetrators. Hence, evidence from inscriptions can be used only with great caution in discussion of problems of recognition, proclamation, dissemination, or cancellation of consulates.

Another factor which tends to undermine the value of epigraphical evidence was first discussed, so far as we know, by De Rossi in his comment on *ICUR* 338 (= n.s. I 3201, 384).[7] Though the lapse of time between death and burial was in antiquity normally brief,[8] that between burial and carving of epitaph is indeterminable. Presumably graffiti and dipinti (which are rare in our evidence) could be incised or carved almost at the time of burial. A tombstone, however, might take anywhere from a few days to a few months to carve and would not be laid until the earth had settled.[9] Hence, an epitaph dated to January or February by the current consuls of the year is not conclusive evidence that the consuls were actually known in January or February. Hence also, the overlap by a few weeks or months of postconsulates with consular dates can usually be explained away: the p.c. may actually have been carved first. It is also possible that in some cases a postconsular formula, once in circulation, did not disappear from use simply because the consuls were later announced; some occurrences, therefore, may reflect failure to know or use the later information (cf. below, p.64).

What class of people are responsible for the dated inscriptions? In the vast majority of cases it is impossible to tell.[10] There are, however, two groups of inscriptions which provide definite evidence about the person(s) who erected them. These are (1) pagan votive and dedicatory inscriptions, most of them from fourth-century Rome; almost all were erected by or for prominent members of the Roman senatorial aristocracy; and (2) epitaphs of members of senatorial families; most of these are from the fifth and sixth centuries and are Christian. They are rather widely scattered geographically. In most cases the persons commemorated on the tombstone, though referred to as v.c. or c.f. (or v.inl. or inl.f., v.sp., etc.) are not otherwise known. These inscriptions have been collected by Diehl in the first volume of *ILCV*.[11]

1. Pagan Votive and Dedicatory Inscriptions

Inscriptions of this type are *a priori* likely to preserve the most accurate versions of consular dating formulas for two reasons: (1) They were erected by people who were in a position to have the best information; and (2) they were set up in public places. Yet there are cases of aristocratic inscriptions which were poorly executed and carved on stones or altars of inferior quality.[12] But of the 58 relevant inscriptions,[13] there are only two outright errors. First *ICUR* n.s. II 5996 giving a false iteration numeral (III for II) for Merobaudes in 383 (see Critical Appendix s.a.); and secondly *CIL* VI 511 (377), which reads DN

---

[7]Ironically, this inscription has been proved by papyri published long after *ICUR* not to require De Rossi's explanation at all; see notes s.a.

[8]E.g., *ICUR* n.s. V 13304, August 359, gives the dates of death and burial: two days intervened.

[9]Modern cemeteries allow anything from one to six months.

[10]Graffiti and dipinti, were they not so rarely found in the Christian catacombs, might provide some kind of indication. But even these are not a sure sign of poverty: see *CIJ* 6-67; *RAC* 52 (1976) 1ff.; *Beth Shearim* II 174-75.

[11]78-266 *passim*.

[12]E.g. *CIL* VI 511, an altar dedicated by Rufius Caeionius, pontifex maior, augur publicus etc. in 377. *CIL* VI 512, an "ara rudis ac male habita," as the editors note, was dedicated by Ceionius Rufius Volusianus, vicarius Asiae, in 390.

[13]From Rome: *CIL* VI: 36954 (284); 2136-2137 (286); 869-871 (290, 290, and 341); 505 (295); 2141 (300); 2143 (301); 507-508 (313, 319); 1684-1689 (321); 315 (321); 36951 (328); 108 (341); 1769 (342, 346); 1768 (346); 498 (350); 1166B (355); 749 (357); 750-752 (358); 753 (362); 31075 (362); 1729 (364); 32422 (364); 499 (374); 504 (376); 510 (376); 511 (377);; 1698 (377); 500 (377); 1751 (378); 31945 (381); 501-502 (383); 1778 (387); 1759 (389); 512 (390); 503 (390). *IGUR* I 191 (299); 128 (377). From Italy: *CIL* XI 5996 (375). From Baetica: *CIL* II 2211 (349). From Lusitania: *CIL* II 191 (336). From Moesia: *CIL* III 8151 (287). From Pannonia: *CIL* III 10406 (290); 10981 (303). From Africa: *AE* 1955, 51 (357). From Arabia: *IGRR* 1268 (301).

Gratiano V et Merobaude conss.[14] The iteration number again is wrong; Gratian shared his fourth consulate with Merobaudes. It might be noted that this is one of the inscriptions already singled out for its poor execution (n.12).

Otherwise there are three cases of omitted iteration numerals (*CIL* VI 36954, 284; III 10406, Aquincum, 290;[15] VI 1689, 321). In no case does this omission affect the intelligibility of the date. There are a few scattered cases of omission of DN, AUG and CAES, obviously all due to the carelessness of either the composer of the text of the inscription or the stonecutter (*CIL* VI 870, 290; 2141, 300; 749, 357; 1751, 378). There are two cases of the common third and early fourth century abbreviated formula without names used in double imperial consulates, i.e. DD.NN., iterational numerals, AUGG. (*CIL* III 10981, Brigetio, 303; VI 1769, Rome, 342; without Augg.). That this was a fully acceptable formula, suitable even for legal documents, is proved by its use in papyri and in laws (cf. below, p.78).

On the other hand, there are several inscriptions which use versions of the consular formula fuller than those found in the other evidence: *CIL* VI 2136 and 2137 (286) give the full names of the consuls; VI 508 (319) uses unusually full titulature for the imperial consuls. The same is true of *CIL* VI 1684-85 and 1687-89 (all 321) and VI 751b and 510 (both 376).

In short, this group of inscriptions displays none of the errors common on the epitaphs--inversion of order of consuls, omission of one consul, confusion of consuls with similar names, use of DN for non-imperial or v.c. for imperial consuls--except for a few cases of omitted and two cases of mistaken iteration numerals. All of the other peculiarities are simple, careless omissions of optional elements in the dating formula.[16]

2. Epitaphs of Senators and Their Families

Of the more than 200 inscriptions collected in *ILCV* pertaining to Christian senators, only sixty, all funerary, bear consular dates (from 346 [*ILCV* 162] to 533 [*ILCV* 135]; the greatest number are in the fifth century). The great majority come from Rome and the rest of Italy, a scattered few from Dalmatia, Gaul and Germany.

Our expectation that senators and their families would be well-informed about and take care to use the most accurate dating formulas available, confirmed in the case of the public inscriptions, is here disappointed. We find the same range and proportion of errors and inaccuracies (to be discussed below) as in the non-senatorial epitaphs. Furthermore, the unusually full use of optional elements--full imperial titulature for imperial consuls, full nomenclature for commoners, etc.--found in the public inscriptions is absent.[17] In private inscriptions, thus, people of senatorial rank usually took no more care with consular dating formulas than anyone else.

---

[14]Even this case is not so unambiguous. The editors of *CIL* report that some authorities read the number as IV. If that reading is correct there is no error. But it is likely to be wrong since 4 is almost always represented on Latin inscriptions of this period as IIII.

[15]The stonecutter is perhaps to blame: initially, he just carved the names of the consuls, then, realizing his error, he squeezed in IIII above Diocletian's name, but left Maximian's without a number.

[16]In fact, the percentage of omitted iteration numerals here is identical with that of the epitaphs of the same period, i.e. 5 per cent, and incorrect iteration numerals are always very rare. But other varieties of error and of abbreviated or misspelled names are absent, and 18 per cent of these inscriptions use unusually full formulas.

[17]The one exception is *ILCV* 200b, 439, which uses the official-sounding "qui de oriente fuerit nuntiatus"--rare in inscriptions; see below, p.66.

3. Formulas and Errors

1. Formulas

For our observations on the prevalence of different formulas and on optional elements (D.N., Aug. and Fl., the last for civilians, princes and occasionally emperors), we have drawn heavily on the excellent indices to *ILCV*. Our more detailed comments on peculiarities and errors in the inscriptions are based on our own investigations.

The standard consular dating formula in the fourth century is X (abl.) *et* Y (abl.) *consulibus* (or some abbreviation thereof). In Greek inscriptions, as in the papyri, the standard formula is ὑπατίας A (gen.) καὶ B (gen.). The formula *consulatu X* (gen.) *et* Y (gen.) makes its first appearance in an African inscription of 338 (*CIL* VIII 796 = *ILS* 5413) and becomes gradually more common thereafter, though even in the fifth century it does not supplant the other formula. Although on the whole the "consulatu" formula is the less "official" one, there is indirect evidence that it was occasionally used in the laws.[18]

In the western inscriptions, the element v.c. hardly appears after the names of non-imperial consuls before the 370's but soon becomes so widespread that by the early fifth century it can be considered a nearly indispensable element of the dating formula.[19] Interestingly enough, the few eastern inscriptions, both Latin and Greek, use the abbreviation (or its Greek equivalent, ὁ λαμπρότατος) throughout the fourth century, as do the papyri.

Economy may explain the tendency to abbreviate the formula as much as possible, usually by shortening the names of the consuls, but sometimes even by omitting them completely; see 303, 305, 342, 357, 360, 373, 409, and 435.

2. Irregularities and Errors

1. Omission of Iteration Numerals

The most common type of irregularity in our period is the omission of an iteration numeral, an irregularity displayed by roughly 2.5 per cent of the total number of inscriptions.[20] Usually the omission does not affect the comprehensibility of the date: e.g., seven of seventeen Roman inscriptions of 371 omit the Emperor Gratian's iteration number, II, yet this never results in ambiguity since all give the name of the second consul, Probus, with whom Gratian shared only the consulate of 371. In some cases, though, ambiguities could arise from such omissions, most notably in the four joint consulates of the emperors Valentinian and Valens (365, 368, 370, 373).[21] It is quite possible, in fact, that several inscriptions which we have dated to 365 really date to one of their later consulates. That the inscriptions are rather evenly distributed over the four years (13 in 365, 11 in 368, 15 in 370, and 17 in 373), however, suggests that such omission did not happen commonly and that people were careful about iteration numerals when the

---

[18]It seems possible that some of the incorrect p.c. dates in the laws are the result of compilers' or copyists' misunderstanding; cf. below, p.83.

[19]There is one early example from Rome in *ICUR* n.s. V 13101 (346), which reads PONSC AMANTI [et Albini v]V CC; PONSC is presumably a bungled p(ost) cons(ulatum). Interestingly, this text is the mate (literally: the two commemorate spouses) of 13102, the remarkable text of 348 which reads CONS SALLIES E[t Philippi], an otherwise unexampled word order.

[20]The percentage is naturally higher--about five per cent--in the fourth century, when there were many iterated consulates, and practically nil after 476. The omission of Zeno's iteration numeral (III) from the inscriptions of 479 is presumably motivated by uncertainty as to whether the emperor held his second or third consulate in that year; see our comments on 475 and 479. In addition to 479, iteration numerals are omitted from some inscriptions in the following years: 290, 291, 297, 298, 301, 321, 363, 371, 373, 375, 378, 383, 393, 398, 406, 407, 417, 425, 426, 435, 437, 440, 443, 450, 476.

[21]Cf. also *ILCV* 4597 (Critical Appendix under 407), where the iteration numerals of both Honorius and Theodosius are omitted, making the date ambiguous.

comprehensibility of the dating formula depended upon it. Incorrect iteration numerals are surprisingly rare: we have found only thirteen cases.[22]

2. Omission of the Name of One Consul

Another common irregularity, with 28 examples before the fifth century, is the omission of the name of one of the consuls. Before then, with the exception of years in which usurpers ruled, the omission of one consul **cannot** be due to the fact that his name had not been announced. The names of both consuls were proclaimed simultaneously:[23] if one was known, both were.

For the earlier period, it is best to abstain completely from political explanations for the omission of one name.[24] Even De Rossi was misled by the search for the politics underlying what is in reality a perfectly conventional epigraphical peculiarity. For example, *ICUR* n.s. VI 16967 = *ILCV* 2941A, 19.viii.360, omits the name of Julian, the second consul of the year. De Rossi (*ICUR* I 143) argued that in August, 360, after Julian's army had proclaimed him Augustus in Gaul, Constantius had not yet decided how to handle him, so his name was omitted from inscriptions pending Constantius' decision. When Constantius decided that Julian be considered a rebel, the latter's name reappeared on inscriptions, but with the title *Caes.*, which was acceptable to Constantius, not *Aug.* Clever as this explanation is, it is completely unnecessary. Of the 14 inscriptions of the year, only this one omits the name of the second consul. If there were some political motivation for it, we should expect Julian's name to be absent from other inscriptions of the summer of 360 as well. That Julian is referred to throughout the year (where any title is given) as CAES. and not AUG. is due only to the fact that all our inscriptions come from areas which were still loyal to Constantius.[25] In 393, since Eugenius obviously wanted parity with the legitimate Augustus, no political significance can be assigned to the omission of Theodosius from a few inscriptions of that year.

If, before the fifth century, politics usually cannot explain the omission of a consul, what can? In some cases it is quite certain that the reason for the omission of a consul is simply that the stonecutter ran short of space. See, e.g., *ICUR* n.s. I 3162, 340; *ICUR* 121 = *ILCV* 4217, 355; *ICUR* n.s. VII 17455 = *ILCV* 2807 adn., 367. In at least one case, the similarity of the names of the two consuls may have caused the stonecutter to omit the second through haplography (*ICUR* n.s. VII 17466 = *ILCV* 2604A, 373; cf. *CIL* III 15023, 321). In other cases, we simply do not know why a consul, sometimes the first one, is omitted, but we may assume that the reasons are no more weighty than ignorance, apathy, economics, or simply a *lapsus calami*.[26]

With time, omission of one consul becomes increasingly common. This reflects in part the fact that after 411 the two consuls were normally appointed and proclaimed separately. But frequently the eastern consul was omitted even though his name was known in the West. For example, in 398, Eutychianus is named on a Roman inscription dated 8.i, and a Sicilian one dated 11.i, yet is absent from Roman inscriptions dated 16.iii and 13.ix. In 401, the easterner Fravitta is absent from two Roman inscriptions dated to August, though attested at Rome in May or June (and again the next year in a p.c.) and at Milan (the emperor Honorius' residence) in a law dated to February. The more frequent omissions of Theodosius and Antiochos in 407 and 431 respectively are still more striking, as are the omissions of

---

[22]These are: 287, 318 (see Critical Appendix on this text), 377, 380, 388, 396 (see Critical Appendix on both relevant texts), 406, 417, 426, 430, 468.

[23]We have already pointed out (p.16) that there was no sudden change (as often assumed) in 395 or even 399; it was really in 411 that separate proclamation began.

[24]As advised already by Mommsen, *Ostgot.Stud.* 229 = *Ges.Schr.* VI 366.

[25]*ICUR* n.s. V 13105 and *P.Oxy.* XIV 1695, both from 19.xii, also refer to Julian as Caes., showing that the old formula was not necessarily made to conform to the new situation.

[26]Note also texts from the following years (underlining indicates that it is the first name which is omitted): 296, 308, 317 or 330, 318, 337, 344 (?), 345, 348, 350, 356, 363, 364, 374, 377, 382, 383, 391.

Asclepiodotus (423), Valerius (432), Eudoxius (442), Ardabur (447) and the emperor Leo (471) from most of the western inscriptions.[27]

The omission of the eastern consul in western inscriptions, merely a tendency between 441 and 476, is almost the rule after 476, or more precisely after about 482, a phenomenon fully discussed in Chapter 2 above. There are too few eastern inscriptions to support any generalizations.

3. Postconsular Dates

More useful for our purposes, especially in the earlier period, is the pattern of postconsular datings (cf. also above, pp.32 ff.).[28] With some reservations, such inscriptions can be used as evidence for the date of the local announcement of the new consuls. Into this category fall most of the p.c. inscriptions from the first two months of any given year, assuming there is no other evidence that the consuls were already known.[29] Two eastern postconsular inscriptions provide important confirmation of papyrological evidence for late dissemination of consuls in the East in 382 and 387. Sometimes the epigraphical evidence for consulates and postconsulates overlaps slightly, anywhere from a few days to a few weeks. In such cases the explanation may often be an interval between death and the erection of the tombstone.

In two fourth-century cases, suspiciously late postconsulates may perhaps be used as evidence of late local announcement of the consuls where there is no unambiguous evidence from the same area to contradict it: *AE* 1927, 138 (Capua, 5.iv.381), where there is much earlier evidence of the consuls from Rome, but not from south-central Italy; and *AE* 1975, 367 (Piano Laroma, 5.v.384), where once again there is earlier evidence of the consuls from Rome, but not from elsewhere in Italy.

In cases where postconsulates occur much later than consular inscriptions from the same area, we must assume that the p.c. is (if not a matter of a delay in erecting the stone) the result of apathy or ignorance.[30] Such inscriptions are *ICUR* n.s. I 2596 = *ILCV* 2940A (10.vii.350; the consuls are attested at Rome--though with one name deviating from the regular formula found later--as early as April and are attested in Egypt in the same month); *ICUR* n.s. I 2087 = *ILCV* 1478 (13.iv.370; the consuls are attested at Rome in January).

Naturally, this phenomenon becomes increasingly common in the fifth, and especially sixth centuries. From 410 to 476, at least seven inscriptions use p.c.'s at a time when one[31] or both[32] of the new consuls were known. After 476, the use of p.c.'s, iterum p.c.'s, and even regional postconsular eras[33] was a common response to the increasing unreliability of dissemination of consular names.

There are several cases in which the use of a p.c. seems to be a response to a confused political situation. These are *ICUR* n.s. IV 9549 = *ILCV* 4428 and *ICUR* 29 = *ILCV* 873 (x and xii.307) and *CIL* IX 6192 = *ILCV* 582 (24.v.393). For 307, no fewer than four consular formulas are attested, and for 393, two. Apparently, the people who had these stones carved wished to ensure that the dates would be comprehensible to everyone and so used the noncommittal postconsulate rather than one of the several

---

[27]There are also some cases of omission of the *western* consul. A Syracusan inscription (27.vi.433) omits Petronius Maximus probably for lack of space (Theodosius, the eastern consul, was named first even in the West); an Italian inscription (*ILCV* 1288, 24.vi.446) omits the second consul in a year when both were western. The omission of the western imperial consul Majorian from the sole Gallic inscription of 458 perhaps reflects local hostility to the conqueror of the Gallic pretender Avitus.

[28]Unusually late p.c.'s occur in the following years: 350, 370, 372, 381, 384, 385, 386, 393, 409, 410, 411, 414, 418, 423, 425, 427, 439, 441, 447, 450, 453, 454 (?), 457, 462, 466, 478, 485, 486, 487, 491, 495, 505, 506, 508, 510, 520, 538-541.

[29]These come from 366, 367, 388, 392, 395, 399, 402, 403, 405, 408, 410, 423, 429, 431, 434, 455, 460, 467, 473, 475, 484, 488, 492, 503, 516, 519, 523, 529, 530.

[30]Cf. Mommsen, *Ges.Schr.* VI 374.

[31]Inscriptions of 439 (Syracuse), 447 (Dertona, Ravenna).

[32]414 (Salona), 423 (Syracuse), 453 (Como--the pertinence of this inscription depends on the reliability of the consular date in a letter of Pope Leo--see s.a.), 466 (Milan).

[33]To be noted are the p.c. Symmachi (cos. 485) era, attested at Arles as late as 495, and the p.c. Paulini (cos. 534) era, attested at Lodi as late as 552 (*CIL* V 6403 = *ILCV* 338b; cf. *ILCV* III p.258); see Critical Appendix, end.

possible consular formulas of the year. Another possible case is *CIL* V 5206 = *ILCV* 2870, near Brixia, 18.iii.425, dated p.c. Castini. A nearly contemporaneous Roman inscription (dated 11.iii) gives the new consul of the first part of the year--Iohanne Aug. cons. By late March, the western usurper John was probably fighting at Ravenna (closer to Brixia than to Rome). The use of the p.c. in the Brixian inscription may reflect the fact that John was on the verge of defeat, so use of his name might be thought unwise, and the names of the legal consuls of the year, the emperor Theodosius and the legitimate western Caesar Valentinian, had not yet been announced, or could not yet be safely used.

4. Less Common Errors; Miscellaneous Oddities

There are several cases (e.g. in 339 and 414) of confusion of imperial consuls who had similar names, Constantius, Constantinus and Constans, for example. This type of error is hardly surprising and is occasionally found also in the papyri and the laws (it is extremely common in the consular lists and chronicles). There are inscriptions in which the conjunction between the names of two consuls has been omitted: e.g., *Rufino Eusebio cons* (*ICUR* n.s. I 3164 = *ILCV* 3831, 347), *Lupicino Iovino cons* (*ICUR* n.s. I 1350 = *ILCV* 1296A, 367), and *Decio Longino* (*I.Lat.Gaul.Narb.* 606, 486). There are sixteen cases in which the order of the consuls has been reversed[34]--three cases occurring in the consulates of emperors named Valentinian and Valens.

Some miscellaneous oddities: Sometimes D.N. is used with non-imperial consuls (e.g. in 362, 377, 384-386, 397-398); emperors are called v.c. in 398 and 474; Tatianus, cos. 391, is given the incorrect praenomen A.; the name of Olybrius, cos. 395, is written *OCNID*; three inscriptions use the "official" sounding formula, "et qui (de oriente) nuntiatus fuerit," one in Latin (Milan, 439) and two in Greek (Sicily, 452--note the odd phraseology; 459, Sardis, using the version common in the papyri, καὶ τοῦ δηλω- θησομένου).

---

[34]These are in 348 (cf. above, n.19), 359, 365, 372, 373, 374, 378, 384, 436, 443, 457, 462 (eastern), 465, 492 (in an iterum p.c.), 494, 516 (see note in text). Except for 462, the post-395 cases all fall in years when both consuls were appointed in the same half of the empire.

Chapter 6

Papyri

The main body of papyrological evidence comes from the eastern part of the empire, more specifically from Egypt. Only six eastern documents have a non-Egyptian provenance, viz. *YCS* 28 (1985) 101 (Caesarea?, 293), *BGU* I 316 (Askalon, 359), *SB* I 5941 (Caesarea?, 510[1]), *P.Ness.* 16 and 18 (Nessana, Palestine, 512 and 537), and *P.Cair.Masp.* II 67126 (Constantinople, 541). Slightly more numerous are those dated papyrus texts which were written in the western part of the empire and which originally belonged to an archive kept in Ravenna.[2] But even these documents number hardly more than ten, whereas the number of papyri from Egypt runs to *ca* 1000.[3] Most of these are written in Greek, but a few are in Latin or even bilingual. They all present us with the names of consuls in dating formulas either for dating the document itself or for dating an event referred to in a text.[4] As these sometimes official documents are authentic, contemporary source material, the nature of which can best be compared with archival material preserved since the Middle Ages, they are unique sources for our better knowledge both of the names of the consuls themselves and for our understanding of the workings of the consular dating system in Late Antiquity.

There are, it is true, certain problems in the use of consular names for dating purposes,[5] and as the professional scribes of the papyri were, of course, liable to human error, the consular formulas as found in the papyri sometimes deviate *in malam partem* from what we find in other sources. It should be noted, on the other hand, that they sometimes present us with information which has otherwise been lost.[6] On the whole, the data from the papyri coincide with the data from our other main source for the consulate in the East, namely the eastern consular lists and chronicles.[7] More problematical is the relationship between the datings found in the eastern laws and the papyrological evidence, whereas our epigraphical evidence from the East is so scanty that one can hardly define the relationship between the papyri and the inscriptions at all.

The papyrological evidence from the East shows only limited coincidence with our western sources for the consulate, especially after 411. Even before that year, there are already single years and strings of years for which the papyri show divergent consular datings, no doubt due to political crises like uprisings by usurpers and even civil war.[8]

In general, the Egyptian papyri show so basically coherent a picture of consular formulas as to suggest that these formulas were published annually within Egypt in a quick, fairly uniform way. That is not to say that variants of any specific consular formula cannot be found, but these variants are mostly idiosyncrasies of minor importance. It seems most natural to assume that each year the office of the

[1]See J.G. Keenan, *ZPE* 53 (1983) 247 n.ll, who is doubtful about the provenance.
[2]Cf. J.-O. Tjäder, *Die nicht-literarischen lateinischen Papyri Italiens aus der Zeit 445-700*, I-II, Lund 1955-Stockholm 1982. (= *Acta Inst. Romani Regni Sueciae*, ser. in 4°, XIX.1,2).
[3]The period between A.D. 337-540 comprises *ca* 600 documents; for a listing see *Misc.Pap.* 13-23; the period A.D. 284-337 contains roughly 400 documents with consular dates. Cf. R.S. Bagnall, K.A. Worp, "Papyrus Documentation in the Period of Diocletian and Constantine," *BES* 4 (1982) 25-33.
[4]Cf. e.g. *SB* XIV 12167, *P.Panop.* 24 and 30. The last document is dated to 5.viii.332 (lines 2-3), but refers to another document dated 23.x.331 (lines 23,34).
[5]Cf. the remarks in *CSBE* 50; cf. also *GRBS* 20 (1979) 279 ff.
[6]Cf. for the consuls of 411-412 the three articles cited in the entry for those years.
[7]Cf. for the eastern fasti the remarks in *BASP* 18 (1981) 69-72 and in *JRS* 72 (1982) 132.
[8]Cf. e.g. the situation in A.D. 321-324, *CSBE* 72 and 108-09.

Praefectus Aegypti in Alexandria issued a kind of generally prescribed dating formula based upon the most recent information from the capital(s) of the Empire, and that this formula was taken over by most of the Egyptian scribes. In appropriate cases the current manner of dating was "updated" in the course of the year, by substituting for postconsular datings the names of current consuls. The fact that we cannot discern in the period under review any regionalistic features among consular datings in the papyri[9] seems a strong indication that the scribes in the various provinces of Egypt used one standard consular dating formula. Though in individual cases a certain amount of idiosyncrasy was exercised by the scribes while penning the datings above contracts or under petitions, they were apparently not at liberty to choose whatever kind of dating method they thought fit. We see this from the use of postconsular dating formulas. For the most part it appears[10] that within Egypt postconsular dating hardly overlapped with the use of consular dating in any given Julian year (any overlap is a matter of days rather than of weeks). This must reflect the issuing of generally prescribed ways of dating by the government in Alexandria on the basis of current information. In other words: if a postconsular dating still occurs in a papyrus from Oxyrhynchos on 30.viii, there is reason to believe that the news of the consuls for the year in question had not yet reached Alexandria about two weeks earlier, i.e. around 15.viii.[11] A few exceptions to this rule have occurred in recently-edited texts; cf. above, p.29. The distribution over the year of postconsulates in the papyri (and elsewhere, especially in the laws) seems to show that new consuls were not always disseminated early enough (i.e., in the previous year) to be known at its start. See Chapter 2 for a full discussion. The papyri seem to show that the publication of these western consuls was sometimes delayed considerably (cf. 502); in a number of cases they were apparently never published at all in Egypt (cf. the period 481-490).

There are a number of aberrations and errors to be noted in the consular datings between 284-541.[12] Among minor aberrations and variants there is the interchange of Σεβαστός and *Augustus*,[13] the omission of an element like *Dominus Noster* preceding an emperor who is consul,[14] the variation in inclusion of the element *Imperator* in the early fourth century,[15] the omission of names like Flavius and Valerius (e.g., in 309 and 313), the omission of various renderings of *vir clarissimus* after names of private consuls or *nobilissimus* with Caesars, and the omission of offices held, such as the praetorian prefecture; examples of these are scattered throughout various years for which the more complete formula is attested. Apart from such relatively trivial variants one finds also:

1. "Wrong" iteration numerals: 371, 392, 426, 508. Wrong iteration numerals are usually mere errors, although there is one case (411-412) where we have an independent tradition preserved in the papyri. In the case of the papyri from 371, four of the five texts have the correct iteration numeral, with only one text apparently having incorrectly I instead of the expected II. In the years 392 and 417 (? see the Crit.App. for the doubtful date of this text), the scribes who wrote *P.Gron.* 9 and *P.Vindob.Sijp.* 9 were not very competent (the scribe of *P.Gron.* 9 even added a superfluous third consul; cf. *infra*), as their texts and writing (we have seen photographs of both) show. The evidence for the p.c. in A.D. 426 is divided: one text

---

[9]For regionalism in the papyri, cf. the remarks in *GRBS* 20 (1979) 288 ff.; for regionalistic features in imperial oath formulas, see *ZPE* 45 (1982) 217; for regionalisms in Christian invocations, cf. *Cd'E* 56 (1982) 112 ff., 362 ff. For regionalism in the consular/postconsular dating formula after A.D. 541, cf. *BASP* 16 (1979) 245-47. Consulates expressed only with numerals occur almost entirely in Panopolitan texts (see years 308, 329, 339, 340, 342, 346)--but there is an exception in *P.Col.* VII 174.56 (342); cf. also 284.

[10]Cf. *CSBE* 50 ff.; *BASP* 17 (1980) 27-36.

[11]On the speed of communication within Egypt, cf. the remarks in *P.Panop.Beatty* introd., p.xx and now D.W. Rathbone, *ZPE* 62 (1986) 101-31.

[12]Even though a substantial amount has been removed recently through revision of the pertinent documents: cf. e.g. the series of "Chronological Notes on Byzantine Papyri" in *BASP* 15 (1978) 233-46; 16 (1979) 221-47; 17 (1980) 5-36, 105-17; 18 (1981) 33-54, and the articles in *ZPE* 28 (1978) 221-30; 46 (1982) 239-47 and 56 (1984) 127-36; cf. also the bibliography in *GRBS* 20 (1979) 279 n.1.

[13]For an attempt to explain this variation by region, see *P.Oxy.* LI 3620.2n.

[14]Cf. *ZPE* 39 (1980) 165-77 for the use of κύριος or δεσπότης. Cf. also *BASP* 16 (1979) 241.

[15]See *P.Rainer.Cent.* 102.2n.

has the correct numeral XI, one text gives wrongly Theodosius X, and a third text is lacunose. *CPR* VI 8 (ed.: 509) should not be taken as evidence for an otherwise unattested fourth consulate of Anastasius Augustus with Fl. Venantius. Rather, it seems likely that the scribe mistakenly wrote Anastasius IV instead of Anastasius III, that he realized his mistake, left the document (a compromissum) unfinished, and started his text afresh on a clean sheet of papyrus. The preservation by chance of the unfinished text thus confuses rather than enlightens.[16]

 2. Superfluous iteration numerals: 314, 464. In the case of 314, the scribe added an iteration numeral after the names of two private persons, though one could not reasonably foresee that the future would bring them a second consulate. There are some thirty documents from this year, of which only one has this peculiarity. For the case of the papyrus from 464, cf. *CSBE* 52 n.4. It should be remarked that the evidence for this year is not unanimous; there is another text from the year which does not have the superfluous numeral.

 3. "Wrong" omission of iteration numerals: 296, 298, 301, 306, 313, 364, 374, 388, 397?, 403, 418, 476, 496, 528. Most of these cases come from years for which we have other papyri which do mention the numeral. As in the case of the wrong iteration numerals, one is dealing with idiosyncratic scribal errors. Only in the case of 298, 301 (both cases of an earlier suffect consulate) and 528 does our total evidence lack the expected numeral. This seems too small a basis for drawing firm conclusions. The case of *P.Stras.* 255 (397; cf. Crit.App.) is questionable because the papyrus is mutilated and the "omission" of the numerals is based on the editor's statement that there is no space for them in the lacuna. Since few characters are involved, one may doubt that such a precise claim is reliable.

 4. "Wrong" combination of consular names: 296, 297, 330, 361, 380, 530; cf. *BASP* 17 (1980) 30. There are only a few combinations of consular names in papyri published to date which are not attested elsewhere (for additional names not found in other sources, cf. infra; for the question of two consuls, one of whom has a "wrong" interation numeral, cf. no. 3 above). In the case of the papyri from 296 and 297 (*P.Mich.* X 593 and *P.Oxy.* XLIV 3184b) one is dealing quite clearly with a scribal error. Likewise, *P.Oxy.* XLIX 3479 may be taken (despite the editor's view) as a product of scribal confusion, not as a kind of evidence for a revised consular dating formula in 361. In the case of the two papyri giving a p.c. reference to the consuls of 379 in 380 and of the papyri dating from 330, it is not so much a matter of the combination of wrong names as of different papyri giving various parts of the full name of a single person. In *P.Rain.Cent.* 116, from 530 (?), one finds the name of the first consul given as Horios instead of Orestes. In *MPER* n.s. XV 95 a nonexistent pair (Fll. Flavianus and Ptolemaeus) is given, and in XV 61 Theodosius' consular partner of 439 is given as Fl. Maximinus, rather than the correct Festus. These are manifestly writing exercises, not real documents.

 5. "Wrong" order of names: 309 (?). With the inversion of the normal order of the consular names from 332 removed in *SB* XII 11024 (*BASP* 17 [1980] 15) there is among the papyri only one (doubtful) example in which the consuls may not follow the traditional order of names, viz. *P.Ryl.* IV 616 (from 309?). For this text see the Crit.App. for 312. (Licinianus Licinius are reversed in one text of 312 [*P.Cair.Isid.* 41.93], but that is a matter of the order within one consul's names.)

 6. "Wrong" omission of names: 343, 358, 372, 507; cf. A.D. 440. The first three cases listed here come from before the division of the empire. In the case of 358, there seems no reason not to think of a scribal error in *P.Ross.Georg.* III 28 (the scribe was a bungler anyway, dating to a consulate instead of a p.c. held by Constantius Augustus [numeral lost]); and in the case of 343 and 372 most papyri (correctly) give the name of both of the consuls. After 411, the late publication and recognition of a western consul in the East is clearly shown in the papyri, when the name of such a consul is lacking or, if both consuls were westerners but did not get disseminated in the East, when a p.c. dating referring to an earlier consulate is used. Illustrative is the situation with the consuls of 440, Valentinianus V and Anatolius. Valentinianus

---

[16]One wonders why the scribe did not cut off the unused portion of the sheet and start afresh on the unused space. Apparently papyrus was not a sufficiently expensive commodity to him to warrant this procedure in an important legal document.

does not appear in the sole papyrus dating from his actual consulate, but he is also lacking in the sole document dated by the p.c. in A.D. 441. On the other hand, in documents attesting Valentinian's consulate in later years (445, 450, 455) the iteration numeral in the papyri is the same as that found elsewhere: in other words, the fifth consulate of 440 was certainly recognized by the government of the East and taken for granted in Egypt *post eventum*. Obviously what happened is that it was so late in the year when Valentinian's consulate was finally promulgated in the East that no one bothered to send out an updated formula to the provinces. As a result, when dissemination was late again next year, naturally Valentinian's name did not appear in the p.c. Compare too the western consul of 525: though missing from both consular and postconsular dates in papyri, he turns up as consul on an inscription from Thessalonica. These cases should serve as a warning not to infer non-recognition too hastily in the later fifth century just because a western name was not disseminated at the time.

It is presumably the breakdown of speedy communications between the various parts of the empire that is (in part) responsible for the disappearance or extremely late acceptances of most western consuls in the papyri from the late fifth and early sixth centuries. In individual cases, westerners were used in consular datings[17] and a papyrus from 502 seems to show the introduction of a western consul into the eastern dating formula during the consular year.

Rather different from this are cases cited above when names of consuls are omitted in backreferences to earlier events. As it seems, these omissions were partly inspired by the wish to be as brief as possible, partly because of political reasons, especially when in the course of time a consul had fallen out of grace, e.g. in the case of Maximianus after 311 (for his *damnatio memoriae* see Barnes, *New Empire* 34; there are no papyri, however, which can be adduced as definite proof of this *damnatio*, as all pertinent documents can be explained in terms of abbreviation of the formula).

7. "Wrong" addition of consul: 368/369, 392; cf. A.D. 501. The few cases of too many names are easily explicable. The papyri from 368 (and p.c., 369) show that the name of the junior emperor Gratian was tagged onto the consular formula for this year, Valentinianus Aug. II and Valens Aug. II, no doubt the result of confusion between regnal and consular formulas. The scribe of *P.Gron.* 9 did more or less the same thing in 392 by adding Theodosius' name before the actual consular formula of this year (and complicated things further by giving the wrong iteration numeral for Arcadius). Lastly, the incompetent scribe in *P.Amst.* I 45 from 501 did not know how to distinguish between the name of the second consul of 500, Hypatius, and the Greek word for consul, ὕπατος; thinking then that he had only one consular name, he made things worse by adding what seemed to him the appropriate formula, et qui fuerit nuntiatus. Cf. above, p.30 n.76.

These errors and omissions are in general not of such a nature as to put the reliability of the papyrological evidence for consular datings between 284 and 541 very much in doubt. Most errors in any given year are balanced by other documents from the same year which give the expected data. But where there is some consistency in the deviation between the data furnished by the papyri and that of other sources of "eastern" information, it has been shown that the papyri are sometimes likely to contain useful information about the consuls. This holds especially true for the situation in 411/412 (cf. those years), but one may also point to *SB* I 4821 (465; cf. *BASP* 17 [1980] 13-14), and *P.Rainer Cent.* 94 (441; cf. A. Cameron, *YCS* 27 [1982] 217 f., esp. 258) as being documents which provide us with important new data on the names of individual consuls. They are also decisive in 381, when the rest of the eastern evidence is divided on the question of the sequence of the consuls' names: the five papyri, ranging from 25.ii to 31.xii, are unanimous for Eucherius et Syagrius.

---

[17]Compare the case of cos. 480 and A. Cameron, *JRS* 72 (1982) 131; cos. 495, cos. 520, and A. Cameron, *ZPE* 48 (1982) 94.

Chapter 7

The Imperial Laws

1. The Sources and their Problems

Imperial laws issued between 284 and 541 are preserved in the following ancient collections:[1]

1) The so-called *Fragmenta Vaticana*, an unofficial (and confused) compilation which perhaps dates from soon after 318. It apparently drew from the regrettably lost *Codex Gregorianus* and *Codex Hermogenianus*. Nos. 33-36 and 274 continue to treat Licinius as Augustus (though contrast 273). Two isolated later laws (nos. 248 and 37, from 330 and 372) were considered additions to the original collection by Mommsen.[2] If they are not, the collection must be later than 372, though certainly pre-Theodosian.[3]

2) The *Mosaicarum et Romanarum legum collatio* contains several laws of Diocletian from the *Cod. Greg.* and *Cod. Hermog.* and one law of Theodosius (5.3.2), an excerpt of which appears as *CTh* 9.7.6 (390). The original work has obviously been adapted and amplified more than once.[4] This and the preceding work were both edited by Mommsen in *Coll. libr. iur. anteiust.* (1890), and texts appear also in *FIRA* II[2] (Florence 1968) 463ff., 543ff.

3) The *Constitutiones Sirmondianae* (in Mommsen's *CTh* I.2, 907-21, cf. I.1 ccclxxx) contain sixteen laws from 333 to 425, preserved not in excerpts but entire. Like nos. 1 and 2, they are also pre-Theodosian; all three have therefore escaped the editorial interference that is the primary subject of this chapter.

4) The *Codex Theodosianus*, containing legislation from 313 to 438, was issued in 438, first in Constantinople and soon after in Rome. It was not compiled from files in Constantinople alone, but from a wide variety of provincial capitals too, in both East and West (see Seeck, *Regesten* 1-17; Gaudemet, 59-61).[5]

5) The *Codex Iustinianus* was issued in 529 and (in a revised edition) in 534. It was almost entirely based on the three earlier Codes and collections of Novels.

6) Various private collections of laws issued between 438 and 529 are published under the general title of Novels (grouped by the issuing emperor) in Mommsen's edition of *CTh* II (Gaudemet 70-73).

---

[1]The basic facts and bibliography up to 1979 are given by J. Gaudemet, *La formation du droit séculier et du droit de l'église aux IVe et Ve siècles*[2] (Paris 1979). Fragments of constitutions not in the ancient collections also turn up occasionally in papyri: (*PSI* I 112 and *P.Laur.* IV 169: see under 354) and on stone (see below, p.76 n.18).

[2]Cf. F. Schulz, *History of Roman Legal Science* (Oxford 1946) 311.

[3]Gaudemet, 75-77. A few dated laws are also preserved in the 5th/6th c. *Consultatio veteris cuiusdam iurisconsulti*, deriving from *Cod.Greg.*, *Hermog.*, and *Theod.*: cf. Schulz, 323-24; *FIRA* II 591f.

[4]Cf. Schulz, 312-14; Gaudemet, 96-98.

[5]See now the wide-ranging study by Tony Honoré, "The Making of the Theodosian Code," *ZSS* 103 (1986) 133-222. A.J.B. Sirks ("Observations sur le Code Théodosien," *Subseciva Groningana* 2 [1986] 21-34 at 22-24) has recently claimed that the compilers used only Constantinopolitan and Roman archives, on the remarkable grounds that Seeck was able to prove provincial origin for only 10 per cent of extant laws, "ce qui n'est pas un nombre suffisant pour sa thèse." As for the many laws that carry the date and place of receipt in the provinces, "pourquoi n'aurait-elle pas été rapportée [i.e. to Constantinople] par les fonctionnaires responsables?" (p.24). At least one of the reasons why not is expounded in detail in section 2 of this chapter, the p.c. dates picked up by laws arriving in the more distant provinces early in the year.

7) Laws of Justinian issued after 534 are published in R. Schoell and W. Kroll's edition of the Novels (*Corpus Iuris Civilis* III, 1895).

The codes of Theodosius and Justinian--hereafter *CTh* and *CJ*--provide the most abundant and (in theory) most precise material for this study.[6] The best preserved laws will be equipped with some or all of the following elements over and above the text of the law itself.

In the heading:
    (1) The name of the issuing authority (the emperor or emperors);
    (2) The name of the official addressed together with his office;

In the subscription:
    (3) The date (day, month and consular year) and place of issue (*data*);
    (4) The date and place (where different) of receipt (*accepta*) or public posting (*proposita, p.p.*). The place of receipt will often be implied rather than stated: i.e. if a law sent from Sirmium on 23.i.321 to the prefect of Rome (*CTh* 6.22.1) was *accepta* on 5.iv, the second date must refer to Rome.[7]

Virtually all laws have (1) and (2), but a great many have only a single date and no place at all. In such cases we have assumed that this is the date of issue, but in any given case the sole date might be the date of receipt or posting several months later at (say) Carthage rather than of issue at Constantinople. By then it might have been another year, and (more relevant for our purposes) the new consular date would be evidence for Carthaginian rather than Constantinopolitan practice.[8]
Of all these elements the most consistently reliable is probably the name of the official addressed. The name itself is almost always present and seldom corrupt, but the office is often missing and not infrequently incorrect. The commonest confusion is PP(O)/PV,[9] but sometimes the office has simply been interpolated to fill a gap. If the name is well known, it will often help to correct (or at least expose) a false date.
Next most reliable are the place name(s) in the subscription. A few obscure names were liable to be corrupted--or supplanted by more familiar names. But since the Theodosian compilers frequently omitted place names as irrelevant for their purpose, they are most unlikely to have bothered to interpolate them. As we shall see, both *data* and *accepta* sites can help to identify and correct false dates.
Next in order come the month and (less so) the day in the date. Numbers (of course) are always liable to be corrupted: III for IIII, VII for VIII or VIIII, III for XIII and the like. Fortunately, such

---

[6]The laws have been collected by years in two irreplaceable and complementary works: Mommsen's preface to his edition of the Theodosian Code and Novels (I.i.ccix-cccvi; II.xcvi-cix); and Seeck's *Regesten*, passim. Mommsen lists the laws (with due warning where appropriate) under the year of their consular formula; Seeck redistributed them in accordance with his own corrections, normally with a reference to the discussion in his long preface. In a more modest way Krüger lists the laws of *CJ* by years (on the Mommsen model) in his edition, pp.494-509. As far as 476 *CJ* is included along with *CTh* in Seeck's *Regesten*. Since anyone who wishes to check our statements will have these works in his hands, we have not thought it worthwhile to list again the many thousands of laws which for many years all present the same official version anyway. Especially in unproblematic years we decided simply to give the (approximate) number of laws for each year, quote the earliest, and list the places of issue. Naturally we quote all provisional, anomalous and otherwise interesting formulas in full. Curious looking figures like "about 16 laws" mean that there are more or less than 16 according to how certain anomalies are solved. We have not attempted to deal with such insoluble problems as the correct distribution of laws dated by one or another of the joint consulates of Valentinian and Valens. For the sake of simplicity we use the general term law to cover every form of imperial constitution. Since most problems concerning the laws involve the careers of individual officials, the reader should throughout refer to *PLRE* I and II and other prosopographical works for documents discussed here.
[7]For the terms data, p.p., acc., lecta, praelata, regesta (= "filed"), see the detailed account in Mommsen's edition of *CTh*, I.i.clv-clvii.
[8]See further below on this point, p.79.
[9]We use the convenient ancient acronyms PPO = *praefectus praetorio*; PV = *praefectus urbi* (R, Rome; C, Constantinople); and CSL = *comes sacrarum largitionum*. A complete list of abbreviations used in the *CTh* is found in Mommsen's edition, I.i.cli-clii.

corruptions produce errors of only a few days or weeks. More serious but probably less common are confusions such as IAN/IVN/IVL, MAR/MAI, or FEB/SEP.

Least reliable are the imperial names in the heading. The standard abbreviations *Idem A., AA.* or *AAA.* took on a different reference once a law was moved from one context to another--and left it wholly undatable if the subscription was missing or defective. The compilers seem often to have merely inferred the emperors from the consular date--sometimes demonstrably, as in the case of emperors who died early in the year, but still appear in the headings to laws from the end of the year.

But if the imperial headings are almost worthless, the consular dates are only a little more reliable. The numerous sources of error were classified with immense skill and detail by Seeck. Many of Seeck's own corrections have not stood the test of time, and there has been a tendency among the more conservative to resist emendation in principle. This is a mistake. A large number of the dates in the laws can be proved to be wrong (e.g., because the addressee did not hold the office named, or not at that time, or the emperor was not at the place named on the day in question); many more are dubious; and we are scarcely entitled to assume that the majority we have no means of checking are all correct.[10] As might have been expected, the proportion of error is at its highest in laws of Constantine, at its lowest in laws of Theodosius II.

An example, initially chosen at random simply to exemplify a law equipped with all these elements, well illustrates most of the problems that arise (*CTh* 11.36.10):

> Idem AA. [in the context of chapter 36, Constantius and Constans, 337-350] ad Proclianum proconsulem Africae:
> > [Text of the law]
> data xv kal. Feb. [18 Jan.] Constantinopoli; accepta x kal. Aug. [23 Aug.] Karthagine Constantio VII A. et Constante Caesare conss. [? 354]

What could be more precise and informative, it might seem, provided we correct a minor slip. For if 354 is meant, the date should read *Constantio A. VII et Constantio Caes. III*; apparently someone was mislead by the Constans in the heading. In fact, however, both heading and subscription must be in far more serious error, since Constans died in 350 and Constantius was not at Constantinople on 18 January of any year of his reign between 342 and 360. Since Seeck it has been generally agreed that the year must be 360 (i.e., Constantius X et Iulianus Caesar III)--and the true heading *Idem Augustus*. It will also be noticed that the law took more than six months to reach its destination.

We may now look at the two other laws on which our knowledge of Proclianus' career rests. First *CTh* 4.13.4:

> Imp. Constantius A. ad Proclianum proconsulem Africae
> > [Text of the law]
> data xiiii k. Feb. [19 Jan.] Co(nstantinopoli) Constantio A. viii et Iuliano C. conss. [356]

The heading looks sound, but, once more, Constantius was not at Constantinople in mid January 356. Again, we must correct the year to 360. Lastly, *CTh* 11.1.1:

> Imp. Constantinus A. ad Proclianum:
> > [Text of law]
> data xv Kal. Iul. [17 June] Constantinopoli Constantino A. IIII et Licinio IIII conss. [315]

---

[10]This is not to say that dates may be changed at will, but neither should they be presumed sound until proved false. E. Stein's "règle fondamentale de la critique historique et philologique, à savoir qu'il n'est pas permis d'apporter une modification quelconque au texte d'une source qu'en cas d'absolue nécessité, quand tous les moyens de le maintenir tel qu'il nous est parvenu ont été épuisés" (*Byzantion* 9 [1934] 329) is no more applicable to *CTh* than to any other ancient text.

Proclianus' office is not here specified, but surely he is the same man, since a reference in the law to Eusebius cos. 347 points unmistakably to the reign of Constantius, not of Constantine. Yet again we must correct the heading to Constantius and the year to 360. If so, then perhaps the month too should be changed.

Certainty is unattainable in such cases, but in all probability we have three laws addressed to the same man on successive days, 18 and 19 Jan. 360.[11] The transmitted consular dates are

> 315 Constantino A. IIII et Licinio IIII
> 354 Constantio VII A. et Constante C.
> 356 Constantio A. VIII et Iuliano C. ·

Whatever be thought of the suggested corrections, all three are demonstrably in error; and, drastic though it might seem to the untrained eye, the simplest and most plausible solution is to change all three to

> 360 Constantio A. X et Iuliano Caes. III.

It is important to understand why. When faced with a corruption, the textual critic will usually (not always wisely) seek a palaeographically close emendation. So too in the Codes, one imperial consulate is often misread for another. The four consular pairs listed above do bear a general similarity to each other, but that is by no means the only explanation for the common substitution of false consulates, non-imperial no less than imperial.

In the first place, it should never be forgotten that what appear in the codes as independent laws are in fact merely excerpts from laws. This we can see from the post-Theodosian Novels and the so-called Sirmondian Constitutions, an independent collection of 16 complete laws from the period covered by *CTh*. They are often several pages long, and as many as three or four excerpts from them appear in the codes as if independent laws. The full text of one of these laws will usually open with an elaborate rhetorical and moralizing preface that the compilers always omitted, and then go on to deal with a number of linked items. These items the compilers distributed between their own more elaborate subheadings.

It is worth trying to form as concrete a picture as possible of the successive processes of copying and excerpting to which the contents of *CTh* were subjected. It is unlikely that the Theodosian commissioners ever saw the original documents dispatched from court. The closest they got will have been file copies, whether in the central archives or the various provincial archives. Presumably they worked from copies made from these file copies. The sixteen[12] commissioners then read the complete texts and indicated on their copies which passages were to be excerpted and under which titles they were to be classified.[13] They or (more probably) their clerks will then have copied each extract onto a separate sheet (or codex) for each title. The extracts will not yet have been in chronological order, so they will all have to have been copied at least once more before even a provisional final draft was possible. So each extract must have been copied at least four or five times by the time the Code was complete, and at every stage there was not merely the possibility of transcriptional error, but the probability of correction (or corruption) of provisional, incomplete, or abbreviated consular formulas.

[11]Barnes (*Phoenix* 39 [1985] 149) assigns *CTh* 11.1.1 to the same Proclianus in a different office, by emending *data* to *accepta*. He argues that the content suits a CSL, but the closing sentence implies a circular to provincial governors.
[12]A commission of nine was appointed in 429, enlarged to sixteen in 435, though not all survived till 438: Honoré, *ZSS* 103 (1986) 161-68.
[13]A.H.M. Jones once neatly solved two separate problems with the hypothesis that two laws exchanged their subscriptions during this process (*Historia* 4 [1955] 229-33). He presupposed that the excerpting was done literally with scissors and paste, which seems unlikely. But errors of this sort may well have happened nonetheless.

The compilers often left explicit indications of their excerpting: many hundreds of items in *CTh* begin with the formula *post alia* and end with *et cetera* (all these formulas[14] were omitted by the Justinianic compilers). It is sometimes possible to piece together as many as nine extracts from the same original law, usually indicated in modern works with a plus sign. For example, *CTh* 1.1.3 + 1.28.4 + 6.3.1 + 6.4.26 + 12.1.130-132 + 15.1.29-30, all addressed to Aurelian on the same day in 393. It is obviously most unlikely that more than one detailed law was sent to the same official on the same sort of topics on one day. In this case the compilers evidently worked with more care than usual, since all nine extracts give the same day, and no fewer than seven call Aurelian PV(C), with only two calling him PPO, an office he did not hold till 399-400 (and again in 414-416).

But many other groups of extracts carry different dates, sometimes such as can be brought into line with the addition or subtraction of an I or a X, but no less often with a different day, month, and year. For example, the nine extracts from the same law addressed to the entire college of prefects. Full details are given by Mommsen ad *CTh* 6.27.1 and Seeck, *Reg.* 42-43. All nine give a different day, and in only one case can the difference be eliminated by correcting a VII to VIII. As to the consular pairs, they offer:

> 7.13.1: Constano A. VI et C. (?320 or 353)
> 7.21.2: Constantio A. VI et Constante II (353)
> 6.27.1: Constantio A. VII et Constante C. (354)
> 8.4.5: Constantino A. VII et Constante II (?326 or 354)
> 8.7.4: Constantio A. VII et Constante II Caesare (354)
> 8.7.5: Constantio A. VII et Constante Caes. II (354)
> 8.7.6: Constantio A. VII et Constante C. II (354)
> 12.1.14: Constantino A. VII et Constantio C. (326)
> 12.1.18: Constantino A. VIII et Constantio IIII (329)

It seems clear that the trouble here began with the common confusion between *Constantinus* and *Constantius*. Indeed all the rest could be seen as attempts to correct the ambiguous and incomplete no. 1, *Constano A. VI et C.* If so, they can hardly all be attributed to the same compilers on the same occasion. More probably, as Seeck argued, the compilers were faced with (at least) two different copies of the complete law. Mommsen saw *Constantio* as original, Seeck *Constantino*. Fortunately we do not need for present purposes to decide between them; we never include such uncertain dates. But it is disturbing to reflect that we have so many variants here only because we happen to have so many witnesses. When we have only one witness, as in the vast majority of cases, perforce we take the only version we have on trust.

Perhaps more disturbing still are the eight different day dates. Here there is no possibility of an illegible or incomplete original being responsible for the six different months, with four kalends, three nones, and one ides. There seems only one solution. As Maas saw, the original had *no* day date at all. *All* the day dates are guesses. As he shrewdly observed, any document the compilers wanted to include had to have a complete consular date in order to be valid. The first law in the Code clearly lays down (1.1.1) "si qua posthac edicta sive constitutiones *sine die et consule* fuerint deprehensae, auctoritate careant."

It is worth emphasizing[15] why this was considered so important. For whereas the Code of Justinian was intended to provide a harmonious body of law, free of all contradictions, the Theodosian commissioners settled for a more modest aim, and knowingly included a large number of contradictory laws. In fact they supplied explicit instructions on how to deal with contradictory rulings:

---

[14]Usefully studied by P. Maas in his review of Mommsen's edition, *GGA* 1906, 641-62 = *Kleine Schriften* (1973) 608-28 and 618-26. "Ces mentions ne signifient pas simplement que le texte reproduit au C.Th. n'est qu'un fragment de la constitution originale, car dans ce cas elles devraient se rencontrer pour chaque texte. Elles signifient que d'autres fragments de la même constitution figurent dans un autre passage du C.Th." (Gaudemet, 62).
[15]See Honoré, *ZSS* 103 (1986) 163-65.

If any diversity shall cause anything to be stated in two ways, it shall be tested by the order of the readings, and not only shall the year of the consulate be considered and the time of the reign be investigated, but also the arrangement of the work itself shall show that the laws which are later are more valid. (*CTh* 1.1.5.5f.)

So some dates may be no more than guesses to fill a blank in a law the commissioners were anxious to include. By contrast, a large number of laws in *CJ* lack a consular date.[16] Since there are so few dateless laws in *CTh*, the presumption is that most of those in *CJ* were already found dateless by the Justinianic commissioners (textual transmission, bad also for *CTh*, surely accounts only for some). If so, we must allow for the possibility that the Theodosian commissioners were faced with a similar proportion of dateless laws.

A great many official documents of the age survive with every element of a complete date *except* the consular pair (e.g. *Collectio Avellana*[17] 14, 15, 16, 18, 19, 23, 24, 28, 29, 33, 35). As Seeck saw (*Reg.* 13-14), such systematic omission is not to be imputed to mere carelessness. Seeck's own explanation was that the documents were copied from the perishable originals into a codex, in batches under successive years. That is to say, the year was written once at the top of each section, and then systematically deleted from individual documents as they were copied in. It is easy to see how one omission in a subsequent copy could leave scores if not hundreds of documents without a consular date. Excerpting from such a collection would also produce the same result. Whatever the cause, it may be that in some cases the day date is sound but the consular pair a guess. We also possess a handful of laws (some known in part from extracts in the Code) inscribed on stone.[18] Not one carries a consular date. But there is no need to paint too bleak a picture. The nine identical dates in the nine excerpts from the law of 393 addressed to Aurelian show that the compilers did not always guess and were not always inaccurate.

Since we are not primarily concerned with correcting erroneous dates, there is no need to spend long on all the mechanical causes of corruption. Confusion between imperial consulates (for which reference may also be made to the law addressed to the college of prefects) may be illustrated by a single example: *CTh* 4.2.1 and 5.1.5 are addressed to Aurelian as PPO Orientis and dated 6.x.396, *Arcadio IIII et Honorio III*. Since another man was PPO at that time, either year or office (or both) must be in error. It cannot be the office alone, since another man was also PVC at the time, and since Aurelian had been PVC in 393-394, he could not have held a lower post than either prefecture in 396. The simplest and most plausible solution is to place both laws in 394, *Arcadio III et Honorio II*, when he was PVC, and to correct the office from PPO to PVC. There are in fact three other laws addressed to Aurelian as PPO in 393 (*CTh* 12.1.131-132; 138), when Rufinus was PPO, and undoubtedly these too must be corrected to PVC. In the case of men who enjoyed long or frequent tenure of (say) the PPO at the end of their careers, this title was liable to be added by guesswork in laws where the office was missing.

For the principle of "ergänzte Konsulate," cases where a law gave only one consul and the other was supplied from the consular fasti by conjecture, it will be enough to refer to the very full discussion in Seeck (*Reg.* 88f.). The danger was particularly acute with imperial consulates: for example, between 411 and 435 the eastern court dated by the name of Theodosius II (usually with *e.q.f.n.* added) alone for all or part of at least seven years. It seems too much to hope that the compilers supplied the correct colleague every time, even supposing that the iteration numbers were always correctly given in their sources. But there are also many examples with citizen consuls: e.g. *Basso* wrongly supplemented *Basso et Philippo* (408) rather than *Basso et Antiocho* (431) (e.g. *CJ* 2.15.1, addressed *Flaviano PPO*, an office he held in 431, not 408).

[16]Krüger's Index constitutionum ad temporis ordinem redactus (pp.489-509) conveniently collects all laws "sine consulibus" at the beginning of each reign.
[17]See below, p.88.
[18]C.G. Bruns, *Fontes Iuris Romani*[7] (1909) nos.94-97; A. Giardina and F. Grelle, *MEFRA* 95 (1983) 258-59). The letter of Honorius to the city of Pamplona (in N. Spain) recently published by H. Sivan (*ZPE* 61 [1985] 273-87) has likewise lost its consular date.

2. Proposita, Accepta, and Postconsulates

Seeck also discussed at length the two other major sources of error, omitted *p.p.* (or *accepta*) date and p.c. (postconsulate) read as consulate. The first error is liable to result in a date one year too late, the second one year too early. Since both are very important for our purposes, and since Seeck was inclined to postulate p.c.'s far too late in the year, a more extended discussion will be necessary. The two cannot easily be separated.

For our purposes, there is no need to distinguish *p.p.* (*proposita*, "posted") from *accepta*; both refer to the arrival of the law at its destination.[19] Omission of *p.p.* may suitably be illustrated by an example from *ConstSirm*. In general the *ConstSirm*, not having been subjected to a process of excerpting and editing, are less prone to error than the laws in *CTh*. But when we are in the position of being able to compare the headings and subscriptions to the same laws in both collections, we seldom find that any of them gets everything correct. In fact, each usually gets a different detail wrong. Two examples will suffice.
First *ConstSirm* 12:

> Impp. Honorius et Theodosius Augg. Curtio PPO ... data VII Kal. Dec. [25.xi] Romae, pp. Carthagine ... Nonis Iuniis [5.vi] Basso et Philippo conss. [408]

Then we have two excerpts in *CTh*, first 16.5.43:

> Idem AA. Curtio PPO ... data XVII Kal. Dec. [15.xi] Romae Basso et Philippo conss.

Then 16.10.19:

> Impp. Arcadius, Honorius et Theodosius AAA. Curtio PPO ... data XVII Kal. Dec. Romae Basso et Philippo conss.

It will be seen that the *CTh* excerpts agree in giving XVII Kal. Dec. [15.xi] for *ConstSirm*'s VII [25.xi]. Since the X was more likely to have been omitted than added, XVII is probably correct. On the other hand, both excerpts omit the *p.p.* date and mistakenly refer the *Kal.Dec.* date to 408 instead of 407. Note too that only the second excerpt preserves the reference to Arcadius in the heading, necessary since Arcadius was still alive in November, 407. But since he was dead by 7 July 408, someone was misled by the *p.p.* date into removing his name from the heading, as already in *ConstSirm*. A similar case is *ConstSirm* 16 and its excerpts *CTh* 5.7.2 and *CJ* 1.4.11, where again both excerpts omit the *accepta* date and so misdate the law by a year (409 instead of 408). In addition, all three give different day dates: *III Non. Dec.; IIII Id. Dec.; III Id. Dec.*

Of more direct concern to a modern consular list is the question of postconsulates. But for reasons which will become clear as we proceed, one other source of error and distortion needs to be discussed as a preliminary, perhaps the most pervasive of all. This is what might be called retroactive normalization: that is to say, bringing the actual dates originally written on the laws into line with the established form of the consular fasti--more particularly the eastern fasti as established in Constantinople where both Codes were compiled. The purpose of this normalization (mainly the work of the Theodosian compilers)[20] was to

---

[19]For more detail, Seeck, *Regesten* 9f.

[20]The Justinianic compilers did their best to eliminate these details more systematically still, though even they missed a few, e.g. two examples of "Licinius A." retained in headings to laws (*CJ* 3.1.8; 7.22.3; cf. Mommsen, *Ges.Schr.* VI 312). In the first two centuries all laws were presumably dated (where appropriate) by suffects as well as ordinary consuls. At some point, all suffect datings were eliminated, probably well before Justinian--perhaps in the early third century, when the chancellery abandoned dating by suffects (p.3 above). On the other hand, if it was the Justinianic editors who did the job, we must view early imperial dates in *CJ* with considerably more skepticism than has usually been done. Was there really a complete list of suffects in sixth-century Constantinople?

eliminate precisely what we are trying to reconstruct in this book, those untidy anomalies and irregularities that constituted the day to day functioning of the consular system.

They naturally expanded or standardized provisional formulas (p.c.'s and *et qui nuntiatus fuerit*) and the often cryptic contemporary abbreviations that still occasionally survive: *II et I* (284); *ipsis IV et III Augg.* (290); *CC. conss.* (? 294); *DD.NN. VIII et VII Augg.* (303); *post VI cons.* (Constantius and Galerius were both cos. VI in 306); *IX et Constantinus* (307, where the IX is Diocletian); *X et Maximianus VII* (308, Max. = Galerius); *p.c. X et VII* (309); *anno II p.c. X et VII* (310); *p.c. II et I* (in fact Constantius II et Constans I = 340); *dnis nostris* (360); *A.A. conss.* (368); *p.c. IX et V* (in fact Honorius IX et Theodosius V = 413).[21] Though no doubt instantly recognizable to contemporaries, some of these formulas must have been wholly ambiguous a century later, even without the almost inevitable corruption of iteration numbers. If such drastic abbreviations of double imperial consulates were at all common,[22] here is yet another rich potential source of error.

Of course from every point of view but ours it was clearly preferable that a law be filed under the final formula *Valerio et Aetio* (432) rather than the cumbersome *Valerio e.q.f.n.* The Theodosian compilers may often have been anticipated here. The lowliest filing clerk must often have eliminated such irritations without even consulting his superior. So too perhaps with the rarer cases of consuls who suffered *damnatio memoriae*, such as Eutropius (399) or Vitalian (520). From the moment of their *damnatio* their names were removed from the formula, and retroactively (though not with complete success) they were removed from earlier laws too. Thus in the case of 399, nine eastern laws earlier than Eutropius' fall have been so corrected. Naturally all references to consuls appointed by usurpers have been similarly eliminated. Since it was hardly possible to strike out all six consulates of a long-reigning defeated Augustus like Licinius (three of them held jointly with Constantine) they were simply stripped of his title Augustus.

It must be the Theodosian compilers who were responsible for the slightly different and more confusing cases of 400 and 405, when Stilicho refused to recognize the consulates of his eastern colleagues Aurelian and Anthemius. In the West the relevant laws (and all other documents and monuments) are dated *Stilichone v.c.* and *Stilichone II.* The eastern compilers routinely added the eastern colleagues Stilicho himself had repudiated, and since (as often happens) the iteration number was often missing, they sometimes added the wrong colleague, transforming mere normalization into downright error. More generally and pervasively still, whenever the compilers included western laws, they routinely reversed the western sequence of names: i.e., laws originally dated *Agricola et Eustathio* (421) appear in the Codes, quite incorrectly, as *Eustathio et Agricola.* So too in 423.

So there must be many hundreds of laws which, while dated to the *correct* consular year, nonetheless carry a consular formula that has been tampered with in one way or another. There must be many cases in

---

[21]Presumably imperial laws would never have borne the despairing formulas we find on the papyri for 322-324: τοῖς μέλλουσιν or ἐσομένοις ὑπάτοις.

[22]Three Italian inscriptions (*CIL* X 3699; XI 4086; XIV 352) and one Dura papyrus all refer to the consular date 251 (Decio III et Herennio) by the cryptic abbreviation III et I cos. According to J.F. Gilliam, "it is clear from the papyrus that the omission of the names of Decius and his son in this context is a form of *damnatio memoriae*" (*Studi Calderini-Paribeni* I 306). The same papyrus also refers to 248 (Philippo III et Philippo II) as III et II, and to 245 (Philippo et Titiano) as simply Titiano. Since both the Philippi and the Decii did suffer *damnatio memoriae*, there can be little doubt that, in the context of the papyrus, the abbreviations do serve the purpose Gilliam suggests. But was that the sole and original purpose of this form of reference? Is this what it meant in all three Italian inscriptions quoted above? Surely not. For there are consular medallions for the year 248 bearing the same formula III et II cos, undoubtedly celebrating the joint imperial consulate rather than damning it to oblivion. So too medallions for 252 (Gallo II et Volusiano) inscribed cos II et cos, and for 257 (Valeriano IIII et Gallieno III) inscribed IIII et III cos. (J.M.C. Toynbee, *Roman Medallions* [New York 1944] 86-87). Gilliam weakly concedes, without further comment, that the formulae on these medallions "must be explained in another way". The explanation is simple and certain. Consular dates were cumbersome, and in the ordinary way could never be abbreviated without risk of confusion. But when both consuls had the same name, we regularly find (e.g.) duo Silani (189) or even just Quintilii (151); see Degrassi's index of "consolati indicati in modo speciale" (*Fasti consolari*, 274). And with joint imperial consulates, the names could be dropped altogether, since the iteration numbers alone would normally suffice: III et I fitted no other year but 251. The style at once reappeared with the frequent joint consulates of the tetrarchy, as the examples quoted above amply illustrate—certainly with no condemnatory connotations. It was merely an incidental advantage that it was a formula that could survive *damnatio memoriae*.

addition to 400 and 405 where this process of normalization has generated actual error. Even when it has not, the fact remains that for all their apparent precision, the consular formulas of imperial laws in the Codes cannot be treated like the formulas of papyri and inscriptions.

The tombstone of a man who died in January may have been erected in July, either with a by then outdated January formula or with a (for January) anachronistic July formula. But there will usually be other inscriptions to serve as a control. The compilers did their best to normalize *every* law, however many there were, thus eliminating this sort of control (except from inscriptions and papyri). It was only rarely that they slipped up, missing (e.g.) just one of the 26 western laws of 400.

So when we find an imposing battery of laws with a consular formula that conflicts with our other evidence or even what seems historically probable, we must not be deceived by its volume and unanimity into treating it with the same respect as a single papyrus.

Thus armed, we are now in a position to turn back to the delicate issue of postconsulates in the laws. There is an important but overlooked distinction between the two sorts of what we call provisional formulas. If a law of 18.ix.420 that the compilers failed to standardize (*CTh* 7.16.3) gives the formula *Theodosio IX e.q.f.n.*, then *CJ* 8.10.10, appearing to attest the final formula *Theodosio IX et Constantio III* on 5.v must be the result of retroactive correction. We may surely take it as axiomatic that no one ever replaced the standard formula of the year with an *e.q.f.n.* We may always infer that the *e.q.f.n.* formula was current *at court itself* up till the latest date in the year it is attested. See our tabulation on p.27.

It has been generally assumed (if only implicitly) that the same axiom applies to postconsulates; that if they are attested late in a year, they were current up till that date. In practice even Seeck operated on this axiom, freely postulating confusion between consulate and postconsulate to explain erroneous dates at any time of the year.

A moment's reflection should suffice to show that the situation cannot have been so simple. To be sure papyri and council acta prove that (at least by the fifth century) p.c.'s were in use during much of the year in the provinces. But that was because it often took six months or more for the news to reach the more remote provinces (whatever the cause of this delay). Imperial laws were issued from court, from wherever the emperor happened to be at the time. In the fourth century this might be some tiny place on the road from Sirmium to Milan, whose name has been dutifully preserved in the subscription. How can the emperor himself *ever* not have known the name of at least one of the consuls (unless both were named by the other part of the Empire)? By the fifth century he often knew *only* one, but then the *e.q.f.n.* formula was used, not the p.c. Under normal circumstances, it is difficult to believe that imperial laws were ever dated by p.c.'s.

How then do we explain (e.g.) *CTh* 10.20.10, dated 14.iii.380 by p.c. from Aquileia; or 1.32.2, dated 8.vii.377 from Trier; or above all 8.5.29, dated 2.xii.368, again from Trier? Given the high degree of inaccuracy demonstrated by the compilers, we may confidently ascribe some of these p.c.'s to mere error of one sort or another. But we cannot explain them all away like this. It was Seeck who saw the way to the solution, though he oddly failed to follow his insight through to its logical conclusion. Of the 41[23] laws equipped with p.c.'s in *CTh* and *CJ*, half (19) are addressed to officials serving in Africa, a part of the Empire whose communications with the other western provinces were often severed between October and April. And another eleven are addressed to officials who could have been in Africa, namely praetorian prefects of Italy-Illyricum-Africa, who normally spent part of their term of office in Africa.

First, subscriptions where all the information is explicitly given:

(1) *CTh* 11.1.13, *Dracontio*[24] *vic. Africae, data* 18 Oct. Parisis; *accepta* 18 Jan. *Karthagine*, p.c. 365 (i.e. 366). Obviously the law was issued in Paris on 18 October 365 and reached Carthage on 18 January

---

[23]A few are extracts from the same law, but since there are numerous cases of extracts from the same law somehow acquiring conflicting consular dates (Seeck, *Reg.* 67-68), we nonetheless list them separately.

[24]For the sake of brevity and consistency we give officials' names in the dative even where the original uses *ad* plus accusative. Seeck improbably argued that these two styles pointed to different sources: but see Gaudemet, 58-59.

366. Presumably when it left Paris the *data* formula closed with a consular date for 365, which was deleted in editing on grounds of economy. There are in addition about 50 double dated subscriptiones[25] which do *not* involve a p.c. Every one (as might be expected) follows the same compendious pattern: *data* formula (day and month, with or without place name), *accepta* or *proposita* formula (day and month, with or without place name) and one consular formula at the end. *data* 18 Oct. *Parisis*, acc. 18 Jan. *Karthagine*, *p.c. Valentiniani et Valentis*, made it as clear as anyone could wish that the law had been dispatched *Valentiniano et Valente conss.* and received early the next year.[26] The p.c. (of course) was the date given in Carthage, where the new consuls had not yet been announced.

(2) *CTh* 10.17.3, *Magnillo vic. Africae, data* 19 June *Aquileiae*; *acc.* 13 Jan. *Hadrumeti*, p.c. 391. Another impeccably preserved subscription on the same pattern.

(3) *CTh* 15.7.13, *Diogeniano tribuno voluptatum, data* 8 Feb. *Ravennae* 414, *acc. a tribuno voluptatum* 23 Jan. *Karthagine*, p.c. Honorii IX et Theodosii V Augg. (= 413). Something has evidently gone astray here: the law could not have been sent a year after it was received! Seeck's solution was that the subscription originally ended *p.c. s(upra) s(criptum)*, and that the formula *Hon. IX et Theod. V* was a poorly executed attempt by the compilers to replace this with a current formula. If so, a nice illustration of the error the process could generate.

In the next five cases, the *data* date has been omitted, but the *accepta* date early in the new year is still undisturbed. In every case it seems clear that the law was dispatched from court in the preceding autumn and received its p.c. in Africa, where the new consuls, as usual, were not yet known.

(4) *CTh* 12.12.8, *Severo PV,*[27] *p.p. Karthagine* 25 March, p.c. 381.

(5) *CTh* 12.1.88, *Syagrio PPO, p.p.* 9 April *Karthagine*, p.c. 381.

(6) *CTh* 11.16.13, *Hypatio PPO,*[28] *p.p. Karthagine* 13 April, p.c. 381.

(7) *CTh* 1.9.2, *Principio mag. off., p.p. Hadrumeti* 9 March, p.c. 385.

(8) *CTh* 10.20.9, *Eucherio <mag. off.>, p.p. Karthagine* 28 Feb., p.c. 379.

So long as the *accepta* (*p.p.*) reference was kept, these cross year datings were in no danger of being misunderstood. But the moment it was dropped, then the one consular date at the end of the subscription was bound to be taken as the year of the *data* date. First, six straightforward examples of simple omission of the *acc.* formula:

---

[25]Conveniently collected by A.H.M. Jones, *Later Roman Empire* III 91-93.

[26]There are also cases of the same compendious formulation over a year change without p.c.: e.g. *CTh* 13.1.1, *data iv non. Dec.*, acc. *Romae viii id. Feb. Constantio A. viii et Iuliano Caes. ii conss.*; also *CTh* 9.7.3 and another six African examples, *CTh* 9.40.1 + 11.30.2 + 11.36.1; 11.28.1; 16.9.1; *ConstSirm* 12.

[27]Very heavy weather has been made of the presence of this law addressed to a prefect of Rome in Carthage: e.g. Mommsen on *CTh* 6.6.1; *PLRE* I 837; Chastagnol, *Les fastes* 209 n.70 (who mistakenly thought that the subscription gave PPO). But it asks for *quaecumque civitas* to send delegates to court after prior approval by the PV. It would therefore be natural for the PV to have circulated a copy to all provincial governors. It is just chance, or rather the better records kept at Carthage (Seeck, *Reg.* 2), that has preserved for us the copy sent to the proconsul of Africa. We may compare the African posting of laws originally addressed to *magistri officiorum* at court, nos. 7 and 8 below.

[28]Hypatius could not have been PPO this early in 382. The usual solution is to change the p.c. to a consulate (*PLRE* I 449). Whatever has happened, the subscription itself is a classic example of a Carthaginian spring p.c.

(9) *CTh* 8.5.10, *Flaviano proc. Africae,*[29] *data* 27 Oct. *Sirmio,* p.c. 357.

(10) *CTh* 12.7.3, *Dracontio <vic. Africae>, data* 4 Aug. *Nemasia,*[30] p.c. 366.

(11) *CTh* 11.1.16, *Dracontio <vic. Africae>, data* 25 Oct. *Nicomedia,*[31] p.c. 366.

(12) *CTh* 1.32.2, *Hesperio proc. Africae, data* 8 July *Treveris* p.c. 376.

(13) *CTh* 11.28.5, *Honoratis et possessoribus per Africam, data* 25 Nov. p.c. 409.

(14) *CTh* 16.2.36, *Pompeiano proc. Africae, data* 14 July *Mediolano,* p.c. 400.

It is simply incredible that a p.c. should have been used at court this late in the year. On the other hand, laws sent to Africa this late in the year would almost certainly not have arrived till the following year. This applies even to no. 12, dated 8 July.[32] Of the 21 double dated African constitutions, no fewer than 12 took more than 6 months from desk to desk, and only 7 of those (including 3 extracts from the same law) involved winter travel.

So since these laws would probably not have reached Africa till the following year anyway, and undoubtedly once possessed an *accepta* date, it seems perfectly reasonable to infer that the p.c. originally applied to that now missing *accepta* date, in the early months of the year after the *data* date. That is to say, in each case the p.c. will (as usual) be the African date and the true *data* date should be a year earlier than the p.c. We can eliminate all these anomalous p.c.'s at court by doing no more than postulating an omission that we know to have taken place anyway.

Next five extracts with *data* dates early in the year. To explain these p.c.'s the same way we should have to postulate the best part of a year in transit. While this is perfectly possible, there is an alternative. It may be that in the process of abbreviation[33] the February and April dates were carelessly transferred from the omitted *accepta* to the *data* date. The key fact remains that all five are once more extracts from laws sent to proconsuls of Africa.

(15) *CTh* 12.6.28, *Pompeiano proc. Africae, data* 26 Feb. *Mediolano,* p.c. 400.

(16,17) *CTh* 11.1.34 + 11.30.68, *Celeri <proc. Africae>, data* 25 Feb. *Ravenna* p.c. 428.

(18,19) *CTh* 12.1.185 + 186, *Celeri proc. Africae, data* 27 April *Ravenna* p.c. 428.

That leaves one other homogeneous batch of p.c.'s, eleven laws addressed to praetorian prefects of Italy-Illyricum-Africa:

(20) *CTh* 11.30.20, *Philippo PPO, p.p.* 9 June p.c. 339 (347?)

(21) *CTh* 10.20.10, *Hesperio PPO, data* 14 March *Aquileia,* p.c. 379

(22) *CTh* 12.1.89, *Syagrio PPO, data* 5 July *Viminacio,* p.c. 381

(23) *CTh* 1.29.6, *Eusignio PPO, data* 25 Jan. p.c. 386

(24) *CTh* 6.30.6, *Probo PPO, data* 26 Oct. *Mediolano,* p.c. 383

(25) *CJ* 1.40.9, *Polemio PPO Illyrici, data* 23 Dec. *Mediolani,* p.c. 389

(26) *CTh* 1.2.12, *Johanni PPO, data* 17 Feb. p.c. 412

(27) *CTh* 2.19.6, *Johanni PPO, data* 14 Feb. *Ravenna,* p.c. 412

(28) *CJ* 6.23.19, *Johanni PPO, data* 18 Feb. *Ravenna,* p.c. 412

[29]On Flavianus' proconsulate see now Barnes, *Phoenix* 39 (1985) 148.

[30]Nemetacum, Seeck (*Reg.* 107.4).

[31]Nicomedia is impossible for a western emperor, whatever the year, clearly a case of a well known place name supplanting a rare one. Seeck suggests Novesia (*Reg.* 107.35).

[32]On the other hand, 8 July *could* be the *accepta* data of a late arriving law from the year before, as perhaps *CTh* 16.2.36 (no. 14).

[33]The compilers normally dropped the accepta date (there are nearly ten times as many data as accepta formulas in *CTh*: cf. Seeck, *Reg.* 81), evidently because they saw the data date as the one from which the law became effective, the essential feature for their purpose (above, p.75). Cf. Gaudemet 66: "pour l'application de l'adage *lex posterior derogat priori,* la première seule importait, car elle seule était indépendante des delais de transmission."

(29) *CTh* 11.1.35, *Volusiano PPO, data* 14 Feb. *Ravenna*, p.c. 428
(30) *CTh* 12.6.32, *Volusiano PPO, data* 27 Feb. *Ravenna*, p.c. 428

Some of these dates are simply wrong, and the assumption of an omitted *accepta* does not always help; but it does solve a couple of problems less drastically than current remedies.[34]

Unfortunately Philippus was not PPO till 344, so drastic measures are here necessary (cf. Seeck, *Reg.* 199 and 41.28; *PLRE* I 696). *CTh* 12.1.89 *could* have been sent to Syagrius in 381 (cf. Seeck, *Reg.* 67.6; *PLRE* I 862), but the problems of the prefectures of the two Syagrii, consuls in 381 and 382 and perhaps both PPO in 382, are too complex to go into here (see ad a. 381). Probus had been succeeded as PPO by 13 March 384. The usual solution has been to correct the date of *CTh* 6.30.6 to 26 Oct. 383 (i.e. consulate for p.c.). But emendation may not be necessary. If Probus spent some time in Africa, 26 Oct. could be the date the law was sent in 383, arriving early in 384 before his tenure ended. *CTh* 10.20.10 to Hesperius from Aquileia is dated 14 March 380. Mommsen changed the month to May, followed by Seeck (*Reg.* 102.22) and *PLRE* (I 428): on 18 March 380 Gratian was in Trier, and could not have been in Aquileia till 18 May. But it might be that Hesperius was in Africa, and that 14 March was the *accepta* date there. It would then have been sent in 379; Gratian was at Aquileia in July 379. The three laws with p.c. 412 may reflect Heraclianus' *damnatio memoriae*; cf. under 413.

However individual problems are solved, it is difficult to believe it coincidence that so many of these anomalous p.c.'s are addressed to PPO's of Italy (to whose number we may add nos. 4 and 6 above). That would make a total of no less than 30 out of the total of 41 addressed to officials who served all or part of their terms of office in Africa.

Of the ten that remain, at least four can be plausibly solved along the same lines. First there is *CTh* 1.6.9 (Milan) of 27 April 385 to Symmachus, called 'praepositus' by the MS, but (as the reference to the election of Pope Siricius shows) undoubtedly dating from his urban prefecture, in fact from Dec. 384-Jan. 385. The month cannot be right, since Symmachus is known to have resigned his office by the beginning of February. The extract preserved in *CJ* (9.29.2) gives 28 Dec. 384 (v kal. Ian.), which seems perfect in itself (Pope Damasus died on 11 Dec.), but does not explain the p.c. We could just dismiss the *CTh* subscription in its entirety, but as Seeck argued (*Reg.* 87.1), it would be preferable to combine the two, 28 Dec. p.c. 384, and infer the omission of an *accepta* date at Rome in early January. As it happens we have one Roman inscription with a p.c. date as late as 10.iii, showing that dissemination was somewhat late.

(32) Then there is *CTh* 4.13.6 of probably 369 (we follow Seeck, *Reg.* 237 rather than *PLRE* I 100), *p.p. Beryto* on 29 Jan. Clearly it must have taken at least a month to come from Valens' court at Marcianopolis.

(33) *CTh* 12.6.17 to Hypatius, *praefectus Augustalis* (*PLRE* I 448), was *data Constantinopoli* on 29 April p.c. 382. We have no papyri from early in the year, but the new consuls are not attested in Egypt till 2.iv.383. Once again, the hypothesis of an omitted *accepta* date will transfer the p.c. from court to a distant province.

(34) *CTh* 8.5.29 to Domnus, *consularis* of Sicily, is dated 2 Dec. p.c. 367 from Trier. A courier from Trier to Sicily might easily have taken four weeks at this time of year, and it seems almost inevitable to infer an omitted *accepta* date and refer the *data* to 367.[35] A close parallel may be adduced. *CTh* 11.29.1 was sent to Plotianus the *corrector* of Lucania-Bruttiorum from Trier on 27 Dec. and *accepta* on 6 Feb. 313 at Rhegium (41 days for a slightly shorter journey at the same time of year). If 313 is (as usual) the year of the *accepta* date, the law would have been sent from Trier in Dec. 312. But in Dec. 312 Constantine was in Rome, though he had moved to Trier by Dec. 313. Mommsen simply referred the consular date to the *data*, but Seeck (*Reg.* 78.22) rightly made the point more systematically established above (p.79): in double dated subscriptions the consular date (which always occurs at the end) always refers to the *accepta*. The

---

[34]This is not the place to review all possible solutions; most can be found easily enough in Seeck and *PLRE*.
[35]It is only surprising that Seeck missed this one: cf. *Reg.* 234, and also *PLRE* I 267.

only alternative (with Seeck) is to insert a p.c. The law was *data* on 27 Dec. 313 and *accepta* at Rhegium on 6 Feb. 314, an exact parallel to *CTh* 8.5.29.

Of what remains, (35) *CTh* 7.18.16 to Gaiso MVM *data* at Ravenna on 14 June p.c. 412 does not count, since all western laws of 413 were retroactively corrected to p.c. 412 following the *damnatio memoriae* of the original consul (see *ad annum*). And (36) *CTh* 15.1.48 (28 Nov. p.c. 410, *data Ravenna*, to the prefect of Rome) hardly counts, since much of 411 was dated by p.c. 410 in the aftermath of the sack of Rome.[36]

That leaves only *five* p.c.'s authentically transmitted by the MSS of the Codes that cannot easily be referred to provincial rather than court usage: (37) *CTh* 6.23.4 to a PPO Orientis, *data Constantinopoli* 16 Mar. p.c. 436; and (38-39) two extracts from the same law (6.4.5-6) *data* at Antioch on 9 Sept. 340 and addressed *ad senatum*. There are also (40-41) *CJ* 5.14.8 and 6.52, addressed to Hormisdas PP (Orientis) and dated to 9 Jan. and 3 Apr. p.c. Protogenis et Asterii (450).[37]

It might not seem easy to explain how a law to a PPO Or., sent from one office in Constantinople to another, could pick up a p.c. In fact there is a perfectly satisfactory explanation. All edicts and dedications of any one PPO always bore the names of the entire college of prefects.[38] A good example of a letter to the PPO Or. from a provincial governor addressed to the whole college is preserved among the Acta of Ephesus II (ed. J. Flemming, *AbhGöttingen* n.f. 15 [1917] 21). *NovTheod* 26 to a PPO Or. in 444 carries a note saying that a copy was sent to the PPO of Illyricum. This explains why *CTh* 15.1.35 to Caesarius PPO Or. in 396 was *p.p.* at Rhegium; and *CTh* 3.1.5 to Cynegius PPO Or. in 384 was *accepta* at Rhegium. Seeck alleged improbable political explanations, often repeated (*Regesten* 80-81). The truth is surely just that copies of both laws were routinely dispatched to the PPO of Italy, who decided to circulate them. By pure chance it was the copies sent to the office of the corrector of Lucania-Bruttium at Rhegium that survived. It will be obvious that laws going the rounds of provincial governors like this were indeed liable to pick up p.c.'s.

More problematic (it might seem) is the one p.c. preserved in the Theodosian Novels (22.2), *data* 9 March at Constantinople *p.c. Dioscori et Eudoxii* (443). It was said earlier that Novels were not edited like the laws in the Codes, and while this is largely true, there are one or two qualifications. Eastern novels have not come down to us in an eastern collection, but in western collections of such laws as eastern emperors sent to the West.[39] This is proved by occasional western formulas: e.g. *NovTheod* 7.2-3 and 20, *Valentiniano V et Anatolio* (440), when Valentinian's name did not appear in eastern formulas of that date. *NovTheod* 22.2 offers two anomalies: not only the improbable p.c. in a law from eastern emperor to prefect of the East; but also the anomalous western sequence of names (the eastern formula was *Eudoxii et Dioscori*). The combination supplies the solution. The p.c. must be an *accepta* date added in the West. The law was no doubt dispatched from Constantinople late in 442 and dated by p.c. on arrival in March the next year.

We do not suggest that the explanations offered in the preceding pages are all compelling, though it is hoped that none fails to be at least plausible. It is surely significant that we were able to eliminate all these apparent p.c.'s at court while refraining almost entirely from emendation--in some cases no doubt the sensible solution. Confusion between consulate and postconsulate must surely have occurred, particularly if, instead of the regular formula X et Y (abl.) *consulibus* the rarer alternative formula *consulatu* (+ gen.) X et Y was used. This formula first appears on inscriptions in 338 (above, p.63), and was presumably adapted from the standard Greek formula ὑπατείας plus genitive. The reverse corruption (p.c. mistaken

---

[36]See comments and Crit.App. s.a.

[37]Probably part of the same law as *CJ* 5.17.8, addressed to the same Hormisdas as PP on the same day but Protogene et Asterio (449). Presumably a p.c. was omitted from *CJ* 5.17.8 rather than added to *CJ* 5.14.8. Hormisdas' tenure cannot be pushed back to the beginning of 449: *PLRE* II 571.

[38]Jones, *Later Roman Empire* III 61 n.10; A. Chastagnol, *REA* 70 (1968) 324; D. Feissel, *Travaux et Mémoires* 9 (1985) 427-33.

[39]Mommsen's *CTh* II, p.xif.

for consulate) was no doubt commoner, but surely not as common as Seeck and his modern followers have supposed. Inserting a p.c. has become a standard crutch, automatically advancing any given date by a year without disturbing the consular formula. Great care should be taken in employing this remedy where the resultant p.c. has to be referred to court rather than the provinces. If the p.c. could really be substituted for the current formula at any place and any time of the year, there would surely be unmistakable proof of this in the codes. In fact the evidence of the codes, if carefully and critically examined, confirms the commonsense conclusion that the emperors themselves always knew who was consul.

This is not the place to review all the p.c.'s created by Seeck, but we may appropriately close by giving a fresh look at a typical example of his method: a nexus of five laws in *CTh* that he redated in this way--apparently to universal approval:

> 1.12.7   *data* 29 Sept. Altino   399
> 11.7.15   *data* 28 Sept. Altini   399
> 14.15.6   *data* 28 Sept. Altino   399
> 14.28.1   *data* 27 March Altino   400
> 1.15.17   *data* 29 Sept. Altino   401

All five are addressed to Messala as PPO of Italy, all seem to deal with abuse of taxes relating to the provisioning of Rome, 4 out of 5 were issued on (more or less) the same day, and all five at the same small place, Altinum. It is a reasonable assumption (accepted by *PLRE* II 760) that all five are extracts from one and the same law. But in which year?

Seeck points out that, since Honorius was at Aquileia on 29 September 400 (*CTh* 6.19), he could have been at Altinum, "an easy day's journey by boat," the day before. He then assumes that all five were originally dated by the p.c. of 399 (*p.c.Theodori*). In three cases (he argues) the p.c. was omitted; in one changed, correctly, to the regular formula for 400 (*Stilichone et Aureliano*); in the last changed, mistakenly, to a year one too late, "obviously through a slip of the compiler, whose eye wandered to a lower line in the consular list he was using" (*Reg.* 68). Granted the p.c., the suggested mechanisms of error, if less than attractive, are not preposterous.

But can we grant the p.c.? It is surely inconceivable that the imperial chancellery would date by p.c. as late as the end of September, particularly when the current consul was none other than Stilicho, the all-powerful regent. There can be no question of anyone at court not knowing who was consul *that* year--no question of those five extracts being originally dated *p.c. Theodori*.

Fortunately there is a far simpler and more plausible alternative. If Honorius was really issuing laws at Aquileia on 29 September 400, it is hardly likely that he was also issuing laws at Altinum the day before,[40] 62 Roman miles away by the Antonine itinerary. The journey itself could have been done in a day, but hardly a working day.[41] Seeck also argued that, since *CTh* 14.15.5 shows Honorius at Altinum on 4 September 399 and he was at Milan by 13 September, he is not likely to have gone to Altinum again for 28/29 September the same year. This would be a fair argument, *if* the date of *CTh* 14.15.5 were secure. In fact it is another law to Messala about tax evasion concerning the provisioning of Rome. Is it credible that Honorius issued different laws to the same prefect on the same subject in the same month at the same town in different years? Clearly this is yet another fragment of the same law, in which case the day date has to be changed to 28/29 September--and Seeck's objection to 399 falls to the ground.[42] We now have four extracts out of six dated to 399, and no possible objection to 399. Honorius was at Milan on 13 September and 20 November that year, but could easily have gone to Altinum and back between those dates. We can forget about those five September p.c.s.

---

[40]And this is assuming that the law to Messala should be dated to 28 rather than 29 September; two extracts say 28, two 29.
[41]We might in fact guess that the imperial entourage broke its journey at Concordia, another of the locations from which imperial laws were occasionally issued (e.g.June 391).
[42]In *Reg.*298 Seeck lists two other laws that appear to attest Honorius at Altinum on 1 and 4 September 399. A closer look reveals that the MSS of 11.1.30 gives the year as 406; Seeck's correction is not to be taken seriously (cf. *PLRE* II 976). And the MSS of 9.42.6 offer 1 December. Seeck corrected to 1 September on the grounds that Honorius was at Milan in December - and (allegedly) at Altinum on 4 September. Perhaps 1 October.

Chapter 8

Literary and Miscellaneous Sources

There are numerous miscellaneous texts and artifacts that help to fill out our dossier.

1. Council acts

The largest single category of dated documents in this group is probably church council acta. They are important for two reasons. 1) Church councils were often held in areas where we have little other evidence of consular dating, such as Ephesus in Asia Minor, or various cities in Gaul and Africa. 2) Though there is always the possibility that a meticulous clerk might routinely standardize a provisional date, in general such indications as there are point the other way. For example, two months after Theodosius II wrote from Constantinople to the Council of Ephesus dating by the new eastern consul of 431, the proceedings of the Council at Ephesus itself continued to be dated by the p.c. of 430 (see *ad annum* and above, p.28). All surviving documents from the Council of Carthage in 411 were left dated by the p.c. of 410.

Not only is it likely that most people were too accustomed to provisional dates by the fifth century to bother to revise them; council acta were normally verbatim records, copied down by teams of stenographers[1] so that there should be no doubt afterwards about who said what. To substitute for the original date one not in use at that time was to run the risk of calling the authenticity of the acta into question.

The acta of the main eastern synods and councils (notably Ephesus and Chalcedon) were edited by E. Schwartz, *Acta Conciliorum Oecumenicorum (ACO)* I-IV (Berlin 1914-1983). For the Gallic Councils there is now C. Munier, *Concilia Galliae a.314-506* (Corp.Christ.Lat. 148, Turnhout 1963) and C. de Clerq, *Concilia Galliae a.511-695* (Corp.Christ.Lat. 148A, Turnhout 1963). For the African Councils, C. Munier, *Concilia Africae a.345-525* (Corp.Christ.Lat. 149, Turnhout 1974), and S. Lancel, *Gesta conlationis Carthaginiensis a.411* (Corp.Christ.Lat. 149A, Turnhout 1974).

Numerals (especially in Latin) being so liable to corruption in a manuscript tradition, the day dates may often be wrong, but there is seldom any doubt about the year, especially since there were relatively few years when councils were held.

2. Martyr Acts and Hagiography

Martyr acts are a quite different and altogether more suspect category of document. A few are contemporary records; the majority were invented long after the event. In itself an authentic looking consular date proves little, since it would be so easy to equip a fictitious document with a genuine date, especially since most of these acta fall in the same two years anyway, 303 or 304, during one of Diocletian's persecutions. But many acts agreed on other grounds to be essentially authentic do offer a consular date,

---

[1]We happen to know that at Carthage in 411 no fewer than 20 stenographers were used working in shifts, with six working at any one time: see E. Tengström, *Die Protokollierung der Collatio Carthaginiensis* (Göteborg 1962) and S. Lancel, *Actes de la conférence de Carthage en 411* (Paris 1972). For more information on stenographers, see now H.C. Teitler, *Notarii et Exceptores* (Amsterdam 1985).

typically in an authentic looking official preamble. For example, *Acta Eupli, recensio latina* 1 (H. Musurillo, *Acts of the Christian Martyrs* [Oxford 1972], p.314): *Diocletiano novies et Maximiano octies consulibus pridie idus Augusti in Cataniensium civitate...extra velum secretarii*. The modest value of these acta for our purpose is that they are set in various provincial centres. But caution is always indicated. The acta of Marcellus, set in Tingis in Mauretania, looked authentic enough--until the discovery of another recension, set in a different year and place, Léon in Spain![2] We use the texts reprinted in Musurillo's edition, cited above.

The very abundant later hagiographical literature contains occasional consular dates. Where these have come to our attention, we include them, but we have not read this body of texts systematically in search of them. In all cases which we have seen, these dates are dependent on other sources (such as Socrates) and thus have no independent value. The matter of these lives, of course, is largely fictional; in many cases the consular date may be the only factual element in the entire work. For example, there are three consular dates in the 6th/8th century *Vita Isacii*.[3] Two (in paragraphs 10 and 12, to 380 and 381) are taken from Socrates (*HE* 5.6 and 5.8), and though the third (paragraph 18), dating Isaac's death to 383, cannot be derived from any known source, that is because it is false; Isaac died at least twenty years later.[4]

3. Coins and Medallions[5]

From the reign of Augustus on, emperors had routinely commemorated their consulates on the coinage, normally as just one title along with all the rest, without any explicit consular imagery: e.g. *Imp t Caes Vesp Avg PM tr p PP Cos VIII* (R.A.G. Carson, *Principal Coins of the Romans* [London 1980], no.503). By the beginning of the fourth century the other titles tend to be dropped while increased emphasis is accorded to the consulate. Up to the mid fourth century, consular coins were struck in all three metals. One category has no consular legend, but shows the emperor on the obverse (and sometimes reverse too) in consular dress. The other has an explicit consular legend, with or without consular imagery of some sort: e.g. *Diocletianus PF Aug Cos VIII* (*RIC* VI 166) or *Felix processus Cos VI Aug N* (*RIC* VII 467). Most of these issues were presumably struck during the year to which they refer, but some were undoubtedly struck in anticipation, some later. Since they can be assigned to specific mints, they sometimes provide evidence from areas otherwise sparsely (if at all) represented in this volume (e.g. Serdica, Nicomedia, Cyzicus, Antioch). In one case they provide information known from no other source about four unrecognized consulates of the British usurper Carausius 287-90.

Up till the mid fourth century emperors also issued consular medallions, in both bronze and gold, with representations of themselves in consular dress and the consular procession. If (as Toynbee plausibly argues) these were struck specifically for personal distribution by the emperor on January 1,[6] they are our most precisely dated consular numismatic evidence.

[2]H. Delehaye, *AnalBoll* 41 (1923) 257-87; B. de Gaiffier, *AnalBoll* 61 (1943) 118-21; Musurillo, pp.xxxviii-ix. See Barnes, *New Empire* 177-78 for the authentic martyr acts.
[3]*Acta Sanctorum 30 May* VII 243-55.
[4]G. Dagron, *Travaux et Mémoires* 4 (1970) 245.
[5]For the period 284-294, we have used *RIC* V.2 (London 1933), edited by P.H. Webb; for 294-313, *RIC* VI (1967), by C.H.V. Sutherland; for 313-337, *RIC* VII (1966), by P.M. Bruun; for 337-364, *RIC* VIII (1981), by J.P.C. Kent; for 364-395, *RIC* IX (1953), by J.W.E. Pearce. In the absence of any systematic study of the coinage for the rest of our period, we also cite from J.P.C. Kent and K. Painter, *Wealth of the Roman World: Gold and Silver 300-700* (London 1977), J.P.C. Kent, *Roman Coins* (New York 1978), and G. Lacam, *La fin de l'empire romain et le monnayage or en Italie 455-493* (1983). For the medallions, the standard work is J.M.C. Toynbee, *Roman Medallions* (New York 1944), reissued in 1986 with additional material by W.E. Metcalf. We are very grateful to Diane Schauer for generously allowing us to draw on her unpublished manuscript *Consular Solidi from Constantius II to Justinian I*, the only attempt so far made to assemble and date all consular solidi. Ms. Schauer is also preparing a study of consular iconography, a large and fruitful topic which we have of necessity set aside. There is of course much material in R. Delbrueck, *Die Consulardiptychen* (Berlin 1929).
[6]J.M.C.Toynbee. *Roman Medallions* (New York 1944) 83-84. On imperial money donatives see also P. Bastien and C. Metzger, *Le trésor de Beaurains (dit d'Arras)* (Wetteren 1977) 202f.; M.F. Hendy, *Studies in the Byzantine Money Economy c. 300-1450* (Cambridge 1985) 193-95.

In *ca* 350 the earlier types of consular coinage and the consular medallions both cease, to be replaced by the long series of consular solidi. Thereafter virtually all consular coins are struck in gold alone. Unfortunately, out of the whole series only two issues directly refer to specific imperial consulates, the seventeenth and eighteenth of Theodosius II. In consequence, though for the most part both dated and localized, they add curiously little to our record. The consular reference normally has to be inferred from a combination of other indications: vota or regnal year numbers, die or type links, historical allusions, identification of imperial colleagues. Furthermore, some issues continued to be minted well beyond the consular year (e.g. Theodosius II in 425). A particularly problematic case is the fairly abundant issue (lacking consular imagery and so not formally classifiable as a consular solidus) with the legend *Imp XXXXII Cos XVII* (Kent, *Roman Coins*, no.749). Theodosius' seventeenth consulate fell in 439, but his forty-second regnal year not till 441. Worse still, the unusual mint mark *COMOB* led Kent to infer that the issue was struck not at Constantinople but from a "mobile mint attached to the imperial entourage" during Theodosius' "Asian expedition" of summer 443.[7] Early specimens may have emanated from Constantinople in 441, but even that was long after the relevant consular year.

Many of these consular solidi include representations of co-emperors in consular dress in years when they were not consuls: e.g. Valentinian II's issues of 387 and 390. On the other hand, we are not entitled to draw inferences about non-recognition from non-representation of co-emperors: e.g., in view of the rest of the evidence, it cannot be significant that Valens is represented alone on both obverse and reverse of his issue of 373. Some issues are represented today by a single coin, and it is likely that many others have not survived at all. Yet in view of the increasing weakness of the link with the consular year, it may be doubted whether every imperial consulate was commemorated, at any rate in gold (e.g. all 18 of Theodosius II). On present evidence it seems that Leo minted only two consular issues, with no way of determining to which of his five consulates they belong. There is a tendency for emperors to mint issues that commemorate vota and consulate together (cf. p.24). There is also a natural tendency for emperors to mint consular issues for distribution where they actually assumed their consulate.[8]

4. Consular Diptychs

If emperors commemorated their consulates with coins and medallions, subjects did so by distributing objects hardly less precious. The largest and best known category is a series of ivory panels generally known as consular diptychs. The standard corpus is R. Delbrueck, *Die Consulardiptychen und verwandte Denkmäler* (Berlin 1929); more recent but less satisfactory is W.F. Volbach, *Elfenbeinarbeiten der Spätantike und des frühen Mittelalters*[3] (Mainz 1976); a new corpus by Cameron and Anthony Cutler is in preparation.

We possess diptychs for 17 different consuls from 406 to 541, some of them in multiple non-identical copies. They consist of two engraved ivory panels each measuring up to 40 x 15 cm. The practice of issuing commemorative diptychs seems to be an innovation of the late fourth century, not originally restricted to consuls.[9] A law of 384 (*CTh* 15.9.1) attempted to restrict the practice to consuls in the East, and though even such minor officials as quaestors and tribunes and notaries continued to issue them for some while in the West, almost all extant official diptychs of the late fifth and sixth centuries are consular, in both East and West.

Like imperial medallions, it seems likely that the new consul distributed his diptychs on the day he assumed his office.[10] But at least one extant diptych seems at any rate to have been inscribed later than

---

[7]Marcellinus, s.a. 443, confirmed by the laws (cf. Seeck, *Regesten* 373).

[8]Thus the mints where consular solidi and medallions were struck often tell us where the emperor was when he assumed his consulate. This can often be discovered from the subscriptions to imperial laws too; the evidence is fully set out in O. Seeck's *Regesten*, revised for the period of the Tetrarchs and Constantine by Barnes, *New Empire*.

[9]The information is collected by Cameron, in *AJA* 86 (1982) 126-29.

[10]There is no basis for the often repeated idea that they were intended as *invitations* to the consular inauguration.

this: that of Boethius, cos. 487, which gives his titles as ex PPO, PVR for the second time, consul *and patrician*. Now the inscriptions on all other diptychs, like cursus inscriptions of every sort and period, list the honorand's offices in either ascending or descending sequence, that is to say so that his latest office is either first or last. On all other diptychs the last office named is always the consulate, as we should expect if he were just assuming the fasces. The sequence on the Boethius diptych implies that he won his patriciate later than his consulate. But since he is still styled *Cons Ord*, not *ex Cons Ord*, the diptych was presumably inscribed before the end of his consular year. There is one other hazard that has to be reckoned with. Nancy Netzer has recently shown that the diptych inscribed with the name of Orestes, western consul in 530, is in fact a reused copy of a diptych issued nearly 20 years earlier in Constantinople by Clementinus, eastern consul in 513.[11]

Symmachus distributed two pound silver bowls together with ivory diptychs in commemoration of his son's quaestorship and praetorship.[12] Not surprisingly, no such silver bowls have survived, but we do know of a set of silver spoons with consular representations, apparently presented to or by Eusebius cos. 347 or 359.[13]

5. Papal Letters

The fourth century was the great age of letter writing. An enormous corpus of correspondence survives, from both pagans (Libanius, Julian, Symmachus) and Church fathers (Basil, Paulinus, Jerome, Augustine). Yet not a single letter in any of these vast collections is equipped with any sort of date, much less a consular date. That this is not simply a feature of the manuscript tradition but the practice of the letter writers themselves seems put beyond doubt by the now fairly substantial corpus of autograph private letters known from Egypt. Virtually all are undated.[14] Whatever the reason, it was evidently not felt important to date private correspondence.

Fortunately, successive bishops of Rome felt that their correspondence was sufficiently official to warrant consular dating, and most surviving papal letters are so dated.[15] While we cannot exclude the possibility that the odd provisional formula was updated when a pope's letters were collected for publication, in general there is no sign of systematic interference with the original dates. There is some uncertainty about the inclusion of the Emperor Leo's name in the formula for 458 in some (but not all) of Pope Leo's letters for that year (see the notes to 456), as also about his use of the eastern consuls early in 454. It looks as if an editor or copyist added the name in some manuscripts to some letters. But in general the consular formulas of Pope Leo's letters mirror the complex process of recognition and non-recognition of consuls at this period faithfully.

Papal letters of the late fifth and early sixth centuries are especially valuable to us precisely because their consular formulas have so clearly not been standardized against a full consular list. For they are invariably dated by the name of the western consul alone, even when we can be sure that the name of the eastern consul was known--and no reason to believe that he was not recognized.

There is no comprehensive, still less authoritative modern corpus of papal letters. A. Thiel's *Epistulae Romanorum Pontificum genuinae* I (1867-8) covers only the period from 461 to 523, and though still useful, is hardly a critical edition. A more reliable edition including many papal letters is O. Guenther's *Epistulae imperatorum pontificum aliorum* (CSEL 35, 1895-8), usually cited as *Avellana Collectio*. Earlier papal letters have to be looked for in Migne or Mansi via P. Jaffé, *Regesta Pontificum Romanorum*[2], rev. G. Wattenbach, S. Loewenfeld, F. Kaltenbrunner, P. Ewald, I (1885).[16]

[11]*Burlington Magazine* 125 (1983) 265-71.
[12]*Epp.* ii.81; vii.76; ix.119-20; v.56.
[13]*PLRE* I 308; cf. K.J. Shelton, *Art Bulletin* 65 (1983) 22.
[14]The contrast between the private letters (all undated) and official petitions and contracts (most with consular dates) in the Abinnaeus archive is a good illustration of the general point.
[15]Many individual letters have lost all or part of these dates, but this can be put down to the hazards of manuscript transmission. Many imperial laws have suffered the same fate.
[16]A new edition and translation of papal correspondence up to 400 is in preparation by Glen Thompson.

We have cited a few dates from the *Liber Pontificalis*, a compilation which seems to have contemporary value for the late fifth and early sixth centuries: see the edition by L. Duchesne, vol. I (Paris 1886), with much additional material in vol. III (Paris 1957), both reprinted in 1981. On chronological questions, see I, pp.ccxlviiif.

6. Literary Texts

We possess a number of panegyrics or *gratiarum actiones* pronounced by or addressed to consuls, presumably on the day of their inauguration. And from time to time there are references to consular dates or to consulates in the literary texts of our period. We have done our best to quote all relevant references-- and any other texts that cast any useful or interesting light on the consulate.

We may assume that a historian like Ammianus had a consular list to hand. The ecclesiastical historian Socrates gives consular dates for virtually every year of his narrative (324-439), always with correct iteration numbers for emperors--and occasional synchronization with Olympiads.[17] He even mentions the cancellation of Eutropius' consulate in 399. Rather later and less systematically Jordanes too gives a number of consular dates, referring those who wanted more information on recent events to "annales consulumque seriem" (*Romana* 388), evidently consular annals that were systematically kept up to date.[18]

Almost deserving to be classified as a consular list in its own right is the index to the *Festal Letters* of Athanasius, patriarch of Alexandria. Every year Athanasius sent out a circular letter announcing the date of Easter and the length of the fast required before it. An early editor, apparently working not long after Athanasius' death, compiled an index to all 45 (from 329 to 373), including (along with much other useful information) the consular date of each letter. For most of the first 20 years, the *Festal Letters* themselves survive in a Syriac translation that also supplies consular dates together with other calendaric material in the form of separable headings. In some cases they give the consular formula in fuller detail: e.g. in 334 Optatus is given the title patrician, and in 335 Constantius is described in full as "Julius Constantius, brother of the Augustus," in both cases agreeing with the papyri (in 333, however, they disagree). But a fragmentary Coptic version of the *Letters* does not give these headings, and it seems likely that they are the work of an editor working after Athanasius' death. The consuls cannot be assumed to be those current at Easter of each year; the letters must in any case have been sent out a couple of months before Easter if they were to achieve their purpose. They reflect rather a consular list carefully maintained at least up till 373, which we cannot identify with any of the surviving ones.

A quite independent work covering Athanasius' life from 346 to 373 and written *ca* 400 is the so-called *Historia Acephala*. This anonymous fragment (extant only in a Latin translation) quotes a large number of exact consular (and postconsular) dates, often making use of uncorrected provisional formulas. When we add in the illustrated Alexandrian chronicles discussed above (pp.53-54), it becomes obvious that accurately maintained consular lists were widely used in fourth and fifth century Egypt.

The fullest and most accurate English translation of the *Festal Letters* and index (which we cite as Fest. and Index respectively) is that by E. Payne Smith in A. Robertson (ed.), *Select Writings and Letters of Athanasius* (Nicene and Postnicene Fathers, 2nd series IV) 1891, 495f. (together with the *Historia Acephala* and a useful introduction). A new text of the Index and *Hist.Aceph.* with valuable commentary and French translation has been published by A. Martin and M. Albert, *Histoire "Acéphale" et index syriaque des lettres festales d'Athanase d'Alexandrie* (Sources Chrétiennes 317, Paris 1985); see too the long and critical review by T.D. Barnes, *JTS* 37 (1986).

[17]It has often been assumed that Socrates used a redaction of what Mommsen called the *consularia Constantinopolitana* (above, p.54): cf. *Chron.Min.* II 45 n.3.
[18]As already remarked in the discussion of eastern consular lists in Chapter 4, it cannot be assumed that there were *official* consular annals of Constantinople.

Biographical Data of Emperors

The following list gives the most important biographical data of emperors and usurpers, from the period 284-541. Usurpers' names are marked with an *.

Emperor/Usurper	Caesar	Augustus	Abdic./Death	Cos(s)
Diocletianus	---	20.xi.284	A 1.v.305	284, 285, 287, 290, 293, 296, 299, 303, 304, 308
Maximianus[1]	21.vii.285	a 1.iii.286 b post 28.x.306*	A,a: 1.v.305 A,b: xi.308 D 310	287, 288, 290, 293, 297, 299, 303, 304, 307
Carausius*	---	*ca* 286	*ca* 293	287, 288, 289, 290
Constantius	1.iii.293	1.v.305	D 25.vii.306	294, 296, 300, 302, 305, 306
Galerius	1.iii.293	1.v.305	D v.311	294, 297, 300, 302, 305, 306, 307
Severus	1.v.305	25.vii.306	A Spring 307, D 15/16.ix.307	307
Maximinus	1.v.305	1.v?.310	D *ca* vii.313	307, 311, 313
Maxentius*	28.x.306	early 307	D 28.x.312[2]	308, 309, 310, 312
Constantinus I	25.vii.306	25.vii.306	D 22.v.337[3]	307/309, 312, 313, 315, 319, 320, 326, 329

Licinius	---	11.xi.308	A ix.324	309, 312, 313, 315, 318, 321
Licinius iun.	1.iii.317	---	A ix.324	319, 321
Crispus	1.iii.317	---	D *ca* v.326	318, 321, 324
Constantinus II	1.iii.317	9.ix.337	D Spring, 340	320, 321, 324, 329
Constantius II	8.xi.324	9.ix.337	D 3.xi.361	326, 339, 342, 346, 352, 353, 354, 356, 357, 360
Constans	25.xii.333	9.ix.337	D post 18.i.350	339, 342, 346
Nepotianus	--	3.vi.350	D 30.vi.350	--
Gallus	15.iii.351	---	D 354[4]	352, 353, 354
Magnentius*	---	18.i.350	D 10.viii.353	351, 353
Decentius*	late 350?	---	D 18.viii.353	352
Iulianus	6.xi.355	3.xi.361	D 26.vi.363	356, 357, 360, 363
Iovianus	---	27.vi.363	D 17.ii.364	364
Valentinianus I	---	26.ii.364	D 17.xi.375	365, 368, 370, 373
Valens	---	28.iii.364	D 9.viii.378	365, 368, 370, 373, 376, 378
Gratianus	---	24.viii.367	D 25.viii.383[5]	366, 371, 374, 377, 380
Valentinianus II	---	22.xi.375	D 15.v.392[5]	376, 378, 387

Theodosius I	---	19.i.379[5]	D 17.i.395	380, 388 393
Arcadius	---	19.i.383	D 1.v.408[5]	385, 392, 394, 402, 406
Maximus*	---	Spring 383	D 28.viii.388	(384), 388
Eugenius*	---	22.viii.392	D 6.ix.394	393
Honorius	---	23.i.393	D 15.viii.423	386, 394, 396, 398, 402, 404, 407, 409, 411/412, 415, 417, 418, 422
Theodosius II	---	10.i.402	D 28.vii.450	403, 407, 409, 411, 412, 415, 416, 418, 420, 422, 425, 426, 430, 433, 435, 438, 439, 444
Constantinus III*	---	407	D 18.ix.411	409
Constantius III	---	8.ii.421	D 2.ix.421	414, 417, 420
Iohannes*	---	20.xi.423	D iv/v.425	425
Valentinianus III	23.x.424	23.x.425	D.16.iii.455	425, 426, 430, 435, 440, 445, 450, 455
Marcianus	---	25.viii.450	D 27.i.457	451
Petronius Maximus*	---	17.iii.455	D 31.v.455	(433, 443)
Avitus*	---	9.vii.455	D 17.x.456	456

Leo I	---	7.ii.457	D 18.i.474	458, 462, 466, 471, 473
Maiorianus	1.iv.457	28.xii.457	D 2.viii.461	458
Libius Severus	---	19.xi.461	D 14.xi.465	462
Procopius Anthemius	25.iii.467	12.iv.467	D 11.vii.472	455, 468
Olybrius	---	?.iv.472	D 2.xi.472	-
Glycerius	---	3.iii.473	D ?vi.474	-
Iulius Nepos	---	19/24.vi.474	A 28.viii.475	-
Romulus Augustulus	---	31.x.475	D ix.476	-
Leo II	x.473	1-18.i.474	D xi.474	474
Zeno	---	9.ii.474	D 9.iv.491	469, 475, 479
Basiliscus*	---	9.i.475	D Fall 476	465, 476
Anastasius	---	11.iv.491	D 9.vii.518	492, 497, 507
Iustinus	---	10.vii.518	D 1.viii.527	519, 524
Iustinianus	---	1.iv.527	D 15.xi.565	521, 528, 533, 534

Notes on the Chart

1. See Barnes, *New Empire* 13; *ZPE* 61 (1985) 99 and n.1.
2. Barnes, *New Empire* 12-13.
3. Barnes, *New Empire* 5-8.
4. See *ZPE* 28 (1978) 243.
5. For the counting of the regnal years of Gratianus, Valentinianus II, Theodosius I and Arcadius, see P.J. Sijpesteijn and K.A. Worp, "Dates with Regnal Years of Three Rulers," *ZPE* 28 (1978) 239-43; R.S. Bagnall and K.A. Worp, *RFBE* 42-44 (where add *P.Rainer Cent.* 87, years 15,7,3 = 381/2 and *P.Laur.* III 70.5 from 367/8, showing Oxyrhynchus era years 44-13 plus regnal year 5 of Valentinianus I and Valens; Gratian's accession was not yet known).

Table of Indictions

The table below shows the year in which indictions *began*; that is, '312' means that an indiction began in 312 and ended in 313. Indiction numbers are given across the top of the chart. For the workings of the indiction system, particularly in Egypt, see *CSBE*.

1	2	3	4	5	6	7	8	9	10	11	12	13	14	15
312	313	314	315	316	317	318	319	320	321	322	323	324	325	326
327	328	329	330	331	332	333	334	335	336	337	338	339	340	341
342	343	344	345	346	347	348	349	350	351	352	353	354	355	356
357	358	359	360	361	362	363	364	365	366	367	368	369	370	371
372	373	374	375	376	377	378	379	380	381	382	383	384	385	386
387	388	389	390	391	392	393	394	395	396	397	398	399	400	401
402	403	404	405	406	407	408	409	410	411	412	413	414	415	416
417	418	419	420	421	422	423	424	425	426	427	428	429	430	431
432	433	434	435	436	437	438	439	440	441	442	443	444	445	446
447	448	449	450	451	452	453	454	455	456	457	458	459	460	461
462	463	464	465	466	467	468	469	470	471	472	473	474	475	476
477	478	479	480	481	482	483	484	485	486	487	488	489	490	491
492	493	494	495	496	497	498	499	500	501	502	503	504	505	506
507	508	509	510	511	512	513	514	515	516	517	518	519	520	521
522	523	524	525	526	527	528	529	530	531	532	533	534	535	536
537	538	539	540	541	542	543	544	545	546	547	548	549	550	551

PART II
THE EVIDENCE

Guide to the Evidence

The section below contains two pages, one for the East and one for the West, for each year from 284 through 541. In those periods when the parts of the empire were not politically under one rule or at least in concord, the separation by regions shows which consul(s) were recognized or disseminated in each part. Where there was division within a region or a change of consuls within a year, multiple versions are given in the heading. Where there was unity or concord, the division is simply one of the provenance of the evidence. *Occidens* includes all primarily Latin regions, regardless of temporary fluctuations of political control, and *Oriens* primarily Greek ones. Inscriptions and papyri may be assumed to be in the language of the part from which they come unless the contrary is indicated.

In order to present a relatively clear picture, certain principles of simplification have been followed: (1) All names and titles are rendered in Latin, whatever the language of the original document; (2) Variations in spelling (especially phonetic renderings) are ignored almost entirely; (3) Variation between (e.g.) Fl. before each name and Fll. (in Latin usually FFLL) at the start or Aug. after each emperor's name and Augg. after both names are usually not reported; (4) Names and titles are given in the nominative regardless of the case in the source, except for p.c. dates, where the genitive is used; (5) Greek epithets with the names of private consuls are usually rendered 'v.c.' even if the evidence shows some deviation from that. (6) Consuls are assigned the name Flavius in the heading to years only if it is independently attested as one of their names (not simply given as a kind of honorific prefix to the principal name) or if no name other than the principal one is known. (7) An asterisk next to a reference indicates that it is discussed, or a reference to a discussion of it is given, in the Critical Appendix.

Some remarks about individual categories of evidence may be helpful (for fuller information, see the pertinent introductory chapters):

1. Fasti. The abbreviations used for chronicles and consular lists are those of Mommsen with modifications (see above, Chapter 4). Minor variants in MSS are ignored unless they seem to be significant. The reader should be cautioned that the magnificent consular index in Mommsen standardizes formulas far more than we have and is not to be relied on for details.

2. Laws. Only a selection is listed here. Full lists may be found in the editio sterotypa of the *CJ* and in Seeck (above, p.72). We give the places of issue, number of laws at each, the earliest law with a formula, the last with any 'provisional' formula (above, p.77), and such other details as seem to us to contribute to the overall picture. 'About' with a number of laws reflects the uncertainty of some attributions to years. We do not include, either in that count or in the references, those instances where modern scholars have restored or substantially emended a formula on the basis of prosopographical or other arguments about the probable date of a law, nor where, though reference to a particular year is certain, a formula with names is not given. This practice does not indicate any doubt about the rightness of such datings or emendations (though many are open to doubt) but only our view that they are not useful evidence for the consular formula in that year.

3. Inscriptions. These are organized by provenance. Outside Rome, a specific place is given where known. (We have not adopted any particular standard for these; modern names are generally given unless the ancient is better known to most modern scholars.) Dates are those (mostly of individuals' birth and death) given in the inscriptions; they are not necessarily (or even probably) those of the actual inscribing. Usually a maximum of two references for a single inscription are given, in most cases the latest major edition plus a convenient collection (*ILS* or *ILCV*). The = sign does **not** mean that the same text is presented in the editions, but only that the same inscription is involved. Elements resting only on editors' restorations are not usually mentioned in the parenthetical remarks. Elements given in the third column **outside** parentheses (round brackets) are found in all inscriptions (so far as preserved) except as noted; those **inside** parentheses are found only when their presence is noted specifically. The choice of what to print inside and outside parentheses rests on the relative frequency of the elements in the evidence for a particular year and place. Deviations from editors' texts (as opposed to restorations), where not wholly trivial, are defended in the Critical Appendix. Texts which may belong either to the consulate or to the postconsulate are listed under the consulate, but those attributable with probability or certainty to the postconsulate are given under the julian year of the postconsulate.

4. Papyri are subject to the most of the remarks made above for inscriptions. We assume all corrections to texts which were made or cited in *CSBE* and those given in the *Berichtigungsliste*; those in publications subsequent to *BL* VII are listed in the Critical Appendix (Part III). Discussions are provided in the Critical Appendix only for items not discussed (or adequately treated) in any of these places. We do not include writing exercises with false consulates (cf. p.69 above).

5. Papal Letters are found in a variety of editions; there is no standard comprehensive edition. We cite the best edition we have found, but in some cases we know of none other than that in Migne, *Patrologia Latina*, drawn in turn from a variety of anterior sources. Where we can compare Migne's texts of letters with modern critical editions, they are almost invariably inaccurate, and we warn the reader against undue reliance on details of the formula (or exact date) in *PL* texts.

Abbreviations for sources cited are given in the Bibliography (Part IV).

Italian (mainland) place names are furnished with the number of the Augustan regions in which they are located. These cover the following territory:

I	Latium and Campania
II	Apulia and Calabria
III	Lucania and Bruttium
IV	Samnium etc.
V	Picenum
VI	Umbria and Ager Gallicus
VII	Etruria
VIII	Aemilia
IX	Liguria
X	Venetia and Istria
XI	Gallia Transpadana

THE EVIDENCE

Occidentis

<u>FASTI</u>:	Chr. 354 (fast.,praef.) VindPr.	Carinus II et Numerianus
	Prosp. Aq. Cass. Hyd. VindPost. (Clarus)	Carus II et Numerianus
<u>LAWS</u>:	7 laws, earliest *CJ* 8.55.3 (no prov., 14.i); *CJ* 8.53.5 (Rome, 27.i)	Carinus II et Numerianus
<u>INSCR.</u>:	**ROME:** *CIL* VI 36954 (27.v)	DD.NN. Carinus Aug. et Numerianus Aug.
	AFRICA: *I.Lat.Alg.* II 2 4557* (Ghar el Djemae)	Carinus et Numerianus
<u>COINS</u>:	Kent, *Roman Coins* no. 557: Bimetallic consular medallion (Rome)	Imp. C. Numerianus P.F. Aug. cos.

<u>NOTES</u>:

The consuls of 284 present problems. Pasch. records Diocletianus et Bassus *between* the consuls of 283 and 284. *PLRE* hesitantly identifies them as suffects of 283 (I 254, 1042), but elsewhere (like other late consular lists) Pasch. records only ordinary consuls, and it would be an odd coincidence that Diocletian should chance to be suffect only one year before he seized the throne. More probably Pasch. inserted the pair a year early, and Diocletian proclaimed himself and Bassus consuls at his elevation on 20 November 284 (so Barnes, *New Empire* 93 n.6). Bassus could then be L. Caesonius Ovinius Manlius Rufinianus Bassus (*PLRE* I 156; Barnes, *New Empire* 97), attested as cos. II by an inscription, both evidently suffect since his name does not appear in the fasti. In favor of this hypothesis is the undoubted fact that in 285 Diocletian was cos. II (and so on up to cos. X in 308), and it is difficult to see how his previous military career could otherwise have brought him even the *ornamenta consularia* (not in any case attested after 222: A. Chastagnol, *Recherches sur l'Histoire Auguste* [Bonn 1970] 51), much less the suffect consulate.[1] [Continued]

---

[1]Oddly enough Carus (283) and Claudius II (269) also both appear as cos. II in their first imperial consulates. Carus, as PPO, may have previously been a suffect (A. Chastagnol, *Recherches sur l'Histoire Auguste* 52), but Claudius' first consulate remains a mystery (mere error, according to *PIR*[2] A 1626; *ornamenta consularia*, implausibly, J.R. Rea, *P.Oxy.* XL, pp.27-28). Perhaps all three took a suffect consulate during the tail end of their first calendar year as emperor.

(a) **Carinus Aug. II et Numerianus Aug.**
(b) **Diocletianus Aug. I et Bassus** (from 20.xi)

Orientis

<u>FASTI:</u>	Heracl. Pasch. (see below)	Carinus II et Numerianus
	Theo	Carinus Aug. et Numerianus
	Pasch.	Diocletianus et Bassus
<u>LAWS:</u>	*CJ* 5.52.2 (Emesa, 18.iii)	Carinus II et Numerianus Augg.
<u>PAPYRI:</u>	*ChLA* XI 499 ii.6	II et I

<u>NOTES:</u>

[Continued from the preceding page]

Yet if this is what happened, it might seem surprising that no attempt was made to eliminate the original consuls from the record; they remain not only in all consular lists (including *Pasch.*) but also in the legal evidence. Perhaps, since Diocletian initially posed as the avenger of Numerian, he felt unable to include him in a blanket *damnatio memoriae* of the original consuls of the year. He was content to allow himself and Bassus to be counted as suffects in the ordinary way. This would explain why Diocletian and Bassus are omitted in all lists save Pasch., where they appear in addition to the ordinary consuls.

(a) **Carinus Aug. III et T. Cl. Aurelius Aristobulus**
(b) **Diocletianus Aug. II et T. Cl. Aurelius Aristobulus**

Occidentis

<u>FASTI</u>:	Chr. 354 (fast.,praef.) Hyd.	Diocletianus II et Aristobulus
	VindPr. Aq. Cass. Prosp. VindPost.	Diocletianus et Aristobulus
<u>LAWS</u>:	About 12 laws, earliest *CJ* 6.34.2 (1.i). 1 law from Atubinum, 3.xi; *Collatio* 3.4.1 (5.xii; Diocletianus III)	Diocletianus Aug. II et Aristobulus
<u>INSCR.</u>:	**PANNONIA:** *AE* 1982, 782 (E. of Carnuntum; 11.vi; frag.)	Diocletianus II et [
<u>OTHER:</u>	Ammianus 23.1.1	Diocletianus et Aristobulus

Orientis

FASTI: Heracl. (om. Aug.) Pasch.   Diocletianus Aug. II et
            Theo (om. II)   Aristobulus

LAWS: none

PAPYRI: none

NOTES:

Hyd. s.a. 285 (Diocletiano II et Aristobulo) records that "his conss. occisus est Carinus Margo, qui ipso anno cum Aristobulo consul processerat." Since Aristobulus is known to have been Carinus' PPO (Victor, *Caes.* 39.15; Barnes, *New Empire* 97), it is plausible enough that he should originally have been Carinus' colleague as consul, subsequently retained, both as consul and PPO, by Diocletian; plausible too that no other trace should survive of this obviously revoked III cos. of the fallen Carinus. Aristobulus was later PVR in 295-96 (*PLRE* I 106).

Occidentis

FASTI:	Chr. 354 (fast.,praef.) Hyd.	Maximus II et Aquilinus
	Prosp. VindPr. Aq. Cass.	Maximus et Aquilinus
	VindPost.	Aquilinus et Maximus
LAWS:	About 38 laws total; cf. East	Maximus II et Aquilinus
INSCR.:	**ROME:** *CIL* VI 2136 (25.ii); *CIL* VI 2137 = *ILS* 4936 (1.iii)	M. Iunius Maximus II et Vettius Aquilinus
	ITALY: *CIL* XIV 2038 (Lavinium, Reg. I; 1.ii)	Maximus II et Aquilinus

Orientis

FASTI: Heracl. Pasch.   Maximus et Aquilinus
                Theo (Maximinus)

LAWS: Nicomedia, 4 laws, earliest   Maximus II et Aquilinus
                CJ 4.21.6 (20.i); Tiberias,
                2 laws, earlier 31.v

PAPYRI: none

NOTES:

    Maximus was PVR in 286-288 and presumably suffect consul at an earlier date (*PLRE* I 587); Aquilinus is otherwise unattested (*PLRE* I 92).

Occidentis

<u>FASTI</u>:	Chr. 354 (fast.,praef.) Hyd. VindPr. (D. II) Aq. (D. II) Prosp. (D. II) Cass. VindPost. (Max.Aug.)	Diocletianus III et Maximianus (Aug.)
<u>LAWS</u>:	About 20 laws total, earliest *CJ* 2.3.18 (7.i), no provenances; *Collatio* 6.6.1 (9.vi)	Diocletianus III et Maximianus Augg.
<u>INSCR.</u>:	**ROME:** *CIL* VI 1117 (1.i); *ICUR* n.s. VII 19946 = *ILCV* 2938* (23.vi; om. DD.NN.; Max. II); *CIL* VI 3743 = 31130 (24.vi)	DD.NN. Diocletianus III et Maximianus I
	ITALY: *AE* 1977, 265b (Ravenna, Reg. VIII; 7.vi; or 290?)	DD.NN. Diocletianus et Maximianus Augg.
	MOESIA SUP.: *CIL* III 8151 = 1660 = *I.Més.Sup.* I 20	DD.NN. Diocletianus III et Maximianus Augg.
	PANNONIA INF.: *Eph.Ep.* 2.678 (Buda)	Impp.DD.NN. Diocletianus III et Maximianus Augg.
	AFRICA: *CIL* VIII 23291* (Byzacena prov., Thala; Max. should be I)	Impp. DD.NN. Diocletianus III et Maximianus II
<u>COINS</u>:	*RIC* V.2, 233, 250, 254 (Rome, Cyzicus, and Antioch)	Diocletian cos. III
	Toynbee, *Rom.Medallions*, p.88: gold consular medallion of Diocletian and Maximian	Impp. Diocletiano et Maximiano ccss
	Toynbee, *Rom.Medallions*, p.88: bronze consular medallion of Maximian	P.M. Tri.p. cos. p.p.

Orientis

FASTI: Heracl. (om. Aug. after Diocl.)   Diocletianus Aug. III et
     Theo (om. III) Pasch (Herc.)   Maximinus (Herculius) Aug.

LAWS: See West.

PAPYRI: none

NOTES:

  While errors of iteration numerals in consulates of emperors are not unparalleled (cf. p.64), it is remarkable that of five inscriptions probably to be assigned to this year, one lacks numerals entirely and two have Diocletian III, Maximian II, while VindPr., Prosp. and Aq. have II and I. Cf. the Critical Appendix. It is hard to escape the conclusion that the consular count here has been contaminated in some way by the regnal: 286/7 was Diocletian's third regnal year, Maximian's second.

  It has been inferred that the usurper Carausius styled himself consul in 287 (II, 288; III, 289; IV, 290) in Britain and parts of northwestern Gaul, but he is absent from the fasti and inscriptions; see Barnes, *New Empire* 11. A billon consular medallion of Carausius may date from this year or the following one (Kent, *Roman Coins*, no.557, perhaps from Boulogne). A coin of his marked cos. IIII (*RIC* V.2, 497, from Camulodunum) was found in a hoard apparently datable to 290.

Occidentis

FASTI: Chr. 354 (fast.,praef. [Aug.])   Maximianus (Aug.) II et
                Hyd. VindPr. Cass. Aq. Prosp.   Ianuarinus

                VindPost.   Ian. et Max. II

LAWS: none

INSCR.:   none

COINS: *RIC* V.2, 275, 290, 292   Maximian cos. II
                (Rome, Cyzicus, Antioch)

SUFFECT CONSULS:

The *Fasti Caleni* record a pair of suffects whose names end in ...]*a* and ...]*ivianus* respectively (*I.Ital.* XIII.1, p.269). These traces do not fit any of the undated suffects listed in *PLRE* I 1046-47.

NOTES:

For Ianuarianus, see Barnes, *New Empire* 98 and Christol, *Essai* 119-20; he was PVR 288-289, *PLRE* I 452-53. On his name, cf. C. Vandersleyen, *Chronologie des préfets* 27-28.

Orientis

FASTI: Heracl. Theo (Aug.; om. II)   Maximianus (Aug.) II et
                                                                Ianuarinus

                Pasch.   Maximianus Herculius II
                                                                et Ianuarius

LAWS: none

PAPYRI: none

INSCR.:   **CILICIA:** *AE* 1972, 636 (Ayasofya,   D.N. Maximianus Aug. II
                25.v)   et Ianuar[ianus]

Occidentis

FASTI:	Chr. 354 (fast.,praef.: B. II)	Bassus (II) et Quintianus
	Hyd. VindPr. Prosp. Aq. Cass.	
	VindPost.	Bassus et Maximianus III
LAWS:	*CJ* 7.56.3 + 9.2.9 (no prov., 19.viii); *CJ* 4.19.8 (no prov., 19.xi)	Bassus et Quintianus
INSCR.:	**ROME:** *ICUR* n.s. III 7376 = *ILCV* 855A (14.viii-1.ix)	Bassus et Quintianus
	ITALY: *CIL* X 3698 = *ILS* 4175 (Cumae, Reg. I; 1.vi); *CIL* X 4631 = *I.Ital.* XIII.1 16 (Calvi; part of list of coss., order reversed)	M. Magrius Bassus et L. Ragonius Quintianus

SUFFECT CONSULS:

The *Fasti Caleni* list three pairs of suffects in addition to the ordinarii (who are given here alone with Quintianus' name first), as follows (*I.Ital.* XIII.1, p.269):

[......L. Ragonius] Quintianus   cos
[..........M.] Magrius Bassus
[............] M. Umbrius Primus   cos
[.........T.] Flavius Coelianus
[.........Ce]ionius Proculus   cos
[..........H]elvius Clemens
[............] Flavius Decimus   cos
[............]ninus Maximus

CIL X 3698 = *ILS* 4175, dated to 17.viii *M.Umbrio T.Fl.Coeliano cos.* (whence the restoration above), incorporates a document of 1.vi still dated by the ordinarii. We might guess that the three pairs of suffects entered office on 1.vii, 1.ix, and 1.xi respectively. A column to the right of this column of names contains the first two or three letters of a series of dates, *k(al) apr.* and the like, which Mommsen originally (on *CIL* X 4631) took to be the dates on which the suffects entered office. This interpretation (abandoned by Mommsen himself at *Röm. Staatsrecht* II.1³ 85-86 n.5) was unfortunately followed in the entries for all six suffects in *PLRE*, who are there alleged to have entered office on 1.ii (Primus and Coelianus together), 1.iii, 1.iv. 1.v and 1.vi. So too W. Kuhoff, *Studien zur zivilen senatorischen Laufbahn im 4. Jhdt. n. Chr.* (Frankfurt 1983). But not only does this necessitate rejecting the 17.viii date for Primus and Coelianus in the contemporary *CIL* X 3698 (so explicitly Kuhoff, p.284, n.94) and splitting up the third and fourth pairs; [Continued]

Orientis

FASTI:	Heracl.	Tiberius Bassus et Dion Quintianus
	Theo (B. II) Pasch.	Bassus (II) et Quintianus
LAWS:	See West.	
PAPYRI:	*P.Mich.* X 593 i.18* (doc. 312)	[Bassus et Quintianus]

[Continued from preceding page]

in other epigraphic lists that give entry dates for suffects (e.g. the *Fasti Ostienses*), the date precedes rather than follows the name, and Degrassi was surely right (*I.Ital.* XIII.1, p.270) to refer these traces to a later year. Kuhoff oddly suggests that the last four names were appointed singly for one month each; yet they are obviously set out in pairs exactly like the first four. None of these suffects is known from any other source.

NOTES:

Neither consul is otherwise known, though apparently of senatorial birth: Christol, *Essai* 120-21. Christol is inclined to accept that Bassus was consul II as listed by Chr. 354 (praef.) and Theo, on the basis presumably of an earlier suffect consulate. Heracl., mixing up the coss. of 289 and 291, has a pair of consuls, the first of whom is a combination of the first consul of 291 and the first of 289, followed by the second of 291 and the second of 289.

Occidentis

FASTI: Chr. 354 (fast.,praef.) Hyd.   Diocletianus IV et
                VindPr. Prosp. (Diocl. Aug., Max.   Maximianus III[2]
                Herc. Aug.) Cass. Aq.

                VindPost.   Diocletianus III et
                                                      Quintianus

LAWS: About 73 laws for the year,   Ipsis IV et III Augg.
                earliest *CJ* 10.3.4 (*p.p.*
                Sirmium, 11.i)[3]

                Collatio 1.10.1 (30.xi)   Diocletianus Aug. IV
                                                      et Maximianus

INSCR.:   **ROME:** *CIL* VI 869 (7.i); *CIL*   DD.NN. Diocletianus Aug.
                VI 870 (16.iv; om. Aug.); *ICUR*   IV et Maximianus Aug. III
                n.s. IV 9546 = *ILCV* 3318B adn.
                (26.viii; om. DD.NN., Aug., III)

                ITALY: *CIL* XI 2573 = *ILCV* 3032
                (Chiusi, Reg. VII; 16.i; om.
                DD.NN., Aug.)

                PANNONIA INF.: *CIL* III 10406*
                (Budapest; om. III)

                AFRICA: *CIL* VIII 8332 (cf. p.
                1897 and suppl. V, p.424 ad
                Index V) (Numidia; 20.vii)

COINS: *RIC* V.2, 260, 290-292   Maximian cos. III
                (Lyons, Cyzicus, Antioch)

                RIC V.2, 250, 222 (Antioch, Lyons) Diocletian cos. IIII

NOTES:

For Carausius' coins dated to his fourth consulate, see 287.

[2]The numerals are corrupt in many fasti: III & IV, VindPr.; III & II, Prosp.; III & III, Cass,. Aq.
[3]Original formula with names is nowhere retained in *CJ*.

Orientis

<u>FASTI:</u>	Heracl. Theo (Aug. 2x, no num.) Pasch.	Diocletianus IV et Maximianus III
<u>LAWS:</u>	See West.	
<u>PAPYRI:</u>	*P.Mich.* X 593 i.7 (doc. 312; much rest.)	Diocletianus IV et Maximianus III

Occidentis

FASTI: Chr. 354 (fast.,praef.[Tib. II])   Tiberianus (II) et Dio
              Hyd. VindPr. Prosp. Aq. Cass.
              VindPost. (rev. order)

LAWS: 11 laws total, earliest *CJ*   Tiberianus et Dio
              5.16.15 (29.i); 1 law from
              Sirmium (13.v), 1 from Triballae
              (?) (4.xii); *Collatio* 6.5.1 (15.iii)

INSCR.:   **ROME:** *ICUR* n.s. V 13886 = *ILCV*   (Gaius Iunius) Tiberianus
              2305 (16.iii-1.iv); *ICUR* n.s.   II et (Cassius) Dio
              VIII 21595 = *ILCV* 4578 (27.xi;
              om. II); *ICUR* n.s. III 8718* =
              ILCV 4366A (C. I[un. Tib.
              II] et Cass. Dio)

NOTES:

Tiberianus was cos. I in 281 and PVR in 291-92 (*PLRE* I 912, with Barnes, *JRS* 65 [1975] 43); Dio was PVR 296 and presumably a descendant of the historian Cassius Dio (*PLRE* I 253). Of the sources, only Chr. 354 (praef.), Heracl., and at least one inscription have Tiberianus' iteration numeral.

Orientis

<u>FASTI:</u>	Heracl.	Tiberianus II et Dio
	Pasch. Theo	Tiberianus et Dio
<u>LAWS:</u>	See West.	
<u>PAPYRI:</u>	*P.Oxy.* IX 1205.14 (14.iv); *P.Mich.* X 593 [i.17]; ii.4,18 (doc. 312)	Tiberianus et Dio

Occidentis

FASTI:	Chr. 354 (fast.,praef.) Hyd. VindPr. Prosp. Aq. Cass. VindPost.	Hannibalianus et Asclepiodotus
LAWS:	*CJ* 7.35.4 (27.ii), 1.23.3 (31.iii), 9.2.11 (6.iv), 10.10.1 (12.iv), no prov.	Hannibalianus et Asclepiodotus
INSCR.:	**ROME:** *ICUR* n.s. VI 16964 = *ILCV* 3996 (18.i)	Hannibalianus et Asclepiodotus

NOTES:

Hannibalianus was PPO between 285 and 292, and PVR 297-98 (*PLRE* I 407); Asclepiodotus was PPO with Hannibalianus before 292 "but not necessarily identical with the Asclepiodotus who was PPO of Constantius in 296" (Barnes, *New Empire* 98). The absence of Asclepiodotus in the papyrus is probably just a result of short-form reference in a military roster referring to years of enlistment; cf. below on 304.

Orientis

FASTI: Heracl. Pasch. Theo   Hannibalianus et
                                                     Asclepiodotus

LAWS: See West.

PAPYRI: *P.Mich.* X 593 ii.12,14   Hannibalianus
                  (doc. 312)

Occidentis

<u>FASTI</u>:	Chr. 354 (fast.,praef.) Hyd. VindPr. Prosp. Aq. Cass. VindPost.	Diocletianus V et Maximianus IV[4]
<u>LAWS</u>:	None in *CJ*;[5] *Consultatio* 1.9 (6.ix; Max. III; om. Aug. 2x); 6.16 (om. Max.'s num.)	Diocletianus V Aug. et Maximianus IV Aug.
<u>INSCR.</u>:	none	
<u>COINS</u>:	*RIC* V.2, 260 (Lyons), 292; VI 613.3-4 (Antioch): consular solidi of Maximian	consul IIII
	RIC VI 613.5-6 (Antioch): consular solidi of Diocletian	consul V

---

[4]The numerals are again corrupt in several of the lists: IV & III, VindPr., Prosp.; IV & IV, VindPost., Aq.; III & IV, Cass.
[5]The formula *Diocletianus V et Maximianus IV Augg.* is not found in any law as preserved. Mommsen assigned to this year all 216 laws which simply use the formula *AA* (*Augustis*), see *Zeitfolge der Verordnungen Diocletians* 433. Cf. note on 294. There is also an example in *Collatio* 10.3.1 (Serdica, 24.vi).

Orientis

<u>FASTI:</u>	Heracl. Theo (om. numerals) Pasch. (Aug., Hercul. Aug.)	Diocletianus (Aug.) V et Maximianus (Hercul. Aug.) IV
<u>LAWS:</u>	See the West.	
<u>PAPYRI:</u>	*P.Lips.* 4.1, 5.1 (10.ix); *YCS* 28 (1985) 101.12 (Caesarea; 6.xii; Lat.); *P.Cair.Isid.* 35.1 (18.xii; om. Aug.); *P.Vindob.Sal.* 7.1 (Impp.)	DD.NN. (Impp.) Diocletianus Aug. V et Maximianus Aug. IV
	P.Grenf. II 110.6* = *ChLA* III 205 = *Rom.Mil.Rec.* 86 (Lat.)	[DD.NN. Diocletianus Aug. V et] Maximianus Aug. IV

Occidentis

FASTI: Chr. 354 (fast.,praef.) Hyd.   Constantius et Maximianus
              VindPr.

              VindPost.   Constantius Caesar et
                                                Maximianus Caesar

              Prosp. Cass. Aq.   Constantius et Maximus

LAWS: None in *CJ*[6]

INSCR.:   None

NOTES:

      Constantius and Galerius were following the normal practice of taking the consulate in the first full year after their (joint) proclamation as Caesars (1.iii.293: Barnes, *New Empire* 4).

---

[6]The formula *Constantius et Maximianus Caesares* is not found in the laws. Mommsen (cf. under 293) 440 assigned all 262 laws in which only *CC* (*Caesaribus*) appears to this year. Cf. also *Collatio* 10.4.1, 10.6.1.

Orientis

FASTI: Heracl. Pasch. (Constantius,   Constantinus Caesar et
        Iovius) Theo   Maximianus (Iovius) Caesar

LAWS: *Consultatio* 5.6 (Nicomedia,   Constantius et Maximinus
        10.xii)

PAPYRI: *P.Oxy.* VI 891.1 (*ca* vi);   DD.NN. Constantius et
        P.Cair.Isid. 34.13 (12.viii);   Maximianus nobb. Caess.
        P.Oxy. I 23 verso (adds Augg.);
        perhaps *BGU* VII 1644.1

        P.Mich. X 593 i.6 (doc. 312;   Constantius et Maximianus
        largely rest.)

Occidentis

FASTI: Chr. 354 (fast.,praef.) Hyd.   Tuscus et Anul(l)inus
              VindPr. Prosp. Cass. Aq.
              VindPost.

LAWS: *Consultatio* 5.7 (*p.p.* Milan,   Tuscus et Aquilinus
              21.iii)

INSCR.:   **ROME:** *CIL* VI 505 = *ILS* 4143   Tuscus et Anullinus
              (26.ii); *ICUR* n.s. VII 17416
              = *ILCV* 2786 (24.viii); *ICUR* n.s.
              VIII 21596

              GERMANIA: *CIL* XIII 8019
              (Bonn; 19.ix)

OTHER: *Acta Maximiliani* 1 (Lanata,   Tuscus et Anullinus
              Atti dei Martiri, p.194)
              (Tebessa, Africa, 12.iii)

NOTES:

Tuscus, perhaps son of M. Nummius Tuscus cos. 258, was PVR in 302-303 (*PLRE* I 927); Anullinus was PVR in 306-307 and perhaps again in 312 (see Barnes, *New Empire* 117; *PLRE* I 79). Christol, *Essai* 122-24, doubts the identification of Tuscus with the PVR of 302-303, with a useful note on the interval between ordinary consulate and PVR.

Orientis

<u>FASTI:</u>	Heracl. Theo Pasch.	Tuscus et Anullinus
<u>LAWS:</u>	*CJ* 5.72.3 (Nicomedia, 18.iii); 3.36.25 (no prov., 13.iv); 5.4.17 = *Collatio* 6.4.1 (Damascus, 1.v); 9.9.27 (no prov., 1.vi)[7]	Tuscus et Anullinus
<u>PAPYRI:</u>	*P.Oxy.* I 43 recto vi.25 (i-ii); *P.Oxy.* I 23 verso; *P.Lips.* 29.19	Nummius Tuscus et Annius Anullinus
	BGU III 858.1* (11.x); *P.Mich.* X 593 ii.3,7,10; iii.4 (doc. 312)	Tuscus et Anullinus

---

[7]Barnes, *New Empire* 54 n.33, suspects that *CJ* 6.20.14 (23.ii) may come from some place near Nicomedia; the place name is perhaps corrupt, and Mommsen rejected the date.

Occidentis

FASTI: Chr. 354 (fast.,praef.,episc.   Diocletianus VI et
            75,32.34) Hyd. VindPr. Prosp.   Constantius II
            Aq. Cass. VindPost.[8]

LAWS: none

INSCR.:   **ROME:** *ICUR* n.s. VII   Diocletianus VI
            17417 = *ILCV* 2807A (29.ii)

            AFRICA: *CIL* VIII 9988 =   Diocletianus Aug. VI
            I.Ant.Maroc II 1 (Tangier)   et Constantius Caesar II

COINS: *RIC* VI 612.1, 614.13 (Antioch):   consul VI
            consular gold solidus and
            multiple of Diocletian

            Toynbee, *Roman Medallions*, p.88   consul VI p.p. procos.
            (Consular medallion of Diocletian)

NOTES:

    There is no reason to think that the omission of Constantius in *ICUR* n.s. VII 17417 reflects
anything except careless drafting of the inscription. More curious is the mistaken identity of the second
consul in Scal. and in the Michigan papyrus.

[8]VindPr. Prosp. Aq. Cass. Chr. 354 (fast.) give V & II; VindPost. gives D. V et C. Caes. II.

Orientis

FASTI: Heracl. Theo (Aug., no VI)   Diocletianus (Aug.) VI et
               Pasch. (Aug., Caes.)   Constantius (Caesar) II

               Scal.   Diocletianus Aug. V et
                                      Maximianus Caes. II

LAWS: none

PAPYRI: *P.Oxy.* XXXVIII 2849.8 (21.v);   DD.NN. (Imp.) Diocletianus
              P.Oxy.Hels. 26.1 (13.vi; Imp.);   Aug. VI et Constantius
              P.Michael. 23a.1 (9.ix; Imp.);   nob. Caesar II
              P.Oxy. XLIV 3184a.1 (x-xi;
              Imp., om. II); *PSI* IX 1071.1
              (29.viii-31.xii; om. Aug., nob.
              Caes.); *SB* VI 9502.1; *P.Stras.*
              261.1

              P.Mich. X 593 iii.1 (doc. 312)   Diocletianus VI et
                                        Maximianus II

Occidentis

FASTI: Chr. 354 (fast.,praef.) Hyd.   Maximianus V et
              VindPr. Prosp. Aq. Cass.   Maximianus II[9]

LAWS: none

INSCR.:   **ROME:** *ICUR* n.s. I 1168 =   (Imp.) DD.NN. Maximianus
              ILCV 286   Aug. V et Maximianus
                                                       (nob.) Caes. II

              ITALY: *CIL* XIV 4562.8 (Ostia)

              MOESIA INF.: *CIL* III 14433[1]*
              (Silistria; Imp.; no numerals;
              [Caes.])

              HUNGARY: *AE* 1926, 72
              (Szentendre; nob.)

              PANNONIA: *AE* 1982, 783 (E. of
              Carnuntum; 11.vi; [nob.])

COINS: *RIC* VI 614.11-12 (Antioch):   consul V
              consular soliduis of Maximian

_____

[9]VI & II, Hyd.; IV & II, VindPr. Prosp. Aq.

Orientis

FASTI: Heracl. Theo (Aug. 2x)   Maximinus (Aug.) V et
Maximianus Caes. II

Pasch.   Maximianus Herculius V
et Maximianus Iovius
Caesar II

Scal.   Max. Caes. V et Max.
Caes. V

LAWS: none

PAPYRI: *P.Oxy.* XLIV 3184b.1 (9.i;   DD.NN. (Imp.) Maximianus Aug. V
Constantius for 2nd Max.);   et Maximianus nob. Caesar II
BASP 22 (1985) 351.1 (3.ii);
P.Cair.Isid. 81.1 (9.iv); *SB*
XIV 12190.1 (17.vii; om. nob.);
P.Oxy. XLV 3245.1 (i-viii; Imp.);
P.Mich. X 592 ii.7 (doc. 311-324;
om. nob.; Lat.); *P.Lond.* III 959
descr. = *BASP* 22 (1985) 351.1

P.Mich. X 593 ii.1,9,19   Maximianus V et
(doc. 312)   Maximianus II

Occidentis

FASTI:	Chr. 354 (fast.,praef.) Hyd.	Faustus II et Gallus
	VindPr. Prosp. Aq. Cass. VindPost.	Faustus et Gallus
LAWS:	none	
INSCR.:	**ROME:** *ICUR* n.s. VII 17418 (21.x; Gk.); *ICUR* n.s. VII 19947 = *ILCV* 3888 (Anicius F. et Virius G.); *ICUR* n.s. I 1416; *ICUR* I 26 (frag.)	(Anicius) Faustus et (Virius) Gallus
	ITALY: *CIL* XVI 156 = IX 261 (Torre d'Agnazzo, Reg. II; 7.i)	Faustus II et Gallus
	RAETIA: *CIL* III 11955 (Eining; frag.)	Faustus II et Gallus
OTHER:	*Acta Marcelli*, 1 (Place unknown, 28.viii), 4 (Tangiers, 30.x) (Lanata, *Atti dei Martiri*, pp.202-203)	Faustus et Gallus

NOTES:

Anicius Faustus, PVR 299-300, was probably the father of Iulianus cos. 322 and grandfather of Paulinus cos. 334; he must previously have been suffect in some year unknown (*PLRE* I 329). Gallus is otherwise known only as *corrector* of Campania (*PLRE* I 384). It is interesting that the Roman inscriptions omit Faustus' iteration numeral, along with the papyri, martyr acts and some fasti, while two provincial inscriptions and other fasti have it.

Orientis

FASTI: Heracl. Theo (II)   Faustus (II) et Gallus

          Pasch.   Anicius Faustus et
                                                Severus Gallus

          Scal.   Faustus et Tatianus cc.

LAWS: none

PAPYRI: *P.Wisc.* II 58.3, 59.3 (5.iv);   Anicius Faustus et
          P.Oxy. XIV 1705.22 (6.vii);   Virius Gallus
          P.Mich. IX 548.22 (6.ix);
          P.Oxy. XIV 1704.24;
          P.Oxy. XII 1469.24*

          P.Oxy. XIV 1643.19 (11.v);   Faustus et Gallus
          P.Panop.Beatty 1.26 (5.viii);
          P.Cair.Isid. 2.25 (1.xii); *SB*
          X 10726.15 (xi-xii); *P.Mich.*
          X 593 ii.8,11; iii.7,(8) (doc. 312)

Occidentis

FASTI: Chr. 354 (fast.,praef.) Hyd.   Diocletianus VII et
             VindPr. Prosp. Prol.pasch.   Maximianus VI[10]
             (1,738,3.25) Cass. Aq.
             VindPost.

LAWS: *CJ* 9.1.17 (9.i); 7.72.9 (19.viii)   Diocletianus VII et
                                            Maximianus VI Augg.

INSCR.:   **ROME:** *IGUR* I 191 = *IG* XIV   DD.NN. Diocletianus Aug.
             1026 (27.iii; Gk.)   VII et Maximianus Aug. VI

             AFRICA: *CIL* VIII 11532 = *ILS*
             5649 (Byzacena, Ammaedara; 1.iv)

---

[10]As usual, the numerals are corrupt in some: VII & VI, Chr. 354 (praef.); VI & VI, Cass. Aq.; VI & V, VindPr., VindPost., Prosp.; VII & V, Hyd.

Orientis

FASTI:	Heracl. Theo (Aug. 2x)	Diocletianus (Aug.) VII et Maximianus (Aug.) VI
	Pasch.	Diocletianus Aug. VII et Maximianus Herculius Aug. VI
	Scal.	Diocletianus et Maximianus cc.
LAWS:	none	
PAPYRI:	*SB* VIII 9833.1 (2.v; Impp.); *P.Laur.* III 67.1 (17.vii; Impp.?); *P.Oxy.* IX 1204.1,11 (19.viii; in 1, Impp.); *P.Cair.Isid.* 3.1, 4.1, 5.1 (all 11.ix); *PSI* XIII 1338.1* (11.x; Impp.); *P.Panop. Beatty* 2.40 (31.xii; cf. index for other refs.); *P.Laur.* IV 154.10 (Impp.?)	DD.NN. (Impp.) Diocletianus Aug. VII et Maximianus Aug. VI
	P.Mich. X 593 ii.16; iii.2 (doc. 312; iii.2 om. Max.)	Diocletianus VII et Maximianus VI
COINS:	*RIC* VI 615.20-22 (Antioch): consular solidi of Diocletian	consul VII
	RIC VI 614-15.17-19 (Antioch): consular solidi of Maximian	consul VI

NOTES:

For the omission of Maximianus in one place in the Michigan papyrus, cf. 304.

Occidentis

FASTI:	Chr. 354 (fast.,praef.) Hyd. VindPr. Prosp. Cass. Aq.	Constantius III et Maximianus III[11]
	VindPost.	Constantinus Caes. et Maximianus
LAWS:	none	
INSCR.:	**ROME:** *CIL* VI 2141 (19.xii; om. DD.NN.); *ICUR* n.s. IV 9547 = *ILCV* 2795	DD.NN. Constantius Caesar III et Maximianus Caesar III
COINS:	*RIC* VI 232 (Trier)	Constantius with cos. bust

[11]IV & III, Aq.

Orientis

FASTI: Heracl. (om. Caes. III after   Constantinus Caesar III et
          Max.) Theo   Maximianus Caesar III

          Pasch.   Constantius Caesar III et
                                              Maximianus Iovius III

          Scal.   Constantius et Max. cc.

LAWS: *CJ* 7.22.2 (Antioch, 26.iii)   Constantius III et
                                              Maximianus III Caesares

PAPYRI: *P.Panop.Beatty* 2.37,58   DD.NN. Constantius et
          (1.i; doc. 30.i); *P.Sakaon*   Maximianus nobb. Caess. III
          2.1 (14.i); 3.1 (i); *P.Col.* VII
          179.1 (5.ii); *SB* IV 7338.3
          (vi-vii); *P.Cair.Isid.* 112
          (i-viii); *P.Oxy.* XLIII 3141.1
          (i-viii); *P.Oxy.* XLVI 3301.1

          P.Mich. X 593 ii.6 (doc. 312)   Constantius et
                                              Maximianus III

COINS: Kent, *Roman Coins*, no.577   Galerius on obv.,
          (Thessalonica; the plural   consul Caess. on rev.
          Caess. points to the joint
          consulate of the Caesars Galerius
          and Constantius in 300 [or 302])

Occidentis

FASTI: Chr. 354 (fast.,praef.) Hyd.   Titianus II et Nepotianus
                VindPr. Prosp. Aq. Cass.[12]

LAWS: None

INSCR.:   **ROME:** *CIL* VI 2143 (6.v)   Titianus II et
                                                         Nepotianus

NOTES:

Titianus' long career is discussed in *PLRE* I 919-20 and Barnes, *New Empire* 99; he was proc. Africae 295-96 and PVR 305-306. He was the last man to be officially styled cos. II on the basis of an early suffect consulate (date unknown). Three papyri are broken at the point where Titianus' iteration numeral would have been given (the fourth, *P.Oxy.* 2859, has a small lacuna which cannot have contained the numeral), but the absence of the numeral from all eastern documents makes us doubt that it actually stood in any of the papyri. Nepotianus is otherwise unknown, but presumably the father of Nepotianus cos. 336.

[12]Only Hyd. and Chr. 354 (praef.) give the iteration numeral.

Orientis

FASTI:	Heracl. Theo Pasch. Scal.	Titianus et Nepotianus
LAWS:	*CJ* 3.28.25 (Antioch, 4.vii); 4.12.4 (no prov., 23.viii)	Titianus et Nepotianus
PAPYRI:	*P.Oxy.* XLVI 3304.3 (6.vi); *P.Flor.* I 3.23* (vii-viii); *PSI* IX 1037.5 (i-viii)	Postumius Titianus et Virius Nepotianus
	P.Oxy. XXXVIII 2859.30 (10.xi)	Titianus et Nepotianus
INSCR.:	**ASIA:** *AE* 1973, 526b (Aphrodisias; 1.ix);	Titianus et Nepotianus
	I.Ephesos VII 2 3803 = *SEG* XXX 1385 (Hypaipa; fragm.)	Postumius Titianus [et Virius Nepotianus]
	SYRIA: *IGRR* III 1268* (Rîmet el Luhf)	Postumius Titianus et Virius Nepotianus

Occidentis

FASTI: Chr. 354 (fast.,praef.) Hyd.   Constantius IV et
                VindPr. Prosp. Aq. Cass.   Maximianus IV

                VindPost.   Const. Caes. IV et
                                                          Max. IV

LAWS: none

INSCR.:   **ROME:** *ICUR* n.s. I 1249* =   DD.NN. Constantius et
                ILCV 4366B (9.ix);   Maximianus (nobb.
                ICUR n.s. III 8717 =   Caess.) IV
                ILCV 4158 (12.xii)

                DALMATIA: *CIL* III 1967
                (Salona; 14.i-1.ii; om. DD.NN.;
                adds nobb. Caess.)

COINS: *RIC* VI 234 (Lugdunum)   Constantius and Galerius
                                                          with cos. busts

Orientis

FASTI: Heracl. (Max. numeral I)   Constantinus Caes. IV et
             Pasch. (Iovius) Theo   Maximianus (Iovius)
                                                   Caes. IV

             Scal.   Constantinus et
                                                 Maximus nobb. Caess. IV

LAWS: none

PAPYRI: *P.NYU* 20.1 = *P.Mich.* XII,   DD.NN. Constantius et
             pp.38-40 (i-iii); *P.Corn.*   Maximianus nobb. Caess. IV
             20.1, etc. (23.ix); *P.Cair.Isid.*
             41.20 (ref. on 31.x to 31.v)

Occidentis

FASTI: Chr. 354 (fast.,praef.)   Diocletianus VIII et
             Hyd. VindPr. Prosp.   Maximianus VII[13]
             Aq. Cass. VindPost.

LAWS: none

INSCR.:   **ITALY:** *AE* 1968, 81* =   DD.NN. Diocletianus VIII
             CIL XIV 132 (Ostia; om.   et Maximianus VII Augg.
             DD.NN.)

             DALMATIA: *CIL* III 1968a (Salona;
             1.ii); *AE* 1922, 47 (Salona)

             AFRICA: *AE* 1942, 81 (Ain-
             Naimia, Algeria)

             PANNONIA SUP.: *CIL* III 10981 =   DD.NN. VIII et VII Augg.
             Röm.Inschr.Ung. III 699 (O-Szöny;
             15.vii)

COINS: *RIC* VI 166.27 (Trier), 457.22,   Consul VIII
             458.29 (Siscia): consular
             solidi and half-solidus of
             Diocletian

             RIC VI 167.28-30 (Trier), 457.21   Consul VII
             (Siscia), 615.27 (Antioch):
             consular solidi of Maximian

OTHER: Excerpts from acts of Munatius   Diocletianus VIII et
             Felix, curator coloniae   Maximianus VII
             Cirtensium, cited in trial of
             Silvanus before Zenophilus
             (*CSEL* 26, p.185) (Cirta, 19.v)

             Passion of St. Felix, Bp. of
             Thibiuca, 1 (Musurillo, *Acts of the
             Christian Martyrs*, p.266) (5.vi)

[13]VII & VII, Aq. Cass.; VII & VI, Prosp., VindPost.; VII & V, VindPr.

Orientis

FASTI: Heracl. Theo (Aug. 2x)   Diocletianus (Aug.) VIII
                                                    et Maximianus (Aug.) VII

        Pasch.   Diocletianus Aug. VIII et
                                                    Maximianus Herculius

        Scal.   Diocletianus et Maximus
                                                    nobb. Augg. VII

LAWS: *CJ* 2.30.4 (Nicomedia, 6.i);   Diocletianus VIII et
        3.3.4 (Joppe [cf. Barnes,   Maximianus VII Augg.
        New Empire 55 n.40]; 22.xi)

PAPYRI: *P.Corn.* 20(a).2,21* (23.v);   DD.NN. (Impp.)
        SB VIII 9917.1 (15.vii);   Diocletianus VIII
        P.Wisc. II 61.1 (24.xii;   et Maximianus VII. Augg.
        Impp.); *SB* XIV 11614.1*;
        P.Oxy. LIV 3727.1 (Impp.);
        P.Mich. X 592 ii.4 (doc. 311-324;
        Lat.); *ChLA* IX 401.4 (Lat.)

INSCR.:   **SYRIA:** *LBW* 2514 (Habiba)   Diocletianus VIII et
                                                      Maximianus VII Augg.

Occidentis

FASTI: Chr. 354 (fast.,praef.,feriale eccl.Rom. 71,12.72, 11, episc. 75,34, gener. 140,19) Hyd. VindPr. Prosp. Aq. Cass. VindPost.   Diocletianus IX et Maximianus VIII[14]

LAWS: None

INSCR.:   **ROME:** *NotScav* 1919, 105   DD.NN. Diocletianus IX et Maximianus Aug. VIII

COINS: *RIC* VI 457.24 (Siscia): consular solidus of Diocletian   Consul VIIII

    RIC VI 457.23 (Siscia), 616.30 (Antioch): consular solidi of Maximian   Consul VIII

OTHER: Augustine, *Breviculus Collationis cum Donatistis* (CSEL 53, p.81) (12.ii, retrosp. ref.)   Diocletianus IX et Maximianus VIII

    Acta Agapes, Irenes et Chiones 7 (Musurillo, *Acts of the Christian Martyrs*, p.292) (Thessalonica, 1.iv; Gk.)   Diocletianus Aug. IX et Maximianus Aug. VIII

    Acta Eupli 1,2 (Lanata, *Atti dei Martiri*, pp.222-23) (Catania, 29.iv, 12.viii; Gk.)   DD.NN. Diocletianus IX et Maximianus VIII

    Passio sanctae Crispinae 1 (Musurillo, p.302) (Thebeste, 5.xii)   Diocletianus IX et Maximianus <VIII> Augg.

[14]VIII & VIII, Aq., Cass.; VIII & VII, Prosp., VindPost.; VIII & VI, VindPr.

Orientis

FASTI: Heracl. Theo (Aug.)   Diocletianus IX et
                Scal. (Diocl. VIII)   Maximianus (Aug.) VIII

                Pasch.   Diocletianus Aug. IX et
                                                       Maximianus Herculius VIII

LAWS: *CJ* 9.1.18 (no prov., 27.ii);   Diocletianus IX et
                3.28.26 (Nicomedia, 28.viii)   Maximianus VIII Augg.

PAPYRI: *P.Oxy.* XVIII 2187.1* (13.i;   DD.NN. Impp. Diocletianus
                frag.); *P.Oxy.* XXXVI 2770.1   IX et Maximianus VIII
                (26.i); *P.Oxy.* XXXIII 2673.1   Augg.
                (5.ii); *P.Oxy.* XII 1551.1 (ii-
                iii)*; *SB* VI 9269.1 (18.ix); *CPR*
                VII 14.8-9* (doc.d. 28.iv.305);
                P.Mich. X 592 ii.11 (doc. 311-
                324; Lat.); *P.Vindob.Bosw.* 5.2

                P.Mich. X 593 iii.3 (doc. 312)   Diocletianus IX

OTHER: Zosimus 2.7

NOTES:

   We do not know if Maximian's absence from *P.Mich.* X 593 is a result of short-form retrospective reference or a reflection of official *damnatio memoriae*; cf. 292, 299, and 308, where the same phenomenon occurs.

Occidentis

FASTI: Chr. 354 (fast.,praef.)   Constantius V et
                Hyd. VindPr. Prosp.   Maximianus V[15]
                Cass. Aq. VindPost.

LAWS: None

INSCR.:   **ROME:** *ILCV* 4366B (14.iv)   DD.NN. Caesares V et V

                CIL VI 497 = *ILS* 4145 (14.iv)   DD.NN. Constantius et
                                                           Maximianus nobb. Caess. V

COINS: *RIC* VI 457.20 (Siscia), 622.65a   Consul V
                (Antioch): consular solidi of
                Constantine

                RIC VI 472.149 (Siscia), 622.65b   Consul V
                (Antioch): consular solidi of
                Galerius

OTHER: Augustine, *Breviculus Collationis*   p. eorundem (Diocl. IX
                cum Donatistis (CSEL 53, p.81)   et Max. VIII) cons.
                (5.iii, retrosp. ref.)

[15]Hyd. omits Max. by haplography.

Orientis

<u>FASTI:</u>	Heracl. (Const. VII) Theo	Constantinus Caes. V et Maximianus Caes. V
	Pasch.	Constantius Caesar V et Maximianus Iovius V
	Scal.	Diocletianus IX et Constantius V nobb. Augg.
<u>LAWS:</u>	*CJ* 5.42.5 (no prov., 22.xii)	Constantius V et Maximianus V Augg.
<u>PAPYRI:</u>	*P.Sakaon* 59.1 (11.iii); *P.Wisc.* I 32.1 (26.iv); *CPR* VII 14.6 (28.iv); *P.Oxy.* XLIII 3143.1 (27.v/14.vi); *P.Oxy.* VI 895.1 (v-vi); *P.Oxy.* XXXVI 2766.1	DD.NN. Constantius et Maximianus nobb. Caess. V
	P.Laur. IV 168; *P.Oxy.* XXXIII 2665.1 (Impp.; or 306)	DD.NN. (Impp.) Constantius et Maximianus Augg. V
<u>INSCR.:</u>	**GREECE:** *IG*[2] II-III 1121 (cf. *CIL* III 12134) (Athens; 19.ix)	Constantius et Maximianus Augg. V

Occidentis

FASTI: Chr. 354 (fast,praef.)   Constantius VI et
                Hyd. VindPr. Prosp.   Maximianus VI[16]
                Aq. Cass. VindPost.

LAWS: none

INSCR.:   **ITALY:** *AE* 1961, 240   DD.NN. Constantius Aug. VI
                (Grosseto, Reg. VII; 7.i)   et Maximianus Aug. VI

COINS: *RIC* VI 492-93 (Serdica)   Constantius (obv.), rev.
                                                          Consul Augg. NN.

                RIC VI 493 (Serdica)   Galerius (obv.), rev.
                                                          Consul Augg. NN.

                RIC VI 623.66 (Antioch):   Consul VI
                consular solidus of Galerius

NOTES:

Constantius and Galerius marked their joint elevation to the rank of Augustus on 1.v.305 by taking another joint consulate in 306.

[16]Hyd. om. Const. VI by haplography.

Orientis

FASTI: Heracl. Theo (Aug. 2x)   Constantius (Aug.) VI et
Maximianus (Aug.) VI

               Pasch.   Constantius Caesar VI et
Maximianus Iovius VI

LAWS: none

PAPYRI: *P.Sakaon* 71.1 (6.iii); *CPR*   DD.NN. (Impp.) Constantius
V 6.1,20 (20.iii; om. in 1   et Maximianus Augg. VI
Augg. VI); *P.Oxy.* LIV 3728.1
(ii-iii; Impp.); *P.Lips.* 6.1
(16.iv); *P.Oxy.* VIII 1104.1 (29.v;
Impp.); *P.Sakaon* 60.2 (25.vi);
P.Oxy. I 102.1 (13.x; Impp.);
BGU I 286.1; *PSI* VI 716.1
(frag., see introd.); possibly
P.Oxy. XXXIII 2665.1 (Impp.;
or 305)

147

307

(a) Galerius Maximianus Aug. VII et Constantinus Caesar (i to *ca* ix)
(b) **Maximianus Aug. IX et Constantinus Caesar** (*ca* ix to xii)
(c) **Galerius Maximianus Aug. VII et Maximinus Caesar** (i-iv)
(d) **post sextum consulatum** (iv-xii)

Occidentis

FASTI:	Chr. 354 (praef.) (1)	Maximianus VII et Maximinus
	Chr. 354 (praef.) (2) (ex mense Aprili)	post VI consulatum quod est novies et Constantinus
	Chr. 354 (fast.) Hyd.	novies et Constantinus... quod est post sextum cons.
	Prosp. Aq. Cass. VindPost.	Diocletianus IX et Constantinus
	VindPr.	Diocletianus IX et Maximianus VII
LAWS:	none[17]	
INSCR.:	**ROME:** *ICUR* n.s. IV 9549 = *ILCV* 4428 (16.x-1.xi); *ICUR* I 29 = *ILCV* 873 (6-8/10-13.xii; om. 'cons.')[18]	post sextum consulatum
COINS:	*RIC* VI 498.27-28 (Serdica): consular gold multiple of Galerius	VII conss.

[17]See however Barnes, *New Empire* 69 n.102.
[18]See Barnes, *New Empire* 94 n.14.

Orientis

FASTI:	Theo Heracl. (om. Aug.)	Severus Aug. et Maximinus Caes.
	Pasch.	Novius Constantinus Aug. solus
LAWS:	none	
PAPYRI:	*P.Sakaon* 64.1 (3.iv; om. nob.; I); *P.Oxy.* LIV 3729.2 (4.v; Imp.); *P.Oxy.* XLIV 3192.1 (9.v); *P.Mil.* I 55.1 (29.ix; Imp.)	DD.NN. (Imp.) Severus Aug. et Maximinus nob. Caes. (I)
	P.Mich. X 593 ii.21 (doc. 312)	Severus et Maximinus
	P.Mert. I 31.12,19 (24.xii); *P.Col.* VII 138.9 (24.xii)	D.N. Maximinus Caesar
COINS:	*RIC* VI 496.16 (Serdica): consular solidus of Severus	Consul(atus) Augg.NN.
	RIC VI 625.78 (Antioch): consular solidus of Severus	Consul

NOTES:

(a) were the consuls originally proclaimed by Constantine; (b) his second proclamation after his alliance with Maximian, emerging from retirement. (c) were the consuls originally proclaimed by Maxentius in Italy but subsequently repudiated after his break with Galerius in April. (d) that is to say, p.c. 306; Maxentius evidently proclaimed no new consuls after repudiating Galerius and Maximinus. The changing situation is well mirrored in the informative note in Chr. 354 (praef.): "Maximiano VII et Maximino. Ex mense Aprili factum est <post> sextum consulatum, quod est novies [sc. Maximiano] et Constantino." The comical error in Pasch. clearly results from a misunderstanding of this entry.

Severus and Maximinus were the consuls recognized by the senior Augustus Galerius in the East, signalling their elevation to the rank of Caesar on 1.v.305. See further Barnes, *New Empire* 93-94. It is not clear why Severus was dropped entirely from the papyri after his death, for this was not the normal practice.

(a) **Diocletianus Aug. X et Galerius Maximianus Aug. VII**
(b) **consules quos iusserint DD.NN. Augusti** (1.i-19.iv)
(c) **Maxentius Aug. et Valerius Romulus** (from 20.iv)

Occidentis

FASTI:	Chr. 354 (praef.) (1)	Consules quos iusserint DD.NN. Augg.
	Chr. 354 (praef.) (2) (ex xii k. Mai.)	Maxentius et Romulus quod est X et Maximianus VII
	Hyd.	Item X et Maximianus quod est Maxentius et Romulus
	Chr. 354 (fast.)	X et Maximianus VII
	Chr. 354 (episc. p.76) VindPr. Prosp. Aq. Cass. VindPost.	Diocletianus Aug. X Maximianus Aug. VII[19]
LAWS:	none	
INSCR.:	ROME: *ICUR* n.s. V 13887 (5.v); *ICUR* n.s. VI 15767 (6.xii; om. Aug.; Gk.)	Maxentius Aug.
COINS:	*RIC* VI 498 (Serdica)	Gal. Maximianus Aug. VII conss.
	RIC VI 295.102-103 (Ticinum): consular bronzes of Maxentius	Imp. Maxentius P.F. Aug. cons.
	RIC VI 325.123-124 (Aquileia): consular bronzes of Maxentius	Consul
	RIC VI 372.167-169, 374.179, 375.188 (Rome): consular gold multiples, solidus, and silver of Maxentius	Felix process. consulat. Aug. N.

NOTES: Galerius' solution to the crisis of authority was to recall Diocletian from retirement and proclaim himself and Diocletian consuls (*pater* stressing seniority to all other members of the imperial college). Constantine recognized this arrangement (a). According to Barnes (*Constantine and Eusebius* 32), Maxentius "adopted a conciliatory posture"; that is to say, he interprets the [Continued on next page]

---

[19]Aq. Cass. Prosp. om. Aug.; VindPr., VindPost., Max. VIII; Chr. 354 (episc.) om. numeral for Max.

Orientis

FASTI: Heracl. Theo (Aug. 2x; Max. IX)   Diocletianus (Aug.) X
et Maximinus (Aug.) VII

    Pasch.   Item X et Maximianus
Galerius

    Scal.   Diocletianus X et
Maximianus VIII
invictissimi

LAWS: none

PAPYRI: *P.Lond.* III 1133 (p.lix)   DD.NN. (Impp.)
(1.i); *P.Grenf.* II 75.19   Diocletianus pater Augg. X
(6.i); *P.Sakaon* 15.8,18,27,36   et Galerius Valerius
(3-26.ii); *P.Grenf.* II 72.11*   Maximianus Aug. VII
(18.ii); *P.Cair.Isid.* 97.15
(iv); *P.Oxy.* XIV 1645.1 (31.viii);
P.Lond.inv. 2226.21 (29.ix; in
J. Lallemand, *L'adm.civ.* 265);
P.Panop. 2.10 (22.x); *P.Mich.*
XV 720.1 (ix-xii); *P.Oxy.* XXXIII
2674.1 (Impp.); *P.Lips.* 18.1;
P.Mich. X 592 ii.15 (doc.
311-324; Lat.)

    P.Mich. X 593 iii.5,(6) (doc. 312)   Diocletianus pater Augg. X

    P.Mich. X 593 iii.9 (doc. 312)   Diocletianus X

    P.Panop. 15.4,11,14 (26 and   X et VII
29.xii)

COINS: *RIC* VI 625.79 (Antioch): consular   Consul VII
solidus of Galerius

NOTES: [continued] formula given by the prefect list of Chr. 354 as implying that Maxentius too initially recognized Galerius' consuls. But if this is all he did, why not just publish their names in the ordinary way-- which would not have prevented him from subsequently proclaiming new consuls of his own (as he had done the previous year)? By the fifth century, when it was normal for one consul to be announced later than the other, the equivalent formula *qui nuntiatus fuerit* normally implies no more than that the name of *one* of the two consuls has not yet been announced but is still expected. It would surely be wrong to [Continued on the next page]

Occidentis

FASTI:	Chr. 354 (praef.) Hyd. (1)	Maxentius II et Romulus II
	Chr. 354 (fast., episc. p.76,2) Hyd. (2) VindPr. Prosp.	p.c. X et VII
	Aq. Cass.	p.c. Diocletiani X et Maximi VII
LAWS:	none	
INSCR.:	none	
COINS:	*RIC* VI 295.104, 107 (Ticinum): consular bronzes of Maxentius	Imp. Maxentius P.F. Aug. cons. II
	RIC VI 326.119-120, 125-126 (Aquileia): Consular bronzes of Maxentius	Cons. II
	RIC VI 382-257 (Rome): posthumous consular bronze of Romulus	Divo Romulo N.V. bis cons.

NOTES: [Continued from preceding page] interpret *coss. quos iusserint DD.NN. Augusti* as an official proclamation by Maxentius himself, implying that he was meekly waiting for the proclamation of his colleagues. In his own domain Maxentius was one of the Augusti here designated. It is surely just one of several provisional formulas, no different in meaning or use from *qui nuntiati fuerint* or even the use of the p.c. of the preceding year, implying rather that Maxentius has not yet made up his mind. It is the orders of Maxentius as much as of the other Augusti that are being awaited. In practice, it amounted to a provisional non-recognition of Galerius' consuls though less final and provocative than proclamation of his own instead, since it left him free to proclaim Galerius' later if he chose. In the event, in April Maxentius broke with his father Maximian and proclaimed himself and his son Romulus consuls. On Romulus, see Barnes, *New Empire* 99. For the omission of Maximianus in *P.Mich.* X 593, cf. 304.

On 11.xi.308, after conferring with Diocletian and Maximian, Galerius appointed Licinius Augustus, implicitly rejecting the claims of Constantine and Maximinus, who were left as Caesars (cf. *ILS* 659) and Maxentius, not recognized at all (Barnes, *New Empire* 6). In an attempt to conciliate Constantine, Galerius proclaimed him consul together with the new Augustus Licinius (c), as Caesar but with the compromise title "filius Augustorum" (shared with Maximinus--cf. Barnes, *Constantine and Eusebius* 33--but not Maxentius). Maxentius replied by proclaiming himself and his son again (b). Less provocatively but nonetheless firmly refusing to accept Galerius' ranking, Constantine simply observed the p.c. of 308 (a). As a consequence, in 312 Constantine styled himself only cos. II, continuing to ignore Galerius' nomination for 309.

Orientis

FASTI: Theo (I with each) Heracl.   Licinius Aug. et
           (adds VII after Const.)   Constantinus

           Scal.   Licinius et Constantinus
                                                   I novv. Augg.

LAWS: none

PAPYRI: *P.Panop.* 15.16 (16.i); *P.Sakaon*   DD.NN. Valerius Licinianus
           89.14 = *P.Stras.* 577 (21.i);   Licinius Aug. et
           P.Cair.Isid. 90.15 (2.iii; om.   Fl. Valerius Constantinus
           Val. 1st time); *P.Sakaon* 16.1   filius Augg.
           (29.iii); *P.Cair.Isid.* 8.1
           (14.vi); *P.Oslo* III 86.5 (19.vi);
           P.Oxy. XXXIII 2667.15 (22.vi);
           M.Chr. 196.15* (2.vii);
           P.Cair.Isid. 47.48 (26.viii);
           P.Hib. II 219.16 (viii-ix);
           P.Cair.Isid. 117.8 (15.x; om. Val.
           2x); *P.Oxy.* XLVI 3270.1 (14.ix-
           15.x); *P.Col.* VII 141.91 (24.xii?);
           P.Berl.Leihg. 21.13 (31.xii);
           P.Cair.Isid. 9.15 (xii); *P.Cair.
           Isid.* 86.13; *YCS* 28 (1985)
           120.10,22,26

           SB XVI 12289.24 (1.viii;   DD.NN. Licinius Aug. et
           formula in line 1 frag.);   Constantinus fil. Augg.
           P.Cair.Isid. 91.15

COINS: *RIC* VI 630.101-102 (Antioch):   Consul
           Consular solidi of Licinius

           RIC VI 513.27 (Thessalonica):   Consul. DD.NN.
           consular solidus of Licinius

           RIC VI 513.28 (Thessalonica):   Consul. DD.NN.
           consular solidus of Constantine

(a) II post consulatum X et VII
(b) Maxentius Aug. III

Occidentis

<u>FASTI</u>:	Chr. 354 (praef.) Hyd. (1)	Maxentius III
	Chr. 354 (fast.) Hyd. (2) Prosp.	anno II p.c. X et VII
	Aq. (om. II) Cass.	II p.c. Diocletiani X et Maximi VII
<u>LAWS</u>:	none	
<u>INSCR.</u>:	**ROME:** *ICUR* n.s. V 13098 = *ILCV* 3355 (6-13.xii)	Maxentius III
	NORICUM: *CIL* III 5565 = *ILS* 664 (Prutting, Bavaria; 27.vi)	Andronicus et Probus
	PANNONIA INF.: *CIL* III 3335 (Duna-Pentale)	
<u>COINS</u>:	*RIC* VI 378.215-217, 383.264 (Rome): consular bronzes of Maxentius	Felix proces. cons. III Aug. N.
	RIC VI 635.127b (Antioch): consular solidus of Constantine ref. to 309	Consul

<u>NOTES</u>:

Once again, Maxentius proclaimed himself (b), this time (his son having died in 309) as sole consul, while Constantine continued to repudiate Galerius' consuls (c) by the less provocative device of a p.c. (a).

Orientis

FASTI:	Theo Heracl.	Andronicus et Probus
LAWS:	none	
PAPYRI:	*P.Cair.Isid.* 95.11 (12.i; cos. for p.c.)	p.c. DD.NN. Valerii Liciniani Licinii Aug. et Fl. Valerii Constantini fil. Augg.
	P.Sakaon 1.1 (27.ii); *P.Cair.Isid.* 50.13,29,44 (16.v); *P.Heid.* IV 323 A.12, B.14, C.14 (15-24.v); *P.Cair. Isid.* 127.14 (29.vii); *P.Cair. Isid.* 118.9 (i-viii); *P.Col.* VII 141.99 (18.x; Statius); *P.Panop.* 3.12 (x-xi); *P.Cair.Isid.* 69.32; *P.Panop.* 20.15 (Statius; om. vv.cc. praeff.); *P.Panop.* 24.4 (doc. *ca* 323-326; Statius; om. praeff.); *SB* XIV 12167.4* (frag.; om. Tatius, Pompeius; doc. 314)	Tatius Andronicus et Pompeius Probus vv.cc. praeff.

NOTES:

Nothing else is known of Andronicus and Probus beyond the prefectures attested for them by the formula of the papyri quoted above. They are otherwise attested only by the two eastern lists Theo and Heracl. and, interestingly, by inscriptions from Noricum and Pannonia. For the political allegiances of these two provinces, cf. Barnes, *NE* 198-99.

311

(a) **Galerius Maximianus Aug. VIII** (until v) et **Maximinus Aug. II**
(b) **consules quos iusserint DD.NN. Augg.** (i-ix)
(c) **Rufinus et Volusianus** (ix-xii)

Occidentis

FASTI:	Chr. 354 (praef.)	consules quos iusserint DD.NN. Augg.
	Chr. 354 (praef.) (ex mense Sept.; confusion with 347?)	Rufinus et Eusebius
	Chr. 354 (episc., p.76)	Maximiano VIII solo, quod fuit m. Sept. Volusiano et Rufino
	Chr. 354 (fast.)	Maximianus VIII solus
	Hyd.	Maximianus VIII...quod est Rufino et Volusiano
	Prosp. Aq. Cass.	Maximianus VIII et Licinius
	VindPr.	Maximianus VIII et Constantius
	VindPost.	Constantinus II et Maximianus IX
LAWS:	none	
INSCR.:	**NORICUM:** *CIL* III 4796 = *ILS* 4197	Divus Maximianus VIII et (D.N.) Maximinus II Augg.
	HUNGARY: *AE* 1937, 158 (date only) and 232* = *FIRA* I 93 (Brigetio; 10.vi; adds D.N. before Maximinus)	

NOTES: Maximinus was finally proclaimed Augustus with Galerius' consent, and both emperors took the consulate together (d), this time recognized by Constantine (a), though if the interpretation given above (under 308) of the formula in Chr. 354 is correct, not by Maxentius. In September, Maxentius nominated two senators, perhaps in a belated attempt to conciliate the aristocracy of Rome (cf. Barnes, *Constantine and Eusebius* 37). Once again, Maxentius' changes of policy are clearly reflected in the Roman Chr. 354. It is interesting to note that Galerius' name was dropped from the eastern formula [Continued]

156

Orientis

FASTI:	Theo (no numerals) Heracl.	Maximianus VIII et Maximinus II
	Pasch.	Maximianus Herculius VIII et Galerius Maximus
LAWS:	none	
PAPYRI:	*Aegyptus* 63 (1983) 58.10* (2-5.i)	[p.c. Tatii Androni]ci et Pompei Probi vv.cc.
	P.Cair.Isid. 119.9 (23.ii); *P.Oxy.* XIV 1708.20 (3.iv; om. Gal. Val. 2x); *P.Cair.Isid.* 146.1 (14.iv); *SB* VI 9214.1 (vii; om. 2nd Aug.); *P.Athen.* 40.3; *P.Coll.Youtie* II 79.15*	DD.NN. Galerius Valerius Maximianus Aug. VIII et Galerius Valerius Maximinus Aug. II
	P.Cair.Isid. 120.10 (26.viii); *P.Mich.* X 592 ii.18 (doc. 311-324; Lat.)	D.N. Galerius Valerius Maximinus Aug. II
	P.Corn. 13.24 (12.vii); *P.Oxy.* XXXIII 2668.23 (22.viii); *BGU* III 928.24; *P.Rainer Cent.* 83.13	D.N. Maximinus Aug. II
	P.Cair.Isid. 13.25,32; 16.3 (both 4.xii)	Maximinus II
COINS:	*RIC* VI 563.62 (Nicomedia); 635.127a (Antioch): consular solidi of Maximinus	Consul
	RIC VI 635.128 (Antioch): consular solidus of Galerius	Consul VIII

NOTES: [Continued] on his death *ca* May, 311 (see the papyri, but contrast "*Divus* Maximianus" on the dedication from Noricum), presumably an act of revenge by Maximinus, who seized Galerius' domains. Rufinus is probably Aradius Rufinus, Maxentius' PVR in 312 (though see Barnes, *New Empire* 100); Volusianus' distinguished career (suff. *ca* 280, PPO 309, PVR 310-311) continued under Constantine (PVR 313-315, cos. II 314): cf. Barnes, *New Empire* 100. "The order of names [Rufinus/Volusianus] cannot be established with certainty": Barnes, *NE* 94 n.18.

312 (a) **Constantinus Aug. II et Licinius Aug. II**
(b) **Maxentius Aug. IV** (until 28.x)

Occidentis

FASTI: Chr. 354 (praef.) Hyd. (Max. III)   Maxentius IV

Chr. 354 (fast., pasch., praef.)   Constantinus II et
Hyd. Prosp. Cass. Aq.   Licinius II

VindPr.   Constantius II et Licinius

LAWS: *FragVat* 32 (no prov., 29.viii)   Constantinus et
Licinius Augg. II

INSCR.: none

NOTES:

Faced with hostility from Maxentius in 311, Constantine offered Licinius his sister's hand in marriage. The result of this compact was the joint proclamation of Constantine and Licinius as consuls, Constantine now not only recognized as Augustus but as the senior of the two. This arrangement was recognized by all the emperors (a, c) save Maxentius (b). Maxentius' IV consulate was naturally abolished after his defeat by Constantine on 28.x.312.

Orientis

<u>FASTI:</u>	Theo Heracl.	Constantinus II et Licinius II
	Pasch.	Constantinus Aug. II Licinius[20]
	Scal.	Licinius et Constantius II
<u>LAWS:</u>	none	
<u>PAPYRI:</u>	*P.Sakaon* 18.1 (28.iv); *P.Princ.Roll* i.19 (22.v); *P.Oxy.* LIV 3732.1, 3733.1, 3734.1, 3735.1 (all 25.v); *P.Cair.Isid.* 41.93,106 (15.viii in 106; in 93, Lic. Lic. rev.); *PSI* VII 820.1 (29.viii); *P.Oxy.* LIV 3737.1, 3738.1, 3739.1, 3740.1 (27.ix); *P.Oxy.* LIV 3736.1	DD.NN. Fl. Valerius Constantinus et Licinianus Licinius Augg. II
	P.Flor. I 31.13 (22.ii; Impp.); *P.Cair.Isid.* 94.17 (4.v); *P.Sakaon* 38.31 (17.viii; Lat.); *P.Sakaon* 5.62 = *P.Stras.* I 45 (22.viii); *P.NYU* 4a.13 (4.xi); *P.Cair.Isid.* 121.11 (17.ix); 52.8 (20.x); *P.Cair.Isid.* 11.69 (4.xii); *P.Princ.Roll* ii.16 (viii-xii); *SB* XVI 12340.10; *P.Athen.* 40.8-9	DD.NN. Constantinus et Licinius (Impp.) Augg. II

[20]Also: Const. Aug. III et Lic. II.; the failure to include two years has messed up the count.

159

Occidentis

FASTI:	Chr. 354 (fast.,pasch.,praef.) Hyd. VindPr. Prosp. Cass.	Constantinus III et Licinius III[21]
	VindPost.	Constantinus III et Anianus
LAWS:	*CTh* 10.10.1, 13.10.1 (Rome, 18.i); 10.8.1 (Milan, 10.iii)	Constantinus Aug. III et Licinius III
	FragVat 34 (21.vii)	Constantinus Aug. III
INSCR.:	**ROME:** *CIL* VI 507 (15.iv)	DD.NN. Constantinus et Maximinus Augg. III
	IG XIV 956B.23 = *IGUR* I 246 (retrosp. ref.; date of doc. uncert.; Gk.)	D.N. Fl. Valerius Constantinus maximus III Aug.
	ITALY: *AE* 1969/1970, 119 (Gaeta, Reg. I; 22.i)	DD.NN. Constantinus Aug. III et Maximinus Aug. III
OTHER:	Augustine, *Epp.* 88.3, quoted at *Gesta Conl.Carth.* 3.220 (15.iv; Barnes, *New Empire* 241, argues for restoring DD.NN. Constantinus et Maximinus Augg. III)	D.N. Constantinus Aug. III
	Synod at Rome (Von Soden, *Urkunden* p.15 no.13) (2.x; p.14 gives Const. IV et Lic. III)	Constantinus ter et Licinius iterum

[21]Lic. II, VindPr.

(a) **Maximinus Aug. III et Constantinus Aug. III** (i-iv)
(b) **Constantinus Aug. III et Licinius Aug. III** (*ca* viii-xii)

Orientis

FASTI: Theo   Constantinus III et
                                                                    Licinius III

                 Heracl.   Constantinus III et
 Maximinus III
 Constantinus IV et
 Licinius III

     Pasch.   Constantinus Aug. IV et
 Licinius III

LAWS: none

PAPYRI: *P.Oxy.* XLVI 3305.1 (16.iii; Gal.   DD.NN. (Galerius Valerius)
Val., Fl. Val.; Impp.); *P.Princ.*   Maximinus et (Fl.
Roll iii.1 (17.vi); *P.Oxy.*   Valerius) Constantinus
XLIII 3144.1 (23.vii; Gal.   (Impp.) Augg. III
Val., Fl. Val.); *P.Sakaon* 6.13 =
PSI IX 1038 (28.vii); *P.Ryl.* IV
619.7 (frag.)

     P.Oxy. LIV 3741 introd.   D.N. Fl. Valerius
                                           Constantinus Aug. III

     P.Cair.Isid. 103.20 (13.ix);   DD.NN. Constantinus et
BGU II 408.19* (22.xi;   (Licinianus) Licinius
Licinianus, om. III); *BGU*   Augg. III
II 409.13 (25.xi; Licinianus?);
I 349.14 (26.xi; Licinianus)

OTHER: Zosimus 2.7

NOTES: To start with, all parties recognized the joint consulate of Constantine and Maximinus, each of the two claiming seniority in his own domains (a). But after Maximinus' defeat by Licinius on 30.iv, both Licinius and Constantine removed his name from the formula. By about August, Licinius' name was added in Maximinus' place, to signal the solidarity of the two remaining Augusti (b). Heracl. remarkably preserves both (a) and (b), though both are a bit garbled. The western laws have been retroactively corrected. VindPost. has combined parts of the formulas for 313 and 314; see 315 for the same thing with 314 and 315.

Occidentis

FASTI: Chr. 354 (fast.,pasch.,praef.,   Volusianus II[22]
              episc. 76,4.6) Hyd. VindPr.   et Annianus
              Prosp. Aq. Cass.

LAWS: 6 laws total, earliest *CJ*   Volusianus et Annianus
              7.32.10 (Trier, 22.i); 2 from Trier

INSCR.:   none

OTHER: Council at Arles: *Conc.Galliae*   Volusianus et Annianus
              (Corp.Christ.Lat. 148), pp.14,
              15,17,19,21

              Report of Proceedings against   Volusianus et Anianus
              Felix of Abtugni (Von Soden,
              Urkunden p.25, no.19) (15.ii);
              p.26 (19.viii)

              Libanius, *Epp.* 1036 (Volusianus)

NOTES:

    Volusianus was cos. I in 311, but since this was Maxentius' appointment, the iteration number is not given in most official documents (contrast *ILS* 1222 and two of the fasti). Petronius Annianus was PPO 315-317 (*PLRE* I 68-69). The addition of the numeral I after the consular formula in *CPR* VIII 22.3 (post 10.ix) is remarkable.

[22]Numeral only in Hyd. and Chr. 354 (fast.); Chr. 354 (pasch.) has Valerianus.

Orientis

<u>FASTI:</u>	Heracl.	Petronius et Rufinus Vusianus (and) Volusianus et Arianus
	Theo Pasch. Scal. (cc.) Berol.	Volusianus et Annianus
<u>LAWS:</u>	See West.	
<u>PAPYRI:</u>	*P.Cair.Isid.* 54.15 (15.i); *P.Lond.* III 975.20 (p.230) (15.i); *PSI* VII 820.43 (17.ii); *P.Amst.* I 44.1	p.c. DD.NN. Constantini et Licinii Augg. III
	P.Cair.Isid. 16.46 (19.ii); *PSI* VII 820.31 (23.ii); *CPR* I 233.11 = *W.Chr.* 42 (19.iii); *PSI* VII 820.46 (16.iv); *SB* XIV 12167.13 (30.iv); *BGU* II 411.9 (27.v); *P.Gen.* 13.8 (9.vi); *Pap.Lugd.Bat.* XIII 7 A.14 (14?.vi); *P.Princ.Roll* iv.20 (24.vi); *P.Cair.Isid.* 128.18 (vi-vii); 13.57 (31.vii); *CPR* VIII 22.3 (post 10.ix; adds I); *P.Princ. Roll* iii.10 (1.viii); *P.Col.* VII 141a.1 (9.viii); *P.Cair.Isid.* 55.7 (20.viii); *PSI* VII 820.81 (14.ix); *ZPE* 50 (1983) 68.1 (17.ix); *P.Panop.* 4.18 (19.x); *P.Cair.Isid.* 122.7 (5.xi); 55.12 (18.xi); *P.Flor.* I 54.16 (2.xii); *P.Cair.Isid.* 92.15 (11.xii); 53.28 (29.viii-31.xii); *P.Cair.Preis.* 40.1 (29.viii-31.xii); *SB* XVI 12705.11; *P.Panop.* 23.15 (date of doc. uncert.)	Rufius Volusianus et Petronius Annianus vv.cc.
	SB XIV 12167.26 (30.iv); *P.Panop.* 21.16 (16.vii; doc. 26.v.315)	Volusianus et Annianus
	PSI VII 820.72 (8.viii)	Rufius et Annianus
<u>INSCR.:</u>	**HELLESPONTUS:** *EpigrAnat* 2 (1983) 99 = *SEG* XXXIII 1051 (Cyzicus)	Volusianus et Annianus vv.cc.

Occidentis

FASTI:	Chr. 354 (fast.,pasch.,praef.) Hyd. VindPr. Prosp. Aq. Cass.	Constantinus IV et Licinius IV[23]
	VindPost.	Volusianus et Licinius II
LAWS:	Total 13 laws, earliest 22.i (*CTh* 8.5.1, no prov.); 1 from Sirmium, 2.vi; 4 from Rome, earliest 13.viii	Constantinus Aug. IV et Licinius (Aug.) IV[24]
INSCR.:	none	
COINS:	*RIC* VII 123.24-25, 124.37 (Lyons); 238.48, 239.69 (Arles): consular bronzes of Constantine	cos. IIII
	RIC VII 164.12 (Trier), 363.26 (Ticinum): consular solidi of Constantine	Felix processus cos. IIII Aug. N.
OTHER:	Optatus of Milevis 1.23, in *CSEL* 26, p.26 (2.x; retrosp. in account of trial of Donatus)	Constantius IV et Licinius III

[23]Chr. 354 (praef.) has Const. III; VindPr. has Lic. III.
[24]In addition to *Frag.Vat.* 32, 33 and 274, *CTh* 11.27.1, though putting Aug. after Constantine and not after Licinius, also preserves Augg. (presumably original) at the end of the formula; all other laws observe the *damnatio memoriae* completely; cf. above, p.71.

Orientis

<u>FASTI:</u>	Heracl. (1)	Constantius et Licinius
	Heracl. (2)	Valerius Constantinus et Valerius et Licinius IV
	Theo Pasch. (Aug. V)	Constantinus (Aug.) IV et Licinius IV
	Scal.	Const. Aug. IV et Lic. Caes. III
<u>LAWS:</u>	*CTh* 8.7.1 (Thessalonica, 8.iii)	Constantinus Aug. IV et Licinius IV
<u>PAPYRI:</u>	*P.Hamb.* I 21.15 (30.i)	p.c. Rufii Volusiani et Petronii Anniani vv.cc.
	P.Princ.Roll v.1 (12.ii); *P.Rainer Cent.* 84.26 (27.iii); *P.Panop.* 21.1 (26.v); *P.Lond.* III 976.11 (p.230) (i-v); *P.Princ.Roll* v.6 (4.vii); vi.10 (27.vii); *P.Cair.Isid.* 122.19 (28.vii); 57.31 (11.ix); 58.20 (16.ix); *P.Sakaon* 19.13 (1.x); *P.Princ.Roll* viii.1 (11.x); *P.Oxy.* XXXI 2585.1 (x-xi); XLV 3255.1 = *P.Coll.Youtie* II 80 (7.xi); *P.Cair.Isid.* 74.21 (27.xii; Lat.); *P.Mert.* II 91.19 (27.xii; doc. 31.i.316); *PSI* VIII 893.1 (or restore p.c.?)	DD.NN. Constantinus et Licinius Augg. IV

<u>NOTES:</u>

Heracl. is confused; it also gives Valerius Constantinus et Valerius et Licinius IV. Cf. 313 for VindPost.

Occidentis

FASTI:	Chr. 354 (fast.,pasch.,praef.) Hyd. VindPr. Prosp. Aq. Cass.	Sabinus et Rufinus
	VindPost.	Const. IV et Rufinus
LAWS:	6 laws total, earliest *CTh* 1.22.1 (Trier, 11.i); 1 law from Vienne (6.v), 1 from Arles (13.viii); *PSI* I 112.8 (Rome)	Sabinus et Rufinus
INSCR.:	**ROME:** *CIL* VI 37122 = *ILCV* 162 (15.vi; ref. to birthdate in inscr. d. 346)	Sabinus et Rufinus
	DALMATIA: *CIL* III 1967 (Salona; frag.)	

NOTES:

Rufinus was PVR 315-316 (*PLRE* I 777), but Sabinus is not attested in any other office. The papyri support "Caecinius" for his middle name over the "Caecina" reconstructed from Heracl. (καί [= et] Κινασαβηνου) and preferred by Mommsen and *PLRE* I 793.

Orientis

FASTI: Heracl. (1)   Antonius Caecina Sabinus

                Heracl. (2) Theo Pasch.   Sabinus et Rufinus

                Scal.   Rufinus et Sabinus cc.

LAWS: See West.

PAPYRI: *P.Oxy.* XVII 2113.27 (i)   p.c. DD.NN. Constantini et
                                                                        Licinii Augg. IV

                P.Princ.Roll ix.1 (22.i);   Caecinius Sabinus et
                P.Cair.Isid. 59.7 (26.i);   Vettius Rufinus vv.cc.
                P.Mert. II 91.4 (31.i); *SB*
                III 6003.14 (21.ii); *P.Oxy.* I
                53.12 (25.ii); *P.Princ.Roll*
                iv.27 (27.ii); *P.Oxy.* VI 896.19,
                35 (1.iv); *P.Cair.Isid.* 59.17
                (14.iv); *SB* XIV 11278.13 (15.iv);
                P.Oxy. XVII 2124.18* (i-iv); *P.Oxy.*
                XIX 2232.16 (v-vi); *P.Princ.Roll*
                vi.21 (1.viii); *P.Gen.* 10.20
                (8.viii); *P.Oxy.* XVII 2114.18
                (10.viii); *P.Oxy.* I 103.22 (13.x);
                P.Mich. IX 573.25 (19.x); *P.Bad.*
                II 27.11 (28.x); *P.Oxy.* I 84.19
                (1.xi); *P.Stras.* 278.1; *P.Laur.*
                IV 176.19; *PSI* VII 771.6 (doc. 321)

                P.Cair.Isid. 76.8, *P.Col.*   Sabinus et Rufinus
                VII 169.3, 170.9 (all ii-iii;   (vv.cc.)
                docs. all 318); *Aegyptus* 66 (1986)
                73.14 (21.v; vv.cc.); *P.Cair.Isid.*
                75.22 (24.x; vv.cc.);
                P.Sakaon 19.29 (vv.cc.)

INSCR.:   **SYRIA:** *Princ.Arch.Exp.*   Sabinus et Rufinus
                Syria III 788 (Wakm)

Occidentis

FASTI:	Chr. 354 (praef.)	Consules quos iusserint DD.NN. Augg.
	Chr. 354 (praef.: ex d. XIII k. Mart.; fast.,pasch.) Hyd. VindPr. Prosp. Aq. Cass.	Gallicanus et Bassus
	VindPost.	Sabinus et Bassus
LAWS:	7 laws total, earliest *CTh* 12.1.4 (pp. 19.i); 1 each from Serdica (17.iv) and Sirmium (6.vi)	Gallicanus et Bassus
INSCR.:	**ROME:** *ICUR* n.s. VIII 23058 = *ILCV* 2763 (13.viii; 330 poss.?)	Gallicanus

NOTES:

According to Chr. 354 (praef.), Gallicanus and Bassus were not proclaimed till 17.ii. They appear to turn up in the papyri already on 8.i and in another January citation. The Giessen text, however, is a retrospective reference; and the absence of other attestations in Egypt before July makes one suspect that the date in *P.Sakaon* 50 on 8.i is a mistake for p.c. Bassus is presumably the son of Caesonius Bassus cos. 285 (*PLRE* I 154); why he is missing in the one Roman inscription is not clear--but neither is its ascription to 317. Gallicanus was PVR 316-317 and perhaps the first Christian consul, cf. E. Champlin, *Phoenix* 36 (1982) 71-76. For this consulate, cf. also J.F. Gilliam, *Historia* 16 (1967) 252-54.

Orientis

FASTI: Heracl. (Suppl.) Theo Scal. (cc.)   Gallicanus et Bassus

            Pasch.   Gallicanus et Symmachus

LAWS: See West.

PAPYRI: *P.Princ.Roll* viii.20 (2.vii);   Ovinius Gallicanus et
            P.Vindob.Worp 8.15 (22.viii);   Caesonius Bassus vv.cc.
            P.Oxy. LIV 3742.14 (26.xi);
            P.Lond. III 1290 (p.lxxi)

            P.Sakaon 50.8 (8.i);   Gallicanus et Bassus
            P.Giss. 102.14 (i); *P.Cair.*   vv.cc.
            Isid. 123.11; *SPP* XX 284 (Lat.)

Occidentis

FASTI: Chr. 354 (fast.,pasch.,praef.)   Licinius V et
              Hyd. VindPr. Prosp. Aq. Cass.   Crispus Caes.[25]

              VindPost.   Gallicanus et
                                                        Licinianus III

LAWS: *CTh* 11.29.2 (Sirmium, 7.ii);   Licinius V et
              CJ 3.11.4 (Sirmium, 9.ii);   Crispus Caes.
              CTh 9.15.1 (no prov., 16.xi)

INSCR.:   **ROME:** *ICUR* n.s. III 8416*   Licinius VI
              (14.ii-1.iii)   [et Crispus]

              ICUR suppl. 1411 = *ILCV* 845   Licinius V et
                                                        Crispus Caesar

NOTES:

   Constantine's son Crispus (born before 300? See Barnes, *New Empire* 44) was proclaimed Caesar together with Constantine iunior and Licinius iunior on 1.iii.317. Cf. 321, notes.

---

[25]Caes. omitted by Aq., Prosp., Cass., Chr. 354 (fast., pasch.). Lic. IV in VindPr.

Orientis

FASTI: Heracl.   Licinius V et Priscus I[26]

         Theo Pasch. Scal. (om. V)   Licinius V et Crispus
                                                     Caes.

LAWS: See West.

PAPYRI: *P.Oxy.* XXXIII 2675.1 (15.i);   DD.NN. Licinius Aug. V
         P.Oxy. XII 1425.1 (13.iv);   et Crispus nob. Caesar I
         SB X 10728.1 (19.iv); *P.Harr.* II
         211.14 (26.iv); *P.Cair.Isid.* 59.25,
         31 (9 and 17.vii); *P.Col.* VII 170.6
         (16.vii); *P.Cair.Isid.* 76.5
         (16.vii); 82.16 (26.vii); *P.Got.*
         5.11 (12.viii); *P.Princ.Roll*
         x.11 (13.viii); *P.Thead.* 21.21
         (7.ix); *P.Oxy.* XLV 3257.1 (10.xi);
         P.Oxy. LIV 3743.1; 3744.1; 3745.1

[26]This formula is followed by Licinius V et Priscus III and then by Priscus IV et Constantinus IV.

Occidentis

FASTI: Chr. 354 (fast.,pasch.,praef.)   Constantinus V et
              Hyd. Prosp. Cass. Aq.   Licinius Caes.[27]

              VindPr.   Constantius V et
                                                    Licinius V

              VindPost.   Crispus et Licinius IV

LAWS: About 24 laws for the year,   Constantinus Aug. V et
              earliest *CTh* 9.1.2 (no prov.,   Licinius Caes.
              [Sirmium?] 13.i); 3 laws from
              Sirmium (earliest, 11.iii); 2
              from Naissus (both 25.vii); 3
              from Serdica

INSCR.:   **ROME:** *CIL* VI 508 = *ILS*   DD.NN. Constantinus
              4146 (19.iv; max., iun.);   (max.) Aug. V
              ICUR n.s. VII 17424 = *ILCV*   et Licinius (iun.) Caes.
              265 (much rest.)

              DALMATIA: *CIL* III 1968b
              (Salona; 1.ii; iun.)

COINS: *RIC* VII 396.28 (Aquileia):   Felix processus cos.
              consular solidus of Constantine   VI Aug. N.

NOTES:

    Licinius Caesar held his first consulate with Constantine. In Egypt, a slight delay in proclamation is
visible; for the slight overlap in Egyptian p.c. and cos. attestations, cf. *BASP* 17 (1980) 28-32.

[27]Chr. 354 (fast., pasch.) om. Caes.

Orientis

<u>FASTI:</u>	Heracl.	Constantinus V et Licinius VI
	Pasch.	Constantinus Aug. VI et Licinius V
	Theo	Constantinus Aug. V et Licinius Caes.
	Scal.	Constantinus Aug. V et Constantius novus Caes.
<u>LAWS:</u>	See West.	
<u>PAPYRI:</u>	*P.Col.* VII 185.17 (21.i)	p.c. DD.NN. Licinii Aug. V et Crispi nob. Caes. I
	P.Sakaon 20.11 (19.i); *P.Oxy.* LIV 3746.18,44 (23-25?.iii); LIV 3748.1, 3749.1, 3750.1, 3751.1, 3752.1, 3753.1 (all 26.iii); *PSI XVII Congr.* 28.1 (prob. i-v); *P.Princ.Roll* x.23 (25.vi); *SB* XVI 12530 = *P.Genova* II p.74.19 (4.vii; invictus); *SB* XIV 11496.13 (16.x); *P.Cair.* *Isid.* 60.17 (2.xii); *P.NYU* 4a.17 (21.xii); *SB* VI 9219.1,7 (27.xii); *P.Sakaon* 21.9,38 (30-31.xii); *P.Oxy.* XLV 3258.1 (Imp. for Aug.), 3259.1 (both 30.viii-31.xii); P.Lond. inv. 2222.1 (Lallemand, *L'adm.civ.* 264); *SB* XIV 12013 (uncert. rest.)	DD.NN. Constantinus (invictus) Aug. V et Licinius nob. Caesar I
<u>INSCR.:</u>	**GREECE:** *Syll.*[3] 901* = *SEG* XII 226 (Delphi; cf. *SEG* XIV 407, frag. perh. to be rest. similarly)	DD.NN. Fl. Valerius Constantinus Aug. V et Fl. Valerius Licinianus Licinius Aug. fil. Caesar

Occidentis

<u>FASTI:</u>	Chr. 354 (fast.,pasch.,praef.) Hyd. VindPr. Prosp. VindPost. Aq. Cass.	Constantinus VI et Constantinus Caes.[28]
<u>LAWS:</u>	4 laws, earliest *CTh* 3.2.1 (Serdica, 31.i)	Constantinus Aug. VI et Constantius Caes.
<u>INSCR.:</u>	**DALMATIA:** *CIL* III 1968c + 8568 (Salona)	DD.NN. Constantinus Aug. VI et Constantinus nob. Caesar
<u>COINS:</u>	*RIC* VII 375.104 (Ticinum), 397.34 (Aquileia), 467.1,4 (Sirmium; no Aug.N. in 1), 683.39,41 (Antioch): consular solidi and multiples of Constantine	Felix processus cos. VI Aug. N.
	RIC VII 185.242,244 (Trier): consular solidus and multiple of Constantine	Cos. VI
	Toynbee, *Roman Medallions*, p.88: consular medallion of Constantine	Cos. VI
<u>OTHER:</u>	Gesta apud Zenophilum (Von Soden, *Urkunden*, p.38 no.28 = CSEL 26, p.185) (Thamugadi, Africa, 8 or 13.xii)	Constantinus maximus Aug. et Constantinus iun. nob. Caes.

<u>NOTES:</u>

The last of the new Caesars had to wait two years before holding his first consulate, with his father this time; see p.23 above.

---

[28]VindPost. (Const. V), Chr. 354 (fast., pasch.) om. Caes.; Prosp. adds Aug. before VI.

Orientis

FASTI: Heracl. (om. VI, Caes.; I)   Constantinus Aug. VI et
                  Theo Pasch. (om. Aug.)   Constantinus Caes. (I)

                  Scal.   Constantinus Aug. VI
                                              et Licinius minimus I

LAWS: See West.

PAPYRI: *PSI* V 454.1 (i-ii); *CPR* VIII   DD.NN. Constantinus
                  23.1 (i-ii); *P.Sakaon* 21.20   (invictus) Aug. VI et
                  (9.ii); *SB* V 7667.20 (17.ii);   Constantinus nob. Caesar I
                  P.Col. VII 188.1 (14.iii);
                  P.Cair.Preis. 4.1 (iii-iv);
                  P.Genova 21.24 (25.vii; invictus);
                  P.Sakaon 7.14 (23.viii; om. nob.);
                  P.Oxy. LIV 3755.19 (27.ix);
                  P.Lips. 19.1 (25.x; rest. uncert.);
                  P.Panop. 11.11 (27.xi); *CPR* V 8.1
                  (29.viii-31.xii); *SPP* XX 99.1;
                  P.Cair.Isid. 77.31 (om. nob.);
                  P.Sakaon 21.55 (rest.);
                  P.Princ.Roll xi.7 (rest.); *P.Oxy.*
                  LIV 3754.1

INSCR.:   **SYRIA:** *OGIS* II 619* =   DD.NN. Constantinus Aug.
                  LBW III 2393 (Deir el-Lében)   VI et Cl. [sic]
                                                  Constantinus nob. Caesar
                                                  perpp. Augg.

Occidentis

FASTI: Chr. 354 (fast.,pasch.,praef.)   Crispus II et
             Hyd. VindPr. Prosp. Aq. Cass.   Constantinus II[29]

LAWS: About 16 laws, earliest *CTh* 2.19.2   Crispus II et
             (Serdica, 6.ii); 2 from Serdica,   Constantinus II Caesares
             4 from Sirmium, 1 from Viminacium

INSCR.:   **ROME:** *CIL* VI 1687 = *ILS* 6111 (13.iii;   DD.NN. Crispus et
             iun.); *CIL* VI 1685 = *ILS* 6111a (9.iv);   Constantinus (iun.)
             CIL VI 1688 = *ILS* 6111b (22.iv);   nobb. Caesares II
             CIL VI 1684 (29.viii; iun.); *CIL* VI
             315 = *ILS* 3409 (20.x; om. DD.NN., nobb.);
             ICUR n.s. VII 20340* (14.ix-7.x; frag.;
             or 324?); *CIL* VI 1689 (iun.; om. II);
             ICUR n.s. IV 9550 (om. DD.NN.; om. nobb.
             Caess.?); *ICUR* n.s. II 5710
             (frag.; Crispus app. omitted)

             DALMATIA: *CIL* III 15023   DD.NN. Imp. Licinius
             (cf. 15022?)   Licinianus Caesar coss.

COINS: *RIC* VII 470.18,20 (Sirmium), 682.37 Crispus et Constantinus
             (Antioch): consular gold multiples   nobb. Caess. coss. II

             RIC VII 470.20A (cf. p.717:   Felix processus cos. II
             Sirmium), 683.40, 685.46 (Antioch):
             consular solidi of Crispus

             RIC VII 131.135-136, 133.175,192   Cos. II
             (Lyons): consular bronze of Crispus

             RIC VII 131.141-142, 133.178-179 (Lyons):   Constantinus iun. cos. II
             consular bronzes of Constantine Caesar

             Toynbee, *Roman Medallions*, p.197:
             gold medallion of Crispus and Constantine
             Caesars as consuls (Nicomedia); with
             legend cos. II from Antioch and Sirmium (p.197)

OTHER: Letter of Constantine to the vicar   Crispus et
             Verinus (Von Soden, *Urkunden*, p.   Constantinus iterum
             51 no.30) (5.v)

[29]Aq. Cass. give Caes. in place of second II; VindPost. has Const. VI et Const. II.

Orientis

<u>FASTI:</u>	Heracl. (Const. III) Pasch. Theo (om. II after Const.; Caes. 2x)	Crispus (Caes.) II et Constantinus (Caes.) II
	Scal.	Crispus et Constantinus nobb. Caess. fill. Aug. II
<u>LAWS:</u>	none	
<u>PAPYRI:</u>	*P.Got.* 6.16 (10.iii); *P.Vindob. Worp* 3.8 (29.iii); *SPP* XX 80.12* (29.v); *SB* XII 11154.1 (v-vi); *P.Princ.Roll* xii.7 (5.vii); *P.Oxy.* VI 900.1 (30.vii); *SB* VI 9544.14 (24.viii); *P.Sakaon* 34.1 (12.xii; Lat.); *SPP* XX 78.1 (20.xii); *P.Sakaon* 67.18* (viii-xii); *PSI* VII 771.1 (year uncert.; 322?); *P.Vindob.Tandem* 7.5 (year uncert.: 322?); *P.Cair. Preis.* 8.1; *SPP* XX 79.4	DD.NN. Licinius Aug. VI et Licinius nob. Caesar II
<u>INSCR.:</u>	**EGYPT:** *SB* I 4223.11* = Milne, *Gk.Inscr.Cairo* 9238 (26.v)	
<u>COINS:</u>	Toynbee, *Roman Medallions*, p.89: bronze medallion of Licinius II with his bust as consul	

<u>NOTES:</u>   It is a clear sign of the deteriorating relations between Constantine and Licinius that from 321 on neither recognized the other's consuls. Constantine proclaimed both his sons, Licinius himself and his son. The minting of medallions of Crispus and Constantine Caesars in Antioch suggests that in late 320 a break had not yet occurred, with Licinius preparing to proclaim Constantine's nominees. On the other hand, it was Licinius' turn to appoint the consuls. Barnes (*New Empire* 96 n.24) points to *ICUR* n.s. III 8416 (= I 34), which gives *Kal. Mar. Licino VI[*, as an indication that Constantine began the year by recognizing the Licinii. On this view, then, each side would show early signs of accepting the other's nominees! This cannot be right, and we have preferred to classify the Roman inscription under 318 (see Crit.App.), albeit with some hesitation. Why Crispus is omitted in *ICUR* n.s. II 5710 we do not know. Dalmatia dated by the Licinii, but the one surviving inscription has evidently suffered from haplography (cf. Barnes, *NE* 199 for Dalmatia's political position). The eastern fasti show retroactive adaptation of the consular formula; cf. 324, notes.

Occidentis

FASTI: Chr. 354 (fast.,pasch.,praef.)   Probianus et Iulianus
              Hyd. VindPr. Prosp. Aq. Cass.

              VindPost.   Crispus II et Iulianus

LAWS: 9 laws, earliest *CTh* 9.1.3   Probianus et Iulianus
              (no prov., 9.ii); 3 laws from
              Sirmium (earliest 23.v);
              1 each from Savaria and Serdica

INSCR.:   **ROME:** *CIL* VI 1686   Petronius Probianus et
              = *ILS* 6111c (31.iii)   Anicius Iulianus

              ITALY: *CIL* XI 2548 = *ILCV* 1027   Probianus et Iulianus
              (Chiusi, Reg. VII; 10/11.xii)

NOTES:

    Probianus was PVR 329-331, father of Probinus cos. 341, grandfather of Probus 371, and great-grandfather of the consuls of 395 and 406 (*PLRE* I 733). Anicius Iulianus was PVR 326-329, probably son of the Anicius Faustus cos. 298 and father of Anicius Paulinus cos. 334 (*PLRE* I 473-74).

Orientis

<u>FASTI:</u>	Heracl.	Crispus III et Constantinus IV
	Pasch. Theo Scal.	Probianus et Iulianus
<u>LAWS:</u>	none	
<u>PAPYRI:</u>	*P.Panop.* 26.15 (28.ii); *P.Oxy.* XLIII 3123.16 (29.iii); *P.Princ.Roll* xii.17 (14.viii); *P.Oxy.* XLIII 3122.1; *P.Harr.* II 212.1 (numeral lost; or 323?); *SB* XIV 11611.1	p.c. DD.NN. Licinii Aug. VI et Licinii nob. Caes. II, qui fuerint (nuntiati) consules II
	P.Col. VII 143.12 (2.vii)	qui fuerint nuntiati consules II

<u>NOTES:</u>

For the formulas in use for "consuls to be announced" in the years 322-324, see *ZPE* 10 (1971) 124 and *CSBE* 108. Licinius reacted during these years in the same way as Maxentius had in 308 and 311 and Constantine in 309 and 310, by not recognizing his colleague's consuls but not proclaiming any of his own. The effect is what has been called a "postconsular era" (*CSBE* 51). Heracl. has simply become confused in these years; cf. his treatment of 321 and 324. For the other eastern fasti, cf. 324, notes.

Occidentis

<u>FASTI</u>:	Chr. 354 (fast.,pasch.,praef.) Hyd. VindPr. Prosp. Aq. Cass.	Severus et Rufinus
	VindPost.	Probianus et Rufinus
<u>LAWS</u>:	7 laws, earliest *CTh* 4.8.6 (Thessalonica, 15.ii); 1 law each from Byzantium (13.iv) and Sirmium (25.xii)	Severus et Rufinus
<u>INSCR.</u>:	**ROME:** *ICUR* n.s. III 6497 (27.iv); *ICUR* n.s. VII 20341 (28.vi); *ICUR* n.s. VII 17425 = *ILCV* 3257 (6-13.ix)	(Acilius) Severus et (Vettius) Rufinus
	ITALY: *AE* 1908, 107 = *ILS* 9420 (Feltre, Reg. X; 28.viii); *CIL* X 407* = *I.Ital.* III.1 17 (Buccino, Reg. III; [Acil.] Sev., Vett. Ruf.)	
	AFRICA: *AE* 1969/1970, 657 (El Ayïda, 8.xi; frag.)	Rufinus et Severus

<u>NOTES:</u>

Constantine continued his new policy of appointing Roman aristocrats to the consulate. Severus is presumably Acilius Severus, PVR 325-326 (*PLRE* I 834), but his name as consul is nowhere preserved as such; if Rufinus was really called Vettius (only in *I.Ital.* III.1 17), then he was evidently related to C. Vettius Cossinius Rufinus, cos. 316, though nothing else is known of him. The order in the African inscription is unparalleled. For the eastern fasti, cf. 324, notes.

Orientis

FASTI: Heracl. (Rufus) Theo Pasch.   Severus et Rufinus
                 Scal.

LAWS: none

PAPYRI: *P.Oxy.* I 42.8 (18.i)   p.c. DD.NN. Licinii Aug.
                                           VI et Licinii nob. Caes.
                                           II, qui fuerint nuntiati
                                           consules III

            P.Col. VII 143.20 (28.ii);   qui fuerint (nuntiati)
            P.Oxy. XXXVI 2767.1 (29.iii);   consules III
            P.Oxy. XLIV 3194.1 (29.iv);
            P.Cair.Isid. 61.7,22 (17.v),
            24,31 (24.v); *P.Panop.* 27.25
            (iv-v); *P.Oxy.* XXXVI 2771.1
            (24.vi); *P.Cair.Isid.* 61.36
            (27.vii); *P.Oxy.* I 60.12
            (17.viii); *P.Herm.* 18.2
            (6.xii); *P.Oslo* III 138.1
            (17.xii); *P.Oxy.* XLV 3260.1
            (30.viii-31.xii); XLI 2969;
            P.Princ.Roll xiii.7 (numeral
            restored); *P.Vindob.Sal.* 8.23
            (1.i; cf. p.203; dubious rest.);
            PSI XII 1233.30 (6/7.ix.323
            or 324)

Occidentis

FASTI:	Chr. 354 (fast.,pasch.,praef.) Hyd. VindPr. Prosp. Aq. Cass.	Crispus III et Constantinus III
	VindPost.	Severus et Const. III
LAWS:	4 laws, *CTh* 12.17.1 (Sirmium, 19.i); 13.5.4 (Thessalonica, 8.iii); 12.1.9 (*p.p.* Carthage, 9.vii); 15.14.1 (16.xii [Seeck], no prov.)	Crispus III et Constantinus III Caess.
INSCR.:	none	
COINS:	*RIC* VII 473.43, 476.57 (Sirmium): consular solidi of Crispus	Felix processus cos. III
	Toynbee, *Roman Medallions*, p.197: medallion of Constantine (obv.) with Crispus as consul and Constantius in military costume. Perhaps struck for 8.xi.324 (Constantius' promotion to Caesar)	

(i-ix) **qui fuerint (nuntiati) consules IV**
(ix-xii) **Crispus Caesar III et Constantinus Caesar III**

Orientis

<u>FASTI</u>:	Heracl.	Crispus IV et Constantinus V
	Pasch. Scal. (Const. Caes. II)	Crispus III et Constantinus III
	Theo	Crispus Caes. et Constantinus Caes.
<u>LAWS</u>:	none	
<u>PAPYRI</u>:	*P.Cair.Isid.* 78.19 (30.i); *P.Ant.* I 39.1 (6.ii); *P.Oxy.Hels.* 44.1* (ii-iii); *P.Sakaon* 51.28 (6.v); *PSI* IV 300.1* (8.v); *P.Mert.* II 92.25 (31.v); *P.Col.* VII 171.21 (6.vi); *P.Princ.Roll* xiv.11 (29.vi); *P.Oxy.* XII 1430.1 (31.vii); *P.Sakaon* 22.1,14,21,33,45 (5-8.ix); *BGU* II 586.29; *P.Oxy.* XLV 3261.1; *P.Panop.* 16.6; *P.Harr.* II 214 i.1 (cf. ii.14)	qui fuerint consules IV
	P.Oxy. VI 889.10 = *SB* XVI 12306 (12.xii; doc. 325); *P.Sakaon* 23.13 (24.xii); *SB* XVI 12673.1 (324 or 325); *P.Oxy.* LIV 3758.203 (retrosp., doc. d. 15.iii.325)	DD.NN. Crispus et Constantinus nobb. Caess. III

<u>NOTES:</u>

In the year of his final conflict with Licinius, Constantine once again proclaimed his sons, while, once again, Licinius made no proclamations at all. After Licinius' defeat, Constantine's consuls were proclaimed in the East as well, and with iteration numerals which implicitly proclaimed their previous consulates which Licinius had not proclaimed at the time. Cf. 326, notes.

Occidentis

FASTI:	Chr. 354 (fast.,pasch.,praef.) Hyd. VindPr. ('Plautianus') Prosp. Beda (3,295 c.415) Aq. Cass.	Paulinus et Iulianus
	VindPost.	Crispus III et Iulianus
LAWS:	See East.	
INSCR.:	**ROME:** *ICUR* n.s. III 7377 = *ILCV* 2568	Paulinus et Iulianus
	ITALY: *AE* 1937, 119 (Amiternum; 7.xii)	
	GERMANIA: Vermaseren, *Corpus* *Inscr. et Monum. rel. Mithr.* II (The Hague 1960) 1315* (Gimmeldingen, 22.i)	Paulinus et Iulianus

NOTES:

The uncorrected formula to *CTh* 2.25.1 of 29.iv and now five papyri make it clear that the original consular pair was Proculus and Paulinus. As Barnes saw (*ZPE* 21 [1976] 280; *New Empire* 102), Proculus must have been deposed and disgraced and Iulianus appointed in his place, with Paulinus moving up in the ranking to prior consul. For the German inscription, see the Critical Appendix. Proculus is perhaps the Proculus proc. Africae in 319-320. Sex. Anicius Paulinus was PVR 331-333, probably son of Anicius Faustus cos. 298 and brother of Anicius Iulianus cos. 322 (*PLRE* I 679-80). Of the fasti, only Theon has preserved any trace of Proculus; the form of his entry, "Proculus or Paulinus and Julian," suggests that the compiler was comparing two different lists rather than simply correcting his own original entry at the time. Most of the laws have been corrected. For Iulianus' first name, see the Critical Appendix.

Orientis

FASTI:	Heracl. Pasch.	Paulinus et Iulianus
	Theo	Proclus sive Paulinus et Iulianus
LAWS:	*CTh* 2.25.1 (no prov., 29.iv)	Proculus et Paulinus
	About 15 laws, earliest *CTh* 15.14.2 (prov.?, 12.ii); Nicomedia, 5 laws (earliest *CTh* 1.15.1, 25.ii); Nicaea, Nassete, Aquae, 1 law each	Paulinus et Iulianus
PAPYRI:	*P.Oxy.* X 1261.1 (13.i)	p.c. DD.NN. Crispi et Constantini nobb. Caess. III
	P.Oxy. LIV 3756.26 (i-ii; om. vv.cc.); LIV 3758.39 (3.iii; om. vv.cc.); LIV 3758.132 (17.iii?); XLIII 3125.9 (iii-iv)	Proculus et Paulinus vv.cc.
	P.Oxy. VI 889.11 = *SB* XVI 12306 (24.v)	V[alerius Proculus et Anicius Paulinus] vv.cc.
	P.Stras. 138.17* (vi-vii); *P.Charite* 13.39* (23.ix); *P.Stras.* 137.19 (27.ix)	Anicius Paulinus et Ionius Iulianus vv.cc.
	P.Oxy. LIV 3757.1 (13.iii; later copy); *P.Oxy.* XIV 1626.23 (26.v); *P.Haun.* III 55.18 (16.vi); *P.Sakaon* 24.11 (28.vi); *P.Col.* VII 176.18 (8.ix); *P.Vindob.Sijp.* 3.18 (21.ix); *P.Sakaon* 68.26 (2.x); *P.Oxy.* I 52.1; *P.Lond.* III 977.17 (p.231) (21.vi; doc. 330)	Paulinus et Iulianus vv.cc.
OTHER:	Socrates, *HE* 1.13	Paulinus et Iulianus
	Extract from Council at Nicaea, quoted at Chalkedon [451]: *ACO* II.1.2, p.79.13 (19.vi)	Paulinus et Iulianus vv.cc.

Occidentis

FASTI:	Chr. 354 (fast.,pasch.,praef.) Hyd. Prosp.	Constantinus VII et Constantius Caes.[30]
	VindPr.	Constantius VI et Constans
	VindPost.	Constantinus VII et Maximus
LAWS:	About 15 laws total; see East for earliest. Milan, 2 laws, earlier *CTh* 9.21.3, 6.vii; 1 law each from Aquileia (*CTh* 9.8.1, 4.iv), Sirmium, Rome, Spoleto	Constantinus Aug. VII et Constantius Caes.
INSCR.:	**ROME:** *ICUR* n.s. V 13892	DD.NN. Constantinus Aug. VII et Constantius nob. Caes.
COINS:	Toynbee, *Roman Medallions*, p.88: consular medallion of Constantius Caesar, prob. fr. 326. Also prob. a consular medallion of Constantine from this year (both from Trier)	

NOTES:

Exceptionally, the new Caesar Constantius (elevated 8.xi.324) had to wait two years for his first consulate. Barnes has already noted that Porfyrius, *carm.* 12.1 and 18.2 seem to imply that Constantine was expected to take the consulate in 325 (*AJP* 96 [1975] 181-82; *New Empire* 96 n.31). He did in fact celebrate his *vicennalia* that year in Nicomedia, but he celebrated it again in Rome in 326 and held the consulate on that occasion instead. Perhaps the civilian consuls of 325 had already been designated by 8.xi.324, and contrary to general expectation Constantine decided to wait a year.

---

[30]Chr. 354 (fast., pasch.), Prosp., Aq., omit Caes.; Cass. adds I at end.

Orientis

FASTI: Heracl.   Constantinus VII et
                                                      Constantinus IV

          Theo (om. Caes.) Pasch. (adds   Constantinus VII et
          IV at end) Berol. (om. VII)   Constantius Caes.

          Scal.   Constantinus Aug. VII et
                                                      Constantius VI

LAWS: Cf. West. Earliest law,   Constantinus Aug. VII et
          CTh 9.3.2 and 9.7.1 (both   Constantius Caes.
          Heraclea, 3.ii); C'polis, 1 law
          (*CTh* 2.10.4, 8.iii)

PAPYRI: *P.Oxy.* LI 3620.1 (2.ii); *P.Oxy.*   DD.NN. Constantinus Aug.
          XLV 3265.1 = *P.Coll.Youtie*   VII et Constantius nob.
          II 81 (vi-vii; om. Aug.);   Caesar I
          P.Stras. 177.23 (19.viii; om.
          nob.); *SB* XIV 11385.1 (7.ix);
          P.Laur. IV 169.4 (14-30.ix; om.
          nob.); *P.Stras.* 296.1 (19.xi);
          P.Col. VII 177.20 (31.xii); *P.Oxy.*
          XLV 3249.1 (ix-xii); *P.Amh.* II
          138.20 (late 326); *P.Stras.*
          316 recto; *P.Princ.* II 79.1

INSCR.:   **EGYPT:** *Baillet* 1889   Constantinus Aug.
          (Thebes)   VII et Constantius
                                                       Caesar I

          SYRIA: *AE* 1936, 148 (Doueire)   DD.NN. Constantinus
                                                      Aug. VII et Constantius
                                                      nob. Caesar I

COINS: Toynbee, *Roman Medallions*, p.197:
          medallion of Constantine and Constantius
          in consular dress (Antioch)

Occidentis

FASTI: Chr. 354 (fast.,pasch.,praef.)   Constantius et Maximus
              Hyd. Cass. VindPr.[31]

              Aq.   Constantius Caesar V et
                                                  Maximus

              Prosp.   Constantinus II et Maximus

              VindPost.   Constantius et Iustus

LAWS: See East.

INSCR.:   **ROME:** *ICUR* n.s. I 1250   Constantius et Maximus
            = *ILCV* 4609 (14.ii-15.iii);
            ICUR suppl. 1419 (16.x-1.xi;
            Constantinus)

---

[31]Hyd. gives Constantinus for Constantius.

Orientis

<u>FASTI:</u>	Heracl.	Constantinus et Maximus
	Pasch.	Constantius Caesar VI et Maximus
	Theo	Constantinus et Maximinus
	Berol.	Constantius IV et Maximus
	Scal.	Const. VII et Const. III Augg.
<u>LAWS:</u>	7 laws, earliest *CTh* 1.5.2 (no prov., 21.i); 1 law each from Thessalonica and C'polis	Constantius et Maximus
<u>PAPYRI:</u>	*P.Oxy.* I 83.23 (16.i; frag.; p.c. poss.?); *PSI* IV 309.17 = *SB* XVI 12543 (11.ii; om. praeff.); Pack[2] 2731* (24.iv); *P.Flor.* I 53.1 (24.vi); *P.Sakaon* 25.11,13 (30.viii, 7.ix; om. Fl., Val., praeff.), 30 (12.ix; om. praeff.); *SB* I 5356.30 (7.xi; om. praeff.); *P.Harr.* II 215 r.1 (29.x-27.xi); *P.Col.* VII 178.16 (20.xii)	Fl. Constantius et Valerius Maximus vv.cc. praeff.

<u>NOTES:</u>

Both Constantius (324-327) and Maximus (327-328; 332-333; 337) served Constantine as praetorian prefects (Barnes, *New Empire* 103).

189

Occidentis

FASTI:	Chr. 354 (fast.,pasch.,praef.) Hyd. VindPr. ('Iulianus' for Ian.) Prosp. Aq. Cass.	Ianuarinus et Iustus
	VindPost.	Ianuarinus et Const. V
LAWS:	5 laws total; for earliest, see East. 1 law from Oescus; 1 law from Trier	Ianuarinus et Iustus
INSCR.:	**ROME:** *CIL* VI 36951 = *ILS* 8943 (1.iii); *ICUR* n.s. III 7378* (6-13.xii)	Ianuarinus et Iustus

Orientis

<u>FASTI:</u>	Heracl. Theo Pasch. Berol.	Ianuarinus et Iustus
	Scal.	Lollianus et Iustus
<u>LAWS:</u>	Cf. West. Earliest law, *CTh* 14.24.1 (Nicomedia, 1.iii)	Ianuarinus et Iustus
<u>PAPYRI:</u>	*P.Sakaon* 62.12 (22.i)	p.c. Constantii et Maximi vv.cc. praeff.
	P.Oxy. XLIII 3126 i.22 (19.viii); *SPP* II p.33.16 (24.viii); *P.Sakaon* 65.21* (11.ix); *P.Sakaon* 73.20 (28.ix); *P.Flor.* I 14.16 (1.x); *PSI* IV 316* (ix-x); *P.Sakaon* 26.1; *SB* XII 11024.21*	Fl. Ianuarinus et Vettius Iustus vv.cc.

<u>NOTES:</u>

Ianuarinus has not been certainly identified and Iustus is otherwise unknown (Barnes, *New Empire* 103). This year is the first of a long series of years in which political turmoil cannot be used to explain the delayed dissemination of the consulate in the Egyptian papyri.

Occidentis

FASTI: Chr. 354 (fast.,pasch.,praef.) Constantinus VIII et
        Hyd. Aq. Cass. Prosp.   Constantinus IV[32]

        VindPr.   Constantius VIII
                                       et Constant

        VindPost.   Constantinus VIII et
                                       Symmachus

LAWS: none

INSCR.: none

[32]Cass. gives VI, Prosp. IV .

Orientis

FASTI: Heracl. (II for IV) Theo   Constantinus VIII et
Berol. (om. numerals)   Constantinus IV
Scal. (Const. Magnus VIII et
Const. Aug. IV)

Pasch.   Constantinus Aug. X
et Constantius Caesar V

LAWS: *CTh* 12.1.17 (Heraclea,   Constantinus Aug. VIII
25.x)   et Constantius Caesar IV

PAPYRI: *P.Oxy.* LI 3621.1 (10.v);   DD.NN. Constantinus Aug.
P.Panop. 28.15 (9.vii);   (Imp.) VIII et
P.NYU 22.19 (1.ix);   Constantinus nob. Caesar IV
P.Oxy. XXXI 2570 ii.1,
iii.1; LIV 3766.23,49,77
(all 27.x); *P.Stras.* 316
V.8; *P.Lond.* III 1291 (p.lxxi;
Imp.); *P.Harr.* II 236.1

P.Panop. 17.5 (ii-iii)   VIII et IV

OTHER: Athan., *Fest.* 1 (6.iv),   Constantinus Aug. VIII et
Index   Constantinus Caes. IV

Occidentis

FASTI:	Chr. 354 (fast.,pasch.,praef.) VindPr.	Gallicanus et Symmachus
	Prosp. Aq. (-ius) Cass. (-ius VII)	Constantinus III et Symmachus
	VindPost.	Gallicanus et Ablabius
LAWS:	7 laws, earliest *CTh* 16.2.7 (Serdica, 5.ii); 1 law from Bessapara, *CTh* 2.26.1 (22.ii; prov. acc. Seeck)	Gallicanus et Symmachus
INSCR.:	**ROME:** *ICUR* n.s. I 1417* = *ILCV* 4667 (4.i)	Fl. Gallicanus et Tullianus
	ICUR n.s. I 2804 = *ILCV* 4941 (14.v) Cf. also under 317.	Gallicanus et Symmachus

NOTES:

Gallicanus is otherwise unknown. Symmachus is the grandfather of Symmachus cos. 391 (for the complicated question of his nomenclature, see Cameron, *Last Pagans of Rome*, forthcoming; meanwhile, Barnes, *New Empire* 103-04 with *ZPE* 53 [1983] 276 n.4). Prosper, Victor of Aquitaine, and Cassiodorus seem to have conflated 329 and 330, perhaps by haplography at some point. The delay in dissemination in Egypt was minor.

Orientis

<u>FASTI:</u>	Heracl.	Gallenus et Symmalius
	Hyd. Theo Pasch. Scal. (adds cc.)	Gallicanus et Symmachus
	Berol.	Gallicanus et Valerius
<u>LAWS:</u>	C'polis, 2 laws, earlier 16.vii (*FragVat* 248)	Gallicanus et Symmachus
<u>PAPYRI:</u>	*P.Oxy.* XLVII 3350.1 (12.i)	p.c. DD.NN. Constantini Aug. VIII et Constantini nob. Caes. IV
	SPP XX 86.26 (31.i; om. Symm.) *BGU* XIII 2252.13 (16.ii; om. Symm.); *P.Sakaon* 26.3 (i-ii; 2nd cos. rest.); *PSI* III 224.5 (4.ix; om. Tull.); *SB* V 7666.9 (27.x; 2nd cos. is Aurelius Symm.); *P.Lond.* III 977.1 (p.231) (2nd cos. rest.)	Fl. Gallicanus et (Aurelius) Valerius Tullianus Symmachus vv.cc.
<u>OTHER:</u>	Athan., *Fest.* 2 (19.iv); *Index* (om. Valerius)	Gallicianus et Valerius Symmachus

<u>NOTES:</u>

Symmachus' name is not fully preserved in some of the papyri. The forms we do find preserved are as follows:

Valerius Tullianus	*SPP* XX 86; *BGU* XIII 2252
Valerius Symmachus	*PSI* III 224
Aurelius Symmachus	*SB* V 7666

195

Occidentis

FASTI:	Chr. 354 (fast.,pasch.,praef.) VindPr. Prosp. Aq. Cass.	Bassus et Ablabius
	VindPost.	Bassus et Hilarianus
LAWS:	See East.	
INSCR.:	**ROME:** *ICUR* n.s. IV 11748 = *ILCV* 450 (5.ix); *ICUR* n.s. VIII 21597 = *ILCV* 1545 (27.ix)	Bassus et Ablabius

NOTES:

Bassus was PPO from 318-332 (*PLRE* I 154); Ablabius from 329-337 (*PLRE* I 3; Barnes, *New Empire* 104).

Orientis

FASTI:	Heracl. Hyd. Pasch. Theo Berol. Scal. (adds cc.)	Bassus et Ablabius
LAWS:	9 laws, earliest *CTh* 4.8.7 (no prov., 28.ii); C'polis, 3 laws, earliest *CTh* 5.9.1, 17.iv	Bassus et Ablavius
PAPYRI:	*P.Stras.* I 43 = *P.Sakaon* 69.26* (14.i); *P.Stras.* 129.15 = 149.17 (23.iii; om. praeff.); *P.Oxy.* XLVIII 3384.1 (14.iv); *SB* XVI 12335.1 (iii-iv); *P.Oxy.* XLIV 3195.1,24 (13-14[?.vi); *P.Oxy.* VI 990 (21.viii); *PSI* VII 767.1 (7.xi; om. praeff.); *P.Bad.* II 28.1 (30.xi); *P.Oslo* II 41.1 (2.xii; much rest.); *P.Lond.* III 978.18 (p.232) (7.xii); *CPR* VII 36.13 (22.xii); *P.Panop.* 30.23,34 (23.x; doc. 5.viii.332)	Iunius Bassus et Fl. Ablabius vv.cc. praeff.
INSCR.:	**ASIA:** *MAMA* VII 305 = *ILS* 6091 (C'polis, 30.vi; Lat.)	Bassus et Ablabius
	PALESTINA: *CIG* III 4593* = *LBW* 2546a (Umm ez-Zeitun)	Bassus et Ablabius vv.cc.
OTHER:	Athan., *Fest.* 3 (11.iv); *Index*	Iunius Bassus et Ablabius

Occidentis

FASTI: Chr. 354 (fast.,pasch.,praef.)   Pacatianus et Hilarianus
              VindPr. Prosp. Aq. Cass.

              VindPost.   Pacatianus et Zenofilus

LAWS: See East.

INSCR.:   none

NOTE:

   Pacatianus was PPO 332-337 (*PLRE* I 656); Hilarianus PVR 338-339 and PPO 354 (*PLRE* I 433;
Barnes, *New Empire* 105).

Orientis

<u>FASTI:</u>	Heracl. Hyd. Pasch. Theo Berol. Scal. (adds cc.)	Pacatianus et Hilarianus
<u>LAWS:</u>	5 laws, earliest *CTh* 3.5.4-5 (Marcianopolis, 12.iv); 2 laws from C'polis, earlier *CJ* 6.1.6, 17.x	Pacatianus et Hilarianus
<u>PAPYRI:</u>	*SB* XIV 11711.25 (i-ii); *P.Panop.* 22.5 (17.iii; doc. 25.iii.336); *P.Oxy.* XLIII 3128.1 (29.vi); *P.Panop.* 29.20 (1-24.vii); 30.2 (5.viii); *P.Oxy.* XII 1426.1, XLIII 3127.1 (both om. sacr. praet.)	Papius Pacatianus v.c. praef. sacr. praet. et Mecilius Hilarianus v.c.
<u>OTHER:</u>	Athan., *Fest.* 4 (2.iv); *Index* (om. Fab., Mec.)	Fabius Pacatianus et Mecilius Hilarianus

Occidentis

FASTI: Chr. 354 (fast.,pasch.,praef.)   Dalmatius et Zenofilus
             VindPr. Prosp. Aq. Cass.

             VindPost.   Dalmatius et Paulinus

LAWS: See East. Aquae, 2 laws (*CTh*   Dalmatius et Zenofilus
             1.32.1 and 1.2.6, ?.x and 11.xi)

INSCR.:   **ROME:** *ICUR* n.s. VI 17247 =   Dalmatius et Zenophilus
             ILCV 2561; *ICUR* n.s. V 13894
             = *ILCV* 3001 adn.; *CIL* VI 30884

NOTES:

Dalmatius was the half-brother of Constantine; he lived at court for several years but held none of the high offices of state, though he was *censor*, residing at Antioch with wide powers close to this date; Zenophilus held three proconsulships (Achaea, Asia and Africa more or less in succession), but apparently no higher office (his career is deduced from an acephalous inscription) (Barnes, *New Empire* 105-07 for both).

Orientis

<u>FASTI:</u>	Heracl. Hyd. Pasch. Theo Scal. Berol.	Dalmatius et Zenophilus
<u>LAWS:</u>	8 laws, 4 from C'polis, earliest *CTh* 3.30.5 (18.iv)	Dalmatius et Zenofilus
<u>PAPYRI:</u>	*P.Oxy.* XIV 1716.1 (9.iv)	Fl. Dalmatius frater D.N. Constantini Aug. et Domitius Zenophilus vv.cc.
<u>INSCR.:</u>	**JORDAN:** *ZPE* 65 (1986) 232 (Qasr el-Azraq; p.c. poss.; Lat.)	Dalmatius et Zenofilus vv.cc.
<u>OTHER:</u>	Athan., *Fest.* 5 (15.iv); *Index*	Dalmatius et Zenophilus

Occidentis

<u>FASTI</u>:	Chr. 354 (fast.,pasch.,praef., gener. 140,21.22) VindPr. Prosp. Aq. Cass.	Optatus et Paulinus
	VindPost.	Optatus
<u>LAWS</u>:	9 laws, earliest *CTh* 14.4.1 (no prov., 8.iii); Singidunum and Naissus, 1 law each	Optatus et Paulinus
<u>INSCR.</u>:	**ROME:** *ICUR* n.s. V 13285 (19-30.viii; frag.)	Optatus et Paulinus
	GAUL: *CIL* XIII 2351 = *ILCV* 3039 (Lyons; 1.ii)	
	AFRICA: *CIL* VIII 5357 = *I.Algérie* 270 (Numidia; frag.)	

<u>NOTES</u>:

Optatus (*PLRE* I 650) held none of the high offices but was influential at court and the first to be honored with the refurbished title of patrician; Anicius Paulinus (*PLRE* I 679) was PVR 334-335, an aristocrat, son of Iulianus cos. 322 and (probably) nephew of Paulinus cos. 325; see Barnes, *New Empire* 107.

Orientis

<u>FASTI:</u>	Heracl. Hyd. Theo Scal. (cc.) Berol.	Optatus et Paulinus
	Pasch.	Optatus patricius et Anicius Paulinus
<u>LAWS:</u>	*CTh* 8.18.3 (C'polis, 30.iii); *CTh* 1.22.2 (C'polis, 17.vi)	Optatus et Paulinus
<u>PAPYRI:</u>	*P.Vindob.Sal.* 12.11 (early in year)	p.c. Fl. Dalmatii fratris D.N. Constantini Aug. et Domitii Zenophili vv.cc.
	P.Lond. VI 1913.1 (19.iii); *P.Oxy.* LIV 3769.1 (ii-iii); *P.Oxy.* LIV 3770.18 (26.iii); *PSI* V 469.1 (18.ix); *P.Panop.* 5.8 (12?.xi); *P.Sakaon* 45.21; 45a.24 (both 7.xii); *SB* VIII 9848.1 (mostly rest.)	Fl. Optatus patricius et Anicius Paulinus vv.cc.
<u>INSCR.:</u>	**TRANSJORDAN:** *AE* 1948, 136	Optatus et Paulinus vv.cc.
<u>OTHER:</u>	Athan., *Fest.* 6 (7.iv); *Index* (om. patr., Anic.)	Optatus patricius et Anicius Paulinus

Occidentis

<u>FASTI</u>:	Chr. 354 (fast.,pasch.,praef.[33] episc. 76,8) VindPr. Prosp. Aq. Cass.	Constantius et Albinus
	VindPost.	Constantius et Egeas
<u>LAWS</u>:	none	
<u>INSCR.</u>:	**ROME:** *ICUR* n.s. I 2721 = *ILCV* 2795A (5.ix); *ICUR* n.s. III 8137*	[ ] Constantius et Rufius Albinus
	ITALY: *AE* 1937, 121 (Amiternum, Reg. IV; 18.xii)	Fl. Constantius et Rufius Albinus

___

[33]Paulinus in place of Albinus.

Orientis

<u>FASTI:</u>	Heracl. ('Ablabius' for Alb.) Hyd. Theo Berol.	Constantius et Albinus
	Pasch.	Constantius Caes. VI et Albinus
	Scal.	Constantinus nob. Aug. I et Savinus
<u>LAWS:</u>	*CTh* 10.10.3 (22.iii) and 8.9.1 (17.iv), both C'polis; *CJ* 1.40.4 (Nicopolis, 23.x)	Constantius et Albinus
<u>PAPYRI:</u>	*CPR* I 247.20 (7.iv); *P.Oxy.* IX 1206.1 (iii-iv); *P.Oxy.* XLIII 3129.10 (14-30.ix; adds v.c. bef. patr.; frag.; Lat.); *PSI* VI 706.1 (26.x); *P.Würzb.* 15.6,16 (Rufinus); *SB* V 8265.16; p.c. poss.)	Iulius Constantius (v.c.) patricius frater D.N. Constantini Aug.et Rufius Albinus vv.cc.
<u>OTHER:</u>	Athan., *Fest.* 7 (30.iii); *Index* (Constantius et Albinus)	Iulius Constantius Aug. frater et Rufinus Albinus
	Letter of the Mareotic clergy to Philagrius, Prefect of Egypt, Athanasius, *Apol.c.Arian.* 76 (*PG* 25.385C) (7.ix)	Iulius Constantius v.c. patricius frater piiss. Imp. Constantini Aug. et Rufinus Albinus v.c.

<u>NOTES:</u>

Constantius was another half-brother of Constantine, the father of the future emperors Gallus and Julian. Albinus was the son of Volusianus cos. 311 and 314, PVR 335-337 (Barnes, *New Empire* 108). The eastern evidence is unanimous that Constantius' first name was Iulius. In the West, both Roman inscriptions are broken in the place in question, but one inscription from Amiternum gives Flavius instead. Since the name Flavius was common in the family, it is plausible enough. But its absence in the abundant Greek sources makes one suppose that the use at Amiternum was an error caused by the presence of Flavius in Constantine's name.

Occidentis

FASTI: Chr. 354 (fast.,pasch.,praef.,   Nepotianus et Facundus
              episc. 76,10) VindPr.
              Prosp. Aq. Cass. VindPost.

LAWS: See East.

INSCR.:   **ROME:** *AE* 1976, 32 (4.ii); *ICUR*   Nepotianus et Facundus
              n.s. I 3159 = *ILCV* 3252 (8.v);
              ICUR n.s. VIII 21598 = *ILCV*
              2562 (1.vi); *ICUR* n.s. II 5930
              (16.vii-13.viii); *ICUR* n.s. I
              1418 = *ILCV* 3648 (5.x)

              ITALY: *AE* 1903, 377 = *ILCV* 3311
              (Aquileia, Reg. X; 16.x);
              AE 1972, 202 (nr. Mantua,
              Reg. Reg. X)

              LUSITANIA: *CIL* II 191 =
              ILS 5699 (Olisipo)

Orientis

<u>FASTI:</u>	Heracl. (Suppl.) Hyd. Pasch. Theo Scal. (adds cc.)	Nepotianus et Facundus
	Berol.	Pompeianus et Facundus
<u>LAWS:</u>	6 laws, earliest *CJ* 3.8.4 (no prov., 15.iii); C'polis, 1 law (*CTh* 12.1.22, 22.viii)	Nepotianus et Facundus
<u>PAPYRI:</u>	*P.Oxy.* XII 1470.1 (ii-iii; om. vv.cc., adds qui fuerint nuntiati consules); *P.Panop.* 22.1 (25.iii); *P.Oxy.* X 1265.1 (26.iii)	p.c. Iulii Constantii patricii fratris D.N. Constantini Aug. et Rufii Albini vv.cc.
	CPR VI 5.8 (22.iv); *PSI* X 1106.1; 1107.1 (both 26.iv); *P.Oxy.* VI 901.1, LIV 3771.1 (both 1.v); *SB* III 6294.1 (25.x); *P.Col.* VII 178a.18 (5.xii; Iurius Nep.); *P.Panop.* 6.12; *P.Laur.* IV 167.1	Virius Nepotianus et Tettius Facundus vv.cc.
	P.Col. VII 142.1,9 (6 and 8.xii); *P.Sakaon* 4.26 (15.xii)	Nepotianus et Facundus vv.cc.
<u>OTHER:</u>	Athan., *Index* (18.iv)	Nepotianus et Facundus

<u>NOTES:</u>

Nepotianus was presumably the son (or grandson) of Nepotianus cos. 301 and possibly brother-in-law of Constantine (Barnes, *New Empire* 108). Facundus is otherwise unknown. The dissemination in Egypt was comparatively late this year. The addition of *qui fuerint...* to the postconsulate in *P.Oxy.* XII 1470 is most unusual (found hitherto only with the era under the Licinii; see 322); but compare Athanasius' usage in 356.

Occidentis

<u>FASTI</u>:	Chr. 354 (fast.,pasch.,praef. episc. 76,12) VindPr. Prosp. Aq. Cass. VindPost.	Felicianus et Titianus
<u>LAWS</u>:	One law from Naissus (*CJ* 5.17.7)	Felicianus et Titianus
<u>INSCR.</u>:	**ROME:** *ICUR* n.s. IV 11088 (16.v-12.vi); *ICUR* n.s. I 2078 = *ILCV* 2805 (1.viii; om. Fabius)	Fabius Titianus [
	ICUR I 47 = *ILCV* 2795A adn. (16.xi)	Felicianus et Titianus
	ITALY: *CIL* X 476 = *ILS* 6112 (Paestum, Reg. III; 30.iv); *AE* 1912, 256 (Fondi, Reg. I; 2.viii; om. Fl., Fab.)	Fl. Felicianus et Fabius Titianus

NOTES:

Felicianus cannot be securely identified; Titianus was PVR 339-341 and 350-351, PPO from 341-349 (*PLRE* I 918-19). Curiously enough, the two Roman inscriptions up to 1.viii give either only Titianus or else reverse the order (in both we have Titianus, then a lacuna), though Felicianus is found in Paestum in the right order on 30.iv. Moreover, there are no papyri with the new consuls still in early March (the first example with them comes from August). Dissemination in Egypt was thus again rather late.

On 9.ix.337, more than three months after Constantine's death, his three surviving sons--Constantine II, Constantius II, and Constans--were all proclaimed Augusti.

Orientis

<u>FASTI:</u>	Heracl.	Felix et Titianus
	Hyd. Pasch. Theo Berol. Scal. (Tatianus; adds cc.)	Felicianus et Titianus
<u>LAWS:</u>	6 laws, earliest *CTh* 3.1.2 (C'polis, 4.ii); 1 law from Thessalonica	Felicianus et Titianus
<u>PAPYRI:</u>	*P.Flor.* I 96.6,13 (18.ii); *PSI* VII 804.14* (4.iii)	p.c. Virii Nepotiani et Tettii Facundi vv.cc.
	P.Oxy. XLV 3266.1 = *P.Coll. Youtie* II 82 (13.viii); *SPP* XX 88.17 (23.xii); *P.Panop.* 12.9 (xi-xii)	Fl. Felicianus et Fabius Titianus vv.cc.
<u>OTHER:</u>	Athan., *Index* (3.iv)	Felicianus et Titianus
	Socrates, *HE* 1.40	Felicianus et Tatianus

209

Occidentis

FASTI:	Chr. 354 (fast.,pasch.,praef.) VindPr. Prosp. Aq. Cass. VindPost. (Polleocius)	Ursus et Polemius
LAWS:	9 laws, earliest *CTh* 10.10.4 (Viminacium, 12.vi); 1 law from Sirmium, *CJ* 10.48.7 (27.vii)	Ursus et Polemius
INSCR.:	**ROME:** *ICUR* n.s. III 8719 = *ILCV* 1266 (7.ii); *ICUR* n.s. III 7379 = *ILCV* 1539 (3.v); *ICUR* n.s. I 221 = *ILCV* 287ab (12.vi); *ICUR* n.s. I 2946 = *ILCV* 4367 (1.iv, 26.viii); *ICUR* n.s. VII 17426 = *ILCV* 4629 (8.xi); *ICUR* n.s. VIII 23059 = *ILCV* 3105G **ITALY:** *CIL* XI 4180 (Terni, Reg. VI; 15.i); *CIL* IX 4215 = *ILS* 6561 (S. Vittorino, Reg. IV; 29.vi); *CIL* XI 2565 (Chiusi, Reg. VII; 11.x?) **AFRICA:** *CIL* VIII 796 = *ILS* 5413 (Buftis, Procons.; 11.iii)	Ursus et Polemius

Orientis

<u>FASTI:</u>	Heracl. Hyd. Pasch. Theo Scal. (adds cc.) Berol.	Ursus et Polemius
<u>LAWS:</u>	See West. Antioch, 2 laws, *CTh* 12.1.23 and 2.6.4, 11.x and 27.xii; Emesa, 1 law, *CTh* 12.1.25, 28.x	Ursus et Polemius
<u>PAPYRI:</u>	*P.Oxy.* VI 892.13 (13.i); *P.Oxy.* I 67.1, 86.1, XLVIII 3386.1 (all 28.iii); *P.Lips.* 97 i.7; xxxiv.23 (25.iv; om. Fl. 2x); *P.Oxy.* XXXI 2571.22 (27.vii); *P.Panop.* 19 viii.a.5 (12.viii; om. Fl. 2x); *P.Ryl.* IV 660.8 (23.viii); *P.Lond.* III 651 (p.xxii) (ix-x); *P.Sakaon* 70.16 (x-xi); *P.Oxy.* I 85 ii.19 = *SB* XVI 12648; iv.18 (26.xi); *P.Vindob.Sijp.* 1 i.20; ii.19 (24.xii; om. Fl. 2x)	Fl. Ursus et Fl. Polemius vv.cc.
<u>OTHER:</u>	Athan., *Fest.* 10 (26.iii); *Index*	Ursus et Polemius

<u>NOTES:</u>

Polemius is otherwise attested as a comes under Constantius in 345 (*PLRE* I 710); Ursus cannot be certainly identified (ibid., 989). "It is probably significant that the ordinary consuls of 338 were not two of the new Augusti, as custom prescribed, but two men who were probably generals--and that they displaced an Italian senator, who had received a formal designation to office before May 337" (Barnes, *Constantine and Eusebius* 262, writing of the crisis precipitated by Constantine's death; the senator is Lollianus, eventually consul in 355). For an explanation, see above, p.19.

Occidentis

<u>FASTI</u>:	Chr. 354 (fast.,pasch.,praef.) VindPr. Prosp. Aq. Cass. VindPost.	Constantius II et Constans[34]
<u>LAWS</u>:	*CTh* 12.1.27 (Trier, 8.i); 11.1.5 (no prov., 3.ii; Aug. only after Constantius)	Constantius II et Constans Augg.
<u>INSCR.</u>:	**ROME:** *ICUR* n.s. I 45 = *ILCV* 4225 (16.iii-1.iv; Constantinus for Constantius); *ICUR* suppl. 1434 = *CIL* VI 31131 (6-13.vi; DD.NN.; om. Aug.?); *ICUR* n.s. VII 17427	(DD.NN.) Constantius Aug. II et Constans Aug.
	ITALY: *CIL* XI 4028 = *ILCV* 3226 (Capena, Reg. VII; 5.xii)	
<u>COINS</u>:	*RIC* VIII 235 (Rome)	Medal of Constantius II and Constans in cos. robes

---

[34]Chr. 354 (fast.) gives Constans II.

Orientis

FASTI:	Heracl. Hyd. (om. I) Theo Scal. (Aug., nob. Caes.)	Constantius (Aug.) II et Constans (nob. Caes.) I
	Pasch.	Constantius iun. IV et Constans Aug. VII
LAWS:	See West.	
PAPYRI:	*P.Panop.* 19 iv.a.4 (10.i; cos. for p.c.); 19 vi.a.3 (3.ii)	p.c. Ursi et Polemii
	P.Panop. 9.10 (20.iii; perpp. Augg.); *P.Col.* VII 175.6 = *SB* XVI 12692 (10.v); 175.2 = *SB* XVI 12692 (17.v); *P.Ant.* I 32.4* (vi); *P.Monac.* III 89.1 (28.ix); *PSI* III 215.1 (8.xii); *P.Panop.* 13.11 (23.xii; perpp. Augg.); *CPR* V 9.1; *BGU* XIII 2296.7; *P.Lond.* III 1257 (p.lxviii)	DD.NN. Constantius (perp.) Aug. II et Constans (perp.) Aug. I
	P.Panop. 19 viii.b.4 (30.iii)	Constantius II et Constans I
	P.Panop. 19 iv.b.3 (3.ix); 19 viii.c.3	II et I
COINS:	Toynbee, *Roman Medallions*, p.199: consular medallion of Constantius and Constans (Thessalonica)	
OTHER:	Athan., *Fest.* 11 (15.iv); *Index* (om. Augg.)	Constantius II et Constans I Augg.

NOTES:

It is not known why Constantine II allowed his two junior colleagues to be the first to assume the fasces as Augusti (see above, pp.13-14), but he was losing the struggle for power among the brothers, perishing in battle with Constans early in 340 (Barnes, *Constantine and Eusebius* 262-63). Dissemination was late in the papyri once again. The first examples in the papyri of *perpp. Augg.* come from this year.

Occidentis

<u>FASTI</u>:	Chr. 354 (fast.,pasch.,praef.) VindPr. Prosp. Aq. Cass. VindPost.	Acindynus et Proculus[35]
<u>LAWS</u>:	12 laws, earliest *CTh* 12.1.29 (Naissus, 19.i); 1 other law from Naissus, 1 each from Aquileia and Milan	Acindynus et Proculus
<u>INSCR</u>.:	**ROME:** *ICUR* suppl. 1435 = *ILCV* 760 adn. (9.i); *ICUR* n.s. VI 15985a (21.i); *ICUR* n.s. VI 15985b = *ILCV* 3019 (21.i); *ICUR* suppl. 1438 = *ILCV* 4399 (22.vi); *ICUR* n.s. I 1419 = *ILCV* 4647 (2-5.viii); *ICUR* n.s. I 3162 (21.viii; om. Proc.); *ICUR* n.s. III 8417; *ICUR* n.s. IV 11089	Acindynus et Proculus

[35]Chr. 354 (fast.) gives 'Aquilinus'.

Orientis

<u>FASTI:</u>	Heracl. Hyd. Pasch. Theo Scal. (adds cc.)	Acindynus et Proculus
<u>LAWS:</u>	*CTh* 6.4.5,6 (Antioch, 9.ix; 6.4.6 adds D.N.)	p.c. (D.N.) Constantii II et Constantis
	CTh 12.1.30 (Edessa, 12.viii); cf. West.	Acindynus et Proculus
<u>PAPYRI:</u>	*P.Panop.* 19 ix.b.4 (16.ii)	p.c. II et I
	P.Col. VII 148.7,22 (21.iii); *CPR* VII 16.13 (3.v); *P.Col.* VII 149.9 (15.vi); *P.Vindob. Sijp.* 4.15 (29.vi); *BGU* I 21 i.14 (13.viii); *P.Cair.Goodsp.* 12 i.19 (15.viii); *P.Vindob.Sijp.* 5.15 (24-28.viii)	Septimius Acindynus v.c. praef. sacr. praet. et Populonius Proculus v.c.
	P.Panop. 19 iii.a.6 (26.viii); 19 vi.b.3	Acindynus et Proculus
<u>OTHER:</u>	Athan., *Index* (30.iii)	Acyndinus et Proclus
	Socrates, *HE* 2.5	Acindynus et Proclus

<u>NOTES:</u>

Acindynus was PPO Or. 338-340 and presumably son of Septimius Acindynus, PVR 293-295 (*PLRE* I 11). Proculus, a man of noble family, was PVR 337-338 and 351-352 (ibid., 747-49). It is curious to find his signum placed before his last name in the way given on the papyri. It is impossible to believe that the eastern court was dating by p.c. in September--especially since the papyri show dissemination by March. There must be some sort of error; cf. above, p.83.

Occidentis

<u>FASTI</u>:	Chr. 354 (fast.,pasch.,praef.) VindPr. Prosp. Aq. Cass. VindPost.	Marcellinus et Probinus
<u>LAWS</u>:	6 laws, earliest cf. East. 1 law from Lauriacum, *CTh* 8.2.1 (24.vi)	Marcellinus et Probinus
<u>INSCR.</u>:	**ROME:** *ICUR* n.s. VIII 20768 = *ILCV* 2999 (6.ii); *ILCV* 1724 (9.iii); *RAC* 44 (1968) 156, fig. 11 (11.iii); *ICUR* n.s. I 1420 = *ILCV* 2816 (12.iv); *CIL* VI 108 = *ILS* 3991 (8.v); *ICUR* n.s. VIII 20769 (16.vi); *ICUR* n.s. V 13895 (18.iii/18.vii); *CIL* VI 871 (16.xi); *ICUR* n.s. VIII 20767 (frag.); *ICUR* I 64; *ICUR* n.s. V 13289 (p.c. poss.)	Marcellinus et Probinus
	ITALY: *CIL* IX 10 = *ILS* 6113 (Nardò, Reg. II; 6.v; Antonius, Petronius); *CIL* XI 4095 = *ILS* 5696 (Otricoli, Reg. VI; 16.xi); *CIL* XI 4096, 4097 = *ILS* 5697 (Otricoli; 16.xi)	(Antonius) Marcellinus et (Petronius) Probinus

Orientis

<u>FASTI:</u>	Heracl.	Tronius et Probinus
	Hyd. Pasch. Theo Scal. (adds cc.)	Marcellinus et Probinus
<u>LAWS:</u>	Antioch, 2 laws, both 12.ii (*CTh* 5.13.1-2)	Marcellinus et Probinus
<u>PAPYRI:</u>	*P.Cair.Goodsp.* 13.16 (1.iv); *P.Oxy.* VI 991 (5.iv); *P.Charite* 26.12 (4.v); *P.Flor.* I 17.19 (30.v?; Probianus); *P.Würzb.* 15.22 (28.vi); *P.Oxy.* XII 1559.1 (13.xi); *P.Nag Hamm.* 63.12 (20.xi); *P.Oxy.* L 3575.1 (x-xi); 3576.1 (30.xi); *P.Panop.* 19 viii.d.2; *P.Oxy.* LIV 3774.1	Antonius Marcellinus et Petronius Probinus vv.cc.
	P.Panop. 10.8 (21.ix)	Marcellinus et Probinus vv.cc.
<u>OTHER:</u>	Athan., *Fest.* 13 (19.iv); *Index*; *De synodis* 25	Marcellinus et Probinus
	Socrates, *HE* 2.8	Marcellus et Probinus

<u>NOTE:</u>

Marcellinus was PPO Ital. 340-341; Probinus was PVR 345-346, son of Probianus cos. 322, father of Probus cos. 371 and grandfather of the consuls of 395 and 406 (*PLRE* I 548-49, 735).

217

Occidentis

<u>FASTI</u>:	Chr. 354 (fast.,pasch.,praef.) VindPr. Prosp. Aq. Cass. VindPost.	Constantius III et Constans II
<u>LAWS</u>:	7 laws, earliest *CJ* 2.57.1 (no prov., 23.i; cf. East); Milan, 1 law, *CTh* 9.7.3 (4.xii)	Constantius III et Constans II Augg.
<u>INSCR.</u>:	**ROME:** *ICUR* n.s. I 1251 (2-5.ix); *ICUR* n.s. IV 12523 = *ILCV* 2978 et (4.xii; om. Aug.); *ICUR* n.s. IV 9556 = *ILCV* 2846 adn.	Constantius Aug. III Constans Aug. II
	CIL VI 1769	DD.NN. III et II

Orientis

FASTI: Heracl. Hyd. Theo (Aug. 2x)   Constantius (Aug.) III et
         Scal. (adds Augg. nobb.)   Constans (Aug.) II

         Pasch.   Constantius Aug. V et
                                          Constans Aug. II

LAWS: Antioch, 4 laws, earliest *CTh*   Constantius III et
         3.12.1 (31.iii); *CJ* 2.57.1 (no   Constans II Augg.
         prov., 23.i) may be from Antioch
         also or from C'polis.

PAPYRI: *P.Panop.* 19 xi.5 (12.i)   p.c. Marcellini et
                                   Probini vv.cc.

         P.Oxy. L 3577.9 (28.i; Lat.);   DD.NN. Constantius III
         3578.1 (ii-iii); *P.Oxy.* I 87.1   et Constans II (perpp.) Augg.
         (ii-iii); *P.Sakaon* 46.21
         (29.iii); *P.Abinn.* 44.20*
         (29.iii); *P.Flor.* I 34.1* (8.iv);
         P.Harr. 65.1 (5.v); *P.Oxy.* LIV
         3775.1 (1.vii); *P.Col.* VII
         150.10 (20.vii); 150.35* (28.vii);
         P.Oxy. XIV 1627.1 (12.viii);
         P.Panop. 19 vi.c.4 (9.ix; om.
         DD.NN.; perpp.); *P.Col.* VII
         181.1 = *P.Coll.Youtie* II 78 (18.x);
         BGU IV 1049.1; *SB* XII 10988.3 (frag.)

         P.Panop. 19 vi.d.3 (23.xi);   III et II
         19 i.a.4; 19 iv.c.4; *P.Col.*
         VII 174.56

OTHER: Athan., *Fest.* 14 (11.iv);   Constantius III
         Index (om. Augg.)   et Constans II Augg.

         Socrates, *HE* 2.13   Constantius III et
                                   Constans II (Augg.)

Occidentis

<u>FASTI</u>:	Chr. 354 (fast.,pasch.,praef.) VindPr. Prosp. Aq. Cass. VindPost.	Placidus et Romulus
<u>LAWS</u>:	6 laws, earliest *CTh* 11.16.5 (Bononia, 25.i); 1 law from Trier, *CTh* 12.1.36 (30.vi)	Placidus et Romulus
<u>INSCR.</u>:	**ROME:** *RAC* 44 (1968) 156, fig. 11 (13.iv); *ICUR* n.s. I 264 = *ILCV* 4393 (5.vii); *ICUR* n.s. VII 17428 = *ILCV* 2563 (14.xi); *ICUR* n.s. III 8720 = *ILCV* 2571 and 2819 (15.xi); *ICUR* n.s. VIII 21599 = *ILCV* 4634A adn.; *ICUR* n.s. VI 16966; *ICUR* n.s. IX 23757	Placidus et Romulus
	ITALY: *CIL* IX 3073 = *ILCV* 3641 (Interpromii, nr. S. Valentino, Reg. IV; 19.ix)	

<u>NOTES:</u>

Placidus was of noble birth, PPO Ital. 342-344, PVR 346-347 (*PLRE* I 705-06); Romulus is otherwise unknown. It has often been argued or assumed that a notorious passage in the *HA* (*Aur.* 15.4, "vidimus proxime consulatum Furii Placidi") refers to this year. Yet whatever the actual date of the *HA*, the *Aur.* purports to have been written in 305-306 (cf. 44), and it is difficult to believe that a forger capable of a hoax of this order would have given himself away by such "childish anachronisms" (Momigliano, *Secondo Contributo* [1960] 140). If the passage has any genuine reference at all, a suffect consulate celebrated by the father or grandfather of the consul of 343 is an obvious possibility.

Orientis

<u>FASTI:</u>	Heracl. ('Placianus') Hyd. Pasch. Theo Scal. (adds cc.)	Placidus et Romulus
<u>LAWS:</u>	Antioch, 1 law, *CTh* 9.21.5, 22.1 (18.ii); Hierapolis, 2 laws (*CTh* 8.1.1, *p.p.* 9.vi; *CTh* 15.8.1, 4.vii)	Placidus et Romulus
<u>PAPYRI:</u>	*P.Oxy.* XLVIII 3389.1 (14.iii; Plac. is v.c. praef. sacr. praet.); *P.Sakaon* 48.27 (6.iv); *P.Harr.* II 216.1 (17?.vi); *P.Abinn.* 45.23 (23.vi; Fl. Plac.); *SPP* II p.34.23 (7.vii); *P.Oxy.* LIV 3776.32 (24.vii); *P.Cair.Goodsp.* 14.13 (11.viii); *P.Panop.* 19 i.b.5 (13.ix); 19 i.c.2 (19.ix; om. 2nd cos.); *P.Abinn.* 46.9 (21.ix; Fromolus); *P.Mil.* I 66.5; *SB* XIV 11548.15 (Fur. not cert.; p.c. also poss.); *P.Leeds Mus.* 25	Furius Placidus et Fl. Romulus vv.cc.
	P.Panop. 19 i.d.3 (6.x)	Placidus et Romulus
<u>OTHER:</u>	Athan., *Index* (27.iii)	Placidus et Romulus

Occidentis

<u>FASTI</u>:	Chr. 354 (fast.,pasch.,praef.) VindPr. Prosp. Aq. Cass. VindPost.	Leontius et Sallustius
<u>LAWS</u>:	*CTh* 12.1.37 (28.v); 8.10.2 (29.vi), both no prov.	Leontius et Sallustius
<u>INSCR.</u>:	**ROME:** *ICUR* I 79 = *ILCV* 3797	Leontius et Bonosus
	ICUR n.s. VIII 21600 = *ILCV* 2817 (17.ix); *ICUR* suppl. 1449 (frag.); *ICUR* n.s. IV 11752; *ICUR* I 80	Leontius et Sallustius
	ITALY: *CIL* XI 4030 = *ILCV* 3227 (Capena, Reg. VII; 21.i); *CIL* XI 4031 = *ILCV* 3227A (Capena; 25.i); *CIL* XI 4032 (Capena; 14.ii-15.iii); *CIL* X 478 = *ILS* 6114 (Paestum, Reg. III; 8.iv; Fll.); *I.Christ.Ital.* IV 12 (Capena)	(Fll.) Leontius et Bonosus
	CIL XI 7788 = *ILCV* 2960 (Capena; 28.vi)	Leontius et Sallustius
	DALMATIA: *CIL* III 9563, 12867 = *ILCV* 3042 (3.v; frag.)	[Leontius et] Bonosus

<u>NOTES</u>:

Leontius was PPO Or. 340-344; Sallustius was (eastern?) magister peditum at any rate during his consular year (*PLRE* I 502-03; 798). In the West, Bonosus is securely attested as Leontius' colleague up till April or May. Why this was so, and why Bonosus was eventually replaced by Sallustius are alike mysterious. Bonosus left no traces in the fasti, and there are no papyri before August to tell us if he was disseminated in the East; the mention of Sallustius in the Index to the Festal Letters is later editorial information. It is usually assumed (e.g., *PLRE* I 164) that Bonosus is the magister militum found in Constantius' service in 347 (*CTh* 5.6.1), but the removal and replacement of an ordinary consul normally implies disgrace and *damnatio memoriae* (e.g. 325, 399, 413, 520). The consul may be another man.

Orientis

<u>FASTI</u>:	Heracl. Hyd. Pasch. Theo Scal. (adds cc.)	Leontius et Sallustius
<u>LAWS</u>:	*CTh* 13.4.3 (6.vii, no prov.); cf. West.	Leontius et Sallustius
<u>PAPYRI</u>:	*P.Princ.* II 81.1 = III 181* (Sall. is comes); *P.Abinn.* 2.10 (Lat.; om. sacr.)	Fl. Leontius praef. sacr. praet. et Fl. Sallustius mag. ped. vv.cc.
	P.Panop. 19 i.e.3; x.a.6 (both viii-ix; om. vv.cc.); 19 iii.b.4 (x-xi)	Leontius et Sallustius vv.cc.
<u>OTHER</u>:	Athan., *Index* (15.iv)	Leontius et Sallustius

Occidentis

<u>FASTI:</u>	Chr. 354 (fast.,pasch.,praef.) VindPr. Prosp. Aq. Cass. VindPost.	Amantius et Albinus
<u>LAWS:</u>	*CTh* 10.10.7 (Trier, 15.v); 3.5.7 (Agrippina, 9.vi/11.vii); 11.30.23 (no prov., 2.vii)	Amantius et Albinus
<u>INSCR.:</u>	**ROME:** *ICUR* n.s. VII 17432 (23.i); *ICUR* n.s. V 13289 (10.iii); *ICUR* n.s. III 8139 = *ILCV* 2967 adn. (14.iv-15.v); *ICUR* n.s. IV 10851 = *ILCV* 589ab (10.vii); *ICUR* n.s. VII 17431 = *ILCV* 4742 (20.vi; only Amant. desp. avail. space); *ICUR* n.s. III 8721 = *ILCV* 4461 (26.viii); *ICUR* n.s. V 13897 (9.ix; [Fl. Am.], Numm. Alb.); *ICUR* n.s. V 13100 (27.ix); *ICUR* n.s. V 13293; *ICUR* n.s. IV 11753 (frag.); *ICUR* n.s. II 4799 (frag.); *ICUR* n.s. II 4798 = *ILCV* 4367 adn.; *ICUR* n.s. V 13292a/b/c (frag.)	(Fl.) Amantius et (Nummius) Albinus

ITALY: *CIL* XI 4033* = *ILCV* 3194 (Capena, Reg. VII; 2.i); Agnello, *Silloge* 88 = *AE* 1933, 29* (Catania; 21.ix); *CIL* XI 4034 = *ILCV* 3035 (Capena; 30.ix); *CIL* XI 4035 = *ILCV* 3035 (Capena; 6.x); *CIL* X 6420 = *ILCV* 4422 (Terracina, Reg. I)

AFRICA: *I.Ant.Maroc* II 16 = *ILCV* 1470 (Tangier)

Orientis

<u>FASTI:</u>	Heracl. Hyd. Pasch. Theo	Amantius et Albianus
	Scal.	Amantius et Savinianus cc.
<u>LAWS:</u>	*CTh* 11.7.5 (Nisibis, 12.v)	Amantius et Albinus
<u>PAPYRI:</u>	*P.Abinn.* 58.1 (1.ii); 59.19 (2.ii; Fl. Sall., praeff.)	p.c. Fl. Leontii et Iulii Sallustii vv.cc. (praeff.)
	P.Wisc. I 12.1 (30.v); *P.Lond.* III 1248.24 (p.226) (vi-vii); *P.Genova* I 22.1 (15.viii); *P.Lond.* III 1246.23 (p.224) (20.viii); 1247.26 (p.225) (25.viii); *P.Harr.* 82.1 (viii-ix); *P.Panop.* 19 ii.4 (15.x; om. Fll.); 19 x.b.4 (30.xi; om. Fll.); *P.Princ.* III 183.1	Fll. Amantius et Albinus vv.cc.
<u>OTHER:</u>	Athan., *Fest.* 17 (7.iv); *Index*	Amantius et Albinus

<u>NOTES:</u>

Amantius is otherwise unknown; Albinus held no identifiable post higher than comes before his consulate. *ILS* 1238 describes him as *consul ordinarius iterum*, which has usually been referred to a suffect consulate held earlier than 345 (*PLRE* I 37). For other possibilities, see above, p.3. Dissemination in Egypt was somewhat late.

Occidentis

<u>FASTI</u>:	Chr. 354 (fast.,pasch.,praef.) VindPr. Prosp. Aq. Cass.	p.c. Amanti et Albini
	Prosp. Aq. VindPost. Cass.	Constantius IV et Constans III
<u>LAWS</u>:	none	
<u>INSCR.</u>:	**ROME:** *ICUR* n.s. IV 11754 (25.ii/27.iv); *ICUR* n.s. VIII 23401 (8.iii); *CIL* VI 1769 (15.iii); *ICUR* n.s. I 3163 -3164 = *ILCV* 3831A (19.vii); *ICUR* n.s. I 1421 = *ILCV* 2627 (27.viii); *ICUR* n.s. I 3126 = *ILCV* 2602 (12.ix); *CIL* VI 37122 = *ILCV* 162 (15.ix); *ICUR* n.s. V 13101 (vv.cc.; frag.); *CIL* VI 1768 = *ILS* 1229; *ICUR* suppl. 1458 = *ILCV* 1126B	p.c. Amanti et Albini (vv.cc.)
	ITALY: *ICUR* I 90 = *CIL* XI 4036 (Capena, Reg. VII; 6-13.vi; cos. possible); *CIL* X 4712 = *ILCV* 1 344 (Calvi, Reg. I; 1.ix)	
	AFRICA: *AE* 1955, 139 (Kherba des Aouisset)	
<u>COINS</u>:	*RIC* VIII 341-42 (Siscia)	Constantius and Constans in cos. robes
<u>OTHER</u>:	Council at Cologne: *Conc. Galliae* (Corp.Christ.Lat. 148), p.27* (12.v)	p.c. Amanti et Albani

Orientis

<u>FASTI:</u>	Heracl. Hyd. Theo Scal.	Constantius IV et Constans III
	Pasch.	Constantius Aug. VI et Constans Aug. III
<u>LAWS:</u>	*CTh* 11.39.4 (C'polis, 27.viii)	Constantius IV et Constans III Augg.
<u>PAPYRI:</u>	*SB* XIV 12088.1 (5.iii); *P.Lond.* III 1249.22 (p.227) (5.v)	p.c. Fll. Amantii et Albini vv.cc.
	P.Abinn. 47.20* (1.v); 48.21* (29.vi); 49.26* (5.vii); *P.Herm.* 21.1 (20.vii); 54.1 (prob. copy); *P.Abinn.* 60.25 (28.vii); 50.26 (30.vii); 61.12 (21.viii); 51.21 (26.viii); 52.23* (29.viii); *P.Nag Hamm.* 64.1 (21.xi); *P.Lond.* III 979.1 (p.234) (22.xii); *P.Abinn.* 53.19 (xii); 54.32; *P.Oslo* III 113.1; *P.Oxy.* VI 897.1; *P.Harr.* II 217.1 (p.c. poss.); *WO* 1309 (confused)	DD.NN. Constantius IV et Constans III Augg.
	P.Panop. 19 vii.4 (x-xi)	IV et III
<u>OTHER:</u>	Athan., *Fest.* 18 (30.iii); *Index*	Constantius IV et Constans III Augg.
	Hist.Aceph. 1.2 [2] (21.x)	Constantius IV et Constans III

<u>NOTES:</u>

The appearance of vv.cc. in *ICUR* n.s. V 13101 is remarkable at this date in a western inscription.

"L'entente entre les deux empires fut rétablie: en 346, Constance et Constant revêtirent ensemble le consulat" (A. Piganiol, *L'empire chrétien*[2] [1972] 93). So they did. But as the varied evidence here assembled makes clear, Constans refused to recognize this joint consulate. What more eloquent proof could there be of the distance between the brothers? Even in the East, the announcement did not reach the Arsinoite Nome until the start of May, when a bit of overlap is found.

Occidentis

FASTI: Chr. 354 (fast.,pasch.,praef.)   Rufinus et Eusebius
                VindPr. Prosp. Aq. Cass.
                VindPost.

LAWS: none

INSCR.:   **ROME:** *ICUR* n.s. I 3164 =   (Vulcacius) Rufinus et
                ILCV 3831 (19.v); *ICUR* n.s.   (Fl.) Eusebius
                VII 17433 = *ILCV* 3001 (22.viii);
                ICUR n.s. V 13294 (Bulc. Ruf.,
                [Fl. Eus.])

                ITALY: *CIL* X 477 = *I.Lat.Paestum*
                107 (Paestum, Reg. III; 1.viii;
                Vulc. Ruf., Fl. Eus.)

                CIL XI 2599 = *ILCV* 4544 adn. (nr.   Rufinus et Eusebius
                Chiusi, Reg. VII; 14.ix-15.x)

                GAUL: *CIL* XIII 299 = *ILCV* 273
                (Valcabrere, Aquitania; 5.vii)

NOTES:

    Rufinus was PPO Ital. 344-347 (*PLRE* I 782-83) and distantly related to the imperial house (his sister was the mother of the future Caesar Gallus: *PLRE* I 382); Eusebius was MVM (East) *ca* 347 or earlier (*PLRE* I 307-08). The order of names in *CTh* 11.36.8 is remarkable but probably not significant.

Orientis

<u>FASTI:</u>	Heracl. Hyd. Pasch. Theo Scal. (adds cc.)	Rufinus et Eusebius
<u>LAWS:</u>	*CTh* 5.6.1 (Hierapolis, 11.v)	Rufinus et Eusebius
	CTh 11.36.8 (Ancyra, 8.iii)	Eusebius et Rufinus
<u>PAPYRI:</u>	*P.Oxy.* XLIII 3146.1 (10.v); *P.Oxy.* IX 1190.15 (22.vi); *P.Ant.* I 31.14 (24.vii); *P.Charite* 7.22 (22.x; om. comes); *P.Athen.* 34.28 (om. v.c. praef. sacr. praet., v.c. after Eus.; perh. vv.cc. at end); *ChLA* XI 472.8 (Lat.; om. sacr., comes)	Volcacius Rufinus v.c. praef. sacr. praet. et Fl. Eusebius v.c. comes
<u>OTHER:</u>	Athan., *Fest.* 19 (12.iv); *Index*	Rufinus et Eusebius
	Socrates, *HE* 2.20	Rufinus et Eusebius

Occidentis

<u>FASTI</u>:	Chr. 354 (fast., pasch., praef.) VindPr. Prosp. Aq. Cass. VindPost.	Philippus et Salia
<u>LAWS</u>:	3 laws, earliest *CTh* 10.1.6 (24.iv); 1 from Milan, 17.vi (*CTh* 10.14.2)	Philippus et Salia
<u>INSCR.</u>:	**ROME**: *ICUR* n.s. I 318 = *ILCV* 3797A (5-13.i); *ICUR* n.s. IV 11755 (30.i); *ICUR* I 97 = *ILCV* 1267 (8.iii); *ICUR* n.s. II 5711 = *ILCV* 4326 (30.iii); *ICUR* n.s. IV 11756* (14.iv-15.v); *ICUR* n.s. VI 15986 (24.vi); *ICUR* n.s. VIII 20773 = *ILCV* 1477 (2.vii); *ICUR* n.s. III 6498 = *ILCV* 3382 (12.vii); *ICUR* I 100 (24.vii); *ICUR* n.s. I 887 = *ILCV* 748 (2.viii; Fl. with each); *ICUR* n.s. I 81 = *ILCV* 2940 (19.xi); *ICUR* n.s. VII 19948; *ICUR* n.s. VII 19949	(Fl.) Philippus et (Fl.) Salia
	ICUR n.s. V 13102 = *ILCV* 4428B adn. (cf. Ferrua, *Nuove corr.* 175)	Sallies e[t Philippi?]

<u>NOTES</u>:

Fl. Philippus was PPO Or. 344-351, *PLRE* I 696-67; Fl. Salia was mag. equitum 344-348, *PLRE* I 796.

Orientis

<u>FASTI:</u>	Heracl. Hyd. Pasch. Theo	Philippus et Salia
<u>LAWS:</u>	none	
<u>PAPYRI:</u>	*BGU* II 405.1 (6.iii); *SB* XIV 11877.1 (1.iv); *P.Charite* 8.20 (27.v); *P.Nag Hamm.* 65.15 (7.x); *SB* XIV 11929.18 (9.xii); *BGU* III 917.1	Fl. Philippus v.c. praef. sacr. praet. et Fl. Salia v.c. magister equitum
<u>OTHER:</u>	Athan., *Fest.* 20 (3.iv); *Index*	Philippus et Salia

Occidentis

<u>FASTI</u>:	Chr. 354 (fast., pasch., praef.) VindPr. Prosp. Aq. Cass. VindPost.	Limenius et Catullinus
<u>LAWS</u>:	16 laws, earliest *CTh* 7.22.6 (= 8.4.4) (2.ii)	Limenius et Catullinus
<u>INSCR.</u>:	**ROME**: *ICUR* n.s. IV 12524 = *ILCV* 2795B (11.i); *ICUR* n.s. VIII 20774 = *ILCV* 2600 (6.v); *ICUR* n.s. III 8418 (14.viii-15.ix); *RAC* 44 (1968) 140 fig. 1 (27.x); *ICUR* n.s. V 13296* = *ILCV* 4328A (21.xi; frag.); *ICUR* n.s. IX 23758 = *ILCV* 2874 (26.xi); *ICUR* n.s. V 13295; *ICUR* n.s. V 13899*; *ICUR* n.s. IV 11090* ([Ulp.] Lim., Ac[on. Cat]ull.); *ICUR* n.s. III 8419 (p.c. poss.)	(Ulpius) Limenius et (Aconius) Catullinus
	ITALY: *I.Christ.Ital.* IV 18 (Capena, Reg. VII; 16.v-13.vi; frag.); Agnello, *Silloge* 89 (Syracuse; cos. or p.c.?; Gk.)	
	BAETICA: *CIL* II 2211* = *ILS* 7222 (9.iv)	

<u>NOTES</u>:

Ulpius Limenius was PPO Ital. and PVR 347-349, *PLRE* I, 510; Catullinus was PPO ?Ital. 341 and PVR 342-344, *PLRE* I, 187-88. His first name appears as Aco in *CIL* II 2635, and Chastagnol, *Fastes* 121, has argued that this is the correct form. But abbreviation there is not impossible, and against Aco must be set Aconius in *CIL* VI 1780 (contrary to *PLRE*, which says that Aco is there), and the postconsular date in *P.Amh.* 139 has Acontius. He had a daughter Aconia. That Acontius in the papyrus is a more familiar name than Aconius is understandable; but such a substitution for Aco would be less likely. The conflation of 349 and 359 in *Hist.Aceph.* is striking.

Orientis

<u>FASTI:</u>	Heracl. Hyd. Pasch. Theo	Limenius et Catullinus
	Scal.	Limenius et Tolinus cc.
<u>LAWS:</u>	Antioch, *CTh* 12.1.39 (1.v); C'polis, *CTh* 12.2.1 (3.x)	Limenius et Catullinus
<u>PAPYRI:</u>	*P.Würzb.* 16.14 (10.x); *P.Amh.* II 140.19 (om. Fll.)	Fll. Limenius et Catullinus vv.cc.
<u>OTHER:</u>	Athan., *Index* (26.iii)	Limenius et Catullinus
	Hist.Aceph. 1.2 [2]	Hypatius et Catullinus

Occidentis

<u>FASTI</u>:	Chr. 354 (fast., pasch., praef.) VindPr. Prosp. Aq. Cass. VindPost.	Sergius et Nigrinianus
<u>LAWS</u>:	*CTh* 7.1.4 (27.vi; but cf. *PLRE* I 231, s.v. Cretio)	
<u>INSCR.</u>:	**ROME**: *ICUR* n.s. I 2596 = *ILCV* 2940A (10.vii)	p.c. Limeni et Catullini
	CIL VI 498 (27.ii/29.iv)	Fl. Anicius et Nigrinianus
	ICUR n.s. VII 19950 = *ILCV* 3996A (30.vii); *ICUR* n.s. I 479 = *ILCV* 3650 (11.viii; Fl. bef. each); *ICUR* n.s. I 1422 = *ILCV* 2628 (15.viii; Sergius om.); *ICUR* n.s. V 13297 (24.xi); *ICUR* n.s. V 13298* [sub 349]; *ICUR* suppl. 1472 (frag.); 1473 = n.s. II 4801	(Fl.) Sergius et (Fl.) Nigrinianus
	ITALY: *CIL* XI 7784 = *ILCV* 2827 (Capena, Reg. VII; 6.iii)	p.c. Limeni et Catullini

<u>NOTES</u>:

   Magnentius was proclaimed Augustus on 18.i.350 (*PLRE* I 532; *RIC* VIII 10-12), though his hold on Italy was briefly shaken by the short-lived seizure of Rome by Nepotianus from 3-30 June (*RIC* VIII 240-41). It is difficult to know whether it is significant that, with the dubious and partial exception of *CIL* VI 498, Sergius and Nigrinianus are not attested at Rome till July. The Roman p.c. of 10 July certainly suggests late dissemination.
   CIL VI 498 (extant in MS only) gives Anicius instead of Sergius. The possibility that Fl. Anicius was the original consul of the year, soon disgraced and replaced (*PLRE* I 67) may surely be excluded. For we have Sergius known as early as 7.iv in Egypt, and disgraced consuls were not normally replaced (though see on 325). There must be some error in *CIL* VI 498: perhaps Anicius is an additional name of Nigrinianus, with Sergius omitted; of the thirty Anicii listed in *PLRE*, not one has the name Anicius in last place (most in first place). Nothing else is known of the careers of either Sergius or Nigrinianus (cf. *PLRE* I 826, 631), though the latter was at any rate an easterner (from Antioch).

Orientis

<u>FASTI:</u>	Heracl. Hyd. Pasch. Theo Scal. (adds cc.)	Sergius et Nigrinianus
<u>LAWS:</u>	none	
<u>PAPYRI:</u>	*P.Abinn.* 62.1 (5.ii); *P.Amh.* II 139.21 (28.ii; Ulpius Limenius, Acontius Catullinus)	p.c. (Ulpii) Limeni et (Acontii) Catullini vv.cc.
	P.Amh. II 141.20 (7.iv); *P.Oxy.* XIX 2233.1 (7.vi); *P.Abinn.* 63 i.1,4 (Lat.; 6.x, 13.xi); *P.Harr.* II 218.1; *P.Oxf.* 6.25 (Fl.)	(Fl.) Sergius et (Fl.) Nigrinianus vv.cc.
<u>INSCR.:</u>	**SYRIA:** *Princ. Arch. Exp. Syria* III 669 (Il-Kefr)	Fl. Sergius et Fl. Nigrinianus vv.cc.
<u>OTHER:</u>	Athan., *Index* (8.iv)	Sergius et Nigrianus
	Socrates, *HE* 2.26	Sergius et Nigrianus

351
(at the time) Magnentius Aug. et Gaiso
(retrospectively) p.c. Fl. Sergii et Fl. Nigriniani

Occidentis

FASTI:	Chr. 354 (praef.)	Magnentius et Gaiso
	Chr. 354 (fast., pasch.) Prosp. Aq. Cass.	p.c. Sergii et Nigriniani
LAWS:	none	
INSCR.:	none	

NOTES:

For Magnentius, see 350. Gaiso was the officer who murdered Constans for him, cf. *PLRE* I 380.

Orientis

<u>FASTI:</u>	Heracl. Hyd.	p.c. Sergii et Nigriniani
	Pasch.	Sergius et Nigrinianus
	Theo	qui fuerint
<u>LAWS:</u>	none	
<u>PAPYRI:</u>	*P.Abinn.* 55.17 (11.ii); *PSI* VI 707.1 (ii-iii); *CPR* V 12.8 (5.vii)	p.c. Fl. Sergii et Fl. Nigriniani vv.cc.
<u>INSCR.:</u>	**ASIA:** J. Ebersolt, *Mission arch. de Constantinople* (1920) 45 (6.i; Lat.)	p.c. Sergii et Nigriniani
<u>OTHER:</u>	Athan., *Index* (31.iii)	p.c. Sergii et Nigriani
	Socrates, *HE* 2.29	p.c. Sergii et Nigriani

<u>NOTES:</u>

Socrates (l.c.) dates the Synod of Sirmium "after the consulate of Sergius and Nigrianus, in which year no consul celebrated the customary consular ceremonials, because of the tumults of war." Sozomen (*HE* 4.6.6) adds that there was no consul in either East or West. Magnentius, to be sure, proclaimed his own; but they were not recognized in the East and disappeared from all of the sources except Chr. 354 (praef.), as happened also in 352; Theo records a stage at which an announcement was still expected.

(at the time) **Magnus Decentius et Paulus**
(retrospectively) **Constantius Aug. V et Constantius Caesar**

Occidentis

<u>FASTI</u>:	Chr. 354 (praef.)	Decentius et Paulus
	Chr. 354 (episc. p.76,13.19) VindPr. Prosp. Aq. Cass. VindPost.	Constantius V et Constantius Caesar[36]
	Chr. 354 (fast., pasch.)	Constantius V et Constantius iunior
<u>LAWS</u>:	*CJ* 6.22.5 (Sirmium, 26.ii); *CTh* 15.14.5 (Milan, 3.xi)	Constantius Aug. V et Constantius Caesar
<u>INSCR.</u>:	**ROME**: *ICUR* n.s. II 4241 = *ILCV* 3252A (3.ii); *ICUR* I 113 = *ILCV* 2941 (12.iii); *ICUR* n.s. VIII 21601 = *ILCV* 2626 (28.iii); *ICUR* n.s. VII 19951 = *ILCV* 3302 (28.iv); *ICUR* n.s. II 4798 = *ILCV* 4367 adn. (20.vii; frag.); *ICUR* n.s. I 2081 (14.vii-13.viii)	Decentius (Caesar) et Paulus
	ICUR n.s. I 1252* = *ILCV* 2967 adn.	Magnentius et Decentius
	ITALY: *AE* 1982, 383 (Aquileia, Reg. X; 28.vii); *ICUR* I 116 = *CIL* XI 4037 (Capena, Reg. VII; 14.vii-13.viii; frag.)	Decentius (Caesar) et Paulus
	GERMANIA: *CIL* XIII 7918 = *ILS* 7069 (Zülpich, Caes.)	
	SPAIN: *Röm.Inschr.Tarraco* 943 (Caes.)	
	DALMATIA: *Forsch.Salona* II 102 (frag.)	
<u>COINS</u>:	Kent, *Roman Coins*, no.673: consular solidus of Decentius Caesar	

[For inscriptions from Illyricum, see next page]

[36]VindPr. gives V and IV.

Orientis

<u>FASTI:</u>	Heracl. (iun. I) Hyd. Pasch. (Aug.) Theo (Aug.) Scal. (adds invv. Augg.)	Constantius (Aug.) V et Constantius Caes. (iun. I)
<u>LAWS:</u>	none	
<u>PAPYRI:</u>	*P.Stras.* I 9.6 (27.iii; frag.); *ChLA* III 210.1* (Lat.)	DD.NN. Constantius Aug. V et Constantius nob. Caesar
<u>INSCR.:</u>	**SYRIA:** *Princ. Arch. Exp. Syria* III 799[1] (Djebil)	Constantius V et Constantius I
<u>OTHER:</u>	Athan., *Index* (19.iv)	Constantius Aug. <V> et Constantius Caesar I

<u>NOTES:</u>

Decentius was a kinsman of Magnentius (*PLRE* I 244-45); Paulus (ib. 683) is otherwise unknown. The fasti were corrected later except, once again (cf. 351), for Chr. 354 (praef.). It is uncertain whether Decentius' elevation fell in 350 or 351; for a full discussion and bibliography (especially of the numismatic evidence), see P. Bastien, *Quaderni ticinesi di numismatica e antichità classiche* 12 (1983) 177-89 (arguing for 350). But (as Seeck saw, *RE* 4.2, 2268) if Decentius was elevated in 350, we should have expected to see him as consul in 351. There are one or two exceptions to this rule, as Bastien pointed out, but there is usually some exceptional circumstance to explain them (see p.23), not present here. It would be anomalous for Magnentius to have preferred a subject to his new coemperor.

Fl. Claudius Constantius was the name taken by Gallus (son of Constantius cos. 335) when he became Caesar.

[Continued from preceding page]

<u>INSCR.:</u>	**ILLYRICUM:** R. Noll, *Griechische u. latein. Inschr. der Wiener Antikensammlung* (Wien 1962) 410 = *Bull.Ist.Corr.Arch.* 1868, 143 no. 2 (Sirmium; 24.iv)	DD.NN. Fl.Iul. Constantius invictus Aug. V et Fl. Constantius nob. Caesar

Occidentis

FASTI: Chr. 354 (fast., pasch., praef.)   Constantius VI et
         VindPr. Prosp. Cass. Aq.   Constantius II[37]
         VindPost.

LAWS: *CTh* 11.36.9 (23.vii, no prov.);   Constantius Aug. VI et
         CTh 16.10.5 (23.xi, no prov.   Constantius Caesar II
         [Arles?]; om. name of Caesar
         but has title)

INSCR.: **ROME:** *ICUR* n.s. V 13299 = *ILCV*   Constantius Aug. VI et
         3239 (14.iii/14.v); *ICUR* n.s.   Constantius II
         V 13902 = *ILCV* 3250A adn. (11.iv?;
         frag.); *ICUR* n.s. V 13900 (26.v);
         ICUR n.s. V 13901 = *ILCV* 2976 adn.
         (11.viii)

NOTES:

   Magnentius committed suicide on 10.viii; but there are no indications that he controlled Rome at all in 353.

[37]Prosp. adds Caes. bef. II; VindPr. gives VI & V.

Orientis

FASTI: Heracl.

Constantius II
et Constans II

Hyd. Pasch. (Aug., Caes.) Theo
Scal. (adds novorum Augustorum,
om. II)

Constantius (Aug.) VI
et Constantius (Caes.) II

LAWS: none

PAPYRI: *P.Oxy.* XIV 1632.1 (25.vii);
P.Coll.Youtie II 83.1 (12.xii)

DD.NN. Constantius Aug. VI
et Constantius nob. Caesar II

OTHER: Athan., *Index* (11.iv)

Constantius Aug. VI et
Constantius Caesar II

Socrates, *HE* 2.32

Constantius VI et
Constantius Gallus II

Hist.Aceph. 1.8 [3]

Constantius VI Aug. et
Constans Caesar II

Occidentis

FASTI:	Chr. 354 (fast., pasch., praef.) VindPr. Prosp. Cycl. VindPost. Pasch.	Constantius VII et Constantius III[38]
	Aq. Cass.	Constantius VII et Constans Caesar III
LAWS:	*CTh* 8.5.5 (no prov., 25.vii)	Constantius Aug. VII et Constantius Caesar III
INSCR.:	**ROME**: *ICUR* n.s. V 13903 (31.viii); *ICUR* n.s. V 13904 (28.x; om. Aug.); *ICUR* n.s. VIII 21602 (om. Caes.); *ICUR* n.s. VIII 20776 (om. Aug.; frag.)	DD.NN. Constantius Aug. VII et Constantius Caesar III
OTHER:	Amm.Marc. 14.10.1 ('Caesaris iterum')	

[38]Prosp. adds Caes. bef. III; Cycl. IV for second consul; VindPr. VII & VI.

Orientis

<u>FASTI</u>:	Heracl.	Constantius VII et Constans III
	Hyd. Pasch. (VII & VI) Theo (Caes.)	Constantius VII et Constantius (Caes.) III
	Scal.	Constantius VII et Constantius novus II Augg.
<u>LAWS</u>:	*P.Laur.* IV 169.4* (Nicomedia; 14.ix-1.x)	[Constantius Aug.] VII et Constantius Caesar [III]
<u>PAPYRI</u>:	*PSI* IX 1077.1* (13.ii; restored, p.c. poss.); *P.Stras.* 329.4 (12.v; om. nob.); *P.Ant.* I 36.1 (6.vi); *P.Laur.* IV 162.1 (v-xii; frag.)	DD.NN. Constantius Aug. VII et Constantius nob. Caesar III
<u>INSCR.</u>:	**TRANSJORDAN:** *AE* 1905, 215* (Es-Sanamen in Hauran)	DD.NN. Constantius Aug. VII et Constantius nob. Caesar III
<u>OTHER</u>:	Athan., *Index* (27.iii)	Constantius Aug. VII et Constantius Caesar III
	Socr., *HE* 2.34	(Constantius VII et Constantius Caesar III)
	Soz., *HE* 4.7.3	

Occidentis

FASTI: Chr. 354 (pasch.) VindPr.   Arbitio et Lollianus
                  Prosp. Cycl. (A. et Iulianus)
                  Aq. Cass.

LAWS: About 14 laws, 9 from Milan,   Arbitio et Lollianus
                  earliest *CTh* 11.34.2 (1.i)

INSCR.:   **ROME**: *ICUR* n.s. IX 23759 = *ILCV*   (Fll.) Arbitio et
                  4217 (22.vi; om. Loll.); *CIL* VI   Lollianus
                  1166B (30.vi); *ICUR* n.s. II 4268 =
                  ILCV 3099 (1.vii; Fll.);
                  ICUR n.s. VII 17424 = *ILCV* 265
                  (31.vii); *ICUR* suppl. 1494 = *ILCV*
                  4435 (18.viii); *ICUR* n.s. II 4802 =
                  ILCV 1735 adn. (9.x); *ICUR*
                  n.s. I 2769 = *ILCV* 2978A (11.x);
                  ICUR suppl. 1485 = *ILCV* 4331
                  (30.xi); *ICUR* I 126 = *ILCV*
                  3002A (10.xii); *ICUR* n.s. IV 11091

OTHER: Amm.Marc. 15.8.17

Orientis

<u>FASTI:</u>	Heracl. Hyd. Pasch. Theo	Arbitio et Lollianus
	Scal.	Arbitio et Iulianus cc.
<u>LAWS:</u>	none	
<u>PAPYRI:</u>	*P.Oxy.* IV, p.202.1* = *M.Chr.* 361 (12.i)	p.c. DD.NN. Constantii Aug. VII et Constantii nob. Caes. III
<u>OTHER:</u>	Athan., *Index* (16.iv)	Arbitio et Lollianus
	Subscription to letter of Constantius II to the Senate about Themistius; one MS date of reading (1.ix), in Themistius, *Orationes*, ed. G. Downey and A.F. Norman III (Leipzig 1974) 122	Arepio et Lollianus
	Hist.Aceph. 1.9 [4] (vii-viii; 23.xii)	Arbetio et Lollianus
	Socr., *HE* 2.34	Arbetio et Lollianus

<u>NOTES:</u>

Arbitio was magister equitum from ?351-361; Lollianus was a prominent aristocrat, PVR 342, PPO 355-356 (*PLRE* I 94-95; 512-14). Lollianus had earlier been designated to the consulate by Constantine in 337 (see p.19).

Occidentis

<u>FASTI:</u>	Chr. 354 (pasch.) VindPr. Prosp. Cass. Aq. Cycl.	Constantius VIII et Iulianus Caesar (I)[39]
<u>LAWS:</u>	6 laws, all from Milan, earliest *CTh* 16.10.6 (19.ii)	Constantius Aug. VIII et Iulianus Caesar
<u>INSCR.:</u>	**ROME:** *ICUR* n.s. V 13906 = *ILCV* 3002 (17.i; om. Iul.); *ICUR* n.s. III 6499 = *ILCV* 3663 (29?.ii); *ICUR* I 129 (16.iii-1.iv); *ICUR* n.s. VIII 20777 = *ILCV* 2600A (18.xii; om. Aug.); *ICUR* n.s. VIII 20766* (Iul. name om.; frag.; could be p.c.)	Constantius Aug. VIII et Iulianus Caesar
	ITALY: Agnello, *Sylloge* 90 = *CIL* X 7167* = *ILCV* 1715 (Syracuse, 27.iv)	
<u>OTHER:</u>	Amm.Marc. 16.1.1	

---

[39]Cycl. and VindPr. om. Caes.; Chr. 354 (pasch.) adds I.

Orientis

FASTI:	Heracl. Hyd. Theo (Aug.)	Constantius (Aug.) VIII et Iulianus Caesar I
	Pasch.	Constantius Aug. X et Iulianus Caesar
	Scal.	Constantius VIII et Constantius III Augg.
LAWS:	none	
PAPYRI:	*P.Oxy.* LI 3622.1 (29.viii; perp.); *PSI* IX 1078.1 (25.xi)	DD.NN. Constantius (perp.) Aug. VIII et Iulianus fortiss. et nob. Caesar I
INSCR.:	**ASIA:** *AE* 1977, 806 (N. Phrygia)	DD.NN. Constantius Aug. VIII et Iulianus Caesar (I)
	SYRIA: *LBW* III 2412k (Mahite; Caes. I)	
OTHER:	*Hist.Aceph.* 1.10 [5] (6.i)	p.c. Arbitionis et Lolliani
	Athan., *HArian.* 81 fin (12.ii)	qui fuerint nuntiati p.c. Arbitionis et Lolliani
	Athan., *Index* (7.iv)	Constantius Aug. VIII et Iulianus Caesar I
	Hist.Aceph. 2.1 [5] (10.vi)	Constantius Aug. VIII et Iulianus Caesar I

NOTES:

Fl. Claudius Iulianus (son of Constantius cos. 335) was proclaimed Caesar on 6.xi.355. The dissemination of the new consuls in the East seems to have been slow, to judge from the presence of a p.c. in the reference in Athanasius; there are no papyri from before August.

Occidentis

FASTI:	Chr. 354 (pasch.) Prosp. Cycl. Aq. Cass.	Constantius IX et Iulianus Caesar II[40]
LAWS:	About 12 laws, earliest *CTh* 9.16.4 (Milan, 25.i); 1 from Rome, 2 from Sirmium	Constantius Aug. IX et Iulianus Caesar II
INSCR.:	**ROME:** *CIL* 749 = *ILS* 4267a (10.viii; om. Aug., Caes.); *ICUR* I 132 = n.s. I 3166* (7.ix; om. Caes.; frag.); *ICUR* n.s. V 13300* (24.ix); *ICUR* suppl. 1489 = *ILCV* 4622 adn. (much rest.)	Constantius Aug. IX et Iulianus Caesar II
	ICUR n.s. III 8722* (8.ii)	VIIII et II
	ITALY: *CIL* X 1191 = *ILCV* 3352 (Atripalda, Reg. I; 18.vii)	Constantius Aug. IX et Iulianus Caesar II
	TUNISIA: *AE* 1955, 51 (Mactar)	DD.NN. Fl. Constantius max. IX et Iulianus nob. Caes. II
COINS:	*RIC* VIII 277.297-298 (all Rome, presumably minted for distribution during his visit to Rome in Spring, 357; no issue is known for Milan, where he entered his consulate)	Constantius, consular image on obv. of solidi
OTHER:	Amm.Marc. 16.11.1	

[40]Cycl. om. Caes. II.

248

Orientis

FASTI: Heracl. Hyd. Theo (Aug.)   Constantius (Aug.) IX et
Iulianus Caesar II

Pasch.   Constantius Aug. XI et
Iulianus Caes. II

Scal.   Constantius IX et
Lollianus

LAWS: none

PAPYRI: *P.Oxy.* I 66.1 (2.vii); *SPP* XX
101.7 (22.ix; om. nob.);
P.Lond. III 1245.12* (p.228;
Cl.); *ChLA* V 285.13* (Cl.; Lat.)   DD.NN. Constantius Aug. IX
et (Claudius) Iulianus
nob. Caesar II

OTHER: *Hist.Aceph.* 2.2 [6] (24.ii)   Constantius IX
et Iulianus Caesar II

Athan., *Index* (23.iii)   Constantius Aug. IX
et Iulianus Caesar II

Occidentis

FASTI: Chr. 354 (pasch.) Prosp.   Datianus et Cerealis
          Cycl. VindPost.

          VindPr.   Datianus et Symmachus

          Aq. Cass.   Titianus et Cerealis

LAWS: 9 laws, 6 from Sirmium, earliest   Datianus et Cerealis
          CTh 9.42.4 (4.i); 1 from Mursa

          CTh 8.5.10 (Sirmium, 27.x)   p.c. Constantii Aug. IX
                                                       et Iuliani Caes. II

INSCR.:   **ROME:** *ICUR* n.s. V 13907   Datianus et Cerealis
          (23.ii/24.iv); *CIL* VI 752* = *ILS*
          4267D (17?.iii); *CIL* VI 750 =
          ILS 4267B (4.iv); *CIL* VI 751a
          = *ILS* 4267C (19.iv); *ICUR* n.s.
          VII 17437 = *ILCV* 2941 adn. (5.vi);
          ICUR n.s. VII 17438 = *ILCV* 2976
          (22.vii); *ICUR* n.s. VIII 20779 =
          ILCV 3141 (18.xi); *ICUR* n.s. IV
          12525 (20.xii); *AE* 1976, 33; *ICUR*
          n.s. VIII 20780a (frag.); 20780b
          (frag.); *ICUR* n.s. IV 12420 =
          ILCV 2690 adn. (frag.)

          ITALY: *CIL* XI 5434 (Asisium, Reg.   Censorius Datianus et
          VI; 25.i)   Neratius Cerealis

          CIL IX 1009 = *ILCV* 3911   Datianus et Cerealis
          (nr. Conza, Reg. II; 10.x)

          DALMATIA: *CIL* III 2654 =
          ILCV 1223 (Salona, 2.xi);
          CIL III 13120A

OTHER: Amm.Marc. 17.5.1   Datianus et Cerealis

Orientis

FASTI:	Heracl. Hyd. Pasch. Theo Scal. (adds cc.)	Datianus et Cerealis
LAWS:	none	
PAPYRI:	*P.Ross.Georg.* III 28.1 (prob. p.c., 24.ii [not indic.])	DD.NN. Constantius Aug. [IX]
OTHER:	Athan., *Index* (12.iv)	Tatianus et Cerealis
	Hist.Aceph. 2.3 [6] (29.viii)	Tatianus et Cerealis
	Socrates, *HE* 2.39	Tatianus et Cerealis

NOTES:

Datianus was a close confidant of Constantius (*PLRE* I 243); Cerealis was PVR 352-353 (ib. 197-99). The western p.c. presumably reflects usage at time of receipt in Carthage rather than at time of issue in Sirmium; it is addressed to the proconsul of Africa; cf. above, p.81.

Occidentis

<u>FASTI</u>:	VindPr. Prosp. Cycl. Aq. Cass.	Eusebius et Hypatius
	VindPost.	Tatianus et Hypatius
<u>LAWS</u>:	8 laws, earliest *CTh* 11.16.9 (no prov., 23.ii); 2 fr. Sirmium (earliest *CTh* 6.4.14,15, 22.v), 1 from Singidunum	Eusebius et Hypatius
<u>INSCR.</u>:	**ROME**: *ICUR* n.s. V 13302 (6.i) ; *ICUR* n.s. V 13301 = *ILCV* 4698 (10.i); *ICUR* n.s. VII 18472* = *ILCV* 4755C (8.ii); *CIL* VI 752 = *ILS* 4267D (11.iii); *ICUR* n.s. V 13307 (8-15.v); *ICUR* n.s. I 1424 = *ILCV* 2807A adn. (9.vi); *ICUR* n.s. V 13305 (14.vi-15.vii; names reversed); *ICUR* n.s. V 13304 (5/7.viii); *ICUR* n.s. II 4164 = *ILCV* 90 (25.viii); *ICUR* suppl. 1494 = *ILCV* 4435 (3.x); *ICUR* n.s. V 13908 (24.xi); *ICUR* n.s. V 13306; 13303* (sub 349); *ICUR* n.s. VIII 20781; 23402b	Eusebius et Hypatius
	ITALY: *CIL* X 1338 = *ILCV* 1356 (Nola, Reg. I; 27.v); *CIL* IX 5012 = *ILCV* 739 (Farfa, Reg. IV; 3.ix); *CIL* XI 3054 + add. p.1321 = *ILCV* 4184 (Polimartium, Reg. VII)	
	DALMATIA: *CIL* III 9503 add. bis = *ILCV* 1505 (Salona, 24.xi + p.c. in 360 on 1.v)	
<u>OTHER:</u>	**TUNISIA**: *AE* 1915,81* (Henchir-Bou-Gornine; ostrakon)	p.c. Datiani et Cerealis
	Amm.Marc. 18.1.1, 29.2.9	Eusebius et Hypatius

Orientis

<u>FASTI:</u>	Heracl. Hyd. Pasch. Theo Scal. (adds cc.)	Eusebius et Hypatius
<u>LAWS:</u>	none	
<u>PAPYRI:</u>	*P.Oxy.* LI 3624.18, 3625.17 (25.i)	p.c. Censorii Datiani patricii et Neratii Cerealis vv.cc.
	BGU III 909.30* (24-29.viii; om. Fl. twice); *P.Oxy.* LI 3623.1 (*ca* 30.viii?); *BGU* I 316.1 (12.x)	Fl. Eusebius et Fl. Hypatius vv.cc.
<u>OTHER:</u>	Socrates, *HE* 2.37; Athan., *De Synodis* 8 (both Sirmium, 22.v)	Fl. Eusebius et Hypatius vv.cc.
	Athan., *Index* (4.iv); *Hist.Aceph.* 2.5 [7] (23.vi); Socrates, *HE* 2.39; Sozom., *HE* 4.17.10;	Eusebius et Hypatius

<u>NOTES:</u>

Eusebius (*PLRE* I 308-09) and Hypatius, PVR 379 and PPO 382-383 (*PLRE* I 448-49), were brothers of Constantius' wife Eusebia.

Occidentis

FASTI: VindPr. Prosp. Aq. Cass.   Constantius X et
                                              Iulianus Caesar III[41]

             Cycl.   DD.NN.

             VindPost.   Eusebius et Iulianus II

LAWS: 3 laws, see East

INSCR.:   **ROME:** *ICUR* n.s. V 13309 (21.i);   DD.NN. Constantius Aug. X
            ICUR n.s. IV 11093 = *ILCV* 2807   et Iulianus Caesar III
            adn. (23.iv); *ICUR* n.s. III 3141 =
            ILCV 2690 adn. (6.v); *ICUR* n.s.
            V 13308* (26.vii; om. Caes.);
            ICUR n.s. VI 16967 = *ILCV* 2941A
            (17,19.viii; only Const. X); *ICUR*
            n.s. VI 16968 (7.ix; frag.; om.
            Caes.); *ICUR* n.s. V 13310 (23.x;
            much rest.); *ICUR* n.s. V 13105*
            = *ILCV* 2883 (19.xii); *ICUR* n.s.
            VIII 20782 (much rest.)

            ITALY: *AE* 1901, 168 = *ILCV* 297
            (Capua, Reg. I, 27.vi)

            CIL X 4485 = *ILCV* 2932 (Capua,   DD.NN. X et III
            Reg. I; 18.x); Agnello, *Sylloge* 91
            = *IG* XIV 112 (Syracuse, 27.xi; Gk.)

            DALMATIA: *CIL* III 9503 add. bis   p.c. (Eusebii et Hypatii)
            = *ILCV* 1505 (Salona; 1.v)

            CIL III 9504 = *ILCV* 240   Constantius Aug. X et
            (Salona, 7.viii)   Iulianus Caesar III

OTHER: Amm.Marc. 20.1.1   Constantius X et
                                              Iulianus III

---

[41]VindPr. om. Caes.

Orientis

FASTI: Heracl. Hyd. Theo (Aug.)   Constantius (Aug.) X et
          Scal. (Aug.; Iul. II)   Iulianus Caesar III

          Pasch.   Constantius Aug. XII et
                                            Iulianus Caes. III

LAWS: *CTh* 11.24.1 (C'polis, 4.ii);   Constantius Aug. X et
          16.2.15 (30.vi); 7.4.6   Iulianus Caesar III
          (Hierapolis, 17.xii)

PAPYRI: *P.Mert.* I 36.1 (early 360);   p.c. Fl. Eusebii et
          P.Oxy. VIII 1103.1 (12.ii)   Hypatii vv.cc.

          P.Oxy. XIV 1695.1 (19.xii);   DD.NN. Constantius Aug. X
          XX 2267.1 (much rest.); perhaps   et Iulianus nob. Caes. III
          P.Ross.Georg. V 29.35

OTHER: Athan., *Index* (23.iv)   Constantius Aug. X et
                                            Iulianus Caes. III

          Socrates, *HE* 2.43   Constantius X et
                                            Iulianus Caes. III

NOTES:

For the situation in 360 see p.64 above.

Occidentis

<u>FASTI</u>:	VindPr. Prosp. Cycl. Aq. Cass.	Taurus et Florentius
	VindPost.	Constantius IX et Florentius
<u>LAWS</u>:	4 laws, see East	
<u>INSCR.</u>:	**ROME**: *ICUR* n.s. VIII 23403 (14.ii-15.iii; frag.); *ICUR* n.s. VII 19952 (11.iii/11.v; frag.; *ICUR* n.s. III 8142 = *ILCV* 288 (22.vii); *ICUR* I 148 = *ILCV* 2967 (25.viii; Fll.); *ICUR* n.s. VI 15443 (5.x); *ICUR* n.s. VIII 22967 (7.x); *ICUR* n.s. I 2979 = *ILCV* 4368 (8.x); *ICUR* n.s. VII 17440 = *ILCV* 3888A (25.x; Fl. 2x); *AE* 1981, 96 (28.x); *ICUR* n.s. V 13309 (frag.); 13910 (frag.); 13911 (frag.; Fl. 2x); 13311* (sub 349); 13312; *ICUR* n.s. II 6023 = *ILCV* 2569	(Fll.) Taurus et Florentius
<u>OTHER</u>:	Amm.Marc. 21.6.5, 22.3.4	

Orientis

FASTI:	Heracl. Hyd. Pasch. Theo	Taurus et Florentius
	Scal.	Constantius Aug. XI et Iulianus Caes. III
	(also)	Paulus et Frorentius cc.
LAWS:	4 laws, earliest *CTh* 16.2.16 (Antioch, 14.ii); 1 from Gephyra (3.v)	Taurus et Florentius
PAPYRI:	*P.Fuad Univ.* 16.7*	[Taurus et Fl]orentius vv.cc.
	P.Oxy. XLIX 3479.1 (ed. 361?; cf. p.69)	Taurus et Eusebius vv.cc.
OTHER:	Athan., *Index* (8.iv); *Hist.Aceph.* 2.6 [7] (26.xi); Socrates, *HE* 2.45, 47; 3.1; Zos. 3.10.4	Taurus et Florentius

NOTES:

Taurus was PPO 355-361 (*PLRE* I 879-80). Sons were coss. in 397 and 400; a grandson in 428 and a more remote descendant in 513. Florentius was PPO in 357-360 and 360-361 (*PLRE* I 365).

A remarkable passage in the Martyrdom of S. Eusignius (*AnalBoll* 100 [1982] 213) tells us that "In the consulate of Julian Constantine Caesar was killed and Julian became emperor on the 8th day before the Ides of November." Not a single item in this statement is accurate, and we cannot tell if the author preserves dimly a memory of Julian's consulate in 360 or in 363.

Occidentis

<u>FASTI:</u>	Comput. (1, 153, 16.18) VindPr. Prosp. Cycl. Aq. Cass. VindPost.	Mamertinus et Nevitta
<u>LAWS:</u>	About 30 laws, earliest *CTh* 7.4.7 (no prov., 6.i)	Mamertinus et Nevitta (vv.cc.)
<u>INSCR.:</u>	**ROME:** *ICUR* n.s. IV 11758 = *ILCV* 3904 (28.i); *CIL* VI 753 = *ILS* 4267E (16.iii-1.iv); *ICUR* n.s. VI 15989 = *ILCV* 4338A (17.v/16.vi); *ICUR* n.s. III 8143 = *ILCV* 1268 (20.v); *ICUR* I 151 = *ILCV* 2390 (10.vii); *ICUR* n.s. I 82 (18.vii); *ICUR* n.s. III 8421 = *ILCV* 2978B (31.viii; Cl. M. et Fl. N.); *ICUR* n.s. VII 17441 = *ILCV* 2602 adn. (4.ix); *ICUR* n.s. IV 9557 (6-13.ix); *ICUR* n.s. III 6500 = *ILCV* 2967 adn. (20.xi); *CIL* VI 31075* (Cl. M.); *ICUR* n.s. I 2805; *ICUR* n.s. II 4804; *ICUR* n.s. VII 17442 = *ILCV* 312 adn. (Fl. N.); *ICUR* n.s. IV 12526* = *ILCV* 4144B (D.N. Kl. M. et Fl. N.); *ICUR* n.s. VI 15444; *ICUR* n.s. V 13313C (frag.) **ITALY:** *Riv.Ingauna e Intemelia* n.s. 36-37 (1981-82) 3 (Liguria; 7.vi); *CIL* IX 5684 (Cingoli, Reg. V; 10.x); *CIL* IX 3921 (Alba, Reg. IV; Cl. M. et Fl. N.) **DALMATIA:** *Forsch.Salona* II 105 (Salona; frag.)	(Claudius) Mamertinus et (Fl.) Nevitta
<u>OTHER:</u>	Amm.Marc. 21.10.8; 21.12.25; 22.7.1; Mamertinus, *Gratiarum actio de consulatu suo* (*Pan.Lat.* 3 = xi)	

Orientis

<u>FASTI:</u>	Heracl. Hyd. Pasch. Theo	Mamertinus et Nevitta
<u>LAWS:</u>	C'polis, 7 laws (earliest *CTh* 8.1.6, 17.i); Antioch, 11 laws (earliest *CTh* 1.16.8, 28.vii)	Mamertinus et Nevitta (vv.cc.)
<u>PAPYRI:</u>	*SB* XVI 12384.16*, 12385.19* (both 22.vii); *P.Cair.Preis.* 2.1, 3.1; *P.Cair.Goodsp.* 15.1	Mamertinus et Nevitta vv.cc.
	P.Flor. I 30.25	Fl. Claudius et Fl. Nevitta vv.cc.
<u>INSCR.:</u>	**THRACE:** Unpubl. inscr. communicated by I. Sevcenko (Selymbria; 23.i; Lat.)	Mamertinus et Nevitta vv.cc.
<u>OTHER:</u>	*Hist.Aceph.* 3.1 [9] (4.ii)	p.c. Tauri et Florentii
	Athan., *Index* (31.iii)	Mamertinus et Nevitta
	Hist.Aceph. 3.4 [10] (24.x)	Mamertinus et Nevitta

<u>NOTES:</u>

Mamertinus was PPO 361-365 (*PLRE* I 540-41); Nevitta a barbarian general, mag. equitum 361-363 (ib. 626-27). The p.c. in the *Hist.Aceph.* stands alone in the documentation, but there are no papyri from before July to check its witness to late dissemination.

Occidentis

FASTI:	VindPr. Prosp. Cycl. VindPost. Cass. Aq.	Iulianus Aug. IV et Sallustius[42]
LAWS:	none	
INSCR.:	**ROME:** *ICUR* n.s. I 2082 (2.ii; om. D.N.?); *ICUR* n.s. I 1425 = *ILCV* 2603 (13.v); *ICUR* n.s. I 1426 = *ILCV* 3359B (29.v; Cl., Fl.); *ICUR* n.s. VII 17443 = *ILCV* 4743 (1.ix; om. D.N.); *ICUR* n.s. I 3167 = *ILCV* 3137 (4.ix); *ICUR* n.s. I 2806 = *ILCV* 4338F (29.ix; om. D.N.); *ICUR* n.s. VIII 23404 (frag.); *ICUR* n.s. I 966 = *ILCV* 4653 (incl. Aug.; pre-Oct.?); *ICUR* n.s. I 2083 (incl. Aug.; pre-Oct.?); *ICUR* n.s. VII 17430C (Cl.; much rest.; pre-Oct.?)	D.N. (Cl.) Iulianus Aug. IV et (Fl.) Sallustius
	ICUR suppl. 1515 = *ILCV* 4410 (14.ix-15.x; Divus); *ICUR* n.s. I 1427 = *ILCV* 2941A adn. (11.x); *ICUR* n.s. V 13314 = *ILCV* 4409 (18.x; Divus; om. Sall.); *ICUR* n.s. IV 9559 = *ILCV* 1327 (8.xii); *ICUR* n.s. IV 11759; *ICUR* suppl. 1517 = *ILCV* 1529 adn. (IV om.; frag.); *ICUR* n.s. I 2807 (Cl. Iul., om. num.)	(Divus) (Cl.) Iulianus IV et (Fl.) Sallustius
	ITALY: *CIL* XI 4038 = *ILCV* 3035B (Capena, Reg. VII; 30.x); *CIL* XI 4039 = *ILCV* 3035A (Capena; 2.xii; IV om.);	Iulianus IV et Sallustius
COINS:	*RIC* VIII 530.204-206 (all from Antioch, where Julian entered his consulate)	Julian, consular image on obv. and rev. of solidi
OTHER:	Amm.Marc. 23.1.1	

---

[42]Aug. om. in VindPr. Cycl. Prosp. Aq. Cass.

Orientis

<u>FASTI:</u>	Heracl. (om. Aug.) Hyd. Pasch. Theo Scal. (adds cc.)	Iulianus Aug. IV et Sallustius
<u>LAWS:</u>	About 15 laws, 6 from Antioch (earliest *Const.Iul. de postulando* [*Abh.München*, n.f. 58 (1963) 7.38], 17.i); *CTh* 9.17.5 (12.ii); Mopsuestia, 1 law (12.xi, *CTh* 11.20.1)	Iulianus Aug. IV et Sallustius
<u>PAPYRI:</u>	*P.Lond.* V 1651.1 (20.iv); *BGU* III 939.1 (7.viii; om. perp., v.c.); *P.Oxy.* VIII 1116.1 (viii-ix; om. D.N., perp. Aug., Fl.); *P.Stras.* 131.1 (frag.)	D.N. Iulianus perp. Aug. IV et Fl. Sallustius v.c. praef. sacr. praet.
	P.Monac. III 90.7	D.N. Iulianus perp. [Aug.]
<u>OTHER:</u>	Athan., *Index* (20.iv); *Hist.Aceph.* 4.1 [12] (19.viii)	Iulianus Aug. IV et Sallustius
	Socrates, *HE* 3.21; Libanius, *Orat.* 12 (cf. 1.127-29): Hypatikos addressed to Julian in Antioch; Iacobus of Edessa p.283 (Brooks, *Chron.Min.*, p.212)	

<u>NOTES:</u>

Sallustius was PPO Gall. in 361-363 (*PLRE* I 797). According to Ammianus (23.1.1), "for a private citizen to be associated with the reigning emperor seemed an innovation which no one recalled to have been made since Diocletian and Aristobulus" [i.e. 285]. If he had checked, he would have noticed Maximianus and Ianuarianus in 288.

Though Julian died on 26 June, the news is not reflected in Roman inscriptions until October; the omission of all titles in *P.Oxy.* VIII 1116 (August-September) may show knowledge of his death in Egypt by then. The Roman inscriptions seem consistently to omit D.N. from October on, often replacing it with Divus.

Occidentis

<u>FASTI</u>:	VindPr. Prosp. Cycl. VindPost. Cass. Aq.	Iovianus et Varronianus[43]
<u>LAWS</u>:	About 54 laws, earliest *CTh* 13.3.6 (11.i); 1 law each from Emona, Verona, Tres Tabernae and Serdica; 6 from Aquileia (7.ix), 5 from Altinum (30.ix), 9 from Milan (9.xi), 2 from Philippopolis (earliest 24.v), 3 from Naissus (earliest 8.vi), 2 from Sirmium (earliest 5.vii)	Divus Iovianus et Varronianus
<u>INSCR.</u>:	**ROME**: *ICUR* n.s. IV 9560* (19.ii or ?21.iv); *ICUR* n.s. II 6024 (frag.)	D.N. Iovianus Aug. I et Varronianus
	ICUR n.s. I 2770 = *ILCV* 3546 (30.iii; frag.); *ICUR* n.s. VI 15587 = *ILCV* 4377 (8.v; Div.; Aug.); *CIL* VI 1729 = *ILS* 1254 (28.v; Div., Aug.); *CIL* VI 32422 = *ILS* 4938 (9.vi; Div.); *ICUR* n.s. V 13912* (15.vi); *ICUR* n.s. IV 11096 = *ILCV* 3099 adn. (29.vi); *ICUR* I 174 = *ILCV* 4342 (19.viii; Div., Aug.); *ICUR* n.s. IV 11760 = *ILCV* 4411 (14.viii-1.ix; Div., Aug.; om. Varr.); *ICUR* n.s. I 2084* = *ILCV* 2941A (14.ix-1.x; Div., Fl.); *ICUR* n.s. VII 19953 = *ILCV* 2631A (12.x); *ICUR* n.s. VIII 21603 (18.x); *ICUR* n.s. IX 23760 = *ILCV* 4689; *ICUR* n.s. VII 17439D (frag.); *ICUR* n.s. II 5789 (frag.); *ICUR* n.s. V 13316 (frag.); *ICUR* n.s. V 13914 (frag.); *ICUR* n.s. VI 15990A; *ICUR* n.s. VI 15990B (frag.); *ICUR* suppl. 1524 = *ILCV* 4411 adn. (frag.; Divus); *ICUR* n.s. III 7381* (frag.; nob. puer; p.c. poss.) [Continued on the next page]	(Divus) Iovianus (Aug.) et (Fl.) Varronianus (nob. puer)

[43]VindPost. has Iurianus.

Orientis

FASTI:	Heracl. (om. Aug.) Hyd. Pasch. Theo ('Iulianus' Aug.)	Iovianus Aug. et Varronianus
	Scal.	Varronianus et Iulianus et Iovianus cc.
LAWS:	*CTh* 9.25.2 (*p.p.* [Seeck] Antioch, 19.ii)	Iovianus Aug. et Varronianus
	Earliest *CTh* 10.1.8 (Mnizus [Seeck], 4.ii); laws also from C'polis, Pantichion, Nicaea or Nicomedia, Hadrianopolis, Herakleia	Divus Iovianus et Varronianus
PAPYRI:	*P.Ryl.* IV 662.1 (13.ii); *PSI* I 90.1 (17.x; om. IV and Sallustius' title; adds vv.cc.)	p.c. Iuliani IV et Fl. Sallustii v.c. praef. sacr. praet.
	CPR X 107 (26.vii)	Iovianus et Varronianus
OTHER:	*Hist.Aceph.* 4.4 [13] (14.ii)	Iovianus et Varronianus
	Athan., *Index* (4.iv)	Iovianus Aug. et Varronianus
	Socrates, *HE* 3.26, 4.1; Iacobus of Edessa p.284 (Brooks, *Chron.Min.*, p.212)	(Iovianus) et Varronianus
	Amm.Marc. 25.10.11,17; Eutropius, 10.18.3; Themistius, *Orat.* 5 (Hypatikos) was addressed to Jovian in Ancyra on 1 January	

NOTES: For notes on 364, see the Critical Appendix.

[Continued from preceding page]
ITALY: *CIL* XI 8086 (Fossembrone; 16.iii-13.iv; Aug.); *AE* 1964, 203 = *Suppl.Ital.* n.s. 1 (1981) 136 no. 13 (Ponto Ritorto; 18.vii; Div.)

Occidentis

FASTI: VindPr. Prosp. Ciz. Cycl. Cass.   Valentinianus Aug. et
             Aq. VindPost.   Valens Aug.[44]

LAWS: About 75 laws, 43 from Milan,   Valentinianus et
             earliest *CTh* 15.1.14 (1.i); 1 law   Valens Augg.
             each from Tres Tabernae, Ticinum,
             Mantala, 3 from Paris (earliest,
             CTh 11.1.13, 18.x)

INSCR.:   **ROME:** *ICUR* n.s. I 2695 = *ILCV*   DD.NN. (Fl.) Valentinianus
             1327A (28.v; om. Augg.); *ICUR* n.s.   et (Fl.) Valens Augg.
             IV 9561 (1.vi); *ICUR* n.s. V 13915
             (8.vi; om. DD.NN.); *ICUR* suppl.
             1531 (14.vi-22.vi; frag.; Augg.);
             ICUR n.s. I 1189 = *ILCV* 2807A adn.
             (6-13.viii; om. DD.NN., Augg.);
             ICUR n.s. III 6501 (1.ix; rev. names);
             ICUR suppl. 1532 = *ILCV* 3996C (15.ix;
             om. DD.NN.); *ICUR* n.s. VII 17444 = *ILCV*
             2611 (16.x-13.xi; om. DD.NN.); *ICUR* n.s.
             I 2085 = *ILCV* 94A adn. (frag.; om. Augg.);
             ICUR n.s. III 7382* (Fl., om. DD.NN.?);
             ICUR n.s. III 9343 (frag.; om. DD.NN.,
             Augg.); *ICUR* n.s. III 8144 (frag.)

             ITALY: *Eph.Ep.* 8 (1899) no. 514
             (Capua, Reg. I; 13.v; om. DD.NN., Augg.)

COINS: *RIC* IX 145.1a (Siscia), 173.3   Valentinian, consular
             (Thessalonica)   image on obv. of solidi

             RIC IX 145.1b (Siscia), 173.1,   Valens, consular
             174.3b (Thessalonica)   image on obv. of solidi

OTHER: Amm.Marc. 26.9.1; 10.15   Valentinianus et Valens

             Valens and Valentinian entered their
             consulates at Constantinople and Milan
             respectively (Amm.Marc. 26.6.1)

---

[44]VindPr., Prosp., Ciz., Aq., Cass., and Cycl. all om. Aug.

Orientis

<u>FASTI:</u>	Heracl. (om. Aug. 2x) Hyd. Pasch. Theo (I) Scal.	Valentinianus Aug. et Valens (Aug.) (I)
<u>LAWS:</u>	5 laws from C'polis (earliest, *CTh* 5.19.1, 27.i), 1 each from Caesarea, Chalcedon	Valentinianus et Valens Augg.
<u>PAPYRI:</u>	*P.Oxy.* XLVIII 3393.1 (8.vi); *SB* III 6612.2 (22.x)	DD.NN. Valentinianus et Valens perpp. Augg.
<u>INSCR.:</u>	**ARABIA:** *SEG* VII 1164 (Dibîn)	DD.NN. Valentinianus et Valens perpp. Augg.
<u>OTHER:</u>	Athan., *Index* (27.iii); *Hist.Aceph.* 5.1 [15] (5.v; om. Augg., I); Socrates, *HE* 4.3	Valentinianus et Valens Augg. I

<u>NOTES:</u>

Valentinian was proclaimed Augustus on 26.ii.364; Valens on 1.iii.364 (*PLRE* I 930-31; 933-94).

Occidentis

<u>FASTI</u>:	VindPost. Prosp. Ciz. Cycl. Cass. Aq.	Gratianus et Dagalaifus
	VindPr.	Gratianus nob. puer et Dagalaifus
<u>LAWS</u>:	*CTh* 11.1.13 (*acc.* Carthage, 18.i; issued 18.x.365 at Paris)	p.c. Valentiniani et Valentis Augg.
	About 11 laws, 6 from Reims, earliest *CTh* 6.1.7 (7.iv); Veromandui, 1 law	Gratianus nob. puer et Dagalaifus
<u>INSCR.</u>:	**ROME:** *ICUR* n.s. II 4269 = *ILCV* 4606 (26.i)	p.c. Valentiniani et Valentis
	ICUR n.s. IV 11097 (14.ii-15.iii; frag.); *ICUR* n.s. IV 11763 = *ILCV* 1126 (21.vi); *ICUR* n.s. I 1429 = *ILCV* 2942 (23.ix); *ICUR* n.s. V 13322 (24.ix); *ICUR* suppl. 1560 = *ILCV* 2629 (7.xi); *ICUR* n.s. VII 17449 (14.xi; Fl. 2x); *ICUR* n.s. III 8723 = *ILCV* 3252B (29.xi); *ICUR* n.s. V 13312, 13321, 13323; *ICUR* n.s. IV 10853 (frag.); *ICUR* n.s. II 4163 (very frag.); *ICUR* n.s. V 13918 (frag.); *ICUR* n.s. VII 17448 = *ILCV* 1477A (nob. puer); *ICUR* n.s. VII 17453A; *ICUR* n.s. VIII 21606a*, 20787 (both frag.)	(Fl.) Gratianus (nob. puer) et (Fl.) Dagalaiphus
	ITALY: *CIL* V 8606 = *ILCV* 3632A (Aquileia, 31.viii); *CIL* X 4487 = *ILCV* 1490 (Capua, 4.ix; Fl. Gr.); *ICUR* I 187 = *ILCV* 4343 (Ostia, 22.xi); *CIL* XI 4328 (Terni, Reg. VI)	
<u>OTHER</u>:	Amm.Marc. 26.9.1, 27.2.1	

Orientis

<u>FASTI</u>:	Heracl. (om. nob.) Pasch. Theo Hyd. (om. nob.)	Gratianus nob. et Dagalaifus
	Scal.	Gratianus fil. Valent. Caes. et Galaifus
<u>LAWS</u>:	1 law at Thyateira (*CTh* 4.12.6, 4.iv; Th. is Seeck's rest. for MS TRIV)	Gratianus nob. puer et Dagalaifus
<u>PAPYRI</u>:	*P.Flor.* I 84.1 = *SB* XIV 12816 (frag.)	Gratianus nob. fil. D.N. Valentiniani Aug. et Dagalaiphus v.c. stratelates
<u>OTHER</u>:	*Hist.Aceph.* 5.6 [16] (1.ii)	p.c. Valentiniani et Valentis
	Hist.Aceph. 5.7 [17] (1.ii)	Gratianus et Dagalaifus
	Athan., *Index* (16.iv)	Gratianus Aug. filius et Dagaiphus
	Socrates, *HE* 4.5, 4.9	Gratianus et Dagalaifus

<u>NOTES:</u>

Gratian was not proclaimed Augustus till 24.viii.367; Dagalaifus was magister peditum 364-366 in the West (*PLRE* I 239). The *Hist.Aceph.* and one Roman inscription indicate a slightly delayed dissemination in both parts of the empire. For the western law with a p.c., see above, p.79.

Occidentis

<u>FASTI</u>:	VindPr. Prosp. Ciz. Aq. Cass. Cycl.	Lupicinus et Iovinus
	VindPost.	Lupicinus et Rufinus
<u>LAWS</u>:	*CTh* 12.7.3 (Nemetacum, 4.viii); *CTh* 11.1.16 (Novesia, 25.x)	p.c. Gratiani n.p. et Dagalaifi
	About 20 laws, 7 from Reims, earliest *CTh* 10.19.4 (8.i); Ambiani, 2 laws (earliest *CTh* 8.14.1, 18.viii); Trier, 2 laws (earliest *CTh* 11.68.4, 13.x)	Lupicinus et Iovinus
<u>INSCR.</u>:	**ROME:** *ICUR* n.s. I 896 = *ILCV* 2943 (16.ii)	p.c. Gratiani et Dagalaifi
	CIG IV 9842 = *ILCV* 2878 (12.iii; Gk.); *ICUR* n.s. I 1350 = *ILCV* 1296A (23.iv); *ICUR* n.s. II 6028 = *ILCV* 3099 adn. (13.v); *ICUR* n.s. IV 9563 = *ILCV* 3253 (18.v); *ICUR* n.s. III 8146* (5.vi); *ICUR* n.s. VII 17456 = *ILCV* 1296 (7.vi; Fll.); *ICUR* n.s. I 3175 = *ILCV* 4311 (5.ix); *ICUR* n.s. VII 17455* = *ILCV* 2807A adn. (14.ix; Iov. om.); *ICUR* suppl. 1579 = *ILCV* 2943 adn. (13.x; frag.); *ICUR* n.s. II 6027 = *ILCV* 2976A (25.x); *ICUR* n.s. I 2086 = *ILCV* 4217a; *ICUR* n.s. II 6026 = *ILCV* 2824; *ICUR* n.s. IV 12529; *ICUR* n.s. VIII 20790 = *ILCV* 4796 adn.; *ICUR* n.s. VII 17454 = *ILCV* 3789D/4612 adn.; *ICUR* n.s. II 4805 = *ILCV* 2807A adn.; *ICUR* n.s. I 1431; *ICUR* n.s. I 2792 (very frag.); *ICUR* n.s. V 13920; *ICUR* n.s. VI 15768 = *ILCV* 4699; *ICUR* n.s. VIII 23408b (frag.)	(Fll.) Lupicinus et Iovinus
	ICUR n.s. I 265; *ICUR* n.s. I 1401; *ICUR* suppl. 1589; *ICUR* n.s. II 4805 = *ILCV* 2609	Iovinus et Lupicinus

[Continued on the next page]

Orientis

<u>FASTI</u>:	Heracl. Hyd. Pasch. Theo Scal. (adds cc.)	Lupicinus et Iovinus
<u>LAWS</u>:	Marcianopolis, 2 laws (earliest *CTh* 12.18.1, 10.v)	Lupicinus et Iovinus
<u>PAPYRI</u>:	*SB* XIV 12099.1*	p.c. Gratiani nob. fil. D.N. Valentiniani Aug. et Dagalaifi v.c. mag. eq.
<u>OTHER</u>:	Athan., *Index* (1.iv)	Lupicinus et Iovinus
	Hist.Aceph. 5.7,11 [17, 18] (24.ix)	Lupicinus et Iovinus
	Socrates, *HE* 4.11	Lupicinus et Iovianus

<u>NOTES</u>:

Fl. Lupicinus was magister equitum in the East 359-360, 364-367 (*PLRE* I 520-2l); Fl. Iovinus was magister equitum in the West from 361-369 (ib. 462-463). It is not at all clear when the consuls were disseminated in the East. The Roman inscriptions have them by 12.iii, but the only papyrus (undated) has a p.c.; the p.c. in two laws in the *CTh* from August and October is no doubt an African *accepta* date, cf. above, p.81. Why four Roman inscriptions have an inverted order, we do not know. One is tempted to imagine that some masons thought Iovinus was the late Iovianus Aug. and so entitled to priority.

[Continued from the preceding page]

ITALY: *ZPE* 63 (1986) 166 (Assisi, Reg. VI; 22.ii); *CIL* X 4724 = *ILCV* 97 (nr. Capua, Reg. I; 10.v; v[v.cc.]); *I.Christ.Ital.* III 3* (Casauria, Reg. IV; 22.ix)	Lupicinus et Iovinus (vv.cc.)

Occidentis

<u>FASTI</u>:	Chr. 354 (pasch.) VindPost. Prosp. Ciz. Cycl. Aq. Cass.	Valentinianus II et Valens II
<u>LAWS</u>:	*CTh* 8.5.29 (Trier, 2.xii)	p.c. Lupicini et Iovini vv.cc.
	6 laws, 3 from Trier, earliest *CJ* 11.62.4 (15.iii)	Valentinianus et Valens II Augg.
<u>INSCR.</u>:	**ROME**: *ICUR* n.s. I 725 = *ILCV* 2603 adn. (1.ii); *ICUR* suppl. 1590 = *ILCV* 3310 (22.ii; om. DD.NN.); *ICUR* suppl. 1593 = *ILCV* 1145 (6.iii/6.v; frag.); *AE* 1977, 143* (6.iii); *ICUR* n.s. II 5931 = *ILCV* 3797B (14.vi-15.vii; frag.); *ICUR* n.s. II 4807 = *ILCV* 2609 (26.ix; frag.; om. DD.NN.); *ICUR* n.s. VII 17457B (14.ix-15.x; frag.; om. Augg.); *ICUR* n.s. I 963 = *ILCV* 2732 (4.x; om. DD.NN.); *ICUR* n.s. I 2808 = *ILCV* 4393A (18.xi; om. DD.NN., Augg.); *ICUR* n.s. V 13326* (30.xi); *ICUR* n.s. I 479 = *ILCV* 3650 (7.xii)	DD.NN. Valentinianus et Valens Augg. II
<u>COINS</u>:	*RIC* IX 15.8a and 17.18a-b (Trier), 76.3a (Milan), 217.29a (C'polis), 254.16a (Nicomedia), 278.23a (Antioch)	Valentinian, consular image on obv. of aureus and solidi, consular image of Valens and Valentinian on rev. of solidi
	RIC IX 15.8b and 17.18c (Trier), 76.3b (Milan), 217.29b (C'polis), 254.16b-c,17 (Nicomedia), 278.23b (Antioch)	Valens, consular image on obv. of aureus and solidi, consular image of Valens and Valentinian on rev. of solidi
<u>OTHER</u>:	Letter of Valentinian to Praetextatus, PVR: *Coll.Avell.* 7 (Trier, 12.i)	

270

Orientis

<u>FASTI:</u>	Heracl. Hyd. Pasch. (Aug. 2x) Theo (Valens Aug.)	Valentinianus (Aug.) II et Valens (Aug.) II
<u>LAWS:</u>	None	
<u>PAPYRI:</u>	*P.Lond.* III 1113 (p.lvii; cf. p.336)	p.c. Fl. Lupicini comitis equit. et ped. et Fl. [ ] Iovini vv.cc.
	ChLA XII 523 = *P.Lips.* 33 ii.1* (before 18.viii)	DD.NN. Valentinianus II et Valens II et Gratianus perpp. Augg.
<u>OTHER:</u>	Athan., *Index* (20.iv)	Valentinianus II et Valens II Augg.
	Hist.Aceph. 5.8 [17] (8.vi)	Valentinianus II et Valens II
	Socrates, *HE* 4.11	Valentinianus II et Valens II

<u>NOTES:</u>

The papyri (cf. 369 for a p.c. dating) show a confusion between regnal and consular dating, including all three emperors in the consular formula. The western p.c. (a law addressed to the consularis of Sicily) is presumably an *accepta* date--certainly not usage at the western court as late as December, cf. above, p.82.

Occidentis

FASTI: Chr. 354 (pasch.) VindPost.   Valentinianus nob. puer
           Prosp. Ciz. Cycl. Cass. Aq.   et Victor[45]

LAWS: About 37 laws, 15 from Trier,   Valentinianus nob. puer
           earliest *CTh* 14.3.13 (1.i *acc.*   et Victor (v.c.)
           Seeck) or *CTh* 12.6.15 (*p.p.* 7.i);
           Confluentes, Mattiacum, Altaripa,
           Brisiacum, 1 law each; Noviodunum,
           2 laws

INSCR.:   **ROME**: *ICUR* n.s. III 8148 = *ILCV*   (Fl.) Valentinianus nob.
           1128 (1.ii, 9.iv, 11.iii, 29.x?,   puer et (Fl.) Victor
           4.x); *ICUR* n.s. V 13106 (16.iv;
           Fl. 2x); *ICUR* n.s. VII 17459 =
           ILCV 2925 (25.vii); *ICUR* n.s. II
           4165 = *ILCV* 1603 (20.viii); *AE*
           1912, 261 = *ILCV* 1128 (3.xi);
           ICUR n.s. VII 17457c (25.xi);
           ICUR n.s. VII 19955 (28.xii; Fl.
           Victor); *ICUR* n.s. IV 11101 =
           ILCV 4213A; *ICUR* n.s. VII 19956

           ITALY: *CIL* XI 3278 (Sutri, Reg.
           VII)

[45]Chr. 354 (pasch.) om. nob. puer; Cycl. has Aug. instead.

Orientis

FASTI:	Heracl. Hyd. Theo	Valentinianus et Victor
	Pasch.	Valentinianus Aug. III et Victor
	Scal.	Valentinianus et Victor Augg. III
LAWS:	Marcianopolis, 4 laws (earliest, *CTh* 9.21.7, 11.iii)	Valentinianus nob. puer et Victor (v.c.)
PAPYRI:	*P.Stras.* 272.1	p.c. DD.NN. Valentiniani et Valentis et Gratiani perpp. Augg. II
OTHER:	Athan., *Index* (12.iv); *Hist.Aceph.* 5.10 [17] (8.vi; om. Aug. fil. I)	Valentinianus Aug. fil. I et Victor
	Themistius, *Orat.* 9 (*Protrepticus Valentiniano novo*)	

NOTES:

Valentinianus Galates was the infant son of Valens; he died *ca* 370 (*PLRE* I 381). Victor was magister equitum in the east 363-*ca* 379 (ib. 957-59). For the superfluous third consul in the papyrus, cf. above, p.70 and the year 368.

Occidentis

FASTI: Chr. 354 (pasch.) VindPr.   Valentinianus III
                Prosp. Ciz. Cycl. Aq. Cass.   et Valens III[46]
                VindPost.

LAWS: 11 laws, 6 from Trier, earliest   Valentinianus et
                CJ 2.6.7 (20.ii)   Valens III Augg.

INSCR.:   **ROME:** *ICUR* n.s. I 2087 =   p.c. Victoris et
                ILCV 1478 (13.iv)   Valentiniani nob. pueri

                ICUR n.s. VII 17460 = *ILCV* 2944   (DD.NN.) Valentinianus
                adn. (27.i; om. Augg.); *ICUR* n.s.   et Valens Augg. III
                I 3179 = *ILCV* 2795B adn. (27.iii;
                DD.NN.); *ICUR* n.s. VI 15769 =
                ILCV 4146 adn. (7.vi; frag.; om.
                Augg.); *CIL* VI 509* = *IGUR* I 129
                (17.v/16.vi; DD.NN.); *ICUR* n.s. II
                4501 = *ILCV* 2603A (21.viii; om.
                Augg.); *ICUR* n.s. VII 17462 = *ILCV*
                2945B (30.viii; om. Augg.); *ICUR*
                n.s. I 3180 (5.ix; DD.NN.); *ICUR*
                n.s. IV 11770 = *ILCV* 3996C (14.ix;
                num. after 1st name only); *ICUR*
                n.s. II 6029 = *ILCV* 2807A adn.
                (2.x; num. after 1st name only;
                om. Augg.); *ICUR* n.s. IV 12530 =
                ILCV 2944 (20.ix/12.x; om. Augg.);
                ICUR n.s. IV 12421 = *ILCV* 1297
                (14.x; DD.NN.); *ICUR* n.s. I 1351*
                (frag.); *ICUR* n.s. VII 17461
                (DD.NN.; om. Augg.); *ICUR* n.s. V
                13922 (frag.; om. Augg.)

                ITALY: *AE* 1908, 219 = *ILCV* 2883
                adn. (Teano, 29.iii; om. Augg.)

                NORICUM: *CIL* III 5670a = *ILS* 774   Cons. eorundem DD.
                (Ips; ref. back to heading of doc.   principumque NN. III
                with all 3 emperors mentioned)

---

[46]Ciz., VindPost. om. second III.

Orientis

<u>FASTI:</u>	Heracl. Hyd. Theo	Valentinianus III et Valens III
	Pasch.	Valentinianus Aug. IV et Valens Aug. III
	Scal.	Valentinianus et Valens Augg. IV
<u>LAWS:</u>	Hierapolis, 2 laws (*CTh* 1.29.5, 10.viii; *CTh* 7.13.6, 18.ix)	Valentinianus et Valens Augg. III
<u>PAPYRI:</u>	*P.Oxy.* XVII 2110.1 (6.x); *P.Flor.* I 43.1	DD.NN. Valentinianus et Valens perpp. Augg. III
<u>OTHER:</u>	Athan., *Index* (28.iii)	Valentinianus et Valens Augg. III
	Hist.Aceph. 5.10 [17] (8.vi); Socrates, *HE* 4.14	Valentinianus III et Valens III
	Amm.Marc. 28.5.1	

<u>NOTES:</u>

It is curious to note that, although the new consuls were known in Rome when an inscription referring to 27.i (*ICUR* n.s. VII 17460) was carved, there is one inscription dated by the p.c. of 369 as late as 13.iv. The inscription dated 27.i may have been carved longer after that date than normal.

Occidentis

<u>FASTI</u>:	Chr. 354 (pasch.) VindPr. Aq. Prosp. Ciz. Cycl. Cass. VindPost.	Gratianus Aug. II et Probus[47]
<u>LAWS</u>:	About 23 laws, earliest *CTh* 15.10.1 (no prov. [Trier?], 1.i); Trier, 4 laws (earliest *CTh* 15.7.1, 11.ii); Contionacum, 5 laws (earliest *CTh* 11.1.17, 12.vii); Mainz, 1 law; *Abh.München* n.f. 58 [1963] 7.39 (Rome, n.d.)	Gratianus Aug. II et Probus (v.c.)
<u>INSCR.</u>:	**ROME**: *ICUR* n.s. VIII 23410 = *ILCV* 4456B (31.i); *ICUR* n.s. I 3181 = *ILCV* 4258 (3.ii; om. II); *ICUR* n.s. VII 17464 = *ILCV* 4218 (22.ii; om. II); *ICUR* n.s. VIII 23061 = *ILCV* 2874A (9.iii; om. II; D.N., Petronius Pr.); *ICUR* n.s. VI 15502 (13.iv/13.viii); *ICUR* n.s. I 1432 = *ILCV* 2968 adn. (30.iv; om. II); *ICUR* n.s. II 6031 = *ILCV* 3253A (18.vii; Aug.); *ICUR* n.s. IV 11102* = *ILCV* 1614 (17.viii); *ICUR* n.s. VII 17463 = *ILCV* 4431B (26.viii); *ICUR* n.s. I 2809 = *ILCV* 4351 (16.ix; D.N., Aug.); *ICUR* n.s. IV 11765 (28.ix; om. II); *ICUR* n.s. II 5712 (vii-xii; Aug.); *ICUR* n.s. I 2088 = *ILCV* 1478A (D.N., Fl., Aug., Petr.); *ICUR* n.s. I 2089 (Aug.); *ICUR* suppl. 1606 (mostly rest.); *ICUR* n.s. II 5933 = *ILCV* 3813A (om. II; p.c. poss.); *ICUR* n.s. V 13327 (om. II; p.c. poss.) **ITALY**: *CIL* X 4488 = *ILCV* 1525 (Capua, Reg. I; 25.vii) [Continued on the next page]	(D.N.) (Fl.) Gratianus (Aug.) II et (Petronius) Probus (v.c.)

---

[47]Ciz., Cass., Aq. Prosp., Cycl., and VindPr. omit Aug.

Orientis

FASTI:	Heracl. (om. Aug.) Hyd. Pasch. (om. Aug.) Theo	Gratianus (Aug.) II et Probus
	Scal.	Gratianus Aug. II cl.
LAWS:	C'polis, 4 laws (earliest, *CTh* 13.10.7, 16.i); Ancyra, 1 law	Gratianus Aug. II et Probus [v.c.]
PAPYRI:	*CPR* VIII 38.1 (10.i)	p.c. DD.NN. Valentiniani et Valentis Augg. III
	P.Stras. 243.5 (23.vii; om. Fl.); *P.Lips.* 46.1 (22.viii); 58.21 (8.x; om. Fl.); 59.1 (has num. I); 45.1	D.N. Gratianus perp. Aug. II et Fl. Probus v.c. praef. sacr. praet.
INSCR.:	**ARABIA:** *CIL* III 88 = *ILS* 773 (Petra)	D.N. Gratianus perp. Aug. II et Probus v.c.
OTHER:	Athan., *Index* (17.iv)	Gratianus Aug. II et Probus
	Hist.Aceph. 5.10 [17] (8.vi; om. II); Socrates, *HE* 4.20;	Gratianus II et Probus

NOTES: Probus was the head of the Anician family and PPO four times: *PLRE* I 736-40; D.M. Novak, *Klio* 62 (1980) 473-93; Cameron, *JRS* 75 (1985) 164-82. For the frequent omission of Gratian's iteration numeral, see p.63.

	[Continued from preceding page] **GERMANIA:** Walser, *RIS* II 202 = *CIL* XIII 11538 = *ILS* 8949 (Schwaderloch; D.N.; v.c.); Walser, *RIS* II 201 = *CIL* XIII 11537 (nr. Koblenz, Aargau; cf. prec. for rest.)	
	PANNONIA INF.: *CIL* III 3653* = *Röm.Inschr.Ung.* III 771 (nr. Gran)	Gratianus Aug. II et Probus v.c.
OTHER:	Ausonius, *Epist.* 10.22; Symmachus, *Epp.* 9.112 (with the comm. of S. Roda, 1981, pp.247-49)	

Occidentis

<u>FASTI</u>:	Chr. 354 (pasch.) VindPr. Prosp. Ciz. Cycl. Aq. Cass. VindPost.	Modestus et Arinthaeus
<u>LAWS</u>:	22 laws, earliest *CTh* 7.22.8 (pp. Rome, 15.ii); Trier, 10 laws (earliest *CTh* 14.3.14, 22.ii); Nasonacum, 3 laws (earliest, *CTh* 8.7.12, 30.v); "Cilicia", 1 law	Modestus et Arinthaeus
<u>INSCR.</u>:	**ROME:** *ICUR* n.s. VIII 23412 = *ILCV* 2795B adn. (19.iii; names in ablative)	p.c. D.N. Gratiani II et Probi
	ICUR n.s. VI 17298 (28.iv); *ICUR* n.s. I 1433 = *ILCV* 2976B (9.v; Fl.); *ICUR* n.s. VII 17457d (14.vii-13.viii; frag.); *ICUR* n.s. I 1434 = *ILCV* 2690 (18.viii; Fl. Domitius et Fl. Ar.); *ICUR* n.s. II 4748 = *ILCV* 2795B adn. (14.viii-13.ix); *ICUR* n.s. VI 15770 (24.ix; Fl. Mod.); *ICUR* n.s. VIII 20778 = *ILCV* 4622 adn. (10.x; order rev.); *AE* 1981, 100 (12.xi); *ICUR* n.s. I 83 = *ILCV* 4670 (2.xii); *ICUR* n.s. VII 17465 = *ILCV* 2976B adn. (Dom.); *ICUR* n.s. VIII 23413; *ICUR* n.s. VI 15503; *ICUR* n.s. II 4809; *ICUR* n.s. I 3183 (frag.); *ICUR* n.s. III 6503 (Dom., Fl.); *ICUR* n.s. IV 11104 = *ILCV* 4461A (frag.); *ICUR* n.s. VIII 20791 (frag.); *ICUR* n.s. V 13328 (p.c. poss.); *ICUR* n.s. I 2090 (frag., p.c. poss.)	(Fl.) (Domitius) Modestus et (Fl.) Arintheus (vv.cc.)
	ITALY: *AE* 1975, 357 (Falerona, Reg. V; Dom., Fl.)	
	DALMATIA: *CIL* III 9505 = *Forsch.Salona* II 107 (Salona, 22.ix; vv.cc.; Gk.)	

Orientis

FASTI: Heracl. Hyd. Pasch. Theo   Modestus et Arinthaeus
              Scal. (adds cc.)

LAWS: Seleucia and Antioch, 1 law each   Modestus et Arinthaeus
              (*CTh* 11.4, 4.iv and *CTh* 6.4.19, 13.iv)

PAPYRI: *P.Vindob.Sijp.* 13.1 (4.i; om.   Domitius Modestus v.c.
              Dom., sacr. praet., Ar. title   praefectus sacro praetorio
              [mag.ped.?] part. om.); *P.Col.*   et Fl. Arintheus v.c.
              VII 182.21 (4.ii; Ar. also mag.   comes
              ped.); *P.Lips.* 47.17 (27.vii;
              Ar. is stratelates; vv.cc. at
              end); 48.20 (28.vii; om. Fl.;
              Ar. is stratelates); 49.22
              (28.vii; om. Fl., comes); *Archiv*
              32 (1986) 36.21 (29.vii; Ar. also
              mag.ped.); *P.Lips.* 50.20 (7.viii;
              om. Dom., v.c.; leaves out Ar.);
              51.19 (17.viii; like *P.Lips.* 48);
              BGU IV 1092.1* (1.ix; om. Fl.; Ar.
              also mag.ped.); *P.Col.* VII 183.1
              (23.xi; Ar. also mag.ped.);
              184.1 (17.xii; Ar. also mag.ped.);
              P.Lips. 52.19 (om. Fl., all
              titles; vv.cc. at end); *P.Lips.*
              53.20 (like prec., also om. Dom.)

OTHER: Athan., *Index* (8.iv); *Passio S.*   Modestus et Arintheus
              Sabae Gothi, in *AnalBoll* 31 (1912)
              221 (12.iv; Fll.? text corrupt)

NOTES:

       Modestus was PVC 362-363 and PPO 369-377; Arintheus was magister peditum in the East *ca* 366-378 (*PLRE* I 605-08; 102-03). It is possible that all three papyri with the new consuls in January and February have cos. by error for p.c. (373); in the case of *P.Lips.* 85, we have considered the probability high enough to move it to 373; cf. *P.Col.* VII, pp.201-03. On the other hand, since both consuls were easterners, they may have been proclaimed by Valens, who was wintering at Antioch (Seeck, *Reg.* 243). This would explain the otherwise improbable combination of early dissemination in Egypt with late dissemination in Rome; cf. above, p.15.

Occidentis

<u>FASTI</u>:	Chr. 354 (pasch.) VindPr. Prosp. Ciz. Cycl. Aq. Cass. VindPost.	Valentinianus IV et Valens IV
<u>LAWS</u>:	5 laws, 3 from Trier, earliest *CTh* 16.6.1 (20.ii); Alteia, 1 law	Valentinianus et Valens IV Augg.
<u>INSCR.</u>:	**ROME:** *ICUR* n.s. V 13107 (1.iii/ 1.v); *ICUR* n.s. III 8724* = *ILCV* 4392 (18.iii; om. IV); *ICUR* n.s. VII 17462 = *ILCV* 2945A (22.v); *ICUR* n.s. III 9344c (8-15.vii; DD.NN.); *ICUR* n.s. I 1254 = *ILCV* 2604 (23.viii); *ICUR* n.s. II 4810 = *ILCV* 3002B (23.viii; DD.NN. Fl. Val. Aug. IV, Fl. Val.); *ICUR* n.s. I 2091 (14.viii-13.ix; Augg.; frag.); *ICUR* n.s. VII 17466 = *ILCV* 2604A (3.x; Augg.; om. Valens); *ICUR* n.s. IV 11766 (28.xi); *ICUR* n.s. VIII 21608* (7.xii); *ICUR* n.s. I 2092 = *ILCV* 4458 (names rev.); *ICUR* n.s. II 4811 (frag.; Augg.)	(DD.NN.) (Fl.) Valentinianus et (Fl.) Valens (Augg.) IV
	ICUR n.s. VII 19957 = *ILCV* 2609A (30.ix)	DD.NN. Augg. IV
	ITALY: *CIL* XI 4629 = *ILCV* 3658 (S. Gemini, Reg. VI; 30.iv; Augg.); *CIL* V 1862 = *ILS* 5885 (Zuglio, Reg. X; DDD. NNN., Augg.); *CIL* XI 2847 (Bolsena, Reg. VII); *CIL* X 7221 (Mazara, Sicily; DD.NN.; frag.; cf. *Kokalos* 28-29 [1982-83] 6 no.11)	(DD.NN.) (Fl.) Valentinianus et (Fl.) Valens (Augg.) IV
<u>OTHER:</u>	**TUNISIA:** *AE* 1912, 62 (Carthage; 16.ii; ostrakon); *AE* 1912, 61 (Carthage; 16.ii?; ostr.); *AE* 1912, 63 (Carthage; 5.iii; ostr.); *AE* 1912, 64 (Carthage; ostr.)	p.c. Modesti et Arinthei

Orientis

<u>FASTI:</u>	Heracl. Hyd. Scal. (num. V)	Valentinianus IV et Valens IV
	Pasch.	Valentinianus Aug. V et Valens Aug. IV
<u>LAWS:</u>	none	
<u>PAPYRI:</u>	*P.Lips.* 85.1* (4.i; Ar. also mag. ped.; cos. for p.c.); *P.Lips.* 86.2 (5.i); *P.Oxy.* XLVI 3308.1 (17.i; Fl. at start, om. titles exc. v.c.); *P.Lond.* V 1648.1 (=1822); 1649.1 (i-iv); 1650.5; 1828; *SB* XIV 11298.1 (Fl. at start, om. Dom. and all titles exc. v.c.)	p.c. Domitii Modesti v.c. praef. sacro praet. et Fl. Arinthei v.c. comitis
	P.Col. VII 168.11 (11.iv); *P.Mert.* I 37.1 (3.ix); *P.NYU* 24.15 (ix-xii); *P.Flor.* III 320.1 (ix-xii); *P.Lips.* 34 verso 13; *P.Oxy.* XLVI 3309.1	DD.NN. Valentinianus et Valens perpp. Augg. IV
<u>COINS:</u>	*RIC* X 276.17 (Antioch)	Valens, consular image on obv. and rev. of solidi
<u>OTHER:</u>	Athan., *Index* (31.iii); *Hist.Aceph.* 5.10 [17] (3.v)	Valentinianus IV et Valens IV

281

Occidentis

FASTI: Chr. 354 (pasch.) VindPr.   Gratianus III et
                Prosp. Ciz. Cycl. Hist.Britt.   Equitius[48]
                (3, 172, 1.2) Aq. Cass.
                VindPost.

LAWS: About 14 laws, earliest *CTh*   Gratianus Aug. III
                15.1.8 (*p.p.* Sirmium, 26.i);   et Equitius
                Milan and Robur, 1 law each;
                Trier, 3 laws

INSCR.:   **ROME:** *ICUR* n.s. I 1937 = *ILCV*   (D.N.) Gratianus Aug. III
                2007 (5.v; om. Aug.); *ICUR* n.s.   et (Fl.) Equitius (v.c.)
                V 13924 (14.vi; order rev.;
                frag.); *CIL* VI 499 = *ILS* 4147
                (19.vii; D.N.; [Fl.] Eq.); *AE*
                1953, 238 (19.vii; D.N.); *ICUR*
                n.s. VIII 20792; *ICUR* n.s. IV
                9566 (D.N.); *ICUR* n.s. IV 12243
                (frag.); *ICUR* n.s. V 13329 (om.
                Aug., III); *ICUR* n.s. V 13331;
                ICUR n.s. I 2093 = *ILCV* 4369 (om.
                Aug.; frag.); *ICUR* n.s. VII
                17468a (om. Eq.)

                374 or 375: *ICUR* n.s. II 4813
                (13.ii); *ICUR* suppl. 1638 = *ILCV*
                1568 (6-13.ii; om. Aug.); *ICUR* n.s.
                VI 15504 (16-30.iii; Fl.; frag.);
                ICUR n.s. V 13923 (14.iv-1.v;
                mostly rest.); *ICUR* n.s. IV 11106
                (14.ix-1.x); *ICUR* n.s. I 1938*
                (mostly rest.; adds v.c.; or 517?);
                ICUR n.s. IV 11767* (i or xii;
                frag.)

                ITALY: *AE* 1913, 227 (Reggio di
                Calabria, Reg. III; 28.vi; D.N.,
                Fl. Eq. v.c.); *EphEp* 8 (1899)
                515 (Capua, Reg. I; 14.viii-1.ix)

                [Continued on the next page]

[48]Cycl. om. III.

Orientis

FASTI: Heracl. Hyd. Pasch. (Aug.) Gratianus (Aug.) III
        Scal. (Aug., clariss.) et Equitius

LAWS: Antioch, 3 laws (earliest, Gratianus Aug. III
        CTh 10.20.8, 16.ii) et Equitius

PAPYRI: *P.Oxy.* XLVI 3310.1 p.c. DD.NN. Valentiniani
        (i-ii; year uncert.) et Valentis perp. Augg. [IV]

        P.Turner 45.9 (ref. to 4 and D.N. Gratianus (perp.)
        10.iv; adds perp.); *SPP* XX 102.1 Aug. III et Fl. Equitius
        (2.v; or p.c.; om. Fl., comes); v.c. comes
        P.Gen. 66.20 (2.v; perp.; om.
        num., comes); *P.Lips.* 23.1*
        (24.ix); *BGU* XIII 2332.1 (12.xi);
        SB VI 9311.1* (late 374, adds perp.,
        om. com.)

NOTES:

Equitius was magister militum 365-375 (*PLRE* I 282). His placement before Gratian in *ICUR* n.s. V 13924 is remarkable (cf. p.66). In Libanius, *Or.* 24.12, an unnamed official in Pannonia is represented speaking of a "year of tears, not the consular robe." Probus cos. 371, according to *PLRE* I 737 and Norman (Loeb ed. p.500 n.); surely rather Equitius (so, with discussion of the campaign involved, C.E.V. Nixon, *JNG* 33 [1983] 53-56).

[Continued from preceding page]

        AQUITANIA: *CIL* XIII 11065 = *ILCV* D.N. Gratianus Aug. III
        3322 (Mediolani Santonum; 5.v) et Equitius v.c.

OTHER: Council at Valence: *Conc.Galliae* Gratianus III
        (Corp.Christ.Lat. 148), p.37 et Equitius
        (12.vii); cf. vol. 148A, p.90
        (quoted in 534, numeral IV in
        most MSS)

        Amm.Marc. 30.3.1

Occidentis

<u>FASTI</u>:	Chr. 354 (pasch.) VindPr. Prosp. Ciz. Cycl. Aq. Cass.	p.c. Gratiani III et Equiti[49]
	VindPost.	Gratianus Aug. IV et Equitius II
<u>LAWS</u>:	*CTh* 12.6.16 (Trier, 9.iv)	p.c. Gratiani Aug. III et Equiti v.c.
<u>INSCR.</u>:	**ROME:** *ICUR* n.s. V 13334* (2.i); *ICUR* n.s. IV 12531 (10.i; frag.); *ICUR* n.s. III 8725 = *ILCV* 4258A (24.ii; om. Aug. III); *ICUR* n.s. II 4814 (14.ii-15.iii; om. Aug. III); *ICUR* n.s. V 13109 = *ILCV* 95 (3.v; D.N.); *ICUR* n.s. I 3184 = *ILCV* 3305 (8-15.v; Fl.); *ICUR* n.s. VIII 20793 (14.viii-1.ix; om. Aug.; frag.); *ICUR* n.s. II 6032 = *ILCV* 4226 (28.x; om. Aug.); *ICUR* n.s. III 8726 (20.xi; D.N.; om. III); *ICUR* n.s. II 6009 = *ILCV* 775 (26.xi; Fl.); *ICUR* n.s. V 13333* (6-11.xii; frag.); *ICUR* n.s. V 13108 (om. Aug.); *ICUR* n.s. V 13332 (frag.); *ICUR* n.s. III 8149 (14.viii-13.ix or 16.x-13.xii; om. Aug. III)	p.c. (D.N.) Gratiani Aug. III et (Fl.) Equiti (v.c.)

Cf. 374 for other documents which may
belong to 375.

ITALY: *CIL* XI 5996 = *ILS* 5519
(Sestinum, Reg. VI; 19.ix; D.N., v.c.)

DALMATIA: *CIL* III 9506 = *ILCV*
78 (Salona; 6.vii; D.N., v.c.);
ILCV 3835B (Salona; D.N., v.c.)

---

[49]Prosp., Cycl. om. III; VindPr. gives IV & IV.

Orientis

FASTI: Heracl. Hyd. (III)   p.c. Gratiani (III)
et Equiti

Pasch.   Gratianus Aug. IV
et Equitius II

LAWS: *CTh* 7.13.7 (2.vi) and 12.1.79   p.c. Gratiani Aug. III
(3.xii), both from Antioch   et Equiti v.c.

PAPYRI: *BGU* XII 2148.1 (rest.; p.c. not   p.c. D.N. Gratiani (perp.)
indic., i-iv); *P.Flor.* I 95.17   Aug. III et Fl. Equiti
(1.iv); 95.2 (5.x; perp.; om. Fl);   v.c.
P.Lips. 61.1 (11.xi)

OTHER: Socrates, *HE* 4.31; *Passio S.*   p.c. Gratiani III
Nicetae (*AnalBoll* 31 [1912]   et Equiti
211.27; 213.7); Iacobus of
Edessa p.284 (Brooks,
Chron.Min., p.213)

NOTES:

It was presumably the distraction of the Pannonian invasion of late 374 (Piganiol, *L'empire chrétien*[2] 216-17) that was responsible for the failure to nominate consuls.

Occidentis

<u>FASTI:</u>	VindPr. Aq. Cass. Prosp. Ciz. Cycl.[50]	Valens Aug. V et Valentinianus iun. (Aug.)
	Chr. 354 (pasch.)	Valens V et Valentinianus Caes. iun.
<u>LAWS:</u>	About 13 laws, 5 from Trier, earliest *CTh* 15.7.3 (10.iii); Valent. I in *CTh* 16.2.23	Valens V et Valentinianus (I) Augg.
<u>INSCR.:</u>	**ROME:** *CIL* VI 751B = *ILS* 4268 (8.iv; Valent. iun. I); *ICUR* n.s. VII 17469* (23.v; Valent. iun.); *ICUR* suppl. 1645 = *ILCV* 4333A (26.vii); *AE* 1971, 35 (13.viii); *CIL* VI 504 = *ILS* 4153 (13.viii); *CIL* VI 510 = *ILS* 4152 (13.viii; Valent.iun.); *ICUR* n.s. IV 9568 = *ILCV* 1328 (27.ix; om. DD.NN., Augg.; Valent. iun.); *ICUR* n.s. IV 11769 = *ILCV* 4219 (11.xii; iun.; om. Augg.); *ICUR* n.s. VIII 20794 = *ILCV* 657 (frag.); *ICUR* n.s. V 13335 (om. Augg.); *ICUR* n.s. VI 15771 (frag.); *ICUR* n.s. IV 9569; *ICUR* n.s. V 13110 (frag.); *ICUR* n.s. V 13336; *CIL* VI 3118; *ICUR* n.s. VII 17457e (frag.; p.c. poss.)	DD.NN. Valens V et Valentinianus (iunior) (I) Augg.
	376 or 378: *ICUR* n.s. I 3186 (16-30.x; frag.); *ICUR* n.s. IV 12244 = *ILCV* 4146 (frag., om. DD.NN.; 15.xi); *ICUR* I 280 = *ILCV* 4248 adn. (frag.); *CIL* VI 1736 = *ILS* 1256 (frag.)	

[Continued on the next page]

---

[50]VindPr., Ciz. give V & V; Prosp. Cass. Aq. Ciz. om. Aug., iun. Aug.; Cycl. om. titles, numerals.

Orientis

FASTI: Heracl. Hyd. (Aug. 2x)   Valens (Aug.) V et
                                                          Valentinianus iun. Aug.

                Scal.   Valentinianus et Valens
                                                          filius eius Augg.

                Pasch.   Valens Aug. V et
                                                          Valentinianus Caes.

LAWS: Antioch 2 laws, earlier *CTh*   Valens V et
                1.28.3 (29.v); *CTh* 6.4.24 (30.v)   Valentinianus (iun.) Augg.
                refers to Valent. as iunior

PAPYRI: *P.Flor.* I 95.29 (21.vi), 53 (v-vi),   DD.NN. Valens V et
                70,90 (x-xi); *BGU* III 941.1   Valentinianus iunior I
                (x-xi); *P.Flor.* I 52.1;   perpp. Augg.
                P.Stras. 596.15 (om. I perpp. Augg.);
                P.Lips. 36.12 (or 378; numerals lost)

OTHER: Socrates, *HE* 4.35   Valens V et
                                                          Valentinianus iunior I

NOTES: The young Valentinian II (born 371) was proclaimed Augustus on 22.xi.375, a few days after the
death of his father (17.xi).

[Continued from preceding page]

ITALY: *CIL* X 4489 = *ILCV* 2932
adn. (Capua, Reg. I; 22.viii;
om. Augg.); *CIL* XI 2834 = *ILCV*
365 (Bolsena, Reg. VII; 12.ix;
om. Augg.); *CIL* XIV 5238 =
ILCV 4660 (Ostia; 6.x); *CIL* IX
5284 = *ILCV* 4807 (S. Benedetto,
Reg. V; frag.)

376 or 378: *CIL* IX 1362* = *ILCV*
4395 adn. (nr. Aeclanum, Reg. II;
om. DD.NN., Augg.)

Occidentis

<u>FASTI</u>:	Chr. 354 (pasch.) VindPr. Prosp. Ciz. Cycl. Cass. Aq.	Gratianus IV et Merobaudes
<u>LAWS</u>:	*CTh* 1.32.2 (Trier, 8.vii)	p.c. Valentis V et Valentiniani Augg.
	About 18 laws, 5 from Trier, earliest *CTh* 9.35.3 (4.i); Mogontiacum and Confluentes (Seeck's emend.), 1 law each	Gratianus Aug. IV et Merobaudes (v.c.)
<u>INSCR.</u>:	**ROME:** *ICUR* n.s. I 3188 = *ILCV* 4289 (7.ii; om. Aug.); *ICUR* n.s. II 4815 = *ILCV* 1269 (1.iii; om. Aug.); *CIL* VI 511 (12.iii; Grat. V); *ICUR* n.s. I 84 (23.iii; DD.NN. Grat. III); *ICUR* n.s. IV 11107 = *ILCV* 2969 (15.iv; D.N.); *CIL* VI 1698 = *ILS* 1257 (29.iv; D.N. Grat. IV); *ICUR* n.s. V 13925 (11.v); *CIL* VI 500 = *ILS* 4148 (13.v; D.N., om. IV); *ICUR* n.s. V 13338 = *ILCV* 4307 (14.iv-15.v; D.N., Fl.); *ICUR* n.s. VIII 23415 (16.v-1.vi); *ICUR* n.s. I 1435 (17.vi); *ICUR* n.s. VIII 23416 (1.vi/1.vii); *ICUR* n.s. VI 15772 (2-5.viii; om. Aug.); *ICUR* n.s. VII 17471 = *ILCV* 4400 (1.ix; D.N.); *ICUR* n.s. VI 17299 (14.ix; Fl.); *ICUR* n.s. II 5790 = *ILCV* 1002 adn. (3.xi; frag.; adds v.c.); *ICUR* n.s. VII 17472 = *ILCV* 1615 adn. (16-30.xi); *ICUR* n.s. VIII 20795 = *ILCV* 2976B adn. (2.xii?; D.N., om. Aug.); *ICUR* n.s. IV 11108 (om. Aug.); *ICUR* n.s. VII 17468c; *ICUR* n.s. V 13111 = *ILCV* 4033 (frag.); *ICUR* n.s. III 8423 = *ILCV* 3598 (D.N.); *ICUR* n.s. IV 12532 = *ILCV* 1515 (only Grat. IV); *ICUR* n.s. I 2094 (frag.); *AE* 1974, 85 (om. Aug. IV); *CIL* VI 30966 = *IGUR* I 128 (D.N., Fl.); *AE* 1976, 35 (D.N.); [Continued on next page]	(D.N.) Gratianus Aug. IV et (Fl.) Merobaudes (v.c.)

Orientis

FASTI: Heracl. Hyd. Pasch. (Aug.)   Gratianus (Aug.) IV
et Merobaudes

Scal. as above, but also: Valentinianus novus
Aug. V et Merobaudes cl.

LAWS: Antioch, 2 laws (earliest *CTh*   Gratianus Aug. IV
8.7.14, 25.i); Hierapolis, 3 laws   et Merobaudes (v.c.)
(earliest *CTh* 10.16.3, 6.vii)

PAPYRI: *SB* XIV 12109.1 (13.ii)   p.c. DD.NN. Valentis V et
Valentiniani iun. I perpp. Augg.

SB XIV 12021.5 (21.iii; doc.   D.N. Gratianus perp. Aug.
prob. later; frag.); *P.Flor.* I   IV et Fl. Merobaudes v.c.
95.82 (17.vi); *P.Lips.* 17.1
(10.ix); *PSI* IV 287.1 (30.xii)

OTHER: *Subsidia Hagiograph.* 69 (1985) 298

NOTES: Merobaudes was magister peditum 375-?388 and cos. again in 383 (see that year). *CTh* 1.32.2 was sent to the proconsul of Africa; the p.c. is presumably the *accepta* date, cf. p.81.

[Continued from preceding page]
ICUR suppl. 1664 (or p.c.?);
ICUR n.s. VIII 21609a (frag.)

ITALY: *CIL* X 1518 = *ILCV* 2275 adn.
(Naples, Reg. I; 29.iii); *AE* 1972,
214 (Milan, Reg. XI; 3.xi); *RendLincei*
26 (1971) 443 no. 59 (Montecassino,
Reg. I; ed. rest. p.c.; om. Aug. IV)

GAUL: *CIL* XII 138 = *ILCV* 281 (Alpes
Poeninae, Narb.; D.N.)

DALMATIA: *Forsch.Salona* II 111 =
CIL III 14663 (p.2328, no. 127)
(Salona; 6-13.viii)

OTHER: Amm.Marc. 31.8.2

Occidentis

FASTI:	Chr. 354 (pasch.) (1)	p.c. Gratiani et Merobaudis
	Chr. 354 (pasch.) (2) VindPr. Prosp. Ciz. Aq. Cass. VindPost. Cycl. Dionys. (1, 754) Aug.	Valens VI et Valentinianus iun. II[51]
LAWS:	11 laws, 4 from Trier, earliest *CTh* 1.15.9 (1.i[52])	Valens VI et Valentinianus II Augg.
INSCR.:	**ROME:** *ICUR* n.s. VIII 23418 = *ILCV* 2807A adn. (23.v); *ICUR* n.s. IV 12533 = *ILCV* 4378 (24.v; om. 2nd Aug.); *ICUR* n.s. I 1436 = *ILCV* 2945A (4.viii; om. DD.NN.; names interchanged; 2nd cos. iun., om. Aug. twice); *CIL* VI 1751 = *ILS* 1265 (8.viii); *ICUR* n.s. IV 11771* = *ILCV* 2945A adn. (4.ix); *ICUR* n.s. V 13112 (5.ix; om. Aug. twice; om. II); *ICUR* n.s. V 13926 (om. 2nd Aug.); *ICUR* n.s. IV 9570* = *ILCV* 4146A (Fl. Valens, om. 1st Aug.); *ICUR* n.s. IV 11772 = *ILCV* 3754A (om. DD.NN., Aug. twice; om. II)	DD.NN. (Fl.) Valens Aug. VI et Valentinianus (iun.) Aug. II

GAUL: *CIL* XIII 2798 = *ILCV* 2814 (Autun; 25.x; om. DD.NN., Aug. twice)

DALMATIA: *CIL* III 9507 = *ILCV* 821 (Salona; 5.ix; Augg.)

---

[51]Chr. 354 (pasch.) om. II; Prosp. Cass. Aq. Aug. Cycl. om. iun.; Cycl. om. VI; VindPr. and VindPost. give VI for both.
[52]Based on Seeck's emendation of the date from KAL IUN to KAL IAN.

Orientis

<u>FASTI:</u>	Heracl.	Valentinianus VI et Valentinus iun.
	Hyd.	Valens VI et Valentinianus II
	Pasch.	Valens Aug. VII et Valentinianus Caes. II
	Scal.	Valens VI et Valentinianus iun. Augg.
<u>LAWS:</u>	none	
<u>PAPYRI:</u>	*BGU* XIII 2339.1 (15.i); *P.Grenf.* I 54.1 (10.xi);	DD.NN. Valens VI et Valentinianus II perpp. Augg.
<u>OTHER:</u>	Socrates, *HE* 4.38	(Valens) VI et Valentinianus iunior II

<u>NOTES:</u>

It is curious that Chr. 354 (pasch.) preserves a p.c. for early in this year; the papyri know the new consuls already by mid-January.

Occidentis

FASTI:	VindPr. Cass. Aq. VindPost. Prosp. Ciz. Cycl. Aug.	Ausonius et Olybrius
	Chr. 354 (pasch.)	Olybrius et Ausonius
LAWS:	About 17 laws, earliest *CTh* 6.30.1 (Sirmium, 24.ii); Aquileia, Milan, Trier, 2 laws each; Scupi, Tricciana?, Tres Tabernae?, 1 law each[53]	Ausonius et Olybrius (vv.cc.)
INSCR.:	**ROME:** *ICUR* n.s. I 1437 = *ILCV* 4354 (3.vii); *ICUR* n.s. I 3191 = *ILCV* 2772 (16.vii); *ICUR* n.s. VII 17473 = *ILCV* 2969A (20.viii); *ICUR* n.s. I 3142 = *ILCV* 1479 (24.xi); *ICUR* n.s. V 13339 (21.xii); *ICUR* n.s. V 13113 (Fl., Cl.); *ICUR* n.s. VIII 23419 (frag.)	(Fl.) Ausonius et (Cl.) Olybrius (vv.cc.)
	ITALY: *EphEp* 8 (1899) 516 (Capua, Reg. I; frag.; vv.cc.)	
	DALMATIA: *CIL* III 9509* = *Forsch. Salona* II 113 (Salona; or p.c., 380?; before 1.iv; vv.cc.)	
OTHER:	Ausonius, *Gratiarum actio*	

[53]The last two names are Seeck's emendations of impossible readings.

Orientis

FASTI: Heracl. Marcell. Hyd. Pasch.   Ausonius et Olybrius
Scal. (adds cc.)

LAWS: *CTh* 10.1.12 (Thessalonica, 17.vi)   Ausonius et Olybrius
(vv.cc.)

PAPYRI: *P.Lips.* 13.1* (23.x)   [p.c. DD.NN. Valentis Aug.
VI et Valentin]iani [II
perp.] Aug. et [----]

              P.Monac. III 78.6 (doc. may   [p.c.] DD.NN. Valentis
be later than 379)   VI et Valentiniani II
perpp. [Augg.]

OTHER: Socrates, *HE* 5.2   Ausonius et Olybrius

NOTES:

    Ausonius was the well known professor-poet, PPO 378-379 (*PLRE* I 140-41); Olybrius was a Roman aristocrat, PVR 369-370, PPO 378; *PLRE* I 640-42; Chastagnol, *Fastes*, 178-84. There is no trace in the other evidence of the late dissemination of the consuls suggested by *P.Lips.* 13.

Occidentis

<u>FASTI</u>:	Chr. 354 (pasch.) VindPr. Prosp. Ciz. Aq. Cass. Cycl. VindPost. (om. V) Beda (3, 299 c.456; Gr. VI) Aug. Hydatius (2, 14 c.45) (Aug., om. V; Th. I)	Gratianus V et Theodosius
<u>LAWS</u>:	*CTh* 10.20.9 (*p.p.* Carthage, 28.ii), 10.20.10 (Aquileia, 14.iii)	p.c. Ausonii et Olybrii
	About 41 laws, 5 from Trier (earliest, *CTh* 14.3.17, *acc.* Seeck 10.i); Sirmium and Milan 1 law each, Aquileia 2 laws	(DD.NN.) Gratianus V et Theodosius I (Augg.)
<u>INSCR.</u>:	**ROME:** *ICUR* n.s. II 4166 (23.vii); *ICUR* n.s. I 1438 (6-13.viii; om. DD.NN., Augg.); *ICUR* n.s. VII 17474 = *ILCV* 2945A adn. (13.viii; Fll.); *ICUR* n.s. VI 15774 (16.vii-13.viii); *ICUR* n.s. V 13343 (17.viii; om. DD.NN., V); *ICUR* n.s. I 3194 = *ILCV* 1464 (18.viii); *ICUR* n.s. V 13341 (25.viii); *ICUR* n.s. VI 15773 = *ILCV* 2976B adn. (15.ix; om. Augg.); *ICUR* n.s. VII 19959 = *ILCV* 3574 (5.x; om. NN., V); *ICUR* n.s. VII 19960 = *ILCV* 2605 (5.x; om. V, Augg.); *ICUR* I 291 = *ILCV* 3035C (20.xi; om. DD.NN., Augg.); *ICUR* n.s. VII 17475 (frag.); *ICUR* n.s. II 6033 = *ILCV* 3754B (om. DD.NN., Augg.); *ICUR* n.s. IV 11774 = *ILCV* 4248A (frag.; numeral VI)	DD.NN. (Fll.) Gratianus V et Theodosius (I) Augg.
	ITALY: *CIL* XI 4040 (Capena, Reg. VII; 20.x; om. DD.NN., Augg.); *CIL* XI 4996 (nr. Spoleto)	
<u>COINS:</u>	*RIC* IX 24.51 (Trier): solidi	Gratian, cons. image on obv., cons. images of Gratian and Val. on rev.

294

Orientis

FASTI:	Marcell. Heracl. (Gr. II, Th. I; om. Aug. 2x) Hyd. Pasch. (Gr. VI) Scal. (Th. I nobb. Augg.)	Gratianus Aug. V et Theodosius Aug.
LAWS:	Thessalonica, 23 laws (earliest *CTh* 9.27.1, 15.i); Hadrianopolis, C'polis, Cosintus, 1 law each	(DD.NN.) Gratianus V et Theodosius I (Augg.)
PAPYRI:	*CPR* VII 19.1 (6.v); *P.Stras.* 749.1 (Hermogen. in place of Olybr.; adds sacr. praet. at end)	p.c. Ausonii et Olybrii vv.cc. praeff. (sacr. praet.)
	P.Flor. I 75.1 (11.x); *BGU* III 974.12 (26.xii); *ChLA* XI 470.1* (om. perp., adds Fll. bef. Gratianus)	DD.NN. (Fll.) Gratianus V et Theodosius I perpp. Augg.
OTHER:	Socrates, *HE* 5.6	Gratianus V et Theodosius I

NOTES:

Theodosius was proclaimed Augustus 19.i.379 and in the usual way took his first consulate in the year following his accession, apparently at Thessalonica (Seeck, *Regesten* 253). The p.c. in *CTh* 10.20.10 must reflect usage at the destination rather than Aquileia (cf. above, p.82). Dissemination was evidently slow.

Occidentis

<u>FASTI</u>:	Chr. 354 (pasch.) VindPr. Aq. Prosp. Ciz. Cycl. Aug. Cass. VindPost.	Syagrius et Eucherius
<u>LAWS</u>:	*CTh* 8.5.36 (Trier, 27.ii); Aquileia, 3 laws (earliest, *CTh* 15.10.2, 22.iv); Milan, 1 law; *CTh* 15.7.6 (Trier, 22.ii) and *CTh* 15.7.7 (Aquileia, 8.v) give rev. order	Syagrius et Eucherius

<u>INSCR.</u>: **ROME:** *ICUR* suppl. 1690 (19.i; om. Fll.); *ICUR* n.s. VIII 20798 = *ILCV* 1129 (24.v); *ICUR* suppl. 1691 (14.vi-1.vii; om. Fll.); *ICUR* n.s. VII 17476 = *ILCV* 4356 (2.viii); *ICUR* n.s. IV 11109 (16.viii); *ICUR* n.s. IX 23761 = *ILCV* 3091 (1.ix; om. Fll.); *ICUR* n.s. II 6034 = *ILCV* 2851 (30.ix); *ICUR* n.s. VIII 22968 (14.ix-1.x; om. Fll.); *CIL* VI 31945 = 3865 (16.x-13.xi; om. Fll.); *ICUR* n.s. V 13344 (6-13.xi; om. Fll.); *ICUR* n.s. II 6035 (om. Fll.; frag.); *ICUR* n.s. IV 9572 (om. Fll.; vv.cc.); *ICUR* n.s. I 2095 = *ILCV* 4332 adn. (vv.cc.); *ICUR* suppl. 1693 (om. Fll.; frag.); *ICUR* n.s. V 13927 (om. Fll.; frag.; p.c. poss.)
    Fll. Syagrius et Eucherius (vv.cc.)

ITALY: *AE* 1927, 138 (Capua, Reg. I; 5.iv)
    p.c. DD.NN. Gratiani et Theodosii I Augg.

RendPontAccad 22 (1946-47) 228 no.2 (Syracuse; Gk.)
    Fll. Syagrius et Eucherius vv.cc.

381 or 382: Rome: *ICUR* n.s. VII 19962 (bef. 1.vii?; frag.); *AE* 1974, 23 (frag.); *ICUR* n.s. II 5995 (frag.); **Italy:** *AE* 1925, 83 = *ILCV* 4165A (Velitrae, Reg. I; 13.iii; v.c.)

<u>OTHER</u>: Gesta Conc. Aquiliensis 1 (CSEL 82, v.III, p.326) (3.ix)
    Syagrius et Eucherius vv.cc.

Orientis

<u>FASTI:</u>	Marcell. Heracl. (Sy. I)	Eucherius et Syagrius
	Hyd. Pasch. Scal. (adds cc.)	Syagrius et Eucherius
<u>LAWS:</u>	C'polis, 15 laws (*CTh* 16.5.6, 10.i, earliest); ; Heraclea, 5 laws; Hadrianopolis, 1 law; four laws from C'polis give order rev.: earliest *CTh* 16.7.1 (2.v), latest *CTh* 6.10.3 (13.xii)	Eucherius et Syagrius
<u>PAPYRI:</u>	*P.Rainer Cent.* 86.1 (25.ii; adds praef.sacr.praet. to Sy.); *P.Lips.* 20.1 (adds praeff.; 2.iv); *P.Oxy.* VII 1041.1 (9.vi); *PSI* X 1108.1 (2.ix); *P.Lips.* 28.1 (31.xii; adds praef. to Sy.)	Fl. Eucherius et Fl. Syagrius vv.cc. (praeff.)
<u>OTHER:</u>	Council at Constantinople: Mansi III 557 (9.vii; Fl., vv.cc.); Benesevic, *Abh.München* n.f. 14 (1937) 213.2; Greg.Naz., *PG* 37.389-90 (31.xii; Fl. 2x); Socrates, *HE* 5.8	(Fl.) Eucherius et (Fl.) Euagrius (vv.cc.)

<u>NOTES:</u>

Eucherius (CSL 377-379) was Theodosius' uncle (*PLRE* I 288). On present evidence it is impossible to separate with certainty the careers of the two Syagrii, consuls in 381 and 382 and both praetorian prefect while consul. In addition to their entries in *PLRE* I 862-63, see J.R. Martindale, *Historia* 16 (1967) 254-56; A. Demandt, *BZ* 64 (1971) 38-45; S. Roda, *Comm. stor. ad libro ix ... di Q. Aur. Simmaco* (1981) 254-55. See the Critical Appendix for discussion.

To judge by the unanimity of Roman inscriptions on the one side and Egyptian papyri on the other, the laws were presumably in origin no less unanimous for the sequence Syagrius-Eucherius in the West and Eucherius-Syagrius in the East. The compilers must have tried to correct them against lists which gave both versions (such a conflict is actually documented in our surviving eastern lists), thus making the confusion worse. The explanation is presumably that Gratian, the senior Augustus, proclaimed his own nominee Syagrius as consul prior, while Theodosius gave his uncle the seniority. It seems to have been agreed that imperial kin automatically received such seniority: see above, p.22. Gratian must have accepted the argument, since the very next year we find another kinsman of Theodosius as undisputed consul prior in both West and East. In 381, however, it is not surprising that a certain amount of confusion resulted.

Occidentis

FASTI:
    Chr. 354 (pasch.) VindPr. Aug.   Antonius et Syagrius[54]
    Prosp. Dion. (1, 755) Cycl.
    Ciz. Cass. Aq.

    VindPost.   Syagrius II et Antonius

LAWS:
    4 laws, earliest *CTh* 12.12.8,   p.c. Syagrii et Eucherii
    25.iii); 3 *p.p.* Carthage (*CTh*
    11.16.13; 12.1.88; 12.12.8),
    1 from Viminacium (5.vii), probably
    p.p. Carthage (*CTh* 12.1.89)

    41 laws, earliest *CTh* 6.6.1 (no   Antonius et Syagrius
    prov., 1.iv); Milan, 3 laws   (vv.cc.)
    (earliest, 3.iv); Padua, 2 laws;
    Brixia, 1 law

INSCR.:
    ROME: *ICUR* n.s. VII 17478 (13.iv); (Cl./Fl.) Antonius et
    ICUR n.s. II 4749 = *ILCV* 2907A (Fl.) Syagrius (vv.cc.)
    (1.vii; vv.cc.); *ICUR* n.s. I 3197
    = *ILCV* 1479A (14.viii); *ICUR* n.s.
    VII 20603 = *ILCV* 2564 (18.viii;
    Cl., Fl.); *ICUR* I 313 = *ILCV* 4278
    (2-5.ix; vv.cc.); *ICUR* n.s. II
    4167 (14.viii-13.ix); *ICUR* n.s.
    V 13115 (18.ix); *ICUR* n.s. I 1439
    = *ILCV* 4700 (26.ix); *ICUR* n.s.
    VII 17479 = *ILCV* 2875 (23.x; Fll.;
    vv.cc.); *ICUR* n.s. II 5791 = *ILCV*
    4146C (4.xii); *ICUR* n.s. VIII
    20799 = *ILCV* 316; *ICUR* n.s. I 2096*
    = *CIL* VI 9787 (Cl.); *ICUR* n.s.
    I 3127 = *ILCV* 2148; *ICUR* n.s. VIII
    20800; *ICUR* n.s. IV 11110; *ICUR*
    n.s. III 6504 = *ILCV* 4333A adn.;
    ICUR n.s. VI 17248 (Fl. with each);
    ICUR n.s. III 8151; *ICUR* n.s. IV
    12259 fr. A; *ICUR* n.s. II 6036
    (Cl.; frag.); *ICUR* suppl. 1698;
    ICUR n.s. II 5995 (Fl. Sy.; vv.cc.;
    frag.); *AE* 1949, 163 (Fl. bef. each)
    [Continued on the next page]

[54]VindPr., identifying the two Syagrii, puts a II after Syagrius here.

Orientis

FASTI:	Marcell. Heracl. (Sy. II)	Antonius et Syagrius (II)
	Hyd. Pasch. (Sy. II)	

LAWS:	C'polis, 26 laws, earliest	Antonius et Syagrius
	12.i (*CTh* 14.10.1)	(vv.cc.)

PAPYRI:	*P.Gen.* 67.1 (19.i); *P.Gen.*	p.c. Fl. Eucherii et
	68.20 (8.v); *SB* IV 7445.1	Fl. Syagrii vv.cc.
	(12.vii); *P.Lond.* III 980	
	descr. (p.l)	
	P.Lips. 21.1	Fll. Antonius v.c. et
		Syagrius v.c. praef. sacr.
		praet.

INSCR.:	*I.Cret.* IV 285* (Gortyn;	p.c. Syagrii et
	18.vi)	Eucherii

NOTES:

Antonius was PPO Ital. 376-378 (*PLRE* I 77) and a relative by marriage of the Emperor Theodosius; for Syagrius, see the previous year.

In this year, as in 380, the laws using postconsulates are *p.p.* dates from Carthage (see Chapter 7). The papyri, the *p.p.* dates in Carthage, and the Cretan inscription all point to the use of p.c. dating as late as June-July.

[Continued from preceding page]

ITALY: *CIL* V 1620 = *ILCV* 4214 (Aquileia, Reg. X; 25.xi; vv.cc.)

DALMATIA: *CIL* III 9508 = *ILCV* 3835C (Salona, 29.xi; om. Sy.)

Occidentis

<u>FASTI</u>:	VindPr. Aq. Cass. Prosp. Ciz. Cycl. Aug. VindPost. (om. II)	Merobaudes II et Saturninus
	Chr. 354 (pasch.)	Saturninus et Syagrius
<u>LAWS</u>:	About 45 laws, earliest *CTh* 6.2.13 (10.i); Milan, 7 laws (earliest, *CTh* 6.1.3, 19.i); Padua, 3 laws; Verona, 2 laws	Merobaudes II et Saturninus
<u>INSCR.</u>:	**ROME:** *ICUR* n.s. II 5996 = *ILCV* 4623 (10.i; Mer. III); *ICUR* n.s. IV 12250 (4.iii; Fl. Theod., om. Aug., v.c.); *ICUR* n.s. II 6044 = *ILCV* 2925A (only Theod. et Mer.); *ICUR* n.s. VIII 23420b*	D.N. (Fl.) Theodosius Aug. II et Merobaudes v.c. II
	ICUR suppl. 1705 (14.ii-15.iii; frag.); *ICUR* suppl. 1711 (14.ii-15.iii; frag.); *CIL* VI 501 = *ILS* 4149 (5.iv); *CIL* VI 502 = *ILS* 4150 (5.iv; both v.c.); *ICUR* n.s. VII 17481* = *ILCV* 3498 (20.iv; om. Fll., II, Sat.); *ICUR* n.s. III 8728 = *ILCV* 3057A (29.iv; om. Fll., II); *ICUR* n.s. IV 12534* = *ILCV* 4571 adn. (2-7.v; om. Fll.); *ICUR* n.s. VIII 20717* = *ILCV* 3390A (14.iv-15.v; om. Sat.); *ICUR* n.s. V 13928 (14.vi; om. Fll.); *ICUR* n.s. VII 17482* = *ILCV* 3797C (28.vii; om. Fll., II, Sat.); *ICUR* n.s. II 6037 (16.vii-13.viii); *ICUR* I 326 = *ILCV* 4191 (14.viii; om. Fll.); *ICUR* n.s. IV 12246 (31.viii); *ICUR* n.s. V 13346 (8.ix; om. Fll.); *ICUR* n.s. II 6038 = *ILCV* 2868 (11.ix; om. Fll.); *ICUR* n.s. I 2097* (14.viii-13.ix; frag.); *ICUR* n.s. III 7383 (14.viii-13.ix); [Continued on the next page]	Fll. Merobaudes II et Saturninus (vv.cc.)

Orientis

FASTI:	Marcell. Heracl. (Sat. I)	Merobaudes II et
	Hyd. Pasch. (om. II)	Saturninus
LAWS:	*CTh* 12.6.17 (C'polis, 29.iv)	p.c. Antonii et Syagrii
	C'polis, 23 laws (earliest,	Merobaudes II et
	CTh 10.3.4, 18.i); Selymbria,	Saturninus
	1 law	
PAPYRI:	*P.Gen.* 12.1 (2.iv);	Fl. Merobaudes II et
	SPP XX 104.5	Fl. Saturninus vv.cc.
OTHER:	Socrates, *HE* 5.10 and 11	Merogaudes II et
	(11 om. II)	Saturninus
	Themistius, *Or.* 16, *Gratiarum*	
	Actio Theodosio ob pacem et	
	consulatum Saturnini	

NOTES: See the Critical Appendix for a full discussion of this year.

[Continued from preceding page]
ICUR n.s. VII 19961 (6-13.xi); *ICUR*
n.s. I 1440 = *ILCV* 3446 (30.xii;
om. II); *ICUR* suppl. 1710; *ICUR*
n.s. I 1169* (frag.; vv.cc.); *ICUR*
n.s. III 8425* (frag.); *ICUR* n.s.
I 2944* = *ILCV* 4144B (frag.; om. Fl.
bef. Mer.); *ICUR* n.s. I 2098* (frag.);
ICUR n.s. IV 12245 (frag.); *ICUR* n.s.
V 13116 (om. Fll.); *ICUR* n.s. II 4818
= *ILCV* 3499 (frag.); *ICUR* n.s. IV 11111;
ICUR n.s. I 504 (frag.; p.c. poss.); *ICUR*
n.s. II 6039; *ICUR* suppl. 1707 (om. Fll.);
ICUR n.s. VIII 21609b (frag.); *ICUR* n.s.
VIII 23420a (frag.); *ICUR* I 1142 (om. II; frag.)

ITALY: *CIL* XI 4041 = *ILCV* 3035D
(Capena, Reg. VII; 27.viii; om. Fll.);
CIJ I 650 = *AE* 1984, 439 (Catania; 21.x; om. Fll.)

GAUL: *Rec.Inscr.Chrét.Gaule* I
211* (Trier; vv.cc.; Gk.)

Occidentis

FASTI: Chr. 354 (pasch.) VindPr. Aq. Ricomer et Clearchus
Prosp. Ciz. Cycl. Aug. Cass. VindPost.

LAWS: *CTh* 6.30.6 (Milan, 26.x) p.c. Merobaudis II et
Saturnini

About 30 laws; Milan, 4 laws (earliest Ricomer et Clearchus
CTh 13.1.12, 13.iii); Aquileia, 1 law

INSCR.: **ROME:** *ICUR* n.s. I 3201 = *ILCV* p.conss. Me[robaude II
2609A adn. (14.iv-7.v) et S]aturnino vv.cc.

ICUR n.s. VII 17486 = *ILCV* (Fll.) Ricomer et
4343C (16.iii-1.iv; frag.); Clearchus (vv.cc.)
ICUR n.s. VII 17485 = *ILCV* 4343B
(16.iii-13.iv); *ICUR* n.s. V 13931
(31.v); *ICUR* n.s. I 2099 = *ILCV*
2782 (24.vi); *ICUR* n.s. II 4167 =
ILCV 4620 (11.vii); *ICUR* n.s.
III 8426 (25.vii); *ICUR* n.s. VI
15775 (16.vii-13.viii; vv.cc.);
ICUR n.s. VI 15776 = *ILCV* 3003
(7.ix); *ICUR* n.s. V 13929 (12.ix);
ICUR n.s. I 62 (6-13.ix); *ICUR*
n.s. VIII 23421 = *ILCV* 4159
(17.ix; Fll.); *ICUR* n.s. VII
19963 = *ILCV* 2819A (20.ix;
DD.NN. C. et R. vv.cc.!); *ICUR*
n.s. II 6040 (16/23.ix); *ICUR*
n.s. V 13930 (28.x); *ICUR* n.s.
I 331 = *ILCV* 4248 (9.xi); *ICUR*
n.s. I 3200 = *ILCV* 1270 (24.xi);
ICUR n.s. II 4750 = *ILCV* 2879 (11.xii);
ICUR n.s. VIII 20801b; 20802; *ICUR* n.s.
VII 17487 (frag.); *ICUR* n.s. I 177 (frag.;
p.c. poss.); *ICUR* n.s. V 13347; 13348
(frag.); *ICUR* n.s. VI 15991;
15992; *ICUR* n.s. II 4480; *ICUR*
n.s. II 5860 (frag.; poss. p.c., 385)

ITALY: *AE* 1975, 367 (Piano p.c. Fl. Merobaudis II
Laroma, nr. Casoli, Reg. IV; 5.v) et Fl. Saturnini
[Continued on next page]

Orientis

FASTI:	Marcell. Heracl. Hyd. Pasch. Scal. (adds cc.)	Ricomer et Clearchus
LAWS:	C'polis, 8 laws (earliest, *CTh* 12.13.5, 18.i); Heraclea, 4 laws (earliest *CTh* 6.30.7, 10.vi)	Ricomer et Clearchus (vv.cc.)
PAPYRI:	*P.Lips.* 62 i.1,15	p.c. Fl. Merobaudis II et Fl. Saturnini vv.cc.
	P.Lips. 62 i.24; ii.1	Ricomer et Clearchus vv.cc.
OTHER:	Socrates, *HE* 5.12	Richomelius et Clearchus

NOTES:

Ricomer was mag.mil. 383 and MVM 388-393 (*PLRE* I 765-66); Clearchus was a wealthy Thesprotian, PVC 372-373, 382-384 (*PLRE* I 211-12).

CTh 6.30.6 probably combines the date of issue at Milan with an *accepta* year, cf. above, p.82. We do, however, find a p.c. of iv/v at Rome and 5.v near Casoli, and an undatable instance in a papyrus.

Magnus Maximus, *comes Britanniarum*, proclaimed himself Augustus in Spring, 383, and, after the death of Gratian in August, ruled in the Gauls (*PLRE* I 588; J.R. Palanque, *Les empereurs romains d'Espagne* [Paris 1965] 255-63). Since four of the ten Roman consular inscriptions of 388 style him "Maximus Aug. II," we may presume (with Seeck) that he took his first consulate in January, 384 in the ordinary way. Since this will have been in the Gauls, unrecognized by Valentinian II and Theodosius, naturally it does not appear in the consular lists compiled or edited after his fall--just as none of his legislation appears in the Codes. It is mere chance that no inscription dated by his first consulate has survived from Gaul. Unlike Carausius and Magnentius, Maximus seems not to have struck any consular coinage; at any rate, none survives.

[Continued from preceding page] *CIL* XI 4968 = *ILCV* 2169 (Spoleto, Reg. VI; 13.x; vv.cc.); *CIL* XIV 1880 = *ICUR* I 352 (Ostia)	Ricomer et Clearchus (vv.cc.)

Occidentis

<u>FASTI</u>:	Chr. 354 (pasch.) VindPr. Prosp. Ciz. Cycl. Aug. VindPost. Cass. Aq.	Arcadius (I) et Bauto (v.c.)
<u>LAWS</u>:	*CTh* 1.6.9 (Milan, 28.xii)	p.c. Richomeris et Clearchi
	About 40 laws; Milan, 11 laws (earliest *CTh* 1.23.5, 1.ii), Aquileia, 10 laws (earliest *CTh* 6.30.10, 31.viii)	Arcadius Aug. et Bauto (v.c.)
<u>INSCR.</u>:	**ROME:** *ICUR* n.s. I 1441 = *ILCV* 4460 (10.iii)	p.c. Ricomeri et Clearchi
	ICUR n.s. VII 17489 = *ILCV* 4258B (27.ii; DD.NN.); *ICUR* n.s. I 3202 = *ILCV* 1480 (22.vi; om. D.N.;Fl. Arc.); *ICUR* n.s. I 3001 = *ILCV* 2945A adn. (12.viii); *EphEp* 8 (1899) 648 = *ILS* 1264 (4.ix; Fl. Bauto v.c.); *ICUR* n.s. II 6041 (18.xii; v.c.); *ICUR* n.s. IV 12247 (v.c.); *ICUR* n.s. VII 19966b (frag.); *ICUR* n.s. VIII 23062 (frag.; p.c. 386 poss.); *ICUR* n.s. VII 19966a (frag.; p.c. 386 poss.)	D.N. (Fl.) Arcadius (Aug.) et (Fl.) Bauto (v.c.)
	ITALY: *CIL* X 4490 = *ILCV* 488 (Capua, Reg. I; 30.vi; om. D.N.; Arc. Aug.); *AE* 1925, 84 = *ILCV* 4599 (Velletri, Reg. I; 20.x; om. D.N.; Arc. Aug.); *CIL* XIV 2934* = *ILS* 8375 (Praeneste, Reg. I; 16.xi/4.iii.386?; D.N. Arc. Aug. et Bauto v.c.); *CIL* IX 5300 = *ILCV* 81 (Civita di Marano, Reg. V; 13.xii; DD.NN.)	
	DALMATIA: *CIL* III 9509 = *ILCV* 2964 (Salona; 12.viii; om. D.N.?; Arc. Aug., Fl., v.c.); *CIL* III 13121 (Salona; frag.; p.c. poss.)	

[Continued on the next page]

Orientis

FASTI:	Marcell. Heracl. (Arc. I) Hyd. (Aug.) Pasch. (Aug.) Gol. (I, v.c.)	Arcadius (Aug.) (I) et Bauto (v.c.)
	Scal.	Arcadius Aug. filius Theodosii et Bauto
LAWS:	C'polis, 14 laws (first, *CJ* 1.55.4, 2-5.i)	Arcadius Aug. I et Bauto (v.c.)
PAPYRI:	*P.Lips.* 62 ii.17 (4.xi)	p.c. Ricomeri et Clearchi vv.cc. praeff.
COINS:	Dumbarton Oaks Collection (C'polis)	Consular image of Arcadius on obv. and rev. of solidi and siliqua
OTHER:	Socrates, *HE* 5.12	Arcadius Aug. I et Bauto

NOTES:

Arcadius was proclaimed Augustus on 19.i.383, and so waited a year longer than usual before taking his first consulate. (Pacatus praised Theodosius for postponing his own sons' consulates in order to honor *amici*: *Pan.Theod.* 16.4.) Bauto replaced the original consul designated for the year, Praetextatus, cf. above, p.19. Bauto was mag. militum *ca* 380-385 (*PLRE* I 159-60).

The one papyrus has a p.c. as late as November, whereas the only epigraphical p.c. from Rome refers to early March, eleven days after the date of the first consular date. The p.c. in the law was added at Rome to a law issued at Milan at the end of the year (see above, p.82).

[Continued from the preceding page]

OTHER:	Letter 1 of Pope Siricius (*PL* 13.1132) (11.ii)	Arcadius et Bauto
	Augustine delivered the panegyric of Bauto on 1.i: *contra litt. Petiliani* 3.25-30 (cf. above, p.19)	

Occidentis

FASTI: Chr. 354 (pasch.) VindPr.   Honorius nob. puer (I)
            Prosp. Ciz. Cycl. Aug. Cass.   et Euodius (v.c.)[55]
            Aq. VindPost.

LAWS: *CTh* 1.9.2 (*p.p.* Hadrumetum,   p.c. Arcadii Aug. I et
            9.iii)   Bautonis v.c.

            About 47 laws; Milan, 9 laws   Honorius nob. puer
            (earliest *CTh* 16.1.4, 23.i);   et Euodius (v.c.)
            Ticinum, 1 law; Aquileia, 2 laws

INSCR.:   **ROME**: *ICUR* n.s. V 13934 = *ILCV*   Fl. Honorius nob. puer
            2631B (7.v; DD.NN., vv.cc.); *ICUR*   et (Fl.) Euodius v.c.
            n.s. II 6043 = *ILCV* 2978C (3.vii;
            om. Fl. bef. Hon.); *ICUR* n.s. V
            13350 = *ILCV* 645 adn. (23.vii;
            Fl. Eu.); *ICUR* n.s. VIII 21610 =
            ILCV 419ab (16.vii-13.viii; Fl.
            Eu.); *ICUR* n.s. VI 15777 (vv.cc.);
            ICUR n.s. I 1257 (om. Fl. bef.
            Hon.; frag.); *ICUR* n.s. I 1353
            (vv.cc.); *ICUR* n.s. I 1443 (frag.);
            ICUR n.s. III 8154 = *ILCV* 1119
            adn. (om. n.p.); *ICUR* n.s. VII
            17493 (om. n.p.); *ICUR* n.s. V
            13351 (om. n.p.); *ICUR* n.s. I
            2101 (p.c. poss.?); *ICUR* suppl.
            1753 (frag.)

            ITALY: *CIL* XI 4329 = *ILCV* 323   p.c. Arcadi et
            (Interamna, Reg. VI; 2.iii)   Bautonis v.c.

            CIL XIV 231 = *ILCV* 398   Fl. Honorius nob. puer
            (Ostia)   et Fl. Euodius

[Continued on the next page]

---

[55]VindPost. Cycl. Aug. and Chr. 354 (pasch.) om. puer or nob. puer.

Orientis

FASTI:	Marcell. Pasch. Hyd. (om. Caes.)	Honorius Caes. et Euodius
	Heracl. Gol. (I, v.c.)	Honorius nob. puer (I) et Euodius (v.c.)
LAWS:	C'polis, 30 laws (earliest, *CTh* 9.34.9, 19.i)	Honorius nob. puer et Euodius v.c.
PAPYRI:	*P.Gen.* 69.1 (i-iv); *ZPE* 61 (1985) 74.1 (26.vi)	p.c. D.N. Arcadii perp. Aug. et Fl. Bautonis v.c.
	P.Oxy. XXXIV 2715.1* (29.viii)	Fl. Honorius nob. puer et Fl. Euodius [v.c.]

NOTES:

Honorius was not proclaimed Augustus till 23.i.393; Euodius was PPO 385-386 (*PLRE* I 297).

The *p.p.* date by p.c. at Hadrumetum, an inscription from Interamna and the p.c. in the papyri all show delay in dissemination.

[Continued from the preceding page]

OTHER:	Letter 5 of Pope Siricius (*PL* 13.1155) (6.i)	p.c. Arcadii Aug. et Bautonis v.c.
	Sulpicius Severus, *V.Martini* 20.4, records how Magnus Maximus, St. Martin and "praefectus idemque consul Euodius" dined together in his palace at Trier.	

Occidentis

FASTI: Chr. 354 (pasch.) VindPr. Aq.   Valentinianus III
              Prosp. Ciz. Cycl. Aug. Cass.   et Eutropius (v.c.)[56]
              VindPost. (IV)

LAWS: *CTh* 1.29.6 (no prov., 25.i)   p.c. Honorii n.p. et
                                                        Euodii v.c.

              About 15 laws, 4 from Milan,   Valentinianus Aug. III
              earliest *CTh* 13.3.13 (22.i)   et Eutropius

INSCR.:   **ROME:** *CIL* VI 1778 (1.ii; Fl.   D.N. (Fl.) Valentinianus
              Val.); *ICUR* n.s. V 13352 (16.vii-   Aug. III et Eutropius
              13.viii); *ICUR* n.s. I 1444 (17.ix;   (v.c.)
              om. D.N., Aug.); *ILCV* 4987 = *CIJ*
              528 (1.x; om. D.N., Aug.); *ICUR*
              n.s. VII 19967 (14.viii-13.xii;
              om. Aug.); *ICUR* n.s. I 1258
              (20.xii?; om. Aug.); *ICUR* n.s. I
              3204; *ICUR* n.s. III 8155; *ICUR*
              n.s. VI 17282; *ICUR* n.s. V 13369
              = *ILCV* 4804 adn. (om. Aug.);
              ICUR n.s. VIII 23063 (om. D.N.,
              Aug. III)

              ITALY: *EphEp* 8 (1899) 516 (Capua,
              Reg. I; 18.v; v.c.); *CIL* V 6243
              = *ILCV* 4398a (Milan, Reg. XI;
              17.ix; om. D.N.); *I.Ital.* XIII.2,
              46 = *ILS* 4918 (Capua; 22.xi; om.
              D.N., Aug.)

              SPAIN: *CIL* II 3222 = 6340 = *ILCV*
              2243 (Oretum, Tarraconensis; v.c.)

COINS: *RIC* IX 78.9 (Milan); Pearce,   Valentinian, cons. image
              NC 5 ser. 18 (1938) 225-28   on obv., cons. image of
                                                        Val. and Theodosius
                                                        on rev. of solidi

[56]Chr. 354 (pasch.): II; Cycl. om. numeral.

Orientis

FASTI:	Marcell. Heracl. Pasch. (IV) Hyd. ('Valerius')	Valentinianus III et Eutropius
	Scal. Gol.	Valentinianus Aug. III et Eutropius v.c.
LAWS:	C'polis, 7 laws (earliest, *CTh* 10.10.19, 2.iii);[57] Thessalonica, 1 law	Valentinianus Aug. III et Eutropius
PAPYRI:	*SB* XIV 11285.1 (28.v)	p.c. Fl. Honorii nob. pueri et Fl. Euodii v.c.
INSCR.:	**GREECE:** *IG* II² 4842 = *Syll.*³ 907 (Attica; 27.v)	p.c. Honorii et Euodii

NOTES:

Eutropius, author of the *Breviarium*, was PPO 380-381 (*PLRE* I 317). The Athenian inscription, the papyri, and the (placeless) law of 25.i from *CTh* all point to late dissemination. The p.c. in the law is presumably an *accepta* rather than a *data* date (cf. above, pp. 81-82).

[57]Following Mommsen's emendation of VI in place of XVI NON MART.

(1) Magnus Maximus Aug. II (through Aug.)
(2) Theodosius Aug. II et Cynegius

Occidentis

<u>FASTI</u>:	Chr. 354 (pasch.) VindPr. Prosp. Ciz. Cycl. (om. II) Aug. Cass. Aq.	Theodosius Aug. II et Cynegius (v.c.)
<u>LAWS</u>:	9 laws; Aquileia, 1 law (*CTh* 15.14.6, 22.ix); Milan, 1 law (*CTh* 15.14.7, 10.x); Stobi and Scubi, 1 law each	(D.N.) Theodosius Aug. II et Cynegius (v.c.)
<u>INSCR.</u>:	**ROME:** *ICUR* n.s. II 4820 = *ILCV* 2795C (11.i; om. Aug.); *ICUR* n.s. VIII 20718 = *ILCV* 4219A (17.i; om. D.N., II); *ICUR* n.s. III 6506 = *ILCV* 3287A (8.ii; only Max.); *ICUR* n.s. VIII 21611* = *ILCV* 3287 (22.ii; only Max. Aug.); *ICUR* n.s. VII 17494 = *ILCV* 3306 (13.v); *ICUR* n.s. II 6045 = *ILCV* 2795C, 4146D (24.vii; om. D.N.); *ICUR* n.s. VIII 23424 (xi; om. II); *ICUR* n.s. IV 9575 (frag.); *ICUR* n.s. VII 17495 = *ILCV* 610; *ICUR* n.s. I 5995	D.N. Magnus Maximus Aug. II
	ICUR n.s. II 4821 = 5713 (12.ix)	[Fl. Theodosius Aug. II et] Cynegius v.c.
	ITALY: *CIL* V 6243 = *ILCV* 4398b (Milan; 29.vi)	D.N. Mag[nus Maximus Aug. II]

Orientis

FASTI: Marcell. Heracl. (om. Aug.)   Theodosius Aug. II
              Hyd. Pasch. Gol. (v.c.)   et Cynegius (v.c.)

LAWS: Thessalonica, 3 laws (earliest,   (D.N.) Theodosius Aug. II
              CTh 16.5.14, 10.iii)   et Cynegius (v.c.)

PAPYRI: *P.Lips.* 63.1 (14.vi); *SB* VIII   D.N. Theodosius perp. Aug.
              9907.1 (19.ix; om num. II);   II et Fl. Cynegius v.c.
              P.Lips. 22.1 (1.x); *SB* VIII
              9825.1? (393 also poss.)

OTHER: Socrates, *HE* 5.13   Theodosius II et Cynegius

              The discovery of the pseudonymous
              Apocalypse of Paul is said to have
              been made in the foundations of a
              house in Tarsus "in the consulate
              of Theodosius Augustus the Younger
              and of Cynegius" (Syriac version:
              New Testament Apocrypha, ed. E.
              Hennecke et al. II [1965] 756, 759)

NOTES:

Magnus Maximus' first consulate presumably fell in 384; see that year for references. After Maximus' defeat on 28.viii, Theodosius and Cynegius (PPO Or. 384-388; cf. *PLRE* I 235-36) were proclaimed in the West (the only inscription is 12.ix; a date by Maximus occurs in November). For the possibility that the original of Hyd. was Cynegius' personal consular list, see above, p.55. For a discussion of the attribution of the inscriptions supposedly referring to a third consulate of Merobaudes with Theodosius, see the Critical Appendix for 383.

Occidentis

FASTI:	Chr. 354 (pasch.) VindPr. Hyd. Aq. Prosp. Cycl. Aug. Cass.	Timasius et Promotus
LAWS:	About 24 laws, 12 from Milan, earliest *CTh* 15.14.8 (14.i); Trier, 2 laws; Rome, 8 laws (earliest *CTh* 16.5.18, 17.vi)	Timasius et Promotus (vv.cc.)
INSCR.:	**ROME:** *ICUR* n.s. IV 12251 (21.iii); *ICUR* n.s. II 4823 = *ILCV* 1130 (2.iv; om. Fll.); *ICUR* n.s. VII 19970 = *ILCV* 2978D (3.iv; om. vv.cc.); *ICUR* n.s. II 5934 = *ILCV* 2777 adn. (23.v; om. Fll., vv.cc.); *ICUR* n.s. I 2771 = *ILCV* 1481 (4.vi; om. Fll.); *AE* 1979, 43 (15.viii; om. Fll., vv.cc.); *ICUR* n.s. VII 17497 = *ILCV* 2970 (18.viii; om. Fll.); *CIL* VI 1759 = *ILS* 1272 (25.viii); *ICUR* n.s. IV 12538 = *ILCV* 2945B (12.ix; om. Fll., vv.cc.); *ICUR* n.s. II 4825 (14.viii-13.ix; om. Fll., vv.cc.); *ICUR* n.s. V 13355 (4.x); *ICUR* n.s. IV 11117 (18.x; om. vv.cc.); *ICUR* n.s. IV 11120 (12/13.xii; om. Fll.); *ICUR* n.s. III 6507 (om. Fll.); *ICUR* n.s. IV 11118 (om. vv.cc.; frag.); *ICUR* n.s. II 4824 (om. vv.cc.; frag.); *ICUR* n.s. VI 15994 (frag.); *RAC* 61 (1985) 20 (frag.)	Fll. Timasius et Promotus vv.cc.

Orientis

FASTI: Marcell. Heracl. Pasch.   Timasius et Promotus
             Gol.

LAWS: none

PAPYRI: *P.Lips.* 37.1 (5.v);   p.c. D.N. Theodosii perp.
             P.Ross.Georg. III 30.1 (om. Fl.)   Aug. II et Fl. Cynegii
                                                  v.c.

             P.Lips. 38.4 (16.xii; doc.   Timasius et Promotus
             19.ix.390); *BGU* III 943.1   vv.cc.

NOTES:

    Timasius was mag. equitum 386 and MVM 388-395; Promotus was mag. peditum 386 and mag. equitum 388-391 (*PLRE* I 914-15; 750-51), both in the East. Dissemination in Egypt was late.

Occidentis

FASTI: Chr. 354 (pasch.) VindPr. Aq.   Valentinianus IV
        Prosp. Cycl. Aug. Cass. Hyd.   et Neoterius

LAWS: *CJ* 1.40.9 (Milan, 23.xii)   p.c. Timasii et Promoti[58]

        About 23 laws, 13 from Milan,   Valentinianus Aug. IV
        earliest *CTh* 6.30.12 (15.i);   et Neoterius (v.c.)
        Verona, 3 laws

INSCR.:   **ROME:** *ICUR* n.s. VIII 20806   D.N. (Fl.) Valentinianus
        = *ILCV* 2974 adn. (5.i; om. Aug.);   Aug. IV et Neoterius v.c.
        ICUR n.s. II 6047 (17.iv; om. D.N.,
        Aug.); *CIL* VI 512 = *ILS* 4154
        (23.v; om. v.c.); *CIL* VI 503 =
        ILS 4151 (23.v; om. v.c.); *ICUR*
        n.s. I 2102 = *ILCV* 3501 (18.vii;
        om. Aug. IV, v.c.); *ICUR* n.s. I
        1445 = *ILCV* 2946 adn. (21.vii;
        Fl. Val.); *ICUR* suppl. 1811
        (23.vii); *ICUR* n.s. II 6049 =
        ILCV 4215 (16.viii; om. D.N.;
        Fl. Val.); *ICUR* n.s. VII 17498 =
        ILCV 4643 (27.ix); *ICUR* n.s. II
        6048 = *ILCV* 2977 (1.x; om. IV);
        ICUR n.s. VIII 23426 (22.x; om.
        v.c.); *ICUR* n.s. II 4770* = *AE*
        1959, 64 (19.xi; rest. as p.c.,
        391); *AE* 1980, 95 (22.xi); *ICUR*
        n.s. VII 19972; *ICUR* n.s. III
        8156; *ICUR* n.s. V 13117; *ICUR* I
        382 (frag.; year uncert.?); *ICUR*
        n.s. IV 11120 (frag., om. v.c.);
        ICUR n.s. V 13936 (om. D.N., Aug.,
        v.c.); *ICUR* n.s. VIII 23425 =
        ILCV 2156; *ICUR* n.s. VII 19973;
        17499; 19971; *ICUR* n.s. II 4778 =
        ILCV 1857C (or p.c.?); *ICUR* n.s.
        IV 11117 (very frag.); *ICUR* n.s.
        V 13356 (frag.; p.c. poss.; om. v.c.)
        [Continued on the next page]

---

[58]The p.c. is presumably an accepta date, though the day date must be wrong anyway (Seeck, *Regesten* 101); above, pp.81-82.

Orientis

FASTI:	Marcell. (Aug.) Heracl. Hyd. Pasch. Gol.	Valentinianus (Aug.) IV et Neoterius
LAWS:	none	
PAPYRI:	*P.Lips.* 38.1* = *ChLA* XII 520 (19.ix; Lat.); *W.Chr.* 434.1 = *P.Monac.* III 99 (prob. v-xii; om. Fl.); *P.Lips.* 39.1 (23.xii); 65.1 (om. Fl.)	D.N. Valentinianus perp. Aug. IV et Fl. Neoterius v.c.
INSCR.:	**PHRYGIA:** *AE* 1984, 849 (Sebaste; Lat.)	Valentinianus Aug. IV et Neoterius v.c.

NOTES:

Neoterius was PPO three times, Orientis, Italiae and Galliarum (380-381, 385, 390), cf. *PLRE* I 623.

[Continued from preceding page]

COINS:	*RIC* IX 31.91 (Trier), 81.21a (Milan); Pearce, *NC* 5 ser. 18 (1938) 225-27	Valentinian, cons. image on obv., cons. image of Val. and Theodosius on rev. of solidi
	RIC IX 81.21b (Milan); Pearce, *NC* 5 ser. 18 (1938) 225-27	Theodosius, cons. image on obv., cons. image of Theod. and Valentinian on rev. of solidi
OTHER:	Council at Carthage: *Conc.Africae* p.12 (20.v)	gloriosissimus Imp. Valentinianus Aug. IV et Neotherius vv.cc.
	Amm.Marc. 26.5.14	

Occidentis

<u>FASTI:</u>	Chr. 354 (pasch.) VindPr. Hyd. Prosp. Cycl. Aug. Aq. Cass.	Tatianus et Symmachus
<u>LAWS:</u>	About 15 laws, 4 from Milan, earliest *CTh* 16.10.10 (24.ii); Vincentia, 2 laws; Concordia, 1 law; Aquileia, 3 laws	Tatianus et Symmachus
<u>INSCR.:</u>	**ROME:** *ICUR* n.s. II 6051 (1.ii); *ICUR* n.s. I 1446 = *ILCV* 2926 (5.v; Tat. et Symm.); *ICUR* n.s. II 6050 (9?/11?.v; T. et S.); *ICUR* n.s. VII 19974 = *ILCV* 197 (16.v-1.vi; om. vv.cc.); *ICUR* n.s. VI 17249 = *ILCV* 4380 (25.vii; T. et S.); *ICUR* n.s. I 2103 (14.ix-1.x; T. et S.); *ICUR* suppl. 1831 (frag.); *ICUR* n.s. I 3209 (T. et S.); *ICUR* n.s. III 8428 = *ILCV* 3821 (Q. Aur. Symm.); *ICUR* n.s. II 4169 = *ILCV* 659 adn. (T. et S.); *ICUR* n.s. VIII 23427 = *ILCV* 4701A (T. et S.; frag.); *ICUR* n.s. III 8158 = *ILCV* 2132 adn. (A. [sic] Tat. et Q. S. vv.cc.); *ICUR* n.s. V 13358 (T. et S.); *ICUR* n.s. II 4751 (T. et S.); *ICUR* n.s. VII 17501 (Fl. T. et Aur. [Symm.]); *ICUR* n.s. V 13118 (frag.); *ICUR* n.s. V 13357 (frag.) **ITALY:** *AE* 1982, 386 (W. of Aquileia, Reg. X; 12.vii; om. Fl., Aur.); *CIL* X 37 = *ILCV* 2837 (Gerace, Reg. III; 26.vii); *CIL* X 5646 = *ILCV* 2935A (S. Giovanni in Carico, Reg. I; 6.xii; T. et S. vv.cc.)	Fl. Tatianus et (Q.) Aur. Symmachus vv.cc.
<u>OTHER:</u>	Symmachus, *Epp.* 2.62-64; 5.15; 9.149, 153	

Orientis

<u>FASTI:</u>	Marcell. Heracl. Hyd. Pasch. Gol.	Tatianus et Symmachus
<u>LAWS:</u>	C'polis, 3 laws (earliest, *CTh* 13.9.4, 18.vii)	Tatianus et Symmachus
<u>PAPYRI:</u>	*P.Lips.* 42.1* (iii-iv); 14.1 (29.v); *P.Ross.Georg.* V 60 recto, p.176 (10.vi; frag.); *PSI* XV 1566.1 (13.x; only vv.cc.); *P.Stras.* 142.1 (16.x; om. sacr., ex-praef.)	Fl. Tatianus v.c. praef. sacr. praet. et Fl. Symmachus v.c. ex-praef.
<u>OTHER:</u>	Socrates, *HE* 5.18	Tatianus et Symmachus
	Libanius, *Epp.* 1021 (acknowledging receipt of Tatianus' consular diptych)	

<u>NOTES:</u>

This was the last year with two pagan consuls: Tatianus was PPO Orientis 388-392 (*PLRE* I 876-78); Symmachus was the famous orator and epistolographer, PVR 384-385 (*PLRE* I 865-71; Chastagnol, *Fastes* 218-29).

Occidentis

FASTI: Chr. 354 (pasch.) (Aug.) VindPr.   Arcadius (Aug.) II
                Prosp. Cycl. (Aug.) Aug. Cass.   et Rufinus (v.c.)[59]
                Aq. Hyd.

LAWS: *CTh* 10.17.3 (*acc.* Hadrumetum,   p.c. Tatiani et
                13.i; issued at Aquileia,   Symmachi vv.cc.
                19.vi.391)

INSCR.:   **ROME:** *ICUR* n.s. III 6508*   p.c. Fl. Tatiani et
                (9.i/9.ii)   Q. Aur. Symmachi vv.cc.

                ICUR n.s. IV 12540 = *ILCV* 2601   D.N. Arcadius Aug. II
                (17.ii); *ICUR* n.s. V 13359   et Fl. Rufinus v.c.
                (20.iii; om. Aug., Fl.); *ICUR*
                n.s. I 1447 = *ILCV* 4339 (23.iii;
                om. Aug., Fl., v.c.); *ICUR* n.s.
                I 986 = *ILCV* 2611 adn. (12.vi
                or 14.vii; om. Aug., Fl.); *ICUR*
                n.s. IV 12539 = *ILCV* 2926 adn.
                (6.v, 4.vi,16.vii-13.viii; om.
                Aug.); *ICUR* n.s. II 4827 = *ILCV*
                3429 (24.viii); *ICUR* n.s. II 4271
                = *ILCV* 3502 (13.ix; om. Fl.,
                v.c.); *ICUR* n.s. VII 17502 =
                ILCV 4219B (23.ix; om. Fl., v.c.);
                ICUR n.s. VIII 23429 = *ILCV* 754
                (5.xi; om. Aug.); *ICUR* n.s I 2980
                = *ILCV* 3727A (om. D.N., Fl.); *ICUR*
                n.s. VII 17434 = *ILCV* 4329A adn.
                (om. Fl.); *ICUR* n.s. I 1355* (om.
                Aug., Fl.); *ICUR* n.s. I 3211 =
                CIL VI 31935 (om. Fl., v.c.);
                ICUR n.s. IV 11777 = *ILCV* 3797D
                (om. D.N., Aug., Fl., v.c.); *AE*
                1953, 224 (om. Aug., Fl.); *ICUR*
                n.s. V 13360 (om. Aug., Fl.);
                ICUR n.s. VII 17503 (om. Fl.;
                p.c. poss.)
                [Continued on the next page]

[59]Cycl. om. II.

Orientis

FASTI: Marcell. (om. Aug.) Heracl. (om.   Arcadius Aug. II
           Aug.) Hyd. Pasch. Gol. (v.c.)   et Rufinus (v.c.)

LAWS: About 29 laws from C'polis   Arcadius Aug. II
           (earliest *CTh* 13.5.21, 15.ii)   et Rufinus (v.c.)

PAPYRI: *PSI* VI 698.1 (25.i)   p.c. Fl. Tatiani et
                                                   Fl. Symmachi vv.cc.

           P.Gron. 9.19 (20.iv; adds   D.N. Arcadius perp. Aug.
           Theod. et bef. Arcad.; om.   II et Fl. Rufinus v.c.
           perp. Aug.; numeral I);   (comes et magister)
           P.Herm. 19.18 (6.x; om. Fl.,
           adds comes et magister);
           P.Oxy. VII 1033.1 (18.x)

NOTES:

   Rufinus was PPO Orientis 392-395 (*PLRE* I 778-81). The western p.c. in *CTh* 10.17.3 is clearly the
date appended in Hadrumetum. Valentinian II died on 15.v.392 and Fl. Eugenius was proclaimed Augustus
by the western MVM Arbogastes on 22.viii.392.

           [Continued from preceding page]

           ITALY: *CIL* V 1622 (Aquileia,   p.c. Tatiani et
           Reg. X; 16.iii-1.iv)   Symmachi [vv.cc.]

           IG XIV 2252* (Pisauri, Reg. VI;   D.N. Arcadius Aug. II
           21.ii; om. D.N., Aug., Fl., v.c.;   et Fl. Rufinus v.c.
           Gk.); *CIL* XIV 3417 = *ICUR* I
           407+408 (Praeneste, Reg. I; cf.
           ILCV 2956 adn.; om. Aug., Fl., v.c.)

Occidentis

FASTI: Chr. 354 (pasch.) (Aug.) VindPr.   Theodosius (Aug.) III
           Prosp. Cycl. (Aug.) Aug. Cass.   et Abundantius[60]
           Aq. Hyd. (Aug.)

LAWS: none (all East)

INSCR.:   **ROME:** *ICUR* n.s. I 1449 = *ILCV*   (DD.NN.) (Fl.) Theodosius
           2971A (14.iv; Eug. Aug.); *ICUR*   Aug. III et (Fl.) Eugenius
           n.s. III 8429 = *ILCV* 4556* (30.v;   (Aug.)
           om. Aug. III); *AE* 1975, 115 (23.ix;
           om. Aug.); *ICUR* n.s. I 727 =
           ILCV 1599 (4.x); *ICUR* n.s. III
           8159 = *ILCV* 4642 adn. (13.x; Fl.
           Th., Fl. Eug. Aug.); *ICUR* n.s. IV
           11123 = *ILCV* 4414 (8.xii; om.
           Aug.); *ICUR* n.s. V 13119 = *ILCV*
           2946 adn. (15.xii; DD.NN., Fl. Eug.
           Aug.); *ICUR* n.s. I 1448 = *ILCV*
           2663 (25.xii; DD.NN., om. Aug.);
           ICUR n.s. VII 17506 = *ILCV* 4664
           (DD.NN.; om. Aug.; Eug. Aug.);
           ICUR n.s. IV 12422; *ICUR* n.s. III
           8430 = *ILCV* 4702 (Fl. Eug.; frag.);
           ICUR n.s. II 4828; *ICUR* n.s. III
           8431; *ICUR* n.s. I 1940 (Eug. Aug.);
           ICUR n.s. V 13939; *AE* 1975, 116
           (om. Aug. III); *ICUR* n.s. VII
           17505 (Augg. at end)

           ITALY: *CIL* X 4491* (Capua, Reg.   p.c. D.N. Arcadii Aug.
           I; 17.v; om. Aug., v.c.); *CIL* IX   et Fl. Rufini v.c.
           6192 = *ILCV* 582 (nr. Canossa,
           Reg. II ; 24.v)

           Röm.Quart. 10 (1896) 25 no. 34   Theodosius III
           (Syracuse; 1.xii; Gk.)   et Eugenius I

           CIL X 4492* = *ILCV* 1491 (Capua;   D.N. Eugenius (Aug.) I
           31.viii, 25.x; Aug.); *IG* XIV 2295
           (Milan, Reg. XI; om. D.N., I; Gk.)
           [Continued on the next page]

---

[60]Cycl. om. III.

Orientis

<u>FASTI:</u>	Marcell. Heracl. Pasch.	Theodosius (Aug.) III et Abundantius
<u>LAWS:</u>	About 42 laws, 40 from C'polis (earliest, *CTh* 1.21.1 and 7.3.1 = 10.19.13, both 12.ii)	(D.N.) Theodosius Aug. III et Abundantius (v.c.)
<u>PAPYRI:</u>	*P.Rein.* II 92.1 (iii-iv)	p.c. D.N. Arcadii perp. Aug. II et Fl. Rufini v.c.
<u>OTHER:</u>	Socrates, *HE* 5.25	(Theodosius) III et Abundantius

<u>NOTES:</u>

On the circumstances behind Eugenius' proclamation of Theodosius, see p.16. Abundantius was eastern MVM 392-393 (*PLRE* I 4-5). The fasti were efficiently corrected after Eugenius' death, but the inscriptions tell a different story. *CIL* IX 6192 and X 4491 show that the p.c. in the papyrus is not a local aberration. For Eugenius, see *PLRE* I 293 and above, p.64.

	[Continued from preceding page]	
	SPAIN: *Röm.Inschr.Tarraco* 944 (Tarragona)	Eugenius Aug. I
<u>COINS:</u>	*RIC* IX 33.100 and 102 (Trier)	Eugenius, cons. image on obv. of aureus and solidi, cons. image of Eug. and Theodosius on rev. of solidi
<u>OTHER:</u>	Council at Hippo: *Conc.Africae* p.182 (8.x)	glorios. Imp. Theodosius Aug. III et Abundantius v.c.

Occidentis

FASTI: Chr. 354 (pasch.) (Aug.) VindPr.   Arcadius (Aug.) III
Prosp. Cycl. Aug. Aq. Cass.   et Honorius Aug. II
Hyd. (Aug.)

LAWS: none

INSCR.: **ROME:** *ICUR* n.s. II 6460 = *ILCV*   (Fl.) Nicomachus Flavianus
3822 (13.v); *ICUR* n.s. III 8648
(11.viii; Fl. N. Fl.); *ICUR* n.s.
V 13364 (30.viii); *ICUR* suppl.
1855 = *ILCV* 1482 (17.ix); *ICUR*
n.s. II 4503 = *ILCV* 4321 adn.;
ICUR n.s. V 13368; *ICUR* n.s. VII
19975; *ICUR* n.s. V 13361

ICUR n.s. II 4487 (9.x);   DD.NN. Arcadius III
ICUR suppl. 1704 = *ILCV* 2907B   et Honorius II Augg.
(24.xi); *ICUR* n.s. I 2811
(om. Augg.)

OTHER: Council at Carthage: *Conc.Africae*   glorios. Impp. Arcadius
p.182 (16.vi)   III et Honorius II Augg.

NOTES:

    For Nicomachus Flavianus, PPO Italiae twice (the details are controversial) see *PLRE* I 347-49 and
D. Vera, *Athenaeum* 61 (1983) 24-64 and 390-426. An appointee of Eugenius, he committed suicide on
Eugenius' defeat and subsequent death (6.ix, cf. *PLRE* I 293).

Orientis

FASTI:	Marcell. Heracl. Pasch.	Arcadius (Aug.) III et Honorius (Aug.) II
LAWS:	About 8 laws, earliest *CTh* 2.29.2 (C'polis, 4.iii); C'polis, 5 laws; Heraclea and Hadrianopolis, 1 law each; one given as Tyre (Cf. Seeck, *Reg.* 11)	Arcadius (Aug.) III et Honorius (Aug.) II
PAPYRI:	*P.Oxy.* XIV 1712.1	p.c. D.N. Theodosii perp. Aug. III et Fl. Abundantii v.c.
	P.Herm. 22.1; *P.Rain.Cent.* 165.9 (Lat.)	DD.NN. Arcadius III et Honorius II perp. Augg.
OTHER:	Synodal judgment: Mansi III 852 (Constantinople, 30.ix)	piiss. et amantiss. Deum Impp. NN. Fl. Arcadius Aug. III et Honorius II
	Socrates, *HE* 5.25	Arcadius III et Honorius II

Occidentis

FASTI: Chr. 354 (pasch.) Hyd. VindPr.   Olybrius et Probinus
            Prosp. Cycl. Aug. Aq. Cass.

LAWS: Milan, 23 laws, earliest 6.i (*CTh*   Olybrius et Probinus
            2.1.8--date *acc.* Seeck, otherwise
            earliest *CTh* 7.24.1, 5.iii); Brescia, 1 law

INSCR.:   **ROME:** *ICUR* n.s. V 13365* (15.i;   (p.c.) DD.NN. Arcadii
            stone has cons., error for p.c.)   III et Honorii II Augg.

            ICUR n.s. II 6053 = *ILCV* 2606   (Fll.) Anicii
            (22.i; om. Anic.); *ICUR* n.s.   (Hermogenianus) Olybrius
            IV 9377 = *ILCV* 3003A (19.ii);   et Probinus vv.cc.
            ICUR n.s. I 3213 = *ILCV* 2946 adn.
            (24.iv; om. vv.cc.); *ICUR* n.s.
            III 8164 = *ILCV* 2146 (13.v;
            Anicio); *ICUR* n.s. III 8729 =
            ILCV 3424 (16.viii; om. Anic.);
            ICUR n.s. V 15354 = *ILCV* 4146E
            (24.viii); *ICUR* n.s. VII 19976
            (14.viii-1.ix; om. Anic.); *ICUR*
            n.s. V 15355 (4.ix; om. Anic.,
            vv.cc.); *ICUR* n.s. I 2105 = *ILCV*
            3099A (14?.ix; Hermogenianus);
            ICUR n.s. III 8161 = *ILCV* 994
            + add. (21.ix; om. vv.cc.); *ICUR*
            n.s. VII 17508 = *ILCV* 2946 adn. (11.xi;
            om. Anic.); *ICUR* n.s. VII 19977 (9.xii;
            om. Anic.); *ICUR* n.s. VII 17507 (i-ii
            or xii); *ICUR* n.s. III 6509 (Flaviis
            Aniciis vv.cc.); *ICUR* n.s. V 13367; *ICUR*
            n.s. V 13368; 15778; *ICUR* I 432* (om.
            Anic., vv.cc.); *ICUR* n.s. III 8149 (om.
            vv.cc.); *ICUR* n.s. I 1212 (om. Anic.;
            frag.); *ICUR* n.s. III 8162 (frag.);
            NotScav 1888, 504 (frag.); *ICUR*
            n.s. III 8163 (frag.; om. vv.cc.);
            ICUR n.s. VIII 20808 (frag.);
            ICUR n.s. II 4829 = *ILCV* 3800A
            (frag.); *ICUR* n.s. II 4510; *ICUR*
            n.s. VII 17509b; *RAC* 60 (1984)
            31 (frag.)
            [Continued on the next page]

Orientis

<u>FASTI:</u>	Marcell. Heracl. Pasch.	Olybrius et Probinus
<u>LAWS:</u>	C'polis, 16 laws (earliest, *CTh* 13.8.1, 9.i)	Olybrius et Probinus
<u>PAPYRI:</u>	*ZPE* 56 (1984) 82.11 (17.iv; Lat.); *P.Rainer Cent.* 165.9 (Lat.)	p.c. DD.NN. Arcadii III et Honorii II perpp. Augg.
<u>OTHER:</u>	Socrates, *HE* 5.26, 6.1 (17.i)	Olybrius et Probinus
	Soz. 7.29.4	

<u>NOTES:</u>

The consuls were brothers, sons of Probus cos. 371, consuls in extreme youth: *PLRE* I 639-40; 734-35.

	[Continued from preceding page]	
	ITALY: *CIL* IX 259 = *ILS* 6115 (Genosa, Reg. II; 27.iii)	p.c. DD.NN. Arcadii III et Honorii II Augg.
	CIL XI 4042 = *ILCV* 3036A (Capena, Reg. VII; 20.ix; Ol.'s name mangled); *CIL* XI 4043 = *ILCV* 3036 (Capena, 9.xii)	Anicii Olybrius et Probinus
	DALMATIA: *CIL* III 12861* = 13122 = *ILCV* 184 (Salona; 4.vii)	Olybrius et Probinus
<u>OTHER:</u>	Subscription in Medic. 68.2 of Apuleius: Zetzel, *Latin Textual Criticism* 213 (3) (Rome)	Olibrius et Probinus vv.cc.
	Claudian, *Panegyricus Olybrio et Probino dictus* (recited at Rome in January)	

Occidentis

FASTI: Chr. 354 (pasch.) Hyd. VindPr.   Arcadius Aug. IV
                Prosp. Cycl. Aug. Cass. Aq.   et Honorius Aug. III[61]

LAWS: Total 59 laws, 14 from Milan   Arcadius Aug. IV
                (earliest *CTh* 8.5.55, 18.ii)   et Honorius Aug. III

INSCR.:   **ROME:** *ICUR* n.s. VIII 20809 =   DD.NN. (Fl.) Arcadius
                ILCV 659 adn. (3.i; Arc. Aug.);   (Aug.) IV et Honorius
                ICUR n.s. V 13370 (1-13.i or   (Aug.) III
                14-31.xii); *ICUR* n.s. VII 17510*
                (23.iii; Arc. V!; or 402?); *ICUR*
                n.s. I 3199 = *ILCV* 4343C adn.
                (16.v-13.vi; om. DD.NN.); *ICUR*
                n.s. VII 17485 = *ILCV* 4343B (16.v-
                13.vi); *ICUR* n.s. VII 17486 =
                ILCV 4343C adn. (vi; om. DD.NN.);
                ICUR n.s. I 2107 = *ILCV* 3057 adn.
                (23.vii; om. D.N.; frag.); *ICUR*
                n.s. VI 15995 (2.ix; om. D.N.); *ICUR*
                n.s. IV 12252* (23.ix; Fl. Arc.;
                Hon. IV!); *ICUR* n.s. I 1450 = *ILCV*
                301 (11.x; Aug. after each); *ICUR*
                n.s. I 2106 (14.ix-15.x); *ICUR*
                n.s. VIII 22969 = *ILCV* 4654 (16.x-
                1.xi; om. DD.NN.); *ICUR* n.s. I
                4073 = *ILCV* 1483 (Augg. at end);
                ICUR n.s. IV 12541 = *ILCV* 4414A;
                ICUR n.s. III 6510 (om. DD.NN.);
                ICUR I 369 = *ILCV* 4804 adn. (Augg.
                at end); *ICUR* n.s. VIII 20810 (om.
                DD.NN.)

                ITALY: *CIL* IX 3601 = *ILCV* 2957A
                (Bazzano, Reg. VIII; 21.viii;
                om. DD.NN.)

COINS: Kent, *Roman Coins* no.732 (Milan):   Honorius, cons. image
                solidus   on obv., cons. image of
                                                             Hon. and Arcadius on rev.

OTHER: Claudian, *Panegyricus de III consulatu
                Honorii Augusti*, delivered in January at Milan

---

[61]Only Hyd. and Chr. 354 have Aug.

Orientis

<u>FASTI:</u>	Marcell. Heracl. Pasch.	Arcadius Aug. IV et Honorius Aug. III[62]
<u>LAWS:</u>	C'polis, 39 laws, earliest 6.i (*CTh* 15.13.1; date disp.) or 17.i (*CTh* 7.6.4)	Arcadius Aug. IV et Honorius Aug. III
<u>PAPYRI:</u>	*P.Oxy.* VIII 1133.1 (24.iii); *P.Rainer Cent.* 88 = *CPR* X 107a.1 (25.vii)	p.c. Fll. Olybrii et Probini vv.cc.
	P.Flor. I 39.1 (29.viii); *ZPE* 56 (1984) 80.9 (Lat.); *CPLat.* 230 (Lat.)	DD.NN. Arcadius IV et Honorius III perpp. Augg.
<u>OTHER:</u>	*PG* 85.713-15 (29.vi)	(Impp. Arcadius IV et Honorius III Augg.)

<u>NOTES:</u>

Dissemination in Egypt was evidently late again.

---

[62]Marcell. and Heracl. om. Aug. 2x.

Occidentis

<u>FASTI</u>:	Chr. 354 (pasch.) Hyd.(A. & C.) VindPr. Prosp. Cycl. Aug. Aq. Cass.	Caesarius et Atticus
<u>LAWS</u>:	Total 38 laws, earliest *CJ* 7.45.12 (no prov., 9.i); 16 from Milan (earliest *CTh* 11.16,21,22, 31.i); 1 from Padua	Caesarius et Atticus (vv.cc.)
<u>INSCR.</u>:	**ROME:** *ICUR* n.s. I 471 (14.i-13.ii; frag.); *ICUR* n.s. VII 17514 (14.i-13.ii); I 941* = *ILCV* 3444 (mid-ii; DD.NN. Fl. C. et Nonius Att. vv.cc.); *ICUR* n.s. VII 17511 = *ILCV* 2777 (25.ii; Fl. C. et Non. Att.); *ICUR* n.s. V 13372 (7.v); *ICUR* n.s. I 2108 = *ILCV* 4146E (15.v; frag.); *ICUR* n.s. VII 19978 = *ILCV* 2927 (29.v; DD.NN. Fl. C. et Non. A. vv.cc.); *ICUR* n.s. V 13371 (4.vi); *ICUR* n.s. I 2812 = *ILCV* 1508 (28.vi; om. vv.cc.); *ICUR* n.s. IV 11779* = *ILCV* 4400A (29.vi; Fl. C. et N. A.); *ICUR* n.s. I 717 = *ILCV* 4671 (4.vii; om. vv.cc.); *ICUR* n.s. II 4830 = *ILCV* 3747 (26.vii; om. vv.cc.); *ICUR* n.s. II 4831 (14/24.viii; Fl. C. et N.A.); *ICUR* n.s. II 6056 = *ILCV* 4988 (24.viii; like preced.); *ICUR* n.s. II 6055* (23.x; Fl. C.); *ICUR* n.s. I 2772 = *ILCV* 3099B (11.xi; Fl. C et N. A.; om. vv.cc.); *ICUR* n.s. IV 12423 = *ILCV* 3091A (om. vv.cc.); *ICUR* n.s. I 2109 = *ILCV* 2609A adn. (om. vv.cc.); *NotScav* 1888, 504 (frag.; Non. A.); *ICUR* n.s. VIII 20811* = *ILCV* 3494 (Fl., Non.); *ICUR* n.s. I 1451* (frag.); *ICUR* n.s. IV 9582 (frag.); *ICUR* n.s. II 4832 (Fl. C.; frag.); *ICUR* n.s. IV 11128 = *ILCV* 4193 adn. (frag.); *ICUR* n.s. I 3214 = *ILCV* 4768; *ICUR* n.s. II 6057 (om. vv.cc.); *ICUR* n.s. VII 17512a; *NotScav* 1888, 703 (frag.; Fl. C.); *ICUR* n.s. II 6058 = *ILCV* 3781 (Fl. C. et [Continued on the next page]	(Fl.) Caesarius et (Nonius) Atticus vv.cc.

Orientis

<u>FASTI:</u>	Marcell. Heracl. Pasch.	Caesarius et Atticus
<u>LAWS:</u>	C'polis, 16 laws, earliest *CTh* 9.26.1, 16.ii; Nicomedia and Ancyra, 1 law each	Caesarius et Atticus (vv.cc.)
<u>PAPYRI:</u>	*SB* XII 10932.1* (6.iii); *P.Stras.* 255.17* (om. numerals?, perpp. Augg.; cf. above, p.69)	p.c. DD.NN. Arcadii IV et Honorii III perpp. Augg.
	P.Oxy. XXIV 2408.5* (16.vii-13.viii); *PSI* I 34.1 (2.ix); *P.Giss.* 52.1* (prob. 27.xii)	Fll. Caesarius et Atticus vv.cc.
<u>OTHER:</u>	George of Alexandria, Life of John Chrysostom, in Halkin, *Douze récits*, pp.123, 321 (27.ix; death of Nectarius, Bp. of C'polis)	Caesarius et Atticus
	Socrates, *HE* 6.2	Caesarius et Atticus
	Subscription to Apuleius codex: Zetzel, *Latin Textual Criticism* 213 (3) (C'polis)	Caesarius et Atticus

<u>NOTES:</u>
    Atticus was PPO It. 384 (*PLRE* I 586, s.v. Maximus 32). For the Maximus in *ICUR* n.s. II 6058 see Cameron, *Epigraphica* 47 (1985) 109-10. Caesarius was PPO Or. 395-397 and 400-403.

	[Continued from preceding page] Maximus vv.cc.); *ICUR* n.s. V 13373 (frag.); *ICUR* n.s. VII 17512b (frag.)	
	ITALY: *CIL* X 4493 = *ILCV* 2932A (Capua, Reg. I; 18.v; Fl. C. et N. A.; om. vv.cc.); *Kokalos* 28-29 (1982-83) 9 no. 19 = Agnello, *Silloge* 87 (Catania, om. vv.cc.)	
<u>OTHER:</u>	Council at Carthage: *Conc.Africae* pp. 193 (26.vi), 28 (13.viii; om. vv.cc.), 182, cf. 329 (28.viii)	Caesarius et Atticus vv.cc.
	Epigrammata Bobiensia 48, on "balnea quae consul Nonius instituit" (line 4)	

Occidentis

FASTI: Chr. 354 (pasch.) Hyd. VindPr.   Honorius Aug. IV
             Prosp. Cycl. Aug. Cass. Aq.   et Eutychianus[63]

LAWS: Total of 39 laws, 17 from Milan,   Honorius (Aug.) IV et
           earliest *CTh* 1.5.11, 11.ii   Eutychianus (v.c.)

INSCR.:   **ROME:** *ICUR* n.s. IV 9583 = *ILCV*   D.N. Honorius Aug. IV
           2946 adn. (8.i); *ICUR* I 461 =   et (Fl.) Eutychianus v.c.
           ILCV 3058 (16.iii; om. Aug.,
           Eut.); *ICUR* n.s. I 309* = *ILCV*
           4400B (26.viii; Arcadius for Hon.);
           ICUR n.s. III 8432 (14.viii-1.ix;
           Fl.); *ICUR* n.s. I 1941 = *ILCV* 2570
           (4.ix; om. Aug., v.c.); *ICUR* n.s.
           II 4834 = *ILCV* 4164 (13.ix; om.
           Eut.); *ICUR* n.s. I 1452 = *ILCV*
           3179 adn. (16.ix; Fl.; om. D.N.,
           Aug.; adds vv.cc.); *ICUR* n.s.
           IV 12542 (16.x-13.xi; om. D.N.);
           ICUR n.s. II 4833 (16.x-13.xi;
           DD.NN.); *AE* 1945, 24 (14.xi; Fl.;
           frag.); *ICUR* n.s. II 4505*; *ICUR*
           n.s. III 8647 (om. Aug., v.c.);
           ICUR n.s. V 13375; *ICUR* n.s. VIII
           23431b (frag.); *RAC* 60 (1984) 30a
           ('Horius', om. Aug., v.c.); *ICUR*
           n.s. V 13933* (om. D.N., numeral);
           ICUR n.s. VII 19979 (om. Eutychi-
           anus?); *ICUR* n.s. IV 12424 (garbled)

           ITALY: *IG* XIV 246 = Agnello,
           Silloge, 92 (Modica; 11.i; om. D.N.,
           Aug., v.c.; Gk.)

COINS: O. Ulrich-Bansa, *Moneta Mediola-*   Cons. image of Honorius on
           nensis (1949) no.87 (Milan)   obv. and rev. of solidus
           [Continued on the next page]

---

[63]III, Hyd.; Prosp., Cass., Aq., VindPr., Aug. om. Aug.

Orientis

<u>FASTI:</u>	Marcell. (om. Aug.) Heracl. Pasch.	Honorius Aug. IV et Eutychianus
<u>LAWS:</u>	C'polis, 16 laws, earliest 28.i (*CTh* 7.1.16); 1 each from Nicomedia, Nicaea, Mnizus	Honorius (Aug.) IV et Eutychianus (v.c.)
<u>PAPYRI:</u>	*P.Lips.* 56.1 (28.i); *P.Flor.* I 66.1 (10.iii); *P.Herm.* 52.1; 53.1 (4.vii)	p.c. Fll. Caesarii et Attici vv.cc.
	BGU III 940.24 (2.xi)	D.N. Honorius perp. Aug. IV et Fl. Eutychianus v.c.
<u>INSCR.:</u>	L. Robert, *La déesse de Hiérapolis Castabala* (Paris 1964) 29-30*	D.N. Honorius Aug. IV et Fl. Eutychianus v.c.
<u>OTHER:</u>	Socrates, *HE* 6.2	Honorius (IV et) Eutychianus
	George of Alexandria, Life of John Chrysostom, in Halkin, *Douze récits*, p.128	(Honorius and Eutychianus)

<u>NOTES:</u>

Eutychianus was PPO Or. 397-399 and 404-405. According to Socrates (whence George of Alexandria), Eutychianus celebrated his consulate in Constantinople, Honorius his in Rome; in fact, Honorius celebrated his in Milan, where Claudian recited his panegyric (Cameron, *Claudian* 95).

OTHER:	[Continued from preceding page] Council at Carthage: *Conc.Africae* p.343 (8.xi; not a genuine council at Carthage, but a Gallic document of *ca* 475 claiming to be such a council)	Augustus Honorius IV et Eutychianus
	Claudian, *Panegyricus de IV consulatu Honorii Augusti*	

Occidentis

FASTI:	Prosp. Cycl. (om. v.c.) Dionys. (1, 755) (om. v.c.) Aug. Aq.	Mallius Theodorus v.c.
	Chr. 354 (pasch.)	Eutropius et Theodorus
	Cass. (om. v.c.) Hyd.	Manlius et Theodorus v.c.
LAWS:	Total of 43 laws, 20 from Milan (earliest 7.i, *CTh* 11.30.58 = *CJ* 7.62.30), 2 from Brescia and Altinum, 1 each from Verona, Padua, Ravenna	Theodorus v.c.
INSCR.:	**ROME:** *ICUR* n.s. IV 12543* = *ILCV* 4539 (18.i?);	p.c. Honori Aug. IV et Eutychiani v.c.
	ICUR I 471 (10.iv); *ICUR* n.s. I 2811B = *ILCV* 4337B (2-5.viii; frag.); *ICUR* n.s. VII 19980a (14.viii-13.ix; dub.); *ICUR* n.s. VII 17513 = *ILCV* 4146F (7.ix); *ICUR* I 475 = *ILCV* 4394 (21.ix; Fl. Mallius Th.); *IGUR* I 65 = *ILS* 1274 (9.xi; Fl. Mallius Th.); *ICUR* I 477 = *ILCV* 120 (27.xi; Fl. Ma. Th.); *ICUR* n.s. I 1453 = *ILCV* 3432 (Fl. Ma. Th.); *ICUR* n.s. III 8166 ([Fl.] Ma. Th.; frag.); *ICUR* n.s. VII 17516a (Fl. Ma. Th.); *ICUR* n.s. I 987 ([Fl.] Ma. Th.; p.c. poss.); *ICUR* n.s. VII 17514 (dub.); *ICUR* n.s. I 524 (frag.)	(Fl.) (Mallius) Theodorus v.c.
	ITALY: *NotScav* 1893, 284 no.22 = *NBC* 1902, 56 (Syracuse; 14.ix; Ma. Th.; Gk.); *IG* XIV 160 = *NotScav* 1895, 521 no.267 (Syracuse; 22.ix; [Fl.] Ma. Th.; Gk.); *CIL* X 4493a = *ILCV* 2958 (Capua?, Reg. I; 7.x; Fl. Ma. Th.); *CIL* XIV 3418 = *ILCV* 2956 (Praeneste, Reg. I; 14.xi; om. v.c.)	
OTHER:	Council at Carthage: *Conc.Africae* pp.193-94 (27.iv) [Continued on the next page]	p.c. glorios. imp. Honorii Aug. IV et Eutychiani v.c.

Orientis

<u>FASTI:</u>	Heracl.	Eutropius et Theodorus
	Marcell.	Theodorus et Eutropius eunuchus
	Pasch.	Theodorus solus
<u>LAWS:</u>	C'polis, 10 laws, earliest *CTh* 11.24.4, 10.iii	Theodorus v.c.
<u>PAPYRI:</u>	*P.Giss.* 104.1 (30.vi); *CPLat.* 199* (om. Fl.; Lat.)	p.c. D.N. Honorii perp. Aug. IV et Fl. Eutychiani v.c.
	CPR X 108.1* (16.viii)	[Fll. Eutropius et] Theodorus vv.cc.
<u>OTHER:</u>	Socrates, *HE* 6.5	(Theodorus)

<u>NOTES:</u>

Theodorus was PPO It. 397-399 and author of many works (*PLRE* I 900-02; Cameron, *Claudian* 323-26). Eutropius was Arcadius' praepositus sacri cubiculi (*PLRE* I 440-44); after his fall from power in August he suffered *damnatio memoriae* and his name was ordered stricken from the fasti--as Prosper says, "ablato honore" (cf. Socrates, *HE* 6.5; *CTh* 9.40.17 of ?17.viii; 17.i, MSS). Stilicho had already refused to recognize Eutropius' consulate at all in the West (Claudian, *In Eutr.* 1.319, "eunuchumque vetat fastis accedere Ianus;" cf. ib. 436, 488f.; 2.127).

Dissemination at the start of the year was slow, as the p.c. inscription from Rome shows, along with the council at Carthage and the papyrus of 30.vi. The papyrus of 16.viii shows, however, that Eutropius was proclaimed in Egypt. The compilers of the fasti had a glorious time. Chr. 354 (pasch.) and Heracl. have the original Eutropius et Theodorus; the rest have just Theodorus (botched in some cases, where Mallius was not recognized as part of his name), but Marcellinus, who started out with just Theodorus, added Eutropius' name out of sequence, evidently from Claudian (whom he actually quotes).

[Continued from preceding page]
Claudian, *Panegyricus dictus Mallio Theodoro consuli* (delivered at Milan)

Occidentis

FASTI: Hyd. (v.c.) Aq. (Q) (v.c.)   (Fl.) Stilicho (v.c.)
              Cycl. (Fl.) Hist. Britt. (3, 207, 5)

              Chr. 354 (pasch.) VindPr. (Fl. St.)   (Fl.) Stilicho et Aurelianus
              Prosp. Aq. (GLS) Aug. Cass.

LAWS: Total about 26 laws, earliest *CTh*   Stilicho et Aurelianus
              7.8.6 (Milan, 17.i); Milan, 19 laws;   (vv.cc.)
              Brescia and Aquileia, 1 law each

              CTh 2.14.1 (Milan, 27.xi)   Stilicho v.c.

INSCR.:   **ROME:** *ILCV* 3347 (8.i; om. v.c.);   Fl. Stilicho v.c.
              ICUR n.s. III 8730 = *ILCV* 2281
              adn. (12.i); *ICUR* n.s. VII 17520
              = *ILCV* 159 adn. (1.iii); *ICUR* n.s.
              VII 17519 (21.iv; om. Fl.); *ICUR*
              n.s. I 528 = *ILCV* 4146F adn.
              (26.iv); *ICUR* n.s. V 13946 (24.v);
              ICUR n.s. VIII 21612 = *ILCV* 2606
              adn. (7.vi); *ICUR* n.s. II 6059 (15.vii);
              ICUR n.s. VII 17517 = *ILCV* 4219C (16.viii);
              ICUR n.s. V 13376 (17.viii); *ICUR* n.s. VII
              17521 = *ILCV* 3754D (23.viii); *ICUR* n.s.
              VIII 22970 (14.ix); *ILCV* 4394A* (13.xi;
              om. Fl., v.c.); *RAC* 61 (1985) 16 (16.xi);
              CIL VI 1706 (19.xi); *ICUR* n.s. VI 15780 =
              ILCV 4942 (om. Fl., v.c.); *ICUR* I 490 = *ILCV* 317

              ITALY: *CIL* X 7115* (Catania; 29.xi); *CIL* XI
              3238 = *ILCV* 3294 (Nepi, Reg. VII; om. Fl.);
              I.Ital. IV.1 543 = *ILCV* 4181 (om. Fl., v.c)

              DALMATIA: *CIL* III 13123 = *SEG* XXXIII
              491 (16.ii; om. Fl.; Gk.)

              For documents dating to 400 or 405, see next page.

OTHER: Sulpicius Severus completed his chronicle
              in 400: he remarks that from the crucifixion
              "in Stiliconem consulem sunt anni CCCLXXII."

Orientis

FASTI:	Marcell. Heracl. Pasch.	Stilicho et Aurelianus
LAWS:	C'polis, 2 laws (*CTh* 1.10.5 and 1.34.1, 26.viii and 8.xii)	Stilicho et Aurelianus vv.cc.
PAPYRI:	*P.Oxy.* XLIV 3203.1 (vi-vii); *MPER* n.s. XV 95.3 (om. v.c.; school exercise)	p.c. Fl. Theodori v.c.
	SB VI 9359.1*	Fll. Stilicho et Aurelianus vv.cc.
OTHER:	Socrates, *HE* 6.6; Zos. 5.18.8	Stilicho et Aurelianus

NOTES: Aurelian was PVC 393-394, PPO Or. 399-400 and 414-416 (*PLRE* I 128-29). Stilicho was MVM 392-408, and father-in-law of Honorius (*PLRE* I 853-58). Stilicho did not accept the eastern consul of the year, and contemporary inscriptions in the West do not include Aurelian's name. Apparently the western laws were revised on the basis of an eastern list, and only *CTh* 2.14.1 escaped revision, presenting the original form with only Stilicho's name. It seems very unlikely either that Aurelian was "designated for the consulship of the year 400, but had been unable to enter upon it in January" (Bury, *LRE* I^2 [1923] 134) or that in the course of the year he "lost and later regained his consulate" (Barnes, *Phoenix* 37 [1983] 255). For such hypotheses, see the forthcoming *Barbarians and Politics at the Court of Arcadius* by Alan Cameron, Jacqueline F. Long, and Lee Sherry. In the East, both consuls were accepted, though dissemination was apparently not very early. Stilicho's name presumably stands first (in East as well as West) because of his kinship (son-in-law) with Theodosius.

[Continued from preceding page]
400 or 405 (uncert. if numeral lost) (all Rome)
ICUR n.s. VIII 23437 = *ILCV* 2609A adn.
(31.vii; om. Fl.); *ICUR* n.s. II 6060
(16.x-1.xi); *ICUR* n.s. II 4844 = *ILCV*
1299 (om. Fl.); *ICUR* n.s. V 13377
(om. Fl., v.c.); *ICUR* n.s. V 13351;
ICUR n.s. VII 17522 = *ILCV* 4146F adn.;
ICUR n.s. IV 11131 (om. Fl.); *ICUR* n.s.
VII 17518 = *ILCV* 4033 adn.; *ICUR* n.s.
VIII 23438 (like prec.); *ICUR* n.s. II
4853; *ICUR* n.s. IV 11132; *ICUR* n.s.
VI 15779; *ICUR* n.s. VII 19980b (om. Fl.);
ICUR n.s. VII 17527b (frag.); *ICUR* n.s.
VIII 20812, 23436a, 23436b (all frags.);
ICUR n.s. III 8168a = *ILCV* 2350a
adn. + add.

Occidentis

<u>FASTI</u>:	Chr. 354 (pasch.) Hyd. VindPr. Prosp. Cycl. Aug. Aq. Cass.	Vincentius et Fravitus
<u>LAWS</u>:	*CTh* 12.6.28 (Milan, 26.ii), 16.2.36 (Milan, 14.vii)	p.c. Stilichonis et Aureliani
	About 16 laws total, 11 from Milan, earliest *CTh* 11.17.2, 13.ii	Vincentius et Fravitus (vv.cc.)
<u>INSCR.</u>:	**ROME:** *ICUR* n.s. VII 17523 = *ILCV* 3003B (11.i; om. v.c.); *ICUR* n.s. II 4835 = *ILCV* 2115 (11.ii); *ICUR* n.s. IV 11134 (6.viii; om. Fl., v.c.); *ICUR* n.s. II 6061 (20.viii)	Fl. Vincentius v.c.
	ICUR n.s. IV 11133 = *ILCV* 1468 (31.v, 4.vi or 12.vi); *ICUR* n.s. III 9365 (4.vi); *ICUR* n.s. V 13381 (14.vi-1.vii; om. Fll.); *ICUR* n.s. I 1942 (18.viii; Gk.); *ICUR* n.s. II II 4506 = *ILCV* 2974 (9.ix; om. Fll., vv.cc.); *ICUR* n.s. I 3174 (14.viii-13.ix); *ICUR* n.s. II 6062 = *ILCV* 3503 (p.c. poss.); *ICUR* n.s. I 349 (p.c. poss.); *ICUR* n.s. V 13121; *ICUR* n.s. V 13380 (frag.); *ICUR* n.s. V 13382; *ICUR* n.s. V 13947; *NotScav* 1888, 450, no. 47 (om. vv.cc.); *ICUR* n.s. V 13379 (p.c. poss.)	Fll. Vincentius et Fravitus vv.cc.
	ITALY: *CIL* XI 6160 = *ILCV* 3055 adn. (Fossombrone, Reg. VI; 27.iv; om. Fll., vv.cc.); *CIL* V p.1060 = *IG* XIV 2300 (Como, Reg. XI; 27.xi; om. Fll.; Gk.); *CIL* X 8139 = *ILCV* 3029 (Castellamare di Stabia, Reg. I)	
	DALMATIA: *CIL* III 9510 = *Forsch. Salona* II 160 (Salona; frag.; or p.c.?)	

[Continued on next page]

Orientis

<u>FASTI:</u>	Marcell. Heracl. Pasch.	Vincentius et Fravitus
<u>LAWS:</u>	C'polis, 3 laws (earliest, 19.i (*CTh* 9.42.17)	Vincentius et Fravitus (vv.cc.)
<u>PAPYRI:</u>	*SB* VIII 9774.1	p.c. Fll. Stilichonis et Aureliani vv.cc.
	SPP XX 113.11 (26.ix); *P.Rain. Cent.* 165 ii.6* (Lat.)	Fll. Vincentius et Fravitta vv.cc.
<u>OTHER:</u>	Socrates, *HE* 6.6; Soz. 7.4; Eun. fr. 82; Zos. 5.21.6	

<u>NOTES:</u>

Vincentius was PPO Gall. 397-400 (*PLRE* II 1169); Fravitta (the eastern consul) the Gothic magister militum who suppressed the rebellion of Gainas (*PLRE* I 372-73). For the numerous different spellings of the name (? best Fravitta), see *PLRE*. The earliest two Roman inscriptions suggest that Fravitta's name was late arriving or perhaps not recognized at first; the former seems more likely. But why two Roman inscriptions from August omit Fravitta, is not clear. The two western laws were addressed to a proconsul of Africa, and the p.c. is presumably the *accepta* date at Carthage (cf. p.81); the p.c. date in the council at Carthage confirms that dissemination there was late.

[Continued from preceding page]

<u>OTHER:</u>	Council at Carthage: *Conc.Africae* p.194, cf. 355 (16.vi)	p.c. Fl. Stiliconis v.c.
	Council at Carthage: *Conc.Africae* p.199 (13.ix)	Vincentius et Fravitus vv.cc.
	Subscription in Martial MSS: Zetzel, *Latin Textual Criticism* 212 bottom (Rome)	Vincentius et Fraguitius vv.cc.

Occidentis

<u>FASTI</u>:	Chr. 354 (pasch.) Hyd. VindPr. Prosp. Cycl. Aug. Aq. Cass.	Arcadius Aug. V et Honorius Aug. V[62]
<u>LAWS</u>:	*CTh* 7.13.15 (Ravenna, 6.xii)	Arcadius Aug. V et Honorius Aug. V
<u>INSCR.</u>:	**ROME:** *ICUR* n.s. V 13950 (13.iii; om. DD.NN.); *ICUR* n.s. V 13949 (12.iv; om. Augg.); *ICUR* n.s. I 718 = *ILCV* 3142A (1.vi); *ICUR* n.s. VII 17525 = *ILCV* 451a (21.vi; om. DD.NN.); *ICUR* n.s. III 8433 (9.vii); *ICUR* I 506 = *ILCV* 3142 (27.vii); *ICUR* n.s. VII 17485 = *ILCV* 4343B (16.vii- 13.viii); *ILCV* 2880a (31.viii); *ICUR* I 507 = *ILCV* 1274A (10.ix; om. DD.NN.?); *ICUR* n.s. I 1943 = *ILCV* 2576 = 2946 adn. (19.ix; om. DD.NN.); *ICUR* n.s. V 15356 = *ILCV* 2974 adn. (9.xi); *ICUR* n.s. V 13383 (21.xi); *ICUR* I 336 = *ILCV* 4343B; *ICUR* n.s. VIII 22971 (om. Augg.); *ICUR* n.s. I 3219 = *ILCV* 3239 adn. (om. Augg.; frag.); *ICUR* n.s. I 4054 (much rest.; om. DD.NN.); *ICUR* n.s. IV 12253* (frag.); *ICUR* n.s. VIII 23432; *ICUR* n.s. VII 19979b; *ICUR* n.s. IX 23763 = *ILCV* 2773 adn. (Fl. Arc. et Hon.; frag.)	DD.NN. (Fl.) Arcadius V et Honorius V Augg.
	ITALY: *AE* 1933, 26 = Ferrua, *RendPontAccad* 22 (1946-47) 230 (Catania; 25.i; Gk.)	p.c. Vincentii
	Atti III Congr.int.arch.crist. 151, fig. 21 (Modica, Sicily; 24.vi; om. DD.NN., Augg.; Gk.); *CIL* V 6224 = *ILCV* 1501 (Milan, Reg. X, 22.viii) [Continued on the next page]	DD.NN. Arcadius et Honorius Augg. V

---

[62]Cycl. omits V; others except Chr. 354 om. Aug.

Orientis

<u>FASTI:</u>	Marcell. Heracl. Pasch. (Augg.)	Arcadius (Aug.) V et Honorius (Aug.) V
<u>LAWS:</u>	*CTh* 14.17.14 (C'polis, 22.iii)	Arcadius Aug. V et Honorius Aug. V
<u>PAPYRI:</u>	*P.Grenf.* II 80.1 (4.viii)	p.c. Fll. Vincentii et Fravitta vv.cc.

<u>NOTES:</u>

It is remarkable that we find Fravitta omitted from the p.c. date from Catania, for he was known in Italy in 401.

[Continued from preceding page]

<u>OTHER:</u>	Council at Milevis: *Conc.Africae* p.205, cf. p.361 (27.viii)	glor. impp. Arcadius et Honorius Augg. V
	Subscription in Persius MSS: Zetzel, *Latin Textual Criticism* 214 (4) (Barcelona)	DD.NN. Arcadius et Honorius V

Occidentis

FASTI: Chr. 354 (pasch.) Hyd. VindPr.   Theodosius Aug. (I)
                Prosp. Cycl. Aug. Aq. Cass.   et Rumoridus[63]

LAWS: 8 laws, all from Ravenna   (D.N.) Theodosius Aug. I
                (earliest *CTh* 12.6.29, 20.ii)   et Rumoridus (v.c.)

INSCR.:   **ROME:** *ICUR* n.s. VIII 23434 = *ILCV*   (D.N.) (Fl.) Theodosius
                732 (29.i; om. Aug., Fl., v.c.);   Aug. (I) et Fl.
                ICUR n.s. IV 12425 = *ILCV* 3811A   Rumoridus v.c.
                (14.iv; only Rumor.; om. Fl.,
                v.c.); *ICUR* n.s. V 13951 (19.v;
                Theod. nob.puer); *ICUR* n.s. II 4507
                (20.vi; frag.); *ICUR* n.s. I 713
                = *ILCV* 4744 (1.vii; D.N.); *ICUR*
                n.s. II 4272 = *ILCV* 2398 (16.x-
                1.xi; om. Aug., Fl.); *ICUR* n.s.
                V 13952 = *ILCV* 2757 (11.xi; om.
                Fl.; Aug. I); *ICUR* n.s. VII 17526
                = *ILCV* 3771 (D.N., om. Fl.); *ICUR*
                n.s. II 4242 = *ILCV* 1605 (om.
                Fl.); *ICUR* n.s. I 1462 = *ILCV*
                3503A (frag.); *ICUR* n.s. I 1460
                = *ILCV* 4703; *ICUR* n.s. I 3220;
                ICUR n.s. I 1459 (frag.); *ICUR* n.s.
                IV 11136 (frag.); *ICUR* n.s. VI
                15996 (frag.); *ICUR* n.s. VI
                16007C (frag.); *ICUR* n.s. VII
                17527a* (Fl. Theod.; frag.)

                ITALY: *NotScav* 1893, 284 #22* =   p.c. Arcadii et
                NBC 1902, 56 (Syracuse, 24.i; Gk.)   Honori Augg. V

                CIL XI 4044 = *ILCV* 3036B (Capena,   Theodosius Aug.
                Reg. VII; 25.vii?); *CIL* XI 4045   et Rumoridus
                = *ILCV* 3036B adn. (Capena, 28.ix;
                om. Aug.);

                CIL V 6196 = *ILCV* 2852   Rumoridus
                (Milan, Reg. XI)
                [Continued on next page]

---

[63]I only in Cass.; Aug. om. by Hyd., VindPr.

Orientis

FASTI: Marcell. (om. Aug. et Rum.)   Theodosius iun. Aug. I
    Heracl. (om. iun. Aug.) Pasch.   et Rumoridus

LAWS: none

PAPYRI: *P.Grenf.* II 81.1 (26.v)   p.c. DD.NN. Arcadi et
                 Honori perpp. Augg.

    P.Oxy. X 1319.1 (7.ix);   D.N. Theodosius perp. Aug.
    P.Grenf. II 81a.13* (27.x)   et Fl. Rumoridus v.c.

NOTES:

  The young Theodosius was born on 10.iv.401 and proclaimed Augustus on 10.i.402 (*PLRE* II 1100); Rumoridus was MVM of Valentinian I in 384 (*PLRE* I 786). The earliest Roman inscription perhaps lacks the 'Aug.' because the news of Theodosius' elevation had not yet arrived; similarly the nob.puer on 19.v was by then long anachronistic. It is odd to find one Roman and one Milanese inscription without Theodosius at all. There is no evidence of a p.c. in use at Rome, but both Syracuse and Egypt attest one.

[Continued from preceding page]

    DALMATIA: *CIL* III 2655   [Theodosius Aug.] et
    (cf. p.1510; frag.)   Rumoridus v.c.

OTHER: Council of Carthage: *Conc.Africae* glor. imp. Theodosius
    p.208 (25.viii)   Aug. et Rumoridus v.c.

    Gesta procons. in *Gesta Conlat.* D.N. Theodosius perp.
    Carth. 3.174, cf. 173 (13.ix;   Aug. et Rumoridus v.c.
    'p.c.' D.N. Theod. perp. Aug.,
    p.169, refers to same date)

Occidentis

FASTI: Aq. Prosp. Cycl. Aug.   Honorius VI

          Chr. 354 (pasch.) Hyd. Haun.   Honorius VI
          Cass. Prosp. (suppl.; 1, 488,491)   et Aristaenetus
          Aug. Aq.

LAWS: Total of about 15 laws; 5 from   Honorius Aug. VI et
          Rome (earliest *CTh* 8.5.65, 27.ii)   Aristaenetus (v.c.)

INSCR.:   **ROME:** *ICUR* n.s. II 4840 = *ILCV*   D.N. Honorius Aug. VI
          3115 (7.vi); *ICUR* n.s. V 15323
          (16.v-13.vi); *ICUR* n.s. V 13384
          = *ILCV* 659 adn. (26.vi; om. D.N.);
          ICUR n.s. VI 15506 (14.vii; om.
          Aug.); *ICUR* n.s. V 17252 = *ILCV*
          2792 (26.vii; om. D.N.); *ICUR*
          n.s. VI 15997 (8.viii; om. D.N.);
          AE 1888, 153 = *ILCV* 755 (12.viii;
          om. D.N.); *ICUR* n.s. II 4841 =
          ILCV 354 (24.viii); *ICUR* n.s. I
          3222 = *ILCV* 3807 (14.ix); *ICUR*
          n.s. V 15357 = *ILCV* 1351 (7.x;
          om. Aug.); *ICUR* n.s. II 4499 =
          ILCV 2144 (22.x); *ICUR* n.s. II
          4843 = *ILCV* 4177 (om. D.N.);
          ICUR n.s. II 4842 (om. D.N.,
          Aug.; Gk.); *ICUR* n.s. I 1402 =
          ILCV 3754E; *AE* 1975, 36 (p.c. poss.)

          ITALY: *AE* 1968, 194 (Aquileia,
          Reg. X; 2-5.xii); *CIL* V 6217 =
          ILCV 4280 (Milan, Reg. XI;
          13.xii; om. D.N., Aug.)

OTHER: Pope Innocent, *Epp.* 2 (*PL* 20.   Honorius Aug. VI et
          469) (15.ii)   Aristaenetus v.c.

          Council at Carthage: *Conc.Africae*   glorios. imp. Honorius
          p.211 (16.vi)   Aug. VI

Orientis

FASTI:	Marcell. Heracl. (both om. Aug.)	Honorius Aug. VI
	Pasch.	et Aristaenetus
LAWS:	C'polis, 7 laws, earliest	Honorius Aug. VI et
	CTh 16.4.4 (29.i)	Aristaenetus (v.c.)
PAPYRI:	none	
OTHER:	Jerome, *Epp.* 108.35: dates	Honorius Aug. VI et
	the burial of Paula to 28.i	Aristaenetus
	Socrates, *HE* 6.18	Honorius VI (et)
		Aristaenetus
	Synesius, *Epp.* 133*;	
	Halkin, *Douze récits* 236 (20.vi)	

NOTES:

Once again, as in 400, the inscriptions make it clear that the eastern consul was not recognized in the West. The letter of Pope Innocent has surely been retroactively corrected from one of the western fasti which entered Aristaenetus. That all of the laws for this year use the formula including Aristaenetus is probably also the result of revision.

Synesius *Epp.* 133 has been held to imply that Honorius' consulate was not recognized in the East at the beginning of the year (Seeck, *Reg.* 307: for detailed refutation, see the Critical Appendix). But unless we postulate retroactive interpolation (improbable in an informal document), Jerome knew the names of both consuls by soon after 28.i in Bethlehem. This long letter was not written on that day, but hardly more than a month or two later (cf. J.N.D. Kelly, *Jerome: His Life, Writings and Controversies* [1975] 278). And while Socrates did not write his date in that year, his source was either contemporary ecclesiastical documents or (at least) a consular list maintained till the year in which he wrote, 439. Honorius' VI consulate appears in all the eastern fasti, and there seems no reason to doubt that it was recognized as soon as known in the East.

Occidentis

FASTI: Geneal. 1,196 (II) Cycl. (Fl.)   (Fl.) Stilicho (II)

Chr. 354 (pasch.) Hyd. Haun.   Stilicho II et Anthemius
Prosp. Aug. (V) Aq. Cass.

LAWS: *CTh* 16.2.35 = *ConstSirm* 2   Stilicho II
(Ravenna, 4.ii)

About 19 laws total, 7 from   Stilicho II et Anthemius
Ravenna (earliest, *CTh* 16.6.4,5,
12.ii)

INSCR.: **ROME:** *ICUR* n.s. VII 17535 = *ILCV*   Fl. Stilicho v.c. II
2128 (29.iv; om. v.c.); *ICUR* n.s.
I 2813 = *ILCV* 2607 (25.v; om. v.c.);
Epigraphica 21 (1959) 110 (9.vii;
om. Fl., v.c.); *ICUR* n.s. V 13954
(28.vii; om. Fl.); *ICUR* n.s. VII
17533 = *ILCV* 2974 adn. (29.iii/
29.vii; om. v.c.); *ICUR* n.s. VII
17534 = *ILCV* 4146F adn. (14.viii-
13.ix); *AE* 1948, 99 (14.ix); *ICUR*
n.s. VII 19981 (26.ix); *ICUR* n.s.
I 1457 = *ILCV* 3502 adn. (14.ix-
15.x); *ICUR* n.s. I 1463* = *ILCV*
693 (26.x; om. v.c.); *ICUR* n.s.
I 729 = *ILCV* 1131 (2.xii; om. Fl.,
v.c.); *ICUR* n.s. V 13955 (14-31.xii
or 1.i; p.c. poss.); *ICUR* n.s. VIII
23435 (om. v.c.); *ICUR* n.s. I
1259 (om. Fl., v.c.); *ICUR* n.s.
IV 11781 (om. v.c.)

ICUR n.s. II 4170 (23.vii); *ICUR*   Fll. Stilicho II et
n.s. II 6066 (22.x); *ICUR* n.s. I   Anthemius vv.cc.
1464 = *ILCV* 3003B adn. (St. is v.
inlustris; om. Fl. bef. Anthemius)

ITALY: *AE* 1924, 100* (Veroli, Reg.   Fl. Stilicho v.c. II
I; 24.iii or 23.vi?); *SEG* XIX 630
(Florence; 1.vii; om. Fl., v.c.; Gk.)

[Continued on next page]

Orientis

FASTI:	Marcell. Heracl. (Anth. I) Pasch.	Stilicho II et Anthemius (I)
LAWS:	Nicaea, 2 laws (earliest, *CJ* 5.4.19; 11.vi); C'polis, 3 laws; Ancyra, 3 laws	Stilicho II et Anthemius
PAPYRI:	*SB* VIII 9931.1 (22.ix)	Fll. Stilicho [II] et Anthemius vv.cc.
OTHER:	Socrates, *HE* 6.20; Halkin, *Douze récits* 245 (around 11.xi)	Stelicho II et Anthemius

NOTES:

It appears that Anthemius was not yet announced in the West in the first half of the year; later revision brought all laws but one into conformity with the final formula. Cf. Seeck, *Regesten* 19-20 on the process. Once again, Stilicho refused to recognize the eastern consul, protesting the deposition of John Chrysostom (E. Demougeot, *De l'unité à la division de l'empire romain: 395-410* [1951] 345 f.). But Roman inscriptions of 23.vii and 22.x suggest that Anthemius was recognized later in the year. The Carthaginian date might thus be original; but the two versions of the formula in Innocentius' letter of February point clearly to interpolation, in one case mistakenly adding Theodosius II from 407. Aquitania has (uniquely) a p.c., but it is early in the year.

	[Continued from preceding page]	
	AQUITANIA: *CIL* XIII 1118 = *ILCV* 4387 (nr. Saintes; 22.i; 'Horius'); *CIL* XIII 912 + add. p.7 = *ILCV* 3040 (nr. Bordeaux; D.N.)	p.c. (D.N.) Honori VI
OTHER:	Innocentius, *Epp.* 6 (*PL* 20.495) (20.ii)	Stilico II et Anthemius vv.cc.[64]
	Council at Carthage: *Conc.Africae* p.214 (23.viii)	Stilico II et Anthemius vv.cc.

[64]Some MSS have "Theodosius II et Stilico II".

Occidentis

FASTI:	Chr. 354 (pasch.) Hyd. Haun. (om. VI) Prosp. Cycl. Aug. Aq. Cass.	Arcadius VI et Probus
LAWS:	About 16 laws total, 5 from Ravenna; earliest *CTh* 13.7.2 (11.i)	Arcadius Aug. VI et Probus (v.c.)
INSCR.:	**ROME:** *ICUR* n.s. VIII 23440 (6-13.iv; app. gives Hon. VII, Anic.; frag.); *ICUR* n.s. VII 20604 = *ILCV* 3727B (20.iv; Petr.); *ICUR* n.s. II 4846 = *ILCV* 2006 (2-5.vii; Arc. VII; Diehl prints VI; om. Probus); *ICUR* n.s. V 13956 = *ILCV* 2824A (2.viii; om. Probus); *ICUR* n.s. IV 11782 (11.viii; frag.; om. v.c.); *ILCV* 2977A (2.ix; Anic.); *ILCV* 4459 (13.ix; Anic.); *ICUR* n.s. II 4847 = *ILCV* 4427 (15.x; Petr.); *ICUR* n.s. VII 17536 = *ILCV* 133 (6.xi; om. VI; Anic.); *ICUR* n.s. VII 17537 = *ILCV* 4704 (Anic.); *ICUR* n.s. I 988 = *ILCV* 2927A adn. (Anic.; om. Aug.); *ICUR* n.s. I 1358 (frag.; Anic. Petr.); *ICUR* n.s. VIII 23439b (frag.); *ICUR* n.s. II 4848 (frag.); *ICUR* n.s. IV 11140 (Anic.); *ICUR* n.s. V 13386 (Anic.); *ICUR* n.s. II 6067	D.N. Arcadius Aug. VI et (Anicius) (Petronius) Probus v.c.
	ITALY: *CIL* XI 2872* = *ILCV* 2258 (Bolsena; 27.ix)	Arcadius VI (et) P. Anicius Probus
	AE 1983, 131 (Isola Sacra, Reg. I)	[D.N. Arcadius] VI et Petronius Anicius Probus v.c.
OTHER:	Archival date on document, at Ravenna: *Gesta conlat. Carth.* 3.141, cf. 170, 173 (30.i)	D.N. Arcadius perp. Aug. VI et Probus v.c.
	Consular diptych of Probus (Volbach 1; Delbrueck 1; *ILS* 8991), where he is styled simply "Probus famulus v.c. cons. ord."	

346

Orientis

<u>FASTI:</u>	Marcell. Heracl. Pasch. (Aug.)	Arcadius (Aug.) VI et Probus
<u>LAWS:</u>	C'polis, 11 laws, earliest *CTh* 7.4.27, 1.iv	Arcadius Aug. VI et Probus (v.c.)
<u>PAPYRI:</u>	none	
<u>OTHER:</u>	Socrates, *HE* 6.20; Zos. 6.3.1; Halkin, *Douze récits* 245 (*ca* iii)	Arcadius VI et Probus

<u>NOTES:</u>

Probus was a brother of the consuls of 395 (*PLRE* II 913-14) and western consul.

Occidentis

FASTI: Chr. 354 (pasch.)   Theodosius II et Honorius VII

                Hyd. (Aug.) Prosp. Cass. Aq.   Honorius (Aug.) VII et
                Cycl. Aug.   Theodosius (Aug.) II

LAWS: Total of 11 laws, 4 from Rome (earliest   (DD.NN.) Honorius VII et
                CTh 16.5.4, 22.ii), 1 from Ravenna   Theodosius II Augg.

INSCR.:   **ROME:** *ICUR* n.s. VII 17540 = *ILCV*   DD.NN. Honorius VII et
                1526 (19.i; om. D.N., II, Augg.);   Theodosius II Augg.
                ICUR n.s. I 3224 = *ILCV* 3652
                (5.iii); *ICUR* n.s. VIII 23443
                (2-5.vi); *ICUR* n.s. I 3225 =
                ILCV 3181A (16.v-13.vi; om. D.N.,
                Theod. II); *AE* 1953, 200 (16.vii-
                13.viii); *ICUR* n.s. IV 12545-12546
                = *ILCV* 2607 adn. (16.x-1.xi; om.
                Theod.); *ICUR* n.s. VII 17539 = *ILCV*
                3504 (4.xi; om. DD.NN.); *ICUR* n.s. VII
                17541b (16.x-13.xi); *ICUR* n.s. IX 23764
                (14.xi-13.xii; frag.); *ICUR* n.s. I 178
                = *ILCV* 2928 (19.xii; om. DD.NN., Aug.
                w. Th.); *ICUR* n.s. VIII 23441 (26.xii;
                om. Theod.); *ICUR* n.s. VIII 23442 = *ILCV*
                3154 (31.xii; om. D.N., Theod.); *ICUR* n.s.
                VIII 23439d (Fl. bef. Hon.?); *ICUR*
                n.s. IV 11141 (om. Theod.?; frag.);
                ICUR I 581 (om. Theod.); *ICUR*
                n.s. III 8169 (frag.; om. Theod.?);
                ICUR n.s. IV 10855 (frag.; om.
                Theod.?); *ICUR* n.s. I 2773* =
                ILCV 4444A (frag.; p.c. poss.)

                ITALY: *AE* 1979, 235 (Arezzo, Reg.
                VII; 6.ii); *CIL* XI 2994 = *ILCV*
                4724 (Toscanella, Reg. VII;
                19.ix); *CIL* XI 4046 (Capena,
                Reg. VII; i or xii; om. Theod.)

                DALMATIA: *CIL* III 14306 (Salona; 9.ix);
                CIL III 9511 = *Forsch.Salona* II 162
                (Salona; 11.x)
                [Continued on the next page]

Orientis

FASTI: Marcell. (om. Aug.) Heracl. (om.   Honorius Aug. VII et
                iun., Aug.) Pasch.   Theodosius iun. Aug. II

LAWS: C'polis, 6 laws, earliest   (DD.NN.) Honorius VII
                CTh 6.26.13 (25.i)   et Theodosius II Augg.

PAPYRI: *P.Oxy.* VIII 1122.1 (9.vi)   p.c. D.N. Arcadii perp.
                                                             Aug. VI et Fl. Probi v.c.

                ZPE 62 (1986) 140.14 (14.ix);   DD.NN. Honorius VII et
                CPR X 110.1 (2.xii);   Theodosius II perpp. Augg.
                P.Rainer Cent. 89.1 (p.c. poss.)

OTHER: Socrates, *HE* 6.21; 7.6;   Honorius (Aug.) VII et
                Halkin, *Douze récits* 262;   Theodosius (Aug.) II
                Zos. 6.2

NOTES:

A substantial minority of the Italian inscriptions omit Theodosius entirely (five Roman and one from Capena); another three Roman inscriptions may omit him but are too fragmentary for us to be certain. See above, p.64, for this phenomenon.

[Continued from previous page]

OTHER: Council at Carthage: *Conc.Africae*   glor. Impp. Honorius VII
                p.214 (13.vi)   et Theodosius II Augg.

Occidentis

<u>FASTI</u>:	Chr. 354 (pasch.) Hyd. Haun. Prosp. Cycl. Aug. Aq. Cass.	Bassus et Philippus
	Aq. (Q)	Bassus v.c. et Philippus
<u>LAWS</u>:	About 26 laws total, 2 each from Rome (earliest *CTh* 14.4.8, 15.i) and Milan; 11 from Ravenna	Bassus et Philippus (vv.cc.)
<u>INSCR.</u>:	**ROME:** *ICUR* n.s. II 5718 = *ILCV* 572 (2-5.i; frag.)	p.c. [DD.NN. Honori VII et The]odosi II Augg.
	ICUR n.s. II 4849 (23.i; Anic.; Gk.); *ICUR* n.s. II 4854 = *ILCV* 411 (17.ii, 19.iv, 19.x); *ICUR* n.s. VII 17542 (16.iii-13.iv; Anic.); *ICUR* n.s. V 13388 = *ILCV* 1352 (27.iv); *ICUR* I 586 = *ILCV* 2631C (9.viii; Anic.; Fl.); *ICUR* n.s. II 6070 (11.ix); *ICUR* n.s. VIII 20815 = *ILCV* 808B (15.x; Anic.; Fl.); *ICUR* I 588 = *ILCV* 411 (20.x); *ICUR* n.s. IV 12254 (Fl.; om. vv.cc.; frag.; p.c. poss.); *ICUR* n.s. VI 15998	(Anicius) Bassus et (Fl.) Philippus vv.cc.
	ITALY: *CIL* IX 1364 (nr. Aeclanum, Reg. II; 16.iii-5.iv; Auch.; frag.; p.c. poss.); *CIL* X 5349 (nr. S. Giorgio, Reg. I; 6.vii); *AE* 1979, 242 (Arezzo, Reg. VII; 16.vii; Anic., Fl., vv.cc.); Agnello, *Silloge* 94 = *I.Gr.Palermo* 9 (Catania; 24.vii; Anic. Auchen., Fl.; Gk.); *CIL* V 6282 = *ILCV* 2735 adn. (Milan, Reg. XI; 7.xi); *ICUR* I 589 = *ILCV* 2801 (Ostia; 6-13.xii)	(Anicius) (Auchenius) Bassus et (Fl.) Philippus (vv.cc.)
<u>OTHER</u>:	Council at Carthage: *Conc.Africae* p.219 (16.vi and 13.x)	Bassus et Philippus vv.cc.

350

Orientis

FASTI:	Marcell. Heracl.	Bassus et Philippus
LAWS:	C'polis, 5 laws, earliest *CTh* 6.30.19, 17.i	Bassus et Philippus
PAPYRI:	none	
OTHER:	Socrates, *HE* 6.23, 7.1; Soz. 9.1.1; Zos. 5.28.1, 5.34.7	Bassus et Philippus

NOTES:

For Bassus, see *PLRE* II 219-20; for Philippus, *PLRE* II 876-77. (The remark there that Philippus was a westerner because *SB* I 1540 [A.D. 409: *PLRE* erroneously describes it as a papyrus] has Bassus first--i.e. an easterner would presumably come first--is erroneous. Cf. 400, where Stilicho is given first in the papyri. We presume that Philippus was an easterner.)

Distinguishing between the homonymous consuls of 408 and 431, presumably father and son, is not easily possible where the other consul is not mentioned. See 431 for the reasons why all inscriptions mentioning only Bassus are listed under that year.

(a) Honorius Aug. VIII et Theodosius Aug. III
(b) Honorius Aug. VIII et Constantinus I (in Gaul)

Occidentis

<u>FASTI</u>:	Chr. 354 (pasch.) (rev. order) Hyd. Prosp. Cycl. Hydatius (2, 17 c.42) Aug. Cass. Aq.	Honorius VIII et Theodosius III
<u>LAWS</u>:	Total about 26 laws, earliest *CTh* 16.2.31 = *ConstSirm* 14 (Ravenna, 15.i); 9 other laws from Ravenna	(DD.NN.) Honorius VIII et Theodosius III (Augg.)
<u>INSCR.</u>:	**ROME:** *ICUR* n.s. VII 17545 = *ILCV* 1722 (3.iv); *ICUR* n.s. IV 9378 = *ILCV* 2974A (6.iv); *ICUR* n.s. II 4851 (14.vi-15.vii; frag.); *ICUR* n.s. VII 20605 = *ILCV* 2634 adn. (3.viii); *ICUR* n.s. VI 15999 (19.viii); *ICUR* n.s. I 86 = *ILCV* 2971A adn. (29.xii); *ICUR* n.s. VII 17544 = *ILCV* 2817 adn.; *ICUR* n.s. III 6512 (frag.; om. Augg.?); *ICUR* n.s. VII 19982 = *ILCV* 3789B (frag.; om. Augg.); *ICUR* n.s. III 6513 (frag.; p.c. poss.); *ICUR* n.s. V 13389 (frag.; p.c. poss.); *ICUR* n.s. IV 11143 (frag.; p.c. poss.)	DD.NN. Honorius VIII et Theodosius III Augg.
	BullCommArch 53 (1926) 220 no.48 (30.xi?)	VIII et III
	ITALY: *CIL* V 6257 = *ILCV* 1500 (Milan, Reg. XI, 13.x)	p.c. Bassi
	RAC 36 (1960) 21 no.2 (Syracuse; 30.vii; Gk.)	p.c. Bassi et Philippi
	NotScav 1929, 84 = *AE* 1951, 89* (Lipari; vi; Gk.; frag.); *IG* XIV 444 (Taormina; 13.x; om. DD.NN.; Gk.); *AE* 1907, 211 (Naples, Reg. I; 16.x-1.xi)	DD.NN. Honorius VIII et Theodosius III Augg.
	AFRICA: *AE* 1953, 39 (Perigotville, Algeria; 18.i)	p.c. Bassi et Philippi vv.cc.

[Continued on next page]

Orientis

FASTI: Marcell. (om. Aug.) Heracl.   Honorius Aug. VIII et
           (om. iun., Aug.) Pasch.   Theodosius iun. Aug. III

LAWS: C'polis, 14 laws (earliest, *CTh*   (DD.NN.) Honorius VIII
           13.11.12, 23.i; prob. *CTh* 13.5.32   et Theodosius III (Augg.)
           [19.i] is from C'polis)

PAPYRI: *SPP* XX 115.1 (very frag.;   DD.NN. Honorius VIII
           uncert. form.; p.c. poss.)   et Theodosius III perpp.
                                           Augg.

INSCR: *SB* I 1540.8 (Alexandria; 19.iii)   p.c. Bassi et Philippi

NOTES:

     For Fl. Claudius Constantinus, Augustus in Gaul 407-411, see *PLRE* II 316. Apart from the remarkable Milanese inscription (a date to 432 for this seems far less likely), the p.c. in Syracuse on 30.vii is striking.

             [Continued from preceding page]

             GAUL: *IG* XIV 2559 = *Rec.*   Honorius VIII et
             Inscr.Chrét.Gaule I 93 (Trier,   Constantinus I
             12.vii; Gk.)

OTHER: Council at Carthage: *Conc.Africae*,   glor. Impp. Honorius
           p.220 (15.vi)   VIII et Theodosius
                                           III Augg.

(1) **p.c. Honorii VIII et Theodosii III Augg.**
(2) **Tertullus**
(3) **Varanes**

Occidentis

FASTI:	Chr. 354 (pasch.) Prosp. Aq. (Q) Prosp. Cycl. Aug.	Varanes (v.c.)[65]
	Hyd.	Honorius VIIII et Varan quod fuit Tertullus
	Aq (GLS)	Varanes v.c. et Tertullus
	Cass.	Varan et Tertullus
	ExcSang.	Varanes et Philippus II
LAWS:	*CTh* 11.28.5 (25.xi [Seeck, 25.vi], to Africa; p.c. presum. *acc.* year, cf. p.81)	p.c. Honori VIII et Theodosi III Augg.
	Ravenna, 11 laws, earliest *CTh* 11.28.6, 25.vi	Varanes (v.c.)
INSCR.:	**ROME:** *ICUR* n.s. VII 19983 (2.vii); *ILCV* 3084 (19.viii; DD.NN. and Augg. rest.)	p.c. (DD.NN.) Honorii VIII et Theodosi III (Augg.)
	NotScav 1888, 450 no.50* = *BullCommArch* 16 (1888) 250 no. 11 (14.iv-1.v); *NotScav* 1893, 118	Tertullus
	ICUR n.s. II 4855 = *CIL* VI 31962 (23.xi; date uncert.; Seeck, *Reg.* 318, rest. p.c., 411)	Barne [v.c.]
	ITALY: *IG* XIV 63 = Agnello, *Silloge* 100 = Manganaro, *Archivio storico siracusano* 5-6 (1959-60) 21 ff. (Syracuse, 4.ii; Gk.)	p.c. Honori VIII et Theodosi III Augg.
OTHER:	Council at Carthage: *Conc.Africae* p.220 (14.vi) [Continued on next page]	p.c. glorios. impp. Honorii VIII et Theodosii III Augg.

[65]Prosp., Aug., and Aq. add v.c.; Chr. 354 gives 'Varana et' [sic].

Orientis

FASTI:	Heracl.	Varanes v.c.
	Marcell. Pasch.	Varanes solus
LAWS:	C'polis, 6 laws, earliest 21.ii (*CTh* 16.5.48)	Varanes (v.c.)
PAPYRI:	*P.Herm.* 69.1 (5.v)	p.c. DD.NN. Honori VIII et Theodosi III perpp. Augg.

NOTES:

Tertullus was sole consul at Rome under Alaric's puppet emperor Attalus (*PLRE* II 1059); described as "umbratilis consul" by Orosius (7.42.8) and popular by Zosimus (6.7.4). The only 'secure' attestation of the eastern consul Varanes during the year is (as sole consul) in Honorius' letter of 14.x (and that depends on accepting the restoration of the name from the extract in *CTh*). In all likelihood Varanes was recognized at the western court in Ravenna, but alone, not with Tertullus. This and *NotScav* 1893, 118 suggest that Aq. (GLS) were wrong to combine "Varanes et Tertullus;" and G has added v.c. after Varanes, suggesting that it reflects an original version like that of Q, with just *Varanes v.c.* Varanes is thus not to be restored in *NotScav* 1888, 450 no.50. Cf. Prosper Tiro s.a. 410 (*Chron.Min.* I 466): "solus fuit Orientalium partium consul, quod et sequenti anno observatum est." The entry in Hyd. seems a despairing attempt to combine a ninth consulate (fictive in this year) based upon a p.c. of Honorius VIII (409) with both Varanes and Tertullus. (ExcSang. has turned Tertullus into Philippus II.) Many contemporaries preferred amidst the confusion simply to use a p.c.

The source of the confusion was Alaric's siege of and eventual capture (24.viii) of Rome (so Prosper, loc.cit.).

Varanes was magister peditum in the West, but after Stilicho's death he returned to the East, where he presumably became MVM (*PLRE* II 1149-50).

[Continued from preceding page]

| Letter of Honorius (in Ravenna) to Carthage: *Gesta conl.Carth.* 1.4, 3.29 (14.x; rest. from *CTh* 16.11.3) | Varanes v.c. |

411

(1) **p.c. Varanae**
(2) **Theodosius Aug. IV**

Occidentis

FASTI:	Hyd. Prosp. Cycl. Aug. (om. Aug.) Aq. Cass. Rav. Haun.	Theodosius Aug. IV
LAWS:	*CTh* 7.13.20 (corr. Seeck, *Reg.* 73) and 15.1.48 (Ravenna, 8.ii and 28.xi)	p.c. Varanae v.c.
	Const.Sirm. 11 (Ravenna, 24.vi)	DD.NN. [sic] Theodosius Aug. IV
INSCR.:	**ROME:** *ICUR* n.s. II 4171* = *ILCV* 4405 (23.ix?; Fl.); *ICUR* n.s. VII 17546 (frag.; om. num.; or 415?); *ICUR* n.s. I 87 (om. D.N., Aug., num.; Fl.; Gk.)	D.N. (Fl.) Theodosius Aug. IV
	ITALY: *CIL* IX 1365 = *ILCV* 4144C (Aeclanum, Reg. II; 21.vii)	Iterum p.c. Honorii VIII et Theodosi III Augg.
OTHER:	Conference at Carthage: *Gesta Conlat.Carth.* 1.14,148,207 (25.v); 1.55 (30.v); 1.1 (1.vi); 2.12 (2.vi); 2.1 (3.vi); 3.4,5 (6.vi); 3.1 (8.vi); p.179 (26.vi)	p.c. Varanis v.c.

NOTES:

In modern consular lists, which follow the ancient ones from the western empire, 411 is designated "Theodosius IV" and 412 "Honorius IX et Theodosius V." That the contemporary situation in the East was different was first shown by Bagnall and Worp (*Mnemosyne* 31 [1978] 287-93). Further evidence for this view was developed by Cameron in two articles (*BASP* 16 [1979] 177 and 18 [1981] 69-71), and the question is discussed again in full by R.W. Burgess, *ZPE* 65 (1986) 211-21.

In the early part of 411, the East dated by Theodosius IV *e.q.f.n.* (attested in June; reading *IAN* for *IVN* would put the date in January instead), but on 17.viii we find *Honorius IX et Theodosius IV* in a Constantinopolitan law; that this formula was disseminated is shown by the papyrus of 9.xii and by the two papyri of the following year with a p.c. of this pair. The three eastern lists all duly record IX et IV for 411. [Continued on the next page]

356

Orientis

FASTI: Marcell. Heracl. (both om. Aug.)   Honorius Aug. IX et
            Pasch. (Th. iun.)   Theodosius (iun.) Aug. IV

LAWS: *CTh* 5.16.33 (C'polis,   D.N. Theodosius Aug. IV
            6-13.vi)   et qui fuerit nuntiatus

            CTh 7.4.32 (C'polis, 17.viii)   Honorius IX et
                                          Theodosius IV

PAPYRI: *SPP* XX 117.1 (9.xii)   DD.NN. Honorius IX et
                                          Theodosius IV perpp. Augg.

NOTES:

    The situation in the West is not so straightforward. There is no contemporary or later evidence for IX et IV. Rather, we find (1) an iterum p.c. VIII et III at Aeclanum in July; (2) a p.c. Varanae in use not only in Carthage (where late dissemination would not be surprising), but also in two laws from Ravenna, bearing dates of 8.ii and 28.xi; and (3) Theodosius IV, found in one Roman inscription (*ICUR* n.s. II 4171; the other two inscriptions listed are doubtful and lack numerals); in *ConstSirm* 11, dated at Ravenna on 24.vi; and in the unanimous listing of the western chronicles and lists. It is true that *ConstSirm* 11 is not without difficulty (see Critical Appendix), and there is thus some possibility that the western court accepted Theodosius IV in retrospect but never disseminated that consulate in 411 itself; but we think the balance of probability is that Theodosius IV was disseminated in the West in 411. Honorius IX, however, the other half of the eastern formula, was not disseminated in the West in 411 nor accepted retroactively into western lists under that year.

    In 412, the eastern court once again used Theodosius (V) *e.q.f.n.* at the start of the year. Socrates and more than 30 laws, however, give 412 as Honorius IX et Theodosius V. We may suppose that at least the earlier laws are corrected (the earliest dates to the same day as the *e.q.f.n.* formula), but this correction shows that the compilers' list gave IX et V for 412. We know from the papyri of 417 and its p.c. in 418 that in retrospect the East [Continued on next page]

Occidentis

FASTI:	Hyd. Prosp. Cycl. (Th. Aug.) Aug. Cass. Aq.	Honorius IX et Theodosius (Aug.) V
LAWS:	About 26 laws total; Ravenna, 15 laws, earliest *CTh* 16.5.52 (30.i)	(DD.NN.) Honorius IX et Theodosius V Augg.
INSCR.:	**ROME:** *ICUR* n.s. II 4857 (or p.c., 413)	DD.NN. Honorius IX [et Theodosius V]
	ICUR n.s. II 4172 = *ILCV* 2609A adn. (10.x)	DD.NN. Honorius Aug. VIII et Theodosius V
	ITALY: *CIL* XI 2898* (Bolsena; 1.ix)	D.N. Theodosius Aug. V
	DALMATIA: *CIL* III 9512 = *ILCV* 3640A (Salona; 14.viii-1.ix)	DD.NN. Honorius IX et Theodosius V perpp. Augg.
OTHER:	Letter of Conc. Cirtense to Donatists (in Augustine, *Epp.* 141) (14.vi)	Honorius Aug. IX
	Innocentius, *Epp.* 13 (*PL* 20.515) (17.vi)	Honorius IX et Theodosius V Augg.

NOTES: [Continued from preceding page]

used a count of Honorius' consulates which agreed with that in use in the West, and the laws using X et VI in 415 (though lacking papyri for confirmation) agree with that. On the other hand, whatever happened clearly confused some people in the East, for the count in Heracl. (alone of the lists) for Honorius' consulates is too high by one to the end of his reign. And we now have the ambiguous evidence of *P.Heid.* IV 306, from 413, dated by a p.c. of Honorius [missing numeral] and Theodosius V. The papyrus shows, on the one hand, that Honorius was disseminated in 412 (or at least retrospectively *for* 412) in the eastern provinces. It also shows that the scribe was confused about the numeral (such a blank is unique in the papyrological documentation). There is no trace of ink here, but the spot is rubbed. Either the scribe wrote a numeral and rubbed it out, or he never wrote anything. The most likely hypothesis is that IX et V was disseminated, and the scribe, remembering that he had been using p.c. IX et IV just the year before, was understandably confused. Marcell. and Pasch. give only Theodosius V, showing at least an instinct for order.

[Continued on next page]

Orientis

<u>FASTI:</u>	Marcell.	Theodosius Imp. V
	Heracl.	Honorius X et Theodosius V
	Pasch.	Theodosius iun. Aug. V solus
<u>LAWS:</u>	*CTh* 7.17.1 (28.i)	D.N. Theodosius Aug. V et qui fuerit nuntiatus
	C'polis, 8 laws, earliest 28.i (*CTh* 14.26.1)	(DD.NN.) Honorius IX et Theodosius V Augg.
<u>PAPYRI:</u>	*P.Oxy.* LI 3639.1 (11.ix); *P.Mich.* XI 611.1 (27.ix)	p.c. DD.NN. Honori IX et Theodosi IV perpp. Augg.
<u>OTHER:</u>	Socrates, *HE* 7.7 (15.x)	Honorius IX et Theodosius V

<u>NOTES:</u>   [Continued from preceding page]

In the West, the evidence for IX et V is adequate, though we do find one inscription of Bolsena with only Theodosius V and one letter quoted in Augustine with only Honorius IX. Of the two Roman inscriptions, one is broken after Honorius IX and the other gets Honorius' numeral wrong (as VIII).

Such is the evidence. How is this puzzling situation to be explained? A full discussion is presented in Chapter 2 above (p.16). On its basis, we offer the following reconstruction: The eastern court had heard nothing in advance from Ravenna (in turmoil because of the Gothic invasion of Italy in 410), and cautiously proclaimed Theodosius IV *e.q.f.n.* while waiting to hear. A communication eventually arrived which was interpreted in Constantinople to mean that Honorius had celebrated his *vicennalia* a year early in January in order to join with Theodosius' *decennalia*, and that he had accordingly taken the consulate with him. Honorius IX et Theodosius IV was proclaimed and disseminated; presumably word had been sent to the West already that Theodosius was taking his fourth consulate. The end of the year came, evidently without further word. Theodosius V *e.q.f.n.* was proclaimed, as in the previous year. Then word arrived that Honorius was *now* celebrating his *vicennalia* and taking his ninth consulate. The eastern court, making the best of an embarrassing situation, proclaimed *Honorius IX et Theodosius V*, which was duly disseminated (though with normal delays), causing confusion to alert scribes and future chroniclers.

Occidentis

FASTI: Hyd.   a) p.c. Honorii IX et
                                                               Theodosi
                                                               b)Lucius

             Prosp. Aq. Cass. Rav. Haun.   Lucius v.c.

             Aug.   p.c. i. e. Teracliano et
                                                               Lucio

             Cycl.   p.c. IX et V

LAWS: Ravenna, 6 laws, earliest   p.c. Honori IX et
             CTh 12.1.176 (27.i);   Theodosii V Augg.
             latest, *CTh* 15.14.13 (3.viii)

INSCR.:   none

NOTES:

Heraclianus was comes Africae from 408-413 as a reward for killing Stilicho. In 413 he collected a large fleet and rebelled. He was defeated on the road to Ravenna and killed on his return to Carthage (*PLRE* I 539-40). His death has hitherto been placed in the late summer (S.I. Oost, *CP* 61 [1966] 240), but a fragment of the Ravenna Annals dates it to 7.iii.411 --perhaps too early, since he is supposed to have begun his revolt by withholding the African grain shipment (Orosius, loc.cit.), not normally dispatched till April. The law striking his name from all records ("Heracliani vocabulum nec privatim nec publice ulla memoria teneat..." *CTh* 15.14.13) is dated 3.viii.413).

Orientis

FASTI:	Heracl.	Lucius v.c.
	Marcell. Pasch.	Lucius solus
LAWS:	C'polis, 4 laws, earliest *CTh* 6.13.1 (21.iii) (plus 4 without prov. but pres. eastern)	Lucius v.c.
PAPYRI:	*P.Heid.* IV 306.1 (16.xii)	p.c. DD.NN. Honorii [ ] et Theodosii V perpp. Augg.
INSCR.:	*AE* 1971, 454 (Lesbos)	Fl. Lucius

NOTES:

PLRE II 692 identifies Lucius as the eastern CSL of 408 (Lucius 3), but others see him as the general who (according to Damascius, fr. 303 Zintzen) made an attempt on the life of Theodosius II (K. Holum, *Theodosian Empresses* [Berkeley 1982] 82 n.17). Western fasti suggest that Lucius' name was known in the West, but in the chaos it was evidently not proclaimed during the revolt. The western p.c.'s in the laws are presumably not original but retroactive *western* corrections after Heraclian's *damnatio memoriae*. Curiously enough the Theodosian compilers left these p.c.'s unaltered. Cf. p.82.

Occidentis

FASTI: Hyd. (v.c.) Prosp. (I; cf. 1, 467;   Constantius (v.c.)
         v.c.) Cycl.

         Prosp. (II; cf. 1, 488,491) Aug.   Constantius et Constans
         Aq. Cass.

         Haun.   Constantius v.c. cons.
                                                     et Constans

LAWS: *CTh* 15.7.13 and 2.16.3   Constantius v.c.
         (Ravenna, 8.ii and 6.iii)

         Ravenna, 6 laws, earliest 8.iii   Constantius et Constans
         (*CTh* 6.29.11); 1 from Rome
         (30.viii); *CTh* 7.8.11
         (prob. Ravenna, 10.i)

INSCR.: **ROME:** *ICUR* n.s. I 2722*, cf.   Constantius et Constans
         ILCV 2938 adn. (20.ix)

         ICUR n.s. VII 17548 + 19864   Constantius comes et
         (20.vii; Gk.; see *RAC* 58   [magister militum]
         [1982] 358-63)

         ICUR n.s. I 3160* = *ILCV*   Constantius et
         4145 (3.iv)   Constantinus

         AE 1945, 133 (1.i); *ICUR*   Fl. Constantius v.c.
         n.s. VII 17547 (15.v)

         DALMATIA: *CIL* III 9513 =   p.c. Luci v.c.
         ILCV 454 (Salona; 23.xii)

OTHER: Innocentius, *Epp.* 17   Fl. Constantius v.c.
         (*PL* 20.526) (13.xii)

Orientis

<u>FASTI:</u>	Marcell. Heracl. Pasch.	Constantius et Constans
<u>LAWS:</u>	C'polis, 5 laws, earliest 9.iv	Constantius et Constans
<u>PAPYRI:</u>	*P.Rainer Cent.* 90.1 (frag.; p.c. poss.)	Fl. Constantius et Fl. Constans v.c. praef. praet.

<u>NOTES:</u>

Constantius was MVM in the West from 411-421, cos. II 417, cos. III 420 and Augustus in 421 (*PLRE* II 321-25). Constans, the eastern consul, was MVM in Thrace in 412 (*PLRE* II 311).

Seeck maintained on the basis of Pope Innocent's letter of 13.xii and the silence of some western fasti that Constans was never proclaimed in the West (*Reg.* 18-19). But the Roman inscription *ICUR* n.s. I 2722 is decisive, and the absence of Constans' name from some fasti is perhaps due to nothing more serious than haplography (the MSS of Prosper are divided: see Mommsen's *app.crit.*, *Chron.Min.* I 467). The fact that one of the two western laws with just Constantius' name is the earliest of the year suggests (*if* the formula is intact and original) no more than that Constans' name was late arriving from the East. The p.c. Luci (an easterner) in Dalmatia so late is curious.

Occidentis

FASTI: Hyd. Prosp. Cycl. (om. VI, adds Aug.   Honorius X et
                p.c. Paulini) Aug. Aq. Cass.   Theodosius VI

LAWS: About 24 laws total, 7 from   (DD.NN.) Honorius X et
                Ravenna (earliest 8.i, *CTh*   Theodosius VI Augg.
                6.29.12)

INSCR.:   **ROME:** *ICUR* n.s. II 4858 =   Honorius X et
                ILCV 3532 (18.iv); *ICUR*   Theodosius VI
                n.s. II 6072 = *ILCV* 2886A adn.
                (only Hon.)

                ITALY: *CIL* V 6398 = *ILCV* 146   DD.NN. Honorius X
                (Lodi, Reg. XI; 10.x); *ILCV* 1358   et Theodosius VI Augg.
                = *I.Lat.Sard.* I 299 (Sardinia;
                27.x; om. DD.NN., Augg.)

                DALMATIA: *CIL* III 2656 = *ILCV*   D.N. Theodosius perp.
                479 (Salona; 23.xi)   VI Aug.

NOTES:

    If the (undated) *ICUR* n.s. II 6072 was engraved early, it may point to a delay in the dissemination of Theodosius' name at Rome.

Orientis

<u>FASTI:</u>	Marcell.	Honorius X et Theodosius VI
	Heracl.	Honorius XI et Theodosius VI
	Pasch.	Honorius X et Theodosius iun. Aug. VI
<u>LAWS:</u>	*CTh* 3.1.9 (C'polis, 17.ii)	Theodosius Aug. VI
	C'polis, 11 laws, earliest *CTh* 9.28.2 (5.iii)	(DD.NN.) Honorius X et Theodosius VI Augg.
<u>PAPYRI:</u>	*SPP* XX 90.1 (15.vi); *P.Mich.* XI 613.1 (19.viii; om. Fll.)	p.c. Fll. Constanti et Constantis vv.cc.
<u>OTHER:</u>	Lucian, *Epistola ad omnem ecclesiam de revelatione Stephani martyris* (*REB* 4 [1946] 192) (nr. Jerusalem, 3.xii; Lat. trans. made at time)	Honorius X et Theodosius VI Augg.
	Socrates, *HE* 7.15	Honorius X et Theodosius VI

Occidentis

<u>FASTI</u>:	Hyd. Prosp. Cycl. (Aug.) Aug. Cass. Aq.	Theodosius (Aug.) VII et Palladius
<u>LAWS</u>:	About 27 laws total, 9 from Ravenna, earliest *CTh* 11.5.2, 7.i	(D.N.) Theodosius Aug. VII et Palladius v.c.
<u>INSCR.</u>:	**ROME:** *NotScav* 1888, 450 = *ILCV* 3179 (22.i)	Fl. Palladius v.c.
	ICUR n.s. II 4859 (14.ii-15.iii)	Iunius Qua[rtus Palladius v.c.]
	ICUR n.s. II 4860 (rest. uncert.); *ICUR* n.s. II 4512 (frag.; or p.c., 417?)	D.N. Theodosius VII et Palladius
	ITALY: *Röm. Quart.* 10 (1896) 47 no.83 (Syracuse; 20.iv; Gk.)	Theodosius VII et Palladius v.c.
	NotScav 1895, 521 no.269 = Ferrua, *RendPontAccad* 22 (1946-47) 231 (Syracuse; rest.; Gk.)	Pal]ladius
<u>OTHER</u>:	Innocentius to Decentius, Bp. "Eugubinus" (*PL* 20.561) (19.iii)	Theodosius Aug. VII et Palladius vv.cc.
	Innocentius to Aurelius, Bp. of Carthage (Mansi III 1050D = *PL* 84.658 = 130.709) (2.vi)	Iulio Quarto et Palladio vv.cc. (sic)

<u>NOTES</u>:

Palladius was PPO Ital. 416-421 (*PLRE* II 822-24). The evidence suggests that Palladius was announced in the West and Theodosius in the East, with dissemination of each slow in the other half and retrospective adaptation the rule in both halves of the empire. Only one text in the *CTh* was not 'corrected'; the letter of Innocent to Aurelius is a hash.

Orientis

FASTI: Marcell. Heracl. (om. Aug.)   Theodosius (iun.) Aug. VII
              Pasch. (iun.)   et Palladius

LAWS: *CTh* 6.32.1 (C'polis,   Theodosius Aug. VII
              8.ii)   et qui fuerit nuntiatus

              C'polis, 12 laws, earliest *CTh*   (D.N.) Theodosius Aug. VII
              6.27.18, 20.i; Eudoxiopolis,   et Palladius (v.c.)
              3 laws; Heraclea, 1 law

PAPYRI: none

Occidentis

<u>FASTI</u>:	Hyd. Prosp. Cycl. (III) Aug. Aq. Cass.	Honorius XI et Constantius II
<u>LAWS</u>:	Ravenna, 4 laws; earliest *Codex Parisinus* 1564 *apud* Haenel, *Corpus legum* p.238 (18.i)	(D.N.) Honorius Aug. XI et Constantius v.c. II
<u>INSCR.</u>:	**ROME:** *ICUR* n.s. I 2111 = *ILCV* 2601A (21.v)	Honorius Aug. XII et Constantius
	ITALY: *CIL* XI 1689 = *IG* XIV 2265 (Florence; 24.iv; Gk.)	Honorius Aug. XI et Constantius II
<u>OTHER</u>:	Innocentius, *Epp.* 29 (*PL* 20.588) (27.i)	p.c. Theodosii Aug. VII et Iunii Quarti v.c.
	Innocentius, *Epp.* 31 (*PL* 20.597 = *Coll.Avell.* 41) (27.i)	p.c. glorios. Theodosii Aug. VII et Iunii Quarti Palladii v.c.
	Innocentius, *Epp.* 30 (*PL* 20.593) (27.i)	Honorius et Constantius vv.cc.
	Zosimus, *Epp.* 1 (*PL* 20.645) (22.iii)	Honorius Aug. XI et Constantius II
	Zosimus, *Epp.* 2 (*PL* 20.649) (date?); 4 (*PL* 20.661) (22.ix); 6 (*PL* 20.668) (26.ix); 7 (*PL* 20.669) (26.ix); 5 (*PL* 20.665) (29.ix)	Honorius Aug. XI et Fl. Constantius

Orientis

<u>FASTI</u>:	Marcell. Pasch.	Honorius XI et Constantius II
	Heracl.	Honorius XII et Constans II
<u>LAWS</u>:	C'polis, 6 laws, earliest *CTh* 8.12.9 (14.iii)	(D.N.) Honorius Aug. XI et Constantius (v.c.) II
<u>PAPYRI</u>:	*P.Got.* 39.1 (8.v); *P.Berl. Zill.* 5.1 (15.vi; adds praef. sacr. praet. Italiae)	p.c. D.N. Theodosi perp. Aug. VII et Fl. Palladii v.c. (praef. sacr. praet. Italiae)
	P.Colon.inv. 5853 (Hebrew in Aramaic letters), in C. Sirat, P. Cauderlier et al., *La Ketouba de Cologne: un contrat de mariage juif* = Pap.Colon. XII (15.xi)	[Honorius] Aug. XI [et Fl. Cons]tantius comes v. magnif. et patricius

<u>NOTES</u>:

For Constantius, see the notes to 414. Apparently diffusion of the consuls' names was simultaneous but delayed in both parts of the empire. Some laws at least in the East received correction later. See the Critical Appendix for *P.Vindob.Sijp.* 9. For Innocentius' letters, cf. Mommsen, *Ges.Schr.* VI 371 n.4.

Occidentis

FASTI:	Hyd. ExcSang. Prosp. Cycl. Aug. Aq. Cass.	Honorius XII et Theodosius VIII
LAWS:	Ravenna, 5 laws, earliest 10.iii (*CTh* 16.8.24)	(DD.NN.) Honorius XII et Theodosius VIII Augg.
INSCR.:	**ROME:** *RAC* 44 (1968) 142 fig. 2 (18.iv); *ICUR* n.s. III 8434 = *ILCV* 2946 adn. (22.iv)	Honorius XII
	ITALY: *Kokalos* 28-29 (1982-83) 15-16 no.46 = Agnello, *Silloge* 87 (Catania, 2.iii/2.v)	p.c. [Honorii Aug.] XI et Constantini [II]
	CIL V 6268 = *ILCV* 200 (Milan, Reg. XI; 28.ix); *ILCV* 2936A* (Syracuse; 19.x)	DD.NN. Honorius XII et Theodosius VIII Augg.
	DALMATIA: *CIL* III 12855 ad 9479 = *Forsch.Salona* II 166 (Salona; p.c. poss.; very frag.)	
OTHER:	Zosimus, *Epp.* 9 (*PL* 20.673) (21.ii)	Honorius XII et Theodosius VIII Augg.
	Zosimus, *Epp.* 10, 11 (*PL* 20.674,675) (5.iii)	Honorius XII et Theodosius VIII Augg.
	Zosimus, *Epp.* 12 (*PL* 20.678) (21.iii)	Honorius Aug. XII
	Council at Thelepte: *Conc.Africae* p.58 (24.ii)	p.c. glor. Honorii XI et Constanti II
	Council at Carthage: *Conc.Africae* p.69 (1.v)	Honorius Aug. XII
	Council at Carthage: *Conc.Africae* p.220 (1.v)	glorios. impp. Honorius XII Aug. et Theodosius VIII Aug.

Continued on the next page]

Orientis

FASTI: Marcell.   Honorius XII et
                                                          Theodosius iun. Aug. VIII

              Pasch.   Honorius XII et Theodosius

              Heracl.   Honorius XIII et
                                                          Theodosius VIII

LAWS: C'polis, 2 laws, 3.ii (*CTh*   (DD.NN.) Honorius XII et
              16.2.43) and 17.iv   Theodosius VIII Augg.

PAPYRI: *P.Köln* II 102.1 (30.iii   p.c. D.N. Honorii perp.
              or 9.iv; om. iteration numeral   Aug. XI et Fl. Constantii
              II for Constantius); *CPR*   v.c.
              X 111.1 (same omission?)

NOTES:

It is not clear whether the texts that omit Theodosius reflect late dissemination, are shortened deliberately, or are simply errors; the Roman inscriptions and the Catanian p.c. suggest late dissemination.

[Continued from the preceding page]

Council at Hippo (signatures):   Honorius XII et
Conc.Africae p.48 (25.v)   Theodosius VIII
                                                          Augg. vv.cc.

Zosimus, *Epp.* 14   Honorius XII et
(*PL* 20.680) (3.x);   Theodosius VIII Augg.
16 (20.686) (16.xi)

Occidentis

<u>FASTI</u>:	Hyd. ExcSang. Prosp. Cycl. Aug. Aq. Cass.	Monaxius et Plinta
<u>LAWS</u>:	Ravenna, 3 laws, earliest 26.vi (*CTh* 5.18)	Monaxius et Plinta (vv.cc.)
<u>INSCR.</u>:	**ROME:** *ICUR* n.s. II 4863 = *ILCV* 3546A (4.ix; frag.); *ICUR* n.s. I 730 = *ILCV* 2635 (30.xi); *ICUR* n.s. I 180 (frag.); *ICUR* n.s. V 13390 (om. vv.cc.); *ICUR* n.s. VIII 20816a (om. vv.cc.; frag.)	Monaxius et Plinta vv.cc.
	ITALY: *IG* XIV 239 = Agnello, *Silloge* 95 (Acrae, Sicily; 14.vi; om. vv.cc.; Gk.); *CIL* XI 3515 = *ILCV* 2962 adn. (Corneto, Reg. VII; 30.xi)	
<u>OTHER</u>:	**TUNISIA:** *AE* 1914, 31 (Ksar-Koutine; 17.vii; ostrakon)	p.c. DD.NN. Honori XII et Theodosi VIII
	Boniface, *Epp.* 2a (*PL* 20.792) (26.iv); 3 (*PL* 20.758) (13.vi); 5 (*PL* 20.763) (19.ix)	Monaxius v.c.
	Council at Carthage: *Conc.Africae* p.89 (25.v); p.229 (30.v)	p.c. glor. impp. Honorii XII et Theodosii VIII Augg.
	Letter of Honorius to Aurelius, Bp. of Carthage (Mansi IV 446E = *PL* 48.394) (9.vi)	Monaxius et Plinta
	Letter of Aurelius, Bp. of Carthage (Mansi IV 447C = *PL* 48.400) (1.viii)	Monaxius et Plinta
	Letter of Atticus, Bp. of C'polis to Aurelius and Valentinus (Mansi III 838D) (26.xi)	p.c. glor. impp. Honorii XII et Theodosii IX Augg.

Orientis

<u>FASTI:</u>	Marcell. Heracl. Pasch.	Monaxius et Plinta
<u>LAWS:</u>	C'polis, 4 laws, earliest *CTh* 11.30.66 (8.iii)	Monaxius et Plinta (vv.cc.)
<u>PAPYRI:</u>	*PSI* XIII 1365.2 (6.vii); *P.Rainer Cent.* 91.13	p.c. DD.NN. Honori XII et Theodosi VIII perpp. Augg.
<u>OTHER:</u>	Socrates, *HE* 7.17	Monaxius et Plintha
	Priscus, frag. 1.14	

<u>NOTES:</u>

Monaxius was PVC 408-409; PPO Or. 414, 416-420 (*PLRE* II 764-65); Plinta was MVM 419-438 and a powerful figure at the eastern court (ib. 892-93). Both consuls were nominated in the East this year. There is substantial evidence for very late dissemination in Egypt, Tunisia, and Carthage. There are no Roman inscriptions before September to inform us of the situation there, but Sicily had the new consuls by June.

Occidentis

<u>FASTI</u>:   Hyd. Prosp. Cycl. (Aug. VIII)   Theodosius (Aug.) IX et
           Cass. Aq. Aug.   Constantius III

<u>LAWS</u>:   Ravenna, 2 laws, *ConstSirm* 10,   (D.N.) Theodosius Aug. IX
           8.v and *CTh* 5.1.6, 27.ix   et Constantius III (v.c.)

<u>INSCR.</u>: **ITALY:** *Nuovo Didaskaleion*   p.c. [Monaxi]o et
           1956, 59 no.17 (Syracuse)   Pli[nta vv.cc.]

           CIL XI 4969, cf. p.1375   Constantius v.c. III
           add. = *ILCV* 4813 (Spoleto, Reg.
           VI; 27.vi)

           DALMATIA: *Forsch.Salona* II 167   Constantius v.c. III
           (p.c. possible?)

Orientis

<u>FASTI:</u>	Marcell. Heracl. Pasch. (iun. Aug.)	Theodosius (iun. Aug.) IX et Constantius III
<u>LAWS:</u>	*CTh* 7.16.3 (C'polis, 18.ix)	D.N. Theodosius Aug. IX et qui fuerit nuntiatus
	C'polis, 2 laws, 5.v and 30.xii (*CJ* 8.10.10 and *CTh* 10.1.17)	(D.N.) Theodosius Aug. IX et Constantius III (v.c.)
<u>PAPYRI:</u>	*P.Oxy.* XVI 1973.1 (15.ii); *PSI* XIII 1340.1 (18.xi); *CPR* X 38.1; *MPER* n.s. XV 63.38 (school text or writing practice; breaks off after Monaxius)	p.c. Fll. Monaxii et Plinta vv.cc.

<u>NOTES:</u>

Seeck argued that Theodosius did not recognize Constantius' III consulate because, being an almost unheard of honor for a private citizen, it foreshadowed his elevation to Augustus next year (*Reg.* 26, with the inconclusive discussion of S.I. Oost, *Galla Placidia* [1968] 166 n.83). But the motive alleged is weak, nor is it likely that the military preparations against the East he was alleged to be making when he died in fall, 421 (Olympiodorus, fr. 34; Philostorgius, *HE* 12.12), were under way before the end of 419. The use of the *e.q.f.n.* formula on 27.v and again as late as 18.ix (*CJ* 8.10.10 is no doubt retroactively corrected) certainly suggests late proclamation in the East, but at the same time it is not a formula which implies a definite decision *not* to recognize. We may contrast the case of 424, where the eastern formula is Victor alone, there is a good motive, and the eastern fasti are divided. Here, the three eastern fasti all list Constantius with correct iteration number, as too did the fasti from which the Theodosian compilers (on Seeck's view) corrected the other laws of the year. Moreover, there are four p.c. papyri with the numeral. There is thus sufficient evidence to prove that Constantius was eventually recognized in the East, even if dissemination of his name was late (in Egypt, late for both consuls).

Occidentis

FASTI:	Hyd. Prosp. Cycl. Aug. Aq. Cass.	Agricola et Eustathius
LAWS:	3 laws from Ravenna, earliest, *CTh* 3.16.2 (10.iii)	Eustathius et Agricola
INSCR.:	**DALMATIA:** *CIL* III 12857 ad 9514 = *Forsch.Salona* II 168 Salona	Agricola et Eustathius vv.cc.
OTHER:	Council at Carthage: *Conc.Africae* p.250 (variant reading in one MS) (13.vi)	Agricola et Eustathius vv.cc.
	Boniface, *Epp.* 9 (*PL* 20.769) (14.vii)	Eustathius et Agricola

Orientis

<u>FASTI:</u>	Marcell. Heracl. Pasch.	Eustathius et Agricola
<u>LAWS:</u>	*CTh* 16.2.45 (no prov., 14.vii)	Eustathius et Agricola
<u>PAPYRI:</u>	*P.Oxy.* VIII 1134.1 (3.iii); *Pap.Lugd.Bat.* XIII 8.1 (22.iv); *Pap.Lugd.Bat.* XIII 13.18 (25.vi; om. patr.); *SPP* XX 114.1 (25.vii)	p.c. DD.NN. Theodosii perp. Aug. IX et Fl. Constantii III v.c. patricii
	SB XVI 12260.1 (20.xii)	Fll. Eustathius et Agricola

<u>NOTES:</u>

Agricola was PPO (II) Gall. 418, the father of Magnus cos. 460, and came from Gaul (*PLRE* II 36-37). Eustathius was PPO Or. 420-422 (*PLRE* II 436). The Theodosian compilers (and the papal chancellery) systematically "easternized" the sequence of names in the formulas to western laws. Dissemination in Egypt was late. This is the first year (apart from the peculiar situation in 381) in which East and West use a different order for the names of the consuls.

Occidentis

FASTI:	Hyd. Prosp. Cycl. Aug. Aq. Cass.	Honorius XIII et Theodosius X
LAWS:	Ravenna, 3 laws, earliest 20.ii (*CTh* 11.28.13); one law no prov. (*CTh* 10.10.31, *p.p.* Rome, 25.viii)	(DD.NN.) Honorius XIII et Theodosius X Augg.
INSCR.:	**ROME:** *ICUR* I 613 (19.iii; om. Augg.); *ICUR* n.s. II 4868 (2-5.viii; frag.); *ICUR* n.s. I 3227 (frag.); *ICUR* n.s. II 6074 (perpp.)	DD.NN. Honorius XIII et Theodosius X (perpp.) Augg.
	GAUL: *CIL* XIII 2353 = *ILCV* 2901 (Lyons; 29.vii; om. DD.NN.; Augg.)	
	SPAIN: *Röm.Inschr.Tarraco* 946 (Tarragona; om. DD.NN., Augg.; retrospective ref. to birthdate on gravestone dated 459)	
COINS:	Kent, *Roman Coins* no.733 (Ravenna)	Honorius, cons. image on obv. and rev. of solidi
OTHER:	Boniface, *Epp.* 12 (*PL* 20.774) (9.ii); 13 (*PL* 20.777), 14 (*PL* 20.779), 15 (*PL* 20.784) (all 11.iii)	Honorius XIII et Theodosius X Augg.

Orientis

<u>FASTI:</u>	Marcell.	Honorius XIII et Theodosius X
	Pasch.	Honorius XIII et Theodosius Aug. X
	Heracl.	Honorius XIV et Theodosius X
<u>LAWS:</u>	C'polis, 5 laws, earliest *CTh* 6.32.2 (12.i)	(DD.NN.) Honorius XIII et Theodosius X Augg.
<u>PAPYRI:</u>	*SPP* XX 118 (29.viii)	p.c. Fll. Eustathii et Agricolae vv.cc.
<u>COINS:</u>	Kent, *NC* 6 ser. 20 (1960) pl.IX, no.2 (Constantinople)	Theodosius, cons. image on obv. of solidus
<u>OTHER:</u>	Socrates, *HE* 7.20	Honorius XIII et Theodosius X (Augg.)

<u>NOTES:</u>

Dissemination in Egypt was again late.

Occidentis

FASTI:	Hyd. Prosp. Cycl. Aug. Aq. Cass. Rav.	Marinianus et Asclepiodotus
LAWS:	Ravenna, 5 laws, earliest 8.ii (*CTh* 11.28.14)	Asclepiodotus et Marinianus (vv.cc.)
INSCR.:	**ROME:** *ICUR* n.s. II 4880 = *ILCV* 1559 (14.i-13.ii; frag.); *ICUR* n.s. VII 17550 (14.iv-15.v); *ICUR* n.s. VII 17549 = *ILCV* 885	Marinianus et Asclepiodotus vv.cc.
	ICUR n.s. II 4881 = *ILCV* 3092 (23.vi; Av.); *ICUR* n.s. II 4273* (23.x; om. Fl.); *ICUR* n.s. I 731 = *ILCV* 4461B (27.x; om. Fl., v.c.); *ICUR* n.s. VII 17551 (12.xii)	Fl. (Avitus) Marinianus v.c.
	ITALY: Agnello, *Silloge* 104* = *ILCV* 2370 (Syracuse; 3.iii)	p.c. DD.NN. Honori XIII et Theodosii X Augg.
	NBC 1902, 59 = *Röm.Quart.* 10 (1896) 40 no.342 (Syracuse, 15.vii; Gk.); *CIL* V 6397 (Lodi, Reg. XI; 17.vii); *CIL* V 1623 = *ILCV* 1061B (Aquileia, Reg. X; 1.xii; vv.cc.); *CIL* XI 1731 = *ILCV* 475 (Florence, Reg. VII; 4.xii)	Marinianus et Asclepiodotus (vv.cc.)
	DALMATIA: *CIL* III 3104 (Brattia; frag.); *CIL* III 14303 (Salona; frag.; p.c. poss.)	

Orientis

<u>FASTI:</u>	Marcell. Heracl. Pasch.	Asclepiodotus et Marinianus
<u>LAWS:</u>	C'polis, 10 laws, earliest *CTh* 7.4.35, 14.ii; Eudoxiopolis, 2 laws; 2 with no prov.	Asclepiodotus et Marinianus (vv.cc.)
<u>PAPYRI:</u>	*PSI* I 87.1 (29.vi); *P.Köln* III 151.1 (24.vii); *PSI* VI 689.1	p.c. DD.NN. Honori XIII et Theodosi X perp. Augg.
	P.Rainer Cent. 92.1	Fll. Asclepiodotus et Marinianus vv.magniff. et eminentt. praeff. sacrr. praett.
<u>OTHER:</u>	Socrates, *HE* 7.22; Iacobus of Edessa p.285 (Brooks, *Chron.Min.*, p.213)	Asclepiodotus et Marianus

<u>NOTES:</u>

Marinianus was a Roman aristocrat and PPO Ital. (?) in 422 (*PLRE* II 723-24); Asclepiodotus, PPO Or. in 423-425, was the Empress Eudocia's uncle (*PLRE* II 160). The compilers of *CTh* have again 'easternized' the order of the consuls in the western laws. It is interesting that where *CTh* 9.6.4 and 4.10.2 have eastern order, the versions of the same laws in *CJ* 4.20.12 and 6.7.3 have the western order. It is not at all clear why so many of the Roman inscriptions (and not only early ones) have only Marinianus: in Rome, unlike Italy elsewhere, there is no inscription dated after June which includes Asclepiodotus. It is difficult to believe this the result of any policy--still more so to connect it with the death of Honorius and the usurpation of John (see next year). Dissemination in Egypt was again late.

Occidentis

FASTI: Hyd. Prosp. Aug. Cass. Castinus et Victor
Aq. (GLS)

Aq. (Q) Castinus v.c.

Cycl. Fl. Castinus v.c.

LAWS: none

INSCR.: **ROME:** *ICUR* n.s. VI 17253 = (Fl.) Castinus v.c.
ILCV 2946 adn. (20.v; om. v.c.);
ICUR n.s. VII 17552 = *ILCV* 3504
adn. (29.ix); *ICUR* n.s. VII
17553 = *ILCV* 3727C (31.xii; Fl.;
frag.); *ICUR* n.s. II 4882; *ICUR*
n.s. IV 11144; *ICUR* n.s. VIII
23444

ITALY: *CIL* XI 1690 = *IG* XIV 2266
(Florence, Reg. VII; iv; Fl.,
om. v.c.; Gk.); *CIL* XI 4047
(Capena, Reg. VII; 1.viii);
CIL XI 4996 = *ILCV* 1209 (nr.
Spoleto, Reg. VI; 5.ix; Fl., om.
v.c.); *AE* 1935, 134 (Milan, Reg.
XI; 7.ix); *CIL* V 6281 = *ILCV* 4440
(Milan; 24.xi)

Orientis

FASTI:	Marcell. Pasch.	Victor et Castinus
	Heracl. (suppl.)	Victor solus
LAWS:	13 laws, all C'polis exc. 1 no prov. (*CTh* 15.1.52 (9.i)); earliest C'polis law is *CTh* 10.21.3 (16.i)	Victor (v.c.)
PAPYRI:	*SB* XII 11023.1	p.c. Fll. Asclepiodoti et Mariniani vv.cc.

NOTES:

Honorius died on 15.viii.423 and a *primicerius notariorum* called John seized power at Rome (20.xi, *Rav.Ann.*). In one of his rare errors, Seeck alleged that the eastern law *CTh* 1.8.2 = *CJ* 1.30.1 (26.iv) bore the formula *Castino et Victore*, and since Marcell. and Pasch. list Castinus as well as Victor, he argued that Castinus' consulate was initially recognized by Theodosius. Castinus was MVM in the West from 422-425 (*PLRE* II 269-70). Not noticing that the law in question is in fact subscribed just *Victore* like all other laws of the year, E. Stein (*Bas-Empire* I 283; 565 n.152) claimed that "son consulat ne fut annulé à Constantinople qu'après le 26 avril 424," and that it was Theodosius who designated Castinus consul, an improbable hypothesis accepted by A. Lippold, *RE* Supplbd. XIII (1972) 973 and S.I. Oost, *Galla Placidia* (1968) 179 n.35: "Theodosius, claiming to rule both parts of the empire, must have named both consuls for 424." But now that we know John seized power as early as 20.xi and with the help (*conivente*) of Castinus (Prosper, s.a.), how can we doubt that Castinus was John's nominee? John negotiated with the East for recognition (Greg. Tur., *HF* 2.8; Philostorgius, *HE* 2.13, p.148 Bidez), but it is unlikely that Theodosius gave even provisional recognition to the consul of a usurper. But his name may have been entered on one or two unofficial eastern consular lists when it arrived, or else picked up from western documents, and never subsequently removed.

Occidentis

FASTI:	Hyd. Prosp. Cycl. (om. Caes.) Aug. Aq. Cass.	Theodosius (Aug.) XI et Valentinianus Caesar
	Hist. Britt. (3,168,24 = 169,1; 209,14)	Theodosius et Valentinianus
LAWS:	Aquileia, 4 laws (all excerpts fr. *ConstSirm* 6), earliest 9.vii	(D.N.) Theodosius Aug. XI et Valentinianus Caes. (I)
INSCR.:	**ROME:** *ICUR* n.s. II 4885 = *ILCV* 4745 (27.i and 11.iii)	Iohannes Aug.
	ICUR n.s. II 6076 (7.v); *ICUR* n.s. III 8727 (frag.)	D.N. Theodosius XI et Valentinianus Caes.
	ICUR n.s. VII 17554 = *ILCV* 2946A (29.x); *ICUR* n.s. II 4884 = *ILCV* 4146F adn. (om. Augg.); *ICUR* n.s. II 4513 = *ILCV* 3504 adn.	DD.NN. Theodosius et Valentinianus Augg.
	ITALY: *CIL* V 5206 = *ILCV* 2870 (nr. Brescia, Reg. XI; 18.iii)	p.c. Castini v.c.
	CIL V 6278 = *ILCV* 4394B (Milan, Reg. XI; 12.viii)	DD.NN. Theodosius Aug. XI et Valentinianus puer florentissimus Caesar
	DALMATIA: *AE* 1922, 42* = *ILCV* 3791C (Salona)	DD.NN. Theodosius XI et Valentinianus vir nobilissimus Caes.
	AE 1973, 403 = *ILCV* 185 (15.xii);	DD.NN. Theodosius XI et Valentinianus perpp. Augg.
COINS:	Bíróné-Sey, *Numizmatikai Közlóny* (1975-76) no.4-28 (Constantinople) (struck in 425-426, perhaps until 430)	Valentinian, cons. image of Theodosius and Val. on rev. of solidi

Orientis

FASTI:	Marcell. Heracl. Pasch. (Aug.)	Theodosius (Aug.) XI et Valentinianus Caesar
LAWS:	C'polis, 6 laws, earliest 1.ii (*CTh* 15.5.5); Topirus, 1 law	(D.N.) Theodosius Aug. XI et Valentinianus Caes. (I)
PAPYRI:	*P.Stras.* 639.1 (24.xii)	DD.NN. Theodosius perp. Aug. XI et Valentinianus nob. Caes. I
COINS:	Kent, *Roman Coins*, no.746 (Aquileia); W. Hahn, *Litterae Vindobonenses, Robert Goebl dedicatae*, 111 no.22-23 (no.23 struck 425-426, perhaps until 430)	Theodosius, cons. image of Theodosius and Val. on rev. of solidi
OTHER:	Socrates, *HE* 7.25	Theodosius XI et Valentinianus Caes. I

NOTES:

The young Valentinian, son of Galla Placidia, was proclaimed Caesar at Thessalonica on 23.x.424 and consul for 425. John was defeated and captured at Ravenna in April/May, 425; the first Roman inscription to attest Theodosius XI et Valentinianus I is dated 7.v. Most western inscriptions which include Theodosius omit his numeral, curiously enough. (Theodosius' numeral is also omitted in one inscription of each of 426 and 430. It seems that Romans were more careful to record Valentinian's numeral than that of the eastern emperor.) All western laws are later than this, and all western fasti eliminated John's name.

Valentinian was elevated from Caesar to Augustus on 23.x (*PLRE* II 1139); a Roman inscription dated six days later shows knowledge of this change. For the p.c. inscription, cf. above, p.66.

Occidentis

FASTI: Hyd. (Aug. 2x) Prosp. (Val. Aug.)   Theodosius (Aug.) XII
     Cycl. Aug. Aq. Cass.   et Valentinianus (Aug.) II

LAWS: Total about 17 laws, earliest   (DD.NN.) Theodosius XII
     CTh 10.10.33 = 10.26.2 (Rome, et Valentinianus II (Augg.)
     3.i); 2 others from Rome, 4 from
     Ravenna, earliest 6.iii

INSCR.: **ROME:** *ICUR* n.s. V 13393 (17.x); DD.NN. Theodosius Aug. XII
     ICUR n.s. II 4274 (13.ix; num. et Valentinianus Aug. II
     XI; om. Aug.); *ICUR* n.s. VII
     17555; *ICUR* n.s. VII 17556 (om.
     Aug.); *ICUR* n.s. II 6077 = *ILCV*
     2137 (om. XII, Aug.); *ICUR* n.s.
     VIII 23445

     ITALY: *Kokalos* 28-29 (1982-83) Theodosius XII et
     17 no.55 (Catania; Gk.; or p.c., Valentinianus II
     427)

Orientis

FASTI:	Marcell. Heracl. Pasch. (Aug., iun. Aug.)	Theodosius (Aug.) XII et Valentinianus (iun. Aug.) II
LAWS:	C'polis, 5 laws, earliest *CTh* 9.42.24, 23.i; Nicomedia, 4 laws	(DD.NN.) Theodosius XII et Valentinianus II (Augg.)
PAPYRI:	*BGU* III 936.1 (30.iv; num. X); *P.Oslo* II 35.1 (6.x); *P.Laur.* IV 159.1	p.c. DD.NN. Theodosi XI et Valentiniani I perpp. Augg.
	BGU XII 2137.1 (2nd half of year); *P.Rainer Cent.* 93.1 (p.c. poss.)	DD.NN. Theodosius XII et Valentinianus II perpp. Augg.
OTHER:	Socrates, *HE* 7.26	Theodosius XII et Valentinianus iun. Aug. II

NOTES:

Valentinian was proclaimed Augustus on 23.x.425 (cf. that year) at Ravenna (Marcell. s.a.; not Rome, as in Seeck, *Reg.* 350) and took the consulate the following year in the traditional fashion. Dissemination was again late in Egypt, and *BGU* XII 2137 presumably dates later than 6.x.

Occidentis

FASTI:	Geneal. (1, 196 c.628a) Rav. Hyd. Prosp. Cycl. Aug. Aq. Cass.	Hierius et Ardabur
LAWS:	Total 6 laws; none has a stated western provenance; earliest *CTh* 6.24.10, 16.iii	Hierius et Ardabur (vv.cc.)
INSCR.:	**ROME:** *ICUR* n.s. V 13394 (2.x; frag.); *ICUR* n.s. II 4886 = *ILCV* 87 (18.x; Hierius only; metrical); *ICUR* n.s. I 4887 = *ILCV* 3310A adn.; *ICUR* I 656; *ICUR* n.s. II 4888 = *ILCV* 2777 adn. (frag.; vv.cc.)	Hierius et Ardabur (vv.cc.)
	ITALY: *AE* 1933, 27* = *SEG* XVII 441 (Catania; 18.vii; Gk.)	p.c. Theodosi XII et Valentiniani II
	IG XIV 159 = Führer, *Forsch. zur Sicilia sotterranea* 150 n.3,5 (Syracuse, 24.xi; Gk.)	Hierius et Ardabur vv.cc.
	AFRICA: *CIL* VIII 11127 = *ILCV* 2683 (Leptis Minor; 24.xi; om. vv.cc.)	
OTHER:	Council at Hippo: *Concil.Africae* p.250 (24.ix)	Piaerius et Ardabur vv.cc.

Orientis

<u>FASTI:</u>	Marcell. Heracl. Pasch.	Hierius et Ardabur
<u>LAWS:</u>	C'polis, 3 laws, earliest 23.iii	Hierius et Ardabur
<u>PAPYRI:</u>	*P.Oxy.* XVI 1880.1 (25.ii); 1881.1 (13.iii); *CPR* X 112.1 (14.iv); *P.Oxy.* XVI 1967.1	p.c. DD.NN. Theodosi XII et Valentiniani II perpp. Augg.
	CPR X 113.1 (14.x [ed. 14.ix]; or p.c., 13.x.428)	Fll. Hierius et Artaburius vv.cc.
<u>OTHER:</u>	Socrates, *HE* 7.28	Hierius et Ardaburius

<u>NOTES:</u>

Hierius was PPO Or. 425-428 and 432 (*PLRE* II 557); Ardabur was an Alan, MVM from *ca* 422-427, and father of Aspar cos. 434 (*PLRE* II 137-38). Ardabur is represented on the consular missorium of his son (Delbrueck, *Consulardiptychen* no.35, pp. 154-56). Both consuls were nominated in the East.

Occidentis

<u>FASTI</u>:	Cycl.	Fl. Felix v.c.
	Hyd. Prosp. subscr. ad Cycl. (1,743) Hist. Britt. (3, 209,17) Aug. Aq. Cass. Rav. ExcSang.	Felix et Taurus
<u>LAWS</u>:	Ravenna, 2 laws, earliest 26.ii (*CTh* 7.13.22)	Felix et Taurus
<u>INSCR.</u>:	**ROME**: *ICUR* n.s. II 6078 = *ILCV* 3318B (15?.iii; p.c. poss.); *ICUR* n.s. II 5721 (ix-xii; p.c. poss.; frag.; Gk.); *ICUR* n.s. I 2111a; *ICUR* n.s. I 732 (vv.cc.; frag.); *ICUR* n.s. V 13395 (p.c. poss.)	Fll. Felix et Taurus
	ITALY: *NotScav* 1893, 289 = *RendPontAccad* 22 (1946-47) 227-28, no.1 (Syracuse; 5.ii; frag.; Gk.)	Taurus et Felix vv.cc.
	RendPontAccad 22 (1946-47) 228 no.1 (Syracuse; frag.; Gk.)	Felix et Taurus
	DALMATIA: *Forsch.Salona* III 20 = *ILCV* 151 (Salona; 9?.x)	Felix et Taurus vv.cc.
<u>OTHER</u>:	Caelestinus, *Epp.* 4 (*PL* 50.436) (26.vii)	Fll. Felix et Taurus vv.cc.
	Consular diptych of Felix (Delbrueck, no.3 = Volbach, no.2)	

<u>NOTES</u>:

Felix was MVM in the West from 425-430 (*PLRE* II 461-62); Taurus was son of Aurelian, cos. 400, and PPO Or. 443-444 and 445 (*PLRE* II 1056-57). That Constantius was not part of Felix's name (contra *PLRE*) was shown already by De Rossi, *ICUR* II, p.307 n.5.

Orientis

<u>FASTI:</u>	Marcell. Heracl. Pasch.	Felix et Taurus
<u>LAWS:</u>	15 laws from C'polis:	
	(1) *CTh* 5.1.9 (20.ii)	Taurus et qui fuerit nuntiatus (some MSS: et Felix)
	(2) *CTh* 6.27.22 (31.i); 2.3.1; 3.5.13; 4.6.8 (all 20.ii);	Taurus et Felix
	(3) 10 laws, of which the earliest (again 31.i) is *CTh* 6.2.26 and three others (*CTh* 3.7.3; 3.13.14; *CJ* 6.61.2) are again 20.ii (the rest later)	Felix et Taurus
<u>PAPYRI:</u>	*P.Flor.* III 314.1 (27.iv); *P.Vindob.Tandem* 6.13	p.c. Fll. Hieri et Ardaburis vv.cc.
<u>OTHER:</u>	Socrates, *HE* 7.29; *ACO* II.5, pp. 99.18 (retrosp.ref.), 101.20 (1.iv; retrosp.ref.)	Felix et Taurus

<u>NOTES:</u>

There could be no clearer illustration of the retroactive correction of laws (cf. Seeck, *Reg.* 22), for this year in at least two stages. (1) It was at least 20.ii before Felix's name was proclaimed in the East. The numerous other laws dated on or before that day by their formulas must all have been "corrected". (2) When Felix was proclaimed, to start with (it seems) his name was simply added to Taurus', in second place (as was to become the norm with late-arriving western consuls in the East). What led to (3), confirmed by all the eastern fasti (including the source of Socrates), eastern concession of Felix's priority? In all probability Felix protested that, as Gratian had laid down in 382 (*CTh* 6.6.1), consuls with the patriciate took precedence over consuls without. As Felix's diptych makes clear, he was already patrician before he became consul, whereas Taurus did not become patrician till 433/4 (*PLRE* II 1057). Only contemporaries would have bothered about such a detail, so this stage of the correction must be contemporary. But neither stage was carried out very systematically. It is possible that Cycl. indicates that Felix was proclaimed alone in the West at the start, but there is no other evidence that this happened, and if the one Syracusan inscription is not just a product of negligence, it suggests there a process like that in the East. For other such disputes over priority, see note on 381.

Occidentis

<u>FASTI</u>:	Hyd. ExcSang. Prosp. Cycl. Aug. Aq. Cass. Rav.	Florentius et Dionysius
<u>LAWS</u>:	*CTh* 11.1.35 (14.ii); 11.1.34 + 11.30.68 (25.ii); 12.6.32 (27.ii); 12.1.185-186 (27.iv)	p.c. Felicis et Tauri (vv.cc.)
	CJ 1.14.4 (11.vi)	Florentius et Dionysius
<u>INSCR.</u>:	**ROME:** *ICUR* n.s. II 4889 = *ILCV* 3504 adn. (26.ii/28.iv); *AE* 1973, 49	p.c. Felicis et Tauri vv.cc.
	ITALY: *CIL* XI 4971 (Spoleto, Reg. VI)	
<u>OTHER</u>:	Caelestinus, *Epp.* 5 (*PL* 50.437) (21.vii)	Fll. Florentius et Dionysius vv.cc.

Orientis

<u>FASTI:</u>	Marcell. Heracl. Pasch.	Florentius et Dionysius
<u>LAWS:</u>	C'polis, 3 laws, earliest *CTh* 1.1.5 (26.iii)	Florentius et Dionysius
<u>PAPYRI:</u>	*PSI* III 245.1 (16.i; pap. has cos. for p.c.); *P.Wash.Univ.* 36.1* (9.v; cos. also poss., but less likely); *P.Rainer Cent.* 122.1 (19.ix)	p.c. Fll. Felicis et Tauri vv.cc.
<u>OTHER:</u>	*ACO* I.5, p.65.38	Florentius et Dionysius vv.cc.

<u>NOTES:</u>

Florentius held six prefectures in the East between 422 and 449 (*PLRE* II 478-80); Dionysius was MVM in the East from 428 to 435/40 (*PLRE* II 365-66).

It is puzzling that the two eastern consuls were apparently disseminated so late in the West, the more so since it must have been by prior agreement that Theodosius designated both (see above, p.18); moreover, they appear so far only as p.c. in the papyri, which use the p.c. of 428 as late as September; so eastern dissemination was also late. No western inscriptions use the consuls of 429 during 429, though none is demonstrably later than 26.ii. Under the circumstances, it is possible that they were actually proclaimed late, and even that the earlier p.c.'s in the western laws reflect authentic usage at Ravenna. Yet it is difficult to believe that the western court was dating by p.c. as late as 27.iv, and when it is added that four of the laws are addressed to the proconsul of Africa and the other two to the PPO of Italy and Africa, the possibility must be allowed that all six reflect usage in Africa, not Ravenna. As was shown in Chapter 7, it was normal for Africa to date by p.c. in the early months of the year.

Occidentis

<u>FASTI</u>:	Hyd. Prosp. Aug. (Val. IV) Aq. Cass.	Theodosius XIII et Valentinianus III
	Cycl.	Theodosius VII et Valentinianus III
<u>LAWS</u>:	Ravenna, 2 laws, earliest *CTh* 12.6.33 (15.ii)	DD.NN. Theodosius XIII et Valentinianus III Augg.
<u>INSCR.</u>:	**ROME:** *ICUR* n.s. II 4890 = *ILCV* 1464 adn. (10.i; Plac.); *ICUR* n.s. II 4514 = *ILCV* 3754F (2-7.v; om. XIII, Augg.; frag.); *ICUR* n.s. II 6079 = *ILCV* 2943 adn. + add. (16.viii; om. DD.NN., Augg.); *ICUR* n.s. I 2113 = *ILCV* 3504 adn. (16.ix); *ICUR* n.s. VII 17558 = *ILCV* 4146F (frag.); *ICUR* n.s. IV 11148 (frag.)	DD.NN. Theodosius XIII et (Placidus) Valentinianus III Augg.
	ITALY: *AE* 1977, 204 (nr. Nola, Reg. I; 24.xii; om. DD.NN., Augg.)	
	DALMATIA: *CIL* III 13124* = *ILCV* 3870 (Salona; 11.ix; numerals do not match up)	D.N. Theodosius Aug. XIII et Valentinianus Aug. II
<u>OTHER</u>:	Caelestinus, *Epp.* 11,13,14,12 = *Coll.Veron.* 1,2,5,6 (*ACO* I.2, pp. 6.31; 12.18; 20.25; 22.20) (10.viii)	Theodosius XIII et Valentinianus III Augg.

Orientis

<u>FASTI:</u>	Marcell. Heracl. Pasch. (Aug., iun. Aug.)	Theodosius (Aug.) XIII et Valentinianus (iun. Aug.) III
<u>LAWS:</u>	*CTh* 10.10.34 (22.ii) and 6.27.23 (16.iv), both C'polis	Theodosius Aug. XIII et qui fuerit nuntiatus
	CTh 12.6.33 (C'polis, 31.xii)	(DD.NN.) Theodosius XIII et Valentinianus III (Augg.)
<u>PAPYRI:</u>	*P.Oxy.* XVI 1957.1 (28.iii); *PSI* XII 1239.1 (18.ix); *BGU* XII 2138.1 (16.xi); *P.Mich.* XV 730.1	p.c. Fll. Florentii et Dionysii vv.cc.
<u>COINS:</u>	W. Hahn (see 425) 112 no.7 (C'polis)	Theodosius, cons. image on obv., cons. image of Theod. and Valentinian on rev. of solidi
<u>OTHER:</u>	Socrates, *HE* 7.30	Theodosius XIII et Valentinianus III
	Theodosius to Cyril of Alexandria (*ACO* I.1.1, p.116.7) (19.xi)	DD.NN. Theodosius XIII et Valentinianus III Augg.
	ACO I.5, p.39.21 (date of sermon of Nestorius: 6.xii)	Theodosius XIII et Valentinianus III Augg.

<u>NOTES:</u>

The consuls were the emperors and thus presumably known to both courts in advance. In the West, dissemination appears to have been prompt. In the East, on the other hand, we find a provisional formula in laws issued as late as the middle of April. And in Egypt, not even a provisional formula had been disseminated by the middle of November, when we still find the p.c. of 429 in use.

Occidentis

<u>FASTI</u>:	Hyd. Prosp. Cycl. Aug. Aq. Cass.	Bassus et Antiochus
<u>LAWS</u>:	*CTh* 11.1.36 (Ravenna, 29.iv)	Bassus et Antiochus
<u>INSCR.</u>:	**ROME:** *ICUR* n.s. I 3232 = *ILCV* 3505 (24.i)	p.c. DD.NN. Theodosi Aug. XIII et Valentiniani III
	ICUR I 672* (18.ii/20.iv); *ICUR* n.s. II 6081 = *ILCV* 2921 (11.iv); *ICUR* n.s. II 6082 (22.iv); *ICUR* I 669 = *ILCV* 2928 adn. (4.viii; om. Auch.; v.c.); *ICUR* n.s. VII 17543 (18.xii); *ICUR* n.s. I 47*; *ICUR* n.s. VII 17541c*; *ICUR* n.s. I 3226* (frag.); *ICUR* I 675*; *ICUR* I 676* (om. Auch.; p.c. poss.)	Anicius Auchenius Bassus (v.c.)
	ICUR n.s. II 6080 (29.i); *ICUR* n.s. VIII 23447 = *ILCV* 1718 (6/7.viii); *AE* 1903, 212 (2.xi; om. v.c.)	Fl. Bassus v.c.
	ICUR n.s. VIII 23446 = *ILCV* 3244 (19.v); *ICUR* n.s. II 4891 = *CIG* IV 9730 (4.vi; Gk.); *AE* 1971, 24 + *CIL* VI 1783 (13.ix; vv.cc.); *ICUR* n.s. II 4892 = *ILCV* 107 adn. (14.ix-15.x)	Bassus et Antiochus
	ITALY: *CIL* X 7168* = *ILCV* 2933B (Syracuse; 21.xi); *AE* 1952, 183 (Milan; ii-iii; or p.c.?; frag.)	Fll. Bassus et Antiochus vv.cc.
	GAUL: *CIL* XIII 2354 = *ILCV* 1703 (Lyons)	p.c. Theodosi XIII
	DALMATIA: *CIL* III 9516 = *ILCV* 745A (Salona; 3.x); *CIL* III 9517 (cf. 12858) = *ILCV* 122 (Salona; p.c. poss.)	Bassus et Antiochus
<u>OTHER</u>:	Caelestinus, *Epp.* 16 = *Coll.Veron.* 10 (*ACO* I.2, p.26.7) (7.v); *Epp.* 18,17,19 = *Coll.Veron.* 7,8,9 (*ACO* I.2, pp.24.31; 25.15; 26.10; 27.7) (8.v)	Bassus et Antiochus (vv.cc.)

Orientis

<u>FASTI:</u>	Marcell. Heracl. Pasch.	Antiochus et Bassus
<u>LAWS:</u>	*CTh* 9.45.4 (C'polis, 23.iii; some MSS give Ant. et Bass.)	Antiochus v.c. et qui fuerit nuntiatus
<u>PAPYRI:</u>	*MPER* n.s. XV 95.21 (6.vii; writing exercise or school text); *P.Köln* V 234.1 (1.ix)	p.c. DD.NN. Theodosii XIII et Valentiniani III perpp. Augg.
<u>OTHER:</u>	Socrates, *HE* 7.34, 37	Bassus et Antiochus
	Letter of Theodosius to the Council of Ephesus (*ACO* I.1.3, p.10.22) (29.vi)	Fl. Antiochus et qui nuntiatus fuerit
	Council of Ephesus: *ACO* I.1.2, p.3.3 = 3, p.60.5 (22.vi)	p.c. Fl. Theodosii XIII et Fl. Valentiniani III
	ACO II.1.1, p.189.31; I.1.3, pp.53.7; 59.9; 15.12; 21.6; I.1.7, pp.84.31; 118.18 (10,11,16,17,22.vii and 31.viii)	p.c. Fl. Theodosii XIII et Fl. Valentiniani III perpp. Augg.
	ACO I.4,p.33.35 (Candidianus comes) (26.vi)	Antiochus

<u>NOTES:</u>

Bassus was a Roman aristocrat and PPO Ital. 426 and 435 (*PLRE* II 220-21); Antiochus was PPO Or. in 430-431 and one of the compilers of the Theodosian Code (*PLRE* II 103-04).

Proclamation was late in the East; the same was presumably true of the West at least for Antiochus. More interestingly, two months after Theodosius wrote from Constantinople to the Council of Ephesus *Fl. Antiocho e.q.n.f.*, and his representative dated by Antiochus in a contribution, documents at the Council in Ephesus itself continued to be dated by the p.c. of 430. Roman inscriptions with only Bassus are assigned to 431 rather than 408 because in 408 Philippus was known in the West by 23 January, whereas Antiochus was disseminated late even in the East. It is more likely that some later Roman inscriptions continued the ingrained habit of using only Bassus than that Philippus was dropped at random in some. In any event Roman omission of an eastern consul is far more normal after 410 than before.

There is no obvious significance in Socrates' use of the western sequence.

Occidentis

<u>FASTI</u>:	Hyd. Prosp. Aq. Cass. Aug. Haun.	Aetius et Valerius
	Cycl.	Antiochus Valerius
<u>LAWS</u>:	*CTh* 6.23.3 (Ravenna, 24.iii)	Aetius et Valerius
<u>INSCR.</u>:	**ROME:** *ICUR* n.s. I 1466* = *ILCV* 412 (10.iii); *ICUR* n.s. II 4173 = *ILCV* 3333 (10.vi; om. v.c.); *ICUR* n.s. II 6083 = *ILCV* 2880 adn. (16.vi)	Aetius v.c.
	AE 1931, 93 (3?.iv; Rome or environs)	Aetius et Valerius
	ITALY: *CIL* V 7530 = *ILCV* 343 (Acqui, Reg. IX; 5.iii)	Aetius et Valerius vv.cc.
<u>OTHER</u>:	Caelestinus, *Epp.* 23,24,25,22 = *Coll.Veron.* 23-26 (*ACO* I.2, pp.90.12; 91.22; 98.4; 101.17) (15.iii)	Aetius et Valerius (vv.cc.)

Orientis

<u>FASTI:</u>	Marcell. Heracl. Pasch.	Valerius et Aetius
<u>LAWS:</u>	*CTh* 9.45.5 (C'polis, 28.iii)	Valerius et qui fuerit nuntiatus
	CTh 6.24.11 (C'polis, 11.vi)	Valerius et Aetius vv.cc.
<u>PAPYRI:</u>	*BGU* XII 2139.1 (v); *PSI* *XVII Congr.* 29.1 (31.viii)	p.c. Fll. Antiochi et Bassi vv.cc.
	BGU XII 2140.1 (xi-xii)	Fl. Valerius [

<u>NOTES:</u>

Aetius was MVM in the West from 433-454, cos. II in 437, cos. III in 446 (*PLRE* II 21-29). Valerius was a brother of the Empress Eudocia and magister officium in 435 (*PLRE* II 1145).

Dissemination was late on both sides, but in Italy we see some overlap of Aetius alone and Aetius with Valerius. In the East, there is no secure (and demonstrably uncorrected) evidence for Aesemination.

Occidentis

FASTI:	Hyd. Prosp. Aug. Aq. Cass.	Theodosius XIV et Maximus
	Cycl.	Maximus II
LAWS:	none	
INSCR.:	**ROME:** *ICUR* n.s. VII 17759 (9.v); *ICUR* n.s. I 1262 = *ILCV* 2608 (17.vi); *ICUR* n.s. V 13957* (24.ix)	Petronius Maximus v.c.
	ICUR n.s. I 223 (8-15.x; much rest.); *ICUR* n.s. II 4895 = *ILCV* 207 (31.xii; frag.); *ICUR* n.s. VII 19985	D.N. Theodosius Aug. XIV et Petronius Maximus v.c.
	ITALY: *IG* XIV 85 (Syracuse; 27.vi; Gk.)	Theodosius XIV
	Siculorum Gymnasium (1961) 196 fig. 21* (Catania; frag.)	Theodosius [Aug. XIV] et Maximus v.c.
COINS:	A. & E. Alföldi, *Die Kontorniat-Medaillons* I no. 461: Contorniate medallion with bust of Valentinian III on obv., consul with mappa on rev.	Petronius Maxsimus v.c. cons.
OTHER:	Tjäder, *Nichtlit.Pap.* II 59 i.10 (post 22.ii; p.c. poss.)	D.N. Theodosius Aug. XIV et Maximus v.c.
	Pope Xystus (*ACO* I.2, pp.108.30; 110.8) (17.ix)	Theodosius XIV et Maximus

NOTES:

In Rome, Maximus was the only consul known through September (and appears alone in an Italian inscription from the p.c. in 434). It is possible that the curious formula of Cycl. represents this as well. It is possible that the Ravenna papyrus is a p.c. date, and in any case the text may well be a retrospective reference which does not reflect contemporary usage.

Orientis

FASTI:	Marcell. Heracl. (om. Aug.) Pasch.	Theodosius (Aug.) XIV et Maximus
LAWS:	*CTh* 11.28.16 (no prov., 22.iv); *CTh* 8.1.17 = *CJ* 1.51.9 (C'polis, 3.vii)	Theodosius Aug. XIV et Maximus
PAPYRI:	none	
INSCR.:	*Corinth* VIII.1 (1931) 145* (Corinth; vi)	p.c. Fl. Valerii v.c.
OTHER:	Socrates, *HE* 7.39	Theodosius XIV et Maximus

NOTES:

Petronius Maximus was a Roman aristocrat, PVR 420-421, PVR II and PPO 421/439, PPO II 439-441, cos. II in 443 and Augustus 455 (*PLRE* II 749-51). The Corinthian inscription suggests that Theodosius' consulate was disseminated late even in the East. Seeck restored *CTh* 7.8.15 as *Theodosio Aug. XIII<I> et qui fuerit nuntiatus* on 22.ii of this year, but there is no other evidence for such a phrase in this year.

Occidentis

FASTI: Hyd. Prosp. Cycl. Aq. Cass. Rav.   Aspar et Areobindus

                Aug.   Areobindus et Aspar

LAWS: none

INSCR.:   **ROME:** *ICUR* n.s. VII 17560 = *ILCV*   (Fll.) Aspar et
                1713 (22.iii); *ICUR* n.s. II   Areobindus vv.cc.
                6084 = *ILCV* 2974A adn. (29.iii;
                om. Areob.); *ICUR* n.s. I 88 =
                ILCV 843* (17.iii/17.vii); *ICUR*
                n.s. I 989 = *ILCV* 2928 adn.
                (28.ix; Fll.); *ICUR* n.s. II 4897
                = *ILCV* 2946A adn. (13.x); *ICUR*
                n.s. V 13398; *ICUR* n.s. V 13397
                (p.c. poss.)

                ITALY: *CIL* IX 1368 = *ILCV*   p.c. Petroni Maximi v.c.
                3027A* (nr. Aeclanum, Reg.
                II; 12.i)

                IG XIV 455 (Catania; Gk.)   p.c. Theodosi perp.
                                                             Aug. XIV et Maximi v.c.

                NotScav 1931, 370 (Catania;   Aspar et Areobindus
                vi-vii; frag.)

                CIL V 7408a = *ILCV* 3527C adn.   Areobindus et Aspar
                (Dertona, Reg. IX; 24.vii; frag.);
                CIL V 6201 (Milan, Reg. XI)

                DALMATIA: *AE* 1912, 40 =   Aspar et Areobindus
                ILCV 250 adn. (Salona; 5.xi)

OTHER: Silver missorium commemorating cos.
                of Aspar (Delbrueck, no. 35)

Orientis

<u>FASTI:</u>	Marcell. Heracl. Pasch.	Areobindus et Aspar
<u>LAWS:</u>	*CTh* 5.12.3 = 11.28.15 (18.vi) and 14.16.3 (26.xi), both C'polis; *CTh* 5.3.1 (no prov., 15.xii)	Areobindus et Aspar
<u>PAPYRI:</u>	*P.Lond.* V 1777.1 (7.ix); *ZPE* 66 (1986) 121 (frag.)	p.c. D.N. Theodosi perp. Aug. XIV et Fl. Maximi v.c.
	P.Oxy. XVI 1879.1* (Lat.)	Fll. Areobindus et Ardabur vv.cc.
<u>OTHER:</u>	Socrates, *HE* 7.40; Jo. Malalas, p.364B	Areobindus et Aspar

<u>NOTES:</u>

Areobindus was MVM in the East from 434-449, father of Dagalaifus cos. 461 and grandfather of Areobindus cos. 506 (*PLRE* II 145-46); Aspar was MVM in the East from (at least) 431-471, son of Ardabur cos. 427 and father of Ardabur cos. 447 (*PLRE* II 164-69).

Although an eastern general, he was campaigning in Africa against the Vandals when he became consul (at Carthage) and was therefore officially reckoned western consul (*PLRE* II 166).

Dissemination was messy all over. Early on, we find a p.c. of Maximus at Aeclanum, but a p.c. of Theodosius and Maximus at Catania and in Egypt. Two inscriptions from Italy give the eastern order. The only papyrus with the new consuls is undated. For the occurrence of an eastern order in Aug. see the notes to 448.

Occidentis

FASTI: Hyd. Prosp. Cycl. (Th. X, Val. II)   Theodosius XV et
          Aug. Reges Vand. (3, 458) Aq.   Valentinianus IV
          Cass. Rav. (Th. XVI)

LAWS: none

INSCR.:   **ROME:** *AE* 1906, 136* (cf. *ILCV*   p.c. Asparis et
          3042A adn.);   Areobindi vv.cc.

          ICUR n.s. II 4174 = *ILCV* 1200   DD.NN. Theodosius XV et
          (11.iii; adds vv.cc.; om. DD.NN.);   Placidus Valentinianus IV
          ICUR n.s. II 4898 (20.v; om.   Augg.
          Augg.; p.c. poss.); *CIL* VI 1724 =
          ILS 2950 (30.vii; om. Plac.,
          Augg.); *ICUR* n.s. I 529 = *ILCV*
          629 (30.xii; om. Plac.); *ICUR* I
          688 (om. Augg.); *ICUR* n.s. VIII
          28017 (om. IV); *ICUR* n.s. I 990
          = *ILCV* 3505A (frag.); *ICUR* n.s.
          VII 17561* (om. Augg.)

          ITALY: *CIL* X 7113 = *ILCV* 1357   Theodosius XV et
          (Catania; 17.iii; Fl. Val.);   (Fl.) (Placidus)
          AE 1933, 25 = Agnello, *Silloge*   Valentinianus IV (Augg.)
          96 (Catania; 1.iv; Gk.); *CIL* X
          3298 = *ILCV* 1018 (Pozzuoli, Reg. I;
          13.v); *CIL* XI 270 = *ILCV* 1308A
          (Ravenna, Reg. X; 29.ix; Plac.;
          om. IV); *CIL* V 6272 = *ILCV* 2828
          (Milan, Reg. XI; 23.x); *Kokalos*
          28-29 (1982-83) 19 no.66
          (Catania; Augg.)

          IG XIV 189 (Syracuse; 6.v; Gk.; see   XV et IV
          Ferrua, *Kokalos* 28-29 [1982-83] 19)

          DALMATIA: *CIL* III 2657 + add.   DD.NN. Theodosius XV
          (p.1032) = III 13962* = *ILCV* 307   et Placidus Valentinianus
          (Salona; 22.xi)   IV perpp. Augg.

          GAUL: *CIL* XII 5494 = *ILS* 806   DD.NN. Theodosius et Valentinianus
          (Arles)   pii felices victores ac triumph.
                                                   semp. Augg. XV [et IV]

          [Continued on next page]

404

Orientis

FASTI:	Marcell. Heracl. (Val. XIV) Pasch. (Aug., iun. Aug.)	Theodosius (Aug.) XV et Valentinianus (iun. Aug.) IV
LAWS:	4 laws from C'polis, earliest *CTh* 6.28.8 (29.i), latest *CTh* 10.8.5 (9.x)	(D.N.) Theodosius Aug. XV et qui fuerit nuntiatus
	CTh 16.10.25 (14.xi) and 1.1.6 (20.xii), both C'polis	(DD.NN.) Theodosius XV et Valentinianus IV (Augg.)
PAPYRI:	*Pap.Lugd.Bat.* XIII 15.1 (26.i); *P.Stras.* I 1.1* (20.viii; cos. for p.c.); *P.Flor.* III 315.1 (ix-x?)	p.c. Fll. Areobindi et Asparis vv.cc.
	CPR X 114.1 (p.c. possible)	[DD.] NN. Theodosius XV et [Valentinianus IV perpp. Augg.]
COINS:	Hahn (see 425) 128 (Bank Leu [Zürich] 28 April 1975, 540) (C'polis)	Theodosius, cons. image on obv. and rev. of solidus
OTHER:	Letter of Proclus, Bp. of C'polis: *ACO* IV.2, p.205.41	Piiss. Theodosius XV et Valentinianus IV

NOTES:

The preservation of four uncorrected laws with *et qui fuerit nuntiatus* in the *CTh* as late as 9.x is curious. One of them, *CTh* 10.8.5, was taken over into *CJ* 10.10.5 in regularized form.

[Continued from preceding page]

COINS:	Biróné-Sey (see 425) no.31 (Rome), no.32 (Ravenna)	Valentinian, cons. image on obv. and rev. of solidi
OTHER:	Xystus, *Epp.* 8 (*PL* 50.612) (8.vii)	Theodosius XV et Valentinianus IV Augg.

Occidentis

FASTI:	Hyd. Prosp. Cycl. Aq. Cass. Rav.	Isidorus et Senator
	Aug.	p.c. id est Isidorus et Senator
LAWS:	none	
INSCR.:	**ROME:** *ICUR* n.s. I 733 = *ILCV* 3115A (18.viii; names inverted); *ICUR* n.s. IX 24316 (10.ix); *ICUR* n.s. VII 17562 = *ILCV* 265 (14.ix-15.x; om. Fll., vv.cc.); *ICUR* n.s. II 4903 (frag.)	Fll. Isidorus et Senator vv.cc.
	ITALY: *CIL* XI 4330 (Terni, Reg. VI)	p.c. DD.NN. Theodosi XV et Plac. Valentiniani IV Augg.
	Arch.Stor.Calabr.Luc. 24 (1955) 17 (Vibo Valentia, Reg. III; vii-viii); *CIL* XI 1691 = *ILCV* 258 (Florence, Reg. VII; 25.ix)	Isidorus et Senator vv.cc.

Orientis

FASTI: Marcell. Heracl. Pasch.   Isidorus et Senator

LAWS: C'polis, 5 laws, earliest 8.iii   Isidorus et Senator
             (*CTh* 10.20.18); Apamea, 1 law

PAPYRI: *PSI* VI 708.1 (2.xi)   p.c. DD.NN. Theodosi XV et
                                                           Valentiniani IV perpp. Augg.

OTHER: Socrates, *HE* 7.44   Isidorus et Senator

             ACO I.1.3, p.67.11
             (letter of Theodosius to Isidorus,
             "PPO et consul")

NOTES:

Anthemius Isidorus, son of Anthemius cos. 405, PPO Or. 435-436 (*PLRE* II 631-33); Fl. Senator, influential adviser of Theodosius II, but never held any high office (*PLRE* II 990-91). Since both were easterners, the order is the same in both parts of the empire (except for one Roman inscription which inverts them). The dissemination of names was probably late throughout the empire, but the evidence is too scanty to be certain.

The peculiar entry in Aug. (cf. 413) presumably reflects a correction of an original p.c. entry.

Occidentis

<u>FASTI</u>:	Hyd. Prosp. Cycl. Aug. Aq. Cass. Rav.	Aetius II et Sigisvultus
<u>LAWS</u>:	none	
<u>INSCR.</u>:	**ROME:** *AE* 1982, 73 (17.vi; only Sigisvultus); *ICUR* n.s. I 443 (18.v/17.vi; frag.); *ICUR* n.s. I 530 = *ILCV* 3058 adn. (14.viii- 13.ix); *ICUR* n.s. IV 11150 (frag.; om. vv.cc.); *ICUR* n.s. I 3234 (frag.; p.c. poss.); *ICUR* n.s. VII 17563 (p.c. poss.)	Fll. Aetius II et Sigisvultus vv.cc.
	ITALY: *CIL* IX 1366 (Mirabella, Reg. II; 14.iv-1.v; frag.)	
	DALMATIA: *CIL* III 9518 = *Forsch.* *Salona* II 172 = *ILCV* 455 (Salona; 15.x; om. Fll.); *Forsch.Salona* II 171 (Salona; om. II; frag.; Gk.)	
<u>OTHER</u>:	Xystus, *Epp.* 9,10 (*PL* 50.613; 618) (18.xii)	Aetius iterum et Sigisvultus

Orientis

<u>FASTI:</u>	Marcell. Heracl. Pasch.	Aetius II et Sigisvultus
<u>LAWS:</u>	*CTh* 6.23.4 (C'polis, 16.iii)	p.c. Isidori et Senatoris vv.cc.
<u>PAPYRI:</u>	none*	

<u>NOTES:</u>

Sigisvultus was MVM in the West from (at least) 440 to 448 (*PLRE* II 1010). Both consuls were western; for Aetius, see 432. It is difficult to believe that the eastern court was dating by p.c. in March; surely an error, cf. above, p.83.

Occidentis

FASTI: Geneal. (1,196 c.628b) Hyd.   Theodosius XVI et Faustus
                VindPost. Prosp. Aug. Aq. Cass.

LAWS: *Nov.Val.* 1.1 (Ravenna, 8.vii)   Theodosius Aug. XVI
                                                         et Faustus v.c.

INSCR.:   **ROME:** *ILCV* 4370 (30.viii;   D.N. Theodosius (Aug.) XVI
                Anic.); *ICUR* n.s. II 4904 =   et (Anicius) (Acilius)
                ILCV 302 (7.x; Aug.); *ICUR* n.s.   (Glabrio) Faustus v.c.
                I 734 = *ILCV* 3737 adn. (Anic.
                Acilius Glabrio Faust.; frag.);
                ICUR n.s. VII 17564 (frag.);
                ICUR n.s. I 2114 (frag.)

                DALMATIA: *CIL* III 14929
                = *ILCV* 3791B (Trogir; 4.vi);
                CIL III 2658* = *ILCV* 4370
                adn. (Salona)

                GAUL: *CIL* XIII 11207 =   Theodosius XVI
                ILCV 2783B (Lyons; 5.ix)   et Faustus v.c.

                TUNISIA: *I.Lat.Tun.* 1126 =   Theodosius XVI et Faustus
                Ennabli, *Inscr.Fun.Chrét.Basil.*
                Carthage 46 (Carthage; p.c. poss.)

OTHER: Gesta Senatus de Theodosiano
                publicando (*CTh* ed. Mommsen I.ii),
                pp. 1-4 passim

Orientis

FASTI:	Marcell. Heracl.	Theodosius (Aug.) XVI
	Pasch. (Aug.)	et Faustus
LAWS:	*NovTheod* 3 (31.i) and 1	Theodosius Aug. XVI
	(15.ii), both C'polis	et qui fuerit nuntiatus
	NovTheod 4 (25.ii) and 5.1	Theodosius Aug. XVI
	(9.v), both C'polis	
	NovTheod 6 (C'polis, 4.xi)	Theodosius Aug. XVI et
		Faustus v.c.
PAPYRI:	*P.Köln* II 103.1 (xi-xii)	D.N. Theodosius perp. Aug.
		XVI et Fl. Faustus v.c.
OTHER:	Socrates, *HE* 6.6, 7.45;	(Theodosius XVI)
	Halkin, *Douze récits* 277 f.	
	(27.i)	

NOTES:

Faustus was a Roman aristocrat, PVR three times and PPO twice between 408/423 and 442 (*PLRE* II 452-54); *ICUR* n.s. I 734 gives his name with unusual fullness.

There is no early evidence from the West. Faustus' name did not reach the East till rather late. Socrates does not give an actual formula; it is thus not clear if he did not bother to mention Faustus or if he did not know of him.

Occidentis

<u>FASTI</u>:	Hyd. VindPost. Prosp. Veron. Aug. Reges Vand. (3,458) Aq. Cass.	Theodosius XVII et Festus
<u>LAWS</u>:	*NovVal* 3, Ravenna, 28.viii	D.N. Theodosius Aug. XVII et Festus
<u>INSCR.</u>:	**ROME:** *ICUR* n.s. II 4905 = *ILCV* 570 (11.x)	[D.N. Theo]dosius Aug. XVII et Festus v.c.
	ITALY: *IG* XIV 130 (Syracuse; 24.v; om. D.N.; Gk.); *NotScav* 1895, 480 no.153* (Syracuse; Gk.; frag.)	p.c. D.N. Theodosi XVI et Fausti
	CIL V 6268 = *ILCV* 200b (Milan, Reg. XI; 28.ii)	Festus v.c. et qui de Oriente fuerit nuntiatus
	DALMATIA: *Forsch.Salona* II 174 (frag.)	Theodosius Aug. XVII et Festus
<u>OTHER</u>:	Council at Riez: *Conc.Galliae* (Corp.Christ.Lat. 148), pp.71-72 (29.xi)	Theodosius Aug. XVII et Festus v.c.

Orientis

<u>FASTI:</u>	Marcell. Heracl. Pasch. (Aug.)	Theodosius (Aug.) XVII et Festus
<u>LAWS:</u>	4 laws, from 20.i (*NovTheod* 7.1) to 19.iv (*NovTheod* 10.1,2), all C'polis	(D.N.) Theodosius Aug. XVII
	NovTheod 9 (C'polis, 7.iv)	Theodosius Aug. XVII et qui fuerit nuntiatus
	About 19 laws, all C'polis or prov. unkn., earliest *NovTheod* 5.2 (8.vi); 3 laws in *CJ*, 20.i-3.iv, all give this formula, presumably by retrosp. corr.	(D.N.) Theodosius Aug. XVII et Festus (v.c.)
<u>PAPYRI:</u>	*P.Haun.* III 58.1 (15.v; om. perp. Aug.); *SPP* XX 121.1 (6.vii); *CPR* VI 6.1 (8.vii)	p.c. D.N. Theodosi perp. Aug. XVI et Fl. Fausti v.c.
<u>OTHER:</u>	Socrates, *HE* 7.48	(Theodosius XVII)

<u>NOTES:</u>

Festus is not otherwise identifiable, but is presumably a Roman aristocrat and father of Rufius Postumius Festus cos. 472 (*PLRE* II 467). Once again, dissemination was late on both sides. The dates by Theodosius and Festus in *CJ* are presumably retrospective corrections. Since Socrates twice refers to the "seventeenth consulate of Theodosius" in what is the final chapter of his history, it seems natural to conclude that he laid down his pen before the proclamation of the western consul.

Occidentis

FASTI:	Hyd. VindPost. (om. V) Prosp. (Aug.) Veron. Aug. Aq. Cass. Rav. ('Valerianus')	Valentinianus (Aug.) V et Anatolius
LAWS:	3 laws each from Rome and Ravenna, earliest *NovVal* 4, 24.i	(D.N.) Valentinianus Aug. V et Anatolius (v.c.)
INSCR.:	**ROME:** *ICUR* n.s. VII 19986 (13.vi); *ICUR* n.s. VII 17566 (p.c. poss.); *ICUR* n.s. V 13400* (frag.)	D.N. Valentinianus (perp.) Aug. V et Anatolius v.c.
	ITALY: *CIL* IX 1367 = *ILCV* 3027 (Aeclanum, Reg. II; 29.viii?; om. Aug.); *Civiltà Cattolica* 1964, I, p.34 (Milan, Reg. XI; 20.ix; mostly rest.); *I.Ital.* XI.2, 58 = *ILCV* 674 (Ivrea, Reg. XI; 1.xi?)	
	DALMATIA: *CIL* III 9519 (Salona; 14.viii-1.ix; perp. Aug.); *CIL* III 2658 = *ILCV* 4370 adn. (or p.c.?; frag.)	
	CIG IV 9426* = *Forsch.Salona* II 175 (Salona; 27.ix; Gk.)	Theodosius Aug. XVII et Anatolius

Orientis

FASTI:	Marcell. (om. Aug.) Pasch.	Valentinianus Aug. V et Anatolius
	Heracl.	Anatolius et Valentinianus
LAWS:	C'polis, 5 laws, earliest *CJ* 8.11.21 (22.i); earliest outside *CJ* is *NovTheod* 20 (21.ix)	(D.N.) Valentinianus Aug. V et Anatolius (v.c.)
	NovTheod 19 (C'polis, 20.v)	Anatolius v.c.
PAPYRI:	*P.Harr.* 87.1 (27.vi)	Fl. Anatolius v.c.
OTHER:	C.B. Welles in C.H. Kraeling, ed., *Gerasa* 467 no.273 (inscr.; Fl. Anatolius stratelates et consul in office); *IGLSyr.* XIII 9118	

NOTES:

Anatolius was MVM in the East from 433 to *ca* 446 and 450-451, also distinguished as an ambassador (*PLRE* II 84-86). Up to May or June, only Anatolius was disseminated in the East; the order in Heracl. reflects the fact that Valentinian was added only subsequently. The laws were all corrected except *NovTheod* 19, but the papyri never do show Valentinian's fifth consulate. When he next holds the consulate, however, in 445, it was counted as his sixth.

Occidentis

FASTI:	Hyd. Prosp. Veron. Aug. Aq. Cass. Rav.	Cyrus v.c.
	VindPost.	Cyrus et Anatolius II
LAWS:	*NovVal* 8.2 (27.i) and 10 (20.ii), both Ravenna	p.c. Valentiniani Aug. V et Anatoli v.c.
INSCR.:	**ROME:** *ICUR* n.s. I 736 = *ILCV* 664 (17.iv; DD.NN.; om. v.c.)	p.c. D.N. (Placidi) Valentiniani V et Anatoli v.c.
	ITALY: *CIL* IX 1366* (Aeclanum, Reg. II; 10.vii; Placidus; frag.)	
	GAUL: *IG* XIV 2492 = *Rec.Inscr.Chrét.Gaule* XV 64 (Vienne; 6,7.ii; DD.NN.; Gk.)	
OTHER:	Council at Orange: *Conc.Galliae* (Corp.Christ.Lat. 148), p.78 (8.xi)	Cyrus v.c.

Orientis

FASTI: Marcell. Heracl. Pasch.   Cyrus solus

LAWS: C'polis, 4 laws, earliest   Cyrus v.c.
             NovTheod 7.4 (6.iii)

PAPYRI: *P.Mil.* I 64.1 (6.xii)   p.c. Fl. Anatoli v.c.

             P.Rainer Cent. 94.1 (4.ix;   Fl. Cyrus (Hierax) v.c.
             Hierax); *BGU* II 609.1* (12.xi;
             or 442?)

NOTES:

Cyrus was a well-known poet, PVC 437-441 and PPO Orientis 439-441. In fall 441 he was relieved of all his offices and banished to the bishopric of Cotyaeum in Phrygia (*PLRE* II 336-39 with Cameron in *YCS* 27 [1982] 217-89). He did not suffer *damnatio memoriae*, though the fact that *P.Mil.* I 64.1 reverts to the p.c. of 440 might be interpreted as a sign of caution. The only direct attestation of Cyrus in the West is the Council at Orange, but the evidence for the p.c. of 440 is all relatively early in the year, and there seems no reason to disbelieve the western fasti. There was, moreover, no western consul appointed. Cyrus was designated as early as 5.iv.440 (*CJ* 1.14.7).

Occidentis

FASTI: Hyd.   Dioscorus

                Aq. (Q)   Dioscorus v.c.

                Prosp.   Dioscorus v.c. cons.
                                                        et Eudoxius

                Aq. (GLS) Veron.   Dioscorus et Eudoxius
                Aug. Cass. Rav.

                VindPost.   Dioscorus et Theodosius

LAWS: *NovVal* 2.2 (Rome, 13.viii)   Dioscorus v.c.

                NovVal 7.2 (Spoleto, 27.ix)   Dioscorus et Eudoxius

INSCR.:   **ROME:** *ICUR* n.s. II 5866 (8-   (Fl.) Dioscorus v.c.
                13.viii; Fl.); *ICUR* n.s. VIII
                20818 (15.viii); *ILCV* 3181
                (13.x; om. v.c.); *ICUR* n.s. VIII
                20819 = *ILCV* 266 (5.xi); *ICUR*
                n.s. I 737 = *ILCV* 2971A (Fl.);
                ICUR n.s. V 13403 (Fl.; p.c. poss.)

                ITALY: *CIL* V 6402 = *ILCV* 770
                (Lodi, Reg. XI; 25.v); *CIL* X
                1340 = *ILCV* 1013 (Nola, Reg. I;
                11.ix; Fl.); *IG* XIV 2350 = *CIL*
                V 1624 (Venice, Reg. X; 2.x; Gk.);
                CIL X 1519 = *ILCV* 1443 (Naples,
                Reg. I; 22.x); *CIL* V 6293 (Milan,
                Reg. XI; p.c. poss.)

                DALMATIA: *CIL* III 12860 right
                = *ILCV* 1245b (Salona; 7.ix); *CIL*
                III 12860 left = *ILCV* 1245a =
                Forsch.Salona II 176 (Salona; 24.viii)

OTHER: Council at Vaison: *Conc.Galliae*   Dioscorus v.c.
                (Corp.Christ.Lat. 148), p.96 (13.xi)

Orientis

FASTI: Marcell. Heracl. Pasch.   Eudoxius et Dioscorus

LAWS: 5 laws, 3 from C'polis;   Eudoxius et Dioscorus
                        earliest *CJ* 10.32.60
                        (C'polis, 25.ii)

PAPYRI: *SB* XIV 11434.1 (ii-iii;   [p.c.] Fl. Cyri v.c.
                        p.c. necessary rest.);
                        cf. 441 for *BGU* II 609*

NOTES:

    Dioscorus is proved by the western inscriptions to be the western consul, but is otherwise totally unknown (*PLRE* II 368); and Eudoxius is hardly better known: either the eastern CRP of 440 or the CSL of 427 (*PLRE* II 412-13, nos. 6 and 5). There seems no good reason why Eudoxius' name should make such a late appearance in the West. Relations between the two courts must have been satisfactory for the East to have agreed to the West's designating both consuls for 443. Dioscorus appears alone except at court in September, and many of the fasti show Dioscorus by himself; even Prosper (not all of whose MSS include Eudoxius) clearly added him later.

Occidentis

<u>FASTI</u>:	Hyd. VindPost. (om. II) Prosp. Aug. Veron. Aq. Cass. Rav.	Maximus II et Paterius
<u>LAWS</u>:	Rome, 2 laws (earlier *NovVal* 11, 13.iii); Ravenna, 3 laws (earliest *NovVal* 6.2, 25.v)	Maximus II et Paterius (vv.cc.)
<u>INSCR.</u>:	**ROME:** *ICUR* n.s. I 3236* = *ILCV* 2971A adn. (19.ix/13.x?; om. II); *ICUR* n.s. I 738 = *ILCV* 511A (20.x; order rev., num., vv.cc. om.);*ICUR* n.s. II 4516 = *ILCV* 3506 (31.x; om. vv.cc.); *ICUR* n.s. VI 15781 = *ILCV* 4387 adn. (19.xii); *ICUR* n.s. II 4907 (om. vv.cc.; p.c. poss.); *ICUR* n.s. VII 17567 (om. vv.cc.)	Maximus II et Paterius vv.cc.
	DALMATIA: *CIL* III 14304 + add. p.2328[127] = *Forsch.Salona* III 22 (Salona; 2-7.v); *CIL* III 9520, 9521, 12860 left = *ILCV* 1245a (Salona; 13.viii; om. vv.cc.); *CIL* III 12850 add. (=9333; cf. p.2328[127]) = *ILCV* 3042A = *Forsch.Salona* II 177 (Salona; 1.xi); *CIL* III 2659 = *ILCV* 245 (Salona; 28.xi); *CIL* III 13126 + 14299[7] + add. p.2328[127] = *ILCV* 1086 adn. (Salona); *CIL* III 14892 (Salona; rev. order; year uncert.); *Forsch.Salona* III 23 (frag.)	
<u>OTHER</u>:	Tjäder, *Nichtlit.Pap.* 1.57 = *ChLA* XX 705 (Ravenna, ix-xii)	Maximus iterum
	Leo, *Epp.* 4 (*PL* 54.614) (10.x)	Maximus II et Paterius vv.cc.

Orientis

FASTI:	Marcell. Heracl.	Maximus et Paterius
	Pasch.	Maximus II et Paterius
LAWS:	*NovTheod* 22.2 (C'polis, 9.iii)	p.c. Dioscori et Eudoxii vv.cc.
	C'polis, 2 laws (earlier *CJ* 1.46.3, 28.i); *NovTheod* 23 (Aphrodisias, 22.v)	Maximus II et Paterius (vv.cc.)
PAPYRI:	*P.Oxy.* VI 913.1 (16.x)	p.c. Fll. Eudoxii et Dioscori vv.cc.
	CPR X 39.1 (13.xi)	Fll. [Ma]x[imus II et Paterius vv.] cc.

NOTES:

Paterius was PPO Ital. in 442 (*PLRE* II 836). For Petronius Maximus, see 433 (cos. I). The evidence for dissemination is again late on both sides (note the Ravenna papyrus). The inscriptions from Rome and Salona with reversed order of names are noteworthy; equally striking is the reversed order of names in the p.c. date in *NovTheod* 22.2. The p.c. was perhaps added in the West (see p.83); it cannot reflect authentic Constantinopolitan usage.

Occidentis

FASTI: Hyd. VindPost. Prosp. (etiam in   Theodosius XVIII
          praescr. 1, 385) Victor Veron.   et Albinus
          Aug. Aq. Cass.

LAWS: *NovVal* 6.3 (14.vii) and 14   (D.N.) Theodosius Aug.
          (11.ix), both Ravenna   XVIII et Albinus v.c.

INSCR.:   **ROME:** *ICUR* n.s. VII 17568 = *ILCV*   Albinus v.c.
          3003C (1.iv); *ICUR* n.s. I 1359*
          = *ILCV* 3468 (4.vi/5.vii); *ICUR*
          n.s. II 4517* (19.viii; frag.);
          ICUR n.s. VIII 20820* = *ILCV*
          3727E (7.ix); *ICUR* n.s. II 4990*
          = *ILCV* 2766 (14.ix-15.x?);
          ICUR n.s. II 4178* = *ILCV* 252a

          ICUR n.s. II 4908 + 5724 = *ILCV*   D.N. Theodosius Aug. XVIII
          3506 adn. (14.ix); *ICUR* I   et Albinus v.c.
          902* (14.ix-1.x; frag.); *ICUR*
          n.s. II 4909 (frag.)

          ITALY: *CIL* V 7772* = *ILCV*   Albinus v.c.
          1243 (Genoa, Reg. IX; 26.iv);
          CIL XI 2585* = *ILCV* 259
          (Chiusi, Reg. VII; 4.vi)

          CIL V 6195 = *ILCV* 2735 (Milan,   D.N. Theodosius XVIII
          Reg. XI; 4.vii); *AE* 1977, 205   et Albinus v.c.
          (nr. Nola, Reg. I; 9.viii; om.
          D.N., v.c.); *IG* XIV 2298 =
          CIL V 6254 (Milan; 7.ix; om.
          D.N., v.c.; Gk.)

OTHER: Tjäder, *Nichtlit. Pap.* 1.67   D.N. Theodosius Aug. XVIII
          = *ChLA* XX 705 (Ravenna, ix-xii)   et Albinus v.c.

          Leo, *Epp.* 5,6,7 (*PL* 54.616,620,622) Theodosius (Aug.) XVIII
          (5 and 6, 12.i; 7, 30.i; Aug., vv.cc.   et Albinus (vv.cc.)
          only in 7)

Orientis

FASTI:	Marcell. Heracl. Pasch. (Aug.)	Theodosius (Aug.) XVIII et Albinus
LAWS:	*NovTheod* 25 (16.i), 17.2 (22.iv), 15.2 (20.vii), all C'polis;; *CJ* 1.24.4 (no prov., 28.iii)	Theodosius Aug. XVIII
	CJ 1.51.11 (no prov., 26.ii); *NovTheod* 26 (C'polis, 29.xi)	Theodosius Aug. XVIII et Albinus (v.c.)
PAPYRI:	*P.Oxy.* VII 1037.2 (11.viii); *P.Harr.* 86.15 (8.x); *P.Oxy.* L 3583.1 (13.xi)	p.c. Fll. Maximi II et Paterii vv.cc.
COINS:	Hahn (see 425) 112 nos.10-11 (C'polis; rev. legend only on no.11)	Theodosius, cons. image on obv. and rev. of solidi, with rev. legend IMP XXXXIIII COS XVIII

NOTES:

Albinus was a leading Roman aristocrat, PVR 426, PPO ?440 and 443-449 and probably to be identified with the PVR of 414 as well (*PLRE* II 50 and 53, nos. 7 and 10), ancestor of a whole line of consuls well into the sixth century (Cameron and Schauer, *JRS* 72 [1982] 143). Theodosius was proclaimed very late in the West, and Albinus was proclaimed late even at court in Constantinople. Neither was known in Egypt as late as November.

Occidentis

<u>FASTI</u>:	Hyd.	Valentinianus VI et [sic]
	VindPost. Prosp. Aq. Cass. Veron. Aug.	Valentinianus VI et Nomus
<u>LAWS</u>:	*NovVal* 16 (Rome, 18.i)	D.N. Valentinianus Aug. VI
	Rome, 5 laws, earliest 14.iv (*NovVal* 20)	D.N. Valentinianus Aug. VI et Nomus (v.c.)
<u>INSCR.</u>:	**ROME:** *ICUR* n.s. V 13404 (25.viii; Plac. Val. perp. Aug.); *ICUR* n.s. VIII 22973 = *ILCV* 4401 (19.x); *ICUR* n.s. II 4917 = *ILCV* 1132 (24.x; om. Aug.)	(Placidus) Valentinianus (perp.) Aug. VI
	ITALY: *RAC* 53 (1977) 108 no.4, fig. 3a (Nola, Reg. I; frag.)	D.N. Valentinianus Aug. VI et Nomus
	GAUL: *CIL* XII 5336 = *ILCV* 1806 (Narbonne; 29.xi)	Valentinianus Aug. VI

Orientis

<u>FASTI:</u>	Marcell. Heracl. Pasch. (Aug.)	Valentinianus (Aug.) VI et Nomus
<u>LAWS:</u>	*CJ* 1.2.11 (C'polis, 17.ii)	D.N. Valentinianus Aug. VI et Nomus v.c.
<u>PAPYRI:</u>	*SPP* XX 123.2 (28.iii; pap. omits *post*)	p.c. D.N. Theodosii perp. Aug. XVIII et Fl. Albini v.c.
	P.Ant. II 102.1* (iv-v)	Valenti[nianus Aug. VI et Fl. Nomus] v.c.
<u>OTHER:</u>	'To Nomus the consul', Theodoret, *Epp.* 58 (xvii), = II p.135 Azema	

<u>NOTES:</u>

Nomus was magister officiorum in the East from 443-446 (*PLRE* II 785-86). Valentinian received Nomus late and inscriptions in Rome never do include him. The papyri, on the other hand, probably (restoration is involved) got Valentinian fairly early. Hyd. has an *et* after Valentinian, but not Nomus' name; perhaps the updated information was not entered, but it may be a scribal error.

Occidentis

<u>FASTI</u>:	Hyd.	Aetius III
	VindPost. Prosp. cum Add. (1, 487,488) Victor Veron. Aug. Aq. Cass.	Aetius III et Symmachus
<u>LAWS</u>:	Rome, 3 laws, earliest *NovVal* 21.1 (21.x; has patr. and Q. Aur.)	Aetius (patricius) III et (Q. Aurelius) Symmachus (vv.cc.)
<u>INSCR.</u>:	**ROME:** *ICUR* n.s. I 1263 (14.xi-1.xii; frag.); *ICUR* n.s. VIII 23448 (19-22.v or 19-22.xii); *ICUR* n.s. II 4920; *ICUR* n.s. I 1144 (frag.); *ICUR* n.s. VII 17569a; *ICUR* n.s. VII 17569b	Aetius III et Symmachus vv.cc.
	ITALY: *NotScav* 1897, 366 = *ILCV* 1288 adn. (Dertona, Reg. IX; 24.vi; om. Symm.); *CIL* XI 4077 (S. Andrea, Reg. VII)	
<u>OTHER</u>:	Leo, *Epp.* 13 (*PL* 54.666) (6.i)	Aetius III et Symmachus vv.cc.

Orientis

<u>FASTI:</u>	Heracl.	Aetius III et Symmachus
	Marcell.	Valentinianus VII et Aetius III[66]
	Pasch.	Leontius III et Symmachus
<u>LAWS:</u>	*CJ* 1.14.8 (C'polis, 17.x)	Aetius III et Symmachus vv.cc.
<u>PAPYRI:</u>	*P.Rainer Cent.* 96.1 (23.ix); *BGU* XII 2141.1 (17.xi; Nom. is excellentissimus et illustriss. mag. sacr. off.); *P.Rainer Cent.* 95.1 (ix-xii; beginning lost)	p.c. D.N. Valentiniani perp. Aug. VI et Fl. Nomi v.c.
	CPR X 116.1 (space makes rest. of p.c. less likely)	Fll. Aetius III et Symmachus vv.cc.

<u>NOTES:</u>

Symmachus was a Roman aristocrat, grandson of the cos. 391 and (?grand)father of the cos. 485 (*PLRE* II 1042-43, with Cameron and Schauer, *JRS* 72 [1982] 144). The error of Marcellinus is explicable only as the product of confusion, continuing Valentinian's numbering from VI in 445 and adding only the first of the new consuls. Cf. *BASP* 18 (1981) 71-72.

[66]One MS. has Symmachus VII et Aetius III.

Occidentis

<u>FASTI</u>:	Hyd. VindPost. (post 448) Prosp. cum Add. (1, 487,488) Ciz. (1,507,17) Victor Veron. Aq. Cass.	Calepius et Ardabur
	Aug.	Ardabur et Calipius
<u>LAWS</u>:	*NovVal* 23 (13.iii), 7.3 (25.iv), 24 (25.iv), all Rome	Calepius v.c.
	NovVal 25 (Rome, 3.vi)	Calepius et Ardabur vv.cc.
<u>INSCR.</u>:	**ROME:** *ICUR* n.s. II 4921 = *ILCV* 3419 (25.ii); *ICUR* n.s. II 4276 = *ILCV* 3112 (13.iv); *ICUR* n.s. II 4922 = *ILCV* 164 (22.ix); *ICUR* n.s. II 4275 (6/7.x; om. v.c.); *ICUR* n.s. II 4519 = *ILCV* 734 adn. (13.x; om. v.c.); *ICUR* n.s. II 4923; *AE* 1940, 87 (20.ii; p.c. poss.); *NotScav* 1888, 437 no.54 (p.c. poss.)	Calepius v.c.
	ITALY: *ILCV* 2829 (Dertona, Reg. IX; 12.iii); *CIL* XI 334 (Ravenna, Reg. VIII; 16.vii-1.viii; frag.)	p.c. Aetii III et et Symmachi vv.cc.
	AE 1981, 373 (Arezzo, Reg. VII; 29.xii)	Calepius et Ardabur
	GAUL: *CIL* XIII 2355 = *ILCV* 1551 (Lyons; 19.iv)	Calepius v.c.
<u>OTHER</u>:	Leo, *Epp.* 15 (*PL* 54.692) (21.vii); 16 (*PL* 54.704) (21.xi); 18 (*PL* 54.710) (30.xii)	Calepius et Ardabur vv.cc.
	Leo, *Epp.* 17 (*PL* 54.706) (21.xi)	Calepius v.c.

Orientis

FASTI:	Marcell.	Ardabur et Calepius
	Heracl. Pasch.	Ardabur et Alypius
LAWS:	*NovTheod* 2 (C'polis, 1.x)	Ardabur v.c. et qui fuerit nuntiatus
PAPYRI:	*P.Rainer Cent.* 97.1 (3.xii)	p.c. Fll. Aetii III et Symmachi vv.cc.

NOTES:

Ardabur was MVM in the East from 453-466 and son of Aspar cos. 434 (*PLRE* II 135-37); Calepius is no more than a name on (mainly western) consular documents--so rare a name that Greek speakers were liable to substitute something more familiar (cf. Heracl., Pasch., and the papyri from p.c. in 448; see *PLRE* II 250). Calepius was not disseminated early in the West outside Rome and was disseminated very late in the East; and Ardabur was received in the court formula in the West only in June (though the p.c. still shows up a month or so later in a Ravenna inscription), and found only in one inscription, that from 29 December in Arezzo. For Aug., see 448.

Occidentis

<u>FASTI</u>:	Hyd. VindPost. Prosp. cum Add. (1, 487,489) Victor Veron. Cass. Aq.	Postumianus et Zeno
	Aug.	Zeno et Postumianus
<u>LAWS</u>:	*NovVal* 26 (Ravenna, 3.vi)	Postumianus et Zeno vv.cc.
<u>INSCR.</u>:	**ROME:** *ICUR* n.s. VIII 22975 = *ILCV* 1240 (11.iv); *ICUR* n.s. I 2116 (3.iii/5.v); *ICUR* I 741 = *ILCV* 734 adn. (26.vii; om. v.c.); *ICUR* n.s. VIII 23449a	Postumianus v.c.
	ITALY: *CIL* V 6283 = *ILCV* 2963 adn. (Milan, Reg. XI)	Postumianus et Zeno
	GAUL: *CIL* XIII 2356 = *ILCV* 4404 (Lyons; 16.i/16.xii)	Postumianus et Zeno vv.cc.
<u>OTHER</u>:	Pope Leo, *Epp.* 19 (in *PL* 54.709) (8.iii)	Postumianus v.c.
	Pope Leo, *Epp.* 20 (in *ACO* II.4, p.3) (1.vi)	Postumianus et Zeno
	Polemius Silvius wrote part of his *Laterculus* in Gaul (*Chron. Min.* 523, cf. 547)	Postumianus et Zeno vv.cc.

Orientis

FASTI:	Marcell. Heracl. Pasch.	Zeno et Postumianus
LAWS:	*CJ* 1.1.3 (C'polis, 16.ii)	Zeno et Postumianus
PAPYRI:	*P.Flor.* III 311.1 (24.vi)	p.c. Fll. Ardaburii et Alypii vv.cc.
	JJurPap 19 (1983) 87.1 (10.x)	Fll. Zeno et Postuminianus vv.cc.
OTHER:	Council at C'polis: *ACO* II.1.1, pp.100.3, 156.10 (8.xi); p.103.5 (12.xi)	Fll. Zeno et Postumianus vv.cc.
	R. Heberdey, A. Wilhelm, *Reisen in Kilikien* 89 no.168* (Olba; ?22.ix-31.xii)	Zeno magister militum filius Longini
	Theodoret, *Epp.* 71 (II p.154 Azema), "To Zeno, general and consul"	

NOTES:

Fl. Zeno was an Isaurian, MVM from 447-451 and a power at the eastern court (*PLRE* II 1199-1200). Rufius Praetextatus Postumianus was a Roman aristocrat, PVR twice (ib. 901-02). It is curious that the in other respects wholly western Fasti Augustani should offer the eastern sequence of names in 447-448; perhaps the man maintaining it happened to be in the East during those years; cf. 434. The Roman inscriptions and one papal letter all lack Zeno, but all of the other western evidence has him.

Occidentis

<u>FASTI:</u>	Hyd. VindPost. (post 450) Prosp. cum Add. (1, 487,489) Victor Veron. Aug. Aq. Cass.	Asturius et Protogenes
<u>LAWS:</u>	*NovVal* 27 (17.vi; *p.p.* Rome, 20.vii), 28 (11.ix), both Ravenna	Asturius et Protogenes
<u>INSCR.:</u>	**ROME:** *ICUR* n.s. I 942 = *ILCV* 1706 (26.iii); *ICUR* n.s. VII 17570	Fl. Asturius v.c.
	GAUL: *CIL* XIII 2357* cf. 10032.2 = *ILCV* 1422 (Lyons)	Asturius v.c.
<u>OTHER:</u>	Pope Leo, *Epp.* 23-24 (18.ii), 27 (21.v), 29-30, 32-35 (13.vi), 36-37 (20.vi), 38 (23.vii), 39 (11.viii), 43-45, 47-51 (13.x), 54 (24.xii) (*ACO* II.4, pp.3-27)	Asturius et Protogenes
	One leaf of Astyrius' consular diptych (Volbach no.3; inscr., *ILS* 1300)	
	Polemius Silvius completed his *Laterculus* (*Chron.Min.* I 547, cf. 513)	Asterius

<u>NOTES:</u>

Protogenes was PPO Or. 448-449 and at an earlier date, and an imperial representative at the Council of Chalcedon in 451 (*PLRE* II 927-28). Astyrius was MVM in the West in 441-443 (*PLRE* II 174-75), and entered on his consulate in Gaul (?Arles) to a panegyric by Nicetius (Sidon. Apoll., *Epp.* 8.6.5). The correct spelling of his name is presumably with a Y, as on the (now lost) front leaf of his diptych, known from an early drawing. Protogenes never occurs in the Roman or Gallic inscriptions.

Protogenes was proclaimed separately first in the East, and the news was at Therallum in May, but still unknown or ignored in Ephesus, Beirut, and Egypt 3-4 months later. The first sign of Astyrius comes in the papyrus of November. It is hard to believe that Theodosius himself ever dated by p.c., much less as late as the end of March; cf. above, p.28.

Orientis

<u>FASTI:</u>	Marcell. Heracl. Pasch. (-erius)	Protogenes et Asturius
<u>LAWS:</u>	*CJ* 5.17.8 (9.i; no prov.)	Protogenes et Asturius
<u>PAPYRI:</u>	*P.Oxy.* VIII 1129.1 (19.i); *P.Flor.* III 313.1 (12.viii); *P.Rainer Cent.* 98.1	p.c. Fll. Zenonis et Postumiani vv.cc.
	P.Mil. I 45.1 (7.xi)	Fll. Protogenes et Austurius vv.cc.
<u>OTHER:</u>	Letters of Theodosius (from C'polis) to the Council of Ephesus: *ACO* II.1.1, p.69.7; *Abh.Gött.* n.f. 15 (1917) 5.7 (both 30.iii)	p.c. Zenonis et Postumiani vv.cc.
	Documents from the Council of Chalcedon: (1) at Ephesus: *ACO* II.1.1, p.77.12 (8.viii); *Abh.Gött.* 1917, 7.20 (22.viii)	p.c. Zenonis et Postumiani vv.cc.
	ACO II.1.1, p.3.2 (14.xii)	Protogenes et Asterius vv.cc.
	(2) at Tyre: *ACO* II.1.3, p.14.10 (25.ii)	p.c. Fl. Zenonis et Postumiani vv.cc.
	(3) at Edessa: *Abh.Gött.* 1917, 15.35 (12.iv); 23.1 (n.d.)	p.c. Fl. Zenonis et Fl. Postumiani vv.cc.
	(4) at Therallum: *ACO* II.1.1, p.71.14 (15.v)	Protogenes v.c. et qui nuntiatus fuerit
	(5) at Constantinople: *ACO* II.1.1, p.150.1 (8.iv); *ACO* II.1.1, p.148.2 (13.iv; om. v.c.); *ACO* II.1.1, p.177.1 (27.iv)	Fl. Protogenes v.c. et qui nuntiatus fuerit
	Abh.Gött. 1917, 13.37 (13.vi)	Protogenes v.c. et qui nuntiatus fuerit
	(6) at Beirut: *ACO* II.1.3, p.19.25* (1.ix)	p.c. Fl. Zenonis et Postumiani vv.cc.

Occidentis

<u>FASTI</u>:	Hyd. VindPost. Prosp. cum Add. (1, 487 [adds vv.cc.],489) Victor Aug. Aq. Cass. Veron. (Aug.)	Valentinianus (Aug.) VII et Avienus
<u>LAWS</u>:	*NovVal* 1.3 (5.iii), 29 (24.iv), 30 (3.x), all Rome	Valentinianus Aug. VII et Avienus
<u>INSCR.</u>:	**ROME:** *ICUR* n.s. I 739 = *ILCV* 490 (23.ii; om. v.c.); *ICUR* n.s. VII 19987 (10.vi; Pl. Val.); *ICUR* n.s. VII 17568 = *ILCV* 3003C (25.vi; om. Aug.); *ICUR* n.s. VII 17571 = *ILCV* 2576A (26.viii; om. D.N., Aug. VII); *ICUR* I 750 = *ILCV* 2936 (15.ix; om. Aug., v.c.); *ICUR* n.s. II 4925 = *ILCV* 216 (10.xi; Plac. Val.; om. Aug.); *ICUR* n.s. VII 17572 (om. Aug.; frag.); *ICUR* n.s. VIII 23450 (om. Aug.)	D.N. (Placidus) Valentinianus Aug. VII et Avienus v.c.
	ITALY: *CIL* V 6284 (Milan, Reg.XI)	p.c. Asturi et Protogenis
	CIL IX 1369 = *ILCV* 4189 (Aeclanum, Reg. II; 14.xi); *CIL* IX 1370 = *ILCV* 3028 (Aeclanum, 27.xi; D.N.)	(D.N.) Valentinianus VII et Avienus v.c.
	DALMATIA: *Forsch.Salona* II 178 (Salona, 17.ix; Gk.; cf. *BCH* 108 [1984] 570)	p.c. Asturi et Protogenis
<u>OTHER</u>:	Sidon.Apoll., *Epp.* 1.9.3	
	Pope Leo, *Epp.* 60-61 (17.iii), 69-71 (16.vii), 74 (13.ix; om. Aug. VII), 75 (9.xi) (in *ACO* II.4, pp.28-33); 67 (= *MGH Epp.* III, p.21) (5.v; v.c.)	Valentinianus Aug. VII et Avienus (v.c.)

Orientis

FASTI:	Marcell. Heracl. (om. VII) Pasch. (Aug.)	Valentinianus (Aug.) VII et Avienus
LAWS:	*CJ* 5.14.8 (9.i), 6.52 (3.iv), both no prov.	p.c. Protogenis et Asturii
	NovMarc 2 (11.x); *CJ* 1.39.2 (18.xii), both C'polis	D.N. Valentinianus Aug. VII et Avienus (v.c.)
PAPYRI:	none	
INSCR.:	**BITHYNIA:** *I.Kalchedon* 22 = *BCH* 108 (1984) 566-71 (v)	p.c. Protogenis et Asturii vv.cc.
OTHER:	Subscription in MSS of Vegetius: Zetzel, *Latin Textual Criticism* 216 (7) (C'polis)	Valentinianus Aug. VII et Abienus
	Documents relating to the Council of Ephesus (redactional date refs.):	
	ACO II.1.1, p.8.16 (22.xi)	D.N. Valentinianus piiss. Imp. VIII (sic) et Abinus v.c.
	ACO II.1.1, p.10.17	D.N. Valentinianus perp. Aug. VII et Avienus

NOTES:

Avienus was the most powerful Roman aristocrat of the age (*PLRE* II 193-94), ancestor of many consuls (Cameron and Schauer, *JRS* 72 [1982] 143). Both consuls were western and (as was becoming usual) disseminated very late in the East.

Occidentis

FASTI:	Aq. Add. ad Prosp. (1, 487)	Adelfius v.c.
	Hyd.	Adelfius et Marcianus
	VindPost. Prosp. cum Add. (1, 490) (Aug.) Aq. Veron. Aug. Cass. Haun.	Marcianus (Aug.) et Adelfius
	Victor	Marcianus Aug.
LAWS:	*NovVal* 31-33 (31.i), 34 (13.vii), all Rome	Adelfius v.c.
INSCR.:	**ROME:** *ICUR* n.s. VIII 23064 = *ILCV* 705 (12.iii); *ICUR* n.s. I 1468 = *ILCV* 3873 (7.viii); *ICUR* n.s. II 4926 = *ILCV* 1196 (24.ix)	Adelfius v.c.
OTHER:	Pope Leo, *Epp.* 78-81 (13.iv), 82 (23.iv), 83-86 (9.vi), 87 (14.vi), 88-89 (24.vi), 89-93 (26.vi), 94-95 (20.vii) (in *ACO* II.4, pp.37-53)	Adelfius v.c.

NOTES:

On the death of Theodosius II on 28.vii.450, Marcian was taken as consort by Pulcheria and proclaimed Augustus in Constantinople on 25.viii.450 (*PLRE* II 714-15). But Valentinian felt slighted not to be consulted about the eastern succession (Oost, *Galla Placidia* 293-94), and did not officially recognize Marcian as Augustus till 30.iii.452 (*Chron.Min.* I, p.490, 21). Not surprisingly, therefore, Marcian's consulate of 451 was not acknowledged in the West (though note the African p.c. of 2.iii.452). It looks as if Marcian retaliated by not acknowledging the western consul of the year (cf. the p.c. papyrus in 452). It is curious, however, that the official formula remained *Marcianus Aug. e.q.n.f.* Perhaps Marcian did not go so far as to repudiate Valentinian's consul altogether (for which he would have had no real justification), but merely showed his irritation by affecting not to have been informed; the eastern fasti suggest that Adelfius was eventually recognized. Adelfius was a Roman aristocrat, PVR some time before 451 (*PLRE* II 8-9). The papyri show an overlap of more than ten weeks.

Orientis

<u>FASTI:</u>   Marcell. Heracl. Pasch.   Marcianus Aug. et Adelfius

<u>LAWS:</u>   *NovMarc* 3 (C'polis, 18.i);   Marcianus Aug. I
5 laws in *CJ*, latest
28.xii

<u>PAPYRI:</u>   *CPR* IX 40 B.1 (7.x)   p.c. D.N. Valentiniani
perp. Aug. VII et Fl.
Avieni v.c.

   P.Rainer Cent. 99.1 (24.vii)   Marcianus perp. Aug. I et
qui fuerit nuntiatus

<u>OTHER:</u>   Letter of Marcian to Bishops   D.N. Marcianus perp. Aug.
in Nicaea: *ACO* II.1.1, p.28.8   et qui fuerit nuntiatus
(C'polis, 23.v)

Letter of Marcian to Pope Leo:
ACO II.1.2, p.56.4 (C'polis, 18.xii)

Acts of the Council at Chalcedon:
ACO II.1.1, p.55.1 (8.x); II.1.2,
p.69.2 (10.x); p.3.2 (13.x; Marc.
piiss. et amator Christ. Imp.);
p.84.8 (17.x); p.101.30 (20.x);
p.99.26 (20.x; like p.3.2); p.121.7
(22.x); p.130.20 (25.x); II.3.2,
pp. 3.1 (om. e.q.n.f.), 7.8, 11.20
(all 26.x); p.86.2 (28.x); p.42.20
(29.x); p.56.4 (30.x); pp.63.2, 83.29
(31.x)

Occidentis

FASTI:	Add. ad Prosp. (1, 487)	Fl. Herculanus v.c. et qui de Oriente fuerit nuntiatus
	Aq. (GLQ) Prosp. (C: 1,482)	Herculanus v.c.
	Comput. (1,153,18)	Herculanus
	Prosp. (H: 1,482) Aq. (S) Haun.	Herculanus v.c. et Sporacius
	VindPost.	Herculianus et Aspar
	Hyd. Cass. Veron. Prosp. (1,482)	Herculanus et Sporacius
	Add. ad Prosp. (1, 490)	Honorius et Asper
	Aug.	Marcianus et Herculianus
LAWS:	*NovVal* 35 (15.iv) and 36 (29.vi), both from Rome	Herculanus v.c.
INSCR.:	**ROME:** *ICUR* n.s. II 4928 = *ILCV* 701 (15.v; Fl.); *ICUR* n.s. I 422 = *ILCV* 3506 adn. (16.vii-1.viii; om. v.c.); *ICUR* n.s. VIII 20821 (26.viii); *ICUR* n.s. VII 19988 (7.ix); *ICUR* n.s. IV 11156 (14.viii-13.ix; Fl. Bassus); *ICUR* n.s. VII 19989* = n.s. I 991 (20.ix); *ICUR* n.s. II 4175 = *ILCV* 165 (28.xi); *ICUR* I 760; *ICUR* n.s. II 5998 = *ILCV* 3506 adn. (p.c. poss.); *ICUR* n.s. I 3237 (p.c. poss.); *ICUR* n.s. II 4927 = *CIL* VI 8407 (p.c. poss.); *ICUR* n.s. VII 17569c* (Fl.; p.c. poss.)	(Fl.) (Bassus) Herculanus v.c.
	ITALY: *ZPE* 24 (1977) 222* = Agnello, *Silloge* 97 (Catania; 10.xi; Gk.)	Herculianus et qui de Oriente nuntiatus fuerit
	CIL IX 1371* (Aeclanum, Reg. II; 14.viii-13.ix; year not certain); [Continued on next page]	Fl. Herculanus v.c.

Orientis

FASTI:	Marcell. Heracl. Pasch.	Sp(h)oracius et Herculanus
LAWS:	C'polis, 2 laws, *CJ* 1.1.4 (7.ii) and *CJ* 1.3.23 (6.vii; rest. on basis of *ACO* II.1.3, p.122.12)	Sporacius v.c. et qui fuerit nuntiatus
	CJ 2.7.10 (C'polis, 18.vi)	Sporacius
PAPYRI:	*P.Rainer Cent.* 100.1 (21.ix)	p.c. D.N. Marciani perp. Aug.
INSCR.:	*I.Kalchedon* 22 = *BCH* 108 (1984) 566-71 (22.ix; Sphor. rest.)	Sphoracius v.c.
OTHER:	Documents from the Council at Chalcedon: *ACO* II.2.2, p.22.27 (7.ii; om. v.c. e.q.n.f.; Lat.); II.1.3, p.120.7 (13.iii; om. v.c.); p.122.12 (6.vii); p.124.23 (18.vii)	Sphoracius v.c. et qui nuntiatus fuerit

NOTES:

Herculanus was the respectable but unambitious husband of Valentinian III's sister Justa Grata Honoria (*PLRE* II 544-45); Sporacius was comes domesticorum peditum in the East 450-451 (ib., 1026-27). On the orthography see Feissel, *BCH* 108 (1984) 566-71: Sporacius is normal in Latin, Σφωράκιος in Greek.

Once again Valentinian did not recognize the consul designated by Marcian. There is no evidence that Marcian recognized Herculanus, either (*et qui fuerit nuntiatus* is still used in ii.453). The fasti became *very* confused. Dissemination in Egypt was late again.

	[Continued from preceding page]	
	AFRICA: *AE* 1967, 595 (Cuicul, Numidia; 2.iii)	p.c. D.N. Marciani Aug. et Adelfi v.c.
	AE 1967, 640 = *ILCV* 2104 (Sitifensis, Mauretania; 3.viii)	Herculanus v.c.
OTHER:	Pope Leo, *Epp.* 102 (27.i), 104-107 (22.v) (in *ACO* II.4, pp.53-62)	Herculanus v.c.

Occidentis

FASTI: Hyd.   Opilio

                Add. ad Prosp. Aq (Q) (om. Fl.)   Fl. Opilio v.c.

                Prosp. (I) Haun.   Opilio v.c. cos. et Vincomalus

                Prosp. (II) cum Add. (1, 490,492)   Opilio et Vincomalus
                Aq. (L) Victor Veron. Aug.
                VindPost. Rav. Cass. Aug.
                (has Leo iun. for Vinc.)

LAWS: none

INSCR.:   **ROME:** *ICUR* I 742   Opilio v.c.

                ITALY: *CIL* V 5414 = *ILCV*   p.c. Herculani v.c.
                147 (Como, Reg. XI; 14.v)

                453 or 524

                ROME: *ICUR* n.s. II 5037 (8.ii;   (Rufius) Opilio v.c.
                Rufius); *ICUR* n.s. I 1951 =
                ILCV 3156 adn. (1.x); *ICUR*
                n.s. VIII 20822; *ICUR* n.s. II
                5038 (om. v.c.); *ICUR* n.s. II
                5039 (Gk.); *ICUR* n.s. IV 11157;
                ICUR n.s. II 5041; *ICUR* n.s.
                II 5042; *ICUR* n.s. VII 17573
                (om. v.c.); *ICUR* n.s. I 2123 =
                ILCV 3079; *ICUR* n.s. II 5036;
                ICUR n.s. IV 11158a-d

                ITALY: *AE* 1977, 228 = 1973,   Opilio
                219 (Venosa, Reg. II; ix-xii)

                GAUL: *CIL* XII 2071 (Vienne;   Opilio v.c.
                22.viii); *CIL* XII 2070 =
                ILCV 1671 (Vienne, 31.viii);
                CIL XII 2069 = *ILCV* 2747 (Vienne;
                24.xi); *CIL* XII 2513 (Rumilly,
                Narb.; p.c. poss.)

[Continued on next page]

Orientis

<u>FASTI:</u>	Marcell. Heracl. Pasch.	Vincomalus et Opilio
<u>LAWS:</u>	none	
<u>PAPYRI:</u>	*P.Vindob.Sijp.* 11.1 (17.ii)	p.c. Fl. Sporacii viri excell. et fortiss. et qui de Italia fuerit nuntiatus
	SPP XX 138.1* (17.xi; p.c. poss.)	[Vincomalus et] Opilio vv.cc.

<u>NOTES:</u>

Vincomalus was magister officiorum in the East 451-452 and imperial representative at the council of Chalcedon (*PLRE* II 1169-70); Opilio was magister officiorum in the West 449-450 and PVR (ib. 807). Even after recognizing Marcian as Augustus, it seems that Valentinian still refused to admit his right to designate a consul acceptable in the West (note particularly the practice of Pope Leo). Marcian, on the other hand, recognized Valentinian's consul. But an understanding was evidently reached in the course of the year, since Marcian was allowed to designate both consuls for 454. The p.c. at Como in May is noteworthy.

For an analysis of the inscriptions dated by Opilio, see the Critical Appendix.

[Continued from preceding page]

	453 or 454 or 524	
	ITALY: *CIL* V 6285 (Milan)	Opilio
<u>OTHER:</u>	Pope Leo, *Epp.* 111-112 (10.iii), 113 (11.iii), 114-117 (21.iii), 118 (2.iv), 119-120 (11.vi), 121-123 (15.vi), 125 (25.vi) (in *ACO* II.4, pp.63-81)	Opilio v.c.
	Council at Angers: *Conc.Galliae* (Corp.Christ.Lat. 148), p.137 (4.x)	Opilio v.c.

Occidentis

FASTI: Add. ad Prosp. (1, 487)   p.c. Opilionis v.c.

          Hyd.   Aetius IV et Studius

          Prosp. cum Add. (1, 490) Aq.   Aetius et Studius
          Cass. Rav. Victor Veron. Haun.

          VindPost.   Aetius III et Vincomalus
                                                           et Studius

          Aug.   Aetius IV et Vincomalus

LAWS: *NovVal* 2.4 (Rome, 28.x)   Aetius et Studius (vv.cc.)

INSCR.:   **ROME:** *ICUR* n.s. I 2117 = *ILCV*   p.c. Opilionis v.c.
          510 (23.i; Fl.); *ICUR* n.s. VIII
          22974 (24.i); *ICUR* n.s. II 5040 =
          CIL VI 32008 (31.i); *AE* 1923, 82
          (23.iii; om. v.c.); *ICUR* n.s. I
          1946 = *ILCV* 3058A (1.vi; om. v.c.)

          NotScav 1888, 704 no.283 (19.v;   Aetius et Studius vv.cc.
          p.c. poss.?); *ICUR* n.s. II 4929
          = *ILCV* 289 (14.vii-13.viii); *ICUR*
          n.s. II 4277 (5.x; om. vv.cc.; Gk.)

          DALMATIA: *Forsch.Salona* II 179   p.c. Opilionis v.c.

          Forsch.Salona II 180 (Salona;   [Aetius et] Studius vv.cc.
          14.viii-1.xii; frag.; p.c.
          poss.?; Gk.)

          GAUL: *CIL* XIII 2359 =   p.c. Opilionis v.c.
          ILCV 3327 (Lyons; 24.i; om.
          v.c.); *I.Lat.Gaul.Narb.* 302
          = *ILCV* 180 (Vienne; 24.ii);
          CIL XIII 2358 = *ILCV* 1588
          (Lyons; 16.viii)

          AFRICA: *AE* 1924, 58   Aetius et Studius
          (Cuicul; 15.x)

[Continued on next page]

Orientis

FASTI:	Marcell. Heracl. Pasch.	Aetius et Studius
LAWS:	*NovMarc* 4 (C'polis, 4.iv)	Aetius et Studius vv.cc.
PAPYRI:	*P.Würzb.* 17.1 (8.i; has cos. by error for p.c.); *SPP* I, p.7 ii.1 (2.iii); *P.Lond.* V 1773.1 (11.iv); *SB* X 10523.1 (4.viii; form. uncert.); *Pap.Lugd.Bat.* XIII 1.1	p.c. Fll. Vincomali et Opilionis vv.cc.
	PSI X 1114.1	Fll. Aetius et Studius [
OTHER:	*Anthol.Pal.* 1.4	

NOTES:

Aetius was comes domesticorum (East) 451 (*PLRE* II 29-30); Studius an eastern civilian whose only documented action is building a church of St. John the Baptist, for which (according to its inscriptional epigram, *AP* 1.4) he was rewarded with the consulate (cf. C. Mango, *Byz.Mod.Gr. Stud.* 4 [1978] 115-22). See the remarks under 453 for the designation of the consuls of 454 and for the allocation of Opilio inscriptions. Dissemination was late in the West, as also in the East. To judge by the inscriptions, Pope Leo can hardly have been using the eastern consuls in January, and the p.c. of July suggests that much if not all of the rest of his letters have been corrected. The lists (ancient and modern) which assign a IV to Aetius are wrong; he is not the same man as the cos. III of 446. See Cameron, *BASP* 18 (1981) 72 and n.1.

[Continued from preceding page]

OTHER:	Pope Leo, *Epp.* 138 (*PL* 54.1102) (28.vii)	p.c. Opilionis
	Pope Leo, *Epp.* 126-127 (9.i), 128 (9.iii), 129-130, 131 (10.iii), 134 (15.iv), 135-137 (29.v), 139 (4.ix), 140 (6.xii) (in *ACO* II.4, pp.81-94)	Aetius et Studius vv.cc.

Occidentis

<u>FASTI</u>:	Add. ad Prosp. (1, 487)	Valentinianus VIII
	Hyd. VindPost. Prosp. cum Add. (1, 490) Aq. (1, 681,12, 682,1) Victor Veron. Cass.	Valentinianus VIII et Anthemius
	Aug.	Valentinianus VIII et Studius
<u>LAWS</u>:	none	
<u>INSCR</u>:	**ROME:** *ICUR* n.s. I 1469 = *ILCV* 4412 (29.xi)	Divus Valentinianus VIII
	ITALY: *Kokalos* 28-29 (1982-83) 21 no.73 (Catania; 2-15.x; Gk. and Lat.; Gk. lacks Div.); *CIL* XI 2583 = *ILCV* 3137D (Chiusi, Reg. VII; 1.xii); *CIL* X 1341 = *ILCV* 3118A (Nola, Reg. I); *CIL* XI 6602 (Sarsina, Reg. VI; frag.)	Divus Valentinianus Aug. VIII
	GAUL: *CIL* XII 4311 = *ILCV* 1807 (Regimond, Narb.)	Valentinianus VIII et Anthemius
	SPAIN: *Röm.Inschr.Tarraco* 945 (Tarragona; 13.i)	p.c. Aeti et Studi vv.cc.
<u>COINS</u>:	G. Lacam, *La fin de l'empire romain et le monnayage or en Italie* I (1983) pll.X-XIV (Rome)	Valentinian, cons. image on obv. and rev. of solidi
<u>OTHER</u>:	Pope Leo, *Epp.* 141-143 (in *ACO* II.4, pp.94-95) (13.iii, 11.v)	Valentinianus Aug. VIII
	Note to Leo, *Epp.* 138 (*PL* 54.1102) giving 24.iv as date of April in 455	Valentinianus VIII et Anthemius
<u>OTHER:</u>	Sidon.Apoll., *Carm.* 2.207-9 (Anthemius)	

Orientis

FASTI: Marcell. Heracl. Pasch. (Aug.)   Valentinianus (Aug.) VIII
                                                       et Anthemius

LAWS: *NovMarc* 5 (C'polis, 22.iv);   Anthemius v.c.
            CJ 1.3.24 (no prov., 24.iv)

            CJ 1.5.8 = 1.7.6 (C'polis,   Divus Valentinianus Aug.
            1.viii)   VIII et Anthemius v.c.

PAPYRI: *SPP* I, p.8 iii.1 (13.ii);   p.c. Fll. Aeti et
            P.Gron.Amst. 1.1 (14.iii)   Studi vv.cc.

            P.Monac. III 102.2 (20.ix)   Divus Valentinianus VIII
                                                      et Fl. Anthemius v.c.

NOTES:

Anthemius was grandson of Anthemius cos. 405, husband of the Emperor Marcian's daughter, MVM (East) 454-467 and western emperor 467-472 (*PLRE* II 96-98).

If the practice of Pope Leo is a reliable guide, Valentinian reverted to his practice of not recognizing the eastern consul. In this case he may have been signalling his disapproval of the honors being paid to Anthemius, heir apparent to the elderly Marcian now that Pulcheria was dead. Valentinian must still have cherished the hope of putting a child of his own on the eastern throne. It is perhaps due to no more than the by now normal delays of dissemination that Valentinian's name is missing from the eastern formula at the beginning of the year, though retaliation should not be excluded. After Valentinian's death (16.iii) it was naturally important for each side to recognize the other, in the hope of staving off usurpations by publicizing imperial solidarity; but the only western evidence for the recognition of the eastern consul is from Gaul.

(1) **Eparchius Avitus Aug.** (to 17.x)
(2) **Fl. Varanes et Fl. Iohannes** (thereafter)

Occidentis

<u>FASTI</u>:	Hyd.	Avitus Aug.
	VindPr. Cass. Aq. Victor Haun. Marius Veron. Add. ad Prosp. (1, 492)	Iohannes et Varanes
	Add. ad Prosp. (1, 490)	Varanes et Iohannes
	Aug.	Baranes et Anthemius
<u>LAWS</u>:	none	
<u>INSCR.</u>:	**ROME:** *ICUR* n.s. VIII 20823 (19.v; om. D.N., Aug.; Eparch.); *ICUR* n.s. I 354 = *ILCV* 2974B adn. (1.xi); *ICUR* n.s. VIII 23451	D.N. (Eparchius) Avitus Aug.
	GAUL: *CIL* XIII 11208 = *ILCV* 1730 (Lyons; 10.vi)	D.N. Avitus
<u>OTHER</u>:	Sidon.Apoll., *Carmen* 7, delivered at Rome on 1.i.456	

<u>NOTES</u>:

On Valentinian III's death (16.iii.455) Petronius Maximus (cos. 433, 443) became Augustus (17.iii), and after his early death (31.v) the Gaul Eparchius Avitus was proclaimed on 9.vii.455 (*PLRE* II 196-98). Avitus was not recognized by Marcian, either as Augustus or as cos. 456 (cf. R.W. Mathisen, *Byz.* 51 [1981] 232-47), but Hyd. shows that in the West not only Italy and Gaul but also Spain accepted his consulate. On 17.x.456 he was defeated at Placentia by the western MVM Ricimer and comes domesticorum Maiorianus, who seized power in Italy. Marcian underlined his non-recognition of Avitus by designating two eastern consuls, Varanes and Iohannes, who were naturally not recognized in the West so long as Avitus ruled. But several p.c.'s of 457 (and all of the western consular lists save Hyd.--on whose entry see R. Mathisen, *CP* 80 [1985] 333) show that Varanes and Iohannes were eventually recognized in the West, presumably very late in the year. The obvious explanation is that Majorian attempted to conciliate the eastern government by damning Avitus' memory, belatedly recognizing Marcian's consuls for 456 and then recognizing the two new eastern consuls that Marcian proclaimed for 457, Constantinus and Rufus.

Orientis

<u>FASTI:</u>	Marcell. (cod.Oxon.) Heracl. Pasch.	Varanes et Iohannes
<u>LAWS:</u>	*CJ* 1.4.13 (25.iii-6.iv) and 10.22.3 (18.vii), both no prov.	Varanes et Iohannes
<u>PAPYRI:</u>	*P.Yale* I 71.1 (28.viii)	p.c. Divi Valentiniani et Fl. Anthemi v.c.

Occidentis

FASTI:	VindPr. Add. ad Prosp. (1, 490, 492) Aq. (1, 682,2,11; 683,22; 722) Dionys. (1, 756) Victor Marius Hist. Britt. (3, 209,1) Veron. Cass. Haun. Isidoriana (2, 493, c.7)	Constantinus et Rufus
	Aug.	Constantinus et Iohannes
LAWS:	none	
INSCR.:	**ROME:** *ICUR* n.s. I 2723 = *ILCV* 4388 (10.iii); *ICUR* n.s. VIII 20824 = *ILCV* 2974B (2.iv)	p.c. Iohannis et Varanae
	ICUR n.s. VI 15895 = *ILCV* 1541 (4.iv; Fl. Const., vv.cc.); *ICUR* n.s. VIII 22976 (8.iv)	(Fl.) Constantinus et Rufus (vv.cc.)
	ITALY: *CIL* V 5429 (Como, Reg. XI; i-viii)	p.c. Varanis et Iohannis
	CIL V 8910 = *ILCV* 1445A adn. (Como; frag.)	Constantinus et Rufus
OTHER:	Pope Leo, *Epp.* 144 (1.vi), 145-147 (11.vii), 148-153 (1.ix), 154-155 (11.x), 156, 158 (1.xii) (in *ACO* II.4, pp.95-105, 138-139)	Constantinus et Rufus

NOTES:

Despite waiting till 28.xii.457 before finally assuming the title of Augustus in the West (Stein, *Bas-Empire* I 374-75; 596; *PLRE* II 703), Majorian never received the recognition and support he had hoped for from either Marcian or (after Marcian's death on 27.i.457) the new eastern emperor Leo. Indeed, the laws suggest that in the early months of 458 Majorian refused to recognize Leo as either Augustus or consul. Majorian's *Nov.* 1-2 (11.i and 10.iii) omit Leo's name from both imperial and consular formulas, while *Nov.* 3-7 (8.v-6.xi) include it in both. The promulgation of Leo's name might date from shortly before 21.iii.458-- if we knew for certain which formulas to Pope Leo's letters were original. The five letters printed in *ACO* II.4, pp.105-19, offer *Leone et Maioriano*, but in two cases some MSS omit *Leone et*, and three other letters of the year give just *Maioriano*. See the notes on 459. The Roman inscriptions have no secure mention of Leo, and an inscription of October definitely lacks it. [Continued]

Orientis

FASTI:	Marcell. Heracl. Pasch.	Constantinus et Rufus
LAWS:	*CJ* 1.5.9 (C'polis, 13.viii)	Constantinus et Rufus
PAPYRI:	*P.Rainer Cent.* 101.1 (29.ix); *BGU* XII 2146.1 (3-13.xi)	Fll. Constantinus et Rufus vv.cc.
OTHER:	L. Robert, *Hellenica* 4 (1948) 45 (honoring Constantinus as consul at Laodicea)	

NOTES:

But there is another possibility, recently defended by G. Lacam (*La fin de l'empire romain*, 238f.) on the basis of solidi minted at Ravenna showing both Majorian and Leo in consular dress. Since (he argues) "le consulat commençait toujours le 1er janvier...l'émission de la monnaie qui nous intéresse ici dut avoir lieu, en toute logique, au début du mois de janvier 458" (p.239). What then of the laws? R.W. Burgess suggests to us that perhaps the notification of Leo's consulate was simply late arriving in Ravenna. But it is difficult to imagine what sort of notification could have justified including Leo's image on the consular coinage in January 458 but not actually proclaiming him consul.[67] Nor would this hypothesis explain the absence of Leo's name from the imperial formula in the laws. For this we should have to postulate scribal error, but then it would be an odd coincidence for the error to be present in only those laws that also omitted Leo's name from the consular formula.[68]

The simplest explanation is that the coins date from March 458, when Majorian had decided to recognize Leo as both emperor and consul. There is no problem with postulating a late consular emission. For example, the only consular solidi issued by Constantius II in 357 were minted at Rome in April (*RIC* VIII 244). Some consular issues were very small, and we should not assume (with Kent and Painter, *Wealth of the Roman World* 186) that they were always "intended for distribution as presents at the consular games" in January rather than for private distribution to a select group of high officials at some other time. On balance, it seems most likely that Majorian did not recognize Leo (as either emperor or consul) until (probably) March 458.

For the p.c. dates and eventual recognition of the eastern consuls, see the notes to 456. Constantinus was PPO (Or.) in 447, 456 and 459 (*PLRE* II 317-18); Rufus (*PLRE* II 959 no.4) is otherwise unknown.

[67]Majorian seems also to have struck non-consular solidi in Leo's name, but whether before or after the consular issue cannot be established (see Lacam, 234, 287-90).

[68]There is no reason why a scribe should have "corrected" the imperial to agree with the consular formula, since they did not normally agree. A scribe who was as alert as this might be expected rather to have corrected both imperial and consular formula to agree with the rest of Majorian's novels.

(1) **Maiorianus Aug. (I)** (beginning of year)
(2) **Leo Aug. (I) et Maiorianus Aug. (I)**

Occidentis

<u>FASTI</u>:	Add. ad Prosp. (1, 492) (om. Aug.) Veron. Aq. Cass.	Leo Aug. et Maiorianus Aug.
	VindPr.	Leo Aug. et Apollonius
	Marius	Maiorianus et Leo
	Hyd. (ante a.460)	Maiorianus Aug. et Ariovindus
	Aug. (and also)	Ardabur et Rufus Matoranus et Maximilianus
	Add. ad Prosp. (1, 490)	Ardabur et Maximianus
<u>LAWS</u>:	*NovMaior* 1 (11.i) and 2 (10.iii), both Ravenna	D.N. Maiorianus Aug. I
	5 laws, *NovMaior* 3-7, earliest 8.v (all Ravenna)	DD.NN. Leo et Maiorianus Augg.
<u>INSCR.</u>:	**ROME:** *ICUR* n.s. VIII 22977 (19.x)	D.N. Maiorianus
	ICUR n.s. II 4943 (19.ii/21.iv?; Gk.)	[DD.NN. Fl. Leo et] Fl. Maiorianus
	GAUL: *CIL* XIII 2363 = *ILCV* 2728A (Lyons, 25.vii)	D.N. Leo v.c.
<u>COINS</u>:	Lacam (see 455) 234-44 (Ravenna): solidi	Maiorianus, cons. image on obv., cons. image of Maior. and Leo on rev.
<u>OTHER</u>:	Pope Leo, *Epp.* 160-162 (in *ACO* II.4, pp.105-09) (21.iii); 164-165 (pp.110-19) (17.viii)	Leo et Maiorianus Augg.
	Pope Leo, *Epp.* 159, 166 (in *PL* 54.1140 and 1195); and *ACO* II.4, p.xxxxiiii (21.iii, 28.iii, 24.x)	Maiorianus Aug.
	Sidon.Apoll., *Carmen* 5, delivered at Lyons late in the year	

Orientis

FASTI:	Victor Heracl. (solus)	Leo Aug. (solus)
	Marcell. Pasch.	Leo Aug. et Maiorianus Aug.
LAWS:	*CJ* 12.35.15 = 4.65.31 (C'polis, 6.vii)	Leo Aug.
PAPYRI:	*P.Oxy.* XXXIV 2718.1 (5.vi)	p.c. Fll. Constantini et Rufi vv.cc.
	PSI IX 1075.14 (3.viii)	D.N. Fl. Leo perp. Aug. I
OTHER:	*PG* 85.716 (29.vi)	(Leo Aug. I)

NOTES:

The omission of Majorian's name from the Lyons inscription is usually explained as a manifestation of Gallic hostility to Majorian, destroyer of the Gallic usurper Avitus: cf. C.E. Stevens, *Sidonius Apollinaris* (1933) 44; R.W. Mathisen, "Majorian and the Gallic Aristocracy," *Francia* 7 (1979) 597-627 at 606 (though his argument from the funerary formula shared with *CIL* XIII 2359 of 454 proves nothing; cf. 2364-2365 of 492-493). But there is another possibility. The consular formula (as T. Drew-Bear has kindly confirmed for us) runs as follows: *dom. nos. Leone vv ccons.* (with supralinear strokes over the vv and the cc). That is to say, not only has the stonemason ignorantly given the emperor the title v.c.; he has also written one *v* too many. Vv.cc. for v.c. is not by any means unique in these times, nor is the writer's belief that cc. stands for "consules" (in whatever case). But it is also possible that the stonecutter misunderstood his original, and that the intended date was *Leone V v.c. cons.*, referring to Leo's fifth consulate in 473. For Majorian's initial non-recognition of Leo, see notes on 456, 457 and 459. Despite Marcell. and Pasch., there is no contemporary evidence that Leo recognized Majorian's consulate (cf. also the p.c. in a papyrus from 459, without Majorian).

Occidentis

<u>FASTI</u>:	Hyd.	Ricimer et qui de Oriente
	VindPr. (Fl. R.) Add. ad Prosp. (1, 492) AqS. Cass. Marius Veron.	(Fl.) Ricimer et Patricius
	Aug.	Ricimer II et Maloranus II
<u>LAWS</u>:	*NovMaior* 9 (Arles, 17.iv)	Ricimer v.c.
<u>INSCR.</u>:	**ROME:** *RAC* 44 (1968) 149, fig.7 (20.i; p.c. poss.); *ICUR* n.s. VI 15783 = *ILCV* 3507 (14.iii; om. v.c.); *ICUR* n.s. I 927 = *ILCV* 1510 (11.vii); *ICUR* n.s. I 3238 (frag.; p.c. poss.)	Fl. Ricimer v.c.
	ITALY: *EphEp* 8 (1899) 517 = *ILCV* 4403 (Capua, Reg. I; 26.iii)	
	DALMATIA: *CIL* III 13127* (Salona; 14.ix-15.x; vv.cc.); *Forsch.Salona* II 181 (frag.; Gk.; Fl.; p.c. poss.)	(Fl.) Ricimer
<u>OTHER</u>:	Leo, *Epp.* 168 (*PL* 54.1211) (6.iii)	Recimer

<u>NOTES</u>:

Ricimer was a barbarian, MVM (West) from 456-472 and maker of emperors (*PLRE* II 942-45); Patricius was the son of Aspar cos. 434 and brother of Ardabur cos. 447 and of Hermenericus cos. 465, elevated to the rank of Caesar in 470-471 (ib. 842-43). The puzzling inconsistency of the consular formula to Pope Leo's letters in 458 (see note on 457) might be explained if Majorian had eventually reverted to his initial policy of non-recognition, for at the beginning of 459 neither emperor recognized the other's consul. The eastern fasti, except for Heracl., cannot be relied upon for the contemporary situation. Dissemination in Egypt was late.

Orientis

FASTI:	Heracl.	Patricius solus
	Marcell. Victor	Patricius et Ricimer
	Pasch.	Ricimer et Patricius
LAWS:	*CJ* 8.53.30 (C'polis, 3.iii); *CJ* 1.3.26 (no prov.,17.ix)	Patricius
PAPYRI:	*P.Rainer Cent.* 102.1 (ix-xii)	[p.c.] D.N. Fl. Leonis perp. Aug. Imp. I
INSCR:	**ASIA:** *Sardis* VII.1, 18 = Grégoire, *Inscr.* 322* (Sardis; 27.iv)	Fl. Patricius v.c. et qui fuerit nuntiatus

Occidentis

<u>FASTI</u>:	Hyd. VindPr. Add. ad Prosp. (1, 493) AqS. Cass. Marius Veron.	Magnus et Apollonius
	Aug.	Apollonius et Patricius
<u>LAWS</u>:	*NovMaior* 11 (Arles, 28.iii)	Magnus et Apollonius vv.cc.
<u>INSCR.</u>:	**ROME:** *ICUR* n.s. II 4276 (7.ix); *RAC* 44 (1968) 149 fig.7 (Fl.; p.c. poss.)	(Fl.) Magnus v.c.
	ICUR n.s. VII 17575a (19.viii; only]onio preserved); *ICUR* n.s. VII 17576 = *ILCV* 134 (25.x)	Magnus et Apollonius
	ITALY: *CIL* IX 1372 = *ILCV* 3185A (Mirabella, Reg. II; 31?.i)	p.c. Ricomeri v.c.
	SPAIN: *Röm.Inschr.Tarraco* 946 (Tarragona; d. 28.xii.459)	Magnus
	DALMATIA: *CIL* III 9522* (Salona; 20.ii; Gk.)	p.c. Fl. Ricomeri et Patricii (?) vv.cc.
<u>OTHER</u>:	Letters of Pope Leo: *Coll.Avell.* 51, 52 (17.vi); 53-55 (18.viii)	Magnus et Apollonius

<u>NOTES:</u>

The evidence from the West is interesting when one considers the sharp divide of the year before, when East and West ignored one another's consuls. But even in this year, some of the western evidence lacks Apollonius (two Roman, one Spanish inscription). De Rossi argued (*ICUR* I, p.351) that Apollonius' name was interpolated in both the law and the letters of Pope Leo, on the grounds that it is missing from the inscription of 7.ix and not promulgated till October. But this is to attach too much importance to the omissions of inscriptions, especially at this date (p.64). It is also noteworthy that the incoming consul for the West was apparently known in Spain at least not long after 1 January.

Orientis

<u>FASTI:</u>	Marcell. Heracl. Pasch.	Apollonius et Magnus
	Victor	Magnus et Apollonius
<u>LAWS:</u>	*CJ* 2.7.11 (C'polis, 1.ii)	Magnus et Apollonius
<u>PAPYRI:</u>	*P.Oxy.* L 3599.1	Fl. Ap[ollonius v.c. (e.q.n.f.?)]

<u>NOTES:</u>

Magnus was a Gallic aristocrat, magister officiorum and PPO Gall. in 458 (*PLRE* II 700-01); Apollonius could be either *PLRE* II 121 no.2, PPO Or. 442-443, or (more probably) no.3, MVM (East) 443-451. It is clear from the Egyptian p.c. dating by Apollonius *e.q.f.n.* as late as 1.ix.461 that Magnus was never disseminated in the East. The retroactive addition of his name to a law and his inclusion in the fasti, however, suggest that he may have been officially proclaimed.

Occidentis

<u>FASTI</u>:	Hyd.	Severianus et qui de Oriente
	VindPr. Add. ad Prosp. (1, 493) AqS. Cass. Marius Veron.	Severinus et Dagalaifus
	Aug.	Dagalaifus et Magnus
<u>LAWS</u>:	none	
<u>INSCR.</u>:	**ROME:** *ICUR* n.s. VII 17579 (3.v); *ICUR* n.s. IV 12426 = *ILCV* 1271 17.vii; om. v.c.); *ICUR* n.s. VI 16001 fr. a + add. p.296 = *ILCV* 1133 (23.vii); *ICUR* n.s. VI 16001b (23.vii); *ICUR* n.s. VII 17578* = *ILCV* 2974B adn. (p.c. poss.)	(Fl.) Severinus v.c.
	ITALY: *I.Ital.* XI.2 41 (Ivrea, Reg. XI; 25.i); *CIL* V 5455 = *ILCV* 1159a (nr. Como, Reg. XI; 20.iv); *CIL* IX 1073 = *ILCV* 3185 (Fontanarosa, Reg. II; 28.viii?); *CIL* X 1342 = *ILCV* 1709a (Nola, Reg. I; 9.xi; Fl. Sev.)	
	GERMANIA: *CIL* XIII 5657 = *ILCV* 220 (Pothières, Germ. Sup.; bef. 22.iv?)	
<u>OTHER</u>:	Council at Tours: *Conc.Galliae* (Corp.Christ.Lat. 148), p.143 (18.xi)	Severinus v.c.
	Sidon.Apoll., *Epp.* 1.11.10	

Orientis

FASTI: Marcell. Victor Heracl. Pasch.   Dagalaifus et Severinus

LAWS: none

PAPYRI: *P.Oxy.* XVI 1878.1 (1.ix;   p.c. Apollonii v.c. et
                Lat.)   qui nuntiatus fuerit

INSCR.:   **ISAURIA:** *CIG* IV 9259 = *SEG* XIV   Dagalaifus
                813 (Alahan; i-viii)

                MACEDONIA: *IG* X 2 1 776* = Feissel,
                Recueil Inscr.Chrét.Macéd. 128
                (Thessalonica; frag.)

NOTES:

   Severinus was a powerful influence in western politics in the 450's, though no office other than the consulate is attested (*PLRE* II 1001). Dagalaifus was son of Areobindus cos. 434, son-in-law of Ardabur cos. 447 and father of Areobindus cos. 506; he is not known to have led an active military career himself (*PLRE* II 340-41).
   Yet again, it looks as if neither emperor recognized the other's consul for most of the year. Eventually, however, the East accepted Severinus, and he appears in all eastern p.c. dates.
   The meager evidence for 482 indicates that Trocundes was included in Roman inscriptional formulas that year. Texts with only Severinus are therefore listed under 461, though some could date to 482.

Occidentis

<u>FASTI</u>:	Hyd.	Severus et Leo Augg.
	VindPr. Add. ad Prosp. (1, 493) (om. II) AqS. Cass. Caesaraugust. (2,222) (om. II) Marius Veron. (Aug.)	Leo (Aug.) II et Severus (Aug.)
	Aug.	Leo Aug. II et Severinus
<u>LAWS</u>:	none	
<u>INSCR.</u>:	**ROME:** *ICUR* I 807 = *ILCV* 115 (26.vii); *ICUR* n.s. II 4944 (19.viii; Libi Sev.); *ICUR* n.s. I 737b = *ILCV* 3179A (22.x; Lib. Sev.; om. Aug.); *ICUR* n.s. II 4945 (om. Aug. I); *ICUR* n.s. II 4946 (frag.; p.c. poss.)	D.N. (Libius) Severus Aug. I
	ITALY: *CIL* IX 1373 = *ILCV* 3028A (nr. Aeclanum, Reg. II; 15.v)	
	DALMATIA: *CIL* III 14623 = *ILCV* 1174 (11.iii)	p.c. Severini v.c.
<u>COINS</u>:	Lacam (see 455) 327-30 (Rome)	Libius Severus, cons. image on obv. and rev. of solidus
<u>OTHER</u>:	Pope Hilary, *Epp.* 4,8 (Thiel I 138, 146 = *MGH Epp.* III pp.23 and 28, nos. 16,18) (25.i, 3.xii)[69]	D. Severus Aug.

[69]All MSS of *Ep.* 8 have "gl.p. Severo Aug." Gundlach (in *MGH*) corrects to "Flavio", which is neither palaeographically plausible nor otherwise persuasive (since Severus did not use this name). Thiel interprets the letters as "gloriosissimo principe", which seems possible, but we may simply have some other confusion not now recoverable. We have omitted Hilary, *Epp.* 5 (Thiel p.138-39), since it is a seventeenth-century forgery (see J. Havet, *Bibliothèque de l'école des chartes* 46 [1885] 205-71).

Orientis

FASTI:	Marcell. Victor (om. solus) Heracl. (om. Aug.)	Leo Aug. II solus
	Pasch.	Leo Aug. II et Serpentius
LAWS:	none	
PAPYRI:	*PSI* III 175.1 (20.ix)	p.c. Fll. Dagalaifi et Severini vv.cc.
INSCR.:	**ISAURIA:** *SEG* XIV 812 (Alahan; 13.ii)	p.c. Fl. Severiani (sic) et Fl. Dagalaifi vv.cc.

NOTES:

After deposing (2.viii.461) and executing (7.viii) Majorian (*PLRE* II 703), Ricimer had Libius Severus proclaimed Augustus, at Ravenna on 19.xi.461 (*PLRE* II 1004-05). Severus reigned till his death on 14.xi.465, but was never recognized by Leo. Naturally Leo did not recognize Severus' own consulate in 462, and the probability is that he did not recognize the rest of Severus' consuls either. The eastern fasti for 463 and 464 are not contemporary evidence, and the one law in *CJ* (for 463) is hardly more reliable. Severus 'recognized' Leo as Augustus, but not (apparently) as consul for 462; despite the western fasti, the inscriptions are decisive.

The order of names in the Isaurian inscription is remarkable. Dissemination in the East was late.

An interesting peculiarity is the appearance of D. in the dating formula of Hilary's letter 4 without N. Papal correspondence in fact habitually does not include the element D.N., and we cannot tell if the simple D. here is (a) corrupt, (b) an incorrect insertion of redaction, or (c) significant in the sense that the Pope might find Dominus Noster an inappropriate term for the emperor. A charter of foundation of a church in 471 also has Domno without nostro. Cf. also the law of 473 as presented in *PL*.

Occidentis

<u>FASTI</u>:	Aq. (Q)	Basilius
	Hyd.	Basilius et Gadaifus
	VindPr. Add. ad Prosp. (1, 493) Aq. (GLS) Cass. Marius Veron.	Basilius et Vivianus
	Aug.	Bibianus et Severus Aug.
	Caesaraugust. (2, 222)	Vibianus et Basilius
<u>LAWS</u>:	*NovSev* 1 (Rome, 20.ii)	Basilius v.c.
<u>INSCR.</u>:	**ROME:** *ICUR* n.s. IV 11160 (27.i; om. Fl., v.c.); II 4520 (16.iii -13.iv); *ICUR* n.s. VI 15895 = *ILCV* 1541 (28.iv); *ICUR* n.s. II 4947 = *ILCV* 246a (14-30.viii)	Fl. Basilius v.c.
	ITALY: *CIL* X 1192 = *ILCV* 3342A (Atripalda/Aiello, Reg. I; 20.vii; om. Fl.); *CIL* V 5420 = *ILCV* 1733C (Como, Reg. XI; 1.ix; om. Fl.); *CIL* X 4613 = *ILCV* 1751 (Cajazzo, Reg. I; 24.ix)	
	DALMATIA: *Forsch.Salona* II 182 (Salona, frag.)	
<u>OTHER</u>:	Hilary, *Epp.* 9 (Thiel 147 = *MGH Epp.* III no.19) (10.x)	Basilius v.c.

Orientis

FASTI:	Victor Heracl. (solus)	Vibianus (solus)
	Marcell.	Vivianus et Felix
	Pasch.	Vibianus et Basilius
LAWS:	*CJ* 2.7.12 (C'polis, 20.ii)	Basilius et Vibianus
PAPYRI:	*SPP* XX 127.1 (3.ii); *P.Vindob.Sijp.* 7.1* (om. D.N.?)	p.c. D.N. Fl. Leonis perp. Aug. II
	P.Rainer Cent. 103.1 (p.c. poss.)	Fl. Vivianus v.c. et qui fuerit nuntiatus
OTHER:	Jo. Lyd., *de magg.* 3.48.2	

NOTES:

Caecina Decius [*not* Maximus] Basilius was PPO Ital. 458 and 463-465, and ancestor of a dynasty of consuls (*PLRE* II 216-17; Cameron and Schauer, *JRS* 72 [1982] 127-28, 143). Vivianus was PPO Or. 459-460 and father of Paul cos. 512 (*PLRE* II 1179-80). Vivianus' consulate was long remembered for its extravagance (Jo.Lyd., l.c.).

'Felix' is Marcellinus' one inexplicable error. The postconsular papyri show that Basilius was never disseminated in at least Egypt and presumably the East; the papal letters and Italian inscriptions that Vivianus was apparently not disseminated in the West. It is curious that, as in the similar case of 460, the retroactive correction of the law in *CJ* has resulted in the western name being put first.

All inscriptions by Basilius, without iun., have been listed under this year; but it is possible that the omission of iun. is a scribal error in some cases, in which event 480 or 541 would be possible.

Occidentis

FASTI: Hyd. Aq. (Q)   Olybrius

Add. ad Prosp. (1, 493) Camp.   Olybrius et Rusticius
Aq. (GLS) Marius

VindPr. Cass. Veron. Aug.   Rusticius et Olybrius

LAWS: none

INSCR.: **ROME:** *ICUR* n.s. VII 17583 =   Rusticius et Olybrius
ILCV 1708 (7.viii); *ICUR* n.s.   (vv.cc.)
VII 17584 = *ILCV* 1708 adn.
(7.viii; partial copy of
prec.); *ICUR* n.s. VII 17582
= *ILCV* 4300 (6.xii; frag.);
ICUR n.s. II 4948 (frag.)

ITALY: *CIL* XI 4331 (Terni,
Reg. VI; frag.; vv.cc.)

OTHER: Hilary, *Epp.* 10 (Thiel 151   p.c. Basilii v.c.
= *MGH Epp.* III no.21) (25.ii)

Orientis

<u>FASTI:</u>	Marcell. Heracl. Pasch.	Rusticius et Olybrius
	Victor	Olybrius et Rusticius
<u>LAWS:</u>	none	
<u>PAPYRI:</u>	*JÖBG* 36 (1986) 19.1 (17.iii);	p.c. Fl. Viviani v.c. et
	BGU XII 2147.1 (7.x);	qui nuntiatus fuerit
	P.Oxy. VI 902.19 (20.xi;	
	adds II after Vivianus)	
<u>OTHER:</u>	Malalas, p.373 Bonn	Olybrius, Rusticius

<u>NOTES:</u>

Both consuls were eastern and evidently recognized in the West. Olybrius was husband to Valentinian III's daughter Placidia, presumably descended from Olybrius cos. 395, resident (after 455) in Constantinople, and finally western Augustus in 472 (*PLRE* II 796-99). Rusticius was MVM in Thrace *ca* 464 (ib. 962); for his name, cf. 465, *SB* I 4821. This papyrus shows that the correct order in the East was Rusticius et Olybrius, as Heracl., Pasch., and Marcell. have it. The West also observed this order; but some fasti have reversed them, no doubt out of habit (Malalas does not give an actual formula).

Occidentis

FASTI: VindPr. Camp. AqS. (GLSN) Cass.   Hermenericus et Basiliscus
            Marius Veron. (Hyd. om.)

            Add. ad Prosp. (1, 493) Aug.   Basiliscus et Hermenericus
            AqS. (Q)

LAWS: *NovSev* 2 (no prov., 25.ix)   Hermenericus et
                                                   Basiliscus

INSCR.:   **ROME:** *ICUR* n.s. VII 17586 (3.ii; Hermenericus et (Fl.)
            om. vv.cc.; p.c. poss.); *ICUR*   Basiliscus vv.cc.
            n.s. VII 17584* = *ILCV* 1708 adn.
            (11.iii; Fl. Bas.; om. vv.cc.;
            p.c. poss.; reverse order)
            ICUR n.s. VII 17585 (25.vii);
            ICUR n.s. II 5722 (7.ix); *ICUR*
            n.s. VII 19990 (20.xii); *ICUR* n.s.
            VI 15784; *ICUR* n.s. II 4949;
            ICUR n.s. VII 20606 = *ILCV* 3782*;
            ICUR n.s. II 4950* (frag.); *ICUR*
            n.s. VIII 23449b (frag.)

            ITALY: *CIL* V 5720* (Milan, Reg.
            XI; 14.ii-1.iii); *CIL* V 6627 =
            ILCV 4370 adn. (Paruzzarro nr.
            Arona, Reg. XI; x-xi; Fl. Basil.)

            DALMATIA: *ILCV* 245 adn.   Basiliscus et
            (Salona; 1.iii; cos. and   Hermenericus [vv.cc.]
            p.c. both poss.)

OTHER: Hilary, *Epp.* 16 (Thiel 169)   Basiliscus et
            (30.xii)   Hermenericus vv.cc.

            Council held in Rome (Hilary,   Fll. Basiliscus et
            Epp. 15, Thiel 159) (19.xi)   Hermenericus vv.cc.

            Liber Pontificalis I 242 (16.xi)   Basiliscus <et>
                                                   Hermenericus

Orientis

<u>FASTI:</u>	Pasch. Marcell. Heracl.	Basiliscus et Hermenericus
	Victor	Hermias et Basiliscus
<u>LAWS:</u>	*CJ* 1.36.1 (C'polis, 9.xi)	Basiliscus et Hermenericus
<u>PAPYRI:</u>	*SB* I 4821.1* (3.iv; adds Nestorii after Rust.); *PSI* VII 768.19 (23.vii); *P.Heid.* IV 331.1 (16.x)	p.c. Fll. Rusticii (Nestorii) et Olybrii vv.cc.

<u>NOTES:</u>

Hermeneric was son of Aspar cos. 434 and brother of Ardabur cos. 447 and Patricius cos. 459 (*PLRE* II 549); Basiliscus was brother-in-law of the Emperor Leo, MVM (in Thrace) *ca* 464-*ca* 467/8 and Augustus 475-476 (*PLRE* II 212-14). Hermeneric was treated as consul prior in the western inscriptions (Dalmatia follows eastern practice) and court, but not by Hilary or the council. Possibly Basiliscus was promoted to consul prior after the original proclamation had been received in the West, because of his kinship to the Emperor Leo (see note on 381). The fasti are not in accord on the order of names.

Occidentis

FASTI:	Camp. Add. ad Prosp. (1, 493) AqS. Cass. (om. Hyd.)	Leo Aug. III
	VindPr. Marius Veron. (Aug. II)	Leo (Aug.) III et Tatianus
	Aug.	Leo Aug. III v.c. et Iohannes
LAWS:	none	
INSCR.:	**ROME:** *ICUR* n.s. I 478 (15.v; p.c. poss.); *ICUR* I 821 (16.vii -13.viii); *ICUR* n.s. I 355 (frag.)	D.N. Leo III
	ICUR n.s. II 5935 (frag.)	[Leonis Aug. II]I et Tatiani
	ITALY: *CIL* V 5685 = *ILCV* 2737 (nr. Milan, Reg. XI; 9.x)	p.c. Ermeri (sic) et Fl. Basilisci
	GAUL: *CIL* XIII 2360 = *ILCV* 2910 adn. (Lyons; 6/7?.iii); *CIL* XIII 1548 = *ILCV* 1504 (Aquitania; 5.xi; om. D.N.)	D.N. Leo III
	I.Lat.3 Gaules 145 (Rions, Gironde; 26.v)	Tatianus

NOTES:

Tatianus is a mystery. *PLRE* identifies him as the grandson of Tatianus cos. 391, himself PVC in 450-452 and sent by Leo as an envoy to the Vandals in 464 (II 1053-54). According to Candidus (*FHG* IV 135), Leo and the MVM Aspar "quarreled about Tatianus and Vivianus (*cos.* 463) shortly before Leo turned for support to Zeno 7 [the Isaurian] (c. 467), and Tatianus may therefore have suffered disgrace through Aspar's influence" (*PLRE* II 1054). This Tatianus certainly was of a standing to have become consul, though (in his 80's) older than normal. But there is one important indicator that Tatianus was not an eastern consul in 466, the use of Leo III *e.q.f.n.* in *P.Rainer Cent.* 104 and probably in *M.Chr.* 71. Such a formula makes no sense in an eastern document unless a *western* consul's proclamation is still viewed as a possibility, for the eastern emperor would hardly have proclaimed himself (or any other consul) and left it open that he might proclaim another later; there is in fact no instance of such use. That is not to say that the emperor bound himself to recognize and proclaim any such eventual western proclamation; in 463, for example, the East apparently never proclaimed Basilius even though an *e.q.f.n.* formula was in use with Vivianus' name. [Continued on the next page]

Orientis

FASTI:	Marcell. Heracl. (om. Aug.) Pasch. Victor (om. solus)	Leo Aug. III solus
LAWS:	*CJ* 1.3.27 (= 1.12.6 = 9.30.2) (C'polis, 6.iii)	Leo Aug. III
PAPYRI:	*M.Chr.* 71.19* (14.vii; numeral and presence of "et qui" uncert.); *P.Rainer Cent.* 104.2 (om. Fl., adds Imp.)	D.N. Fl. Leo perp. Aug. (Imp.) III et qui fuerit nuntiatus

NOTES:

[Continued from previous page]

While caution is in order in any year with such limited evidence, we ought therefore to consider the possibility that Tatianus is instead a western consul. His appearance in the three unrelated western lists certainly favors this view. It is true that we have several Roman inscriptions with just Leo, and two from Gaul again with just Leo. But there is also the inscription of 26 May with just *Tatiano consule* from Rions (Gironde), *Inscr. lat. des trois Gaules* 145. It could belong to 391, when Tatianus the grandfather was consul prior with Symmachus, but there is no other example of the omission of Symmachus in an inscription of that year,[70] and since the inscription is both carefully composed and complete, the assumption of the omission of the western consul of the year in favor of the eastern is unattractive. The editors of the inscription have assumed that 466 was the correct date, and this assumption appears justified. Then there is *ICUR* n.s. II 5935, which reads *]i et Tatiani*: perhaps a unique instance of 391 with order reversed, but more likely instead *[Leonis Aug. II]I et Tatiani*.

Tatianus may therefore have been a western consul, proclaimed alone at some point but never universally recognized, perhaps out of office early in the year. Our knowledge of the West in this period is so poor that the fact we do not otherwise know of him means little. There was no western emperor in 466, but of course he would have been designated in 465, when Libius Severus (died 14.xi) was still ruling; eastern nonrecognition of Severus would naturally extend to this as to his other nominees, and areas under eastern control would have followed eastern views. Whatever the actual situation, it does not seem that we can dismiss Tatianus as an error nor accept him as an eastern consul.

[70]*ICUR* n.s. V 13118 and 13357 are fragmentary and could have contained Symmachus' name, though it is now lost. Despite the editor's comment to 13118 ("De Tatiano...466...ne cogites quidem."), however, a date to 466 is not inconceivable.

Occidentis

<u>FASTI</u>:	VindPr. Camp. AqS. Cass. Marius Veron. (Hyd. om.)	Pusaeus et Iohannes
	Aug.	Pusaeus et Mauricianus
<u>LAWS</u>:	none	
<u>INSCR.</u>:	**ROME:** *ICUR* n.s. VIII 20827 (14.ix); *ICUR* n.s. II 5723* (frag.)	Pusaeus et Iohannes vv.cc.
	ITALY: *CIL* V 6210 = *ILCV* 2737A (Milan, Reg. XI; 16.i; om. vv.cc.)	
	GAUL: *CIL* XII 1791 = *ILCV* 2830 (St. Romain d'Albon; 21.ii)	p.c. III Leonis

Orientis

FASTI:	Marcell. Heracl. Pasch. Victor	Pusaeus et Iohannes
LAWS:	none	
PAPYRI:	none	
OTHER:	*Chron.Pasch.* p.496 (judicial activity of Pusaeus as consul)	
	Anth.Pal. 7.697-698 (Iohannes)	

NOTES:

Pusaeus was PPO Or. 465 and 467 (*PLRE* II 930); Iohannes was magister officiorum 467 and PPO Ill. 479 (*PLRE* II 600-01).

On 12.iv.467 Anthemius was proclaimed (western) Augustus at Brontotae (near Rome) and, as normal, took the consulate in the next year.

Occidentis

FASTI: Hyd. VindPr. (D.N.) Camp. AqS.   (D.N.) Anthemius Aug. II
              Cass. Marius (om. II) Veron.

              Aug.   Anthemius Aug. II et
                                                          Severus

LAWS: *NovAnth* 1-3 (20.ii,   D.N. Anthemius Aug. II
              19.iii), all from Rome

INSCR.:   **ROME:** *ICUR* n.s. VII 17588b   D.N. Anthemius (perp.)
              (16.vii-13.viii; om. Aug.);   Aug. II
              ICUR n.s. II 4953 = *ILCV*
              3115B (18.x; frag.); *ICUR* n.s.
              II 4952; *ICUR* n.s. I 741* =
              ILCV 4370 adn.

              ITALY: *CIL* X 1539 = *ILCV* 1643
              (Naples, Reg. I; 9.v; num. is
              III; om. Aug.); *RAC* 29 (1953)
              228 (Teanum, Reg. I; 10.vi;
              om. D.N., Aug.); *CIL* XI 4332
              = *ILCV* 1556 (Terni, Reg. VI;
              perp.)

470

Orientis

<u>FASTI:</u>	Marcell. Heracl. (om. II) Pasch.	Anthemius Aug. II solus
	Victor	Leo IV et Anthemius II
<u>LAWS:</u>	9 laws, all from *CJ*; earliest *CJ* 1.14.10 (no prov.; 8.ii); 4 laws from C'polis, earliest *CJ* 1.4.15 = 2.6.8, 31.iii	D.N. Anthemius (perp.) Aug. II
<u>PAPYRI:</u>	*P.Wisc.* I 10.1 (10.x)	p.c. Fll. Pusaei et Iohannis vv.cc.

<u>NOTES:</u>

Dissemination in Egypt was late.

Occidentis

<u>FASTI</u>:	VindPr. (Zeno II) Camp. AqS. Cass. Veron.	Marcianus et Zeno
	Marius	Marcianus et Leo
	Aug.	Zeno et Probianus
<u>LAWS</u>:	none	
<u>INSCR.</u>:	**ROME:** *ILCV* 3114 (14.viii-1.ix)	Fl. Marcianus et Zeno vv.cc.
	ITALY: *CIL* XI 4078 = *ILCV* 256 (Capena, Reg. VII; 17.i); *CIL* V 6627 = *ILCV* 4370 adn. (Paruzzarro nr. Arona, Reg. XI)	Marcianus v.c.
	GAUL: *CIL* XIII 2361 = *ILCV* 1750 (Lyons; 18.i)	Marcianus vv.cc. (sic)

Orientis

<u>FASTI:</u>	Marcell. Victor Heracl. Pasch.	Zeno et Marcianus
<u>LAWS:</u>	*CJ* 8.52.3 (no prov., 7.ix)	Zeno
	C'polis, 4 laws, earliest *CJ* 1.3.30 (8.iii)	Zeno et Marcianus
<u>PAPYRI:</u>	*P.Oxy.* XXXIV 2724.1 (19.x)	Fll. Zeno et Marcianus vv.cc.
<u>INSCR.:</u>	Feissel, *Rec.Inscr.Chrét.Macéd.* 130 = *IG* X 2 1 779 (Thessalonica, 2.ii); Feissel 101 (Thessalonica)	Zeno et Marcianus
<u>OTHER:</u>	*V.Dan.Styl.* 65; Jo.Ant., fr. 206.2 (both Zeno)	

<u>NOTES:</u>

Marcianus was son of Anthemius and Marcian's daughter Euphemia, husband of Leo's daughter Leontia and MVM (East) *ca* 471/4 (*PLRE* II 717-18). Zeno was the husband of Leo's other daughter Ariadne, MVM 467-474 and Augustus 474-491 (*PLRE* II 1200-02). It is not obvious why Zeno is attested in one Roman inscription but not elsewhere in the West; it is not clear either whether the vv.cc. in *CIL* XIII 2361 should be seen as reflecting knowledge of (but omission of) Zeno's consulate or is just a careless error. The dissemination of Zeno's name could, however, simply have been late; the evidence is thin.

Occidentis

<u>FASTI:</u>	Camp. AqS. (GNQ [Q om. v.c.])	Severus v.c.
	VindPr. (Vind.) AqS. (LS) Cass. Marius Veron.	Severus et Iordanes
	Aug.	Iohannes et Festus
<u>LAWS:</u>	none	
<u>INSCR.:</u>	**ROME:** *ICUR* n.s. II 4954 (25.ii; om. v.c.); *ICUR* n.s. I 2118 = *ILCV* 4370A (14.ix-1.x); *ICUR* n.s. I 3211 = *ILCV* 300 (6.x); *ICUR* n.s. I 90; *ICUR* n.s. II 6085 (p.c. poss.)	Severus v.c.
	ICUR n.s. II 4955 (frag.); 6086 (frag.); *ICUR* n.s. VIII 20828 (frag.)	[Severus et] Iordanes
	ITALY: *CIL* V 6732 = *ILCV* 208 (Vercelli, Reg. XI; 17.ii); *CIL* X 1343 = *ILCV* 248 adn. (Nola, Reg. I; 8.iv; Fl., v.c.)	(Fl.) Severus (v.c.)
	NotScav 1929, 84 = *AE* 1951, 89* (Lipari; vi-vii; p.c. poss.; frag.; Gk.)	Severus et Iordanes
	GAUL: *CIL* XIII 2362 = *ILCV* 2830 adn. (Lyons; 25.ix; DD.NN.); *CIL* XII 1497 = *ILCV* 1927 (Vaison, Narb.; 19?.x; om. vv.cc.)	(DD.NN.) Severus et Iordanes vv.cc.
<u>OTHER:</u>	One leaf of a consular diptych giving Severus' name in full (Volbach no.4, with p.39 above)	

Orientis

FASTI:	Marcell. Victor (Iohannes) Heracl. Pasch.	Iordanes et Severus
LAWS:	*CJ* 5.27.4 (C'polis, 1.i); 1.23.6 (no prov., 27.iii); 1.2.14 (C'polis, no date)	Iordanes et Severus
PAPYRI:	*BGU* XII 2149.2 (19.ix); *SB* XVI 12486.2 (30.ix)	p.c. Fll. Zenonis et Marciani vv.cc.
	P.Herm. 61.1 (3.xii)	Fll. Iordanes et Severus vv.cc.
OTHER:	Jo.Ant., fr. 206.2, 208 (*FHG* 4.617)	

NOTES:

Severus was a Roman, PVR 470, a pagan and a philosopher (*PLRE* II 1005-06); Iordanes was MVM (East) 466-469 (*PLRE* II 620-21). According to Jo.Ant. fr. 206.2, it was Iordanes' designation as consul that led to the revolt of the MVM *per Thracias* Anagastes (*PLRE* II 75-76). Nonetheless, things seem fairly normal: Iordanes is disseminated in the West rather late (though perhaps earlier in Lipari and Gaul than in Rome), and both consuls are known late in Egypt.

Occidentis

<u>FASTI</u>:	VindPr. Camp. AqS. (Aug.) Cass. Marius Veron.	Leo (Aug.) IV et Probianus
	Aug.	Leo IV
<u>LAWS</u>:	none	
<u>INSCR.</u>:	**ROME:** *ICUR* n.s. II 4958 = *ILCV* 1762 (9.v; om. D.N.); *ICUR* n.s. II 4957 (16.vi; om. v.c.; Gk.); *ICUR* n.s. II 4947 = *ILCV* 246b (2.xii; om. D.N., Aug.); *ICUR* n.s. II 4961 (Leo Aug. IV rest.); *ICUR* n.s. II 5867 (om. Aug.)	D.N. Leo Aug. IV et Probianus v.c.
	ICUR n.s. I 1471 = *ILCV* 2650 (2.ix); *ICUR* n.s. II 5725 = *ILCV* 597 (4.x); *ICUR* n.s. II 4956; *ICUR* n.s. II 4959 = *ILCV* 1708 adn. (p.c. poss.)	Probianus
	ITALY: *IG* XIV 2290 and add., p.704 (Pavia, Reg. XI; 6.ix; Gk.)	D.N. Leo IV et Probianus v.c.
	CIL V 6749 (Vercelli, Reg. XI; viii-ix; om. v.c.); *CIL* V 6741 = *ILCV* 1698A (Vercelli, Reg. XI; 25.xii)	Probianus v.c.
	SPAIN: *Röm.Inschr.Tarraco* 947 (Tarragona; 30.vi)	p.c. Severi et Iordanis vv.cc.
<u>OTHER</u>:	*Liber Pontificalis* I, p.cxlvii (Charter of a church near Tivoli; 17.iv)	Domnus Leo perp. Aug. IV et Probianus v.c.

Orientis

FASTI: Heracl.   Leo IV solus et Probianus

              Marcell. Pasch. (om. Aug.)   Leo Aug. IV et Probianus
              Victor (num. V; Probinus)

LAWS: *CJ* 1.3.29 (1.vi) and 1.40.14   Leo Aug. IV et Probianus
              (7.viii), both C'polis

PAPYRI: *P.Bad.* IV 91 b.14 (24.iii)   p.c. Fll. Iordanis et
                                                     Severi vv.cc.

NOTES:

   Probianus was a Roman aristocrat and PPO 461/463 (*PLRE* II 908). The Roman and Italian inscriptions with Probianus alone presumably reflect a stage before Leo's name was added to the formula, but it is curious that they are not earlier than some of the inscriptions that include Leo. Heracl. shows that Leo was proclaimed first in the East, with Probianus added later; cf. its practice for 472 and 476. For the formula in the *Liber Pontificalis*, cf. notes to 462.

Occidentis

<u>FASTI</u>:	Marius	Festus
	VindPr. Camp. AqS. (LSQN) Cass. Veron.	Festus et Marcianus
	Aug.	Marcianus
	AqS. (G)	Marcianus et Festus
<u>LAWS</u>:	none	
<u>INSCR.</u>:	**ROME:** *ICUR* n.s. I 355 (14.i-13.ii?); *ICUR* n.s. V 15358 = *ILCV* 2634 (4.vii; Ruf.Post.); *ICUR* n.s. II 4964 = *ILCV* 167 (5.x); *ICUR* n.s. I 743 = *ILCV* 199 (9.x); *ICUR* n.s. I 735 (Ruf.Post.)	(Rufius Postumius) Festus v.c.
	ICUR n.s. VII 17589 = *ILCV* 166; *ICUR* n.s. II 4963 (frag.); *ICUR* n.s. V 13405 (Fll.; p.c. poss.)	(Fll.) Festus et Marcianus vv.cc.
	ITALY: *CIL* IX 1374 (Mirabella, Reg. II; 2-5.i; or p.c.?)	Festus
	GAUL: *CIL* XII 1724 = *ILCV* 2454 (Aouste, Narb.; 16.xi)	Festus et Marcianus

478

Orientis

FASTI:	Heracl.	Marcianus solus et Festus
	Marcell. Pasch.	Marcianus et Festus
LAWS:	At least 19 laws, 10 from C'polis: earliest *CJ* 8.37.10, 1.i, latest *CJ* 1.3.31,34, 23.xii	Marcianus
	CJ 2.7.15 (16.xii)	Marcianus et Festus
PAPYRI:	*P.Stras.* 148.1 = *SB* V 8752.1 (i-ii); *P.Rainer Cent.* 105.1 (24.vii); *P.Lond.* V 1793.2* (1.xii)	p.c. Fl. Leonis perp. Aug. IV et Probiniani v.c.
	BGU XII 2150.1 (8.xi)	Fl. Marcianus v.c. et qui nuntiatus fuerit

NOTES:

Marcianus is usually identified with Marcianus cos. 469 the son of Fl. Anthemius, but none of our sources gives an iteration number. He must surely be another man (so A. Demandt, *RE* Supplbd. XII 775). The name is not uncommon (see *PLRE* II 713-19, nos. 1-20); no. 9, an eastern MVM, is a possible candidate (but could be the son of Anthemius). Festus was a Roman aristocrat who served on several embassies (*PLRE* II 467-69).

The curious form of the entry in Heracl. (so too under 471 and 476) suggests that the second name was added late in the year after it had already been assumed that Leo was to be the sole consul, as does *BGU* 2150. Dissemination was in any case late in Egypt. In the West, Roman inscriptions with Marcianus are undated, and the Gallic one is late.

Occidentis

<u>FASTI</u>:	VindPr. Camp. AqS. Cass. Marius (om. Aug.) Veron. Aug.	Leo Aug. V
<u>LAWS</u>:	1 law from Ravenna, *PL* 56.898 (11.iii)	D. Leo perp. Aug. V
<u>INSCR.</u>:	**ROME:** *ICUR* n.s. I 224 = *ILCV* 4401 adn. (5.i?)	p.c. Fl. Festi v.c.
	ICUR n.s. IV 11164; *ICUR* n.s. II 4967 = *ILCV* 697 adn.	Leo Aug. V

Orientis

FASTI:	Marcell. Heracl. Pasch. (om. Aug.)	Leo Aug. V solus
	Victor	Leo VI et Probinus
LAWS:	*CJ* 6.61.5 (no prov., 1.vi)	Leo Aug. V
PAPYRI:	*Mneme G. Petropoulos* (Athens 1984) II 204.1* = P.Lond.inv. 869 descr. (14.ix)	[p.c. Fl. Marciani] v.c. et qui fuerit nuntiatus

NOTES:

By Anthemius' death on 11.vii.472, Olybrius had already been proclaimed western Augustus by Ricimer (probably in April), but on 2.xi he too died. On 3.iii.473 the comes domesticorum Glycerius (*PLRE* II 514) was proclaimed at Ravenna, but Leo refused to recognize him and in June, 474, proclaimed instead Iulius Nepos (*PLRE* II 777), magister militum of Dalmatia. 'Probinus' in Victor is probably a misplaced misspelling of Probianus (cos. 471). See 458 for an inscription which could belong to 473.

Occidentis

<u>FASTI</u>:	VindPr. Camp. AqS. Cass. Marius (om. Aug.) Veron. Aug. (ad a.453) Haun. (om. Aug.)	Leo iunior Aug.
	AqS. (S)	Leo iun. et Zeno
<u>LAWS</u>:	none	
<u>INSCR.</u>:	**ROME:** *ICUR* n.s. VI 16002 = *ILCV* 1138 adn. + add. II p.512 (31.i); *ICUR* n.s. I 738* = *ILCV* 511b (13.ii; D.N.; om. iun. Aug. I); *ICUR* n.s. II 4926 = *ILCV* 1196 (9.v; om. Aug.); *ICUR* n.s. II 4973* (14.viii-13.ix; frag.); *ICUR* n.s. VII 17590 (26.ix; om. Aug.)	(D.N.) Leo iun. Aug. I
	ITALY: *I.Ital.* XI 2 42 = *ILCV* 2738 (Ivrea, Reg. XI; 12.viii; om. Aug. I)	
	DALMATIA: *Forsch.Salona* II 183 (frag.)	
	GAUL: *CIL* V 7978 = *ILCV* 250 (Cimiez; 25.v)	D.N. Leo iunior v.c.
<u>OTHER</u>:	Tjäder, *Nichtlit. Pap.* 4-5 B.iii.8 (Ravenna, 13.xi; doc. 552-575)	Leo iun. perp. Aug.

Orientis

FASTI:	Marcell. Heracl. (Aug.) Pasch.	Leo iunior (Aug.) solus
	Victor	Leo iunior Aug.
LAWS:	3 laws: *CJ* 2.7.16 (C'polis, 16.iii); 1.14.11 (22.iv) and 10.15 (10.x), no prov.	Leo iunior Aug.
PAPYRI:	none	

NOTES:

Leo iunior (*PLRE* II 664-65) was the infant son of Zeno and grandson of Leo I, apparently proclaimed Augustus between 1.i and 18.i (when Leo I died). On 9.ii Zeno was proclaimed co-Augustus with his son, who died in November, leaving Zeno sole Augustus.

Occidentis

FASTI:	VindPr. Camp. (om. iun.) Haun. Cass. Veron.	p.c. Leonis iun. Aug.
	AqS. (G)	p.c. Leonis iun.
	AqS. (N) Camp.	p.c. Leonis Aug.; Zeno Aug. II
	AqS. (L,S)	Leoni iun. et Zenoni
	AqS. (Q)	Zeno
LAWS:	none	
INSCR.:	ROME: *ICUR* n.s. V 13958 (25.ii)	p.c. Leonis iun.
	ITALY: *CIL* V 6183a (cf. p.620 n.7) = *ILCV* 1043 (Milan, Reg. XI)	p.c. D. N. Divi Leonis iun.
OTHER:	Pope Simplicius, *Epp.* 1 (Thiel 177) (19.xi)	p.c. Leonis Aug.

NOTES:

On 28.viii Nepos was driven from Italy by the patrician Orestes (*PLRE* II 811-12), who proclaimed his son Romulus Augustus (*PLRE* II 949-50), on 31.x.475.

On 9.i.475 Zeno, who had proclaimed himself consul for this year, was driven from Constantinople by Basiliscus, who proclaimed himself Augustus and abolished Zeno's consulate. As a consequence, the year--at the time--was officially known as *p.c. Leonis iunioris Aug.* There is no way of telling whether *Zeno Aug. II* in Marcell. and Pasch. is original or retroactive correction after Zeno's restoration in 476. Naturally enough Zeno counted 475 when numbering his next consulate (479) III, but hardly any documents from the year 475 itself can ever have used Zeno's consulate. For Heracl.'s entry, see above, p.57.

Orientis

<u>FASTI:</u>	Marcell. Pasch..	Zeno Aug. II solus
	Victor	p.c. Leonis iun. Aug.
	Heracl.	anhypata
<u>LAWS:</u>	*CJ* 5.5.8 (C'polis, 1.ix)	p.c. Leonis iun.
<u>PAPYRI:</u>	*CPR* V 14.1 (25.i); *P.Rain.Cent.* 106.1	p.c. D.N. Fl. Leonis iun. perp. Aug. I
	P.Oxy. XVI 1899.1* (8.v)	p.c. Divi Leonis iun. I

475 or 476:
SB XIV 11425 (frag.)

Occidentis

<u>FASTI</u>:	VindPr. (om. Aug.) Camp. AqS. Marius Veron. (both om. Aug. II) Aug. Cass. Haun. (om. Aug.)	Basiliscus Aug. II et Armatus
<u>LAWS</u>:	none	
<u>INSCR.</u>:	**ROME:** *ICUR* n.s. II 4975 (15.v; frag.); *ICUR* I 863 = *NotScav* 1888, 451 no.56 (14.viii-1.ix); *ICUR* n.s. IV 11165 = *ILCV* 485a (18.viii); *ICUR* I 1164 (om. II; p.c. poss.); *ICUR* n.s. VI 16003 (om. II; p.c. poss.); *ICUR* n.s. II 4974* (frag.; p.c. or p.c. iterum, 478, poss.); *ICUR* n.s. VII 17591 (frag.; p.c. or p.c. iterum, 478, poss.)	D.N. Basiliscus (perp. Aug.) II et Armatus v.c.
	ITALY: *CIL* V 6404 = *ILCV* 1041 (Lodi, Reg. XI; 1.v; adds perp. Aug. after Bas.); *NotScav* 1897, 367 (Dertona, Reg. IX; 14.xi-13.xii)	
	GAUL: *AE* 1965, 332 (Antibes; 29.xii; om. D.N.)	
<u>OTHER</u>:	Pope Simplicius to Basiliscus, *Epp.* 3 (Thiel 183 = *Coll. Avell.* 56, p.129) (10.i)	Basiliscus Aug.

Orientis

FASTI:	Marcell. Pasch.	Basiliscus et Armatus
	Heracl.	Basilius Aug. et Armatius solus
	Victor	Basiliscus tyrannus et Armatus
LAWS:	*CJ* 1.2.16 (no prov., 17.xii)	Armatus v.c.
PAPYRI:	*P.Oxy.* XVI 1958.1 (19.viii; om. I); *BGU* XII 2151.2 (19.x)	p.c. Divi Leonis iun. I

NOTES:

Armatus was MVM from 469/74 to 477/8 and a nephew of Basiliscus (*PLRE* II 148-49). On Zeno's restoration (end of August 476) Basiliscus was imprisoned and starved to death. His name was evidently stricken from the record; whence the appearance of Armatus' name alone in official documents such as laws (*CJ* 1.2.16) (cf. Heracl. and p.c.'s of 477).

The omission of Armatus' name by Pope Simplicius is probably to be put down to more than MS error, since the next letter, written one day later (11.i), is dated *consule supra scripto* (cf. too *Coll.Avell.* no.58, with Guenther's note on p.133.3), implying deliberate reference to one consul. The probability is that, writing so early in the year, Simplicius did not yet know whom Basiliscus had designated as his colleague--or indeed if there was to be a second consul. Not since 467 had there been two eastern consuls. On the other hand, it must long have been obvious--and prescribed by tradition--that Basiliscus would take the consulate himself. The principal MS mistakenly addresses the letter to Zeno (cf. O. Guenther, *Coll.Avell.* p.124.12, note), but the truth is preserved in the earlier MS B.

Occidentis

FASTI:	VindPr. AqS. (GLSN) Cass. (II) Marius Veron. Haun.	p.c. Basilisci (II) et Armati
	Camp.	p.c. s(upra) s(criptorum)
	AqS. (Q)	Zeno III
LAWS:	none	
INSCR.:	none	
OTHER:	Pope Simplicius, *Epp.* 6 (Thiel 189) (9.x)	p.c. Basilisci et Armati

NOTES:

As Thiel observes (p.189, n.16), the omission of *Aug.* after Basiliscus' name is probably deliberate and original. Victor records (between his accounts of 476 and 477): "Inter haec quae gesta sunt, quia nullus consul accessit et Basiliscus tyrannus a consulatu recessit, Armatus praesenti anno consul remansit."

Orientis

FASTI:	Pasch.	Basiliscus et Armatus
	Heracl. Marcell.	anhypata
	Victor	p.c. Armati
LAWS:	*CJ* 5.27.5 (no prov., 20.ii); 8.4.9 (15.xii) and 1.23.7 (23.xii), both C'polis	p.c. Armati v.c.
PAPYRI:	*P.Köln* III 152.1 (28.i; pap. has cos. for p.c.)	p.c. D.N. Fl. Basilisci II et Armati v.c.
	SB III 7167.2 (4.x)	p.c. D.N. Fl. Zenonis et Armati v.c.

NOTES:

For the remarkable versions in the papyri, see *P.Köln* 152 introd. Zeno was properly iterum p.c. II in this year, 475 being his second consulate. Pasch., who did not understand p.c.'s, gives Basiliscus et Armatus two years running. See above, p.57, for Heracl.'s entry.

Occidentis

<u>FASTI</u>:	VindPr. Camp. AqS. Cass. Haun. Marius (om. v.c.) Veron. Aug.	Illus v.c.
<u>LAWS</u>:	none	
<u>INSCR.</u>:	**ROME:** *ICUR* n.s. I 3241	p.c. iterum Armati v.c.
	ITALY: *I.Ital.* IV.1 544 = *ILCV* 251 (Tibur, Reg. I; 1.iii);	p.c. iterum Armati v.c.
	CIL IX 2073 = *ILCV* 1029A (Beneventum, Reg. II; 7.x)	Illus v.c.
<u>OTHER</u>:	Simplicius, *Epp.* 9,10,11, 12,13 (Thiel 195-201 = *Coll. Avell.* 61-65, with improved text) (13.iii, 8.x, 21.x)	Illus v.c.

Orientis

FASTI: Marcell. Heracl. Pasch.   Illus solus
        (Victor om.)

LAWS: *CJ* 5.9.7 (1.iii) and 9.35.11   Illus v.c.
        (prob. 28.x/9.xi), both C'polis

PAPYRI: *CPR* V 15.1 = *P.Rainer Cent.*   p.c. Armati beatae
        123 (15-23.vi)   memoriae

NOTES:

Illus was an Isaurian and close friend of Zeno; magister officiorum 477-481, MVM 481-483 (*PLRE* II 586-90). The consular reference in the papyrus should properly be *iterum p.c. Armati*, although such indications are normally not given in papyri. It is not clear if Illus was ever disseminated in Egypt.

491

Occidentis

FASTI: Camp. AqS. Aug.   Zeno Aug. III

        VindPr. Haun. (one hand   Zeno (perp.) Aug.
        adds perp.)

        Cass.   Zeno Aug. II

        Marius   Zeno

        Veron.   Zeno v.c.

LAWS: none

INSCR.: **ROME:** *ICUR* n.s. II 6462 add.   D.N. Zeno [
         (14.ii-15.iii)

         ITALY: *CIL* V 6730 = *ILCV* 3195   D.N. Zeno perp. Aug.
         (Vercelli, Reg. XI; 13.x;
         simply Zeno); *CIL* XI 2584
         (Chiusi, Reg. VII; ix-xii)

         DALMATIA: *Forsch.Salona* II 184   D.N. Zeno perp. Aug.

OTHER: Pope Simplicius to Zeno, *Epp.*   p.c. Illi v.c.
        15 (Thiel 240 = *Coll.Avell.*
        66) (22.vi)

Orientis

FASTI:	Marcell. Heracl. (om. III, adds solus) Pasch. Victor (om. III)	Zeno Aug. III (solus)
LAWS:	*CJ* 3.28.29 (no prov., 1.v); 5.31.11 (C'polis, 1.ix); 1.49.1 (no prov., 11.x)	Zeno Aug. II
	CJ 6.34.4 (C'polis, 30.v)	Zeno Aug.
PAPYRI:	none	

NOTES:

The formula *Zeno Aug. II* offered by the laws can hardly be correct (see above on 475). The Justinianic compilers were probably misled by a consular list that gave 475 (*Zeno Aug. II*) as *p.c. Leonis iunioris* and so counted 479 only as Zeno II. There may have been confusion, as evidenced by the omission of the numeral altogether in one law, two Italian inscriptions, and a number of fasti. The papyrus in 480 has it right.

Occidentis

<u>FASTI</u>:	VindPr. AqS. Cass. Veron. Haun.	Basilius iun. v.c.
	Marius Aug.	Basilius iun.
<u>LAWS</u>:	none	
<u>INSCR.</u>:	none	

Orientis

FASTI:	Marcell. Heracl. Pasch.	Basilius solus
	Victor	p.c. Zenonis III
LAWS:	*CJ* 6.23.22 (C'polis, 1.v)	Basilius iunior
	CJ 2.21.9, 5.12.28, 5.75.6 (no prov., 1.i or 28.xii)	Basilius (v.c.)
PAPYRI:	*PSI* VI 703.2 (28.i)	p.c. D.N. Fl. Zenonis perp. Aug. III

NOTES:

Basilius was a prominent Roman aristocrat, son of Basilius cos. 463, father of four consuls, and PPO Ital. 483 (*PLRE* II 217, with Cameron and Schauer, *JRS* 72 [1982] 127 f.). He was the first consul designated by a barbarian king. For the widespread but inexplicable modern view that Basilius' consulate was not recognized in the East, see *JRS* 72 (1982) 132. Dissemination may have been late (though we have no papyri after January this year), and the laws and fasti could have been corrected, but the three papyri with p.c.'s in 481 and 482 show certain contemporary dissemination.

We have put all inscriptions dated by Basilius iun. (v.c.) under 541; in those cases where there is no other evidence to indicate 541, however, these inscriptions could be from 480.

Occidentis

FASTI: VindPr. Camp. AqS. Cass. Aug.   Placidus v.c.
                Marius (om. v.c.) Veron.
                Haun.

LAWS: none

INSCR.:   **ROME:** *ICUR* n.s.VII 17592a   (Fl.) (Rufius) Placidus
                (ix-xii; Fl.); *ICUR* n.s. II 4980;   v.c.
                ICUR n.s. I 3243 (frag.); *ICUR*
                n.s. II 4982* (Rufius Pl.; dub.);
                ICUR n.s. VII 17592b (Ruf. Pl.;
                p.c. poss.)

                ITALY: *CIL* V 4117 = *ILCV*
                2778 (Cremona, Reg. X;
                17.ix); *CIL* V 7415 =
                ILCV 1693 (nr. Dertona,
                Reg. IX; 28.xii)

                GAUL: *CIL* XII 2055
                (Vienne; om. v.c.); *I.Lat.*
                Gaul.Narb. 294 (Vienne; p.c.
                poss.)

Orientis

<u>FASTI:</u>	Marcell. Heracl. Pasch. (Victor om.)	Placidus solus
<u>LAWS:</u>	none	
<u>PAPYRI:</u>	*P.Princ.* II 82.1 (27.iii)	p.c. D.N. Fl. Zenonis perp. Aug. III
	P.Lond. III 991.1* (p.258) (22.vi); *BGU* XII 2155.2 (18.x; pap. has cos. for p.c.; om. e.q.f.n.)	p.c. Fl. Basilii v.c. et qui fuerit nuntiatus

<u>NOTES:</u>

The situation in the papyri is remarkable. One early text keeps referring to the p.c. of the cos. of 479; the next gives Basilius, the cos. of 480, *et qui fuerit nuntiatus*; the third gives only Basilius. The dropping of *e.q.f.n.* is paralleled in 451-452; but it reappears in a p.c. date in 482. The testimony of the eastern fasti suggests that Placidus was ultimately recognized in the East, but the papyrus from 482 does not support them.

Placidus was a Roman aristocrat (*PLRE* II 891).

Occidentis

FASTI:	Cass. Marius	Severinus iunior
	AqS. (GSQN) Veron.	Severinus iun. v.c.
	Aug.	Severinus
	Camp. VindPr.	Severinus v.c.
	AqS. (L) Haun. (iun.)	Severinus (iun.) et Trocondus
LAWS:	none	
INSCR.:	**ROME:** *ICUR* n.s. II 4983 (19.x); *CIL* VI 37741 = *ILCV* 451 (om. vv.cc.; Diehl's rest.; uncertain)	[Severinus et] Trocondes vv.cc.
OTHER:	Pope Simplicius, *Epp.* 14, 17,18,20 (Thiel 202f., cf. *Coll.Avell.* 68-69) (20.v, 15.vii, 6.xi)	Severinus v.c.

Orientis

FASTI:	Victor (v.c.) Heracl. (solus)	Trocondus (v.c.) (solus)
	Marcell. Pasch.	Trocondus et Severinus
LAWS:	none (see notes to 483)	
PAPYRI:	*CPR* X 118.2 (13?.x)	[p.c.] Fl. Basilii v.c. et qui nuntiatus fuerit

NOTES:

Severinus iunior was presumably the son of Severinus cos. 461, but nothing else is known of him (*PLRE* II 1001); Trocundes (spelling as on the Syrian inscr. *AE* 1969/1970, 609, that gives his full name) was Illus' brother and MVM 476/7-482 (*PLRE* II 1127-28). The actual contemporary situation is obscure, given the lack of laws and shortage of papyri, but the papyri of 483 suggest that Severinus was not recognized or disseminated in the East (as Heracl. also indicates). The one papyrus (an indiction shows that 482 is meant) shows Basilius still in use in October. Trocundes, on the other hand, seems to have been disseminated at least in Rome; but the Pope does not mention him in his formulas.

Occidentis

<u>FASTI</u>:	VindPr. Camp. AqS. Cass. Marius (om. v.c.) Haun.	Faustus v.c.
	Veron. (v.c.) Aug.	Faustus iunior (v.c.)
<u>LAWS</u>:	none	
<u>INSCR.</u>:	**ROME:** *ICUR* n.s. II 4985 = *ILCV* 1347 (24.i; Aginantius Faustus); *ICUR* n.s. IV 11166 = *ILCV* 1615 (7.iii); *ICUR* n.s. I 1105* (26.vii)	(Aginantius) Faustus v.c.
	ITALY: *CIL* V 6210 = *ILCV* 2737A (Milan, Reg. XI; 2.xii)	
	GAUL: *CIL* XII 2056 = *ILCV* 250 adn. (Vienne; ix-x)	

<u>NOTES</u>:

Faustus was PVR twice at uncertain dates (*PLRE* II 451-52).

Orientis

<u>FASTI:</u>	Victor	p.c. Trocondi v.c.	
	Heracl.	anhypata	
	Marcell. Pasch.	Faustus solus	
<u>LAWS:</u>	none (see notes)		
<u>PAPYRI:</u>	*P.Lond.* V 1896.1 (vi-vii); *BGU* XII 2156.2 (27.viii)	p.c. Fl. Trocondi v.c. et qui fuerit nuntiatus	

<u>NOTES:</u>

In *CJ* 4.59.2 the sixth or seventh cent. Veronensis offers 16.xii aa. conss. Troconde, an abbreviation which should represent the obviously inappropriate *Augustis consulibus*. The usual correction is p.c. Trocondi, which, so late in the year, would strongly suggest non-dissemination of the western consul of 483. But it is equally possible that the corrupt phrase refers to 482 (so Mommsen, *Ges.Schr.* VI 382 n.4), in which case the possibility remains open that Faustus was proclaimed late in the East in 483, as Marcell. and Pasch. imply. As pointed out above (p.70), the continuing use of p.c. 482 in 484 does not necessarily exclude late proclamation of Faustus in 483. ἀνύπατα is no more than Heracl.'s normal way of indicating a p.c. (cf. p.57). It was presumably through no more than force of habit that the *e.q.f.n.* formula was repeated in the papyri of 483 (dropped in those of 484).

Occidentis

FASTI:	VindPr. (v.c.) AqS. (S)	Venantius (v.c.)
	AqS. (N)	Venantius v.c. et Theodericus
	Haun. Marius Veron. Aug. AqS. (QL)	Venantius et Theodericus
	Camp.	Venantius v.c. cons. et Theodericus
	Cass.	D.N. Theodericus et Venantius
	AqS. (G)	Theodericus et Venantius
LAWS:	none	
INSCR.:	**ROME:** *ICUR* n.s. II 4964 = *ILCV* 167b (26.viii); *ICUR* n.s. I 1472* (1.x?); *ICUR* I 933* = *ILCV* 708; *ICUR* n.s. VII 17593 = *ILCV* 842	Venantius v.c.
	ITALY: *CIL* X 1344 = *ILCV* 1014 (Nola, Reg. I; 9.ii); *RAC* 26 (1950) 233-34 (Milan, Reg. XI; 14.iv-1.v)	p.c. Fausti v.c.
	CIL IX 1375 (nr. Aeclanum, Reg. II; 21.i; Fl.); *CIL* V 5241 (Gravedona, Reg. XI; 25.v/24.vi); *CIL* V 6247 = *ILCV* 3171A (Milan, Reg. XI; 1.xii?)	(Fl.) Venantius v.c.
	GAUL: *I.Lat.3 Gaules* 270 (Lyons; 19.v); *AE* 1978, 485 (Lyons; 28.xi)	
OTHER:	Tjäder, *Nichtlit. Pap.* 47-48A.27* (Ravenna; doc. 510 or later)	Venantius
	Pope Felix, *Epp.* 6,8 (Thiel 247, 250)(28.vii, 1.viii)	Venantius v.c.

Orientis

<u>FASTI:</u>	Victor (v.c.) Heracl. (solus)		Theodericus (v.c.) (solus)
	Marcell. Pasch.		Theodericus et Venantius
<u>LAWS:</u>	*CJ* 1.3.36 (C'polis, 28.iii); 1.3.37 (1.iv) and 12.21.8 (1.ix), no prov.		Theodericus
<u>PAPYRI:</u>	*P.Rainer Cent.* 107.1 (14.ii); *P.Oxy.* VIII 1130.1 (4.v)		p.c. Fl. Trocondi v.c.
	P.Oxy. XVI 1969.1 (20.ix); *PSI* III 183.1 (ix-x); *P.Rainer Cent.* 108.1 (p.c. 485 or 486 poss.)		Fl. Theoderichus v.c.
<u>OTHER:</u>	*Anon.Val.* 49		

<u>NOTES:</u>

The East did not disseminate Venantius (*PLRE* II 218), nor the West Theoderic (*PLRE* II 1077-84). Venantius was the son of Basilius cos. 463 and brother of Basilius cos. 480 and Decius cos. 486. He was presumably known by his third rather than (as usual) last name to avoid confusion with his father and elder brother (cf. *JRS* 72 [1982] 127).

Occidentis

FASTI:	Camp. AqS. Cass. Marius (om. v.c.) Aug.	Symmachus v.c.
	Haun. Veron.	Symmachus iunior v.c.
LAWS:	none	
INSCR.:	ROME: *AE* 1969/1970, 86 (14.ii-15.iii); *ICUR* n.s. I 514 = *ILCV* 3112A (6.vii; om. v.c.); *ICUR* n.s. II 4964 = *ILCV* 167, cf. *AE* 1969, 86 (9.ix); *ICUR* n.s. II 4986; *ICUR* n.s. II 5799; *ICUR* n.s. VII 17484c	Symmachus v.c.
	ICUR n.s. II 5869	Symmachus iun.
	ITALY: *CIL* V 5425 = *ILCV* 3170b (Como, Reg. XI; 12.v; om. v.c.); *CIL* V 6237 = *ILCV* 2738A (Milan, Reg. XI; 8.xii)	Symmachus v.c.
	GAUL: *I.Lat.Gaul.Narb.* 297* = *ILCV* 1678 (Vienne; 8?.v); *CIL* XII 1498* = *ILCV* 2256 (Vaison, Narb.; 1.vi; Veri? Ven. v.c.?); *CIL* XII 2062 = *ILCV* 1665 (Vienne; 18.ix; v.c.)	p.c. Venanti (v.c.)
	CIL XII 2057 = *ILCV* 2888 adn. (Vienne; 18.v)	Symmachus v.c.
OTHER:	Synod at Rome (Thiel 257 = *Coll.Avell.* 70) (5.x)	Symmachus v.c.

Orientis

<u>FASTI:</u>	Victor	p.c. Theoderici v.c.
	Marcell. Heracl. Pasch.	Symmachus solus
<u>LAWS:</u>	none	
<u>PAPYRI:</u>	*P.Coll.Youtie* II 89.1 (28.vi); *BGU* XII 2157.1 (21.ix); 2159.1 (4.xii); *P.Laur.* IV 141 verso (or 486)	p.c. Fl. Theoderichi v.c.
<u>OTHER:</u>	Procopius, *BG* 1.1.32 implies eastern recognition of Symmachus' consulate	

<u>NOTES:</u>

Despite most fasti, the papyri with p.c. of Theoderic, continuing in 486, indicate that Symmachus (*PLRE* II 1044-46) was not disseminated in at any rate Egypt. In Gaul, his name was apparently known in May in Narbonne, yet ignored in later inscriptions from the area. For a postconsular era of Symmachus, cf. above, p.65 n.33.

For the years 485, 487, and 488, Marcell., Pasch., and Heracl. all list the western consul of the year. The contemporary eastern evidence, however, unanimously points to continuous use of p.c. dating rather than dissemination of these western names. In 483, 484, 486 and 490, only some of this trio of fasti preserve the western consul, while again the documents use only the eastern consul. Our lemmata reflect contemporary usage in the East without implying non-recognition at the imperial court.

Occidentis

FASTI:	Veron.	Decius iun. v.c.
	VindPr. Camp. AqS. (LNS [S om. v.c.]) Hist.Britt. (3,209,22) Aug.	Decius v.c.
	Haun. AqS. (GQ) Cass. Marius	Decius et Longinus
LAWS:	none	
INSCR.:	**ROME:** *ICUR* I 1021 (22.iii); *ICUR* n.s. VIII 20830 = *ILCV* 592 (9.vii); *ICUR* n.s. I 743 = *ILCV* 199 (18.vii); *ICUR* n.s. I 2119 (16.vii-13.viii); *ICUR* n.s. II 4987 (27.x); *ICUR* n.s. II 5049* (13.xii; Fl.); *ICUR* n.s. VII 17594	(Fl.) Decius v.c.
	ITALY: *I.Ital.* XI.2 43 = *ILCV* 1055 (Ivrea, Reg. XI; 29.iii); *CIL* V 6228 = *ILCV* 2739 (Milan, Reg. XI; 2.iv); *CIL* V 5423 = *ILCV* 1445A adn. (Como, Reg. XI; 24.iv); *NotScav* 1897, 364 = *ILCV* 2829A adn. (Dertona, Reg. IX; 19.ix)	
	GAUL: *CIL* XIII 1656 = *ILCV* 1340 (Anse, nr. Lyons; 22.iii); *CIL* XII 2485 = *ILCV* 2765 (Gresy-sur-Aix, Narb.; 19.v)	p.c. Symmachi
	I.Lat.Gaul.Narb. 606* (Narbonne; 30.i; cos. error for p.c.?)	Decius <et> Longinus
	CIL XIII 2454 = *ILCV* 3565A (nr. Lyons; 17.iii)	Decius v.c.

Orientis

FASTI:	Marcell. (solus) Victor (v.c.)	Longinus (v.c.) (solus)
	Heracl.	Longinus II solus
	Pasch.	Longinus et Decius
LAWS:	*CJ* 4.20.14 (21.v); 9.5.1 (1.vii), both C'polis	Longinus (v.c.)
PAPYRI:	*P.Oxy.* VI 914.1 (30.i); *CPR* V 16.2 (16.ix)	p.c. Fl. Theoderichi v.c.
	SB I 4481.1 (prob. post 16.ix)	Fl. Longinus v.c.
OTHER:	Jo.Ant., fr. 214.7 (*FHG* IV 621)	

NOTES:

Longinus was MVM 485 and brother of the Emperor Zeno (*PLRE* II 689-90); it was presumably to this relationship that he owed his second consulate in 490, an otherwise hitherto unparalleled honor in the East. Decius was son of Basilius cos. 463 and brother of Basilius cos. 480 and Venantius cos. 484 (*PLRE* II 349). Decius does not appear in eastern laws (though the latest is 1.vii) or even in Egyptian p.c.'s of 487; he is even absent from all the fasti save Pasch. He was clearly not disseminated, though it is difficult to think of any reason for complete non-recognition. What is more peculiar is the Gallic situation, where both consuls were evidently known in Narbonne in January or soon after (unless an error for p.c. is supposed; cf. the Critical Appendix), yet Decius is used alone near Lyons in March, and the p.c. of Symmachus still in Narbonensis in May! One has the distinct impression that all centralized dissemination has collapsed.

Occidentis

FASTI:	Haun. Camp. AqS. Cass. Veron. Aug.	Boethius v.c.
	VindPr.	Vetius v.c.
LAWS:	none	
INSCR.:	**ROME:** *ICUR* n.s. VIII 20831 = *ILCV* 342 (14.vi-1.vii); *ICUR* n.s. VII 17595 = *ILCV* 355 (9.x); *ICUR* n.s. I 744; *ICUR* n.s. II 5011 (p.c. poss.)	Boethius v.c.
	ITALY: *CIL* V 6286 = *ILCV* 4727 (Milan, Reg. XI; 31.i)	p.c. Deci v.c.
	CIL XI 1019 = *ILCV* 1359 (S. Ilario, Reg. VIII; 1.vii); *CIL* V 6238 = *ILCV* 3171 (Milan; 17.xi)	Boethius
	GAUL: *CIL* XII 2702 = *ILCV* 1118 (St. Thomé, Narb.; vi); *CIL* XII 933* = *ILCV* 2889A (Arles, Narb.; 25.vii)	iterum p.c. Symmachi v.c.
	CIL XIII 2472 = *ILCV* 1749 (nr. Lyons; 11.ii)	Boethius v.c.
OTHER:	Tjäder, *Nichtlit. Pap.* 47-48A.13 (Ravenna; doc. 510 or later)	Boethius
	Consular diptych giving Boethius' full name (Volbach no.6; inscr. *ILS* 1301 [giving his first name as Nar.], with Cameron, *ZPE* 44 [1981] 181-83)	

NOTES:

Boethius was PPO Ital. and PVR II before his consulate, and father of the philosopher Boethius, cos. 510 (*PLRE* II 232-33). The situation in Gaul is again peculiar, with the new consul known earlier than iterum p.c. Symmachi dates appear. In the East, Boethius was apparently never disseminated, as the two years of p.c. Longini in the papyri and inscription show.

Orientis

FASTI:	Victor	p.c. Longini v.c.
	Marcell. Heracl. Pasch.	Boethius solus
LAWS:	*CJ* 1.51.13 (C'polis, 26.vi); 7.51.5 (C'polis, 26.iii) is acc. Krueger part of 1.51.13	p.c. Longini
PAPYRI:	*P.Oxy.* XVI 1961.2 (14.iv); *SPP* XX 128.1 (23.v); *P.Amh.* II 148.1 (19.viii); *CPR* IX 36.1 (487 or 488); *P.Laur.* II 27.1 (487-491, year uncert.)	p.c. Fl. Longini v.c.
INSCR.:	**ISAURIA:** *AE* 1911, 90* (Zenonopolis; ix.487-viii.488)	p.c. Fl. Longini v.c.

Occidentis

FASTI:	VindPr. Camp. AqS. Cass. Marius Veron. Aug. Haun.	Dynamius et Sifidius
LAWS:	none	
INSCR.:	**ROME:** *ICUR* n.s. VIII 23452* (12.viii; frag.); *ICUR* n.s. V 13407; *ICUR* n.s. II 5729 = *ILCV* 2576A adn. (p.c. poss.; frag.)	Dynamius et Sifidius vv.cc.
	ITALY: *CIL* XI 1142 = *ILCV* 324 (nr. Fiorenzuola, Reg. VIII; 13.i)	p.c. Boethi v.c.
	CIL V 7528 = *ILCV* 1059 (Acqui, Reg. IX; 26.i); *CIL* X 7329 = *ILCV* 1667 (Palermo; 4.ii); *CIL* V 8958* = *ILCV* 3454 (Chieri, Reg. IX; 8.vi); *RAC* 53 (1977) 110 no.7 (Nola, Reg. I; frag.)	Dynamius et Sifidius vv.cc.
	GAUL: *CIL* XIII 2473 = *ILCV* 306 (Lyons; 19.vi)	Dedamius (sic) v.c.
OTHER:	Felix, *Epp.* 13 (Thiel 266) (15.iii)	Dynamius et Sividius vv.cc.
	Consular diptych of Sividius, giving his full name and the correct spelling of his last name (Volbach no.7; inscr. *ILS* 1302)	

510

Orientis

FASTI:	Marcell. Heracl. Pasch.	Dynamius et Sifidius
	Victor	p.c. II Longini v.c.
LAWS:	none	
PAPYRI:	*P.Lond.* V 1794.2 (21.vi); *BGU* XII 2160.1 (21.ix)	p.c. Fl. Longini v.c.

NOTES:

Both consuls were western: Dynamius was PVR *ca* 488 (*PLRE* II 382); Sividius PVR twice by then (ib. 1017-18). Once again (cf. 486, notes), the western names do not appear even in the p.c.'s in Egypt, but they do make all three regular eastern fasti. And in all other cases where one court proclaimed *both* consuls in the fifth and sixth centuries, there is reason to believe that it was done with the prior consent of the other court (see p.18). So here J. Sundwall inferred from the "Doppelkonsulat" that there was no break between East and West this year (*Abhandlungen zur Geschichte des ausgehenden Römertums* [Helsinki 1919] 186). The one Gallic inscription omits Sividius, for no apparent reason.

Occidentis

<u>FASTI</u>:	Camp. AqS. (GN [G om. v.c.]) Aug.	Probinus v.c.
	VindPr. AqS. (LSQ) Cass. Haun. Marius Veron.	Probinus et Eusebius
<u>LAWS</u>:	none	
<u>INSCR.</u>:	**ROME:** *ICUR* n.s. VII 19991 = *ILCV* 3766A (5.v); *ICUR* n.s. II 4988 (14.ix-15.x); *ICUR* n.s. II 4964 = *ILCV* 167 (9.xii); *ICUR* n.s. I 745 (xi-xii?); *ICUR* n.s. VII 17596 (om. v.c.); *ICUR* n.s. I 531; *ICUR* n.s. VII 17597a*	Probinus v.c.
	ITALY: *RAC* 59 (1983) 318 + fig.1 (p.315) (Revello, Reg. XI; 28.ii); *CIL* X 4494 = *ILCV* 3375 (Capua, Reg. I; 28.iv); *CIL* XI 4972 = *ILCV* 1033 (Spoleto, Reg. VI; 23.vii); *CIL* XI 1290 = *ILCV* 1667 adn. (Placentia, Reg. VIII)	
	GAUL: *CIL* XII 487 = *ILCV* 446A adn. (Marseille)	Probinus et Eusebius
<u>OTHER</u>:	Tjäder, *Nichtlit.Pap.* 10-11 ii.5-6 (Ravenna, 18.iii)	Probinus v.c.

Orientis

FASTI: Victor (v.c.) Heracl. (suppl.)   Eusebius (v.c.) (solus)
(solus)

        Marcell. Pasch.   Eusebius et Probinus

LAWS: *CJ* 6.49.6 (pp. C'polis, 1.ix)   Eusebius

PAPYRI: *SB* XIV 11601.1 (3.iii);   p.c. Fl. Longini v.c.
P.Flor. III 325.1 (20.v)

NOTES:

Eusebius was magister officiorum (East) 492-497 and cos. II in 493 (*PLRE* II 433); his two consulates prompt the guess that he was kin to the emperor, like Longinus cos. 486, cos. II 490. Probinus was an aristocrat, son of Placidus cos. 481 and father of Cethegus cos. 504 (*PLRE* II 909-10). Probinus was not disseminated in the East, as one can see from the p.c. of Eusebius alone in 490 and the entry in Heracl. In Gaul, as occasionally happened, the eastern consul was disseminated even though his name was not used at Rome.

Occidentis

FASTI: Haun. (v.c.) AqS. (N)   Faustus iun.
           Camp. Cass.

           Aug.   Faustus Niger

           Veron.   Faustus alius et Longinus

           AqS. (Q)   Faustus et Longinus

           AqS. (G)   Faustus et Areobindus

           AqS. (LS)   Longus et Faustus iun.

           VindPr.   Faustus v.c.

           Marius   Longinus et Faustus

LAWS: none

INSCR.:   **ROME:** *ICUR* n.s. VIII 20832   (Probus) Faustus iun. v.c.
           = *ILCV* 2971B (9.i; om. v.c.);
           ICUR n.s. VIII 20833 = *ILCV* 3727D
           (1.ix); *ICUR* n.s. VII 17598
           (Probus; p.c. poss.)

           ITALY: *CIL* V 6742a (Vercelli,   (Fl.) (Probus) Faustus
           Reg. XI; 14.viii-13.ix); *CIL*   iun. v.c.
           V 7742 = *ILCV* 2908 (Genoa, Reg.
           IX; 28.ix); *CIL* V 1858 = *ILCV*
           1060 (Zuglio, Reg. X; 16.x-13.xi);
           CIL XI 4333* = *ILCV* 304 (Terni,
           Reg. VI; 11.xi; P. Faust. v.c.);
           CIL X 1345 = *ILCV* 1015 (Nola,
           Reg. I; 7.xii; Fl. F.)

OTHER: Pope Felix, *Epp.* 16   Probus et Faustus vv.cc.
           (Thiel 274) (1.v)

           Pope Gelasius, *Epp.* 4   Faustus v.c.
           (Thiel 323) (25.vii)

           Anon.Val. 53   Faustus et Longinus

Orientis

FASTI:	Victor	p.c. Longini v.c.
	Heracl. (suppl.)	Longinus II solus
	Marcell. Pasch. (Faustus II)	Longinus II et Faustus
LAWS:	none	
PAPYRI:	*P.Rainer Cent.* 109.1 (bef. 1.ix)	p.c. Fl. Eusebii v.c.
	P.Rainer Cent. 110.2 (16.xii)	Fl. Longinus v.c. II
OTHER:	Malalas 386B; Theophanes AM 5983 (δὶς ὑπατεύσας)	

NOTES:

Faustus was a prominent aristocrat, son of Gennadius Avienus cos. 450, PPO Ital. 509-512 (*PLRE* II 454-56). To distinguish him from Faustus cos. 483 he was also known (in consular contexts) as Faustus iunior or Faustus niger (cf. pp.42-43).

Marcell. and Pasch., along with some western lists, suggest that each consul was recognized in the other half, but there is no contemporary evidence for dissemination (though Longinus appears in western p.c.'s in 491), and Heracl. has "Longinus alone." The text of Pope Felix's letter is corrupt.

Occidentis

FASTI:	Haun. AqS. Camp. Cass. (om. v.c.) Aug. (om. v.c.)	Olybrius iun. v.c.
	Marius Veron.	Olybrius (v.c.)
LAWS:	none	
INSCR.:	**ITALY:** *CIL* V 5210* (Garlate, Reg. XI; 14.i; adds iun.?); *CIL* V 5656* (nr. Milan, Reg. XI; iterum p.c., 492, also poss.)	p.c. Longini II et Fausti vv.cc.
	CIL IX 1376 = *ILCV* 3028B (Mirabella, Reg. II; 14.iv)	p.c. Probi Fausti v.c.
	GAUL: *CIL* XII 2487 = *Rec.Inscr.Chrét. Gaule* XV 5 (Arles, Narb.; 14.i-1.ii; rest. septies, 492, poss.?)	sexies p.c. Symmachi iun. v.c.
	Inscr.Lat.3 Gaules 305 = *AE* 1965, 141 (Briord nr. Lyons; 17.vii); *CIL* XII 2058 = *ILCV* 1587 (Vienne; 12.viii; Long. bis)	p.c. Longini (II) et Fausti
	CIL XII 2384 = *ILCV* 1734 (Vezeronce, Narb.; 28?.xi)	Olybrius iun. v.c.
OTHER:	Tjäder, *Nichtlit.Pap.* 12 ii.5 (Ravenna, 2.i)	p.c. Fl. Fausti iun. v.c.
	Anon.Val. 54	Olybrius v.c.

Orientis

FASTI:	Marcell. Pasch.	Olybrius solus
	Heracl.	Olybrius iunior solus
	Victor	Olybrius v.c.
LAWS:	CJ 7.39.4 (C'polis, 30.vii [or 29.vii])	Olybrius v.c.
PAPYRI:	BGU XII 2162.1 (20.ii); CPR X 119.1 (16.iii); P.Flor. I 94.1 (18.x)	p.c. Fl. Longini v.c. II

NOTES:

Olybrius was son of Areobindus cos. 506 and Anicia Iuliana (*PLRE* II 795; for the iunior, Chapter 3, above). He was an easterner, yet never appears in the papyri, which still give p.c. Longini in 492, then go on to the new consuls of 492. This must be a fault of dissemination, not of recognition. Note that in both Gaul and Italy, a p.c. of Longinus and Faustus is found, even though Longinus was not attested in 490. The Gallic situation is confusing, with two different p.c. datings plus the consul in use; all centralized control over dissemination seems to have broken down. For the postconsular era of Symmachus, cf. above, p.65 n.33. For possible Roman inscriptions with a dating to Olybrius v.c., see under 526.

Occidentis

FASTI:	AqS. (GS) Aug.	Anastasius Aug.
	Camp. AqS. (LQN) Cass. Marius Veron. (both om. Aug.) VindPr. (adds D.N., perp.) Haun. (adds perp.)	(D.N.) Anastasius (perp.) Aug. et Rufus
LAWS:	none	
INSCR.:	**ITALY:** *CIL* V 7531 = *ILCV* 339 (Acqui, Reg. IX; 1.i)	p.c. iterum Longini et Fausti vv.cc.
	Civiltà Cattolica 1953, III, p.392 (Cales, Reg. I; 5.ii)	p.c. Olibri iun.
	CIL IX 3568 = *ILCV* 3162A (Barisciano, Reg. IV; 15.xi); *CIL* V 6221* = *ILCV* 4815 (Milan, Reg. I; om. perp.)	D.N. Anastasius perp. Aug.
	P.Rugo, *Le iscrizioni dei secoli VI-VII-VIII esistenti in Italia* IV (1978) no.58 (Beneventum; 1.xii)	D.N. Anastasius et Rufus v.c.
	GAUL: *CIL* XIII 2364 = *ILCV* 3559 (Lyons; 22.xi)	Anastasius et Rufus vv.cc.

NOTES:

Anastasius (*PLRE* II 78-80) was proclaimed Augustus on 11.iv.491 (Zeno died on 9.iv) and took his first consulate in 492 in the usual way; Rufus is an otherwise unknown easterner (*PLRE* II 959). The last Italian inscription for the year includes him; he also appears in the one Gallic inscription and in two texts with p.c.

Orientis

FASTI:	Marcell. Heracl. Pasch. Victor	Anastasius Aug. et Rufus
LAWS:	*CJ* 12.35.18 (1.i); 1.30.3 (1.iii), both C'polis	Anastasius Aug. et Rufus
PAPYRI:	*P.Oxy.* XLIX 3512 (27.ii)	p.c. Longini v.c. II
	ZPE 62 (1986) 133.1 (25.iii; to be restored like *P.Rainer Cent.* 124); *SB* VI 9152.1 (17.vi); *CPR* VII 40.1 (2.ix; adds Imp. after Aug.); *P.Rainer Cent.* 124.1 (9.x; om. D.N., perp., Fl.)	D.N. Fl. Anastasius perp. Aug. (Imp.) et Fl. Rufus v.c.
INSCR.:	Feissel, *Rec.Inscr.Chrét.Macéd.* 64 (Beroia, 1.ix)	D.N. Anastasius I et Rufus v.c.

Occidentis

FASTI:	VindPr. Haun. AqS. (LS [S om. v.c.]) Cass. Veron.	Albinus v.c.
	AqS. (G)	Anastasius Aug. II
	Camp. AqS. (Q [om. v.c. cons.] N)	Albinus v.c. cons. et Eusebius
LAWS:	none	
INSCR.:	**ROME:** *ICUR* n.s. II 4987 (10.x)	Albinus v.c.
	ITALY: *CIL* XI 4163 = *ILCV* 1030 (Narni, Reg. VI; 5.x)	Albinus iun.
	GAUL: *CIL* XIII 2365 = *ILCV* 3560 (Lyons; 6.iii); *CIL* XIII 2366 (Lyons)	p.c. Anastasi et Rufi vv.cc.
OTHER:	Pope Gelasius, *Epp.* 6 (Thiel 335) (1.xi)	Albinus v.c.

Orientis

FASTI:	Heracl.	Eusebius II solus
	Marcell. Pasch.	Eusebius II et Albinus
LAWS:	none	
PAPYRI:	*P.Grenf.* I 55.1 (25.ii);	p.c. D.N. Fl. Anastasi
	P.Lond. V 1855.1 (26.iv)	perp. Aug. et Fl. Rufi v.c.

NOTES:

For Eusebius, see 489. Albinus (*PLRE* II 51-52) was PPO Ital. ?500-503. Once again there is no contemporary evidence for dissemination beyond each consul's own half of the empire, even in p.c.'s. For the styling of Albinus as iunior in the one Italian inscription, see above, p.41 n.28.

Occidentis

FASTI:	Haun. Camp. AqS. Cass. Marius Veron.	Asterius et Praesidius
	Aug.	Praesidius et Asterius
LAWS:	none	
INSCR.:	**ROME:** *ICUR* n.s. I 1473 = *ILCV* 246A (20.iii); *ICUR* n.s. II 4992 (23.iii); *ICUR* n.s. I 3246 = *ILCV* 4427A (8-15.v; rev. order; om. vv.cc.); *ICUR* n.s. V 13409 (19.vii); *ICUR* n.s. II 4993 (frag.); *ICUR* n.s. VIII 20834 (Fll.); *ICUR* n.s. V 13408 (27.i; p.c. poss.)	(Fll.) Asterius et Praesidius vv.cc.
	ITALY: *CIL* IX 1377 = *ILCV* 1276 (Aeclanum, Reg. II; 8.v; Fll.); *CIL* XI 304 = *ILCV* 1036 (Ravenna, Reg. VIII; 5.vi)	
OTHER:	The subscription to the Medicean Vergil was written by Asterius on 21.iv of his consular year, together with a poem in which he complains of the expense of his consular games (cf. Zetzel, *Latin Textual Criticism* 217-18).	
	Pope Gelasius, *Epp.* 14,17,18,19 (Thiel 379, 382, 385, 386) (11.iii, 15.v, 2.viii, 23.viii)[71]	Asterius et Praesidius vv.cc.

NOTES:

   Asterius was an aristocrat, descended from the Turcii Aproniani of the fourth century, PVR and patrician (*PLRE* II 173-74); Praesidius is otherwise unknown (ib. 903). The reversed order in one Roman inscription (and in Aug.) is noteworthy.

[71]*Epp.* 13 is a forgery; see p.46 n.46.

Orientis

FASTI: Marcell. Heracl. Pasch. Victor   Asterius et Praesidius

LAWS: none

PAPYRI: *BGU* XII 2164.1 (13.xii)   p.c. Fl. Eusebii v.c. II

NOTES:

Despite the fasti, Asterius and Praesidius never appear in the papyri, with Eusebius being used until mid-496. Cf. on 485 for our practice here.

Occidentis

FASTI:	Haun. Camp. (om. v.c.) AqS. Cass. Marius Aug. (both om. v.c.)	Viator v.c.
LAWS:	none	
INSCR.:	**ROME:** *ICUR* n.s. VII 17602 (23.i; om. v.c.); *ICUR* n.s. VII 17601* = *ILCV* 3154A (14.viii-13.xii); *ICUR* n.s. I 2120; *ICUR* n.s. VII 19993 (p.c. poss.); *ICUR* n.s. IV 12427 (p.c. poss.); *ICUR* n.s. VIII 20835 (p.c. or iterum p.c. poss.); *ICUR* n.s. II 4996 (like prec.); *ICUR* n.s. I 1949 (like prec.; om. v.c.); *ICUR* n.s. VIII 23453 (frag.; p.c. poss.)	Viator v.c.
	GAUL: *CIL* XII 932 = *ILCV* 4420 (Arles; i-ii)	X p.c. Symmachi iun. v.c.
	CIL XII 2059 = *ILCV* 3471 adn. (Vienne; 16.iii-1.iv; frag.)	p.c. Asteri [et Praesidi vv.cc.]
	CIL XII 931 = *ILCV* 2888 adn. (Arles; 21.x); *I.Lat.3 Gaules* 271 (Lyons; 9.xii)	Viator v.c.
OTHER:	Synod at Rome (Thiel 437) (3.iii)	Fl. Viator v.c.

NOTES:

Viator is otherwise unknown (*PLRE* II 1158), presumably a westerner. He was disseminated late in the East, as his p.c. attests. The situation in Gaul is again confused; cf. notes on 491.

Orientis

FASTI:	Marcell. Heracl. (om. solus) Pasch.	Viator solus
	Victor	Viator v.c.
LAWS:	none	
PAPYRI:	*P.Oxy.* XVI 1891.1 (29.xi)	p.c. Fl. Eusebii v.c. II

Occidentis

FASTI: Haun. (v.c.) Camp.   p.c. Viatoris (v.c.)
            AqS. (GNQ [om. Viat.]) Marius

            AqS. (L)   Eusebius v.c.

            Aug.   Speciosus

            VindPost. post a.497 (om. v.c.)   Paulus v.c.
            AqS. (L ad a.497) Cass.

LAWS: none

INSCR.:   **ROME:** *ICUR* n.s. I 292   p.c. Viatoris v.c.
            = *ILCV* 482 (6.vi); *ICUR* n.s.
            II 4179 = *ILCV* 3727F (om. v.c.)

            ITALY: *CIL* V 6468 = *ILCV* 1162
            (Pavia, Reg. XI; 20.i)

            GAUL: *CIL* XII 1724* =
            ILCV 2454 (Aouste, Narb.;
            25.xii)

NOTES:

For Speciosus, see *PLRE* II 1024, where it suggested that he was an appointee of Theoderic and soon removed; he was PVR three times. On the other hand, there are no epigraphical attestations, and only Aug. records him. The eastern consul Paulus was not disseminated in the West, even in his p.c.

Orientis

FASTI:	Victor (v.c.) Heracl. Pasch. Marcell.	Paulus (v.c.) solus
LAWS:	*CJ* 6.21.16 (C'polis, 13.ii); 10.16.13 (1.iv), 8.53.22 (30.iv), 10.19.9 (21.vii), no prov.	Paulus v.c.
PAPYRI:	*SB* VIII 9776.1 (15.i)	p.c. Fl. Eusebii v.c.
	P.Oxy. XVI 1889.2 (22.xi); 1975.1 (30.xi)	p.c. Fl. Viatoris v.c.
OTHER:	Marcell. s.a., *fratre consule*	

NOTES:

Paulus was the Emperor Anastasius' brother (*PLRE* II 853). *SB* 9776 omits any indication that this was the p.c. of Eusebius' second consulate; cf. above, p.69.

Occidentis

FASTI:	Haun. (v.c.) Camp. AqS. (GNQ [Q om. Viat.])	iterum p.c. Viatoris (v.c.)
	Marius	Viatoris [sic]
	AqS. (S)	Viator III
	VindPost. Cass. Aug. (om. II)	Anastasius Aug. II
LAWS:	none	
INSCR.:	**ROME:** *ICUR* n.s. II 4997; *ICUR* n.s. I 2793	p.c. iterum Viatoris v.c.

NOTES:

There is no contemporary evidence for the dissemination of Anastasius in the West, but there are only two undated inscriptions, and by now it was normal for westerners to date by their own consul alone.

Orientis

FASTI: Marcell. Heracl. (om. solus)   Anastasius Aug. II solus
             Pasch. Victor (om. solus)

LAWS: *CJ* 5.17.9 (no prov., 15.ii);   Anastasius Aug. II
             2.7.20 (C'polis, 31.xii)

PAPYRI: *SPP* XX 129.17 (4.ii)   p.c. Fl. Pauli v.c.

             SB V 7758.2 (20.viii; adds Imp.   D.N. Fl. Anastasius perp.
             after Aug.); *P.Oxy.* XVI 1982.1   Aug. (Imp.) II
             (1.x); *P.Oxy.* X 1320.1 (23.x)

Occidentis

FASTI:	Haun. VindPost. AqS. Aug. Camp. Marius (both om. v.c.)	Paulinus v.c.
	Cass.	Paulinus et Iohannes
LAWS:	none	
INSCR.:	**ROME:** *ICUR* n.s. II 4998 = *ILCV* 1306 (1.iii); *ICUR* n.s. I 994 (28.iii; p.c. poss.); *ICUR* n.s. IV 12428 (21.iv; om. v.c.); *ICUR* n.s. V 13410 (26.v/25.vi; p.c. or it. p.c. poss.); *ICUR* n.s. II 5000 (p.c. poss.)	Paulinus v.c.
	GAUL: *CIL* XIII 1655 = *ILCV* 3488 (Anse, nr. Lyons; 13.x)	
OTHER:	Pope Anastasius, *Epp.* 6 (Thiel 637) (23.viii)	Fl. (?) Paulinus v.c.
	Liber Pontificalis I 261 (22.xi)	Paulinus
	Subscription in MSS of Martianus Capella, Rome (Zetzel, *Latin Textual Criticism*, p.218; hitherto generally assigned to 534, but the absence of a *iunioris* points to 498: Cameron, *CP* 81 [1986] 320-28)	Paulinus v.c.

NOTES:

Paulinus was a prominent westerner, but nothing specific is known of his career (*PLRE* II 847); Iohannes was MVM (East) 483-498 (*PLRE* II 602-03). The West, as usual, ignored Iohannes (of the lists, only Cassiodorus includes him), but Paulinus was disseminated more promptly and efficiently than usual in the East.

Orientis

<u>FASTI:</u>	Victor Marcell. Pasch.	Iohannes Scytha et Paulinus
	Heracl.	Iohannes et Paulinus
<u>LAWS:</u>	*CJ* 10.19.10 (31.iii) and 5.30.4 (1.iv), no prov.	Iohannes et Paulinus
<u>PAPYRI:</u>	*P.Oxy.* XIX 2237.1 (15.i); *P.Lond.* I 113, 5a.1 (p.210) (23.iii); *BGU* XII 2173.17 (iii-iv)	p.c. D.N. Fl. Anastasi perp. Aug. II
	SB XIV 12050.1 (xi-xii?); *P.Lond.* III 1303 (p.lxxii descr.)	Fll. Iohannes et Paulinus vv.cc.
<u>OTHER:</u>	Theoph. AM 5988, p.140.6 de Boor	

Occidentis

FASTI: Haun. (v.c.) Camp. AqS. (GSQN)   p.c. Paulini (v.c.)
             Marius VindPost.

             AqS. (L) Cass.   Iohannes v.c.

LAWS: none

INSCR.:   **ROME:** *ICUR* n.s. VII 17604   p.c. Paulini v.c.
             (5.ix); *ICUR* n.s. II 4999

             ITALY: *ILCV* 2829A adn.
             (Dertona, Reg. IX; 20.iv)

OTHER: Tjäder, *Nichtlit.Pap.*   p.c. Paulini
             47-48A.4,6 (Ravenna, doc. 510
             or later)

             Pope Symmachus, *Epp.* 1,2   p.c. Paulini v.c.
             (Thiel 642,655) (1.iii, 21.x)

Orientis

<u>FASTI:</u>	Marcell. Pasch.	Iohannes Gibbus solus
	Heracl.	Iohannes alius solus Gibbus
	Victor	Gibbus v.c.
<u>LAWS:</u>	*CJ* 5.62.25 (no prov., 1.i)	Iohannes
<u>PAPYRI:</u>	*P.Mich.* XV 731.1 (vi-vii)	p.c. Fl. Iohannis et Paulini vv.cc.
	P.Oxy. XVI 1959.1* (30.viii)	Fl. Iohannes v. illustr. et excellent. mag. militum
<u>OTHER:</u>	Theoph. AM 5988, p.140.6 de Boor	

<u>NOTES:</u>

Iohannes qui et Gibbus ('the hunchback') was MVM (East) from 492-499 (*PLRE* II 617); there is no evidence that he was disseminated in the West.

Occidentis

<u>FASTI</u>:	VindPost. Camp. AqS. (NL)	iterum p.c. Paulini
	AqS. (GSQ) Cass. Marius	Patricius et Hypatius
	Haun.	item tertio Paulino v.c.
<u>LAWS</u>:	none	
<u>INSCR.</u>:	**ROME:** *ICUR* n.s. II 5001 = *ILCV* 3783 (17.iv)	iterum p.c. Paulini
<u>OTHER</u>:	Pope Symmachus, *Epp.* 3 (Thiel 656 = *MGH Epp.* no.24) (28.ix)	iterum p.c. Paulini iunioris v.c.

Orientis

<u>FASTI:</u>	Victor Marcell. Heracl. Pasch.	Patricius et Hypatius
<u>LAWS:</u>	*CJ* 2.4.43 (no prov., 17 or 20.xi)	Patricius et Hypatius
<u>PAPYRI:</u>	*P.Herm.* 79.2 (14.i)	p.c. Fl. Iohannis v.c.
	SB XVI 12583.1 (15.ix); *P.Stras.* 273 = 471.1 (3.xii; Patr. also mag. militum)	Fll. Patricius et Hypatius vv.cc.

<u>NOTES:</u>

Patricius was MVM (East) 500-518; Hypatius, MVM on and off from 503 to 529, was a nephew of the Emperor Anastasius (*PLRE* II 840-42; 577-81). The two eastern consuls were not proclaimed in the West. The iunior in the letter of Pope Symmachus must be "a slip by a copyist writing later than 534" (Cameron, *CP* 81 [1986] 321, discussing the formulas for 498 and 534).

Occidentis

FASTI: Haun. (v.c.) Camp.   Avienus (v.c.)

         AqS.   Avienus iun. v.c.

         VindPost. ExcSang. Cass.   Avienus et Pompeius
         Victor Marius

LAWS: none

INSCR.: **ROME:** *ICUR* n.s. VII 17605 =   Avienus v.c.
         ILCV 2391D (22.xii); *ICUR* n.s.
         I 480; *ICUR* n.s. I 2118 =
         ILCV 4370A (or p.c.?)

         ITALY: *CIL* V 5241 (Gravedona,
         Reg. XI; 30.iii)

         GAUL: *CIL* XIII 2474 = *ILCV* 1616a
         (nr. Lyons; 24.iv); *CIL* XIII
         2395 = *ILCV* 1070b (Lyons; 25.iv;
         om. v.c.); *CIL* XIII 2367 = *ILCV*
         3561 (Lyons; 17.v); *CIL* XIII
         2475 = *ILCV* 2903 (nr. Lyons;
         12.vi); *CIL* XIII 2368 = *ILCV*
         3561A (Lyons; 24.viii); *CIL* XII
         930 = *ILCV* 2888 (Arles; 2.ix;
         om. v.c.); *I.Lat.Gaul.Narb.* 295*
         (Vienne; 16.x-13.xi; Av. iun.,
         502, poss.)

NOTES:

The document published by Thiel (pp.656-57) as *Epp.* 4 of Pope Symmachus and dated 13.x, *Avieno et Pompeio* is a seventeenth-century forgery (see above, p.46).

Orientis

FASTI:	Marcell. Heracl. Pasch.	Pompeius et Avienus
LAWS:	*CJ* 8.36.4 (C'polis, 20.xii)	Pompeius et Avienus
PAPYRI:	*P.Amst.* I 45.2 (7.vii)	p.c. Fl. Patricii v.c. mag. militum et cos. et qui nuntiatus fuerit
	BGU XII 2174.1 (23.ix)	Fl. Pompeius v.c.

NOTES:

Pompeius was a nephew of Anastasius, MVM *ca* 517 and 528 (*PLRE* II 989-99). Avienus was (probably) a son of Basilius cos. 480 and brother of the western coss. of 493, 505, and 509 (*PLRE* II 193). *P.Amst.* I 45 has confused Hypatios and ὕπατος, hence the blunder of adding *e.q.f.n.* to the two consuls. It is not clear if Avienus was ultimately disseminated in the East, but the law, if uncorrected, may reflect very late proclamation.

537

Occidentis

FASTI:	Camp. AqS. (G [v.c.] N) Victor	Avienus iun. (v.c.)
	AqS. (L)	Albinus v.c.
	Haun.	Avienus alius iun. v.c.
	VindPost. ExcSang. Cass. Marius	Avienus iun. et Probus
	AqS. (QS)	Avienus et Probus v.c.
LAWS:	none	
INSCR.:	**ROME:** *ICUR* n.s. V 13959 = *ILCV* 4874 (22?.iv); *ICUR* n.s. II 4180 = *ILCV* 3115C; *ICUR* n.s. IV 12428 (p.c. poss.?)	Avienus iun. v.c.
	GAUL: *I.Lat.Gaul.Narb.* 296 (3.i)	
OTHER:	Synod at Rome: Mommsen, *Cassiodori Senatoris Variae* pp.420.14; 422.15; 426.6 (8.viii, 27.viii, 23.x)	Rufius Magnus Faustus Avienus v.c.
	ib. p.438.4 (6.xi)	Fl. Avienus iunior v.c.
	Ennodius, *Epp.* 1.5 (*novellus consul ... quem coepisse videmus a fascibus*)	

Orientis

FASTI:	Marcell. Heracl. Pasch. (Av. II)	Probus et Avienus
LAWS:	*CJ* 3.13.7 (C'polis, 15.ii)	Probus et Avienus
	CJ 6.20.18 (C'polis, 21.vii)	Probus et Avienus iun.
PAPYRI:	*Archiv* 29 (1983) 29.1 (v-viii)	Fl. Probus v.c.
	P.Stras. 229.1 (prob. viii); *P.Oxy.* L 3600.1 (1.xii)	Fll. Probus et Avienus vv.cc.

NOTES:

Probus was the third of Anastasius' distinguished nephews, MVM *ca* 526 (*PLRE* II 912-13); Avienus was grandson of Avienus cos. 450 and son of Faustus cos. 490; he must have been very young when he became consul (*PLRE* II 192-93). The East eventually disseminated Avienus, but the West, as usual, did not disseminate Probus.

Occidentis

FASTI: Haun. (v.c.) Camp. AqS. (v.c.)   Volusianus (v.c.)
               Marius VindPost.

LAWS: none

INSCR.:   **ROME:** *ICUR* n.s. II 5002 =   Volusianus v.c.
               ILCV 217b ([v.c.])

               ITALY: *AE* 1981, 266 (Venusia, Reg. II; 28.i); *CIL* XI 4334 = *ILCV* 3165 (Terni, Reg. VI; 4.xii); *CIL* XI 4335 = *ILCV* 3122 (Terni; 30.xii; om. v.c.)

               GAUL: *CIL* XIII 2370 =   p.c. Avieni iun. v.c.
               ILCV 3561B (Lyons; 1.i)

               CIL XII 1787 = *ILCV* 2889   Volusianus v.c.
               (St.-Vallier, Narb.; 19.i)

               SPAIN: *Röm.Inschr.Tarraco* 948   ] Volusianus [v.c.]

OTHER: Tjäder, *Nichtlit.Pap.* 47-48A.26 (Ravenna; doc. 510 or later)   Volusianus

Orientis

<u>FASTI:</u>	Marcell. Heracl. Pasch.	Dexicrates et Volusianus
<u>LAWS:</u>	none	
<u>PAPYRI:</u>	*P.Ross.Georg.* V 31.1 (8.iii)	p.c. Fll. Probi et Avieni vv.cc.
	P.Herm. 28.1 (x-xi; p.c., 504, also poss.?)	[... Fl.] Volusiani vv.cc.

<u>NOTES:</u>

The eastern consul Dexicrates is not otherwise known (though see *PLRE* II 357); Volusianus was a Roman noble (ibid., 1183-84). The West did not disseminate Dexicrates; the East apparently proclaimed Volusianus but dropped him in the p.c. *P.Herm.* 28 is odd, but 314 is not possible.

Occidentis

FASTI: Haun. (v.c.) Camp. AqS. Cass.   Cethegus (v.c.)
          Victor (v.c.) Marius VindPost.

LAWS: none

INSCR.:   **ROME:** *ICUR* n.s. I 1950   (Fl.) Cethegus v.c.
          (6-13.vi)

          ITALY: *CIL* IX 1376 = *ILCV* 3028B
          (Aeclanum, Reg. II; 26.viii; Fl.)

          GAUL: *AE* 1976, 450b* (Lyons;
          12.vii); *AE* 1945, 73 (betw.
          Vienne and Geneva; 17.xii
          or 16.i?); *CIL* XIII 2371
          = *ILCV* 1615 adn. (Lyons)

OTHER: Tjäder, *Nichtlit. Pap.*   Cethegus v.c.
          47-48A.7,8 (Ravenna, doc.
          510 or later)

          Tjäder, *Nichtlit.Pap.* 29.8   Rufius Petronius
          (Ravenna; 5.ii)   Nicomachus Cethegus v.c.

Orientis

FASTI: Marcell. Heracl. Pasch.   Cethegus solus

LAWS: none

PAPYRI: *P.Ross.Georg.* III 32.1 (12.ix);   p.c. Fl. Dexicratis v.c.
              BGU XII 2180.1 (25.ix); *SB* XVI
              12378.1 (12.x; Dexicratoris!);
              P.Oxy. XVI 1884.16 (27.x)

              Pap.Lugd.Bat. XVII 17.1 = *SB*   Fl. Cethegus v.c.
              X 10287 (29.x); *P.Oxy.* XVI
              1883.12 (21.xii)

NOTES:

     Cethegus was the son of Probinus cos. 489, mag. off. and *caput senatus*; evidently he was consul very young, since he was still alive in 558 (*PLRE* II 281-82). The full citation of his names in one Ravenna papyrus (as for Avienus in the synod of 502) is remarkable.

Occidentis

<table>
<tr><td>FASTI:</td><td>Haun. Camp. (om. v.c.) AqS.
Victor VindPost. (om. v.c.)</td><td>Theodorus v.c.</td></tr>
<tr><td></td><td>Cass.</td><td>Theodorus et Sabinianus</td></tr>
<tr><td></td><td>Marius</td><td>Sabinianus et Theodorus</td></tr>
<tr><td>LAWS:</td><td>none</td><td></td></tr>
<tr><td>INSCR.:</td><td>**ROME:** *ICUR* I 929 = *ILCV* 107
(16.iii-13.iv; Fl.); *ICUR* n.s.
I 897 = *ILCV* 736 (23.vii)</td><td>(Fl.) Theodorus v.c.</td></tr>
<tr><td></td><td>**ITALY:** *CIL* V 5417 (Como, Reg.
XI; 22.vii)</td><td></td></tr>
<tr><td></td><td>**GAUL:** *CIL* XII 2644 = *ILCV* 2910
adn. (Geneva; iii-iv)</td><td>p.c. Cethegi v.c.</td></tr>
</table>

Orientis

<u>FASTI:</u>	Marcell. Heracl. Pasch.	Sabinianus et Theodorus
<u>LAWS:</u>	*CJ* 2.7.22 (C'polis, 1.i/1.vii); 1.4.19 (no prov., 19.iv)	Sabinianus et Theodorus
<u>PAPYRI:</u>	*P.Rainer Cent.* 111.1 (13.i?); *P.Oxy.* XVI 1966.1 (24.v); *SPP* XX 130.1 (26.v); *P.Stras.* 578.2 (3.vii); *P.Stras.* 471 bis = *P.Flor.* I 73.1 (16.vii)	p.c. Fl. Cethegi v.c.
	P.Oxy. XVI 1994.1 (17.vii); *P.Ryl.* IV 609.8 (Lat.; om. Fll.)	Fll. Sabinianus et Theodorus vv.cc.

<u>NOTES:</u>

Sabinianus was MVM (Illyr.) in 505 and the son of Sabinianus Magnus, MVM Illyr. in 479-81 (*PLRE* II 967). Theodorus was son of Basilius cos. 480 and brother of Inportunus cos. 509, Albinus cos. 493, and Avienus cos. 501; PPO Ital. 500 (*PLRE* II 1097-98). The East accepted Theodorus, but as usual there is no trace of Sabinianus in contemporary documents from the West.

Occidentis

<u>FASTI</u>:	Haun. Camp. (om. v.c.) AqS. Victor VindPost. (om. v.c.)	Messala v.c.
	Cass. Marius	Messala et Areobindus
<u>LAWS</u>:	none	
<u>INSCR.</u>:	**ROME:** *ICUR* n.s. VII 17606 (2-5.ii); *ICUR* n.s. VI 16004 (17.ii; om. Fl., v.c.); *ICUR* n.s. II 5003 (p.c. poss.)	Fl. Messala v.c.
	ITALY: *CIL* IX 1363* = *ILCV* 3601 (Aeclanum, Reg. II; 1?.ix)	p.c. Theodori v.c.
	AE 1977, 206 (nr. Nola, Reg. I; 18.iv)	Fl. Messala v.c.
	GAUL: *CIL* XII 631 = *ILCV* 3438 (nr. Arles; 28.x)	Messala v.c.
<u>OTHER:</u>	Tjäder, *Nichtlit.Pap.* 47-48A.21 (Ravenna; doc. 510 or later)	Messala
	Ennodius, *carm.* 2.32, on Messala's consulate	
	Council at Agde: *Conc.Galliae* (Corp.Christ.Lat. 148) p.213 (10.ix)	Messala v.c.
	CIL XIII 2372 (Lyons) has a reference to Messalae consulis annus.	

Orientis

<u>FASTI:</u>	Marcell. Heracl. (Ar. iun.) Pasch.	Areobindus et Messala
<u>LAWS:</u>	*CJ* 4.35.22 (23.vii) and 2.7.23 (20.xi), both C'polis	Areobindus et Messala
<u>PAPYRI:</u>	*Cd'E* 59 (1984) 137.1 (20.iii); *P.Cair.Masp.* I 67100.1 (27.vii); *P.Stras.* 656.1 (30.viii); *MPER* n.s. XV 62.6 (om. Theodorus; school text)	p.c. Fll. Sabiniani et Theodori vv.cc.
<u>OTHER:</u>	All or part of no fewer than seven consular diptychs of Areobindus survive (Volbach, nos. 8-14, Taff. 5-7)	

<u>NOTES:</u>

Areobindus, MVM per Orientem 503-504, was son of Dagalaifus cos. 461 and grandson of Areobindus cos. 434; on his mother's side he was grandson of Ardabur cos. 447 and greatgrandson of Aspar cos. 434 (*PLRE* II 143-44). He thus had a grandfather and greatgrandfather sharing the fasces in the same year (434). Ennodius Messala was son of Faustus cos. 490, grandson of Avienus cos. 450, and brother of Avienus cos. 502 (*PLRE* II 759-60).

Despite a law attesting Messala as well as Areobindus by 23.vii, the papyri continue to show p.c.'s till 30.viii, and there are no papyri with the p.c. in 507. The West shows no contemporary evidence for dissemination of Areobindus.

Occidentis

FASTI:	Victor (transp. 507 & 508)	Venantius iun.
	Camp. Marius (transp. 507 & 508) VindPost.	Venantius
	AqS.	Venantius v.c.
	Haun.	Venantius iun. v.c.
	Cass.	Anastasius Aug. III et Venantius
LAWS:	none	
INSCR.:	**ROME:** *CIL* VI 9942 add. p.3471* = *ILCV* 604 (1.i); *ICUR* n.s. II 4181 (14.i-13.ii; v.c.); *ICUR* n.s. V 13412 (29.v); *ICUR* n.s. I 3248	Venantius iun. (v.c.)
	ITALY: *CIL* IX 1378 = *ILCV* 248 (Aeclanum, Reg. II; 12.xi)	Venantius iun. v.c.
OTHER:	Letter of Theoderic to Senate at Rome (Cassiodorus, *Var.* [ed. Mommsen], p.392) (11.iii)	Venantius v.c.
	Tjäder, *Nichtlit.Pap.* 47-48A.24 (Ravenna; doc. 510 or later)	Venantius iun.

Orientis

FASTI: Marcell.   Anastasius Aug. III

        Heracl. Pasch.   Anastasius Aug. III
                                                    et Venantius

LAWS: none

PAPYRI: *P.Lond.* III 992.1 (p.253)   D.N. Fl. Anastasius
         (vi-vii); *P.Lond.* III 1313.2*   perp. Aug. Imp. III
         (p.256) (1.xii)

         ZPE 62 (1986) 137.1 (1.x)   D.N. Fl. Anastasius
                                                    perp. Aug. III et
                                                    Venantius v.c.

INSCR.: *SEG* XXIX 641 = Feissel,   D.N. Fl. Anastasius III
         Rec.Inscr.Chrét.Macéd. 131
         (Thessalonica, i-viii)

NOTES:

Venantius was son of Liberius (PPO Gall. *ca* 510-534 and patrician 500-554) and consul very young (*PLRE* II 1153).

Anastasius was proclaimed alone in the East early in the year, but a papyrus shows that Venantius was added by fall. Despite Cassiodorus, however, Anastasius was not disseminated in the West during the year; as sometimes happens, he is attested in a p.c. from Gaul.

Occidentis

FASTI:	Camp.	Basilius Venantius
	Haun.	alius Venantius v.c.
	AqS. (cf. above, p.43)	Venantius Basilius iun. v.c.
	Cass. (iun.) Marius (transp. 507 & 508) Victor (transp. 507 & 508)	Venantius (iun.) et Celer
LAWS:	none	
INSCR.:	**ROME:** *ICUR* I 935 = n.s. II 4278 (11.iii)	Venantius alius iunior
	RAC 44 (1968) 154, fig.10 (13.iv)	Venantius iter.
	ITALY: *CIL* XI 4978 add.* (p.1376) (Spoleto, Reg. VI; 19.x)	Venantius alius
	GAUL: *CIL* XIII 2373 (cf. 2393) = *ILCV* 1553 (Lyons?; 1.x)	p.c. iterum Messalae v.c.
	CIL XII 5339 = *ILCV* 3555 (Narbonne; 1.vi)	p.c. Anastasi et Venanti

Orientis

FASTI:	Marcell.	Celer et Venantius
	Heracl.	Celer et alius Venantius
LAWS:	none	
PAPYRI:	*P.Oxy.* XVI 1890.1 (27.xi); *CPR* VI 8.2 (Aug. Imp. IV, Fl. Ven., om. v.c.)	p.c. D.N. Fl. Anastasi perp. Aug. (Imp.) III et (Fl.) Venantii v.c.
	Papyrus with Greek text under Coptic text (Crum, *Short Texts* 405) (21.ix; we owe to R.A. Coles a copy of Grenfell's transcript)	Fll. Celer [et Venantius vv.cc.]

NOTES:

Venantius was probably son of Venantius Basilius cos. 484, grandson of Basilius cos. 463 and cousin of many other Decian consuls, and father of Paulinus and Decius, coss. 534 and 529 (*PLRE* II 1153-54). Celer was mag. off. (East) from 503-518 (*PLRE* II 275-77). In Gaul once again we find a sort of consular era (based on 506).

Occidentis

FASTI:	Haun. (v.c.) Cass. Marius AqS. (GLSQ) (v.c.) VindPost.	Inportunus (v.c.)
	Victor	Inportunus iun.
	Camp.; AqS. (N)	Anastasius Inportunus
LAWS:	none	
INSCR.:	**ROME:** *ICUR* n.s. I 3250 = *ILCV* 168A (18.iii); *ICUR* n.s. II 5006 (16.vii-13.viii); *ICUR* n.s. II 5007 (17.ix); *ICUR* n.s. II 5009; *ICUR* n.s. II 5008 (p.c. poss.)	Inportunus v.c.
	ITALY: *CIL* IX 1379 (nr. Aeclanum, Reg. II; 14.xi- 13.xii; om. v.c.); *CIL* V 6307 (Milan, Reg. XI; p.c. poss.?)	

Orientis

<u>FASTI:</u>	Marcell. Heracl.	Opportunus solus
<u>LAWS:</u>	none	
<u>PAPYRI:</u>	*BGU* XII 2181.1* (4.v)	p.c. Fll. [Celeris] et Venantii vv.cc.
	P.Vindob.Sal. 9.2 (25.ix); *P.Lond.* III 1307 (p.lxxii) (30.ix); *P.Oxy.* XVI 1885.19 (29.xi); *P.Rainer Cent.* 112.1 (5.xii)	Fl. Opportunus v.c.

<u>NOTES:</u>

Inportunus was a member of the Decii, son of the consul of 480, brother of the consuls of 493, 501, and 505 (*PLRE* II 592). For the possibility that his name was Anastasius Inportunus, see above, p.50. The unanimity of the eastern sources leaves little room for doubt that Inportunus' name was incorrectly disseminated from a high level; for a discussion, see *P.Vindob.Sal.* 9.1n. Where the iunior in Victor comes from, we have no notion (cf. above, p.42).

Occidentis

FASTI: Haun.   Boethius iun. v.c.

              Camp. AqS. Cass. Victor   Boethius v.c.
              Marius (om. v.c.) VindPost. (om.
              v.c.)

LAWS: none

INSCR.:   **ROME:** *ICUR* n.s. II 5010   Boethius iun. v.c.
              (14.viii-13.ix); *ICUR* n.s.
              VII 17609 = *ILCV* 3109 (om.
              v.c.); *ICUR* n.s. VII 17608
              (p.c. poss.)

              ITALY: *CIL* V 6816 = *I.Ital.*
              XI.2 44 = *ILCV* 1669 (Ivrea,
              Reg. XI; 22.iv); *CIL* V 7408
              = *ILCV* 4551 (Dertona, Reg. IX;
              14.iv-1.v); *CIL* V 6229 = *ILCV*
              2739 adn. (Milan, Reg. XI;
              1.xii; om. v.c.)

              GAUL: *CIL* XIII 2374 = *ILCV*   p.c. Inportuni v.c.
              4823 (Lyons; 2.xii)

OTHER: Tjäder, *Nichtlit.Pap.* 47-48A.14,   Boethius iun.
              15,16,17,20,23,25 (Ravenna; doc.
              510 or later)

OTHER: Ennodius, *Epp.* 8.1 (letter
              of congratulation to Boethius)

Orientis

FASTI:	Marcell.	Boethius iun.
	Heracl.	Boethius solus
LAWS:	*CJ* 1.5.11 (no prov., 9.viii; Krueger dates 487 or 510)[72]	Boethius v.c.
PAPYRI:	*P.Berl.Frisk* 5.1 (14.v); *BGU* XII 2182.1 (2.vi); *SB* I 5941.7 (practice text; one party comes from Caesarea, but prov. of wooden tablet unknown: see Keenan, *ZPE* 53 [1983] 247 n.11; 21.ix)	p.c. Fl. Opportuni v.c.

NOTES:

Boethius was an aristocrat, son of Boethius cos. 487, father of the two consuls of 522, and the well-known philosopher (*PLRE* II 233-37).

[72]The absence of iun. is not a conclusive argument for 487, since *CJ* does not consistently include this element; and the name of the addressee is lost. Moreover, *CJ* uses p.c. Longini in 487. The index to *CJ* shows that Krüger regarded 510 as the true date.

Occidentis

<table>
<tr><td>FASTI:</td><td>Haun. Camp. AqS. Victor
VindPost. (om. v.c.)</td><td>Felix v.c.</td></tr>
<tr><td></td><td>Chr. Gall. (vol. 1 p.666 c.695)
Cass. Marius</td><td>Felix et Secundinus</td></tr>
<tr><td>LAWS:</td><td>none</td><td></td></tr>
<tr><td>INSCR.:</td><td>**ROME:** *ICUR* n.s. II 4182 (13.x);
ICUR n.s. VII 17610; (Fl.);
ICUR n.s. II 5013; *ICUR* n.s. I
2112; *ICUR* n.s. II 5017 = *ILCV*
3768A (p.c., 512, poss.)</td><td>(Fl.) Felix v.c.</td></tr>
</table>

ITALY: *CIL* IX 1380 = *ILCV* 3185B
(nr. Aeclanum, Reg. II; 4.ii;
Fl.); *IG* XIV 2310a (p.704)
(Verona, Reg. X; 10.viii; Gk.;
om. v.c.); *CIL* XI 4336 = *ILCV*
256 adn. (Terni, Reg. VI;
18.viii); *CIL* IX 1381 = *ILCV*
1260 (Aeclanum, Reg. II; 6?.xii;
Fl.); *CIL* X 3299 = *ILCV* 1019
(Pozzuoli, Reg. I; 11.i; Fl.;
p.c. poss.); *CIL* X 1389 = *ILCV*
1710 adn. (Nola, Reg. I; 30.ix;
p.c. poss.)

GAUL: *CIL* XII 2064 = *ILCV* 1673
adn. (St. Laurent-de-Mure, Narb.;
i-ii); *AE* 1976, 397 (Valence,
Narb.; 30.viii); *CIL* XII 2066 =
ILCV 3415 (Vienne; 14.viii-
13.ix/16.x-13.xii; p.c. poss.);
CIL XII 2063 = *ILCV* 3550 (Vienne;
28.x)

DALMATIA: *Forsch.Salona* II 250;
(Salona; before 1.ix);
Forsch.Salona II 248 = *CIL* III
9525 (Salona)

[Continued on next page]

Orientis

FASTI:	Marcell. Heracl.	Secundinus et Felix
LAWS:	none	
PAPYRI:	*P.Ness.* 15* (30.v); *SPP* XX 135.1 (vii-viii); *P.Oxy.* XVI 1960.1 (17.viii); *P.Cair.Masp.* I 67101.2 (29.x)	Fll. Secundinus et Felix vv.cc.
OTHER:	John Lyd. *de mag.* 3.26	Secundianus

NOTES:

Secundinus was brother-in-law of the Emperor Anastasius and father of Hypatius, Pompeius, and perhaps Probus (cf. Cameron, *GRBS* 19 [1978] 261-62), the eastern consuls of 500, 501, and 502; Felix was a Gallic noble (*PLRE* II 986 and 462-63). The East disseminated both consuls, but the West, as usual, only its own.

[Continued from preceding page]

OTHER:	Council at Orléans: *Conc.Galliae* (Corp.Christ.Lat. 148A), pp. 13-15 (10.vii)	Felix v.c.
	Cassiodorus, *Var.* 2.2 (Theoderic's letter of appointment to Felix); *Var.* 2.1 (Theoderic's letter notifying Anastasius)	

Occidentis

FASTI: Haun. (v.c.) Camp. AqS. (L [v.c.;   p.c. Felicis (v.c.)
         om. p.c.] Q [om. name] N)

         AqS. (G) Cass. Victor Marius   Paulus et Moscianus

LAWS: none

INSCR.: **ROME:** *ICUR* n.s. II 5015   p.c. Felicis
         (14.iv-15.v); *ICUR* n.s.
         VII 17611 (29.ix)

         ITALY: *CIL* V 6176 = *ILCV*
         116 (Milan, Reg. XI; 3.ix)

Orientis

FASTI: Marcell. Heracl.   Paulus et Moscianus

LAWS: none

PAPYRI: *BGU* XII 2185.1 (27.vi; frag.);   Fll. Paulus et
              P.Ness. 16.1 (Nessana, Palestine;   Moschianus vv.cc.
              11.vii); *SB* IV 7369.2 (viii-ix; om.
              vv.cc.?); *SB* I 5174.2 (7.ix);
              P.Stras. 483.1

NOTES:

     Both consuls were easterners. Paulus (*PLRE* II 854) was son of Vivianus cos. 463; Moschianus was either the MVM of 482 (*PLRE* II 766) or more probably his son, perhaps father of Magnus cos. 518 (Cameron, *GRBS* 19 [1978] 261). Paulus had to borrow 1000 lbs. of gold to cover his consular expenses and was given another 1000 by Anastasius (John Lyd., *de mag.* 3.48). The two consuls were not disseminated in the West.

Occidentis

FASTI: Haun. Camp. (om. v.c.)   Probus v.c.
                AqS. (LSQN) Victor VindPost.
                (om. v.c.)

                AqS. (G) Cass.   Probus et Clementinus

                Marius   Clementinus et Probus

LAWS: none

INSCR.:   **ROME:** *ICUR* n.s. I   Probus v.c.
                2121 = *ILCV* 590

                ITALY: *CIL* V 6266 = *ILCV*
                1668 (Milan, Reg. XI; 11.i)

Orientis

FASTI:	Marcell.	Clementinus et Probus
	Heracl.	Clementinus et alius Probus
LAWS:	*CJ* 1.42.2 (8.ii; cf. Krüger's note)	Clementinus et Probus
PAPYRI:	*SB* I 5175.1 (9.vii)	p.c. Fll. Pauli et Moschiani vv.cc.
	P.Coll.Youtie II 90.2 (4.ix); *SB* XIV 11373.1 (19.ix); *CPR* VII 43.1 (19.ix; rest.); *P.Erl.* 78.1 (8.x)	Fll. Clementinus et Probus vv.cc.
OTHER:	Consular diptych giving Clementinus' full name (Volbach no.15; inscr., *ILS* 1304)	

NOTES:

Clementinus was CSL at the eastern court and perhaps a descendant of Taurus cos. 361, Aurelian cos. 400, and Taurus cos. 428 (*PLRE* II 303); Probus came of a distinguished but unidentified western family (*PLRE* II 913). Once again, the western consul was disseminated in the East, but not the reverse.

Occidentis

<u>FASTI</u>:	Haun. Camp. (om. v.c.) AqS. Cass. Victor Marius (om. v.c.) VindPost. (om. v.c.)	Senator v.c.
<u>LAWS</u>:	none	
<u>INSCR.</u>:	**ROME:** *ICUR* n.s. VIII 20836 = *ILCV* 1650 (8.v); *ICUR* n.s. VII 17609 (16.vii-13.viii); *CIL* VI 9613 = *ICUR* n.s. II 5018 (p.c. poss.); *ICUR* I 945 = *ILCV* 3109B (p.c. poss.)	Senator v.c.
	ITALY: *CIL* XI 4337 = *ILCV* 4681 (Terni, Reg. VI; 5.ii); *CIL* XI 5021 = *ILCV* 3166 (Trevi, Reg. VI; 13.ix; om. v.c.)	
	GAUL: *I.Lat.Gaul.Narb.* 607 (Narbonne)	p.c. Probi
	CIL XII 1692 = *ILCV* 1432 adn. (Luc, Narb.; 16.v-13.vi)	Senator v.c.
<u>OTHER</u>:	Pope Symmachus to Caesarius of Arles (Thiel, p.729) (11.vi)	Fl. Senator v.c.
	Liber Pontificalis I 269 (19.vii)	Senator

Orientis

<u>FASTI:</u>	Marcell. Heracl.	Senator solus
<u>LAWS:</u>	none	
<u>PAPYRI:</u>	*P.Lond.* III 993 (p.li) (8.i); *P.Mich.* XI 612.1 (27.vi); *P.Flor.* III 279.1 (15.x); *P.Wash.Univ.* 17.1 (viii-xii); *BGU* XII 2186.1	p.c. Fll. Clementini et Probi vv.cc.
	P.Cair.Masp. I 67001.2 (28.xii); *P.Flor.* III 280.1 (29.xii)	Fl. Senator v.c.
<u>OTHER:</u>	*Coll.Avell.* 109 (letter of Anastasius to Pope Hormisdas), *data* 28.xii	Senator v.c.

<u>NOTES:</u>

'Senator' is Cassiodorus, bureaucrat, historian, and monk: *PLRE* II 265-69. He was PPO Ital. 533-537 after many other positions.

Occidentis

<u>FASTI</u>:	Haun. Camp. (om. v.c.) AqS. (LSQN) Victor VindPost. (om. v.c.)	Florentius v.c.
	AqS.(G) Cass. Marius	Florentius et Anthemius
<u>LAWS</u>:	none	
<u>INSCR.</u>:	**ITALY:** *AE* 1975, 406 = *AE* 1961, 284 (Albenga, Reg. IX; 24.vi); *CIL* IX 1382 = *ILCV* 3185C (Mirabella, Reg. II; 29.x)	Florentius v.c.
	GAUL: *CIL* XII 2067 = *ILCV* 3278 (Vienne; 14.ii-15.iii); *Rec.Inscr.Chrét.Gaule* XV 253 (viii-xii)	Florentius et Anthemius vv.cc.
<u>OTHER</u>:	*Coll.Avell.* 105 (Dorotheus, Bp. of Thessalonica, to Pope Hormisdas), *accepta* 28.iii	Florentius v.c.
	Coll.Avell. 108, 109, 110, 115 (Hormisdas to Anastasius), *data* 4.iv, 14.v, 8.vii, 11.viii	Florentius v.c.

Orientis

FASTI:	Marcell. Heracl.	Anthemius et Florentius
LAWS:	none	
PAPYRI:	*SPP* XX 126.1 (14.ix); *P.Cair.Masp.* III 67306.1 (11.x)	Fl. Anthemius v.c.
OTHER:	*Coll.Avell.* 107 (Anastasius to Pope Hormisdas), *data* 12.i *Constantinopoli et accepta* *A. et F. vv.cc. conss.* 28.iii	Anthemius et Florentius vv.cc.
	Half of a now lost consular diptych of Anthemius giving his full name (Volbach, no. 16)	

NOTES:

Florentius was an otherwise unidentifiable westerner (*PLRE* II 477); Anthemius (the eastern consul) was the son of the western emperor Anthemius (467-472) and greatgrandson of Anthemius cos. 405 (*PLRE* II 99). Anthemius was, so far as the inscriptions show, disseminated only in Gaul of the western provinces, and Florentius is not found in any contemporary eastern documents, though Marcell. and Heracl. include him. Given the positioning of the two day and month dates and the inclusion of Anthemius' name in the composite formula of Anastasius' letter to Hormisdas, it looks as if "*accepta*...28.iii" was inserted into the original eastern formula.

Occidentis

FASTI: Haun. Cass. Victor AqS.(all v.c.)   Petrus (v.c.)
            Camp. Marius VindPost.

LAWS: none

INSCR.:   **ROME:** *ICUR* n.s. II 5020 = *ILCV*   Fl. Petrus v.c.
717 (2-5.ii); *ICUR* n.s. II 5019
(14.vi-15.vii; om. Fl.); *ICUR*
I 963 (14.viii-15.ix); *ICUR* n.s.
II 5021 (31.x/4.xi/12.xi; om.
Fl.); *ICUR* n.s. II 4183; *ICUR* n.s.
I 2122 (om. Fl.); *ICUR* n.s. VIII
23454a' (frag.; om. Fl.; p.c. poss.)

ITALY: *CIL* XI 3566 (Civitavecchia,
Reg. VII; 14.viii-15.x)

GAUL: *CIL* XII 2421 = *ILCV*   p.c. Florentii et
1434 (Sainte Mixte, Narb.;   Anthemii vv.cc.
14.i; rev. order); *CIL* XII 1792
= *ILCV* 2779 (St. Romain d'Albon,
Narb.; 22.ii)

ILCV 1648B (Agaunum [St. Maurice]   Petrus
in Switzerland: epitaph of
Hymnemodus, abbot of Agaunum, in
life of abbots; died 31.i)

OTHER: Council at Tarragona: Mansi VIII 541   Petrus
(6.xi)

Coll.Avell. 118 (Hormisdas   Petrus
to John Bp. of Nicopolis); cf.
120, 121: 14-19.xi

NOTES:

Petrus was a westerner of distinguished but unidentified family (*PLRE* II 871).
The order of names in the p.c. in the Gallic inscriptions is not consistent, with one maintaining the 'western' order found in 515, the other giving Anthemius first.

Orientis

<u>FASTI:</u>	Marcell. Heracl.	Petrus solus
<u>LAWS:</u>	none	
<u>PAPYRI:</u>	*P.Lond.* V 1797.1* (12.vii; frag.)	p.c. Fl. Anthemii v.c.
<u>OTHER:</u>	*Coll.Avell.* 111 (Anastasius to Hormisdas), *data C'poli* 16.vii	Petrus v.c.
	Coll.Avell. 113 (Anastasius to Senate of Rome), *data Chalcedone* 28.vii	Petrus

Occidentis

FASTI:	Haun. Camp. (om. v.c.) AqS. Victor VindPost. (om. v.c.)	Agapitus v.c.
	Cass. Marius	Anastasius et Agapitus
LAWS:	none	
INSCR.:	**ROME:** *ICUR* n.s. I 897 = *ILCV* 736 (25.vii); *ICUR* n.s. II 5022 = *ILCV* 4415A (frag.; inl[ustr. v.]); *ICUR* n.s. I 995 = *ILCV* 4146F adn.; *ICUR* n.s. VII 17613	Agapitus v.c.
	ITALY: *CIL* X 1347 = *ILCV* 1147A (Nola, Reg. I; 18.i or 15.xii); *Riv.Stud.Luguri* 22 (1956) 228 (Pieve del Finale, Reg. IX; 30.iv); *CIL* IX 1383* = *ILCV* 3185D (Aeclanum, Reg. II; 2?.xi); *CIL* X 4495 = *ILCV* 3188 (Capua, Reg. I; 12.xii; Fl.); Agnello, *Silloge* 98* (Syracuse; p.c. poss.)	
	GAUL: *CIL* XIII 2375* = *ILCV* 1255 (Lyons; 28/29.vii); *CIL* XII 2353 (Bourgoin, Narb.; 6-13.xii)	
	CIL XII 590 + add. p.815 = *ILCV* 1552 (Aix, Narb.; 24.xii)	Anastasius v.c.
	DALMATIA: *Recherches à Salona* I (Copenhagen 1928) 174 no.81 (11.iii)	Agapetus v.c.
	CIL III 9526 = *ILCV* 3842 adn. (Salona; p.c. poss.)	[?Anastasius] et Agapi[tus
	[Continued on next page]	

Orientis

<u>FASTI:</u>	Marcell. Heracl.	Anastasius et Agapitus
<u>LAWS:</u>	*CJ* 4.29.21 (1.iv), 5.27.6 (1.iv), 2.7.24 (1.xii), all no prov.	Anastasius et Agapitus
<u>PAPYRI:</u>	*P.Lond.* III 994.2 (p.259) (24.ii)	p.c. Fl. Petri v.c.
	P.Flor. III 281.2 (14.ix)	Fl. Anastasius v.c.
<u>OTHER:</u>	*Coll.Avell.* 138 (Anastasius to Hormisdas), C'polis, 11.vii	Anastasius et Agapitus v.c.
	Portions of 6 consular diptychs (only one complete) giving Anastasius' full name (Volbach, nos. 17-22)	

<u>NOTES:</u>

Agapitus was a Roman senator, PVR 508-509 (*PLRE* II 30-32); Anastasius was a greatnephew of the Emperor Anastasius, perhaps son of Sabinianus cos. 505 (*PLRE* II 82 with Cameron, *GRBS* 19 [1978] 281). Anastasius' letter to Hormisdas and the laws (unless retroactively corrected) show timely proclamation at court, but the papyri (including a p.c. in 518) suggest a failure to disseminate. The only two inscriptions purporting to show two consuls are both restored (see 518 for the p.c.).

As usual, the Gallic evidence is not consistent, even within Narbonensis: two inscriptions with only the western consul, one with only the eastern.

[Continued from preceding page]

<u>OTHER:</u>	Council at Gerona: Mansi VIII 549 (8.vi)	Agapetus
	Council at Epaône: *Conc. Galliae* (Corp.Christ.Lat. 148A), pp. 24,35 (10.vi, 15.ix)	Agapitus
	Coll.Avell. 116, 123-124, 126, 126, 129, 131-134, 136-137 (Hormisdas)	Agapitus
	Coll.Avell. 136 (Avitus of Vienne), 30.i	

Occidentis

FASTI: Haun. (v.c.) Camp. AqS. VindPost.   p.c. Agapiti (v.c.)

              Victor   **Agapitus II et Magnus**

              Cass. (v.c.) Marius   **Magnus (v.c.)**

LAWS: none

INSCR.:   **ROME:** *ICUR* n.s. V 13413   p.c. Agapiti v.c.
              (1.v); *ICUR* n.s. II 5024 =
              ILCV 4559 adn. (16.x-13.xi)

              ITALY: *CIL* Suppl.Ital. I 863   [p.c. Agapiti] et
              (Lodi, Reg. XI; 20.i?)   Anastasi vv.cc.

              GAUL: *I.Lat.Gaul.Narb.*   p.c. Agapiti
              301 = *ILCV* 2440 (Vienne;
              4.iii); *CIL* XIII 2376 =
              ILCV 3562 (Lyons; 4.xii)

OTHER: *Coll.Avell.* 140, 146   p.c. Agapiti v.c.
              (Hormisdas), 10.ii, 20.xii

Orientis

<u>FASTI:</u>	Marcell. Heracl. Pasch.	Magnus
<u>LAWS:</u>	*CJ* 7.63.3 (C'polis, 1.xii)	Magnus
<u>PAPYRI:</u>	*SPP* XX 131.1 (3.ii)	p.c. Fl. Anastasi v.c.
	PSI V 466.1 (ix-x)	Fl. Magnus v.c.
<u>INSCR.:</u>	*CIG* IV 9449* = Froehner, *I.Louvre* 280 (prov.unkn., 10.vii; Fabius M., stone)	Fl. Magnus v.c.
<u>OTHER:</u>	*Coll.Avell.* 141, 143 (Iustinus to Hormisdas), C'polis, 1.viii and 7.ix	Magnus v.c.
	ACO III 62.34: Synod to John, Bp. of C'polis (20.vii)	Magnus v.c.
	Malalas 410	Magnus
	Portions of 3 original consular diptychs (lacking inscriptions) and 2 medieval copies (Volbach, nos. 23-24 bis), the inscription being preserved only by one of the copies (no. 24 bis, with Cameron, *AJA* 88 [1984] 400-01)	

<u>NOTES:</u>

Magnus was a greatnephew of the Emperor Anastasius and perhaps son of Moschianus cos. 512 (*PLRE* II 701, with Cameron, *GRBS* 19 [1978] 261).

Occidentis

FASTI:	Haun. (Fl., v.c.) Camp. AqS. (N) VindPost.	(Fl.) Eutharicus Cillica (v.c.)
	Cass.	D.N. Eutharicus Cillica et Iustinus Aug.
	AqS. (SQ)	Eutharicus
	AqS. (GL)	Iustinus Aug.
	Marius	Iustinus et Eutharicus
	Victor	Iustinus Aug. et Heraclius
LAWS:	none	
INSCR.:	**ROME:** *ICUR* n.s. IV 11171 (29.viii/2.ix/10.ix; frag.; om. v.c.); *ICUR* I 968 = *ILCV* 112 (Fl.); *ICUR* n.s. VII 17614; *ICUR* I 1169 (frag.); *ICUR* I 970 (frag.; p.c. poss.); *RAC* 44 (1968) 147 no.7 (Cillicanis v.c.)	(Fl.) Eutharicus Cillica v.c.
	ITALY: *CIL* IX 410 = *ILCV* 4678 (Canossa, Reg. II; 14.i-13.ii); *CIL* V 6589 = *ILCV* 2740 (Sizzano, Reg. XI; 15.vii; Fl. Euth., om. Cil.); *ILCV* 3188A (Campania?; 16.ix; Fl.; om. v.c.); *CIL* V 7408 = *ILCV* 4551 (Dertona, Reg. IX; 19.x; om. Cil.); *CIL* V 5426 = *ILCV* 1158A (Como, Reg. XI; 13.xii; om. Euth.; garbled)	
	GAUL: *CIL* XII 1500 = *ILCV* 1166 (Vaison, Narb.; 25.i)	p.c. iterum Agapiti v.c.
OTHER:	*Coll.Avell.* 166, 168, 190, 219-220, 224-227 (Hormisdas), 25.iv-3.xii	Eutharicus
	Anon.Val. 80; Cassiod., *Var.* 8.1.3	

Orientis

FASTI:	Marcell. Heracl. Pasch.	Iustinus Aug. et Eutharicus
LAWS:	*CJ* 5.27.7 (9.xi) and 2.7.25 (1.xii), both C'polis	Iustinus Aug. et Euthericus
PAPYRI:	*P.Stras.* 133.1 (frag.)	D.N. Fl. Iustinus perp. Aug. Imp.
INSCR.:	**THRACE:** A. Dumont-Th. Homolle, *Mélanges d'arch. et d'épigr.* (Paris 1892) 414 no. 86y (Panion; xi)	D.N. Fl. Iustinus perp. Aug. Imp. I et Fl. Eutharichus v.c.
	MACEDONIA: *SEG* XXIX 642 = Feissel, *Rec.Inscr.Chrét.Macéd.* 132 (Thessalonica, ix-xii)	D.N. Iustinus
OTHER:	*Coll.Avell.* 159 (John, Bp. of C'polis), 28.iii	Domnus Iustinus perp. Aug. et Eutharicus v.c.
	Coll.Avell. 212, 232 (Iustinus), *data C'poli* 17.xi, 17.xi	Domnus Iustinus perp. Aug.

NOTES:

Iustinus (*PLRE* II 648-51) succeeded Anastasius on 10.vii.518, taking his first consulate in the usual way in the following year. Eutharicus (*PLRE* II 438) was the husband of Theoderic's daughter Amalasuntha. The texts offer a considerable variety of formulas. Iustinus is not known in the western inscriptions, while Eutharicus appears in some, but not all, eastern texts. Cf. above, p.35.

Occidentis

<u>FASTI</u>:	Haun. (v.c.) Camp. AqS. (QN) Victor (v.c.) VindPost.	Rusticius (v.c.)
	AqS. (GLX) Marius	Rusticius et Vitalianus
<u>LAWS</u>:	none	
<u>INSCR.</u>:	**ROME:** *ICUR* n.s. IV 12255 (13.v); *ICUR* n.s. II 5025 = *ILCV* 3787; *ICUR* n.s. II 5026 = *ILCV* 622 adn.; *ICUR* n.s. IV 11172 (p.c. poss.)	Rusticius v.c.
	ITALY: *CIL* V 5219 = *ILCV* 1156 (nr. Lago di Como, Reg. XI; 24.i); *CIL* V 7412 = *ILCV* 1664 (Dertona, Reg. IX: om. v.c.)	
	GAUL: *I.Lat.Gaul.Narb.* 260 (Baume-Cornillane; 2.viii); *I.Lat.Gaul.Narb.* 293* (519 poss.?)	p.c. Iustini Aug.
	CIL XIII 2377 = *ILCV* 1674 (Lyons; 19.ix; Rustiano); *Rec.Inscr.Chrét.Gaule* XV 236 = *ILCV* 1166A (Grenoble; 2.xi; Rusticiano)	Rusticius et Vitalianus vv.cc.
<u>OTHER</u>:	*Coll.Avell.* 201, 209, 212 (*acc.*), 222, 228-229, 232 (*acc.*) (Hormisdas), 7.iv-30.xi	Rusticius v.c.
	Coll.Avell. 231 = *ACO* IV.2, p.46.18 (13.viii)	Fl. Rusticius v.c.

Orientis

FASTI:	Marcell. Heracl. Pasch.	Vitalianus et Rusticius
LAWS:	*CJ* 7.63.4 (C'polis, 28.v)	Rusticius
PAPYRI:	*P.Lond.* V 1699.1 (11.viii); *P.Flor.* III 282.1 (3.ix); *PSI* IV 296.1	Fl. Vitalianus v.c.
	BGU XII 2187.1 (3.x)	Fl. Rusticius v.c.
INSCR.:	**ASIA:** Grégoire, *Inscr.* 255* (Aphrodisias; 5.iv, but in a back reference to ind. 15 [=522], inscr. dated to 551)	Rusticius
OTHER:	*Coll.Avell.* 181-182 (19.i), 192-193 (9.vii) (Iustinus and John, Bp. of C'polis to Hormisdas; all C'polis)	Vitalianus et Rusticius (vv.cc.)
	ACO IV.1, p.200.28 (Iustinus to Hypatius, MVM Orientis; C'polis, 7.viii)	Rusticus (sic) v.c.
	Coll.Avell. 196, 199 (Iustinus), C'polis, Chalcedon, 31.viii-17.ix	Rusticius v.c.
	Coll.Avell. 195, 233 (Epiphanius, Bp. of C'polis), 17.ix and 30.xi	Rusticius v.c.
	Evagrius, *HE* 4.3	

NOTES:

Rusticius was an otherwise unknown westerner (*PLRE* II 963); Vitalianus was a rebellious MVM murdered in the palace at Constantinople during his consular year (*PLRE* II 1171-76), according to Marcellinus (s.a. 520) in July. Documents from later in the year reveal that he suffered *damnatio memoriae*, though the news did not reach Egypt till September (the law of 28.v must have been retroactively corrected: Cameron, *ZPE* 48 [1982] 93-94) and Gaul not at all.

575

Occidentis

<u>FASTI</u>:	VindPost. Camp. AqS. (GLSQN)	Valerius
	AqS. (X)	Valerius et Iustinianus vv.cc.
	Marius	Iustinus II et Valerius
	Victor	Valerius et Iustinianus
<u>LAWS</u>:	none	
<u>INSCR.</u>:	**ROME:** *ICUR* n.s. II 4279 = *ILCV* 1137 (3.vii); *ICUR* n.s. II 5029 (2-5.ix; om. v.c.)	Valerius v.c.
	ITALY: *CIL* V 5192* = *ILCV* 3169A (Bergamo, Reg. XI; 17.iv; Val. Aug.); *CIL* V 6464 = *ILCV* 1046 subscr. (Pavia, Reg. XI; 17.vii); *Puglia paleocristiana e medioevale* IV (Bari 1984) 43-44 (Venusia, Reg. II; 24.ix; om. v.c.); *AE* 1973, 218 (Venusia; 14.ix-1.x; om. v.c.)	
	GAUL: *CIL* XIII 300 = *ILCV* 3040 adn. (15.ii); *Rec.Inscr.Chrét.Gaule* XV 285 (15.xi; om. v.c.); *CIL* XII 4083 = *ILCV* 2021 (Bellegarde, Narb.; om. v.c.)	
<u>OTHER</u>:	Tjäder, *Nichtlit.Pap.* 4-5 B.iv.6 (Ravenna, 3.vi; doc. 552-575)	
	Coll.Avell. 236-240 (Hormisdas), 26.iii	Valerius v.c.

Orientis

<u>FASTI:</u>	Marcell. Heracl. Pasch.	Iustinianus et Valerius
<u>LAWS:</u>	*CJ* 6.22.8 (C'polis, 1.vi)	Iustinianus et Valerius
<u>PAPYRI:</u>	*P.Stras.* 579.1 (24.v); *P.Cair.Masp.* III 67328 passim (5-14.vii)	Fl. Iustinianus v.c.
<u>INSCR.:</u>	**CILICIA:** *AE* 1973, 542 (Silifke)	Iustinianus
<u>OTHER:</u>	*Coll.Avell.* 241 (Iustinus to Hormisdas), C'polis, 1.v	Iustinianus et Valerius vv.cc.
	Two and a half consular diptychs of Justinian, giving his full name (Volbach, nos. 25-27)	

<u>NOTES:</u>

Valerius is an otherwise unknown westerner (*PLRE* II 1145); he was proclaimed at court (by 1.v), but apparently not disseminated in the East. Justinian is the future emperor, at the time MVM praesentalis (*PLRE* II 645-48). He was ignored in the West.

Occidentis

<u>FASTI</u>:	VindPost. Camp. AqS. Marius Haun.	Symmachus et Boethius
<u>LAWS</u>:	none	
<u>INSCR.</u>:	**ROME:** *ICUR* n.s. II 4280* = *ILCV* 694 (4.vi); *ICUR* n.s. II 5030 = *ILCV* 242 (17.vii); *ICUR* n.s. II 4281 = *ILCV* 4419 (11.viii); *ICUR* n.s. I 1193 = *ILCV* 3000 (6-13.viii); *ICUR* n.s. I 749 = *ILCV* 840 (5.xi; Fl. S.); *ICUR* n.s. I 3251 = *ILCV* 3155 (17.xii); *ICUR* n.s. II 5031 = *ILCV* 3156; *ICUR* n.s. II 5033; *ICUR* n.s. I 54 = *ILCV* 4145 adn.	Symmachus et Boethius (germani) vv.cc.
	ITALY: *CIL* V 5430 = *ILCV* 2740 adn. (Como, Reg. XI; 13.v); *CIL* X 4496 = *ILCV* 4254 (Capua, Reg. I; 23.x; Fll.); *AE* 1975, 407 = *AE* 1961, 284 (Albenga, Reg. IX; 25.x; S. et B. germanis); *CIL* IX 2074 = *ILCV* 363 (Benevento, Reg. II; 2.xi; Fll.)	
	GAUL: *CIL* XII 2309 = *ILCV* 2904 (Grenoble; 8.vii)	
<u>OTHER</u>:	*Liber Pontificalis* I 269	Symmachus et Boethius
	Boethius, *Cons.Phil.* 2.3	

Orientis

<u>FASTI:</u>	Marcell. Heracl. Pasch. Victor	Symmachus et Boethius
<u>LAWS:</u>	none	
<u>PAPYRI:</u>	*ZPE* 52 (1983) 261.2 (23.x.522 [cos.] or 24.x.523 [ind.]); *SPP* XX 137.1 (23.xi); *P.Ross.Georg.* III 33.1	Fll. Symmachus et Boethius vv.cc.

<u>NOTES:</u>

Both consuls were the sons of Boethius cos. 510, grandchildren of Boethius cos. 487 and Symmachus cos. 485, evidently very young at the time since their father was barely 30 when he became consul in 510 (*PLRE* II 233).

Occidentis

<u>FASTI</u>:	Haun. VindPost. Camp. (both om. v.c.) AqS. Marius (om. v.c.)	Maximus v.c.
	ExcSang.	Florentius et Maximus
<u>LAWS</u>:	none	
<u>INSCR.</u>:	**ROME:** *ILCV* 3508 (20.iv); *ICUR* n.s. II 5029 (6/10/11.ix); *ICUR* n.s. II 4184 = *ILCV* 110 (Fl.); *ICUR* n.s. I 1474 = *ILCV* 3156 adn.	(Fl.) Maximus v.c.
	ITALY: *AE* 1947, 68 (Milan, Reg. XI; 15.i); *CIL* V 5737 = *ILCV* 326a (Gropelli nr. Milan; 8.ii); *CIL* X 1348 = *ILCV* 1016 (Nola, Reg. I; 26.ii; Fl.); *CIL* V 6264 = *ILCV* 2740 adn. (Milan; 22.v); *CIL* XI 549 = *ILCV* 351 (Ariminum, Reg. VIII; 1.vii); *CIL* V 7137 = *ILCV* 2740 adn. (Torino, Reg. XI; 21.iii/vii?); *CIL* XI 308 = *ILCV* 1193 (Ravenna, Reg. VIII; 5.xii)	
	GAUL: *CIL* XII 2404 = *ILCV* 3281 (Aosta, Narb.; 3.ii)	p.c. Symmachi et Boethi vv.cc.
	CIL XIII 2378 = *ILCV* 3563 (Lyons; 16.iv); *CIL* XII 1781 = *ILCV* 2904 adn. (Bourg-les-Valence, Narb.; 25.vii)	Maximus v.c.

[Continued on the next page]

Orientis

<u>FASTI:</u>	Marcell. Heracl. (Maximinus) Pasch. Victor (v.c.)	Maximus (v.c.) solus
<u>LAWS:</u>	none	
<u>PAPYRI:</u>	*CPR* X 120.1 (21.i)	p.c. Fll. Symmachi et Boethii vv.cc.
	P.Oxy. XVI 1984.1 (28.x); *P.Lond.* V 1687.2 (16.xii); 1688.1 (25.xii)	Fl. Maximus v.c.

<u>NOTES:</u>

Maximus was a western aristocrat, an Anician descended from Petronius Maximus cos. 433, 443, and emperor 455 (*PLRE* II 748-49). The iunior in *Liber Pontificalis* is perhaps influenced by the case of Olybrius iunior cos. 526, mentioned in the same passage.

[Continued from the preceding page]

<u>OTHER:</u>	Marini, *Pap.Dipl.* 85.14 p.132 (Ravenna, 11.xi); listed in Tjäder, *Nichtlit.Pap.* I, p.53, as P †4	Maximus v.c.
	Liber Pontificalis I 100, 104 (6.viii)	Maximus iun.
	Liber Pontificalis I 272 (6.viii)	Maximus
	Cassiodorus, *Var.* 5.42	

Occidentis

<u>FASTI</u>:	Camp. AqS. (GQN) (v.c.)	Opilio (v.c.)
	VindPost.	Opilio et Filoxenus
	AqS. (X)	Opilio et Iustinus Augg. vv.cc.
	Marius	Iustinus et Opilio
<u>LAWS</u>:	none	
<u>INSCR.</u>:	**ROME:** *CIL* VI 32942 = *ILCV* 469 (30.vii)	Venantius Opilio
	ITALY: *ILCV* 2736A (Oriolo, Reg. IX; 15.iii; om. v.c.); *CIL* V 5737 = *ILCV* 326b (Gropelli nr. Milan, Reg. XI; 8.iv); *AE* 1947, 67 (Milan; 23.vii); *CIL* V 1822 = *ILCV* 1701 (Gemona, Reg. X; 6.viii)	Opilio v.c.
<u>OTHER:</u>	Council at Arles: *Conc.Galliae* (Corp.Christ.Lat. 148A), p.45 (6.vi)	Opilio v.c.

Orientis

FASTI:	Marcell.	Iustinus Aug. II et Opilio
	Heracl.	Iustinianus Aug. et Opilio
	Pasch.	Iustinianus Aug. II et Opilio
	Victor	Iustinus et Apio
LAWS:	*CJ* 2.7.26 (13.ii), 1.3.40 (17.xi), and 12.33.5 (25.xii), all C'polis; 2.7.27 (no prov., 20.xi)	Iustinus Aug. II et Opilio
PAPYRI:	*SB* V 8264.1 (5-14.iv)	p.c. Fl. Maximi v.c.
	P.Cair.Masp. I 67117.27 (vi-vii); *P.Flor.* III 342.1 (5.x; adds Imp. after Aug.; Opilianus); *PSI* VIII 931.1 (6.x; adds Imp.; Opilianus); *P.Vatic.Aphrod.* 14.2 (23.x)	D.N. Fl. Iustinus perp. Aug. II et Fl. Opilio v.c.
INSCR.:	*Travaux et Mémoires* 9 (1985) 277 no.14 (Corinth; ix-xii)	[Fl. Iust]inus II [et Fl. Opilio] v.c.

NOTES:

Opilio was a former PPO at the western court (*PLRE* II 808-09), disseminated consistently in the East. Iustinus, on the other hand, was not disseminated in the West. For the allocation of Opilio dates, see the Critical Appendix for 453.

Occidentis

<table>
<tr>
<td>FASTI:</td>
<td>Camp. AqS. (GSQN) (v.c.)</td>
<td>Probus iun. (v.c.)</td>
</tr>
<tr>
<td></td>
<td>Dionys. (1, 756) Beda (3, 307 c.512)</td>
<td>Probus</td>
</tr>
<tr>
<td></td>
<td>VindPost.</td>
<td>Probus et Iustinianus Aug.</td>
</tr>
<tr>
<td></td>
<td>AqS. (X)</td>
<td>Probus et Filoxenus vv.cc.</td>
</tr>
<tr>
<td></td>
<td>Dionys. (1, 752) Marius</td>
<td>Probus et Filoxenus</td>
</tr>
<tr>
<td>LAWS:</td>
<td>none</td>
<td></td>
</tr>
<tr>
<td>INSCR.:</td>
<td>**ROME:** *ICUR* n.s. VII II 4279 =*ILCV* 1137 (1.ii); *ICUR* n.s. II 5043 = *ILCV* 243 (25.v); *ICUR* n.s. VI 17284 = *ILCV* 1469 (23/24.vi; Fl.); *ICUR* n.s. V 15359 (14.viii-1.ix; Fl.)</td>
<td>Probus iun. v.c.</td>
</tr>
<tr>
<td></td>
<td>**ITALY:** *I.Ital.* I 109 (Salerno, Reg. I; 25.i); *CIL* V 4843 = *ILCV* 3168 (Brescia, Reg. X; 28.i; om. iun. v.c.); *CIL* V 5683 = *ILCV* 1162A (nr. Milan, Reg. XI; 23.vi)</td>
<td></td>
</tr>
<tr>
<td></td>
<td>**GAUL:** *I.Lat.Gaul.Narb.* 135 = *ILCV* 2890 (Arles; 10.i); *Rec.Inscr.Chrét.Gaule* XV 86 = *CIL* XII 2072 (Vienne; 5.i or 5.ii)</td>
<td></td>
</tr>
</table>

Orientis

<u>FASTI:</u>	Victor	p.c. II Iustini et Apionis
	Marcell. Victor Heracl. Pasch.	Filoxenus et Probus
<u>LAWS:</u>	*CJ* 7.39.7 (C'polis, 1.xii)	Philoxenus et Probus
<u>PAPYRI:</u>	*P.Flor.* III 323.1 (15.iv); *P.Cair.Masp.* II 67125.2 (14.vii); *BGU* II 673.1 (18.ix); *BGU* IV 1094.17 (29.ix); *P.Lond.* III 1306 (p.lxxii) (5.ix); *P.Iand.* III 43.1 (14.x); *P.Cair.Masp.* II 67254 (30.x); *P.Rainer Cent.* 113.1 (p.c., 526, poss.); *P.Mert.* 134.1 (= *SB* XVI 12472) (p.c., 526, poss.)	Fl. Philoxenus v.c.
<u>INSCR.:</u>	*SEG* XXVI 778 = Feissel, *Rec.Inscr.Chrét.Macéd.* 134 Thessalonica, i-viii)	Fll. Philoxenus et Probus vv.cc.
<u>OTHER:</u>	Two inscribed consular diptychs of Philoxenus giving his full name (Volbach, nos. 28, 30) and another (no.29) identical to no.30 but uninscribed. For the inscr., *ILS* 1308.	
	Ps.-Dorotheos' date for Pope John's visit to C'polis: T. Schermann, *Prophetarum Vitae Fabulosae* (Leipzig 1907) 151	Philoxenus et Probus
	Malalas 411B	

<u>NOTES:</u>

Probus is an unidentifiable westerner (*PLRE* II 913); it is interesting that he is missing from the papyri but turns up in an inscription from Thessalonica. Philoxenus was an eastern MVM (*PLRE* II 879-80). There is no contemporary evidence for Philoxenus in the West.

Occidentis

FASTI:	VindPost.	Olybrius et Hilarus
	AqS. (iun. in GN; v.c. in GX)	Olybrius iun. v.c.
	Dionys. (1, 752) Marius	Olybrius
	Camp.	Olybrius iun.
LAWS:	none	
INSCR.:	**ROME:** *ICUR* n.s. II 5044 = *ILCV* 1305 (22.i); *ICUR* n.s. I 746 (14.ix-15.x); *ICUR* n.s. I 714 (Fl.); *ICUR* n.s. I 747; *ICUR* n.s. VII 17509c =? *ICUR* n.s. I 3244; *ICUR* n.s. VII 17617 = *ILCV* 110 adn. (Fl.); *ICUR* n.s. I 883	(Fl.) Olybrius v.c.
	ITALY: *CIL* V 5405 add. extr. (p.1095) = *ILCV* 1157 (Como, Reg. XI; 31.i); *CIL* V 5428 = *ILCV* 1262A (Como; 29.iv); *CIL* IX 5011 = *ILCV* 3117 (Farfa, Reg. IV; 24.vii)	
	GAUL: *CIL* XII 2073 = *ILCV* 3471 (Vienne; 19.xii)	
OTHER:	*Anon.Val.* 94 (26.viii)	Olybrius
	Liber Pontificalis I 104-05	Olybrius iunior
	Liber Pontificalis I 276 (27.v)	Olybrius

NOTES:

Four of the Roman inscriptions with Olybrius listed above could belong to 491: *ICUR* n.s. I 714, 746, 747, 3244 (=? n.s. VII 17509c); nothing compels a 526 date. We list them here, rather than under 491, because there is indisputable evidence for datings by Olybrius in Roman inscriptions of 526, whereas there is none for 491. But this fact provides only a probability, no certainty.

Orientis

<u>FASTI:</u>	Marcell. Heracl. Pasch.	Olybrius solus
<u>LAWS:</u>	*CJ* 9.19.6 (C'polis, 1.xii)	Olybrius v.c.
<u>PAPYRI:</u>	*P.Michael.* 43.1 (8.vi); *BGU* XII 2188.2 (18.vii); *P.Cair.Masp.* I 67102.1 (25.vii); 67103.1 (16.ix); *PSI* III 246.2 (19.ix); *P.Rainer Cent.* 114.1 (ind. points to 528/9!)	p.c. Fl. Philoxeni v.c.
<u>OTHER:</u>	Subscription to MSS of Priscian, *Inst.gramm.*: Zetzel, *Latin Textual Criticism* 220 (14), C'polis, 1.x	Olybrius v.c.
	Malalas 419B	Olybrius

<u>NOTES:</u>

Since Olybrius' consulate appears so early in the West and so late in the East, he is thought to have been a westerner, but there is no positive information (*PLRE* II 798). Moreover, there are no papyri after 19.ix, and it is not often in this period that a new consul was disseminated in Egypt sooner than then anyway.

Occidentis

FASTI: Camp. AqS. (v.c.) Marius   Mavortius (v.c.)

        VindPost.   Mavortius et Vittellianus

LAWS: none

INSCR.:   **ROME:** *ICUR* n.s. I 4074   (Fl.) Mavortius v.c.
(14-27.ii); *ICUR* n.s. II 5046
= *ILCV* 1609 adn. (5.iii);
ICUR n.s. VI 15896 = *ILCV*
3157 (4.v); *ICUR* n.s. VIII 22979
= *ILCV* 344 (3.x; Fl.); *ICUR*
n.s. II 6088 = *ILCV* 3768 (or p.c.
or iterum p.c.); *ICUR* n.s. I 751
(or p.c.); *ICUR* n.s. I 750
(or p.c.; om. v.c.)

        ITALY: *CIL* V 6212 = *ILCV* 2740
adn. (Milan, Reg. XI; 27.ii);
NotScav 1892, 364 = *ILCV* 2829A
adn. (Dertona, Reg. IX; 13.vi);
CIL V 5219b = *ILCV* 1716 (nr. Lago
di Como, Reg. XI; 27.vii); *CIL*
X 1349 = *ILCV* 3030 (Nola, Reg.
I; 5.ix); *CIL* XI 411 cf. comm.
(p.761) = *ILCV* 4677 (Canossa,
Reg. II; 11.ix; om. v.c.);
CIL V 5208 (nr. Bergamo,
Reg. XI; p.c. poss.)

        GAUL: *CIL* XII 5340 = *ILCV*
2891 (Narbonne; 1.vii);
CIL XII 2584 = *ILCV* 47
(Lugrin, Narb.; 23?.viii); *CIL*
XII 2193 = *ILCV* 1687 (Pornans,
Narb.; 6.xii)

OTHER: Council at Carpentras: *Conc.*   Mavortius v.c.
Galliae (Corp.Christ.Lat. 148A),
p.49 (6.xi)

        Liber Pontificalis I 279 (12.vii)   Mavortius

Orientis

<u>FASTI</u>:	Marcell. Heracl.	Mavortius solus
	Victor	Mavortius
	Pasch.	Mavortius Romanus solus
<u>LAWS</u>:	*CJ* 1.31.5 (C'polis, 22.iv)	Mavortius v.c.
<u>PAPYRI</u>:	*P.Cair.Masp.* III 67300.2 (12.vi; cos. instead of p.c.); *P.Lond.* V 1689.1 (13.vi); *P.Michael.* 44.1 (19.vii); *P.Lond.* V 1690.1 (30.viii); *P.Mich.* XIII 670.1 (after 1.v)	p.c. Fl. Olybrii v.c.
<u>INSCR.</u>:	**ASIA:** Grégoire, *Inscr.* 314.26 = *ILCV* 23 ii.9 (C'polis, 1.vi; Lat.)	Mavortius v.c.
<u>OTHER</u>:	Subscriptions in MSS of Priscian, *Inst.gramm.*: Zetzel, *Latin Textual Criticism* 220-221, C'polis, 11.i-30.v	Mavortius v.c. ac patricius

<u>NOTES</u>:

Mavortius was a member of the Decii, presumably son of Caecina Mavortius Basilius Decius cos. 486, grandson of Basilius cos. 463 and kin of numerous other western consuls (*PLRE* II 736-37). He may well have been disseminated in Egypt late in the year, since there are no papyri securely dated after August.

Occidentis

FASTI:	VindPost.	p.c. Mavorti et Iustiniani II
	Camp. AqS. (GSQN)	p.c. Mavorti
	AqS. (X; adds v.c.)	Iustinianus Aug. II
	Marius	Iustinus
LAWS:	none	
INSCR.:	**ROME:** *ICUR* n.s. I 3250 = *ILCV* 168b subscr. (26.i); *ICUR* n.s. VII 19994 = *ILCV* 1272 (9.vii); *ICUR* n.s. I 752 = *ILCV* 119 (18.xi); *ICUR* I 1015; *ICUR* n.s. IV 12256c (frag.)	p.c. Mavorti v.c.
	ITALY: *CIL* V 6742 = *ILCV* 3360 subscr. (Vercelli, Reg. XI; 28.v); *CIL* X 178 = *ILCV* 3867 (Potenza, Reg. III; 15.vii; om. v.c.)	
	GAUL: *CIL* XII 2061 = *ILCV* 3550A (Vienne; 18.x; om. v.c.)	
OTHER:	Letter of Pope Felix IV to Bp. Caesarius (*Conc.Galliae*, Corp. Christ.Lat. 148A, p.52) (3.i)	p.c. Mavortii v.c.

Orientis

<u>FASTI:</u>   Marcell. (om. II) Heracl.   Iustinianus Aug. II solus
                   Pasch. (III) Victor (om. II solus)

<u>LAWS:</u>   *CJ C.haec* (13.ii); 1.3.41-42   D.N. Iustinianus perp.
                   (1.iii), 1.4.21 (1.vi); 1.53.1   Aug. II
                   (11.xii), all C'polis

<u>PAPYRI:</u>   *P.Cair.Masp.* I 67091.27 (2.ix;   D.N. Fl. Iustinianus
                   adds Imp.); *P.Oxy.* XVI 1900.1   perp. Aug. (Imp.)
                   (24.x)

<u>COINS:</u>   M. Caramessini-Oeconomides,   Justinian, cons. image
                   ANSMusNotes (1966) 75-77, pl.   on obv. of solidus
                   XXVII (C'polis)

<u>NOTES:</u>

Justinian was made co-Augustus by his uncle Justin on 1.iv.527 and became sole emperor when Justin died on 1.viii.527. He was thus following normal practice in taking the consulate (his second) in the first full year after his accession. The absence of the iteration numeral in both papyri is striking. The West did not disseminate his name.

Occidentis

<u>FASTI:</u>	Camp. AqS. (v.c.) Marius	Decius iun. (v.c.)
	VindPost.	Decius iun. et Vittellianus
<u>LAWS:</u>	none	
<u>INSCR.:</u>	**ROME:** *ICUR* n.s. I 2124 = *ILCV* 1692	(Fl.) Decius iun. v.c.
	ITALY: *CIL* XI 6942a (p.1253) = *ILCV* 2827A (Piacenza, Reg. VIII; 18.v; om. v.c.); *CIL* IX 1384 = *ILCV* 3186 (nr. Aeclanum, Reg. II; 3.vi; Fl.; om. v.c.); *CIL* IX 1385 = *ILCV* 1252 (Aeclanum, Reg. II; 1.ix; Fl.); *CIL* X 6218 = *ILCV* 1024 subscr. (Formia, Reg. I; 19.x; om. v.c.)	
	GAUL: *CIL* XII 934 = *ILCV* 2891A (Arles; 4.i); *Rec.Inscr. Chrét.Gaule* XV 244 = *CIL* XII 2326 (nr. Grenoble, Narb.; 25.iv)	p.c. iterum Mavortii
<u>OTHER:</u>	Council at Oranges: *Conc.Galliae* (Corp.Christ.Lat. 148A), pp. 64-65 (3.vii)	Decius iun. v.c.
	Council at Vaison: *Conc.Galliae* (Corp.Christ.Lat. 148A), p.80 (5.xi)	Decius iun. v.c.

Orientis

<u>FASTI:</u>	Marcell. Heracl. Pasch.	Decius solus
	Victor	Decius v.c.
<u>LAWS:</u>	*CJ* 1.4.22 (18.i), 3.28.32 (31.iii), 1.20.2 (1.iv), 2.44.3 (6.iv), *C.summa* (7.iv), all C'polis; *CJ* 1.3.43 (no prov., 18.i); *CJ* 1.4.24 (17.ix), 7.63.5 (17.xi), both Chalcedon	Decius (v.c.)
<u>PAPYRI:</u>	*P.Stras.* 317.1 (13.iii; indiction points to 530; perh. cos. is error for p.c., 530); *P.Rainer Cent.* 115	Fl. Decius v.c.

<u>NOTES:</u>

The consul was a member of the Decii, probably son of Venantius, western consul of 508 (Cameron and Schauer, *JRS* 72 [1982] 129-30).

Occidentis

<u>FASTI</u>:	VindPost. Camp. AqS. (vv.cc.) Marius	Lampadius et Orestes
<u>LAWS</u>:	none	
<u>INSCR.</u>:	**ROME:** *ICUR* n.s. II 5050 = *ILCV* 3158 (12.ix; om. vv.cc.); *ICUR* n.s. II 5051 (14.ix-1.x; frag.); *ICUR* n.s. II 5053 = *ILCV* 591 (24.xi; Fl.); *ICUR* n.s. VIII 23454b (frag.)	(Fll.) Lampadius et Orestes vv.cc.
	ITALY: *CIL* V 5428 = *ILCV* 1262B (Como, Reg. XI; 21.viii); *CIL* V 6742b (Vercelli, Reg. XI); *CIL* XI 336 = *ILCV* 617 (Ravenna, Reg. VIII; ix-xii.530 or p.c., i-ix.531)	
	GAUL: *CIL* XII 936 = *ILCV* 1808 (Arles; 19.i)	p.c. Deciti iun. v.c.
	CIL XII 935 = *ILCV* 2891A adn. (Arles; 23.x)	Lampadius et Orestes vv.cc.

See under 531 for inscriptions mentioning Lampadius and Orestes in the genitive where either cons. or p.c. or iterum p.c. could be restored.

<u>OTHER</u>:	Letter of Pope Boniface II to Bp. Caesarius (*Conc.Galliae*, Corp. Christ.Lat. 148A, p.69) (25.i)	Lampadius et Orestes vv.cc.
	Liber Pontificalis I 279 (12.x); I 108 (18.xi)	Lampadius et Orestes
	ACO IV.2, p.98.1; cf. *Lib.Pontif.* I 282 n.8 (60 priests to Pope Boniface; 27.xii)	Fll. Lampadius et Orestes vv.cc.
	Complete consular diptych of Orestes, giving his full name (Volbach no. 31), though apparently a reinscribed diptych of Clementinus, eastern cos. 513 (N. Netzer, *Burlington Magazine* 125 [1983] 265-71)	

594

Orientis

<u>FASTI:</u>	Marcell. Heracl. Pasch. Victor	Lampadius et Orestes
<u>LAWS:</u>	C'polis, 10 laws, earliest *CJ* 1.2.23 (18/27?.iii); 1 law each from Chalcedon and no prov.	Lampadius et Orestes (vv.cc.)
<u>PAPYRI:</u>	*P.Lond.* V 1722.1* (7-15.iii); *P.Wash.Univ.* 25.1 (25.iii)	p.c. Fl. Decii v.c.
	P.Cair.Masp. I 67104.1 (19.viii); *P.Cair.Masp.* III 67301.2 (20.viii); *P.Rainer Cent.* 116 (30?.x; first name Horius!); *P.Oxy.* XXXVI 2779.1 (30.xii); *BGU* II 369.1 (after 1.vii);	Fll. Orestes et Lampadius vv.cc.
<u>INSCR.:</u>	**THRACE:** Dumont-Homolle, *Mélanges d'arch. et d'épigr.* (Paris 1892) 415 no. 86z = *Bull.épigr.* 1951, 141 (Panion; frag.; p.c. poss.)	Fll. Lampadius et Orestes vv.cc.
	ARABIA: *SEG* XXVII 1019 (Nebo; viii)	

<u>NOTES:</u>

Both consuls were westerners, Lampadius unknown, Orestes probably son of Avienus cos. 502 and grandson of Faustus cos. 490 (Cameron and Schauer, *JRS* 72 [1982] 143). The order of names in the papyri reverses the correct western order, as if whoever disseminated the names was used to reversing the order to put the easterner first. The Epirot inscription of 531 agrees, but nothing else does.

Occidentis

<u>FASTI</u>:	VindPost. AqS. (vv.cc.) Marius Beda (3, 307 c.519)	p.c. Lampadi et Orestis
	Camp.	p.c. s(upra) s(criptorum)
<u>LAWS</u>:	none	
<u>INSCR.</u>:	**ROME:** *ICUR* n.s. II 5054 = *ILCV* 318 adn. (om. vv.cc.)	p.c. Lampadi et Orestis vv.cc.

ITALY: *I.Ital.* VII 1 78 = *ILCV* 3166A (Pisa, Reg. VII; 9.i); *CIL* V 3896* = *ILCV* 1037 (Verona, Reg. X; 24.vii); *CIL* V 5411 = *ILCV* 1157 adn. (Como, Reg. XI; 11.viii)

GAUL: *CIL* XII 937 = *ILCV* 2891A adn. (Arles; 14.ii-15.iii)

Cos. 530; p.c. 531; iterum p.c. 532; or et iterum p.c. 533

ROME: *ICUR* n.s. II 5057 (Fll.); *ICUR* n.s. VII 17618a; *ICUR* n.s. I 2125; *ICUR* n.s. I 3253 (om. vv.cc.); *ICUR* n.s. II 5058 = *ILCV* 3000A; *ICUR* n.s. II 5061a; *ICUR* n.s. II 5061b; *ICUR* n.s. II 5059; *ICUR* n.s. II 5060; *ICUR* n.s. II 5062 = *ILCV* 3508 adn.; *ICUR* n.s. II 5063; *ICUR* n.s. VI 15785 = *ILCV* 2139 (7.ix); *ICUR* n.s. II 5874; *ICUR* n.s. II 5875; *ICUR* n.s. VII 17618b (26/27.ii); *ICUR* n.s. II 5052 (14.ix-15.xi); *ICUR* n.s. VIII 22978b (frag.)

ITALY: *CIL* XIV 3992a (Nomentum, Latium)

p.c. 531, iterum p.c. 532, or et iterum p.c. 533

ROME: *ICUR* I 1033, 1034; *ICUR* n.s. I 1475; *ICUR* n.s. II 5055 (532 not poss.); *ICUR* n.s. VIII 20838; *ICUR* n.s. I 3254

Orientis

<u>FASTI:</u>	Marcell. (om. Pasch.)	p.c. Lampadi et Orestis
	Victor	p.c. II Lampadi et Orestis
	Heracl.	anhypata
<u>LAWS:</u>	C'polis, 9 laws, earliest *CJ* 2.58.2 (20.ii)	p.c. Lampadii et Orestis vv.cc.
<u>PAPYRI:</u>	*P.Hamb.* III 233.2 (22.v [?]); *SB* X 10524.2 (8.vi); *SPP* XX 139.1 (20.vi)	p.c. Fll. Orestis et Lampadii vv.cc.
<u>INSCR.:</u>	**EPIRUS:** L. Heuzey-H. Daumet, *Miss.arch.de Macéd.* (Paris 1876) 390 no. 177 (17.ix)	p.c. Fll. Orestis et Lampadii vv.cc.

Occidentis

FASTI: VindPost. AqS. (vv.cc.) Marius   iterum p.c. Lampadi et
Orestis (vv.cc.)

Camp.   iterum p.c. s.s.

LAWS: none

INSCR.:   **ROME:** *ICUR* n.s. I 753 = *ILCV*   iterum p.c. Lampadi et
356 (11.ii); *ICUR* I 1029 =   Orestis vv.cc.
ILCV 987 (17.x; Fl.); *ICUR* n.s.
II 5056

ITALY: *CIL* V 3897 = *ILCV* 223
(nr. Verona, Reg. X; 11.x)

GAUL: *CIL* XII 938 = *ILCV*
2891A (Arles; 30.xi)

598

Orientis

<u>FASTI:</u>	Marcell. Pasch.	item p.c. Lampadi et Orestis
	Victor	p.c. Lampadi et Orestis anno tertio
	Heracl.	anhypata
<u>LAWS:</u>	*CJ* 1.44.2 (8.iii) and 3.10.3 (18.x), both C'polis	p.c. Lampadii et Orestis vv.cc. anno secundo
<u>PAPYRI:</u>	*P.Lond.* V 1691.2 (8.iii); *P.Cair.Masp.* I 67105.2 (ix-x)	p.c. Fll. Orestis et Lampadii vv.cc.
<u>INSCR.:</u>	*SEG* XXIX 643 = Feissel, *Rec.Inscr.Chrét.Macéd.* 133 (Thessalonica, i-viii, prob. 25.v or 15.vi)	II p.c. Fll. Lampadii et Orestis vv.cc.

Occidentis

FASTI:	VindPost.	et iterum p.c. superiorum
	AqS. (GSQ)	tertio p.c. Lampadii et Orestis
	Camp. AqS. (N)	et iterum p.c. s.s.
	AqS. (X) Marius	Iustinianus Aug. III
LAWS:	none	
INSCR.:	**ROME:** *ICUR* n.s VII 17619 . = *CIL* VI 32080 (2-7.iii); *ICUR* n.s. I 175 = *ILCV* 135 (22.iv); *ILCV* 1780	et iterum p.c. Lampadii et Orestis vv.cc.
	CIL VI 36967 = *ILCV* 25A	Imp. D.N. Iustinianus piiss. Aug. III
	ITALY: *CIL* X 4497 = *ILCV* 3189 (Capua, Reg. I; 17.vi); *CIL* IX 1384* = *ILCV* 3186 (nr. Aeclanum, Reg. II; 20.xii; om. vv.cc.)	et iterum p.c. Lampadii et Orestis vv.cc.
OTHER:	Council at Marseilles: *Conc.Galliae* (Corp.Christ.Lat. 148A), p.85 (26.v)	p.c. tertium Lampadi et Orestis

Orientis

<u>FASTI:</u>	Marcell. Heracl. Victor Pasch. (IV; solus)	Iustinianus Aug. III (solus)
<u>LAWS:</u>	C'polis, 7 laws, earliest *NovIust* 155 (1.ii; om. III)	D.N. Iustinianus perp. Aug. III
<u>PAPYRI:</u>	*P.Rainer Cent.* 117.1 (23.iii); *SPP* XX 140.1 (18.iv); *SB* I 4663.1 = *CPR* X 27.1 (8.x)	p.c. Fll. Orestis et Lampadii vv.cc.
	P.Stras. 472.2* (xi-xii; 16.xii?; or p.c., 534?)	D.N. Fl. Iustinianus perp. Aug. et Imp. III, aureus annus
	See *BASP* 18 (1981) 47 for an unpublished papyrus of 20.x with Justinian's third consulate	
<u>INSCR.:</u>	**GREECE:** *Arch.Eph.* 1977, 67* no. 6 = *SEG* XXIX 310 (Corinth; 17.ix)	Iustinianus Aug. III
<u>OTHER:</u>	Letter of Justinian to Pope John II (*CJ* 1.1.8.24) (C'polis, 6.vi)	D.N. Iustinianus perp. Aug. III

601

Occidentis

FASTI: VindPost. (om. iun.) Camp. AqS.   Paulinus iun. (v.c.)
         (GSQN) (v.c.; GS om. iun.)
         Marius

         AqS. (X)   Iustinianus Aug. IV
                                                et Paulinus

LAWS: None

INSCR.: **ROME:** *ICUR* n.s. I 3255   Paulinus iun. v.c.
         = *ILCV* 247 (28.v); *ICUR*
         n.s. II 5064 (30.ix/31.x/
         30.xi; Gk.); *ICUR* n.s. II 5065

         ITALY: *CIL* V 7416 (nr.
         Dertona, Reg. IX; 3.viii);
         RAC 29(1953) 229 (Teanum, Reg. I:
         8.x); *CIL* V 6269 = *ILCV* 2740
         adn. (20.xii; or p.c., 13.i.535?);
         CIL V 5431 (Como, Reg. XI)

OTHER: Letters of Pope John II (*Conc.*   Fl. Paulinus iun. v.c.
         Galliae, Corp.Christ.Lat. 148A,
         pp.86-87) (6-7.iv)

         Letter of Pope John II to   D.N. Iustinianus perp.
         Justinian: *CJ* 1.1.8.39 (Rome,   Aug. IV et Paulinus
         25.iii)   iun. v.c.

Orientis

<u>FASTI:</u>	Victor	Iustinianus Aug. IV
	Marcell. Pasch. (V) Heracl.	Iustinianus Aug. IV et Paulinus
<u>LAWS:</u>	C'polis, 9 laws, earliest *CJ* 1.27.2 (13.iv)	D.N. Iustinianus perp. Aug. IV et Paulinus v.c.
<u>PAPYRI:</u>	*PSI* III 216.1 (17.ii; om. Imp.); *SB* XIV 11539.1* (i-vii)	p.c. D.N. Fl. Iustiniani perp. Aug. et Imp. III, aureus annus
	SB VIII 9876.1 (16.vii)	D.N. Fl. Iustinianus perp. Aug. IV
<u>INSCR.:</u>	**ASIA:** *I.Smyrna* 560 = Grégoire, *Inscr.* 69 (Smyrna; 8.ii)	Fl. Iustinianus piissimus rex noster IV

<u>NOTES:</u>

Paulinus was a Decian, son of Basilius Venantius cos. 508, and brother of Decius cos. 529 and at least one other western consul (Cameron and Schauer, *JRS* 72 [1982] 128). He appears in the papyri in the p.c. and was thus disseminated, if somewhat late, in the East. The date in Pope John's letter was presumably "corrected" by the compilers of *CJ*, who completed the second edition in this year.

Occidentis

FASTI: AqS.(X) Marius (om. v.c.)   Belisarius v.c.

             VindPost. Camp. AqS. (GN)   p.c. Paulini

             AqS. (SQ)   Paulinus II et Belisarius

LAWS: none

INSCR.:   **ROME:** *ICUR* n.s. V 13123 =   p.c. (Fl.) Paulini iun.
ILCV 1139 (29.iii; om. v.c.)   v.c.

             ITALY: *Arch.stor.Calabr.Luc.* 24 (1955) 15 (Tropea, Reg. III; 8.ii; om. v.c.); *CIL* V 5214 = *ILCV* 1155 (Lecco, Reg. XI; 13.ii; om. iun.); *CIL* X 786 = *ILCV* 3029A (Castellamare, Reg. I; 24.ii); *ILCV* 1211 adn. (Pavia, Reg. XI; vii-viii; could be later year); *CIL* V 5419 = *ILCV* 1431 (Como, Reg. XI; 10.viii); *Rend.Accad.di Arch., di Napoli* 30 (1955) 203 Tav. II.1 (Nola, Reg. I; 19.ix; om. v.c.); *CIL* V 5692 = *ILCV* 1254 (nr. Milan, Reg. XI; 15.x; later year poss.: Monday would be correct in 540 or 546); *CIL* V 5232 (Lenno, Reg. XI; later year poss.)

             GAUL: *CIL* XII 2077 (Vienne; frag.; or cos.?; later year also poss.)

             DALMATIA: *CIL* III ad 2659* (Salona; xii; Fl.; Gk.)

OTHER: Letter of Pope Agapitus I to Bp.   p.c. Paulini iun. v.c.
Caesarius (*Conc.Galliae*, Corp. Christ.Lat. 148A, p.97) (18.vii)

             Council at Arverna: *Conc.Galliae*   p.c. Paulini iun.
(Corp.Christ.Lat. 148A), p.105 (8.xi)

Orientis

FASTI:	MarcellS. Heracl. Pasch.	Belisarius solus
	Victor	Belisarius v.c.
LAWS:	35 novellae, all from C'polis; earliest *NovIust* 1.4 (1.i)	Belisarius v.c.
PAPYRI:	*P.Giss.* I 121.1 (17.iii)	p.c. D.N. Fl. Iustini Aug. IV et Paulini v.c.
	P.Oxy. XVI 1893.1 (18.vii); *P.Cair.Masp.* III 67296.2 (23.vii); 67297.2 (23.vii); *P.Oxy.* XVI 1983.1 (28.vii); *P.Erl.* 75.1	Fl. Belisarius v.c.
INSCR.:	**MACEDONIA:** *IG* X 2 1 403 = Feissel, *Rec.Inscr.Chrét.Macéd.* 135 (Thessalonica; 21.xi); *IG* X 2 1 804 = Feissel, *Rec.Inscr.Chrét. Macéd.* 134 (Thessalonica; ix-xii; om. Fl.)	Fl. Belisarius v.c.
OTHER:	Procopius, *BV* 2.9.15-15; *BG* 1.5.18-19	

NOTES:

Belisarius was Justinian's great general and victor in his Persian, African, and Italian wars. His consulate was disseminated in the West only after the conquest of Italy in 536 (q.v.).

For the postconsular era of Paulinus, see Critical Appendix, end.

Occidentis

FASTI: Camp. AqS. (N)

iterum p.c. Paulini quod
est cons. Vili[

AqS. (SQ)

Paulinus III et Belisarius

AqS. (G)

iterum p.c. Paulini

AqS. (X) Marius

p.c. Belisari v.c.

LAWS: none

INSCR.:   **ROME:** *ICUR* I 1054

iterum p.c. Paulini

ICUR n.s. II 4185 = *ILCV* 713
(23.v; or 537?); *ICUR* n.s. VII
20607 (om. v.c.; or 537?)

p.c. Belisari v.c.

536 or 537[73]
ICUR n.s. II 5072 (14.x); *ICUR*
n.s. I 754; *ICUR* n.s. VI 15683;
ICUR n.s. VII 17621; *ICUR* n.s.
II 5073; *ICUR* n.s. VII 17620b =
(?) *ICUR* n.s. VI 15684; *ICUR* n.s.
II 5074

ITALY: *CIL* XI 1692 = *ILCV* 4459A
(Florence, Reg. VII; 16.iv);
CIL XI 1540 = *ILCV* 2170 (Lucca,
Reg. VII; 1.v); *RAC* 29 (1953) 230
(Teanum, Reg. I; 27.xii); *CIL* XI
309 = *ILCV* 1152 adn. (Ravenna, Reg.
VIII; or 500?)
[Continued on next page]

iterum p.c. Paulini iun.
v.c.

---

[73]Datings by Belisarius do not appear at Rome during the year of his consulate, 535; and one inscription of (apparently) 537 dates simply p.c. Belisarii; the pope mentioned in it did not become pope until 537. The inscriptions listed here are presumably all references to p.c. Belisarii, but in no case is it possible to say whether these refer to 536, his proper p.c., or to 537, iterum p.c.; the condition of the stone prevents knowing in almost all cases, and in addition uncertainty about which year is meant even by simple p.c. remains a problem.

Orientis

FASTI: MarcellS.   p.c. Belisari

        Heracl.   anhypata

        Pasch.   Belisarius II solus

        Victor   p.c. Belisari anno secundo

LAWS: 16 novellae, earliest   p.c. Belisari v.c.
        NovIust 23.4 (3.i), all C'polis

PAPYRI: *P.Grenf.* II 85.1 (21.vi);   p.c. Fl. Belisari v.c.
        P.Lond. V 1841.1 (10.ix);
        P.Flor. III 283.2 (9.xii);
        SPP XX 141.1

INSCR.: **CILICIA:** R. Heberdey, A. Wilhelm,   p.c. Fl. Belisarii v.c.
        Reisen in Kilikien 36 no. 86
        (Anazarbus; ix-xii)

OTHER: *ACO* III 126.1, 159.6 (2.v);   p.c. Fl. Belisarii v.c.
        161.4 (10.v); 166.6 (6.v);
        177.15 (15.v); 169.17 (21.v);
        27.11 (4.vi), all C'polis;
        123.16 (19.ix), Jerusalem

        Order of Justinian: *ACO* III   p.c. Belisarii v.c.
        123.14 (6.viii)

        Coll.Avell. 90, heading: date   iterum p.c. Paulini
        of installation of Menas as Bp.   v.c. iun.
        of C'polis (13.iii): a western
        editorial insertion

        [Continued from preceding page]
        536-538: *CIL* XIV 2766 (Tusculum,   ] Vilisari v.c.
        Reg. I

        GAUL: *CIL* XII 1501 = *ILCV*   iterum p.c. Paulini
        1213 (Vairon, Narb.; 11.i;   iun. v.c.
        om. v.c.); *CIL* XII 2078 =
        ILCV 3038 (Vienne; 8.vi)

Occidentis

<u>FASTI</u>:	AqS. (G)	tertio p.c. Paulini
	AqS. (SQ)	Paulinus IV et Belisarius III
	AqS. (N) Camp.	p.c. Belisarii
	AqS. (X) (v.c.) Marius	iterum p.c. Belisari (v.c.)
<u>LAWS</u>:	none	
<u>INSCR.</u>:	**ROME:** *ICUR* n.s. II 4283 = *ILCV* 3764 (14.vi-15.vii; Vigilius became pope in 537; hence inscr. cannot date to 536)	p.c. Belisari v.excell. atque patrici
	ITALY: *NotScav* 1897, 368 (Dertona, Reg. IX; 16.iii-13.iv; indiction gives year); *CIL* V 4118 = *ILCV* 1278 (Cremona, Reg. X; 12.xii; indiction)	et iterum p.c. Paulini iun. v.c.
	GAUL: *CIL* XII 1693 = *ILCV* 2909 adn. (St. Julien-Quint; Narb.; 20.iii; om. v.c.); *CIL* XII 2405 = *ILCV* 3282 (Aosta, Narb.; 30.x)	p.c. III Paulini iun. v.c.

Orientis

<u>FASTI:</u>	MarcellS. (om. Pasch.)	iterum p.c. Belisari
	Victor	p.c. Belisari v.c. anno III
	Heracl.	anhypata
<u>LAWS:</u>	16 novels, earliest *NovIust* 43 (17.v), all from C'polis	p.c. Belisarii v.c. anno II
<u>PAPYRI:</u>	*P.Amst.* I 47.1 (1.ii); *P.Grenf.* I 56.1 (20.iv); *P.Ness.* 18.1 (Nessana, Palestine; v-vi); *SB* V 8029.1 (6.viii); *P.Stras.* 473.1 (17.ix); *P.Ross.Georg.* III 36.1 (7.x); *P.Cair.Masp.* I 67123.1 (30.x)	p.c. Fl. Belisarii v.c.

Occidentis

FASTI:	AqS. (SQ)	Paulinus V et Iohannes
	Camp. AqS. (GNX) (v.c.) Marius	Iohannes
	VindPost.	et Iohannes
LAWS:	none	
INSCR.:	**ROME:** *ICUR* n.s. II 5731 (25.iv)	iterum p.c. patrici Belisari
	ICUR n.s. VI 15786 (16.iii-13.iv); *ICUR* n.s. I 997 = *ILCV* 4645 adn. (i-viii [indiction); *ICUR* n.s. I 1476 = *ILCV* 318 (20.xii; Fl. Ioh. Orientalis); *ICUR* n.s. II 5076; *ICUR* n.s. I 3256 = *ILCV* 217 (cons. per Oriente; frag.)	(Fl.) Iohannes (Orientalis) v.c.
	ITALY: *CIL* X 1350 = *ILCV* 260 (Nola, Reg. I; 18.i [indict.])	p.c. Belisari v.c.
	CIL IX 1386 = *ILCV* 3186A (Mirabella, Reg. II; 1.i)	Fl. Iohannes
	GAUL: *CIL* XII 1530 (Narb.; ix-xii); *CIL* XII 2080a (Vienne; 16.vii-13.viii; p.c. poss.)	Iohannes v.c.
OTHER:	Council at Orléans: *Conc.Galliae* (Corp.Christ.Lat. 148A), pp. 127-28 (7.v)	quarto p.c. Paulini iun.

Orientis

<u>FASTI:</u>	MarcellS. Pasch.	Iohannes solus
	Heracl.	Iohannes solus et praef. praet.
	Victor	Iohannes v.c.
<u>LAWS:</u>	13 novels, earliest *NovIust* 64.2 (19.i), all from C'polis	Iohannes v.c.
<u>PAPYRI:</u>	*SB* III 6266.1 = 6704.1 (23.i); *P.Michael.* 126.1 (26.ii)	p.c. Fl. Belisarii v.c.
	P.Oxy. XVI 1887.1 (15.iv); *P.Oxy.* XVI 1974.1 (27.iv; adds praef. sacr. praet.); *PSI* VIII 933.1 (24-28.viii); *P.Stras.* 481.1 (23.ix); *P.Flor.* III 284.2 (28.ix); *SB* XVI 12488.2 (2.xii); *P.Cair.Masp.* II 67252.1	Fl. Iohannes v.c. (praef. sacr. praet.)
<u>INSCR.:</u>	**BULGARIA:** Besevliev, *Spätgriech. u. Spätlat. Inschr. aus Bulg.* (Berlin 1964) 231 (Elesnica, 12.vi)	Fl. Iohannes v.c.
	ASIA: Grégoire, *Inscr.* 219 = *Milet* I 7 (1924) 303-04 no.206 (Miletos)	Fl. Iohannes v.c. praef. sacr. praet. II et patricius

<u>NOTES:</u>

John the Cappadocian was Justinian's controversial praetorian prefect: Stein, *Histoire du Bas-Empire* II 443-49, 463-83.

Occidentis

FASTI:	AqS. (SQ)	Paulinus VI et Apio
	AqS. (G)	p.c. Iohannis
	Camp. AqS. (NX) (v.c.) Marius	Apio (v.c.)
	VindPost.	et Apio
	ExcSang.	p.c. Belisarii IV et Stratici IV
LAWS:	none	
INSCR.:	**ITALY:** *CIL* V 5410 = *ILCV* 1040 (Como, Reg. XI; 5.vi); *CIL* V 4998 = *ILCV* 848 (Riva, Reg. X; 24.xii)	p.c. Iohannis v.c.
	CIL V 6467 = *ILCV* 1238 (Pavia, Reg. XI; 22.vii); *CIL* V 5211 = *ILCV* 2741 (Garlate, Reg. XI; 1.ix)	p.c. V Paulini iun. v.c.
	DALMATIA: *Forsch.Salona* II 252 (Salona; 18.viii)	Apio v.c.

Orientis

<u>FASTI:</u>	MarcellS. Heracl. Pasch. (adds son of Strategius)	Apion solus
	Victor	Apio v.c.
<u>LAWS:</u>	27 novels, earliest *NovIust* 78.5 (18.i; Gk. version), all C'polis	Apion v.c.
<u>PAPYRI:</u>	*P.Lond.* III 1001.2 (p.270) (14.ii)	p.c. Fl. Iohannis v.c.
	P.Harr. II 238.4 (4.iv); *P.Cair.Masp.* I 67106.1* (10.x); *P.Cair.Masp.* II 67255.1 (v-xii)	Fl. Apion v.c.
<u>INSCR.:</u>	**CRETA:** *I.Cret.* IV 460 = Bandy, 31 (Gortyn; i-viii)	Fl. Apion v.c.
<u>OTHER:</u>	Consular diptych of Apion giving his full names (Volbach no.32)	

<u>NOTES:</u>

For the Apion family and its landholdings, cf. J. Gascou, *Travaux et Mémoires* 9 (1985) 61-90 and *P.Heid.* IV 331. Dalmatia used his consulate, but the West otherwise not.

613

Fl. Mar. Petrus Theodorus Valentinus Rusticius Boraides Germanus Iustinus

Occidentis

<u>FASTI</u>:	AqS. (SQ)	Paulinus VII et Apio II
	AqS. (G)	bis iterum cons. Iohannis
	AqS. (NX)	Iustinus iun. v.c.
	Camp. Marius	Iustinus
<u>LAWS</u>:	none	
<u>INSCR.</u>:	**ROME:** *ICUR* n.s. II 5077 = *ILCV* 704 (16.iii-1.iv; om. Fl.; frag.); *ICUR* n.s. II 5078 = *ILCV* 411 adn. (8.ix); *ICUR* n.s. II 5079 = *ILCV* 345	Fl. Iustinus v.c.
	ITALY: *CIL* V 4084 = *ILCV* 673 (Mantua, Reg. X; 19.ii)	sexies p.c. Paulini iun.
	CIL XI 4973 (Spoleto, Reg. VI; xi-xii; frag.)	Fl. Iustinus [
	GAUL: *CIL* XII 2081 = *ILCV* 1672 (Vienne; 11.vi)	iterum p.c. Iohannis v.c.
<u>OTHER</u>:	Tjäder, *Nichtlit. Pap.* 31 ii.11 (3.i); 32.15 = *ChLA* XX 708 (21.iii)	VI p.c. Paulini iun. v.c.

Orientis

FASTI:	MarcellS. Pasch.	Iustinus iun. solus
	Heracl.	Iustinus solus
	Victor	Iustinus v.c.
LAWS:	*NovIust* 106.1 (C'polis, 7.ix; Lat. vers.: 9.ix)	Iustinus v.c.
PAPYRI:	*P.Berl.Möller* 3.3 = *SB* IV 7340 (27.iii); *SB* XVI 12267.2 (13.vii); *PSI* III 188.2	p.c. Fl. Apionis v.c.
	P.Michael. 45.1 (vii-viii); *SB* VIII 9773.4 (17.x)	Fl. Iustinus v.c.
OTHER:	Consular diptych of Iustinus, giving full name (Volbach no.33); cf. Feissel, *Travaux et Mémoires* 9 (1985) 403 for resolving Mar. as Marianus	

NOTE:

Iustinus was the son of Germanus, not his cousin Iustinus the son of Vigilantia; both were nephews of Justinian. On his postconsular era in the West, see *Rec.Inscr.Chrét.Gaule* XV, pp.56ff.

Occidentis

FASTI:	AqS. (G)	III p.c. Iohannis
	Camp.	Basilius iun.
	AqS. (GX) Marius (om. v.c.)	Basilius v.c.
	AqS. (SQN)	Basilius iun.
LAWS:	none	
INSCR.:	**ROME:** *ICUR* n.s. V 13406 (22.i); *ICUR* n.s. II 5728	Basilius iun. v.c.
	ITALY: *CIL* V 7414 = *ILCV* 2829B (nr. Dertona, Reg. IX; 13.i); *CIL* IX 5347 = *ILCV* 4216 (Città di Marano, Reg. V; 9.ii; om. iun. v.c.); *CIL* XI 310 = *ILCV* 226 (Ravenna, Reg. VIII; 12.iii)	Basilius iun. v.c.
	GAUL: *CIL* XIII 2380 = *ILCV* 3563A (Lyons; 30.iv)	p.c. Iustini
	CIL XII 939 (Arles; 4.ix)	Basilius v.c.
OTHER:	Tjäder, *Nichtlit.Pap.* 33.10 (Ravenna; 16.vii)	Basilius iun. v.c.
	Council at Orléans: *Conc.Galliae* (Corp.Christ.Lat. 148A), pp.132, 142 (14.v; om. v.c.)	Basilius v.c.

Orientis

FASTI:	MarcellS.	Basilii solius annus primus
	Heracl. Pasch.	Basilius solus
	Victor	Basilius v.c.
LAWS:	9 novels, earliest *NovIust* 107.3 (1.ii), all from C'polis	Basilius v.c.
PAPYRI:	*SB* XVI 12639.4 (ii-iii); *ZPE* 62 (1986) 145.1 (3?.iv); *SB* XIV 12051.1 (ix)	p.c. Fl. Iustini v.c.
	P.Cair.Masp. II 67126 (written in C'polis; 7.i); *P.Stras.* 598.1 (10.ix); *P.Stras.* 597.2* (ix-xii)	Fl. Basilius v.c.
INSCR.:	**ASIA:** *I.Smyrna* 561 = Grégoire, *Inscr.* 71 (Smyrna; 13.iv; indict. points to 540); *I.Smyrna* 562 = Grégoire, *Inscr.* 70 (Smyrna; 9.vi)	Fl. Basilius v.c.
OTHER:	One nearly complete consular diptych, once mistakenly assigned to Basilius cos. 480 (Volbach no.5; Cameron and Schauer, *JRS* 72 [1982] 126-42).	

NOTES:

Though eastern consul, Basilius came from the old western family of the Decii, son, cousin, nephew, grandson and greatgrandson of western consuls (Cameron and Schauer, *JRS* 72 [1982] 143). His p.c. was widely used as the basis of an era.

PART III

CRITICAL APPENDIX

In a work using thousands of documents as evidence, one can hardly avoid some comments on individual texts. Except for a small number of vital texts, however, the format of the main part of this book does not give any scope for discussion of problems in the inscriptions and papyri--particularly the inscriptions, as the papyri have already been subjected to extensive critical work by Bagnall and Worp as well as others. The following Critical Appendix is an attempt to provide some of the needed commentary on inscriptions.

For each year, as needed, there are two parts: (a) a list of documents sometimes attributed to this consulate, together with our reasons for excluding each from our list; and (b) a series of notes on texts where we differ from editors in reading, restoration, date, or interpretation. It is in the nature of the enterprise that neither part can hope to be exhaustive. We have ignored erroneous datings of inscriptions in antiquated editions which we do not cite.

In the exclusions list, we use the following short phrases to give our reasons for omission without extended argument:

Cos. date?: The remains do not seem to us sufficient to establish that we are dealing with a consular date as opposed to some other element of an inscription.

Name doubtful: The likelihood of a consular date is adequate, but we do not consider the remains of names sufficient to make an identification secure or even highly probable. This note is used particularly where the remaining letters offer a choice of several names belonging to different consulates.

Person(s) doubtful: The name(s) are clear enough, but more than one consul bore this name or these names and we cannot find any indication which one is meant. (Where there are only two choices, inherently hard or impossible to distinguish between, and the number of texts is substantial, we have generally listed all examples in the main section under one of them and placed a cross-reference at the other. The material is relegated to the Critical Appendix in all cases where there are three or more bearers of the name.)

Year doubtful: The consul is identifiable (or a pair is), but he/they held office in multiple years, using iteration numbers which are not preserved on the stone or which are insufficiently preserved to allow any degree of probability in assigning a date. Most of these cases are imperial consuls.

Dubious cases are not relisted under every other possible year. The index of texts discussed will allow easy finding of particular texts.

In the case of the papyri, corrections and redatings which are already found in *BL* I-VII, *CSBE* and *RFBE* are not given here; cf. the Guide to the main part of the book. We wish to point out, however, that every papyrus text cited has been reexamined for this book, and the remarks which are made in this Appendix come from that reexamination.

284

Excluded

I.Lat.Alg. II 2 4558, from Ghar el Djemae, gives *Imp. C. Num(eriano) et SEVVAERO cos.* The editors argue that the text comes from a point after a renunciation of the consulate by Carinus, and that Numerian took a new colleague. We know of no other evidence for this course of events, however, and given the doubt about the name of the second consul, we have preferred to relegate the text to the Appendix.

287

Excluded

ICUR n.s. VIII 20716 (year doubtful)

Critical Notes

ICUR n.s. VII 19946 gives Diocletian III, Maximian II, a combination which did not occur, as Diocletian was consul jointly with Maximian in 287 (III and I) and 290 (IV and III). The same combination is found in *CIL* VIII 23291. For some reason, Ferrua prefers 290 as a date for this inscription, though neither numeral matches in that year. At all events, we prefer to follow the iteration number for the senior Augustus.

289

Excluded

ICUR n.s. VIII 23648b (cos. date?)

Critical Notes

The editor of *P.Mich.* X 593 does not indicate reasons for printing the restoration *[Quintianus et Bassus]* instead of the correct order, which we print.

290

Critical Notes

Diocletian's iteration numeral in *CIL* III 10406 was added in small letters as an afterthought. The stonecutter did not go on to add a numeral for Maximian, however.

291

Critical Notes

The restoration in *ICUR* n.s. III 8718 leaves line 3 much shorter than lines 1 and 4, but we do not see a solution which is better.

293

Critical Notes

We see no reason of space not to restore DD.NN. at the start of the formula in *P.Grenf.* II 110.

294

Excluded

ICUR n.s. VIII 20764 (person doubtful)

295

Excluded

ICUR n.s. VIII 20765 (cos. date?)

Critical Notes

For *BGU* III 858, see *BASP* 17 (1980) 6.

297

Critical Notes

CIL III 14433[1] omits both emperors' numerals and abbreviates them *Max* and *Ma* (followed by a small lacuna), leaving open the possibility that Maximianus (i.e. Galerius) VIII et Maximinus Aug. II (311) are the consuls. Slightly in favor of the editor's date of 297, however, is the placement of Aug. after the first consul.

298

Excluded

IGRR I 1291 = *SB* V 8393 (not cos. date); cf. Barnes, *New Empire* 55.

Critical Notes

The editor of *P.Oxy.* XII 1469 restores the numeral II after Paulinus' name, but we see no basis for this restoration.

299

Critical Notes

For *PSI* XIII 1338, see K.A. Worp in *ZPE* 61 (1985) 99.

300

Excluded

ICUR n.s. III 8136 (year doubtful; 302 also possible)

301

Excluded

ICUR n.s. VII 17420. De Rossi, *ICUR* I 27, assigns to 301, correcting stone's *NEPO[* to *NEPO[*. The stone lacks a II after the putative first consul (*Titian]o et*), though the only other Roman inscription of the year, *CIL* VI 2143, has it. On balance, the evidence seems insufficient to date the inscription.

Critical Notes

In *IGRR* III 1268, published earlier in *AJP* 6 (1885) 213, the first name of the second consul was restored as Οὐιρ[γιυἱ]ου, an excessively long restoration as can now be seen. Οὐιρ[ἱ]ου is the correct restoration. In line 1, the editor's T is presumably the first half of the pi of Postumius.

For *P.Flor.* I 3, see *ZPE* 56 (1984) 128.

302

Critical Notes

ICUR n.s. I 1249 was carved in 305 when the boy died; the consular date to 302 refers to his birth and was thus not inscribed contemporaneously with the event.

303

Critical Notes

AE 1968, 81 prefers Diocletian III, Maximian I (287 but error for III and II, see note under 287) in the commentary (p.35); but dates the inscription to 303 in the index (p.237); the latter seems to us correct.

For *P.Corn.* 20a and *SB* XIV 11614, see *ZPE* 56 (1984) 131.

304

Critical Notes

P.Oxy. XVIII 2187.1, if restored correctly (as seems likely), dates by the consulate of Diocletian and Maximian for the ninth time; it was in fact Diocletian's ninth consulate, but only Maximian's eighth. It is possible that the assimilation of their regnal years at this time influenced the scribe.

The editors of *CPR* VII 14 omit Αὐτοκρατόρων from their restoration of lines 8-9, but it is a normal part of the formula for this year, and we believe that it should be restored.

For *P.Oxy.* XII 1551 see *ZPE* 56 (1984) 130.

306

Excluded

CIL XIV 3416 = *ICUR* I 147 (person, year doubtful)

307

Excluded

AE 1967, 442 (Thasos): the suggestion of 307 as a date comes from *AE*; the editio princeps in *BCH* 91 (1967) 588 no. 35 dates it only to the fourth century. We consider the precise date given in *AE* to be speculative.

AE 1964, 226 (Battina, Pannonia): the consuls are entirely restored on the basis of the editor's hypothesized date for the text, and they thus have no evidentiary value.

308

Critical Notes

For *P.Grenf.* II 72 see *BASP* 17 (1980) 108.

309

Critical Notes

For *M.Chrest.* 196, see *BASP* 17 (1980) 16-17; cf. *BL* VI 90.

For *P.Ryl.* IV 616, see the discussion under the year 312, below.

310

Excluded

I.Lat.Paestum 110 presents only *Pomp[* of what is apparently a consular date. The order would be wrong for Pompeius Probus (the second consul of 310), and we cannot suggest another possibility.

Critical Notes

In *SB* XIV 12167.4, the name of the second consul can be restored as just Probus. It is not clear whether there was originally vv.cc. or vv.cc. praeff. at the end of the formula.

311

Critical Notes

AE 1937, 232, gives the text of the editio princeps; 1937, 158, gives a corrected text. Unfortunately, it is the text of 232 which was taken up in *FIRA* I 93 (where the date is also given wrongly as 9.vi).

For *P.Coll.Youtie* II 79, see *ZPE* 56 (1984) 131.

The editor of *Aegyptus* 63 (1983) 58 assigns it to 310, restoring the consulate. But the p.c. of 309 was still in use as late as 12.i of that year, and a date to 311 seems to us more plausible.

312

Excluded

ICUR suppl. 1409 = *ILCV* 258 adn. (cos. date? person doubtful)

ICUR n.s. I 513 = *ILCV* 3492B (year doubtful)

P.Ryl. IV 616: In a note published in *BASP* 17 (1980) 10-12, Bagnall and Worp advanced arguments against the editors' date of 312 for *P.Ryl.* IV 616 and in favor of a date in 309 (or early 310) instead. The text in question contains a reference to the indiction of the present kanon of the consulate of our lords Constantinus and Licinius Augusti I. Arguing that the numeral ($\tau\grave{o}$ α) could not be taken to refer to an indiction, they interpreted it as a consular interation number.

While the arguments against 312 advanced several years ago remain solid, there were a number of objections against 309 raised in the same article, and these warrant further exploration. That concerning the use of an iteration numeral with the first consulate of a given consul or consuls is not substantial, and another instance has now turned up in *CPR* VIII 22.3-5 (with a pair of consuls who did not have a second consulate, moreover). Furthermore, a date to 309 raises problems in administrative history: cf. Thomas, *BASP* 21 (1984) 230 n.30. On the other hand, the fact that the order of the consular names would be the reverse of that found in other documents is still a major problem.

A restudy of the photograph persuades us that the faint traces of $\Sigma\epsilon\beta\alpha\sigma\tau\tilde{\omega}\nu$ are insufficient to compel that reading.

Taking these considerations together (along with the fact that the archive to which this text belongs dates in the main to 317-323), we have examined the possibility that the date might actually be 319, with Constantine (V) and Licinius Caesar I. But to this also objections may be raised: Constantine's iteration numeral would be lacking, and neither consul would have an indication of imperial rank. We therefore think that 319 presents difficulties as formidable as those which 309 offers, and we prefer to regard this papyrus for the present not as evidence for any particular year.

313

Excluded

IGUR I 246 = *IG* XIV 956A.1 (year doubtful)

SbWien, Phil.-hist. Kl. 335 (1978) 27 no.4 = *AE* 1982, 784 (year doubtful; 342 or 346 possible)

Critical Notes

For *BGU* II 408, see *BASP* 16 (1979) 227-28.

314

Excluded

P.Köln V 232.1 (doubtful restoration)

315

Excluded

After describing the pact of 1.iii.317 at Serdica by which Crispus, Constantine iunior and Licinius iunior were simultaneously proclaimed Caesars (Barnes, *Constantine and Eusebius*, 67), *Origo Constantini Imperatoris* 19 adds "itaque Constantinus et Licinius simul consules facti." Commentators assume a reference to 315, the last occasion on which Constantine and Licinius held a joint consulate (before then in 309, 312, and 313). But it would make no sense for the writer to refer to an event of 315 as a consequence of one in 317. Could it be that he mistakenly inferred that the consuls of 319 were Constantine and Licinius *senior* instead of Licinius *iunior*? If so, this would be a surprisingly early misinterpretation of the fasti.

316

Excluded

ICUR n.s. V 13888 (name doubtful)

Critical Notes

For *P.Oxy.* XVII 2124 see *RFBE* 39.

318

Excluded

ILCV 4634A (name doubtful)

Critical Notes

ICUR n.s. III 8416 preserves only Licinius' name but in the form *LICINO . VI*. Licinius' sixth consulate was recognized only in the East (in 321). De Rossi (*ICUR* I 34) suggested emending to *LICINIO . V* (i.e. a misplaced I). Ferrua reads *LICIN(I)O V<I>*. Barnes, *New Empire* 96 n.24, takes it as evidence that "Constantine recognized Licinius and his son as consuls at the beginning of the year." This seems to us an insecure basis for such a conclusion.

319

Critical Notes

Syll.[3] 901 was dated to 312-315 by Dittenberger, meaning 312 *or* 315 (313 and 314 being impossible). See *SEG* XII 226 for the date to 319.

320

Excluded

P.Ryl. IV 653 i.1 = *P.Sakaon* 33 (year doubtful; see *BASP* 21 [1984] 227 n.17)

Critical Notes

OGIS II 619 is restored with Constantine Caesar's epithet as ε[ὑγε]νεστάτου; but ἐ[πιφα]νεστάτου is normal and to be restored here.

321

Critical Notes

ICUR n.s. VII 20340 is restored *kalend]as* by Ferrua, but *non]as* seems equally possible. The consuls are *Cri[spo et Constant]ino*; the line is painted rather than incised, and a numeral could be effaced at the end. There is thus a slight possibility that the year is 324, but the absolute lack of inscriptions from that year makes 321 the more likely date.

SB I 4223 = Milne, *Greek Inscr. Cairo* 9238, was dated by Milne to 323, by *SB* to 322.

For *SPP* XX 80, cf. *CSBE* 8 n.3.

For *P.Sakaon* 67.18, cf. *RFBE* 40, dating to viii-xii.

322

Excluded

ICUR n.s. IV 9551 and 9552 (person doubtful)

323

Excluded

ICUR suppl. 1416 (person doubtful)

Critical Notes

In *CIL* X 407 = *I.Ital.* III.1 17, the reading given derives from Renaissance copies. Mommsen saw only one T of the Vettius. Cf. *PLRE* I 781.

324

Critical Notes

For *P.Oxy.Hels.* 44, see *BASP* 17 (1980) 116.

For *PSI* IV 300, see *BASP* 17 (1980) 16.

325

Critical Notes

P.Stras. 138.17 would appear to be an exception to the rule of consuls' having either one name each or two names each, for it gives Paulinus et Ionius Iulianus. But the space before Paulinus is lost; adding Ἀνικίου to the restoration does make ecthesis a necessary assumption, but we see nothing improbable in that.

There is a larger problem with Iulianus' first name. *P.Stras.* 137.20, where the consular phrase is well preserved, reads ὑπατείας Ἀνικίου Παυλίνου καὶ Ἰωνίου Ἰουλιανοῦ τῶν λαμπροτάτων. The editor corrects to Καιωνίου, supposing haplography, and cites examples of the name Caeionius. Barnes (*New Empire* 102-03) and Chastagnol (*Les fastes de la préfecture* 85 n.89) prefer to emend to Iulius. Barnes rejects the other view, that M. Ceionius Iulianus, proc. Afr. after 325 and praef. urbi 333 (*PLRE* I 476) is the man. *PLRE* I 478-79 lists the man as Iulius Iulianus, alleging that this full name occurs in *SB* 8019 (= *P.Stras.* 137) and 8020 (= 138); in fact, of course, Ionius stands there, as we have seen. The other citations for Iulius Iulianus given refer to the prefect of Egypt, and it is a matter of argument, not of fact, whether he is the same as the consul. There is, in other words, no evidence that the consul of 325 is the prefect and PPO.

In *P.Stras.* 138.17, however, the same reading is found as in 137; unlike 137 (a lease), 138 is a letter from the logistes of Hermopolis, an official of standing. On the month in *P.Stras.* 138, cf. *Aegyptus* 20 (1940) 295 n.2. In *P.Charite* 13.40, the line is lost before -ωνίου, but the editor restores Και]ωνίου. The space, however, seems better suited to just Ἰ]ωνίου than to the longer name. (The letters are in any event not well preserved.)

A corruption of Iulius into Ionius seems to us unlikely. Iulius was a very common and well-known name, whereas the examples of Ionius (whether in Rome or in Egypt) can be counted on one's fingers. Given now that we have (probably) three documents with the name Ionius, from three different writers, it appears that the name must have been disseminated (at least in the Hermopolite) as Ionius. We do not have evidence from elsewhere in Egypt of the first name of this consul. That the logistes would make an error on this point seems to us implausible. In the present state of the evidence, therefore, we think that printing Ionius is the only acceptable procedure; new evidence may one day tell us whether Ionius, Caeionius, or Iulius is the true name of the man in question. It is worth noting that *ICUR* n.s. II 4947 seems to attest the name Ionius for a prominent Roman (v.s.) in the fifth century (cf. *PLRE* II 619), and there are other parallels for such fanciful names.

The inscribed votive monument from a Mithraeum in Gimmeldingen in the Pfalz region of Germany, listed under this year from Vermaseren, *Corpus Inscriptionum et Monumentorum Religionis Mithraicae* II (1960) no. 1315, appears to attest Paulinus and Iulianus as consuls already on 22.i.325, something which would cause serious difficulties for the interpretation offered by us of this year's events:

in h(onorem) d(omus) d(ivinae) deo inviht[o] Midre
Maternin[i]us Faustinu(s) carax fan[um] cum solo inviht[o]
in suo fecit c[onsac]ratus XI k(alendis) Feb(ruariis).
Fanus consacrat(us) per Potentianum patrem co(n)s(ulibus)
Paulino et Iuliano l(ibens) l(aetus) m(erito).

Yet a closer look at the inscription indicates that we must dissociate the consulate from the date of 22 January. Two separate dates are given, one (Faustinus' consecration) being dated by day but not by year, and the other (the consecration of the Mithraeum) being dated by year but not by day.

A number of other reliefs and altars survive from the same Mithraeum, at least two dedicated by the same Faustinus (Vermaseren 1319, 1320; same concluding formula in the fragmentary 1321 and 1322). Obviously the sanctuary as a whole is likely to have taken months if not years to complete, and there is no reason to believe that this particular inscription was cut on or even soon after the day of Faustinus' consecration on 22 January. It might seem natural to infer from the sequence of the sentences that Faustinus' consecration fell before that of the Mithraeum. But the inscription also implies a further distinction, between the actual building (*fecit*) of the Mithraeum by Faustinus and its consecration by his father. Following normal usage, the site will have been consecrated before the building was built, and it was presumably in the completed building that Faustinus was consecrated. Since Faustinus was consecrated in a January, the Mithraeum must have been consecrated in the previous year. Perhaps then it is not just a balancing day date that has been omitted, but another year date as well. Faustinus' date of consecration would then have fallen on 22.i.326. Whatever the correct interpretation, the inscription is hardly secure evidence for knowledge of these consuls in January of 325.

327

Excluded

ILCV 4697 (name/person doubtful)

Critical Notes

For Pack[2] 2731, see *BASP* 17 (1980) 17.

328

Excluded

Bosio, *Roma sotterranea* (1632) 560a (ed. 1650, p.506) = *ILCV* 2379 adn. (cos. date?)

Critical Notes

ICUR n.s. III 7378: the first consul's name is misrestored (a misprint?) by Ferrua as *Ian[uario* instead of the correct *Ian[uarino*.

For the date of *PSI* IV 316 see *BASP* 18 (1981) 53.

For *P.Sakaon* 65, see *RFBE* 76.

For *SB* XII 11024, see *BASP* 17 (1980) 15.

330

Critical Notes

The actual reading of *ICUR* n.s. I 1417 is ETIULLIANO, with the I written very close to the T, an obvious error for ETTULLIANO. See the plate in Marucchi, *I monumenti del museo cristiano Pio-Lateranense* (Milan 1910), pl. XLVII. The appearance of two names for one consul and only one for the other is unusual (cf. p.37).

331

Excluded

ICUR n.s. VIII 23400a (names doubtful)

ICUR n.s. VIII 23399 (person doubtful)

Critical Notes

CIG III 4593 is erroneously dated by the editor to 289? A.D. (corrected by Waddington). In line 1, perhaps ἐπ[άρχων] should be restored.

For *P.Sakaon* 69, see *BASP* 17 (1980) 13.

333

Excluded

ICUR n.s. II 6022 (names doubtful; ed. restores coss. of 358)

335

Critical Notes

ICUR n.s. III 8137 has D.N. restored erroneously before Constantius' name. The editor offers 345 as a less probable date, but this is certainly excluded by the arguments he gives.

336

Excluded

ICUR n.s. VIII 20807a (person doubtful)

337

Excluded

ICUR n.s. IV 11750 (name doubtful)

ICUR n.s. V 13286 (name doubtful)

Critical Notes

For *PSI* VII 804, see *P.Oxy.* XLVI 3304.

338

Excluded

ICUR n.s. I 1647 = *ILCV* 3758 (reading uncertain, despite Ferrua, *Nuove corr.* 122)

339

Excluded

CIL V 876* = C. Gazzera, *Iscr. Crist. del Piemonte*, p.19 (cit. by De Rossi, *ICUR* I 52 note) (forgery)

ICUR n.s. IV 9555 (names/persons doubtful)

Critical Notes

For *P.Ant.* I 32, see *ZPE* 56 (1984) 131.

340

Excluded

CIL XI 4029 (name doubtful)

P.Stras. 817 (restoration gratuitous)

341

Excluded

ICUR n.s. V 13290 (person doubtful)

ICUR n.s. VIII 20770 and 20771 (persons doubtful)

342

Excluded

ICUR n.s. I 983a (names doubtful)

Critical Notes

P.Abinn. 44.20 gives Κωνσταντίνου instead of Κωνσταντίου. Cf. 346.

P.Flor. I 34 has at the start a date to the consuls of 342; the editor restores (with a sign of doubt) the date (Pharmouthi 13) found in line 15, where there stands μετὰ τὴν ὑπατείαν, Pharmouthi 13 (= 8.iv). On the basis of this discrepancy, *CSBE* sub anno says "year uncertain." But in 343, the consuls of that year were known already on 14.iii. The date is therefore virtually certain to be 342, and probably the p.c. is just an error for ὑπατείας τῆς προκειμένης. The restoration of the month and day at the start of the document is probably wrong; many texts of this period have the consulate but no month and day at the start, then the ὑπατείας τῆς προκειμένης plus month and day at the end. (For the reverse phenomenon--a p.c. date followed by ὑπατείας τῆς προκειμένης--cf. e.g. *SB* XIV 12088.1,28.)

In *P.Col.* VII 150.35, for the editors' ἐωνίων read δεσποτῶν.

343

Excluded

ICUR n.s. I 2080 = *ICUR* I 69 has (in Greek) 9 kal. Sept., followed by Ρωμουλι. De Rossi took this as a consular date to 343, because of the position and for want of a better idea. But the omission of the first consul is not normal (cf. above, p.64 n.26), and there is no word to indicate the consulate. The date could be right, but it seems to us insufficiently secure to include.

ILCV 662 adn. = *ICUR* suppl. 1416 (person doubtful).

344

Excluded

ICUR n.s. III 8138 (name doubtful)

ICUR n.s. VII 17430b = suppl. 1447 (uncertain if second consul is Bonosus [as ed.] or Sallustius)

ICUR n.s. VIII 20772 (person doubtful)

Critical Notes

For *P.Princ.* II 81 = III 181 see *ZPE* 56 (1984) 132.

345

Excluded

ICUR I 85 = n.s. VII 20602 (cf. Ferrua, *Nuove corr.* 82-83)

ICUR n.s. VII 17962 (person doubtful, as well as cos. vs. p.c.; 444/445 possible)

ICUR n.s. I 1104 (cos. date?)

Kokalos 28-29 (1982-83) 4 no. 3 (cos. date?)

Critical Notes

The two editions of Agnello, *Silloge* 88 (= *AE* 1932, 72) = *AE* 1933, 29, record the date variously as X or XI kal. Oct. Ferrua reads XI, cf. *Kokalos* 28-29 (1982-83) 4.

The date in *CIL* XI 4033 is read in *ILCV* 3194 as III, but *CIL* has IIII. We suppose the date in *ILCV* is a typographical error.

346

Excluded

I.Christ.Ital. IV 17 (names doubtful)

Critical Notes

CIL VI 37122 was published earlier in *AE* 1907, 133, which dates the inscription erroneously to 345. See Ferrua, *Nuove corr.* 10, for the date.

P.Abinn. 47.20, 48.21, 49.26, and 52.33 give Κωνσταντίνου in place of Κωνσταντίου. Cf. 342.

The Cologne council is probably a forgery of the eighth century, but much of its material seems to derive from fourth-century documents. Cf. the editor's introduction. The date quoted here is thus of rather doubtful pedigree.

347

Excluded

ICUR n.s. VII 17504a (name/person doubtful)

AE 1969/1970, 68a (name doubtful)

ICUR I 406 (person doubtful)

348

Excluded

ICUR n.s. II 4800 (cos. date?)

Critical Notes

The editor of *ICUR* n.s. IV 11756 restores the date as *[kalenda]s Maias*. There seems, however, no reason to exclude a restoration of, e.g., *[viii idu]s* or *[iiii nona]s*; it therefore seems better to us to refrain from restorng the date in the lacuna in any precise way. The inscription refers to the period 14.iv-15.v, but we cannot be more exact.

349

Critical Notes

CIL II 2211 = *ILS* 7222 is dated Limenio et Catullino conss.; the editor gives 348 as the date, presumably by a misprint.

ICUR n.s. V 13296 likewise is dated to Limenius and Catullinus, but the editor gives 409 as the date.

ICUR n.s. V 13899.6 is restored as follows:

Novemb]r consulatu Lim[eni e]t Catulli[ni vvcc

The sketch of the stone, however, shows that this restoration is impossible, as there is no room at the beginning of this line for anything but the R, of which only a trace remains. On the other hand, the diagonal trace at the start seems to exclude

] p(ost) consulatu(m) Lim[eni e]t Catulli[ni

(The stone would, in this case, date from 350). Ferrua tells us that the plate (Tav. XXII c5) is more reliable for this fragment; but that does not help with its placement. Any month ending in R would be possible, perhaps the shorter the better. The restoration of vv.cc. at the end of the formula is very dubious. There is only one example of this epithet in western inscriptions from the period before the 370's (cf. above, p.63), although it appears in inscriptions and papyri from other parts of the empire much earlier. (One should eliminate vv.cc. from the restorations also of *ICUR* n.s. V 13298 (350), 13303 (359), 13311 (361).)

ICUR n.s. IV 11090 is restored (following *ICUR* suppl. 1467) as:

Li]menio et Ac[one Cat]ulino [vv.cc.]

We have pointed out before (cf. p.37), however, that inscriptions almost always give either one name for each consul or two names for each, not one for one and two for the other. And vv.cc. is, as noted above, not generally found in Roman inscriptions of this date. We therefore suggest for this text the following restoration (substituting Aconius for Aco, cf. commentary to the year):

Ulpio Li]menio et Ac[onio Cat]ulino [coss]

350

Excluded

ICUR n.s. VIII 20775 (name doubtful)

RAC 22 (1946) 91 + 36 (1960) 14 (reading doubtful)

352

Excluded

ICUR suppl. 1475 (name doubtful)

ICUR n.s. III 8140 (cos. date? name doubtful)

ICUR suppl. 1477 (name doubtful)

CIL IX 2639 = *ILS* 1248 (year doubtful)

ICUR n.s. VIII 20849c (cos. date?)

Critical Notes

For *ChLA* III 210, see *BASP* 17 (1980) 113.

ICUR n.s. I 1252 = *ILCV* 2967 adn.: This inscription, apparently attesting a joint consulate for Magnentius and Decentius, has caused problems. It seems unlikely to be an error for 351 (so *PLRE* I 245). Degrassi rather oddly lists a joint consulate of Magnentius II and Decentius II in the Gauls in 353. Though wholly undocumented, this is certainly a possibility--but no help in explaining the use of the formula (without iteration numbers) in Rome, which had been in Constantius' hands since September, 352 (Piganiol, *L'empire chrétien*[2] 98). The simplest explanation is that the stonemason miscopied a formula for 352 that gave the first name in full as *Magno Decentio*, not so surprising if he had been carving *Magnentio* all the preceding year.

354

Critical Notes

AE 1905, 215 is dated by the editor as 345; but this is a misprint for 354, the consuls of which stand in the text.

For *PSI* IX 1077 see *RFBE* 76.

P.Laur. IV 169 has been discussed in *ZPE* 59 (1985) 89-90 by J.G. Keenan, who shows that it is probably "the end of a Greek copy in translation of a *constitutio* issued ... in Nicomedia." He dates it to 14-30.ix.326, restoring [Constantino Aug.] VII et Constantius Caesar [I] (in Greek). As T.D. Barnes points out to us, however, this date is impossible. In September, 326, Constantine was at Spoletium, en route from Rome to Milan. He did not reach Nicomedia until summer of the following year (see Barnes, *New Empire* 77). The only possible restoration which does not conflict with what we know of imperial movements is what we print, Constantius Aug. VII et Constantius Caesar III, i.e. 354, with the issuing emperor Gallus.

355

Excluded

ICUR n.s. VII 17435c is restored as

FFLL Arb]itio(ne) [et Ma]vor(tio)

The editor notes that Mavortius was the signum-name of Lollianus, the second consul of 355. Normally, however, such names are not used for indicating consuls in dating formulas (cf. Cameron, *JRS* 75 [1985] 172); moreover, the known inscriptions from 355 invariably use the name Lollianus to designate the second consul. It therefore seems to us far from obvious that this inscription refers to the consuls of 355.

Critical Notes

For *P.Oxy.* IV, p.202, see *BASP* 15 (1978) 235-36.

356

Excluded

ICUR n.s. VIII 23402 (names doubtful)

Critical Notes

CIL X 7167 preserves a month date which is read by the editors as IAN. A plate of this inscription is published in Agnello, *Silloge*, pl. III.3 (and cf. his text 90); on that plate one can see clearly that the month name is to be read as MAI. The date of the inscription, therefore, is 27.iv.356 rather than 28.xii.356. Cf. Ferrua, *Kokalos* 28-29 (1982-83) 5.

In *ICUR* n.s. VIII 20766, the editor suggests 329 as an alternative date (thinking that the Augustus' name was also omitted), but neither the distribution of such numerals-only dates nor that of inscriptions in this cemetery generally favors this idea.

357

Critical Notes

The dating clause in *ICUR* n.s. III 8722 is read

DP IES VI IDVS FEBR CC ꟼIII.T II

The editors note: "Lege D(E)P. ES(T) vel (D)IE<S> et in fine fortasse CO(NSTANTIO) ꟼIII I(VLIANO) II, a. 357." We think that there is an alternative which offers the same year but a far more convincing reading, viz. *CC* (= *consulibus*) ꟼ*III (E)T II*, i.e. *VIIII et II*. One may compare for the indication of a consulate by just the iteration numbers (always of imperial consuls) e.g. a few inscriptions from 360 (*CIL* X 4485, *IG* XIV 112) where one finds the consulate indicated by the numerals X et III. The same practice is found earlier in some papyri, cf. *CSBE* 111 s.a. 339, 340, 342, 346 (see above, p.68); and cf. our pages for 307 and 342 for similar practice in inscriptions (cf. also above, p.62).

The consular dating formula in *ICUR* I 132 is restored as

> *Constantio IX] et Iul. II cons.*

It is rather remarkable that Constantius' name is thought to be given in full but Julian's abbreviated. Moreover, in consular formulas in inscriptions from Rome we normally find the title Augustus following Constantius' name, and the numeral 9 is normally in this period given as VIIII, not as IX (we do not recall an exception in any consular date). We restore therefore:

> *Const. Aug. VIIII] et Iul. II cons.*

The text is reprinted as *ICUR* n.s. I 3166, but in that edition with no restoration at all.

ICUR n.s. V 13300 is restored (line 3) as follows:

> *Constantio Agusto VI[III et] Iuliano I[I conss]*

One would expect the regular *Iuliano [Caes. II]*. The trace of I on the break ("nella frattura", Ferrua) is not visible on the plate, but Ferrua affirms its existence. Is it conceivably *K[aes.]*? If we are correct about *ICUR* n.s. I 3166 (above), it is possible for Aug. to occur without a balancing Caes.

In *P.Lond.* III 1245.12, the editor omits τοῦ ἐπιφανεστάτου before Καίσαρος in the restoration, but there seems to be no reason for doing so.

For *ChLA* V 285 see *BASP* 17 (1980) 114.

358

Critical Notes

CIL VI 752 restores *XVI K]al* on the basis of earlier witnesses. In *ILS* 4267D, the editor has restored *XVII*. We have followed *CIL*.

359

Critical Notes

The ostrakon from Henchir-Bou-Gornine (Tunisia) printed in *AE* 1915, 81, is dated there to 358. The Latin text, however, gives a date to the postconsulate of Datianus and Cerealis rather than their consulate, and 359 is therefore the date.

ICUR n.s. VII 18472 was erroneously dated by Diehl, *ILCV* 4755C, to 490/494, cf. Ferrua, *Nuove corr.* 188.

For *BGU* III 909, see *BASP* 17 (1980) 116.

360

Excluded

ICUR I 145 = *ILCV* 4622 adn. (name doubtful)

ICUR I 146 = *ILCV* 3503 adn. (name doubtful)

Critical Notes

In *ICUR* n.s. V 13308.3, in place of the editors' *[Const(antio) X]* we restore the more regular formula *[DD.NN. Const(antio) Aug(usto) X]*, for which we believe the space would have been adequate; line 4 would seem much shorter, but lines 6 and 7 can have been as long:

> 6 Polocroniae q[uae vixit annos]
> 7 XXIIII fecit cum m[arito annos ...]
> 8 dep. VII Kal. Aug. [

ICUR n.s. V 13105 = *ILCV* 2883 was earlier published as n.s. II 5932 = 5858, with a date of 370, evidently a misprint.

361

Excluded

ICUR n.s. V 13313 (cos. date? name doubtful)

I.Ital. X.4 381 preserves a reference to a consulate of the emperor Julian in a milestone from near Trieste. The editors read the numeral (line 6) as IIII. In their comments, however, they refer to several other stones "eiusdem anni 361/2" though the fourth consulate of Julian fell only in 363. A check of the drawing of the stone reveals, however, that an error has crept into the comment, for one should read *Con[sul]i III*, or a reference to Julian's third consulate in 360. The title is part of the general titulature, however, and not a consular date; it is therefore not taken up in our main part.

ICUR n.s. VIII 20783a (cos. name?), 23403 (name doubtful)

Critical Notes

P.Fuad Univ. 16.7 reads as edited]τερεντίου τῶν λαμπροτάτων; the date assigned is the 4th or 5th century. This looks like a consular date. The only second consul whose name ended in -rentius is Florentius of 361, and since the editor calls attention to his doubt about τε, we have no hesitation in restoring [ὑπατείας Ταύρου καὶ Φ]λωρεντίου τῶν λαμπροτάτων.

362

Excluded

ICUR suppl. 1505 = n.s. IV 9558 (= *ILCV* 1563), lines 5-6, reads:

> quiescet id ivl
> palumbo sine felle m et n

De Rossi already proposed to resolve the end of line 6 as *M(amertino) et N(evitta)*, i.e. the consuls of 362. This resolution seems to us rather dubious. Abbreviation of personal names of consuls in dating formulas is found, but it generally involves abbreviations to three letters or more. We have seen no examples of the use of just one letter to abbreviate a consul's only name. We have no better explanation of the text to offer.

ICUR n.s. I 2282 = *ILCV* 2807A adn. (cos. date?)

Critical Notes

In the commentary to *ICUR* n.s. IV 12526 it is noted that the text presents *DN KL [Mamertino et]/FL Nev[itta vc conss]*, where the editor takes *KL* as an error for *FL*. The first consul of this year, however, was Claudius Mamertinus, and we may have a simple example of the use of K in place of C. Ferrua has argued (e.g. *ICUR* n.s. IV 12495; *Nuove corr.* 154) that K is sometimes written for F, and that FL is to be read here. That K is found for F sometimes does not to our thinking mean that it is always so used.

In accordance with the rule that consuls in pairs have the same number of names each, Fl. should be restored before Nevitta in *CIL* VI 31075.

SB XVI 12384 and 12385 both spell the second consul's name Eouitta (i.e. Evitta). This error is not found in any inscription. For the spelling of the name in the papyri, cf. *WB* III 75 a.362.

363

Excluded

ICUR n.s. III 7380 (name doubtful)

364

Excluded

ICUR suppl. 1522 (cos. date?)

ICUR suppl. 1526 (cos. date?)

ICUR n.s. VIII 20784a = suppl. 1528 (persons doubtful)

ICUR n.s. VIII 20801 (name doubtful)

Critical Notes

Jovian died on 17 February at Dadastana; the news had evidently not reached Rome by 30 March. *CTh* 9.25.2 is the only law without *divus*, bearing a date at Antioch two days after Jovian's death elsewhere. Seeck's conjecture that *dat.* is an error for *p.p.* seems the most likely solution. (*CTh* 13.3.6 and 10.1.8 were corrected so that they give Divus even though dating from Jovian's lifetime.) *Hist.Aceph.* 13 gives 19 Hathyr (read Mechir), Iov. et Varr., i.e. 14.ii. Varronianus was the infant son of Jovian (*PLRE* I, 946).

The editor of *ICUR* n.s. IV 9560 restores the date of this inscription as *XI Kal M[artias*, arguing that the absence of "Divus" in the inscription shows that the news of Jovian's death (16.ii; Seeck, *Regesten* 214, gives 17.ii) had not yet reached Rome at the time of the inscription (cf. also the note to *ICUR* n.s. IV 11096). This reasoning is not compelling, because there are several inscriptions from later in 364 which also omit Divus, e.g. *ICUR* n.s. VII 19953 of 12.x. A restoration of *XI Kal M[aias*, or 21.iv, therefore seems possible.

In *ICUR* n.s. V 13912, the restoration of *Aug.* after *Iovian[o* is not likely, as this element is never found without either D.N. or Divus preceding the name, and neither occurs in this case.

ICUR n.s. I 2084 = *ILCV* 2941A adn. is restored as *[VII Ka]l Octobres*, but the restoration of the precise day depends on emendation of corrupt readings in old witnesses and does not seem to us probative.

ICUR n.s. III 7381 restores D.N. before Iovianus, but Divus would be equally possible (and is found more often).

The dissemination of the consulate in the papyri was late. On the other hand, the scribe of *PSI* 90, the October witness, writes p.c. Iuliani et Sallustii vv.cc., which does not suggest great competence. As the Index to the Festal Letters has been compiled retroactively, it does not help in this matter.

365

Excluded

ICUR n.s. III 8144 (year doubtful)

ICUR suppl. 1533, 1534 (year doubtful)

ICUR n.s. V 13317 (year doubtful)

ICUR n.s. III 8646 (year doubtful)

ICUR n.s. I 3169 (year doubtful)

ICUR n.s. VIII 21604 (year doubtful)

AE 1976, 34 (year doubtful)

ICUR I 184 (persons doubtful)

ICUR I 388 (person doubtful)

ICUR suppl. 1554 = *ILCV* 1316 (person doubtful)

ICUR suppl. 1786 = *ILCV* 3500 (person doubtful)

CIL X 4486 = *ILCV* 4720 (person doubtful)

ICUR n.s. VIII 20784, 20785, 20786, 23406 (persons doubtful)

In all of the "year doubtful" cases, the part of the inscription where an iteration numeral would be found is lost.

ICUR n.s. III 8147 might date to 365, 368, 370 or 373 if one assumes the loss at the right of the iteration numeral; but even this expedient would not reconcile the date with the day of the week (Friday) in any of those years; Gatti (in *ICUR* suppl. 1592) suggested that if the burial occurred after sunset on Thursday, the ecclesiastical calendar would have reckoned the day as Friday (thus agreeing with 368). We do not know if such a reckoning would be represented in inscriptions; there are enough errors of the day of the week vs. date in funerary inscriptions of the period to make datings on this basis rather hazardous. Diehl (*ILCV* 4399A) includes Gatti's restoration *[Augg II conss]* in line 3, which is possible from the point of view of space. But III and IIII also seem possible, and there is Fl. in one text of the fourth consulate of the pair, 373 (*ICUR* n.s. II 4810). It also seems likely that the lacuna in line 2 had Fl. at the end, since Fl. is given before Valens' name in 3. From the above considerations, the following text emerges:

> prid(i)e nonas Martias die Ve[neris DD.NN. Fl.]
> Valen(t)iniano [e]t Fl. Valens [Augg. ..(..) conss.]

Critical Notes

In *ICUR* n.s. III 7382, it is possible that Fl. should be restored before Valens' name, cf. n.s. III 8147, dealt with above.

366

Excluded

ICUR suppl. 1566 (year doubtful)

ILCV 4369A (year doubtful)

ICUR I 293-301 and 1141 = *ILCV* 4188 adn. contain fragments of Gratian's name and cannot be assigned to any particular consulate of his.

ICUR n.s. VIII 20788, 20789, 21605, 23407, 23408a (year doubtful)

Critical Notes

In *ICUR* n.s. VIII 21606a, the editor restores *[Gratiani Aug. et Da]galaifo*. Gratian was not Augustus at this time, however, and *nob. puero* (however abbreviated) is the correct restoration.

367

Excluded

ICUR n.s. III 6502 (cos. date?)

The dating formula in *CIL* X 672 + auct. (p.1005) = *I.Ital.* I² 230 reads

X Kal. Maias post consecrationem Fl. Gratiani Augusti

The date is given as 22.iv.367? on the basis of a proposal of Th. Mommsen, who suggested changing *consecrationem* to *consulatum* in order to make a more regular dating formula of this. Apparently Mommsen took the view that the stone originally had only *post cons.*, wrongly expanded by the first editor of the stone, Camera. Though this idea is not without attractions, caution is in order. Gratian was consul five times, in 366, 371, 374 (+ p.c. in 375), 377, and 380. If the inscription in question dates from 371 or a later year, one expects an iteration numeral following Gratian's name and title. The omission of the numeral I, however, is common, and Mommsen for that reason apparently connected the stone with the consulate of 366. In this year, however, Gratian was not yet an Augustus when he took the consulate in January, but only a nobilissimus puer; he became Augustus on 24.viii.367. Mommsen's date is therefore anachronistic.

Now a well-attested meaning of the word is deification of the emperor, and one might conjecture that the stone was dated after the death of Gratian on 25.vii.383. Christian emperors often have the epithet Divus applied to them after death, the force of the word being attenuated in the course of time (cf. Cagnat, *Cours d'épigr.lat.* 247). The date of the stone would then be 22.iv.384. This dating in turn may be open to the objection that it is unique and suspect.

Faced with this choice of unattractive options, one may be attracted to Mommsen's view of an incorrect expansion of an abbreviation. In that case, however, one must assume that the editor also omitted an iteration numeral, given the impossibility of 367. Given that no colleague apparently is mentioned (though we cannot be certain that nothing is lost at the foot), and given that the one consulate of Gratian which commonly is referred to in postconsular datings is that of 374, which was the standard means of referring to 375, the omission of the numeral III is the most plausible supposition.

Critical Notes

The restoration of the month as Iu[niis in *ICUR* n.s. III 8146 rests on the mention of Tuesday, which in 367 coincided with the nones of June but not those of July.

In *ICUR* n.s. VII 17455, it seems that the lapicide simply ran out of room before Iovinus' name.

In *I.Christ.Ital.* III (Bari 1986) 3, the editor, G. Pani, publishes an inscription with a consular formula given as *Jno et Io*, about which he says, "la data consolare non è precisabile." Study of the index and reverse index of consular names, however, indicates that only Lupicinus and Iovinus are possible.

For *SB* XIV 12099 see *BASP* 17 (1980) 9.

368

Excluded

ICUR n.s. IV 11764 (year doubtful)

ICUR n.s. VII 17458 (person doubtful)

ICUR suppl. 1544 = *ILCV* 565 adn. = *CIL* VI 32952 (name doubtful)

ICUR n.s. VIII 23408c, 21607 (persons doubtful)

ICUR n.s. VIII 21606b (name doubtful)

Critical Notes

In *AE* 1977, 143, the lacuna before Valentinian's name permits the restoration of DD.NN. The same is true in *ICUR* n.s. V 13326.

The editors of *P.Lips.* 33 added Fll. before the emperors' names in restoration, but papyri of this period do not use Flavius for emperors, and we have therefore not accepted the restoration. Cf. 390.

369

Excluded

ICUR I 759-763, 765-794 are fragments containing parts of the name Valentinianus and apparently assignable to any of numerous years in the period 369-445.

Kokalos 28-29 (1982-83) 6 no. 10 (cos. date?)

ICUR n.s. VIII 23409 (year doubtful)

370

Excluded

ICUR n.s. IV 9564 (person doubtful)

ICUR n.s. I 442 (could be 360, *X et III*, or 430, *Theodosius XIII et Valentinianus III*)

ICUR n.s. II 6030 = *ILCV* 3808 (year doubtful: 387 possible)

Critical Notes

CIL VI 509 = *IGUR* I 129 is restored as *XVI Kal Iu[lias]*, but we see no reason that *Iu[nias]* is not equally possible.

ICUR n.s. I 1351 is restored (line 3) as

> [Valentiniano Aug. III et Va]lente Aug. III co[nss.].

It seems to us a more normal formula to restore

> DD.NN. Valentiniano et Va]lente Aug. III co[nss.].

371

Excluded

ICUR I 564 = n.s. I 726 (name doubtful)

ICUR n.s. II 4502 (person doubtful)

ICUR n.s. I 3182 (person doubtful)

ICUR n.s. I 222 (person doubtful)

ICUR n.s. VI 17394a (person doubtful)

CIL XI 4162 (year doubtful)

ICUR n.s. VIII 23411 (year doubtful)

Critical Notes

In *CIL* III 3653 the text gives Divus Noster; but cf. Dessau's note: the reading rests on one fifteenth-century MS and is surely false.

ICUR n.s. IV 11102 = *ILCV* 1614 (person doubtful). If, following De Rossi (*ICUR* I 563, cf. suppl. 1614), one had to restore v.c. (not vv.cc.) after Probus' name, 406 would be preferable to 371, as v.c. is not yet used in Roman inscriptions of 371. But we are not persuaded that this restoration is justifiable. We have therefore followed *ICUR* IV in dating to 371.

372

Excluded

ICUR suppl. 1623 = n.s. VIII 23414a (cos. date?)

ICUR n.s. VIII 20783b (cos. date?), 20791 (name doubtful)

ICUR n.s. II 4808 (name doubtful)

Critical Notes

BGU IV 1092 is wrongly dated by its editor to 2.ix.

373

Excluded

ICUR n.s. VII 17467 (person doubtful)

Critical Notes

ICUR n.s. III 8724 is dated to 373 by De Rossi (*ICUR* I 235) on the grounds that XV kal. Apr. coincides with Monday only in 373 of the years of joint consulates of Valentinian and Valens. We are uncertain that a failed day-date match is more uncommon than the omission of such an iteration numeral. Cf. our discussion of *ICUR* n.s. III 8147 under the Critical Appendix for 365.

ICUR I 220, edited from a bad copy, gave Valentinian and Valens III, pridie kal. Dec. The reedition as *ICUR* n.s. VIII 21608 shows that the year is 373, the date 7.xii.

P.Lips. 85 is dated by the editor to 372, in accordance with the consulate. The close similarity and connection with *P.Lips.* 86, dated 373 (i.e. p.c. where 85 has cos.), persuades us that a date to 373 is very probable.

374

Excluded

NotScav 1895, 521 no. 266 = *Kokalos* 28-29 (1982-83) 6-7 (names doubtful)

Critical Notes

In *ICUR* n.s. IV 11767 the editor restores at the start of line 2:

> .... kalendas Ian]uarias, etc.

This restoration is based on considerations of space, given that the restoration of a postconsular formula would bring us to the month of December in 375. Such considerations do not seem to us compelling in this case. There is, however, no inherent reason to think only of a postconsular formula, since genitives of names with a preceding consulatu are known. Furthermore, restoring kalendas written in full is not necessary. A restoration of *[dep. VIII Id. Ian]uarias* (6.i) seems perfectly possible. In short, either cos. or p.c. is possible, and one has the possibility of dating to p.c. plus kalends (xii.375), p.c. + ides/nones (i.375), or cos. + ides/nones (i.374).

ICUR n.s. I 1938 has only *]iti*, which would leave Agapitus cos. 517 in consideration. Silvagni, however, excluded that consulate on palaeographical grounds, and we follow him, though not without some doubt.

For *P.Oslo* II 38 = *SB* VI 9311, see *BASP* 17 (1980) 110.

For *P.Lips.* 23 see *BASP* 17 (1980) 6-7.

375

Excluded

ICUR n.s. VII 19958 (person doubtful)

Critical Notes

In *ICUR* n.s. V 13334, the editor does not restore *Aug.* at the start of line 8; but it is normally part of the formula in this year, and we consider it likely that instead of *[ter]* we should restore *[Aug III]*.

ICUR n.s. V 13333 is restored

pos. cons. Gra[t. ter et Equiti],

but there is no reason not to restore a more normal

pos(t) cons(ulatum) Gra[tiani Aug. III et (Fl.) Equiti].

376

Excluded

ICUR I 254 (person doubtful)

ICUR I 649 (person doubtful)

ILCV 1772A (year doubtful)

ICUR n.s. VII 17470 (year doubtful)

ICUR n.s. VIII 23409.4 reads *iJun. v.c. cons.* The editor assigns this text to 376 and Valentinian iunior, on the grounds that no private consul before 480 was called iunior. But v.c. is wholly inappropriate for Valentinian. We do not think that there is sufficient evidence to date this inscription.

ICUR n.s. VIII 23414 (person doubtful)

Critical Notes

The consular date in *CIL* IX 1362 = *ILCV* 4395 adn. is printed as *Valente a[c] Valentiniano*. This formula presents an anomaly in that *ac* is hardly found as a copula instead of *et* in these consular dates. We suggest rather that it would be reasonable to restore *Valente A[ug. - et] Valentiniano*. Valens was consul for the 5th time with Valentinian for the 1st time in 376; in 378 their iteration numerals were VI and II. As it is more likely that the numeral I is omitted than that II is, the odds are in favor of assigning this inscription to 376 by restoring V as the iteration numeral in the lacuna.

ICUR n.s. VII 17469: the editor's alternative date of 378 seems very unlikely, given the absence of an iteration numeral for Valentinianus junior.

377

Excluded

ICUR n.s. I 3187 (cos. date?)

ICUR n.s. VIII 23417a (persons doubtful)

378

Critical Notes

ICUR n.s. IV 11771 has Fl. restored before Valentinianus; we know of no preserved example of this consulate in which Flavius occurs in this position, and its restoration therefore incurs some suspicion. We do not, however, have another restoration to offer.

For *ICUR* n.s. IV 9570 see Ferrua, *Nuove corr.* 155.

379

Excluded

ICUR n.s. VIII 23417b (person doubtful)

Critical Notes

The editor of *CIL* III 9509 restores *p.c. A]uxonii et Olybri vv cc*, but the simple *cons. A]uxonii* is equally possible. The use of the *consulatu* plus genitive formula is found as early as 338 (*CIL* VIII 796).

At the end of a discussion of the remains of the fragmentarily preserved consular dating in *P.Lips.* 13.1-4 (see *ZPE* 28 [1978] 222-25) Bagnall and Worp offered the following restoration:

1 [Μετὰ τὴν ὑπατείαν τῶν δεσποτῶν ἡμῶν]
2 [Οὐάλεντος Αὐγούστου τὸ ϛ καὶ Οὐαλεν-]
3 [τιν]ειανοῦ [νέου αἰωνίου] Αὐγούστου καὶ [.......]
4 [..]αυ.ο.[τὸ β´] vacat

4:]αυτο.[?

Subsequently, Cameron pointed out (*ZPE* 56 [1984] 169 n.33) that the restoration of νέου in line 3 was suspect (no papyri from 378 dated by the consular formula for this year show this element). νέου should therefore be cancelled, and τὸ β´ moved from line 4 to line 3. Even so, problems remain. One would expect the formula to have run

1 [Μετὰ τὴν ὑπατείαν τῶν δεσποτῶν ἡμῶν]
2 [Οὐάλεντος τὸ ϛ καὶ Οὐαλεν-]

3 [τιν]ειανοῦ [τὸ β΄ τῶν αἰωνίων] Αὐγούστων

without any other element following. The papyrus definitely reads Αὐγούστου in line 3, however. Furthermore, the copula καὶ followed by αυτο.[seems to suggest that one should continue after Αὐγούστων with καὶ αὐτοκρατόρων; but at this period the element αὐτοκράτωρ does not normally occur in imperial titulature (cf. *P.Rainer Cent.* 102.2n.). We cannot be certain, therefore, just what the original formula in this papyrus was.

380

Excluded

CIL XI 7924 (year doubtful)

ICUR n.s. VIII 20796, 23417 (year doubtful)

ICUR n.s. VIII 20797 (cos. date?)

Critical Notes

For *ChLA* XI 470 see *BASP* 17 (1980) 114-15.

381

Excluded

ICUR n.s. V 15268 (name doubtful)

ICUR n.s. I 482 (name doubtful)

ICUR n.s. I 3196 = 1209 (cos. date?)

ICUR n.s. I 3195 = *ILCV* 4146B (cos. date?)

Critical Notes

The Syagrii: The main difference between Martindale (whence *PLRE*) and Demandt is the latter's refusal to accept that both Syagrii were PPO's. That Syagrius cos. 381 was PPO is expressly attested by three papyri with consular formulas; that Syagrius cos. 382 was also PPO is attested by only one papyrus, *P.Lips.* 21.1, with the formula Φλ. ᾿Αντωνίου τοῦ λαμπροτάτου καὶ Συαγρίου τοῦ λαμπροτάτου ἐπάρχου τοῦ ἱεροῦ πραιτωρίου. This would seem to be strong evidence, but Demandt argues that the last four words are 'interpoliert' (p.4), resting his case on Mitteis' note ad loc. that "lin. 3 ist offenbar nachträglich eingeschoben." But this is not at all the same as interpolation. Unfortunately Mitteis supplied no photograph, but presumably all he meant was that the scribe did not write the last four words at the same time as what precedes them, and did not leave himself enough room to add them, with the result that he squashed them in later. He certainly did not say or imply that it was added later by another hand--an almost inconceivable eventuality in the case of a routine formula in a papyrus document. There is in fact a clear indication that this did *not* happen in the way the scribe set out his formula. If he had intended to give nothing but the bare consular formula, he would normally have written Φλαουίων ᾿Αντωνίου καὶ Συαγρίου τῶν λαμπροτάτων, that is to say with one λαμπροτάτων in the plural agreeing with both names. As it is, he wrote Φλαουίου Ἀντωνίου τοῦ λαμπροτάτου καὶ Συαγρίου τοῦ λαμπροτάτου. We now have many scores of such consular formulas on fourth-century papyri and can say with confidence that scribes wrote a separate λαμπρότατος for each name only when they were planning to give one or both an additional title which they did not share. Clearly in this case the original scribe of *P.Lips.* 21.1 was already intending to give Syagrius another title, although he may have forgotten momentarily and squeezed it in later.

382

Excluded

ICUR n.s. III 8150 (cos. date?)

Critical Notes

I.Cret. IV 285 refers (lines 30 ff.) to a date xiv kal. Iul., in the consulate after Syagrius and Eucherius. The editor computes this date as "die XXVIII mensis Iunii a. 381, Syagrio et Eucherio consulibus," and she remarks in the note to line 31 f. that "casus accusativus post μετά serioris aetatis usui tribuendus est (cfr. *Syll.*³ 907.1 sq.: μετὰ τὴν ὑπατ(είαν) Ὀνωρίου καὶ Εὐοδίου, a. 387). Anno igitur 381, non insequenti, decretum factum est." There are two errors in these remarks: xiv kal. Iul. is 18 June; and the remark concerning the use of μετά followed by an accusative is irrelevant. The postconsulate of Syagrius and Eucherius fell in 382, just as that of Honorius and Euodius fell in 387 (cos. 386).

The consular formula in *ICUR* n.s. I 2096 = *CIL* VI 9787 has been restored (line 2) as

Cl. Antonio et [Syagrio conss.].

It seems likely, however, that as we have noted several times, the consuls are given the same number of names. The formula for this year is thus either Claudius Antonius and Fl. Syagrius or Antonius and Syagrius. The correct restoration is therfore surely *[Fl. Syagrio conss.]*, perhaps also with vv.cc. before conss.

383

Excluded

ICUR n.s. VII 17483 (cos. date?)

ICUR n.s. I 3043 (cos. date?)

ICUR n.s. IX 23762 (cos. date?)

ICUR n.s. VIII 22751a (name doubtful)

Critical Notes

The fasti and the eastern evidence are unanimous that the consuls this year were Merobaudes II and Saturninus (the p.c. of 382 in *CTh* 12.6.17 [addressed to the prefect of Egypt] is presumably an Egyptian accepta date, but it would be late even so, given the papyrological attestation of Merobaudes and Saturninus in early April). Merobaudes had been cos. I 377; Saturninus was mag. equitum 377-378 and mag. militum 382-383, concluding an important settlement with the Goths in 382 (*PLRE* I 807-08). A group of inscriptions attesting a consulate of Theodosius and Merobaudes has caused extensive discussion of this year and 388. We have listed them under 383, for reasons set out below.

One of these inscriptions has a preserved date of Theodosius II et Merobaudes III (*ICUR* I 370 = n.s. II 5996 = *ILCV* 4623), 10.i. If this date is taken seriously and assigned to 388, it would seem that Maximus initially proclaimed this pair hoping that Theodosius would acknowledge the consulate of so distinguished a public servant, especially when linked to his own. Yet by 11.i we find Maximus as sole consul. Since Pacatus alleges that Maximus forced Merobaudes to commit suicide (*Pan.Theod.* 28.4), it might be inferred that Merobaudes refused to continue as consul once repudiated by Theodosius (so *PLRE* I 598-99; B.S. Rodgers, *Historia* 30 [1981] 82-105). And it is true that Theodosius did implicitly repudiate any such original nomination by proclaiming himself and Cynegius. But this news cannot have reached Maximus as early as 10.i, and Merobaudes' death, if it took place in this year at all (see below), has no necessary connection with this allegedly cancelled consulate.

Moreover, there are at least three further problems with this scenario. (1) The intrinsic improbability of a third consulate for a private citizen (without precedent in the fourth century), especially as colleague to an emperor still only on his second, is striking. (2) If Maximus' second proclamation is to be interpreted as a final defiant break with Theodosius, why did he not proclaim *two* consuls of his own (as Theodosius did)? The fact that he proclaimed only himself gives the appearance rather of a conciliatory move, allowing Theodosius to fill the other vacancy. Such a move would make sense only as a first proclamation. (3) *ICUR* n.s. IV 12250 of 4.iii is dated by Theodosius II et Merobaudes II. Quite apart from the necessity of postulating an error in Merobaudes' iteration number, it would be surprising (and imprudent under the circumstances) to find this cancelled consulate in use so late in the year.

According to Seeck (*Regesten* 272), who likewise accepted this third consulate of Merobaudes in 388, Merobaudes died before entering office. But then why did Maximus not simply appoint another consul in his place as Theodosius' colleague? Why cancel the consular pair and proclaim himself alone? Moreover, while it is possible that the news of the consul designate's death had not reached Rome by 10.i, what of the other inscriptions dated by Theodosius and Merobaudes, one as late as 4.iii? Maximus was now in Italy, perhaps in Rome itself.

These difficulties make it much more attractive to refer all of the Theodosius et Merobaudes inscriptions to 383. With M. Waas, *Germanen im römischen Dienst im 4 Jhdt. n. Christus* (Diss. Bonn 1965) 54-56 (approved by T.D. Barnes, *Phoenix* 29 [1975] 160), we would then have to postulate an error in the iteration number for Merobaudes in *ICUR* n.s. II 5996. We know from Themistius (*Or.* 16.202D-203A; 205C-D) that Theodosius had originally been expected to take one of the consulates for 383 himself, and it is possible that the news of a change of plan (which had to come from Constantinople in winter) did not reach Rome until too late, so that the consular pair proclaimed in January in Rome was "Theodosius II and Merobaudes II." It should be emphasized that *ICUR* n.s. IV 12250 (4.iii) gives exactly that formula. It is remarkable that an incorrect formula should last so long, but at any rate less problematic if the inscription is placed in 383 rather than 388, since the correct formula, "Merobaudes II et Saturninus," is not attested before late February or early March. *ICUR* n.s. II 6044 has no iteration numerals; and *ICUR* n.s. VIII 23420b preserves only M]erobaude II[, thus not contributing anything. (The editors restored *[Fl. Saturnino et M]erobaude II[...]*, quite impossibly, since Merobaudes as consul II should have been named first.) Our interpretation requires only one stonecutter's error, the numeral III for II in *ICUR* n.s. II 5996.

There is thus no secure evidence for a third consulate in 388 for Merobaudes. There is even some evidence that he died in the course of his second in 383 (so Barnes, l.c.).

An inscription from Trier in Greek presenting a consular formula connected with the consulate of 383 has recently been republished by N. Gauthier in the *Recueil des inscriptions chrétiennes de la Gaule* I 211. She presents the text with three alternatives for restoration, none of which seems to us quite acceptable. We present our own version of the fully restored text:

[ὑπ(ατείας) Φλ]α(ουίου) Μεροβαύδ[ου τὸ δεύτερον]
[καὶ] Φλα(ουίου) Σατορν[ίνου τῶν λαμ-]
[προτάτ]ων μηνὶ [

In *ICUR* n.s. I 2097, the editor has not restored the iteration number II. Since this is found in the vast majority of cases where the pertinent part of the inscription is preserved, it should be restored here. The same is true in *ICUR* n.s. I 1169, 2098, 2944; III 8425; IV 12534.

ICUR n.s. I 3198 (line 3) preserves the date as *Mai Merobaud[e cons]*. Diehl, *ILCV* 3390A, restores *Merobaud[e II et Saturnino Conss]*, but there is simply not enough room for a restoration of this length; the line should be lacking about the same number of letters as the preceding one, where about 7 letters are missing (the precise number is unclear, since the day is unknown; editors have quite arbitrarily, as it seems, restored various numbers). In the reedition as *ICUR* n.s. VIII 20717, the editor restores *Merobaud[e II cons.]*, which fits the space well. We are not confident that the restoration of the day as *[XVI Kal.] Mai.* must be correct; Ferrua supplies it on the grounds that the Octave of Easter was the day for confirmation, and that it fell on this date in 383.

There are two other inscriptions with only Merobaudes (*ICUR* n.s. VII 17481, 17482). Theoretically it is possible that the cos. of 377 is meant, but omission of an imperial consul in the first place seems less likely than that Saturninus, the second consul of 383, is left out.

384

Excluded

AE 1969/1970, 82 (names doubtful)

ICUR n.s. I 481 = *ILCV* 4763 (name doubtful)

ICUR n.s. VIII 20801a, 20803a, 20803b (name doubtful)

385

Excluded

ICUR n.s. IV 9573 (year doubtful)

ICUR n.s. VII 17490 (year doubtful)

ICUR n.s. I 984, 1256, 1442, 2100, 3203 (year doubtful)

ICUR n.s. III 8152 (year doubtful)

ICUR I 570 (year doubtful)

CIL XI 3239 (year doubtful)

AE 1903, 174 (year doubtful)

ICUR n.s. VIII 20801b, 23439c (year doubtful)

Critical Notes

The gravestone from Praeneste, *CIL* XIV 2934 = *ILS* 8375 = A.E. and J.S. Gordon, *Album of Dated Latin Inscriptions* III 338, indicates that the person commemorated died on *XVI Kal Dec / DN Arcadio Aug et Bautoni / vc conss*, i.e. on 16.xi.385. The stone was dedicated *die IV Nonas / Mar coss SS*. As is remarked by the editors in *CIL*, one normally resolves the letters *SS* as *s(upra) s(criptis)*, though this presupposes a slight chronological error in that a stone for somebody cannot have been dedicated on 4.iii of the same year as that in which the person died on 16.xi. The Gordons try to avoid accepting this error by assuming that *SS* stands for *S(ub)s(equentibus)*, but this resolution of the abbreviation appears to be unique. It is more likely that the stone was set up in the March following the death and burial and assume that the phrase should be taken as meaning "post consules suprascriptos."

386

Excluded

ICUR n.s. I 3178 (name doubtful)

ICUR n.s. II 4819 (name doubtful), 6042 (name doubtful)

ICUR I 365 (name doubtful)

ICUR suppl. 1760 = *ILCV* 2946 (year doubtful)

ICUR n.s. V 13932 (year doubtful)

CIL XI 4970 (year doubtful)

ICUR n.s. VIII 20804, 23423 (year doubtful)

Critical Notes

For *P.Oxy.* XXXIV 2715 see *P.Oxy.* XLV, p.xvii.

387

Excluded

ICUR n.s. III 6734, IV 11116 (name doubtful)

RAC 61 (1985) 19 (year doubtful)

388

Excluded

ICUR I 1143 (person doubtful)

ICUR n.s. VIII 21891b (person doubtful)

ICUR suppl. 1792 = *ILCV* 3737; 1796 = *ILCV* 3335 adn. (year doubtful)

CIL III 14890 (year doubtful)

ICUR n.s. II 6046 (year doubtful: 371 possible)

Critical Notes

Diehl dates *ICUR* suppl. 1790 = *ILCV* 3287 to either 388 or 384. The dating formula reads:

Consulatu Maximo Augusto consulatum

Since Maximus' first consulate was not recognized at Rome in 384, the thought of some confusion of cos. for p.c., referring to 385 does not deserve serious consideration. The only possible date is therefore 388, Maximus' second consulate, as *ICUR* n.s. VIII 21611 recognizes.

389

Excluded

ICUR n.s. IV 11119 (cos. date?)

ICUR n.s. VIII 23063 (cos. date?)

390

Excluded

ICUR I 387 (name doubtful)

ICUR I 390 = *ILCV* 3820 = *ICUR* n.s. VIII 20805 (year doubtful)

ICUR n.s. VII 17500 (person doubtful)

Critical Notes

The fragmentarily preserved Roman inscription *ICUR* n.s. II 4770 has been restored by A. Chastagnol (cf. *PLRE* I 697, Fl. Philippus 8) as:

x[iii kal. Dec. post consulat. d.n.] Valentin[i]ani Aug.
iiii et Neoteri v.c., administrante Fl. Filippo [v.c.
praef. urbi --].

The restoration of the month and day is inspired by the fact that the stone contains a dedication of the basilica of S. Paolo fuori le mura, celebrated in later times on 19 November and by the fact that the remaining parts of the consular formula are in the genitive.

But there is a problem in this restoration. The year 391 is consistently indicated in Roman inscriptions by the use of the consuls of that year, Tatianus and Symmachus; a postconsular reference to 390 as late as 19.xi.391 is very unlikely. There is, moreover, no exactly dated evidence for the urban prefecture of Fl. Philippus, and in itself it appears more plausible to restore 'consulatu' (possibly abbreviated to *cons.*). But a problem would be created by this restoration, in that Philippus would in this case not fit into the fasti for this office presented by Chastagnol, *Les fastes*, 236f. and *PLRE* I 1055. Ceionius Rufius Albinus is attested between 17.vi.389 and 24.ii.391 (though the source for this last date, *CTh* 16.10.10, is a correction of the MSS which give his function as PPO, fairly clearly an error). The penultimate date for Albinus' tenure as PVR is 4.iv.390, cf. *CTh* 15.1.27 and *PLRE* I 38. One might conclude that the MSS in *CTh* 16.10.10 were correct, and that Philippus was indeed the immediate successor to Albinus as PVR, with the latter being promoted to PPO between 4.iv and 19.xi.390. On the other hand, Virius Nicomachus Flavianus is already in office as PPO on 18.viii.390 (*CTh* 9.40.13), still attested as such on 8.iv.392 (*CTh* 10.10.20). Though the date of *CTh* 9.40.13 rests on a correction (the consular date is to 382), Seeck (*Regesten* 92) thinks that the error was limited to an incorrect indication of the year. The law was, as Seeck points out, promulgated in Verona, where other laws attest the presence of Theodosius between 23.viii and 8.ix.390. It is not a very attractive notion to date Nicomachus Flavianus' prefecture from 18.viii.391. In any case, we must almost certainly accept that *CTh* 16.10.10 attests Albinus as PVR rather than PPO (an office he is not otherwise attested to have held) on 24.ii.391, in which case Philippus cannot have been praefectus urbi on 19.xi.390. The solution is not clear to us, but the easiest way out may be that Philippus in the inscription was not PVR but held some other office.

The editor of *P.Lips.* 38 restores Fl. before Valentinian's name, but such use is not found in papyri of this period, and we have therefore not accepted the restoration. Cf. 368.

391

Excluded

ICUR n.s. III 8157 (cos. date? person doubtful)

ICUR n.s. V 13937 (person doubtful)

ICUR n.s. VIII 23428 (person doubtful)

NotScav 1888, 449, nos. 44 (cos. date?) and 45 (person doubtful)

Critical Notes

P. Wuilleumier, *Inscr. Lat. des 3 Gaules* 145, dated this inscription from Rions (Gironde) to 26.v.466, on the basis of a date to *VII Kal Iun Tatiano consule*. The consul Tatianus of 466, however, was an easterner, whose consulate was apparently never accepted in the West, which dated to the 3rd consulate of Leo; cf.

PLRE II 1054. There is, moreover, another possible date, that of 391, when the consuls were Tatianus and Symmachus. Though one normally finds both consuls in datings, and though Gallic inscriptions of this period are not numerous, the date to 391 seems preferable to 466 for this inscription.

For *P.Lips.* 42 see *BASP* 17 (1980) 7.

392

Excluded

ICUR n.s. I 2104 (person doubtful)

Critical Notes

The editors of *ICUR* n.s. I 1355 restore the consular dating formula as

> [Pall]adio II et Rufino vc c[onss].

This is a careless error, as the imperial colleague of Rufinus was Arcadius for the 2nd time. The indices to *ICUR* n.s. I have the name correct.

In a note to *ICUR* n.s. III 6508 (= suppl. 1835), the editors note, "supplevit de Rossi v.5: "IDUS [IANUARIAS, quod post eum mensem iure sumeret consules huius anni Arcadium AUG II et Fl. Rufinum Romae iam esse nuntiatos." The earliest dated consular inscription with the consuls of 392, however, is from 17.ii (*ICUR* n.s. IV 12540 = *ILCV* 2601), and *Februarias* therefore seems equally possible.

IG XIV 2252 contains a formula published in the form (line 9)

> ΚΑΛ ΜΑΡ. ΥΠΑΤ ΑΡΚΑΔ ΚΑΙ ΡΟΥΦΗΝ.

On the drawing of the inscription, however, one can see that this text is not correct. On the basis of the drawing we read the date as follows:

> καλ(ανδῶν) Μαρ(τίων) ὑππατ(είας) τῶ(ν) <δεσποτῶν
> ἡμῶν> Ἀρκαδ(ίου) <τὸ> β καὶ Ῥουφήν(ου)

393

Excluded

ICUR n.s. I 1211 = *ILCV* 4111C (year uncertain)

ICUR n.s. II 4901 (year uncertain)

NBC 1899, 29 (cos. date?)

ICUR n.s. VIII 23430 (persons doubtful)

Critical Notes

In *CIL* X 4491 the dating formula is given as follows:

> XVI Kal Iun[
> consulat[u D.N.
> Arcadi II et [Rufi

The name of the second consul in this year was Rufinus, not Rufus. Moreover, the restoration of a postconsular formula fits the space better (4, 4 1/2, and 5 letters, respectively, counting the two I's in Rufinus as a half each) and is otherwise unobjectionable. We restore therefore

> xvi Kal Iun [post]
> consulat[um D.N.]
> Arcadi II et [Rufini]

This is not the only instance of a p.c. date in 393 this late. The present inscription, from Capua, may be compared with *CIL* IX 6192 = *ILCV* 582, from Canossa, dated to 24.v (cf. *ILCV* ad loc. for the exact date of this text).

In *ILCV* 4556, a reedition of *ICUR* I 411 = n.s. III 8429, Diehl thinks that it is possible to restore [post] conss Theodosi et Eugeni, giving a date of 394 (30.v) rather than 393. The other evidence from Rome from 394, however, is dated consistently to the consulate of Nicomachus Flavianus; Diehl's restoration therefore seems to us quite unlikely.

The editor of *CIL* X 4492 = *ILCV* 1491 gives the dating formula as

> VIII Kal Noben. d. <n.> Eugenio Aug. prim(um)

and dates this to 392. This is an error for 393. De Rossi, *ICUR* I 410, remarks that Eugenius was recognized only in Rome. Our evidence shows that this is not quite accurate, as attestations are known from Milan and Tarragona. There is no reason to think that *CIL* X 4492 gives a regnal rather than a consular date.

394

Excluded

ICUR I 512 = *ILCV* 2773 adn., 513, 514, 515 (year doubtful)

AE 1969/1970, 80 (year doubtful)

CIL V 8768 = *ILCV* 545 (year doubtful)

CIL XI 802 = *ILCV* 1494 (year doubtful)

ICUR n.s. IV 9580 = *ILCV* 3769A (year doubtful)

Agnello, *Silloge* 93 (year doubtful)

ICUR I 616-633 (year doubtful; cos. date doubtful in some)

IG XIV 949a (year doubtful)

ICUR n.s. VIII 20807 (year doubtful)

RAC 60 (1984) 306 (year doubtful)

RAC 61 (1985) 15 (year doubtful)

ICUR n.s. VIII 23431a (person doubtful)

Conc.Galliae (Corp.Christ.Lat. 148), p.50 (year doubtful)

395

Excluded

ICUR n.s. II 4504 (person doubtful)

ICUR n.s. V 13941 (person doubtful)

Critical Notes

The dating formula in *ICUR* n.s. V 13365 is presented as follows:

XVII Kal Febr DD NN Arcadio III et Honorio II Augg conss.

The implied date is 15.i.394. There is a problem, however, in that Nicomachus Flavianus, the protege of Eugenius, was the consul recognized at Rome in 394 as late as 17.ix (*ICUR* suppl. 1855 = *ILCV* 1482). The recognition of the imperially-recognized consuls for this year (the emperors themselves) is found at Rome first on 9.x (*ICUR* n.s. II 4487). A single example of these consuls in January is most unlikely, and we suppose that this must be an error for postconsulate. Less likely, the date could be a retroactive anachronistic use of the formula recognized in October.

It is not noted in *CIL* III that 12861 (ad 9523) is in fact taken up in the same volume as 13122. Cf. R. Egger, *Forschungen in Salona* II 116.

We include *ICUR* I 432, but we note that Silvagni, *ICUR* n.s. I, p.369, thought it a forgery.

396

Excluded

ICUR n.s. I 1357 (year doubtful)

ICUR n.s. V 13120, 13942 (year doubtful)

Critical Notes

ICUR n.s. VII 17510 was first published as giving the consuls as Arcadius V, Honorius IV (*ICUR* I 434). Ferrua, however, states that IV (IIII) is an error of De Rossi for III. The combination V and III, however, is not found; Ferrua considers 396 (therefore an error for IV and III) the best hypothesis, rejecting 402, which was V and V.

ICUR n.s. IV 12252, on the other hand, has IV and IV (i.e. IIII and IIII).

397

Excluded

ICUR n.s. IV 11778 (person doubtful)

Critical Notes

This year is normally designated, in the customary way, with the same number of names for each consul, i.e. either Caesarius and Atticus or Flavius Caesarius and Nonius Atticus. Those inscriptions where exceptions to this rule are alleged by editors can virtually all be seen to be erroneously restored. In *ILCV* 4400A, Diehl adds to Atticus the praenomen T(itus), but this appears to be an error for *(e)t* between the consular names, which in Diehl's version are in asyndeton. Nonius may be restored before Atticus in *ICUR* n.s. II 6055.

ICUR n.s. I 941 is dated *die VIIIX KL Mart*. There is, to be sure, no 18 kal. March. Diehl, *ILCV* 3444, remarks "debuit prid. id. Febr.," assuming the least possible error; there is no way of being sure that this is correct, but it is the most economical assumption and we have followed it.

ICUR n.s. I 1451 gives the consular date as *]Caesario et [Attico conss.]* The question might arise whether two names could be restored for each consul. De Rossi (*ICUR* I 456) notes that the A at the start of Attico was present in Marini's transcription, along with a few letters in the previous line, but that these letters are now lost. If Marini's transcription was accurate, the use of one name per consul rather than two is secure.

ICUR n.s. VIII 20811 = *ILCV* 3494: the editor omits the information that this text is *ICUR* I 455, but his concordance shows that this is just a slip.

The editor argues that there is no space to restore the iteration numerals in *P.Stras.* 255; this may be doubtful, cf. p.69 above. Their loss, however, even if they were written, leaves the year in doubt, with a choice of 397 and 403. The oath formula in lines 12-13, however, clearly included only Arcadius and Honorius, and not Theodosius, who would have been named in third place. Theodosius became an emperor on 10.i.402, and in a document of 403 he should have been named. We therefore assign this document to 397.

We see no reason not to restore Fll. in the consular formula in *P.Giss.* I 52.

Critical Notes

ICUR n.s. VII 17510 was first published as giving the consuls as Arcadius V, Honorius IV (*ICUR* I 434). Ferrua, however, states that IV (IIII) is an error of De Rossi for III. The combination V and III, however, is not found; Ferrua considers 396 (therefore an error for IV and III) the best hypothesis, rejecting 402, which was V and V.

ICUR n.s. IV 12252, on the other hand, has IV and IV (i.e. IIII and IIII).

397

Excluded

ICUR n.s. IV 11778 (person doubtful)

Critical Notes

This year is normally designated, in the customary way, with the same number of names for each consul, i.e. either Caesarius and Atticus or Flavius Caesarius and Nonius Atticus. Those inscriptions where exceptions to this rule are alleged by editors can virtually all be seen to be erroneously restored. In *ILCV* 4400A, Diehl adds to Atticus the praenomen T(itus), but this appears to be an error for *(e)t* between the consular names, which in Diehl's version are in asyndeton. Nonius may be restored before Atticus in *ICUR* n.s. II 6055.

ICUR n.s. I 941 is dated *die VIIIX KL Mart.* There is, to be sure, no 18 kal. March. Diehl, *ILCV* 3444, remarks "debuit prid. id. Febr.," assuming the least possible error; there is no way of being sure that this is correct, but it is the most economical assumption and we have followed it.

ICUR n.s. I 1451 gives the consular date as *]Caesario et [Attico conss.]* The question might arise whether two names could be restored for each consul. De Rossi (*ICUR* I 456) notes that the A at the start of Attico was present in Marini's transcription, along with a few letters in the previous line, but that these letters are now lost. If Marini's transcription was accurate, the use of one name per consul rather than two is secure.

ICUR n.s. VIII 20811 = *ILCV* 3494: the editor omits the information that this text is *ICUR* I 455, but his concordance shows that this is just a slip.

The editor argues that there is no space to restore the iteration numerals in *P.Stras.* 255; this may be doubtful, cf. p.69 above. Their loss, however, even if they were written, leaves the year in doubt, with a choice of 397 and 403. The oath formula in lines 12-13, however, clearly included only Arcadius and Honorius, and not Theodosius, who would have been named in third place. Theodosius became an emperor on 10.i.402, and in a document of 403 he should have been named. We therefore assign this document to 397.

We see no reason not to restore Fll. in the consular formula in *P.Giss.* I 52.

For *SB* XII 10932 see *BASP* 17 (1980) 28.

For *P.Oxy.* XXIV 2408 see *RFBE* 44.

398

Excluded

ICUR n.s. III 7384 (name doubtful)

ICUR n.s. III 8165 = *ILCV* 1269 adn. (year doubtful)

Critical Notes

In *La déesse de Hiérapolis Castabala* 29-30, one must restore at the start of the consular formula (line 8) ὑπ(ατείας) and at the end [νοῦ τοῦ λαμ(προτάτου)] (line 11).

ICUR n.s. I 309 is restored by the editors as *[post]/ consulatu DN Herchadi IIII et Euty/chiani vc conss*. Post was first restored by De Rossi (*ICUR* I 473) because the date, 26.viii, fell on a Friday (as the inscription tells us) not in 398 but in 399, which is the p.c. of this pair (or, rather, of Honorius and Eutychianus!). But days are often wrong, or at least do not match dates; and there is no example of the p.c. so late in 399. Moreover, the restoration of *post* or even *p* would be rather long for the place. We have therefore assigned the text to 398.

ICUR n.s. V 13933 is dated, in the editor's text (line 2), by

Hono[rio Aug]usto et E[uodio conss],

and thus to 386. This cannot be correct, however, as Honorius was not an Augustus at this time, but only nobilissimus puer. There is, moreover, another consulate held by Honorius and a private person whose name starts with E, namely the consulate of 398. We restore the text therefore as

Hono[rio Aug]usto <IV> et E[utychiano v.c. conss.]

In *ICUR* n.s. II 4505, it would be possible to restore Fl. in line 1, but nothing compels the restoration.

399

Excluded

ICUR n.s. V 13943 (name doubtful)

The editors of *AE* 1969/1970, 77 write in their note that a restoration of the name of the consul as *Th[eodoro* (cos. 398) is more convincing than a restoration of *Th[eodosio*. We fail to see why this is so, and we consider it safer not to restore any specific name.

The abbreviations in a consular dating in an inscription from Spain, republished by J.M. Iglesias Gil, *Onomastica Preromana en la epigrafia Cantabra* (Santander 1974) 37 no. 6 (published earlier in J. Vives,

Inscripciones Latinas de la España Romana [Barcelona 1971] no. 851, cf. pp.553-54), are read and resolved as

x K(al) b. Augu(stas) Ma(llio) Eu(tropio) co(n)s(ulibus)

or 399. This is, however, impossible, as the eastern consul Eutropius was never recognized in the West (cf. *PLRE* II ad loc. where this inscription is correctly omitted). Moreover, the western consul for this year is never styled Mallius in the inscriptions, but always either Mallius Theodorus or just Theodorus. The quality of the photograph does not allow us to suggest a better reading of our own; the original must be rechecked to see if an acceptable reading can be found.

Critical Notes

ICUR n.s. IV 12543 was dated by De Rossi (*ICUR* I 478) and then Ferrua to *XV Kal Ia[n*, or 18.xii. Diehl (*ILCV* 4539) read *XV Kal D[ec*. Ferrua buttressed his reading with *Satu[rni]* before XV, but on the plate in Marucchi, *Museo Lat.* 49,17, one can see that this reading is very uncertain and that there is very little of the first letter of the month name, which could as well be *F[eb* as either of the other readings. A plate also appears in Diehl, *Inscriptiones Latinae* (Tabulae in usum scholarum 4, Bonn 1912) Pl. 34, no. 17.

For *CPLat.* 199 see *BASP* 18 (1981) 51.

In the introduction to *CPR* X 108, two possible dates were considered for this fragment, 399 and 505/6. The case for 399 is strengthened by the discovery that Arsinoite documents later than 439 always include indiction dates (*Archiv* 33 [1987] 91-96, esp. 93). There is no space for an indiction numeral in line 2 of this papyrus, and there is no other likely place for it in the text. Though palaeographic considerations cannot be decisive in such a matter, the absence of the indiction strongly favors 399 as the date. Given the virtually invariable usage of the papyri, restoration of Fll. seems warranted.

400

Excluded

ICUR n.s. I 2110 = *ILCV* 3696 (name doubtful)

BC 3.6 (1881) 158 (name doubtful)

ICUR n.s. I 3218 has *et Mallio Sthillicon[e v.c. cons.]* Stilicho was not a Mallius, and De Rossi (*ICUR* I 553) thought that Winghius, the copyist, misread one of the names, as well as correcting Winghius' *ET* to *FL*. If he did not misread a name, the proximity to the consulate of 399 makes 400 a more likely bet than 405. But we cannot assign any date with confidence.

Critical Notes

ILCV 4394A has *ISTILCOS*, which Diehl corrects to *Istilco<ne v.c. co>s*. (The prothetic I or E on Stilicho's name is common.) It seems to us more attractive to read *Istil(ichone) co(n)s(ule)*.

For *CIL* X 7115 = *ILCV* 3735 see *Kokalos* 28-29 (1982-83) 10 no.23; cf. Critical Appendix for 453, no.11.

For *SB* VI 9359 = *P.Lund* VI 10 see *BASP* 17 (1980) 15.

401

Excluded

ICUR n.s. II 4837 (cos. date?)

ICUR n.s. III 8167 (cos. date?)

ICUR n.s. II 4836 = *ILCV* 4669 adn. (name doubtful)

ICUR n.s. VII 17516b (name doubtful)

NotScav 1893, 299 no. 79 (cos. dating doubtful, *pace* Ferrua, *Rend.Pont.Accad.* 1946-47, 230)

Critical Notes

P.Rainer Cent. 165 ii.6 contains the consular names, but without Fll. (see also *ZPE* 56 [1984] 79 ff., esp. 84). The lacuna in line 5, however, makes it possible that Fll. stood at the end of that line.

402

Excluded

ICUR n.s. I 3125 = *ILCV* 4414A adn. (person doubtful)
ICUR n.s. II 4968 = *ILCV* 4391A (person doubtful)
ICUR n.s. II 6064 = *ILCV* 4415 = 2927A (year doubtful)
ICUR n.s. IV 12544 (year doubtful)
ICUR n.s. VIII 23433 (persons doubtful)
Kokalos 28-29 (1982-83) 10 no. 25 (consular date doubtful)

Critical Notes

In *ICUR* n.s. IV 12253, the formula gives *Aug.* after Arcadius' name, but the editor has omitted it after Honorius in the restoration. It should be restored.

The editor of *Atti III Congr. int. arch. crist.* 151 wrongly dates the inscription to 399.

403

Critical Notes

The inscription published in *NotScav* 1893, 284, is dated to *VIIII Kal Feb.*, p.c. Arcadii et Honorii Augg. V, i.e. to 24.i.403, not to 24.i.402 as the publication gives it. The correct date is given in the republication of the same stone in *NBC* 1902, 56.

ICUR n.s. VII 17527a has *FL Theodosio e[t Rumorido cons.* De Rossi (*ICUR* I 1158 = suppl. 1793) dated the stone to 388-444, but Ferrua argues that the absence of an iteration numeral makes 403 the best date. (The presence of Fl., however, is no argument for this year against others.)

For *P.Grenf.* II 81a see *ZPE* 56 (1984) 129.

404

Excluded

ICUR I 599 (year doubtful)

ICUR n.s. I 1461 = *ILCV* 358 adn. (name doubtful)

ICUR n.s. II 4919 (name doubtful)

ICUR n.s. VII 17528, 17529, 17531, 17532b, 17532c (year doubtful)

CIL V 8607 (year doubtful)

ICUR n.s. VIII 22972 (year doubtful)

ICUR n.s. VII 17530 (cos. date?)

ICUR n.s. VIII 21613 (person doubtful)

Critical Notes

Synesius, *Epp.* 133 (p.229 Garzya) opens with the words: "It was only just the other day, under the recent [?new] consuls (ἐπὶ τῶν ἔναγχος ὑπάτων), one of whom is Aristaenetus (his colleague I do not know), that I received your letter ..." Seeck (*Reg.* 307) argued that this letter was written at the beginning of 405 and that Honorius' consulate was therefore not recognized all year in the East. But despite Stilicho's occasional non-recognition of eastern consuls, the eastern court had always so far recognized western consuls, and it would be surprising if Arcadius had repudiated his brother's consulate (which was in any case counted in the iteration number of his next in 407 and included in fasti and laws). Surely the letter was in fact written at the beginning of 404. Synesius goes on to remark that his correspondent's letter looked "very ancient," being worm-eaten and largely illegible, and reproaches him for writing only once a year. He quotes the *new* consuls to prove to the man how long his letter (evidently undated like most correspondence of the age) had been in the mail. So at most his ignorance of the name of Aristaenetus' colleague proves merely that the name of the eastern consul reached Cyrene separately.

405

Excluded

ICUR n.s. VIII 23439a (cos. date?)

Critical Notes

De Rossi restores in *ICUR* I 558 (later republished as n.s. I 1463 = *CIL* VI 9161 = *ILCV* 693) the following:

> post] consulatum Istilichonis
> secundo cc.   septimu
> Kal Nobembres die Beneris

in order to have the indication of Friday match with a date to 26.x (7 kal. Nov.). There is, however, a difficulty in that there is hardly enough space for restoring [post] written out in full. Now one may solve this problem by restoring only *[p(ost)]*, as Diehl does. On the other hand, it is not certain that one must restore anything at all, as it occurs often enough that cases of *consulatus* are incorrect, e.g. ablative for accusative in *ILCV* 1500b (cf. generally *ILCV* III, pp. 221 ff., esp. 221 col. a, II), and it is commonplace for the day of the week and date not to match.

In 406, the consuls of that year are attested at Rome already in April. It would be surprising to find a p.c. dating by Stilicho also in use at Rome as late as October. Such overlaps are not unknown (cf. introduction, p.65), but they are rare in cases where there is not some good explanation. If we take the present inscription to refer to the consulate rather than p.c., the problem is eliminated.

AE 1924, 100 is dated to *IX Kal* (month lost), said to be a Friday. The dates we give are the only possibilities for the coincidence of these two items; they do assume the correctness of the day of the week, which is uncertain.

It should be noted that in the texts from 405 both v.c. II and II v.c. occur, but the latter is relatively rare as a word order.

406

Excluded

CIL V 6288 (cf. 6305) presents the curious text

> S. Iovi et Probo
> v.c. con.

The dedication to a consul baffles us, but the edition gives no sign that this is only a fragment of a larger text. (We considered reading *[Arca]dio VI et Probo v.c. con.*, but the edition provides no basis for this.)

Critical Notes

The editor of *CIL* XI 2872 (= *ILCV* 2258) dates his text to 401. This must (as Diehl notes) be a misprint, as the consulate of Arcadius for the 6th time and Anicius Probus was 406. The editor prints *cosulam Arkadio VI P Anicio Probo*. The only other name starting in P in Probus' nomenclature is Petronius, which *follows* Anicius. The same order, Petronius Anicius Probus, however, has now turned up in *AE* 1983, 131, and we have been able to verify the reading in *CIL* XI 2872 in *Inscriptiones Christianae Italiae vii saecolo antiquiores* I (Bari 1985) no.55. It appears that a wrong order of names was put into circulation at least in Italy.

407

Excluded

NotScav 1888, 450 no. 49 (cos. date?)

ICUR I 580 = *ILCV* 4597 = *ICUR* n.s. VIII 20814 (year doubtful)

ICUR n.s. VII 19962b (name doubtful)

Critical Notes

In *ICUR* n.s. I 2773 = *ILCV* 4444A the editors print *IUN* after Theodosius' name; this element is never found in any preserved formula for this year, however, and it should not be restored. (It is absent from the index in *ILCV* III, p.242.)

408

Excluded

ICUR n.s. II 4850 = *ILCV* 4262 (cos. date?)

ICUR n.s. IV 9584 (person doubtful)

CIG IV 9771 = *ICUR* n.s. II 5701a (person doubtful)

409

Excluded

D. Feissel, *RAC* 58 (1982) 369-71, restores *ICUR* I 1289 = n.s. II 5100b = n.s. II 5656 = *CIG* IV 9748 to show a consulate of 409. He notes, however, that a restoration of the consulate of 412 cannot be excluded (370 n.66), and the uncertainty seems to us sufficient to omit this text from the list for 409.

Critical Notes

In *AE* 1951, 89 the editor has omitted Honorius VIII from the restoration, incorrectly in our opinion; cf. *Kokalos* 28-29 (1982-83) 12 no. 36.

410

Critical Notes

NotScav 1888, 450 (= *BullCommArch* 16 [1888] 250 n.11) is restored by the editor as *[? Varane et Ter]tullo*. There are, however, no inscriptions in which both Varanes and Tertullus appear, and this restoration must be rejected. The only other attestation in epigraphy for Tertullus is *NotScav* 1893, 118, which reads Tertullo cos. The second line is obscure to us, and we remain uncertain about these two examples; it seems clear enough that the first of them refers to the Roman consul of 410.

411

Excluded

Feissel, *Rec.Inscr.Chrét.Maced.* 129 (year doubtful; restoration of Theodosius IX and Constantius III, 420, with month date in August seems equally possible; Theodosius IX et qui fuerit nuntiatus also seems possible.)

Critical Notes

The proclamation of Honorius IX two years running in the East must have been puzzling to contemporaries, but hardly a problem. After all, contemporaries are not likely to confuse this year with last year, whatever they are called. But there was a serious possibility of confusion in the future.

For although contemporary eastern documents carried Honorius IX in both 411 and 412 (as the papyri prove), it is not likely that two Honorius IX's would be allowed to survive on consular fasti. One was sure to be deleted, and there was no obvious way of deciding which.[1] Pasch. and Marcell. preserve a version in which the second was deleted, while Heracl. shows Honorius consul in both years, but (incorrectly, if understandably) renumbered 412 as Honorius X--inevitably leading to an incorrect numbering of all Honorius' subsequent consulates. The list used by the Theodosian compilers may have preserved Honorius IX in both years, since in addition to eight laws of 412 dated *IX et V*, there is also one law of 411 with IX et IV. But the one *IX et IV* could be seen as an uncorrected original date, in which case we should perhaps allow the possibility that the compilers' list deleted the first Honorius IX; one thing we can say for certain is that Honorius' subsequent consulates are correctly numbered in the Code.

No other pair of years has left so many laws with so many different uncorrected formulas. In the East, in addition to *IX et IV* and *IX et V*, we find Theodosius IV *e.q.f.n.* and V *e.q.f.n.*; in the West two laws (of 8 Feb. and 28 Nov.) with a p.c. Varanae and one (*ConstSirm* 11 of 24 June) with just Theodosius IV. The western laws pose a problem of their own, since, if the new eastern formula Theodosius IV was in use by June, we should not expect to find a law dated by a p.c. again as late as November. The puzzle is compounded because an excerpt from *ConstSirm* 11 appears in *CTh* (16.2.40, dated 25 May) with the formula for 412, *Honorius IX et Theodosius V*. Formulas aside, which is the correct year? The law is addressed to Melitius as PPO of Italy, who was certainly replaced by June 412 (Seeck, *PLRE*) and perhaps by January (Burgess). At all events, no law would have been despatched to him on 24 June[2] 412; *ConstSirm* 11 must belong in 411. If so, then it must be the original formula. Unlike the edited excerpts in *CTh*, Sirmondian laws are preserved unexcerpted and unedited (Mommsen, I.i, p.ccclxxviii): note, for example, the original western *Stilichone II* in *ConstSirm* 2, a formula the compilers misguidedly brought into line with the eastern formula *Stilichone II et Anthemio*.

The strongest grounds would be required to impugn *Theodosius IV* in *ConstSirm* 11. Yet Burgess changes it to *p.c. Varanae*, insisting, against the evidence of the Roman inscription *ICUR* n.s. II 4171, that *Theodosius IV* was not disseminated in the West during 411. His starting point was the false consular date for 412 given in the *CTh* extract (16.2.40) and three other laws to Melitius as PPO (5.9.2; 11.16.23; 16.2.41), all of which have to be corrected to 411. He makes the improbable suggestion that, when routinely translating the (for him) original p.c. into the formula for 411, the compiler looked at the wrong line in his consular list and mistakenly wrote the formula for 412 instead. But whether or not this is the most satisfactory way of explaining the undoubted error in the four extracts in *CTh*, that has nothing to do with the formula of *ConstSirm* 11, an unexcerpted law contained in a western collection unknown to the Theodosian compilers. There is no reason to believe that it is in error at all.

[1]A further potential source of confusion was western lists, which gave Theod. IV alone in 411.
[2]In principle, Sirmondian dates are always to be preferred; but 25 May is scarcely less impossible (Seeck, *Reg.* 87, 39).

Burgess naturally also assumed that the formula *p.c. Varanae* in *CTh* 6.26.15 of 28 Nov. was original. But a p.c. at court in November must always be viewed with the deepest suspicion (Chapter 7, section 2). *Theodosius IV* may have been proclaimed very late in Ravenna, but it must have arrived by the end of November, and Honorius, in desperate need of eastern support in his hour of need, can have had no possible motive to repudiate it. An explanation on the lines suggested in Chapter 7 above seems the simplest solution. The law is addressed to Bonosianus, prefect of Rome. If issued at Ravenna on 28 Nov., even in ordinary times it was not likely to be posted at Rome before the New Year, and with communications imperilled by barbarian marauders, we may safely assume no rapid passage. The only other extant law addressed to Bonosianus is dated 25.ix.410 (*CTh* 14.1.6). We suggest that 6.25.15 was issued at Ravenna on 28.xi.410, and that *p.c. Varanae* is the *accepta* date added at Rome early the following year. It would therefore cease to be evidence for November 411.

In fact we should then have no law with the transmitted formula of p.c. Varanae for 411 at all, because 7.13.20 is assigned by MSS to Varanes' consulate, namely 410. Since the law so obviously refers to the sack of Rome (24.viii.410), Seeck changed it (assuming the omission of a p.c.) to 411. The correction is well nigh certain; if the news of Theodosius IV had not yet arrived, even court would have had no alternative but to date by p.c. But at any rate the latest of the three other Theodosian extracts that Burgess assigns to 411 (16.2.41 of 11 Dec.) must originally have carried the formula *Theodosius IV*. Indeed, the simplest explanation of the corruption of an original 411 to 412 in the *CTh* extracts is that *all* of them were originally dated by *Theodosius IV*. Eastern compilers naturally corrected this western formula to its eastern equivalent, *Honorius IX et Theodosius IV*, which was later corrected again against a list which only gave *Honorius IX et Theodosius V*.

In *ICUR* n.s. II 4171, the date is preserved as *Nonu Ka[l. Oct]/ die Satur*. The only ante 9 kal. on a Saturday in 411 was 23.ix, as De Rossi (*ICUR* I 546) noted; but of course the day may have been incorrectly recorded.

412

Critical Notes

CIL XI 2898 is known only from a manuscript copy; it is difficult to know if the reading is right, and if so whether in fact this would, in Italy, be the correct year.

414

Excluded

ICUR n.s. I 1944 (name doubtful)

Nuovo Didaskaleion 1950, 54 no. 6 (see *Kokalos* 28-29 [1982-83] 13 no.39) (year uncertain)

I.Chrét.Mactar X 67 (year doubtful; 432 also possible)

Critical Notes

ICUR n.s. I 2722 (= *ICUR* I 54) was dated by the editors to 339; but those consuls would usually have Aug. with their names, and Constantius would have the iteration numeral II. Hence, Diehl (*ILCV* 2938 adn.), correctly in our opinion, put the inscription in 414. (Ferrua's rejection of 414, *Nuove corr.* 82, rests on circular reasoning, cf. our note *ad annum*.) The same is true of *ICUR* n.s. I 3160 = I 53 = *ILCV* 4145, where the second consul is called Constantino instead of Constante.

415

Excluded

CIL V 1621 (year doubtful)

417

Excluded

ICUR n.s. IV 12259 (name doubtful)

P.Vindob.Sijp. 9.19-22 presents a gross anomaly which we record here rather than listing in the main section for reasons which will be obvious. The text presents a consular date by p.c. D.N. Theodosii perp. Aug. VII et Fl. Constantii v.c. II. There is no month and day. The text is a lease for the crop of the 12th indiction. The readings have been verified by us on photographs. Theodosius' seventh consulate fell in 416; the p.c. would be 417. Constantius was cos. II in 417, and the p.c. of that consulate would be 418. They do not make a pair; but there is worse. The nearest 12th indiction is 413/4, the crop falling in 413 (and the document, by implication, in the fall of 412 or early part of 413).

No solution will save all of the data. It is quite impossible for any competent scribe to have supposed in 412 or 413 that Theodosius had held a 7th consulate or was currently holding one (VI fell in 415, and even if the 411-412 confusion had caused problems [which is not demonstrable], VII in 412 or 413 is impossible. In any case, 412 in the East was p.c. Honorius IX and Theodosius IV.). The numeral for Constantius is doubtfully read, but his **first** consulate fell in 414 and will not have been known earlier than the start of that year. Since Egyptian scribes are hardly likely to have guessed a consulate for someone in the West who had **never** held one, the indiction simply cannot be correct.

If the indiction is wrong, the matter is thrown open. The best bet seems to be that p.c. Theodosii VII is right, and that the cos. of the current year (417), very recently announced perhaps, has been substituted for the true 2nd consul for 416, Palladius. The use of p.c. instead of cos. had become very common in this period, and a reversion to p.c. shortly after the announcement of the consuls is not inconceivable. But a scribe who botched an indiction number was a bungler, and the combination is perhaps not so astonishing for such. The placement of the date at the end rather than the start of such a contract is in itself remarkable. Fall, 417, seems the best guess, but it remains uncertain. It is worth remarking that the harvest following such a date would be that of the second indiction. An error of writing $\iota\beta = 12$ for $\beta = 2$ is at least conceivable.

418

Critical Notes

ILCV 2936A (*NotScav* 1895, 485 no.163) is corrected by Ferrua, *Kokalos* 28-29 (1982-83) 15 from XVI Kal. to XIV Kal.

419

Excluded

CIL V 6227 (cos. date?)

420

Excluded

ICUR n.s. II 4865 = *ILCV* 598 (person doubtful)

ICUR n.s. V 13391 (person doubtful)

RAC 22 (1946) 92 (year doubtful)

422

Excluded

ILCV 3504 adn. (should be same as 2943 adn., included under 430 as *ICUR* n.s. II 6079)

RAC 36 (1960) 31 n.22; cf. *Kokalos* 28-29 (1982-83) 16 (year doubtful; κυρίων not found in inscriptions after 360 in consular formulas, despite Agnello's assertion that writing is not earlier than Honorius; for "dominus noster" in the papyri, cf. *ZPE* 39 [1980] 165-77)

423

Excluded

ICUR n.s. V 13392 (cos. date?)

Ferrua, *RendPontAccad* 22(1946-47) 231 no. 8 (year doubtful)

Critical Notes

Agnello, *Silloge* 104, was earlier published as *AE* 1906, 67, with an erroneous date to 422.

ICUR n.s. II 4273 is restored as *Mariniani [v.c.]*. It is by no means clear that the restoration of *[v.c.]* is warranted in this case. *ICUR* n.s. I 731 = *ILCV* 4461B lacks v.c.

424

Excluded

CIL XI 4047 (name doubtful)

NotScav 1895, 520 no. 266 (rest., attributed to 424) = *RendPontAccad* 1946-47, 231 no. 6 (rest., attributed to 374)

425

Critical Notes

The editor of *AE* 1922, 42 (= *ILCV* 3791C) assigns it to October, 425; but we see no indication in this inscription of the month to which it refers.

427

Excluded

ICUR n.s. IV 11147 (cos. date?)

Critical Notes

AE 1933, 27 and *SEG* XVII 441 both publish the same inscription, but they give the numerals differently: *AE* gives ι(?) for Theodosius, *SEG* ιβ′. Since 12 is the correct figure, presumably the latter is right.

429

Excluded

CIL III 13125 (+ 14239^8, p.2326?) (person doubtful)

CIL VIII 11129 = *ILCV* 3232 adn. (name doubtful)

ICUR n.s. VIII 20837a (person doubtful)

Critical Notes

P.Wash.Univ. 36.1 is dated 9.v, referring to Felix and Taurus: but their consulate or p.c.? The latter seems more likely, for our only evidence to date from 428 is from 27.iv, only 12 days earlier, and it has the p.c. of Hierius and Ardabur. This is not conclusive (cf. the situation in 445, where one has a consulate already early in the year), but it does make 429 a more probable date.

430

Critical Notes

CIL III 13124 has Theodosius XIII, Valentinian II; we consider it more likely that the senior Augustus' numeral is right than that it is wrong and that of the junior consul right.

431

Critical Notes

Ferrua, *Kokalos* 28-29 (1982-83) 18 argues that *Flb. Basso et Antioco* in *CIL* X 7168 means that only Bassus was a Flavius. The rule of two plus two in names makes it inherently probable that *FLL* was meant, and in any case the sources are very inconsistent about indicating singular and plural. Furthermore, contrary to Ferrua's claim that "che Antioco fosse un Flavio non consta da nessuna parte," Fl. is added for him in *PSI XVII Congr.* 29 and in *ACO* I.i.3, p.10. The controversy is in any event not very meaningful: anyone of high status was called Fl. when no other name was provided or known. Cf. Chapter 3.

ICUR n.s. VII 17541c has been placed under the formula with Bassus alone, as the other Roman examples with Auchenius in his name do not include Philippus. The editor, however, restores *et Fl. Philippo*. The editor of *ICUR* n.s. I 3226, apparently in the same class, restored *et* after *Bassi*, in the lacuna. *ICUR* I 672, 675 and 676 and n.s. I 47 also have lacunae after Bassus' name.

432

Excluded

ICUR n.s. VIII 21068a (cos. date?)

Critical Notes

ICUR n.s. I 1466 is known from older copies. De Rossi, *ICUR* I 677, points out that some read *AETIO*, others *APPIO*. He favors *AETIO* because there was no 5th century consul named Appius. Diehl (*ILCV* 412) suggests the possibility of the consul's being Apion (cos. 539); presumably De Rossi did not think it was that late. At all events, Aetius' appearance without his colleague Valerius is shown by all the other inscriptions of this year to be normal at Rome.

433

Critical Notes

ICUR n.s. V 13957 = n.s. I 332 = I 712 was dated by the editors to 443, and restored as

cons. Petroni M[aximi II et Paterii]

Ferrua notes (*ICUR* n.s. VII 17559) that the inscriptions of 443 always call Maximus only Maximus, never Petronius Maximus. Since we have in n.s. I 1262 an unequivocal example of Petronius Maximus without Theodosius and in n.s. VII 17559 another Petronius Maximus with no preserved colleague; and since Theodosius is not attested until October in Rome, we accept this argument. We restore v.c. in the lacuna instead of II et Paterii.

D. Feissel, *BCH* 105 (1981) 491, restores Βαλ[εντινιανοῦ] in *Corinth* VIII.1 (1931) 145. But (1) Fl. before Valentinianus without any imperial title (for which there is no room) is very odd, and (2) we do not see a sti, as Feissel does, in line 7, but rather a leaf. We therefore restore instead

Κοιμητήρ[ιον τῆς]
ὄντος σεμν[ῆς τὴν]
μνήμην Σελή[νης]
μηνὸς Ἰουνίο[υ ....]
τῇ μετὰ τὴ[ν ὑπατίαν]
Φλ. Βαλ[ερίου τοῦ λαμ.]
(leaf)

4

Feissel takes this view into account in *Travaux et Mémoires* 9 (1985) 277, but without altering his text.

Siculorum Gymnasium (1961) 196 is restored by Ferrua, *Kokalos* 28-29 (1982-83) 7 no.15 as Θεο[δοσίου Αὐγ. τὸ β] κὲ Μαξίμου λα[μπρ. ἀνδρὸς τὸ β ΄], dating to 388. No such formula is ever found, whereas what we restore is normal for 433.

<h2 style="text-align:center">434</h2>

Critical Notes

Diehl (*ILCV* 843) restores the month in *ICUR* n.s. I 88 as *A[priles* without explanation; August seems to us equally possible.

CIL IX 1368 = *ILCV* 3027A (Aeclanum) was dated by the editors to 444 on the basis of p.c. Petroni (M)aximi v.c.; cf. under 433 for arguments which make 434 a more attractive date for this text.

PLRE II 164 proposes to restore Aspar after Ardabur in *P.Oxy.* XVI 1879, thus giving him his "full name." But, as we have often observed, formulas usually give an equal number of names to both consuls, and with Fll. papyri never give more than one name each. We therefore reject the restoration.

<h2 style="text-align:center">435</h2>

Excluded

NotScav 1888, 451 no.53 (name doubtful)

ICUR n.s. II 4902 (year doubtful)

ICUR n.s. I 3230 = *ILCV* 2804 (year doubtful)

ICUR n.s. IV 11149 (year doubtful)

Critical Notes

AE 1906, 136 is dated by the editor to 434; but it is actually a p.c. to the consuls of 434, thus 435.

For *P.Stras.* I 1 see *BASP* 17 (1980) 29.

ICUR n.s. VII 17561 has *Decem]bres* restored (by De Rossi, *ICUR* I 686), but we see no reason to exclude September, October, or November.

CIL III 13962 fails to notice that the text had already been published as III 2657; the best text is in fact in the addenda to 2657, p.1032.

437

Excluded

CIL X 1339 (year doubtful)

ICUR n.s. II 4176 (year doubtful)

P.Wash.Univ. 37, which the editor presents as having a date to Aetius II and Sigisvultus, is shown in *BiOr* 39 (1982) 566 to be of very doubtful reading and restoration, so that its secure assignment to any year seems impossible.

438

Critical Notes

The editors of *CIL* III 2658 = *ILCV* 4370 adn. restore the consulate as

D.N. Theodo[sio Aug. XVI et Glabrione] Fausto v.c.

In the other cases in which Faustus has two names, however, we find Anicius (*ILCV* 4370), and Glabrio appears only in *ICUR* n.s. I 734, where the full Anicius Acilius Glabrio Faustus appears; presumably *Anicio* should therefore be restored here also. (So already Diehl in *ILCV* 4370 adn.) For this inscription see also *Forsch.Salona* II 173.

439

Excluded

ICUR n.s. I 735 = I 847 (person doubtful)

ICUR n.s. I 742 = I 845 (person doubtful)

ICUR n.s. II 4975 = I 848 (person doubtful)

ICUR n.s. IV 11151 (person doubtful)

ICUR n.s. V 15358 = I 846 (person doubtful)

CIL VI 33716 = *ILCV* 715 (person doubtful)

ICUR n.s. VIII 20816 (person doubtful)

Critical Notes

For *NotScav* 1895, 480 no. 153 cf. Ferrua, *RendPontAccad* 22 (1946-47) 231 no. 7, who restores Theodosius VI and Palladius; but the numeral should be VII. D. Feissel suggests that equally attractive epigraphically and not requiring assumption of an error would be ς[ι] as the numeral, thus 439.

440

Excluded

CIL XIII 6248 (apparently a forgery)

Critical Notes

CIG IV 9426 (= *Forschungen Salona* II 175) presents the curious formula [Theod.] Aug. XVII et Anatolius (in Greek). Anatolius is the eastern consul of 440, known also in the West, while Theodosius XVII is the consul of 439. It is a priori more plausible to assign the text to 440, since Anatolius' consulate of 440 is unlikely to have been known already in Salona in 439 on 27.ix.

ICUR n.s. V 13400 appears to contain two inscriptions, with line 3 beginning a new one after the consular date, as the editor indicates. There is a space between lines 2 and 3, and given the partial preservation of the stone, it seems to us possible that Anatolius' name stood in a lacuna between these two lines.

441

Critical Notes

For *BGU* II 609 see *BASP* 17 (1980) 29 and *P.Rainer Cent.* 94.1n.

CIL IX 1366 is restored as dated to *p.[c.] D.N. Placidi Valentiniani Au[g. V et Anatoli]*, on 10.vii. The alternative date of 446, a p.c. of 445, seems to us just possible (restoring Nomus instead of Anatolius), but since Aetius is known at Dertona by June, it seems much less likely.

443

Excluded

ICUR I 1171 = *ILCV* 1748 adn. (person doubtful)

ICUR n.s. IV 11154 (person doubtful)

AE 1977, 796 (= 1961, 190) (no cos. dating)

Critical Notes

Immediately before the consular date in *ICUR* n.s. I 3236 = *ILCV* 2971A adn. there stands XIII CC, which conveys no sense to us. If we read XIII OC, however, the date might be ante 13 kal. Oct. or 13 Oct., i.e. 19.ix or 13.x; the former seems to us more likely, given patterns of dating days at this time.

444

Excluded

NotScav 1896, 33 no. 334 (cf. *Kokalos* 28-29 [1982-83] 20 no. 70) (person doubtful)

Critical Notes

Several inscriptions dated by Albinus have been assigned by editors to 493, though they lack the 'iunior' normally found in the inscriptions of that year. We think that they belong under 444. These are *ICUR* n.s. VIII 20820 (= I 900), n.s. II 4990 (= I 901), and n.s. II 4178 (= I 903) (= *ILCV* 3727E, 2766, and 252, respectively; for the first and third *ICUR* n.s. also allowed 444 as possible); *CIL* V 7772 (= *ILCV* 1243) and XI 2585 (= *ILCV* 259). In the case of *ICUR* I 901, the editor argued for 493 on the grounds of a date in October, after the earliest occurrence of Theodosius with Albinus. But we are not persuaded that the letters in question **are** a month name--they are at least out of place.

In *ICUR* n.s. I 1359, iunior is restored; but the space seems to us insufficient, and v.c. would fill it better. We thus prefer 444 again.

ICUR n.s. II 4517 is restored as *[DN Theodosio] / [Aug XVIII et (?) A]lbino vc co[nss*. The restoration of Theodosius is completely gratuitous, and at this date (19.viii) no other Roman attestation of Theodosius is yet known. In *ICUR* I 902, there is space enough to restore Theodosius, and at this date (14.ix-1.x) we think the odds favor it.

445

Critical Notes

For *P.Ant.* II 102 see *ZPE* 46 (1982) 239, where αἰώνιος is wrongly omitted from the restoration.

446

Excluded

AE 1914, 78 (name doubtful)

447

Excluded

NotScav 1893, 389 = *NBC* 1902, 63 (cf. *AE* 1940, 88) (name doubtful)

448

Excluded

RAC 26 (1950) 234 (reading and name doubtful)

Critical Notes

CIL XIII 2356 (cf. *ILCV* 4404) is dated to Friday, *XVII Kal. [ ]arias*, restored by the editor as *Febru]arias*. We do not think that this is a necessary restoration. The date proposed, 16.i.448, fell on a Saturday, not a Friday. *[Ianu]arias* is no better, since 16.xii.448 was a Thursday. We see no way of choosing between two errors. It may be noted that Zenon was added later in smaller characters.

For the date of *Reisen in Kilikien* 89 no. 168, see D. Feissel, *BCH* 108 (1984) 564-66.

449

Excluded

ICUR I 910 = *ILCV* 3206 is too fragmentary and the persons are uncertain.

Critical Notes

There are serious objections to the month of the Beirut date cited in the acts of Chalcedon (*ACO* II.i.3, p.19.25); cf. R.V. Sellers, *The Council of Chalcedon* (1961) 54 n.3.

450

Excluded

CIG IV 9762 (name doubtful)

Vives, *ICERV* 190 (no cos. dating, see *Röm.Inschr.Tarraco* 674)

452

Excluded

CIL VIII 8192 = 19914 = *ILCV* 190 adn. (name doubtful)

Critical Notes

ICUR n.s. VII 17569c is assigned by Ferrua to 452 (or 453, since we see no way of excluding a p.c.), arguing that FL. HER[cannot be Heraclianus (413) or Hermenericus (465) because they are never called Flavius. Heraclianus has no inscriptions at all, in fact, and suffered *damnatio memoriae*, so it is rather hard to know if he was called Flavius. Hermenericus always appears with his colleague Basiliscus. On balance, 452/453 does seem the best possibility but not quite certain. The same arguments apply to *CIL* IX 1371, where again *Fl Her[* is preserved. We might add, however, that the argument from the appearance or not of Flavius seems to us of dubious merit, as it has more the function of a title or prefix for any person of reasonably high degree in this period, and its omission or inclusion seems to have little to do with a person's actual nomenclature; cf. Chapter 3.

ZPE 24 (1977) 222 is the stone mentioned by Dessau in Mommsen, *Ges. Hist. Schr.* III 369 n.1.

ICUR n.s. VII 19989 is the same as I 758 = n.s. I 991, a fact the editor of n.s. VII 19989 omits.

453

The consuls of 453, one western and one eastern, were both announced in the East, but Vincomalus was not announced in the West. Independently of the dating of the inscriptions which come into question here, Pope Leo's correspondence makes this fact clear. In 524, again, the East used two consuls, but there is no trace in the West of the dissemination of the name of Justinus. In both cases, therefore, the only name one anticipates in inscriptions is that of Opilio, the western consul. Can we distinguish the inscriptions of these two years?

(1) *CIL* VI 32942 (*ILCV* 469) is dated *co]ns Venanti Opilionis*. As *PLRE* II 808-09 indicates, the grandson of the consul of 524 was called Venantius. This text should therefore probably be connected with the consul of 524, whether cos. or p.c. is to be restored (see below).

(2) Three northern Italian inscriptions dated to Opilio v.c. add the 2nd indiction, confirming that 524 is the correct year. They bear dates from 8.iv, 23.vii, and 6.viii (*CIL* V 5737, *AE* 1947, 67, and *CIL* V 1822).

(3) In 453, there is a postconsular date by Herculanus cos. 452 on 14.v in Como (*CIL* V 5414). The balance of probability therefore favors the assumption that northern Italian dates by Opilio before May/June refer to the cos. of 524. *ILCV* 2736a (15.iii, from Oriolo in Liguria) is therefore to be assigned to 524.

(4) Probus iun. cos. 525 is attested in Rome as early as 1.ii, in Salerno on 25.i, in Brescia on 28.i, and in Arles on 10.i. It seems a justifiable inference that there were **no** dates by the p.c. of Opilio cos. 524, and that Probus was promulgated right at the start of the year or even known in advance. *CIL* VI 32942 thus belongs to 524, not 525 (as we already demonstrated above in point 1), and we can assign to 454 the following: *ICUR* n.s. I 2117 = *ILCV* 510 (23.i); *ICUR* n.s. VIII 22974 (= I 764) (24.i); *ICUR* n.s. II 5040 (= *CIL* VI 32008) (31.i); *AE* 1923, 82 (23.iii); *ICUR* n.s. I 1946 (1.vi), all from Rome. In 454, the new consuls are first attested at Rome in July-August, though May is possible: one cannot tell if *NotScav* 1888, 704 no.283 refers to cos. or p.c.

(5) For the Gallic inscriptions, likewise, which show p.c. Opilionis, a date in 454 is necessary: *CIL* XIII 2359 (Lyons, 24.i); *I.Lat.Gaul. Narb.* 302 (Vienne, 25.ii); *CIL* XIII 2358 (Lyons, 16.viii).

(6) It is not safe to assume that because Como still dated p.c. Herculani on 14.v.453, Rome did not yet know Opilio.

(7) *ICUR* I 742 is, according to De Rossi, to be assigned to 453 in all probability because it is carved immediately below an inscription dated by Calepius to 447. Unfortunately, dates from January to December are possible.

(8) De Rossi assigned the texts listed here as *ICUR* n.s. I 2123 and II 5036 to 524, on the grounds that their cross to the left of the first line is only a sixth century phenomenon. Such a judgment, even by De Rossi, is not infallible; we have seen such a cross in *ICUR* n.s. I 1946, placed above under 454 (with the palaeographic affirmation of A.E. and J.S. Gordon, *Album of Dated Latin Inscriptions* III 361).

(9) *ICUR* n.s. II 5037 is dated *cons. Rufi Opil(ionis)*. Unfortunately, no other evidence so styles either consul.

(10) We see no secure basis for dating the remainder of the inscriptions dated to Opilio (v.c.). Because we still hope that a search for better dating criteria on the basis of future discoveries may be worthwhile, we list this material here under 453 with the caution that 524 is also possible.

(11) *CIL* X 7115 = *ILCV* 3735 was dated by Mommsen to 453 or 524. The reading is doubtful and Ferrua, *Kokalos* 28-29 (1982-83) 10 no. 23, proposes a reading of Stilicho, 400. We are not completely persuaded but have listed it under 400. Cf. Critical Appendix for 400.

Critical Notes

It should be noted that despite the restoration of Vincomalus' name, *SPP* XX 138 must, because of the plural vv.cc. at the end, refer to this year, since the other possibility (524) would require only v.c., and the papyri are in general reliable in such matters.

458

Excluded

IG XIV 2271 = *CIG* IV 9863 (cos. date?). D. Feissel tells us that J. Gascou has confirmed his suspicion that this text is Coptic; cf. S. de Ricci, *RevArch* 1904, 99-101.

ICUR I 856-860 (year doubtful)

ICUR n.s. VII 17587 (year doubtful)

ICUR n.s. VIII 20825 (year doubtful)

NotScav 1897, 366 (cos. date?)

Critical Notes

In *CIL* XIII 2363, the anomalous v.c. with Leo is correctly read (checked on the original by T. Drew-Bear). The absence of iun. appears to exclude 474.

459

Critical Notes

Grégoire dates his no.322 to 26.iv; the correct date is 27.iv.

CIL III 13127 restores Patricius et Ricimer vv.cc., but the restoration of Patricius (an eastern consul) at the start of this inscription is not at all likely in light of *CIL* III 9522; cf. the following year.

460

Excluded

ICUR n.s. VII 17575b (name doubtful)

Critical Notes

CIL III 9522 has, according to the editors, Φλ(αουίου) Ῥεκ(κομέρου) κ(αὶ) Ἰου(λίου) Π[ατ]ρικ(ίου) τ(ῶν) λαμπ[ροτάτων]. From *PLRE* II 842 we find that this is the only basis for the name Iulius for Patricius. Feissel instead reads ΜΕΤΑ Τ[Η]Ν Υ. ΦΛ/ ΡΕΚΙΜΟΥS ΠΑ[Τ]ΡΙΚS ΤΩΝ ΛΑΜΠS (and we have verified on the photograph he kindly lent us). What remains unclear is whether the scribe intended the S after ΡΕΚΙΜΟΥ as punctuation or as (καὶ), i.e. whether he thought *patricius* was a name or a title. (In favor of the latter is the fact that we do not find Fll. at the start.) Cf. *P.Amst.* I 45 (501), where a scribe thought that ὕπατος was a title, when in fact Hypatius was the consul's name.

461

Excluded

ICUR I 880 (name doubtful)

ICUR n.s. I 1264 (name doubtful)

ICUR n.s. VII 17580 (name doubtful)

CIG IV 9759 (name doubtful)

Critical Notes

In *AE* 1914, 68, the inscription now listed as *ICUR* n.s. VII 17578 is restored as *consulatu] Fl. Severin[i et Fl. Dagalaiphi*. This restoration is certainly wrong, as Dagalaifus never appears in western inscriptions. But a restoration of Trocundes and the consulate of 482 seems possible (cf. that year). Unfortunately, comparative material is scarce.

For *IG* X 2 1 776 = Feissel, *Recueil Inscr.Chrét.Macéd.* 128, see *Classical Journal* 77 (1981-82) 184.

463

Excluded

ICUR n.s. VIII 20826 (person doubtful)

ICUR n.s. I 1947 = *ILCV* 4384 (person doubtful)

Critical Notes

For *P.Vindob.Sijp.* 7 see *BASP* 16 (1979) 241.

464

Excluded

CIL III 9523 (person doubtful)

465

Excluded

CIG IV 9770 (name doubtful)

Critical Notes

For the reading of *ICUR* n.s. VII 17584 = *ILCV* 1708 adn. see Ferrua, *Nuove corr.* 39.

Gatti restored the ed.pr. of *ILCV* 3782 (*ICUR* n.s. I 3240, now = *ICUR* n.s. VII 20606) as *Erm[ogeniani Olybri et Probini vv.cc.]*, the consuls of 395, but this sequence of names is never found, and if a first name is given it is Anicii, referring to both consuls. Gatti later came also to prefer 465.

For *SB* I 4821 see *BASP* 17 (1980) 13-14.

ICUR n.s. II 4950 is dated to '465 vel 466' by Silvagni, following De Rossi (*ICUR* I 819). The one preserved name, however, is *Basi]lisco*, and the ending in -o favors the consulate, though space for post could be found in the preceding line.

CIL V 5720 offers no date for this inscription, but *Her. et Bal. vvcc* must be Her(menericus) et Ba-(si)l(iscus).

466

Excluded

ICUR n.s. II 4177 (name doubtful)

Critical Notes

For *M.Chr.* 71 see *BASP* 17 (1980) 30.

467

Excluded

CIL VIII 9313 = 20923 = *ILCV* 4848 (name doubtful)

Critical Notes

Silvagni restores *ICUR* n.s. II 5723 as *Prisco et Io]anne vv cc* instead of De Rossi's correct *Puseo et Io]anne vv.cc.* (*ICUR* I 1161). This is presumably simply a slip.

468

Excluded

ICUR n.s. VIII 20813 = I 1163 (cos. date?)

Critical Notes

ICUR n.s. I 741 = *ILCV* 4370 adn. has the date to Anthemius (II is restored, but inevitable) in line 2. In lines 5-6 we find

> Kal Dec[embres cons]
> DN FL M[arciano (?)],

which De Rossi (*ICUR* I 825) took to be the date of death (line 2 being birth) and thought perhaps to refer to 469. Silvagni reads *[DN] Fl. M[arciani et Zenonis]*, Diehl *<D>N Fl [Marciani et Zenonis]*. *ILCV* 3114 shows that Marcianus et Zeno is an acceptable dating formula at Rome in 469, but DN is definitely out of place, since Marcianus was a private citizen at this date, as Silvagni pointed out. The copyist actually gives *HN*, and Ferrua suggests (*per litt.*) that this might be a sloppy writing of *CN* for *CONS*. We cannot feel much certainty about the reading and restoration of this text.

469

Excluded

ICUR n.s. VII 17588a (person doubtful)

ICUR n.s. I 741 = *ILCV* 4370 adn. (cf. under 468, Critical Notes)

470

Excluded

LeBlant, *Inscr.Gaule* II 627 (forgery; see *CIL* XII, p.8*, no.66*)

Critical Notes

The month and day of *AE* 1951, 89 are presented as follows:

> τῇ πρὸ]ς ᾿Ιουλίων

The editor comments: "le terminus *post quem non* de la *terminatio* de Jordanes dans l'Occident se trouve ramene au 25.vi ou au 6.vii." The comment indicates that a space after the bracket has been lost in typesetting; though ante 6 kal. Iul. is 26.vi, not 25.vi. But this restoration is hardly of much value. Not only is the understood alternative] ς ᾿Ιουλίων (6 July) possible (though the order would be atypical); we cannot know if some form (not the correct genitive) of kalends, nones, or ides stood there--or, for that matter, ις or κς. For that matter, the 'sti' could even be a numeral marking (as Ferrua, *Kokalos* 28-29 [1982-83] 22 no.75 suggests). There are simply too many possibilities.

471

Critical Notes

For *IG* XIV 2290, see *RAC* 58 (1982) 379 n.102.

472

Critical Notes

For *P.Lond.* V 1793, see *BASP* 17 (1980) 30.

473

Critical Notes

P.Lond. III 869 descr. is published in *Mneme G. Petropoulou* (Athens 1984) II, 203 ff. The editor of this lease of part a house in Hermopolis reads the consular dating formula as follows:

1 [*ca* 25   τ]οῦ λαμπροτ[ά]του καὶ το[ῦ]
         δηλωθησομένου, Θὼθ ιζ, ιβ ἰνδικ(τίονος)

In his note *ad loc.*, he comes to the conclusion that three restorations are possible:

[μ.τ.ὑ. Φλ. Μαρκιανοῦ τ]οῦ κτλ. (473p)
[μ.τ.ὑ. Φλ. Λογγίνου τ]οῦ κτλ. (488p)
[μ.τ.ὑ. Φλ. ᾿Αναστασίου τ]οῦ κτλ. (518p)

The first possibility entails restoring 26 letters in the lacuna before τ]οῦ the second 25 letters, and the third 27 letters. The length of restoration is therefore not a criterion for choice among these, and the editor renounces making a choice. We believe that other criteria lead to a preference for 473.

The text has been signed by a notary whose name (not transcribed by the editor) must be read as Aphous, as we see on a microfilm; line 18 is to be read

+ δι᾿ ἐμοῦ ᾿Αφοῦτος ἐγράφη διὰ Φοιβάμμωνος βοηθ(οῦ).

Now a notary Aphous at Hermopolis also occurs in *BGU* XII 2158 and *CPR* IX 23. The dating clauses in both texts are lost, but their editors date them in both cases to *ca* 485. If this date, imprecise though it be, is roughly correct, a date to 518 for the London papyrus is not very likely (though not quite excluded; long careers for notaries are known). A comparison with the extant dating formulas from papyri of 518 shows that there is no instance of καὶ τοῦ δηλωθησομένου in them. In fact, there is no later occurrence of that phrase than in 501, and that one is inappropriately inserted; the last correctly used instance known so far comes from 483.

There are good grounds, therefore, for supposing our choice to be narrowed down to 473 and 488. Now we do not have any papyri of 473 itself to see what we might expect in Hermopolis on 14.ix. There is, however, a papyrus of 8.xi.472 with the consulate of *Fl. Marcianus et qui fuerit nuntiatus*; this model supports the possibility of 473. In 486, 487, and 488, on the other hand, the years in which p.c. Fl. Longini was in use as a dating formula in papyri, there is no instance of this phrase. It seems thus more likely that 473 is the correct date than that 488 is, and 518 seems much less likely than either.

474

Critical Notes

For the date of *ICUR* n.s. II 4973 = I 861, cf. D. Feissel, *RAC* 58 (1982) 379 n.107.

ICUR n.s. I 738 = *ILCV* 511A has *Cons D N Leonis*. We have classified this as Leo iun. and in this year, but the absence of iunior is disquieting. The other first consulate of a Leo, however, was 458, and Maiorian was ruling at this point in 458 and did not recognize Leo as consul (see under 456). If the consul here is Leo senior, therefore, we would have to assume omission of an iteration numeral.

475

Critical Notes

J. Rea, *P.Rainer Cent.* 123.16n., prefers a date of 476 for *P.Oxy.* XVI 1899.

476

Critical Notes

ICUR n.s. II 4974 is read

[Basilisco II] et Armat[o conss];

there is nothing to prevent a p.c. dating (cf. Pope Simplicius' letter in 477), or even *[p.cons.] et(erum) Armat[i v.c.]* (478); the spelling *eterum* is found elsewhere, cf. *ILCV* III, p.223, col. a, top.

477

Excluded

P.Stras. 655 presents only]σκου τοῦ λαμπρο(τάτου); of the indiction number in line 9 only]άτης survives. The editor, dating to the 2nd half of the 5th century, noted that a date to 465 or 466, restoring Fl. Basiliscus, would not agree with any possible indiction (that is, without supposing scribal or editorial error). In 477, Basiliscus would have been called Augustus, not v.c. Neither date thus suits. We cannot find any other date which will work.

479

Excluded

CIL XIII 2601 = *ILCV* 1077 (name doubtful)

CIL XIV 1948 = *ILCV* 4654 adn. (year doubtful)

Critical Notes

The editor of *ICUR* n.s. II 6462 add. restores [III] after Zeno's name. That this is indeed his third consulate, 479, is not in doubt; but no preserved western inscription actually has the numeral, and Aug. or perp. Aug. may be an equally attractive restoration.

481

Excluded

ICUR n.s. I 394 (person doubtful)

ICUR n.s. II 4981 (name doubtful)

Critical Notes

For *P.Lond.* III 991 (p.258) see *BASP* 17 (1980) 7-8.

The element of doubt in *ICUR* n.s. II 4982 is whether this is a consular date at all; on balance we think it likely.

483

Excluded

AE 1940, 86 = *ICUR* n.s. VIII 20829 (name doubtful)

ICUR n.s. IV 11167 (name doubtful)

CIG IV 9783 (name doubtful)

ICUR n.s. I 1948 (person doubtful)

CIL V 5417 (person doubtful; see 490, Critical Notes)

Critical Notes

ICUR n.s. I 1105 presents *Cons Favi vc*, which De Rossi (*ICUR* I 1373) took to be a slip for *Fausti*. This seems on balance the best possibility, but we are not sure that *F<r>avi<tta>* is quite excluded (cos. 401; though the absence of the first consul, Vincentius, plus the character of the letters weigh against it). One could even envisage *F<l>avi vc* with omission of a name, but this is unparalleled.

484

Excluded

ICUR n.s. I 943, 992 (person doubtful)

ILCV 393A (person doubtful)

Critical Notes

The month in *ICUR* n.s. I 1472 is read as *O[ctobr]*, but from the plate it seems possible that the letter was an F, I, or N, offering other dates (1.ii, 1.vi, 1.vii, 1.xi).

ICUR I 933 appears also as *CIL* VI 9704, where its *ICUR* publication is not noted and where the date is given mistakenly as 506.

Tjäder dates his *Nichtlit. Pap.* 47-48A.27 to 507, but the dating simply *Venantio* seems to us to belong to 484 instead. See Chapter 3, p.44.

485

Critical Notes

I.Lat.Gaul.Narb. 297 (now *Rec.Inscr.Chrét.Gaule* XV 78; cf. also *ILCV* 1678) has a month date given as *VIIII Mai*. Espérandieu offers as possibilities *VIIII Mai* (9 May) or *VIII [K(al.)] Mai*. Descombes adopts the second of these. The first is certainly less likely, in view of contemporary usage, and we prefer instead of emding I to K to understand an omitted *Kal.*, thus 9 kal. Mai.; alternatively, one might think of VIII *I(dus) Mai*, which is 8.v. Cf. the same phenomenon in *Rec.Inscr.Chrét.Gaule* XV 286, of 504.

CIL XII 1498 (cf. *ILCV* 2256, esp. line 6n.) is assigned by *PLRE* II 1154 to Venantius cos. 508, with what justification we cannot see (*CIL* says 509?, citing approvingly--"recte opinor"--Allmer). Before his name there appears *VERI*, which *CIL* and Diehl (*ILCV* III, p.225a top) think means *VIRI*. It is hard to see what this is doing between *Consolatum* and *Venanti* (*CIL*: "male ... positum est"). Is this conceivably meant to be *Mari*, the second name (Venantius is the third) of the consul of 484 (cf. *PLRE* II 218)?

486

Excluded

CIL X 6850 (no consular formula)

Critical Notes

ICUR n.s. II 5049 is broken, so that one cannot tell if it had iun. (thus 529). The rarity of Roman inscriptions from 529 (and absence of Flavius from the existing one) argues (but hardly conclusively) for 486.

I.Lat.Gaul.Narb. 606 is dated by the editor to 486 or 487, but it shows no signs of a postconsulate. The date is admittedly early in the year; it could have been cut later.

487

Excluded

CIL V 5741 = 6253a = *ILCV* 2739 adn. (person doubtful)

Critical Notes

CIL XII 933 has the indiction number 7, which does not match with 487, when it should be 10. Diehl, *ILCV* 2889A, dated the text to 524, but this does not help, since the indiction should then be 2. There are also no examples of iterum p.c. Symmachi for that consulate known.

AE 1911, 90, is dated by the editor to 488, but either 487 or 488 is possible; indiction 11 would be 1.ix.487-31.viii.488. *PLRE* II 349 unaccountably cites this inscription as evidence for the consulate of Decius, cos. 486.

488

Excluded

ICUR n.s. I 1265 (cos. name?)

Critical Notes

There is ample room to restore the name of Sividius in *ICUR* n.s. VIII 23452.

PLRE II 1018 wrongly cites *CIL* V 8958 as *CIL* V 8950.

489

Critical Notes

ICUR n.s. VII 17597a is dated *VI Nonas A[*. Both April and August, however, have the nones on the 5th, and ante VI is thus impossible. Ferrua notes, however, that Arieti and Schmidt saw the foot of the A, which Ferrua dots, "conspicuum." Ferrua (per litt.) indicates that the preserved foot could also belong to M, thus 2 March or 2 May.

490

Excluded

ICUR I 897, 898, 899 (person doubtful)

ICUR n.s. I 91 (person doubtful)

ICUR n.s. VII 17599a (person doubtful)

CIL X 1231 (person doubtful)

CIL XI 4338 (person doubtful)

Critical Notes

CIL XI 4333 = *ILCV* 304, from Terni, is dated 11.xi, *P.Fausto vc*. The Faustus who is normally called Faustus, without iunior, cos. 483, has no P. in his name, whereas Anicius Probus Faustus cos. 490 was iunior rather consistently. We have preferred to accept 490 as the date, albeit with some hesitation, given the rarity of abbreviation of names to a single letter, apart from the traditional praenomina. In *CIL* V 5417, the editor restores *[Longino II et] Fausto vv cc*. The plural vv.cc. does not signify much in this period (cf. *ILCV* III p.224b, foot), and Longinus **never** appears in inscriptions of 490 from Italy. On the other hand, Faustus elsewhere has iunior. (Longinus does show up in p.c. and p.c. iterum dates in Italy in 491 and 492, but the form Fausto opposes a restoration of p.c. or p.c. iterum.) We are attracted by the possibility instead of restoring *[Probo] Fausto*, comparing *CIL* XI 4333, discussed above. It appears that the consul of 490 could be distinguished from the consul of 483 either by adding iunior to his name or by prefixing Probus to it; in the p.c., of course, the combination with Longinus offered another form of distinguishing the two. It is also possible that one should restore *[Aginantio] Fausto* and date to 483. We have therefore excluded it.

Critical Notes

The editors of *CIL* XI 4163 date it to 444, but with iunior it belongs certainly to 493, as Diehl points out, *ILCV* 1030.

494

Excluded

CIL XII 591 = *ILCV* 1066 adn. (name doubtful)

CIL XII 2060 (cos. date?)

ICUR I 907, 908 (cos. date?)

ICUR I 910 = *ILCV* 3206 (name doubtful)

495

Critical Notes

ICUR n.s. VII 17601 preserves the end of a month name *BRIS*. The period from 14.viii-13.xii is therefore possible; we cannot see any basis for preferring one of the months involved.

496

Critical Notes

The stone of *CIL* XII 1724 = *ILCV* 2454 reads ꟼII (= VIII) Kal. Ian., about which the *CIL* editors for some reason say "potius est VIIII quam VII." We cannot see why, and we do not agree. Diehl prints VIII, which we follow.

497

Excluded

P.Stras. 470 (person doubtful)

499

Critical Notes

For *P.Oxy.* XVI 1959 see *P.Mich.* XV 731.1n.

500

Excluded

CIL XII 2074 = *ILCV* 1690 adn. (cos. date?)

Critical Notes

The editors of *CIL* XI 4163 date it to 444, but with iunior it belongs certainly to 493, as Diehl points out, *ILCV* 1030.

494

Excluded

CIL XII 591 = *ILCV* 1066 adn. (name doubtful)

CIL XII 2060 (cos. date?)

ICUR I 907, 908 (cos. date?)

ICUR I 910 = *ILCV* 3206 (name doubtful)

495

Critical Notes

ICUR n.s. VII 17601 preserves the end of a month name *BRIS*. The period from 14.viii-13.xii is therefore possible; we cannot see any basis for preferring one of the months involved.

496

Critical Notes

The stone of *CIL* XII 1724 = *ILCV* 2454 reads CII (= VIII) Kal. Ian., about which the *CIL* editors for some reason say "potius est VIIII quam VII." We cannot see why, and we do not agree. Diehl prints VIII, which we follow.

497

Excluded

P.Stras. 470 (person doubtful)

499

Critical Notes

For *P.Oxy.* XVI 1959 see *P.Mich.* XV 731.1n.

500

Excluded

CIL XII 2074 = *ILCV* 1690 adn. (cos. date?)

IG XIV 2255a+d (cos. date?)

501

Critical Notes

I.Lat.Gaul.Narb. 295 is broken at the right, and it is possible to restore iun. after Avienus' name.

502

Excluded

CIL XIII 2369 = *ILCV* 3516A adn. (name doubtful)

503

Excluded

NotScav 1888, 451 no. 57 (name doubtful)

CIL VI 33841 (name doubtful)

504

Critical Notes

AE 1976, 450b, is dated by the editors to 11.vii; but 12.vii is the correct date (4 Id. Iul.).

Rec.Inscr.Chrét.Gaule XV 286 is dated *XVI Ian.* The editor interprets this as *XV Kal Ian.*, which seems to us an arbitrary emendation. More likely, we think, is the simple omission of *Kal.* Cf. 485 for an analogous case, and now Ferrua, *RAC* 61 (1985) 61-75.

506

Excluded

CIL XIII 2372 (not a consular formula)

Critical Notes

CIL IX 1363 = *ILCV* 3601 was assigned ("videtur") by the editor to 400. Stilicho was known in Rome in January, and the Theodorus of 399 never appears elsewhere in a p.c. In 506, Messala appears in Rome in February, in Nola in April. In either case, therefore, the new consul is known long before September in Rome. What was happening in Aeclanum, we do not know. We think such poor communication is more likely in 506, but we conclude that certainty does not seem attainable.

507

Excluded

CIL XI 7019 = *ILCV* 325 (name doubtful)

Critical Notes

CIL VI 9942 is reread by Ferrua, *Nuove corr.* 16-17, as *V(en)a(ntio) iun. cons.* He dates to 508, but this is the consul of 507.

For *P.Lond.* III 1313 see *ZPE* 62 (1986) 139, notes to lines 1-2.

508

Critical Notes

CIL XI 4978 add. has a date as XIII kal. Nov. (20.x); but the original has XIIII kal. Nov.: Bracceschi, *Magl.*, fol. 366, n.46, cf. *ILCV* 3448.

509

Critical Notes

For *BGU* XII 2181 see *BASP* 17 (1980) 106.

510

Excluded

ICUR n.s. II 5012 (person doubtful)

511

Excluded

CIL XII 2065 (cos. date?)

ICUR n.s. I 1465 (cos. date?)

ICUR n.s. II 5014 (person doubtful)

Critical Notes

We have preferred to date *P.Ness.* 15 in 511 rather than 512 (contra *ZPE* 26 [1977] 283-84) on the grounds that the fifth indiction is more likely reckoned in Rhinocolura on the Pachon indiction (as in Alexandria and Memphis) than the Thoth indiction, plus the fact that in both 511 and 512 only consulates appear in the papyri, disseminated fairly early.

512

Excluded

CIL XII 2860 = *ILCV* 148 (person doubtful)

ICUR n.s. II 5016 (person doubtful)

513

Excluded

I.Lat.Gaul.Narb. 298 (cos. date?)

Agnello, *Silloge* 98, cf. *Kokalos* 28-29 (1982-83) 24-25 no. 78 (reading of name doubtful)

515

Excluded

CIL XII 1499 = *ILCV* 211 (no real consular date, just an allusion)

516

Critical Notes

For *P.Lond.* V 1797 see *BASP* 16 (1979) 246; cf. already *ZPE* 12 (1973) 286.

517

Excluded

CIL XII 2068 = *ILCV* 3631 (cos. date?)

Forsch.Salona II 251 (cos. date?)

NotScav 1897, 367 (name doubtful)

I.Lat.Gaul.Narb. 299 (names doubtful)

ICUR I 1114 (name doubtful)

Critical Notes

CIL IX 1383 = *ILCV* 3185D has *VI Nonas Nobenb* as its date; there is no such date. Vaglieri (*Diz.epigr.* II.2, 1103) dates to 8.xi, taking *Nonas* as error for *Idus*; but one could as well suppose an error for *Kal.* More likely, we think, is inversion of numerals: *VI Nonas* in place of *IV Nonas* (2.xii).

CIL XIII 2375 = *ILCV* 1255 gratuitously restores *Aga[pet]o* instead of the correct *Aga[pit]o*.

Agnello, *Silloge* 98, is dated

>   X Ka[l Iuni]
> [a]s con Agapiti ind d[ecima]

by the editor. But the restoration of June rests on nothing; *[po]s. con.* is possible; and *d[odecima]* could be the indiction number. We see no way of providing a precise date for this stone.

518

Excluded

ICUR I 1168 (name doubtful)

ICUR n.s. I 3247 (name doubtful)

Critical Notes

CIG IV 9449 = *I.Louvre* 280 restores ὑπατίας Φαβίου Μάγνου [μόνου] τοῦ μεγαλοπρεπεστάτου. This restoration is no doubt borrowed from the Fasti, but there is no example of the use of μόνος in this fashion in any inscription (from **any** year). J. Gascou has kindly checked the original stone at our request, and there is no room for the word, which is to be stricken from the text. 'Fabius' is probably just a slip for 'Flavius' (Φλαβίου); cf. *PLRE* II 701 for the full name which does not include Fabius.

519

Excluded

ICUR n.s. I 1215 (cos. date?)

CIL IX 5807 (cos. date?)

520

Excluded

ICUR I 974 (name doubtful)

ICUR n.s. I 3239 = n.s. VIII 22978a (person doubtful)

Critical Notes

I.Lat.Gaul.Narb. 293 was restored by Espérandieu as *[p.c. Constan]tini Aug.* and dated to 410; but as such it would be a unicum, and *I.Lat.Gaul.Narb.* 260, which gives p.c. Iustini, makes a good parallel, also from Vienne. We therefore restore *[p.c. Ius]tini Aug.* in 293 as well. A date to 519 cannot quite be excluded, but the parallel to 260 makes a date in 520 more attractive.

For the date of Grégoire, *Inscr.* 255, see Feissel, *BCH* 105 (1981) 495-96.

521

Critical Notes

CIL V 5192 = *ILCV* 3169A has *Aug* where *vc* is expected after Valerius' name. We suspect a misreading, but the stone is not preserved, and only older copies survive.

522

Excluded

ICUR I 984: De Rossi makes a good case for 522 as the year, but the total loss of the names makes the witness useless for our purposes.

ICUR n.s. I 993 (person doubtful)

Critical Notes

ICUR n.s. II 4280 = *ILCV* 694 gives an amusing view of what some contemporaries thought vvcc meant. The names of the consuls (in the genitive after *consulatu*) are followed by "viris consulibus." Cf. *ILCV* III, p.225 col. a, bottom.

523

Excluded

CIL V 5654 (name doubtful)

525

Excluded

P.Cair.Masp. I 67107 (540 equally possible), cf. *CSBE* s.a. 525

SEG XXIX 643 = Feissel, *Rec.Inscr.Chrét.Macéd.* 133 (person doubtful)

526

Excluded

ICUR I 1009 (cos. date?)

527

Excluded

CIL XII 2099 (name doubtful)

ICUR I 1012 = *ILCV* 686 (name doubtful)

530

Excluded

NotScav 1897, 367 (name doubtful)

Critical Notes

P.Lond. V 1722 was dated by the editor to 573, restoring the consular name as Iustinus (II, the emperor), and it is listed in *CSBE* under that year. Joel Farber, however, informs us that a recent examination of the papyrus at his request by H. Maehler shows that there are sufficient traces to identify the consul as Decius, and the indiction numeral is not sixth but eighth, allowing the year to be identified as 530, p.c. Decii. Maehler reads μετὰ τὴν ὑπατείαν Φλ(αουίου) Δεκ[ίου τοῦ μεγαλοπρεπ(εστάτου)] Φαμεν[ὼ]θ ι. [τ]ῆς [ὀγ]δ[ό]η[ς].

531

Critical Notes

CIL V 3896 is misdated by the index (p.1164) to 20.vii.

533

Critical Notes

For *P.Stras.* 472 see *BASP* 17 (1980) 31; 18 (1981) 46 ff.

CIL IX 1384 is dated to 532 by the editor.

ArchEph 1977, 67, was not recognized by its editor as consular, as he restored it as a regnal year of Justinian. We take it that lines 3-6 should read

μη(νὸς) Σεπ-]
τεμβρ(ίου) ζι ἰν[δ(ικτίονος) ιβ ὑπατείας]
'Ιουστινιαν[οῦ Αὐγ(ούστου) τὸ]
γ

The same conclusion was reached independently by D. Feissel, *Travaux et Mémoires* 9 (1985) 277-78.

534

Critical Notes

For *SB* XIV 11539 see *BASP* 18 (1981) 46-47.

535

Excluded

CIL XII 974 = *ILCV* 1165 adn. (name to be restored is doubtful)

S.J. Saller, B. Bagatti, *The Town of Nebo* (1949) 140 (person doubtful)

Critical Notes

In *CIL* III ad 2659, Mommsen's indiction 15 would imply 536, iterum p.c. Paulini. Revision of the stone by D. Feissel shows that 13 must be read and taken as an error for 14. For the occurrence of Paulinus in the province of Dalmatia, see Mommsen's comments *ad loc.*

538

Excluded

SB III 7201 (see *BASP* 17 [1980] 14-15)

539

Critical Notes

For *P.Cair.Masp.* I 67106 see *ZPE* 26 (1977) 272.

540

Excluded

ICUR I 1070 (name doubtful)

ILCV 1244 adn. (date to p.c. Iustini Aug. cannot refer to Iustinus cos. 540, who was not Aug. Reference must be to cos. 566.)

An early Christian inscription from Penmachno (Caernarvonshire) in Wales has been restored as "in te(m)po[re] Iusti[ni] con[sulis]": V.E. Nash-Williams, *The Early Christian Monuments of Wales* (Cardiff 1950) 93 no.104. A consular date would be unique to all Britain, but that is not in itself reason to reject the restoration; someone from Gaul could well have transmitted the information. And the combination of *Iusti* and *con* is not easy to explain convincingly in any other way. There is, however, no reason to prefer the consulate to the long-used postconsular era of Iustinus, and one can easily envisage a restoration "in te(mpore) po[st cons(ulatum)] etc."

541

Excluded

ICUR I 1072 (person doubtful)

ICUR I 1073-1085, 1087-1126 (Basilius fragments, probably many later than 541, not exactly datable)

ICUR n.s. VIII 20839 = I 1086 (person doubtful)

CIG IV 9279 (completely restored)

AE 1977, 209a-b (person and year doubtful)

Critical Notes

The papyri show p.c. Iustini as late as September. Given this fact, and that *P.Stras.* 597 is a lease (normally contracted in Thoth or later), it seems likely that this papyrus dates from the last four months of the year.

Paulinus

Excluded

A number of inscriptions referring to Paulinus may concern the consul of 499 (with p.c. in 500) or that of 534, p.c. 535. In the latter case, there existed a postconsular 'era' dating well after the consulate (cf. the pages for 535 to 540; but examples go on at least to 552; see Diehl, *ILCV* III, pp.258-59). The following inscriptions are excluded or unplaceable.

CIL V 6287, 7417

CIL X 1346

CIL XI 2586

CIL XII 2075 (= *ILCV* 2891A adn.), 2076, 2077 (= *Rec.Inscr.Chrét.Gaule* XV 161), 2079 (= *ILCV* 1687 adn.)

ICUR I 921, 1051, 1052, 1053 (= *ILCV* 2795C adn.)

ICUR n.s. VII 17603

Miscellany

Excluded

AE 1898, 105 (consulate of one or two emperors, *C[* and (?) *]ino*)

AE 1972, 351 (*]o iuniore v.c.*)

PART IV

BIBLIOGRAPHY

Select List of Works on the Consulate

in the Later Roman Empire

T.J. van Almeloveen, *Fastorum Romanorum consularium libri duo* (Amsterdam 1705, 1740²)

R.S. Bagnall and K.A. Worp, "The Consuls of A.D. 411-412," *Mnemosyne* 31 (1978) 287-93

R.W. Burgess, "The Ninth Consulship of Honorius, A.D. 411 and 412," *ZPE* 65 (1986) 211-21.

A. Cameron, "The Consuls of A.D. 411-412," *BASP* 16 (1979) 175-77

A. Cameron, "The Consuls of A.D. 411-412 Again," *BASP* 18 (1981) 69-72

A. Cameron, "Junior Consuls," *ZPE* 56 (1984) 159-72

A. Cameron and D. Schauer, "The Last Consul: Basilius and his Diptych," *JRS* 72 (1982) 126-43

H.F. Clinton, *Fasti Romani. The Civil and Literary Chronology of Rome and Constantinople from the Death of Augustus to the Death of Justin II*, 2 vols. (Oxford 1845)

A. Degrassi, *I fasti consolari dell'impero Romano dal 30 av. Cristo al 613 d. Cristo* (Rome 1952 = Sussidi eruditi 3)

A.H.M. Jones, "The Constitutional Position of Odoacar and Theoderic," *JRS* 52 (1962) 126-30 (= *The Roman Economy* [Oxford 1974] 365-74)

B. Kübler, "Consul," *RE* 4, 1112 ff., esp. 1133-38

W. Liebenam, *Fasti consulares imperii Romani, von 30 v.Chr. bis 565 n.Chr.* (Bonn 1909 = Kleine Texte für theologische und philologische Vorlesungen und Übungen, 41-43)

A. Lippold, "Consul," *Reallexikon für Antike und Christentum* 3, 390 ff., esp. 398-404

A. Menzer, "Die Jahresmerkmale in den Datierungen der Papsturkunden," *Römische Quartalschrift* 40 (1932) 33-39: Konsulatsjahre

Th. Mommsen, "Ostgotische Studien," *Neues Archiv für ältere deutsche Geschichtskunde* 14 (1889) 225-49 (= *Historische Schriften* III [*Gesammelte Schriften* VI] [Berlin 1910] 362-87)

D. Vaglieri, "Consules," *Dizionario epigrafico* 2, 869 ff., esp. 933-1181

Abbreviations for Works Cited

This list aims principally to include abbreviations and short titles for works cited in the body of this book in other than full bibliographic form, especially corpora of evidence. Papyri are cited according to J.F. Oates et al., *A Checklist of Editions of Papyri and Ostraca*[3] (BASP Suppl. 4, Atlanta 1985), and journals according to the practice of the *American Journal of Archaeology* 80 (1976) 3-8, with minor deviations which should be transparent.

ACO = *Acta Conciliorum Oecumenicorum*, ed. E. Schwartz, 4 vols. (Berlin 1914-1983)

AE = *L'année épigraphique* (Paris, 1888-)

Agnello, *Silloge* = S.L. Agnello, *Silloge di iscrizioni paleocristiane della Sicilia* (Rome 1953)

A. Alföldi, *Die Kontorniaten* = A. Alföldi and E. Alföldi, *Die Kontorniat-Medaillons* (Berlin 1976 = Deutsches Archäologisches Institut, Antike Münzen und Geschnittene Steine 6)

Atti III Congr.int.arch.crist. = *Atti del III Congresso internazionale di archeologia cristiana* (Rome 1934 = Studi di antichità cristiana 8)

Baillet = J. Baillet, *Inscriptions grecques et latines des tombeaux des rois ou syringes à Thèbes* (Cairo 1926 = *Mémoires* de l'Institut français d'archéologie orientale 42)

Bandy = A.C. Bandy, *The Greek Christian Inscriptions from Crete* (Athens 1970)

Barnes, *Constantine and Eusebius* = T.D. Barnes, *Constantine and Eusebius* (Cambridge, Mass. 1981)

Barnes, *NE* (or) *New Empire* = T.D. Barnes, *The New Empire of Diocletian and Constantine* (Cambridge, Mass. 1982)

Besevliev, *Spätgriech. u. spätlat. Inschr. aus Bulg.* = V. Besevliev, *Spätgriechische und spätlateinische Inschriften aus Bulgarien* (Berlin 1964 = Berliner Byzantinistische Arbeiten 30)

BES = *Bulletin of the Egyptological Seminar* (New York)

Beth Shearim = *Beth She'arim* (Jerusalem 1973-) II: *The Greek Inscriptions*, ed. M. Schwabe and B. Lifshitz

Brooks, *Chron.Min.* = *Corpus Scriptorum Christianorum Orientalium* Scriptores Syri, 3 ser. 4, *Chronica Minora* 3, ed. E.W. Brooks (Paris 1905)

Bull.épigr. = J. and L. Robert, "Bulletin épigraphique," in *REG* (cited by year and item number)

Chastagnol, *Les Fastes* = A. Chastagnol, *Les fastes de la préfecture de Rome au Bas-Empire* (Paris 1962 = Etudes prosopographiques 2)

Christol, *Essai* = M. Christol, *Essai sur l'évolution des carrières sénatoriales* (Paris 1986)

Chron.Min. = *Chronica Minora*, ed. Th. Mommsen (Berlin 1892-1898 = Monumenta Germaniae Historica, Auctores Antiquissimi 9, 11, 13)

CIG = *Corpus Inscriptionum Graecarum*, ed. A. Boeckh et al. (Berlin 1828-1877)

CIJ = *Corpus Inscriptionum Judaicarum*, ed. J.B. Frey (Rome 1936 = Sussidi allo studio delle antichità cristiane 1)

CIL = *Corpus Inscriptionum Latinarum* (Berlin 1863-)

CIL, Suppl.Ital. = E. Pais, *Supplementa Italica Corporis Inscriptionum Latinarum,* fasc. I: *Additamenta ad volumen V, Italiae Cisalpinae* (Rome 1888)

Civiltà Cattolica = *Civiltà Cattolica. Pubblicazione periodica per tutta l'Italia* (Napoli 1850-)

CJ = *Codex Justinianus*, ed. P. Krüger (Berlin 1877)

CLA = E.A. Lowe, *Codices Latini Antiquiores. A Palaeographical Guide to Latin Manuscripts Prior to the ninth Century*, 11 vols. (Oxford 1934-1966)

Collatio = *Mosaicarum et Romanorum Legum Collatio* in *FIRA* II 543-89

Coll.Avell. = *Epistulae imperatorum pontificum aliorum inde ab a. CCCLXVII usque ad a. DLIII datae, Avellana quae dicitur collectio*, ed. O. Günther (Wien 1895 = CSEL 35)

Conc.Africae = C. Munier, *Concilia Africae a. 345-525* (Turnhout 1974 = Corp.Christ.Lat. 149)

Conc.Galliae = C. Munier, C. de Clerq, *Concilia Galliae a. 314-506, a.511-695*, 2 vols. (Turnhout 1963 = Corp.Christ.Lat. 148, 148A)

Const.Sirm. = *Constitutiones Sirmondianae*; cf. *CTh*

Consultatio = *Consultatio Veteris Cuiusdam Iurisconsulti*, in *FIRA* II 593-613

Corinth VIII.1 = *Corinth. Results of the Excavation Conducted by the American School at Athens* VIII.1: *Greek Inscriptions 1896-1927*, ed. B.D. Meritt (Cambridge, Mass. 1931)

Corp.Christ.Lat. = Corpus Christianorum, Series Latina (Turnhout 1953-)

CSBE = R.S. Bagnall and K.A. Worp, *The Chronological Systems of Byzantine Egypt* (Zutphen 1978 = Studia Amstelodamensia ad epigraphicam, ius antiquum, et papyrologicam pertinentia 8)

CSEL = Corpus Scriptorum Ecclesiasticorum Latinorum (Vienna 1866-)

Crum, *Short Texts* = W.E. Crum, *Short Texts from Coptic Ostraca and Papyri* (London 1921)

CTh = *Codex Theodosianus cum constitutionibus Sirmondianis et leges novellae ad Theodosianum pertinentes*, ed. Th. Mommsen and P.M. Meyer (Berlin 1905)

Delbrueck = R. Delbrueck, *Die Consulardiptychen und verwandte Denkmäler; Studien zur spätantiken Kunstgeschichte* II (Berlin 1929)

Dumont-Homolle = A. Dumont, *Mélanges d'archéologie et d'épigraphie*, ed. by Th. Homolle (Paris 1892)

Ebersolt, *Mission arch. de Constantinople* = J. Ebersolt, *Mission archéologique de Constantinople* (Paris 1921)

Ennabli, *Inscr.Fun.Chrét.Basil.Carthage* = L. Ennabli, *Les inscriptions funéraires chrétiennes de la basilique dite de Sainte Monique à Carthage* (Rome 1975 = Collection de l'Ecole Française de Rome 25)

Epigr.Anatol. = *Epigraphica Anatolica. Zeitschrift für Epigraphik und historische Geographie Anatoliens* (Bonn 1983-)

Feissel, *Recueil Inscr.Chrét.Macéd.* = D. Feissel, *Recueil des inscriptions chrétiennes de Macédonie du IIIe au VIe siècle* (Athens 1983 = *BCH* Suppl. 8)

Ferrua, *Nuove corr.* = A. Ferrua, *Nuove correzioni alla Silloge del Diehl "Inscriptiones Latinae Christianae Veteres"* (Città del Vaticano 1981)

FHG = *Fragmenta Historicorum Graecorum*, ed. C. Müller (Paris 1841-1851)

FIRA = *Fontes Iuris Romani Anteiustiniani*, edd. S. Riccobono et all. (Florence 1968-1972^2)

Forsch.Salona = *Forschungen in Salona veröffentlicht vom Österreichischen Archäologischen Institut/Archäologischen Institut des Deutschen Reiches* (Vienna 1917, 1926, 1939)

Frag.Vat. = *Fragmenta quae dicuntur Vaticana*, in *FIRA* II 463-540

Führer, *Forsch. zur Sicilia Sotterranea* = J. Führer, *Forschungen zur Sicilia Sotterranea* (München 1897 = *AbhMünchen* 20.3)

Grégoire, *Inscr.* = H. Grégoire, *Recueil des inscriptions grecques-chrétiennes d'Asie Mineure* I (Paris 1922)

Grumel, *La chronologie* = V. Grumel, *La chronologie* = Traité d'études byzantines 1 (Paris 1958)

Haenel, *Corpus Legum* = G. Haenel, *Corpus Legum ab imperatoribus Romanis ante Iustinianum latarum* (Leipzig 1857)

Halkin, *Douze récits* = F. Halkin, *Douze récits byzantins sur Saint Jean Chrysostome* (Brussels 1977 = Subsidia Hagiographica 60)

R. Heberdey and A. Wilhelm, *Reisen in Kilikien* = R. Heberdey and A. Wilhelm, *Reisen in Kilikien* (Vienna 1896 = DenkschrWien 44.6)

Heuzey-Daumet = L. Heuzet and H. Daumet, *Mission archéologique de Macédoine* (Paris 1876)

I.Ant.Maroc II = *Inscriptions antiques du Maroc* II: *Inscriptiones latines*, ed. J. Gascou (Paris 1982)

I.Chrét.Mactar = *Recherches archéologiques franco-tunisiennes à Mactar* V: *Les inscriptions chrétiennes*, ed. F. Prévot (Coll. de l'Ecole Française de Rome 34, Rome 1984)

I.Christ.Ital. = *Inscriptiones Christianae Italiae VII s. antiquiores* (Bari 19??-)

I.Cret. = *Inscriptiones Creticae*, ed. M. Guarducci (Rome 1935-1950)

ICUR = G.B. De Rossi, *Inscriptiones Christianae urbis Romae septimo saeculo antiquiores*, 2 vols. (Rome 1857-1861, 1886); *Supplementum* to vol. 1 by J. Gatti (Rome 1915)

ICUR n.s. = A. Silvagni and A. Ferrua, *Inscriptiones Christianae Urbis Romae*, nova series, 9 vols. to date (Rome 1922-)

I.Ephesos = *Die Inschriften aus Ephesos*, ed. R. Merkelbach et al. (Bonn 1979- = Inschriften Griechischer Städte aus Kleinasien 11-17)

IG = *Inscriptiones Graecae* (Berlin 1873-)

I.Gr.Palermo = *Iscrizioni greche lapidarie del Museo di Palermo*, ed. M.T. Manni Piraino (Palermo 1972)

IGRR = *Inscriptiones Graecae ad Res Romanas pertinentes*, ed. R. Cagnat, G. Lafaye (Paris 1911-1927)

IGUR = *Inscriptiones Graecae Urbis Romae*, ed. L. Moretti (Rome 1968-1979 = Studi pubblicati dall'Istituto Italiano per la storia antica 17,22,28)

I.Ital. = *Inscriptiones Italiae* (Rome 1931-)

I.Kalchedon = *Die Inschriften von Kalchedon*, ed. R. Merkelbach et al. (Bonn 1980 = Inschriften Griechischer Städte aus Kleinasien 20)

I.Lat.Alg. = *Inscriptions latines de l'Algérie*, ed. S. Gsell and H.G. Pflaum (Paris/Alger 1922-)

I.Lat.Gaul.Narb. = *Inscriptions latines de Gaule (Narbonnaise)*, ed. E. Espérandieu (Paris 1929)

I.Lat.Paestum = *Le iscrizioni latine di Paestum*, ed. M. Mello and G. Voza (Naples 1968)

I.Lat.Sard. = *Iscrizioni latine della Sardegna*, ed. G. Sotgiu (Padua 1961-1968)

I.Lat.3 Gaules = *Inscriptions latines des Trois Gaules*, ed. P. Wuilleumier (Paris 1965 = Gallia Suppl. 17)

I.Lat.Tun. = *Inscriptions de la Tunisie*, ed. A. Merlin (Paris 1944)

ILCV = E. Diehl, *Inscriptiones Latinae Christianae Veteres*, 3 vols. (Berlin 1924-31); v.4 by J. Moreau and H.I. Marrou (Berlin 1967)

I.Louvre = *Musée Impérial du Louvre. Les inscriptions grecques*, ed. W. Froehner (Paris 1865)

ILS = *Inscriptiones Latinae Selectae*, ed. H. Dessau (Berlin 1892-1916)

I.Més.Sup. = *Inscriptions de la Mésie Supérieure* (Belgrade 1976-)

I.Smyrna = *Die Inschriften von Smyrna* I, ed. G. Petzl (Bonn 1982 = Inschriften Griechischer Städte aus Kleinasien 23)

Jaffé, *Regesta* = Ph. Jaffé, *Regesta Pontificum Romanorum*, 2nd ed. by F. Kaltenbrunner et al. (Leipzig 1885)

Jones, *LRE* = A.H.M. Jones, *The Later Roman Empire* (Oxford 1964)

Kent, *Roman Coins* = J.P.C. Kent, *Roman Coins* (London 1978)

Kent and Painter, *Wealth of the Roman World* = J.P.C. Kent and K.S. Painter, *Wealth of the Roman World, A.D. 300-700* (London 1977)

Kraeling, *Gerasa* = C.H. Kraeling, ed., *Gerasa, City of the Decapolis* (New Haven 1938)

Lanata, *Atti dei Martiri* = G. Lanata, *Gli atti dei martiri come documenti processuali* (Milan 1973)

LBW = Ph. LeBas and W.H. Waddington, *Voyage archéologique en Grèce et en Asie Mineure pendant 1834-1844* III (Paris 1870)

Liber Pontificalis = *Le Liber Pontificalis*, ed. L. Duchesne (Paris 1886 ff.; new ed. with additional volume, Paris 1955)

MAMA = *Monumenta Asiae Minoris Antiqua* (Manchester 1928-)

Mansi = *Sacrorum conciliorum nova et amplissima collectio*, ed. J.D. Mansi (Florence 1759 ff.)

Marini, *Pap.Dipl.* = *I papiri diplomatici raccolti ed illustrati dell'Abate Gaetano Marini...* (Rome 1805)

Marucchi, *Museo Lat.* = O. Marucchi, *I monumenti dell museo cristiano Pio-Lateranense* (Milan 1910)

MGH = Monumenta Germaniae Historica

Migne: see *PG, PL*

Milne, *Gk.Inscr.Cairo* = Catalogue général des antiquités égyptiennes du Musée du Caire, Nos. 9201-9400, 26001-26123, 33001-33037: *Greek Inscriptions*, by J.G. Milne (Cairo 1905)

Misc.Pap. = *Miscellanea Papyrologica*, ed R. Pintaudi (Florence 1980 = Papyrologica Florentina 7)

Mommsen, *Ges.Schriften* = Th. Mommsen, *Gesammelte Schriften* I-VIII.1 (Berlin 1905-1913)

Mommsen, *Hist.Schriften* = Th. Mommsen, *Historische Schriften* in *Ges.Schriften* IV-VI

Mommsen, *Staatsrecht* = Th. Mommsen, *Römisches Staatsrecht* I-III (Leipzig 1887-1888)

Mommsen, "Zeitfolge der Verordnungen Diokletians," = Th. Mommsen, "Über die Zeitfolge der Verordnungen Diokletians und seiner Mitregenten," in *AbhBerlin* 1860, 349-447 (= *Ges.Schriften* II 195-291)

Musurillo, *Acts of the Christian Martyrs* = H. Musurillo, *The Acts of the Christian Martyrs* (Oxford 1972)

Nov = *Novella* (cited for the novels of the predecessors of Justinian after the edition in the *CTh*; Justinian's novels cited after the edition by R. Schoell and W. Kroll [Berlin 1895])

OGIS = *Orientis Graecae Inscriptiones Selectae*, ed. W. Dittenberger (Leipzig 1903-1905)

PG = *Patrologiae cursus completus, series Graeca*, ed. J.P. Migne (Paris 1857 ff.)

PL = *Patrologiae cursus completus, series Latina*, ed. J.P. Migne (Paris 1844 ff.)

Princ.Arch.Exp.Syria = *Syria. Publications of the Princeton University Archaeological Expeditions to Syria in 1904-5 and 1901, Division III: Greek and Latin Inscriptions*, by E. Littman, D. Magie et al. (Leiden 1921)

PLRE = *The Prosopography of the Later Roman Empire*, ed. A.H.M. Jones, J.R. Martindale, J. Morris (Cambridge 1971-)

Rav.Ann. = *Annals of Ravenna* (cf. p.00 for bibliographic details)

RE = *Real-Encyclopaedie der klassischen Altertumswissenschaft*, ed. A. Pauly, G. Wissowa, W. Kroll et al. (1893-)

Rec.Inscr.Chrét.Gaule = *Recueil des Inscriptions chrétiennes de la Gaule antérieures à la Renaissance carolingienne* I: *Première Belgique*, ed. N. Gauthier (Paris 1975); XV: *Viennoise du Nord*, ed. F. Descombes (Paris 1985)

RIC = *Roman Imperial Coinage*

Robert, *Hellenica* = L. Robert, *Hellenica. Recueil d'épigraphie, de numismatique et d'antiquités grecques* (Paris 1940-1965)

Röm.Inschr.Tarraco = G. Alföldy, *Die römischen Inschriften von Tarraco* (Berlin 1975 = Madrider Forschungen 10)

Röm.Inschr.Ung. = *Die römischen Inschriften Ungarns*, ed. L. Barkóczi et al. (Amsterdam/Budapest 1972-)

Röm.Quart. = *Römische Quartalschrift für christliche Altertumskunde und für Kirchengeschichte* (Rome 1887-)

Rugo, *Le iscrizioni dei sec. VI-VII-VIII esistenti in Italia* = P. Rugo, *Le iscrizioni dei sec. VI-VII-VIII esistenti in Italia* (Cittadella 1974-)

Sardis VII.1 = *Sardis. Publications of the American Society for the Excavations of Sardis* VII.1: *Greek and Latin Inscriptions*, ed. W.H. Buckler and D.M. Robinson (Leiden 1932)

Seeck, *Regesten* = O. Seeck, *Regesten der Kaiser und Päpste für die Jahre 311 bis 476 n.Chr.* (Stuttgart 1919)

SEG = *Supplementum Epigraphicum Graecum* (Leiden 1923-)

Stein, *Bas-Empire* = E. Stein, *Histoire du Bas-Empire* (Paris-Bruges 1949-1959)

Studi Calderini-Paribeni = *Studi in onore di A. Calderini e R. Paribeni*, 3 vols. (Milan 1956)

Suppl.Ital. = *Supplementa Italica*, published by the Unione Accademica Nazionale (Rome 1981-)

Syll.[3] = W. Dittenberger, *Sylloge Inscriptionum Graecarum*, 3rd ed. (Leipzig 1915-1924)

Thiel = A. Thiel, *Epistulae Romanorum Pontificum genuinae* I (Braunsberg 1867-1868)

Tjäder, *Nichtlit.Pap.* = J.O. Tjäder, *Die nicht-literarischen lateinischen Papyri Italiens aus der Zeit 445-700* I (Lund 1954), II (Stockholm 1982) (= Acta Instituti Romani Regni Sueciae, ser. in 4o, 19.1-2)

Toynbee, *Roman Medallions* = J.M.C. Toynbee, *Roman Medallions* (New York 1944; 1986[2] with additional bibliography)

Vandersleyen, *Chronologie des préfets* = C. Vandersleyen, *Chronologie des préfets d'Egypte de 284 à 395* (Brussels 1962 = Collection Latomus 55)

Vermaseren, *Corpus Inscr. et Monum.rel.Mithr.* = M.J. Vermaseren, *Corpus Inscriptionum et Monumentorum religionis Mithriacae* (The Hague 1956-1960)

Vives, *ICERV* = José Vives, *Inscripciones cristianas de la España romana y visigoda* (Barcelona 1942)

Volbach = W.F. Volbach, *Elfenbeinarbeiten der Spätantike und des frühen Mittelalters*, 3rd ed. (Mainz/Rhein 1976 = Röm. Germ. Zentralmuseum zu Main. Kataloge Vor- und Frühgeschichtlicher Altertümer 7)

Von Soden, *Urkunden* = H. von Soden, *Urkunden zur Entstehungsgeschichte des Donatismus*, 2nd ed. (Berlin 1950 = Kleine Texte für Vorlesungen und Übungen 122)

Walser, *RIS* = G. Walser, *Römische Inschriften in der Schweiz* II: *Nordwest- und Nordschweiz* (Bern 1980)

WB = F. Preisigke, *Wörterbuch der griechischen Papyrusurkunden* (Berlin 1925 ff.)

Zetzel, *Latin Textual Criticism* = J.E.G. Zetzel, *Latin Textual Criticism in Antiquity* (New York 1981)

PART V

INDICES

Index 1

Index of Names of Consuls

The list below gives in alphabetical order the names of all persons who served as consuls between A.D. 284 and 541. The purpose of the list is primarily to facilitate the study of documents (papyri and inscriptions) in which a consulate is partly preserved. In general, only one spelling of each name is given, except in the case of very divergent forms used in documents from the East compared with those of the West. After each name is given the year in which the name occurs (sometimes as part of a fuller nomenclature) in the consular formula. One should check following years in order to see whether there are any attestations of a given name in a postconsular formula. The name Flavius is not indexed, as it is found commonly throughout most of this period.

Ablabius	331
Abundantius	393
Achilius	481, 488
Acilius	323, 438, 483
Acindynus	340
Aconius	349, 471
Adelfius	451
Aetius	432, 437, 446, 454
Afranius	382
Agapitus	517
Aginantius	483
Aginatius	444
Agricola	421
Albinus	335, 345, 444, 493
Alypius	447
Amantius	345
Anastasius	492, 497, 507, 517
Anatolius	440
Andronicus	310
Anicius	298, 322, 325, 334, 350, 395, 406, 408, 431, 438, 483, 490, 510
Annianus	314
Annius	295
Anthemius	405, 436, 455, 468, 515
Antiochus	431
Antonius	316, 341, 382
Anullinus	295

Index 2

Reverse Index of Consular Names

Cillica
Salia
Messala
Agricola
Caecina
Plinta
Fravitta
Nevitta

Leo
Stilicho
Dio
Opilio
Apio
Glabrio
Arbitio
Zeno
Gaiso
Bauto

Aspar
Celer
Ricimer
Ricomer
Beator
Viator
Senator
Dexicrator
Victor
Ardabur

Trocundes
Merobaudes
Iordanes
Varanes
Protogenes
Iohannes

Dexicrates
Orestes
Crealis
Constans
Valens
Phoebus
Probus
Andronicus
Eutharicus
Theodericus
Hermenericus
Atticus
Marcus
Basiliscus
Tuscus
Seleucus
Placidus
Rumoridus
Areobindus
Facundus
Pusaeus
Arintheus
Dagalaifus
Rufus
Cethegus
Symmachus
Nichomachus
Antiochus
Clearchus
Dagalaiphus
Gaius
Fabius
Ablabius
Eusebius
Libius
Volcacius
Sporacius

Maecius	Caecinius
Decius	Licinius
Anicius	Ovinius
Patricius	Annius
Rusticius	Aconius
Turcius	Ragonius
Lucius	Ionius
Arcadius	Caeionius
Palladius	Apollonius
Gennadius	Populonius
Lampadius	Nonius
Praesidius	Petronius
Sividius	Caesonius
Clodius	Ausonius
Euodius	Faltonius
Claudius	Antonius
Studius	Iunius
Pompeius	Papius
Adelfius	Calepius
Rufius	Ulpius
Cynegius	Eutropius
Sergius	Alypius
Eparchius	Marius
Adelphius	Caesarius
Eustathius	Belisarius
Boethius	Olybrius
Appalius	Eucherius
Caelius	Hierius
Aurelius	Galerius
Acilius	Valerius
Mecilius	Paterius
Achilius	Neoterius
Basilius	Asterius
Mallius	Magrius
Manlius	Syagrius
Anatolius	Virius
Iulius	Honorius
Dynamius	Nestorius
Anthemius	Furius
Polemius	Astyrius
Septimius	Timasius
Eutolmius	Anastasius
Memmius	Maesius
Nummius	Ecclesius
Postumius	Theodosius
Afranius	Cassius
Eugenius	Messius
Auchenius	Dionysius
Limenius	Dalmatius

Egnatius
Aginatius
Hypatius
Naeratius
Tatius
Statius
Aetius
Domitius
Equitius
Abundantius
Amantius
Venantius
Aginantius
Constantius
Decentius
Vincentius
Magnentius
Florentius
Maxentius
Leontius
Mavortius
Sallustius
Tettius
Vettius
Flavius
Monaxius
Eudoxius
Vincomalus
Zenophilus
Gallus
Illus
Tertullus
Paulus
Aristobulus
Proculus
Romulus
Decimus
Maximus
Nomus
Gallicanus
Probianus
Felicianus
Marcianus
Moschianus
Eutychianus
Hannibalianus
Vitalianus
Heraclianus

Aurelianus
Opilianus
Lollianus
Tullianus
Iulianus
Maximianus
Postumianus
Hermogenianus
Sabinianus
Ianuarianus
Tiberianus
Numerianus
Maiorianus
Volusianus
Pacatianus
Datianus
Gratianus
Tatianus
Diocletianus
Titianus
Quintianus
Nepotianus
Flavianus
Vivianus
Iovianus
Herculanus
Romanus
Avienus
Philoxenus
Magnus
Sabinus
Albinus
Probinus
Lupicinus
Secundinus
Rufinus
Longinus
Aquilinus
Marcellinus
Anullinus
Catullinus
Paulinus
Maximinus
Saturninus
Carinus
Ianuarinus
Severinus
Constantinus

Clementinus
Mamertinus
Castinus
Iustinus
Iovinus
Inportunus
Licinianus
Marinianus
Nigrinianus
Valentinianus
Iustinianus
Annianus
Apronianus
Varronianus
Hilarianus
Petrus
Taurus
Cyrus
Bonosus
Ursus
Bassus
Armatus
Optatus
Praetextatus
Aristaenetus

Agapitus
Avitus
Sigisvultus
Quintus
Opportunus
Acindynus
Philippus
Crispus
Severus
Dioscorus
Isidorus
Theodorus
Cassiodorus
Asclepiodotus
Promotus
Quartus
Modestus
Festus
Faustus
Iustus
Sextus

Hierax
Felix

Index 3

Index of Subjects

References to the introduction are given to page numbers (not otherwise designated); references to the commentaries to the year-by-year are given by the *year number* followed by the # sign; references to the Critical Appendix are given by the *year number* followed by the * sign. Misc.* and Paulinus* refer to the sections at the end of the Critical Appendix.

Abbreviations in consular dates: 62, 77-78
--in imperial laws: 72
Abolition of consuls: see Repudiation
Accepta dates in imperial constitutions: 72, 76
Acclamations, in Senate at acceptance of Theodosian Code: 6; against Bp. Ibas of Edessa: 29
Achaea: 333#
Aco, Aconius, Acontius: 349#
Add. ad Prosp.: 50
Adnotationes antiquiores ad cyclos Dionysianos: 57
Aeclanum: 434#, 506*
Africa: 301#, 325#, 323#, 333#, 358#, 367#, 401#, 413#, 429#, 434#, 451#, 535#
--lack of inscriptions with consular dates from: 60
--late dissemination to: 33
--postconsular dates in imperial constitutions sent to: 79, 81
Alani: 427#
Alaric: 410#
Alexandria: 511*
Alexandrian chronicles: 52
Alius, alius iunior in consular nomenclature: 43
Amalsuntha, d. of Theoderic: 519#
Ammianus Marcellinus: 89
Anagastes, Thracian MVM: 470#
Anicia, gens: 371#, 465*, 523#
Anicia Juliana: 491#
Annales Ravennates: 49
Annals, consular: 48, 54
--of Ravenna: 49
Annullment of consuls: see Repudiation
Anonymus Valesianus: 50
Anticipare, meaning of: 21
Antioch: 333#
Aq., AqS: 51
Aquileia: 380#, 382#
Aquitania: 405#

Canusium (Canossa): 393*
Capena: 407#
Capua: 381#, 393*
Carausius: 287#, 290#
Carthage: 358#, 373#, 382#, 399#, 401#, 405#, 413#, 419#, 434#, 435#
Cassiodorus: 52
Cassius Dio (the historian): 291#
Catania: 402#, 434#
Ceionius Rufius Albinus, PVR *ca* 389: 390*
Chalcedon, Council of: 85, 449#, 449*, 453#
Christians, Christianity: 317#, 367*
Chronica Caesaraugustana: 57
Chronica Gallica (*Chr.Gall.*): 57
Chronica Minora of Mommsen: 47
Chronicon Paschale: 47, 56
Chronographer of 354: 47-48, 307#, 308#, 311#, 317#, 351#, 352#, 378#, 399#
Ciz.: 51
Claudian: 398#, 399#
Codex Gregorianus: 71
Codex Hermogenianus: 71
Codex Iustinianus: 71
Codex Theodosianus: 71; editorial process: 74
Coins and medallions, consular: 86
Collectio Avellana, omission of consular names in: 76
Cologne (Colonia Agrippinensium): 346*
Communication between imperial capitals: 27, 30
Como (Comum): 453#, 453*
Computatio anni 452 (*Comput.*): 57
Confusion between imperial consulates: 76
Constans, consular nominations by: 14; status of: 14
Constantine I, appointed high proportion of aristocrats as consuls: 5
--sons of, consular nominations by: 14
Constantinople: 381#, 383#, 411#, 437#, 443#, 444#, 451#, 464#, 520#
--Different political situation from Rome: 9
Constitutiones Sirmondianae: see Sirmondian Constitutions
Consul II on basis of cos. I suff.: 3
Consul suffectus: 284#, 289#, 298#, 301#, 311#, 343#, 345#; see also suffect consulate
Consular annals: 48, 54; illustrated: 55
--career: 3
--dates in laws, reliability of: 73
--diptychs: 11, 87
--distributions of money: 10; 457#
--dynasties: 5-6
--fasti, gaps in: 7; correction to reflect winning side: 25
--formulas: 17-18, 63, 83; with numerals only: 68, 78
--games: 9-10
--medallions: 86
--panegyric: 19
--solidi: 86, 457#

Dissemination (promulgation), 25-35
--late: 328#, 330#, 336#, 337#, 339#, 345#, 350#, 356#, 359#, 360#, 362#, 364#, 366#, 367#, 368#,
    373#, 379#, 380#, 386#, 387#, 389#, 396#, 399#, 400#, 401#, 411#, 415#, 416#, 417#, 418#,
    419#, 420#, 421#, 423#, 426#, 427#, 429#, 432#, 433#, 434#, 436#, 439#, 443#, 447#, 450#,
    452#, 453*, 454#, 459#, 460#, 462#, 463#, 466#, 468#, 469#, 470#, 472#, 478#, 480#, 482#,
    484#, 489#, 491#, 493#, 495#, 496#, 499#, 502#, 506#, 526#, 527#, 535#;
--collapse of: 486#, 491#, 497#, 512#, 513#, 515#, 517#, 521#, 528#
--failure of: 25
--fitfulness of in fifth century: 25
--lack of eastern names in West: 25
--official formula sent out: 26
--slowness to Egypt in fifth and sixth centuries: 30
Divus: 364#, 364*, 367*, 371*
D(omino) N(ostro), DD.NN.: 293*, 335*, 360*, 363#, 364*, 368*, 383*, 393*, 417*, 422*, 462#, 468*
Documents, imperial, transmission of: 28
Double dates in laws: 28, 79, 81
Duration of consulate: 20-22
--entire year by mid fourth century: 20

East, attempt to keep consulate in civilian hands: 5
--differences from West in use of Flavius: 39-40
--lack of inscriptions with consular dates: 28, 60
Eastern consuls, omission in western inscriptions: 34, 64-65; in other western sources: 34
Egypt: 319#, 325*, 328#, 330#, 336#, 337#, 345#, 346#, 350#, 359#, 360#, 363#, 373#, 383#*, 389#,
    396#, 403#, 417*, 419#, 420#, 421#, 422#, 423#, 426#, 444#, 449#, 452#, 459#, 466#, 468#,
    470#, 472#, 478#, 488#, 520#, 526#, 527#
--abundance of original documents from: 29
--quick and uniform dissemination of formulas within: 67
Emperors, eastern, contribution to consular expenses: 9
Emperors, taking of consulates: 23-24; right to nominate consuls: 13-14; see also Augusti
Entertainment, expenditures on: 9
Ephesus: 449#
Ephesus, Council of: 28-29, 431#
Epiphanestatos (as consular epithet): 320*, 357*
Epirus: 530#
Epitaphs of members of senatorial families: 61
Equestrian order, assimilation to senatorial: 2
"Ergänzte Konsulate": 76
Errors in consular datings
--In papyri: 68
--In votive and dedicatory inscriptions: 61
--Iteration numerals: 68-69, 287#, 287*, 291#, 298*, 298#, 298*, 301#, 303*, 312*, 314#, 318*, 321#, 343*,
    361*, 365*, 367*, 371#, 373*, 376*, 383*, 396*, 411#, 414*, 420#, 425#, 427*, 430*, 439*, 440#,
    446#,   454#, 474*, 479#, 479*, 486#, 528#
--False p.c.'s in the laws: 368#
--Omission of or confusion in names: 66, 298# (cf. 291#), 292#, 296#, 304#, 307#, 311#, 315#, 318*,
    321#, 337#, 342*, 346*, 350#, 403#, 405#, 407#, 414#, 423#, 447#, 448#, 449#, 456#, 458#,
    460#, 463#, 471#, 473#, 476#, 483*, 488#, 501#, 509#

Hermopolis: 325*, 473*
Hilary, Pope: 465#
Historia Acephala: 89
Historia Brittonum cum add. Nennii (*Hist.Britt.*): 57
Holder-Egger, O.: 49
Honorius, ninth consulate of: 16-17; vota celebrations of: 17
Hormisdas, Pope: 34, 515#, 517#, 521#
Hyd.: 54

Ibas, Bp. of Edessa: 29
Illustrated chronicles and consular annals: 53, 55
Illyricum: 467#, 505#
Imperial consulates, proportion of: 4; confusion between: 66, 76; occasions for: 23-24
Imperial laws, elements of: 72; issuance from court: 79
Indictions: 7, 482#, 312*, 417*, 453*, 477*, 487*, 491*, 517*, 535*
Innocentius, Pope: 404#, 405#, 414#, 416#
Inportunus: 42
Interamna (Terni): 386#, 489*
Isauria: 448#, 462#, 478#
Ital. (*Consularia Italica*): 48
Italian nationalism: 34
Italy: 350#, 353#, 402#, 406*, 407#, 411#, 412*, 423#, 432#, 433#, 434#, 453*, 456#, 475#, 479#, 489*,
    491#, 491*, 492#, 493#, 514#, 535#
Iteration numerals, errors in papyri with: 68-69
--omission of: 61, 63
Iunior: 40-46, 53; as alternative to full name: 45; use in *Fasti Veronenses*: 42-43

Jerome, St.: 404#
John, western usurper: 424#
John Chrysostom: 405#
John Lydus: 512#
Judicial functions of consuls: 1
Julius Nepos, mag.mil.Dalm., western Aug. in 473: 475#
Justa Grata Honoria, sister of Valentinian III: 452#
Justin II, consulate in 566: 12

Late distribution of consular solidi: 457#
Laterculus Regum Vandalorum: 57
Laws, correction of dates in: 27
--excerpts from: 74
Lecta: 72
Leo, Pope: 453#, 453*, 455#, 459#
Leontia, d. of Leo Aug.: 469#
Liber genealogus: 57
Liber paschalis codicis Cizensis: 51
Liber pontificalis: 88
Liberius, father of Venantius: 507#
Lipari: 470#
Local eras in Africa and the Orient: 60

Pannonia: 307*, 310#, 375#

Papal letters: 88; forged: 46

Papyri: 67ff.; errors in datings in: 68

Pasch.: 56

Paschal Chronicle, see *Chronicon Paschale*

Paschale Campanum: 50

Patricians, patriciate: 334#, 428#, 460*, 466#, 475#, 507#

Perpetui Augusti (pp.Augg.): 339#, 417*

Persia: 535#

Philostorgius: 420#, 424#

Phrygia: 441#

Piano Laroma: 384#

Placentia (Piacenza): 456#

Placidia, d. of Valentinian III: 464#

Polemius Silvius: 21, 57, 449#

Political explanations for omitted names in inscriptions: 64

Porfyrius: 326#

Post alia, formula: 74

Postconsulate: 65-66, 76ff., 307#, 308#, 310#, 311*, 317#, 319#, 322#, 340#, 342*, 345*, 349*, 350#,
    356#, 358#, 359#, 359*, 360#, 362#, 364#, 367#, 367*, 368#, 370#, 372#, 373*, 374*, 375*, 377#,
    378#, 379*, 380#, 381#, 381*, 382#, 382*, 383*, 384#, 385#, 386#, 388#, 388*, 390*, 392#, 393#,
    393*, 395*, 398*, 399#, 401#, 402#, 403#, 403*, 405#, 405*, 409#, 410#, 413#, 414#, 417*, 419#,
    420#, 429#, 429*, 430#, 431#, 433#, 434#, 434*, 435*, 436#, 437#, 441#, 441*, 443#, 447#, 449#,
    451#, 452*, 453#, 453*, 454#, 456#, 457#, 458#, 460#, 461#, 473*, 474*, 475#, 476#, 476*, 479#,
    480#, 481#, 485#, 486#, 486*, 487#, 488#, 489#, 489*, 490#, 490*, 491#, 495#, 496#, 503#,
    505#, 506*, 507#, 508#, 516#, 517#, 517*, 520*, 530#, 534#, 541*

--confusion with consulate: 83

--iterum p.c.: 474*, 476*, 477#, 478#, 487#, 487*, 489*, 490*, 491*, 530#, 535*

--et iterum p.c.: 533*

--overlap with consular dates: 29, 68

P.p. = proposita: 72

PPO = Praefectus praetorio: 72

Praeneste: 385*

Prefectures, ranked below consulate in later fourth century: 3; importance of urban prefecture to arist-
    ocracy: 8

Praefecti praetorio, edicts of: 83

Praelata: 72

Praetextatus, Vettius Agorius, consular designation and death: 15, 18

Praetorian games: 19

Praetors, advance designation of: 19

Probus, PPO before 384: 384#

Proclamation: 13-18

--late: 308#, 317#, 319#, 324#, 350#, 366#, 380#, 387#, 411#, 413#, 414#, 420#, 428#, 429#, 431#,
    444#, 450#, 455#, 456#, 500#, 502#, 506#, 507#, 513#, 515#, 527#

--role of emperors: 13

--separate in East and West after 411: 16-17

--simultaneous until 411: 13, 16-17; after 411: 18

Proconsul: 301 (Africae), 325#, 325* (Africae), 333#

Prologus Paschae: 57

Proposita dates: 72, 76
Prosper Tiro (*Prosp.*): 50
Prosperi Continuatio Hauniensis: 48
Provincial eras: 60
Provisional formulas: 27, 30, 79
Pulcheria: 451#, 455#
PV = Praefectus urbi: 72

Quinquennalia: 383#

Rav.: 49
Ravenna: 25, 410#, 413#, 425#, 426#, 429#, 433#, 443#, 447#, 462#, 473#, 504#
Recognition: 25, 307#, 308#, 311#, 312#, 313#, 318*, 321#, 322#, 324#, 346#, 351#, 384#, 388*, 393*,
    395*, 399#, 401#, 404#, 405#, 410#, 420#, 424#, 440#, 445#, 451#, 452#, 453#, 455#, 456#,
    458#, 459#, 460#, 461#, 462#, 464#, 474*, 481#, 482#, 485#, 488#, 490#, 491#, 508#
Reges Vand.: see *Laterculus Regum Vandalorum*
Regesta: 72
Regionalistic features in papyri: 68
Repudiation of consuls: 284*, 307#, 308#, 310#, 312#, 313#, 325#, 350#, 383*, 388#, 411#, 424#, 441#,
    466#, 475#, 476#
Retroactive normalization: 77
Rhinocolura (El Arish): 511*
Ricimer: 456#, 473#
Rions (France): 391*
Rome: 298#, 301*, 311#, 317#, 323#, 325*, 337#, 340#, 350#, 354*, 357*, 360#, 363#, 364#, 366#,
    367#, 370#, 371*, 372#, 379#, 384#, 385#, 388#, 388*, 393*, 395*, 398#, 399#, 402#, 403#, 405#,
    405*, 407#, 408#, 408*, 410#, 410*, 414#, 415#, 418#, 419#, 423#, 424#, 425#, 426#, 430#,
    431#, 432*, 433#, 433*, 436#, 438#, 439#, 443#, 444#, 444*, 446#, 447#, 448#, 449#, 450#,
    451#, 453*, 456#, 460#, 468*, 469#, 470#, 471#, 472#, 480#, 481#, 482#, 482#, 486*, 489#,
    491#, 503#, 506*, 517#, 526#
--importance of good relations with people of: 8
--large number of dates from: 32
--postconsular dates: 33

Sabinianus Magnus, MVM Illyr.: 505#
Salerno: 453*
Salona: 443#
Sang.: 48
"Scaliger's Barbarian" (*Scal.*): 52-53
Scribes, identity: 26
Second consulate in early empire: 3
Senate, initiative of in appointment of consul: 19
--presidency of: 1
Senatorial career: 1
--embassy to Zeno about recognition of western consuls: 8
--order, assimilation with equestrian: 2
--wealth, destruction in Gothic wars: 8
Seniority of consuls: 22-23
--by relation to emperor: 22

Index 4

Index of Texts Discussed

References to the introduction are given to page numbers (not otherwise designated); references to the commentaries to the year-by-year are given by the *year number* followed by the # sign; references to the Critical Appendix are given by the *year number* followed by the * sign. Misc.* and Paulinus* refer to the sections at the end of the Critical Appendix. Given the very large number of texts cited in the book, this index can include only those discussed, corrected (including references to corrections by others), or rejected.

A. INSCRIPTIONS

AE 1969/1970, 80: 394*
AE 1969/1970, 82: 384*
AE 1969/1970, 609: 482#
AE 1972, 351: Misc.*
AE 1974, 24: 493*
AE 1976, 34: 365*
AE 1976, 450b: 504*
AE 1977, 143: 368*
AE 1977, 209a-b: 541*
AE 1977, 796: 443*
AE 1982, 784: 313*
AE 1983, 131: 406*
Agnello, *Silloge* 88: 345*
Agnello, *Silloge* 93: 394*
Agnello, *Silloge* 98: 513*, 517*
Agnello, *Silloge* 104: 423*
AJP 6 (1885) 213: 301*
Arch.Eph. 1977, 67: 533*

BC 3.6 (1881) 158: 400*
BullCommArch 16 (1888) 250 no.11: 410*

CIG III 4593: 331*
CIG IV 9279: 541*
CIG IV 9426: 440*
CIG IV 9449: 518*
CIG IV 9748: 409*
CIG IV 9759: 461*
CIG IV 9762: 450*
CIG IV 9770: 465*
CIG IV 9771: 408*
CIG IV 9783: 483*
CIG IV 9863: 458*
CIL II 2211: 349*
CIL II 2635: 349#
CIL III 2657: 435*
CIL III 2658: 438*
CIL III ad 2659: 535*
CIL III 3653: 371*
CIL III 4023: 435*
CIL III 9509: 379*
CIL III 9522: 459*, 460*
CIL III 9523: 464*
CIL III 10406: 290*
CIL III 12861 (ad 9523): 395*
CIL III 13122: 395*
CIL III 13124: 430*
CIL III 13125: 429*
CIL III 13127: 459*

CIL VIII 19914: 452*
CIL VIII 20923: 467*
CIL VIII 23291: 287*
CIL IX 1362: 376*
CIL IX 1363: 506*
CIL IX 1366: 441*
CIL IX 1368: 434*
CIL IX 1371: 452*
CIL IX 1383: 517*
CIL IX 1384: 533*
CIL IX 2639: 352*
CIL IX 5807: 519*
CIL IX 6192: 393#, 393*
CIL X 407: 323*
CIL X 672: 367*
CIL X 1231: 490*
CIL X 1339: 437*
CIL X 1346: Paulinus*
CIL X 3698: 289#
CIL X 4485: 357*
CIL X 4486: 365*
CIL X 4491: 393#, 393*
CIL X 4492: 393*
CIL X 4613: 289*
CIL X 6850: 486*
CIL X 7115: 400*, 453*
CIL X 7167: 356*
CIL X 7168: 431*
CIL X 7169: 492*
CIL XI 802: 394*
CIL XI 2585: 444*
CIL XI 2586: Paulinus*
CIL XI 2872: 406*
CIL XI 2898: 412*
CIL XI 3239: 385*
CIL XI 4029: 340*
CIL XI 4033: 345*
CIL XI 4047: 424*
CIL XI 4162: 371*
CIL XI 4163: 493*
CIL XI 4333: 490*
CIL XI 4338: 490*
CIL XI 4339: 491*
CIL XI 4970: 386*
CIL XI 4978: 508*
CIL XI 7019: 507*
CIL XI 7924: 380*
CIL XII 591: 494*
CIL XII 933: 487*

ICUR I 69: 343*
ICUR I 85: 345*
ICUR I 132: 357*
ICUR I 145: 360*
ICUR I 146: 360*
ICUR I 147: 306*
ICUR I 184: 365*
ICUR I 220: 373*
ICUR I 235: 373*
ICUR I 254: 376*
ICUR I 293-301: 366*
ICUR I 365: 386*
ICUR I 370: 383*
ICUR I 387: 390*
ICUR I 388: 365*
ICUR I 390: 390*
ICUR I 406: 347*
ICUR I 410: 393*
ICUR I 411: 393*
ICUR I 432: 395*
ICUR I 434: 396*
ICUR I 455: 397*
ICUR I 456: 397*
ICUR I 473: 398*
ICUR I 478: 399*
ICUR I 512/515: 394*
ICUR I 513: 394*
ICUR I 546: 411*
ICUR I 553: 400*
ICUR I 558: 405*
ICUR I 563: 371*
ICUR I 564: 371*
ICUR I 570: 385*
ICUR I 580: 407*
ICUR I 599: 404*
ICUR I 616-633: 394*
ICUR I 649: 376*
ICUR I 672: 408*
ICUR I 675, 676: 408*
ICUR I 677: 432*
ICUR I 686: 435*
ICUR I 712: 433*
ICUR I 742: 453*
ICUR I 758: 452*
ICUR I 759-763: 369*
ICUR I 764: 453*
ICUR I 765-794: 369*
ICUR I 819: 465*
ICUR I 825: 468*

ICUR Suppl. 1554: 365*
ICUR Suppl. 1566: 366*
ICUR Suppl. 1592: 365*
ICUR Suppl. 1614: 371*
ICUR Suppl. 1623: 372*
ICUR Suppl. 1760: 386*
ICUR Suppl. 1786: 365*
ICUR Suppl. 1790: 388*
ICUR Suppl. 1792: 388*
ICUR Suppl. 1793: 403*
ICUR Suppl. 1796: 388*
ICUR Suppl. 1835: 392*
ICUR Suppl. 1855: 395*
ICUR n.s. I 47: 408*
ICUR n.s. I 85: 345*
ICUR n.s. I 88: 434*
ICUR n.s. I 91: 490*
ICUR n.s. I 222: 371*
ICUR n.s. I 309: 398*
ICUR n.s. I 332: 433*
ICUR n.s. I 394: 481*
ICUR n.s. I 442: 370*
ICUR n.s. I 481: 384*
ICUR n.s. I 482: 381*
ICUR n.s. I 513: 312*
ICUR n.s. I 714: 526#
ICUR n.s. I 726: 371*
ICUR n.s. I 731: 423*
ICUR n.s. I 734: 438#, 438*
ICUR n.s. I 735: 439*
ICUR n.s. I 738: 474*
ICUR n.s. I 741: 468*
ICUR n.s. I 742: 439*
ICUR n.s. I 746: 526#
ICUR n.s. I 747: 526#
ICUR n.s. I 941: 397*
ICUR n.s. I 943: 484*
ICUR n.s. I 983a: 342*
ICUR n.s. I 984: 385*
ICUR n.s. I 991: 452*
ICUR n.s. I 992: 484*
ICUR n.s. I 993: 522*
ICUR n.s. I 1104: 345*
ICUR n.s. I 1105: 483*
ICUR n.s. I 1169: 383*
ICUR n.s. I 1209: 381*
ICUR n.s. I 1211: 393*
ICUR n.s. I 1215: 519*
ICUR n.s. I 1249: 302*

ICUR n.s. I 3226: 408*
ICUR n.s. I 3230: 435*
ICUR n.s. I 3236: 443*
ICUR n.s. I 3239: 520*
ICUR n.s. I 3240: 465*
ICUR n.s. I 3244: 526#
ICUR n.s. I 3247: 518*
ICUR n.s. II 4171: 411*
ICUR n.s. II 4176: 437*
ICUR n.s. II 4177: 466*
ICUR n.s. II 4178: 444*
ICUR n.s. II 4273: 423*
ICUR n.s. II 4280: 522*
ICUR n.s. II 4487: 395*
ICUR n.s. II 4502: 371*
ICUR n.s. II 4504: 395*
ICUR n.s. II 4505: 398*
ICUR n.s. II 4517: 444*
ICUR n.s. II 4770: 390*
ICUR n.s. II 4800: 348*
ICUR n.s. II 4808: 372*
ICUR n.s. II 4810: 365*
ICUR n.s. II 4819: 386*
ICUR n.s. II 4836: 401*
ICUR n.s. II 4837: 401*
ICUR n.s. II 4850: 408*
ICUR n.s. II 4865: 420*
ICUR n.s. II 4901: 393*
ICUR n.s. II 4902: 435*
ICUR n.s. II 4919: 404*
ICUR n.s. II 4947: 325*
ICUR n.s. II 4950: 465*
ICUR n.s. II 4968: 402*
ICUR n.s. II 4973: 474*
ICUR n.s. II 4974: 476*
ICUR n.s. II 4975: 439*
ICUR n.s. II 4981: 481*
ICUR n.s. II 4982: 481*
ICUR n.s. II 4990: 444*
ICUR n.s. II 5012: 510*
ICUR n.s. II 5014: 511*
ICUR n.s. II 5016: 512*
ICUR n.s. II 5036, 5037: 453*
ICUR n.s. II 5040: 453*
ICUR n.s. II 5049: 486*
ICUR n.s. II 5100b: 409*
ICUR n.s. II 5656: 409*
ICUR n.s. II 5701a: 408*
ICUR n.s. II 5710: 321#

ICUR n.s. IV 9570: 378*
ICUR n.s. IV 9573: 385*
ICUR n.s. IV 9580: 384*
ICUR n.s. IV 9584: 408*
ICUR n.s. IV 11090: 349*
ICUR n.s. IV 11096: 364*
ICUR n.s. IV 11102: 371*
ICUR n.s. IV 11116: 387*
ICUR n.s. IV 11119: 389*
ICUR n.s. IV 11147: 427*
ICUR n.s. IV 11149: 435*
ICUR n.s. IV 11151: 439*
ICUR n.s. IV 11154: 443*
ICUR n.s. IV 11167: 483*
ICUR n.s. IV 11750: 337*
ICUR n.s. IV 11756: 348*
ICUR n.s. IV 11764: 368*
ICUR n.s. IV 11767: 374*
ICUR n.s. IV 11771: 378*
ICUR n.s. IV 11778: 397*
ICUR n.s. IV 12250: 383*
ICUR n.s. IV 12252: 396*
ICUR n.s. IV 12253: 402*
ICUR n.s. IV 12259: 417*
ICUR n.s. IV 12495: 362*
ICUR n.s. IV 12526: 362*
ICUR n.s. IV 12534: 383*
ICUR n.s. IV 12540: 392*
ICUR n.s. IV 12543: 399*
ICUR n.s. IV 12544: 402*
ICUR n.s. V 13101: 346#
ICUR n.s. V 13105: 360*
ICUR n.s. V 13120: 396*
ICUR n.s. V 13286: 337*
ICUR n.s. V 13290: 341*
ICUR n.s. V 13296: 349*
ICUR n.s. V 13298: 349*
ICUR n.s. V 13300: 357*
ICUR n.s. V 13303: 349*
ICUR n.s. V 13308: 360*
ICUR n.s. V 13311: 349*
ICUR n.s. V 13313: 361*
ICUR n.s. V 13317: 365*
ICUR n.s. V 13326: 368*
ICUR n.s. V 13333: 375*
ICUR n.s. V 13334: 375*
ICUR n.s. V 13365: 395*
ICUR n.s. V 13391: 420*
ICUR n.s. V 13392: 423*

ICUR n.s. VII 17587: 458*
ICUR n.s. VII 17588a: 469*
ICUR n.s. VII 17597a: 489*
ICUR n.s. VII 17598: 490*
ICUR n.s. VII 17599a: 490*
ICUR n.s. VII 17601: 495*
ICUR n.s. VII 17603: Paulinus*
ICUR n.s. VII 17962: 345*
ICUR n.s. VII 18472: 359*
ICUR n.s. VII 19946: 287*
ICUR n.s. VII 19953: 364*
ICUR n.s. VII 19958: 375*
ICUR n.s. VII 19962b: 407*
ICUR n.s. VII 19989: 452*
ICUR n.s. VII 19992: 493*
ICUR n.s. VII 20340: 321*
ICUR n.s. VII 20602: 345*
ICUR n.s. VII 20606: 465*
ICUR n.s. VIII 20716: 287*
ICUR n.s. VIII 20717: 383*
ICUR n.s. VIII 20764: 294*
ICUR n.s. VIII 20765: 295*
ICUR n.s. VIII 20766: 356*
ICUR n.s. VIII 20770: 341*
ICUR n.s. VIII 20771: 341*
ICUR n.s. VIII 20772: 344*
ICUR n.s. VIII 20775: 350*
ICUR n.s. VIII 20783a: 361*
ICUR n.s. VIII 20783b: 372*
ICUR n.s. VIII 20784a: 364*
ICUR n.s. VIII 20784-20786: 365*
ICUR n.s. VIII 20788, 20789: 366*
ICUR n.s. VIII 20791: 372*
ICUR n.s. VIII 20796: 380*
ICUR n.s. VIII 20797: 380*
ICUR n.s. VIII 20801: 364*
ICUR n.s. VIII 20801a: 384*
ICUR n.s. VIII 20801b: 385*
ICUR n.s. VIII 20803a,b: 384*
ICUR n.s. VIII 20804: 386*
ICUR n.s. VIII 20805: 390*
ICUR n.s. VIII 20807: 394*
ICUR n.s. VIII 20807a: 336*
ICUR n.s. VIII 20811: 397*
ICUR n.s. VIII 20813: 468*
ICUR n.s. VIII 20814: 407*
ICUR n.s. VIII 20816: 439*
ICUR n.s. VIII 20820: 444*
ICUR n.s. VIII 20825: 458*

ICUR n.s. VIII 20826: 463*
ICUR n.s. VIII 20829: 483*
ICUR n.s. VIII 20837a: 429*
ICUR n.s. VIII 20839: 541*
ICUR n.s. VIII 20849c: 352*
ICUR n.s. VIII 21068a: 432*
ICUR n.s. VIII 21604: 365*
ICUR n.s. VIII 21605: 366*
ICUR n.s. VIII 21606a: 366*
ICUR n.s. VIII 21606b: 368*
ICUR n.s. VIII 21607: 368*
ICUR n.s. VIII 21608: 373*
ICUR n.s. VIII 21611: 388*
ICUR n.s. VIII 21613: 404*
ICUR n.s. VIII 21891b: 388*
ICUR n.s. VIII 22751a: 383*
ICUR n.s. VIII 22972: 404*
ICUR n.s. VIII 22974: 453*
ICUR n.s. VIII 22978a: 520*
ICUR n.s. VIII 23063: 389*
ICUR n.s. VIII 23399: 331*
ICUR n.s. VIII 23400a: 331*
ICUR n.s. VIII 23402: 356*
ICUR n.s. VIII 23403: 361*
ICUR n.s. VIII 23406: 365*
ICUR n.s. VIII 23407: 366*
ICUR n.s. VIII 23408a: 366*
ICUR n.s. VIII 23408c: 368*
ICUR n.s. VIII 23409: 376*
ICUR n.s. VIII 23411: 371*
ICUR n.s. VIII 23414: 376*
ICUR n.s. VIII 23414a: 372*
ICUR n.s. VIII 23417: 380*
ICUR n.s. VIII 23420b: 383*
ICUR n.s. VIII 23417a: 377*
ICUR n.s. VIII 23417b: 379*
ICUR n.s. VIII 23423: 386*
ICUR n.s. VIII 23428: 391*
ICUR n.s. VIII 23430: 393*
ICUR n.s. VIII 23431a: 394*
ICUR n.s. VIII 23433: 402*
ICUR n.s. VIII 23439a: 405*
ICUR n.s. VIII 23439c: 385*
ICUR n.s. VIII 23452: 488*
ICUR n.s. VIII 23648b: 289*
ICUR n.s. IX 23762: 383*

IG X 2 1 776: 461*
IG XIV 112: 357*

IG XIV 949a: 394*
IG XIV 956A: 313*
IG XIV 2252: 392*
IG XIV 2255a + d: 500*
IG XIV 2271: 458*
Iglesias Gil, *Onomastica preromana* 37 no.6: 399*
IGRR I 1291: 298*
IGRR III 1268: 301*
IGUR I 129: 370*
IGUR I 246: 313*
I.Ital. I² 230: 367*
I.Ital. III.1 17: 323*
I.Ital. X.4 381: 361*
I.Ital. XIII.1 p.269: 288#, 289#
I.Lat.Alg. II 2 4558: 284*
I.Lat.Gaul.Narb. 260: 520*
I.Lat.Gaul.Narb. 293: 520*
I.Lat.Gaul.Narb. 295: 501*
I.Lat.Gaul.Narb. 297: 485*
I.Lat.Gaul.Narb. 298: 513*
I.Lat.Gaul.Narb. 299: 517*
I.Lat.Gaul.Narb. 302: 453*
I.Lat.Gaul.Narb. 606: 486*
I.Lat.Paestum 110: 310*
I.Lat.3 Gaules 145: 391*

ILCV 148: 512*
ILCV 190 adn.: 452*
ILCV 211: 515*
ILCV 252: 444*
ILCV 258 adn.: 312*
ILCV 259: 444*
ILCV 304: 490*
ILCV 325: 507*
ILCV 358 adn.: 404*
ILCV 393A: 484*
ILCV 412: 432*
ILCV 469: 453*
ILCV 510: 453*
ILCV 511A: 474*
ILCV 545: 394*
ILCV 565 adn.: 368*
ILCV 582: 393*
ILCV 598: 420*
ILCV 662 adn.: 343*
ILCV 686: 527*
ILCV 693: 405*
ILCV 694: 522*
ILCV 715: 439*

ILCV 3114: 468*
ILCV 3169A: 521*
ILCV 3185D: 517*
ILCV 3194: 345*
ILCV 3206: 449*, 494*
ILCV 3232 adn.: 429*
ILCV 3287: 388*
ILCV 3335 adn.: 388*
ILCV 3390A: 383*
ILCV 3448: 508*
ILCV 3492B: 312*
ILCV 3494: 397*
ILCV 3500: 365*
ILCV 3503 adn.: 360*
ILCV 3504 adn.: 422*
ILCV 3516A adn.: 502*
ILCV 3601: 506*
ILCV 3631: 517*
ILCV 3696: 400*
ILCV 3727E: 444*
ILCV 3735: 400*, 453*
ILCV 3737: 388*
ILCV 3758: 338*
ILCV 3769A: 394*
ILCV 3782: 465*
ILCV 3791C: 425*
ILCV 3820: 390*
ILCV 4111C: 393*
ILCV 4145: 414*
ILCV 4146B: 381*
ILCV 4188 adn.: 366*
ILCV 4262: 408*
ILCV 4369A: 366*
ILCV 4370: 438*
ILCV 4370 adn.: 438*, 468*
ILCV 4384: 463*
ILCV 4391A: 402*
ILCV 4394A: 400*
ILCV 4395 adn.: 376*
ILCV 4399A: 365*
ILCV 4400A: 397*
ILCV 4404: 448*
ILCV 4414A adn.: 402*
ILCV 4415: 402*
ILCV 4444A: 407*
ILCV 4461B: 423*
ILCV 4539: 399*
ILCV 4556: 393*
ILCV 4597: 407*

NotScav 1895, 485 no.163: 418*
NotScav 1895, 520 no.266: 424*
NotScav 1895, 521 no.266: 374*
NotScav 1896, 33 no.334: 444*
NotScav 1897, 366: 458*
NotScav 1897, 367: 517*, 530*
Nuovo Didaskaleion 1950, 54 no.6: 414*

OGIS II 619: 320*

RAC 22 (1946) 91: 350*
RAC 22 (1946) 92: 420*
RAC 26 (1950) 234: 448*
RAC 36 (1960) 14: 350*
RAC 36 (1960) 31 n.22: 422*
RAC 60 (1984) 306: 394*
Recueil Inscr.Chrét.Gaule I 211: 383*
Recueil Inscr.Chrét.Gaule XV 78: 485*
Recueil Inscr.Chrét.Gaule XV 161: Paulinus*
Recueil Inscr.Chrét.Gaule XV 286: 485*, 504*
Reisen in Kilikien 89 no.168: 448*
Rend.Pont.Accad. 22 (1946-47) 231 no.6: 424*
Rend.Pont.Accad. 22 (1946-47) 231 no.7: 439*
Rend.Pont.Accad. 22 (1946-47) 231 no.8: 423*
J. and L. Robert, *La déesse de Hiérapolis Castabala* 29-30: 398*

Saller and Bagatti, *The Town of Nebo* (1949) 140: 535*
SB I 1540: 408#
SB I 4223: 321*
SB V 8393: 298*
SEG XII 226: 319*
SEG XVII 441: 427*
SEG XXIX 643: 525*
Siculorum Gymnasium (1961) 196: 433*
*Syll.*³ 901: 319*
*Syll.*³ 907: 382*

Vermaseren, *Corpus Inscr. et Monum. Rel. Mithr.* II 1315, 1319-1322: 325*
Vives, *Inscripciones latinas de la España Romana* 851: 399*

ZPE 24 (1977) 222: 452*

B. PAPYRI

BGU II 408: 313*

P.Lips. 13: 379#, 379*
P.Lips. 21: 381*
P.Lips. 23: 374*
P.Lips. 33: 368*
P.Lips. 38: 390*
P.Lips. 42: 391*
P.Lips. 85: 372#, 373*
P.Lips. 86: 373*
P.Lond. III 869: 473*
P.Lond. III 991: 481*
P.Lond. III 1245: 357*
P.Lond. III 1313: 507*
P.Lond. V 1722: 530*
P.Lond. V 1793: 472*
P.Lond. V 1797: 516*
P.Lund VI 10: 400*

P.Mich. X 593: 289*, 304#, 308#
P.Mil. I 64: 441#
P.Ness. 15: 511*

P.Oslo II 38: 374*
P.Oxy. IV, p.202: 355*
P.Oxy. VI 889: 325#
P.Oxy. VIII 1116: 363#
P.Oxy. XII 1469: 298*
P.Oxy. XII 1470: 336#
P.Oxy. XII 1551: 304*
P.Oxy. XVI 1879: 434*
P.Oxy. XVI 1899: 475*
P.Oxy. XVI 1959: 499*
P.Oxy. XVII 2124: 316*
P.Oxy. XVIII 2187: 304*
P.Oxy. XXIV 2408: 397*
P.Oxy. XXXIV 2715: 386*
P.Oxy.Hels. 44: 324*

P.Princ. II 81: 344*
P.Princ. III 181: 344*

P.Rainer Cent. 94: 441*
P.Rainer Cent. 102: 379*
P.Rainer Cent. 104: 466#
P.Rainer Cent. 165: 401*
P.Ryl. IV 616: 309*, 312*
P.Ryl. IV 653: 320*

P.Sakaon 33: 320*
P.Sakaon 50: 317#

Tjäder, *Nichtlit.Pap.* 47-48A: 44, 484*

C. LEGAL SOURCES

AbhGöttingen n.f. 15 (1917) 21: 83
CJ 1.2.16: 476#
CJ 1.5.11: 510#
CJ 1.30.1: 424#
CJ 4.20.12: 423#
CJ 5.14.8: 83 n.37
CJ 6.7.3: 423#
CJ 6.20.14: 295#
CJ 6.23.22: 44 n.40
CJ 8.10.10: 420#
CJ 10.10.5: 435#
ConstSirm 11: 411*
ConstSirm 12: 77
CTh, senatorial acceptance of: 6
CTh 1.6.9: 82
CTh 1.8.2: 424#
CTh 1.12.7: 84
CTh 1.15.17: 84
CTh 1.32.2: 377#
CTh 2.14.1: 400#
CTh 2.25.1: 325#
CTh 4.10.2: 423#
CTh 4.13.4: 73
CTh 4.13.6: 82
CTh 5.16.33: 17
CTh 6.6.1: 22, 428#
CTh 6.27.1: 75
CTh 6.30.6: 384#
CTh 7.8.15: 433#
CTh 7.17.1: 412#
CTh 8.5.29: 82, 368#
CTh 9.6.4: 423#
CTh 9.25.2: 364#
CTh 9.40.13: 390*
CTh 9.40.17: 399#
CTh 9.42.6: 84 n.42
CTh 10.1.8: 364#
CTh 10.8.5: 435#
CTh 10.10.20: 390*
CTh 10.20.10: 380#
CTh 11.1.1: 73
CTh 11.1.13: 79
CTh 11.1.30: 84 n.42

D. LITERARY AND SUBLITERARY SOURCES

E. COINS AND OTHER OBJECTS